Kenneth L. Teegarden

The Man,

The Church,

The Time

KENNETH L. TEEGARDEN

The Man, The Church, The Time

by D. Duane Cummins

A joint project of the
Disciples of Christ Historical Society
and TCU Press

TCU Press / *Fort Worth, Texas*

Library of Congress Cataloging-in-Publication Data

Cummins, D. Duane.
Kenneth L. Teegarden : the man, the church, the time / by D. Duane
Cummins.
p. cm.
Includes bibliographical references and index.
ISBN-13: 978-0-87565-339-6 (alk. paper)
ISBN-10: 0-87565-339-1 (alk. paper)
1. Teegarden, Kenneth L. 2. Christian Church (Disciples of Christ)--
Biography. I. Title.

BX7343.T44C86 2006
286.6092--dc22
[B]
2006027540

TCU Press
P.O. Box 298300
Fort Worth, TX 76129
817-257-7822
http://www.prs.tcu.edu/
To order books: 800-826-8911

In Memory of

KENNETH L. TEEGARDEN

I think continually of those who were truly great. . . .
The names of those who in their lives fought for life,
Who wore at their hearts the fire's center.
Born of the sun they traveled a short while towards the sun,
And left the vivid air signed with their honor.

Stephen Spender

CONTENTS

ACKNOWLEDGMENTS

T wo years of research and writing along with the final publication of the manuscript were made possible by the generous and timely philanthropy of Mildred Harbaugh. She and the trustees of her estate, George and Sheryl McClain, deserve high tribute and abiding appreciation from the Christian Church (Disciples of Christ) and its historical society for envisioning the educational value of this biography for Disciples in particular and Protestantism in general. A grateful church expresses an enormous thank you to the generous spirit of Mildred Harbaugh for her major financial gift to the historical society establishing the publications endowment fund to underwrite the research and publication of major historical writings.

This work is drawn primarily from the documentary sources housed at the Disciples of Christ Historical Society in Nashville, Tennessee. Included in that archive are the Kenneth L. Teegarden papers comprised of two library filing boxes covering his four years as administrative secretary of the Commission on Brotherhood Restructure; and seven library filing boxes encompassing the twelve years he served as general minister and president. Also quite valuable were the interviews conducted by James Seale, former president of the society, with two dozen leading figures of the restructure era. These interviews are part of the archival collections. The staff of the historical society: Sara Harwell, vice president; curators Elaine Philpott, May Reed, and Sharman Hartson; administrative assistant Marlene Patterson; chief financial officer, Jean Arnold; and the president, Glenn Carson, were extremely helpful, understanding and encouraging in locating materials and supporting the work and purpose of this writing. My indebtedness to them is gratefully acknowledged.

The Disciples' headquarters building in Indianapolis, Indiana, houses a small quantity of Teegarden materials, and I extend my appreciation to Wilma Shuffitt and Mary Collins for their time and effort in locating specific letters and reproducing them for my use. Appreciation is also expressed for the work of Toni Imbler, curator of the Phillips Theological Seminary archives, who kindly assisted by locating catalogues and transcripts from the 1940-1943 era, and of Newell Williams, who graciously supplied copies of catalogues and transcripts from the former Brite College of the Bible covering 1947-1949.

Wanda Teegarden's unstinting cooperation was profoundly important to the development of this book. She patiently and graciously subjected herself to many hours of interviews in which she shared candidly, both in person and by telephone. In addition, the Teegarden personal collection of correspondence, photo albums, scrapbooks, sermons, news-reports, and other documents fill five four-drawer filing cabinets in her home. She generously allowed open access to these materials, a rich treasure of resource data for the book. Furthermore, Wanda read every chapter in rough draft form, identifying errors of dates, sequence of events, spelling of names, and correcting any misstatement of family activities. This was an invaluable service helping to make the second and third drafts more accurate before they were handed to the manuscript editor.

Many other persons were interviewed for this work, including all members of the immediate Teegarden family: David, Kirk, Grant, Matthew, Sloan, and Blake. The insights they provided into Kenneth as a father and grandfather were exceptionally valuable. Also interviewed were Howard Dentler, William Howland, T. J. Liggett, Robert Friedly, John Humbert, James Suggs and Harold Johnson, all of whom served as colleagues with Kenneth during his years as general Minister and president. In addition, I conducted interviews with Roy Kemp, a resident of Cushing during Kenneth's boyhood; Don Pittman, associate dean at Brite during Kenneth's years on the faculty; and Mrs. Cleo LeVally, administrative assistant at First Christian Church in Healdton, Oklahoma.

I acknowledge with great pleasure the multitude of persons along the research journey who provided advice, information, favors, professional services, and gracious cooperation. This indispensable group included Ruth Ann Johnson, librarian for the Cushing Public Library; Cheryl Wells, administrative assistant at First Christian Church in Cushing, Oklahoma; Almadene Herd, administrative assistant at First Christian Church in Chandler, Oklahoma; Samantha Johnson, librarian at the Moore Memorial Library in Texas City, Texas; Marjorie Grady, administrative assistant at First Christian Church in Texas City, Texas; Mrs. Henry (Willie-Dee) Criss, long-time member of First Christian Church in Texas City, Texas; Bret Coe, pastor of First Christian Church in Vernon, Texas; Randy Jay, pastor of First Christian Church in Fort Smith, Arkansas; Tina Jones, administrative assistant in the office of the Christian Church (Disciples of Christ in the Great River Region; Coretha Loughridge, administrative assistant in the regional office of the Christian Church (Disciples of Christ) in the Southwest; and to Judy Alter and Susan Petty, along with their excellent staff who gave the manuscript its final editorial review. Judy and the TCU press staff have partnered with me on several editorial ventures and my gratitude for their professionalism runs exceedingly deep.

I am especially grateful to a group of scholars and friends who read this manuscript prior to its completion, helping me avoid historical errors and correcting punctuation and grammatical errors. They include Newell Williams, Lester McAllister, Mark Toulouse, James Suggs, Robert Friedly, William Howland, Peter Morgan, Larry Steinmetz, and Larry Grimes. Any errors in the manuscript are totally my own.

Finally, and most significantly, I express abiding appreciation to my wife Suzi for her patience, interest, and unflagging support of this work. Without her warm companionship, personal charm, and cheerful spirit this work would likely never have been started.

D. Duane Cummins
April 15, 2006

PREFACE

It has been two decades and four general ministers since Kenneth L. Teegarden gave leadership to the Christian Church (Disciples of Christ) as its general minister and president. Many of the current generation of Disciples did not know Kenneth; most did not have the opportunity to meet him. As his time recedes into history, there is a growing Disciples multitude who are unaware of his extraordinary contributions, of his leadership qualities or the texture of the time in which he served.

The compelling purpose of this work is to remind us of a major figure in the history of the Christian Church (Disciples of Christ) and in the twentieth century history of mainline Protestantism. The book seeks to embrace the many stages of his sixty year ministry—local pastor, regional minister, architect of restructure, general minister and president, and distinguished minister in residence at Brite Divinity School. His ministry covered the last two-thirds of the twentieth century, 1940–2000. His life, of modest origins, covered eight decades. This writing seeks to tell the story of the man, the church and the time.

It is not meant to be adulatory, but it is meant to be an appreciative biography of Kenneth Teegarden. It strives to present his exceptional qualities and talents as a leader. In that generation of design-makers, heavily populated with exceptional leadership, Kenneth became a leader of leaders. Eminent historian Gordon Wood noted in his recent book, *Revolutionary Characters*, that the very egalitarian democracy the nation's founding fathers created all but guarantees that we will never again replicate the extraordinary generation of the founders. There are those who look back on the Disciples restructure generation—Ronald Osborn, Granville Walker, Dale Fiers, Kenneth Teegarden, T.J. Liggett, Virgil Sly, Spencer Austin, James Moak, Williard Wickizer,

William Blakemore, W. A. Welsh, Stephen J. England, Perry E. Gresham, Raph Miller Jr., Loren Lair, Herold Monroe, Orville Ware, Paul Stouffer, Frank Mabee, Art Wenger, Lester Richman, Mae Yoh Ward, Harlie Smith, and a host of others—and believe they too created an egalitarian polity that may well prevent Disciples from replicating the range and depth of leadership found among those progenitors of the edification of church. Occasional individual leaders of blazing talent will continue to appear among Disciples, but the election or appointment of a full generation of such talent seems, to some, to be less likely. It is important, therefore, to chronicle the life of one who emerged as the pre-eminent leader of that storied generation, a generation that transformed the life of the Christian Church (Disciples of Christ).

Kenneth quickened the heart and mind of that generation. They stood shoulder to shoulder with him during the creation and implementation of The Design, a document that restructured Disciples into a "community in covenant." And it should not be forgotten that his leadership ranged far beyond structure and polity. As a persistent Disciples' advocate for "peace with Justice," he led the church in a vigorous search for God's peace in the nuclear age. He helped the church understand religion as a source of personal and public morality, and how to use its voice as a powerful force for social change. And most important of all, he taught us all how to join hands and become a church. He was not free of imperfection; in fact he was often criticized. But his contributions to the life of our church were enormous, and they are remembered with appreciation in this book.

Other historians will write of Kenneth Teegarden in future years. They, too, will seek to tell his story in the light of their time. It is my fervent hope that this volume will help advance their task.

D. Duane Cummins
April 15, 2006

Kenneth L. Teegarden

The Man,

The Church,

The Time

✠

The Swordmaker's Descendant

The church was all I knew.
Kenneth L. Teegarden

Prologue-*September 26, 2002*

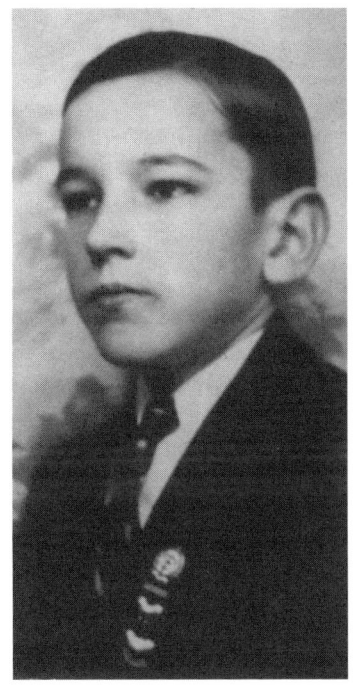

Chords of the Bach aria, "Suite in D" filled the sanctuary. In the tile-roofed tower above, bells tolled their requiem. A thousand and more were gathered in Fort Worth's University Christian Church—both the eminent and the plain. Absorbed in grief, they faced a reality that for many did not as yet seem real. Death had claimed Kenneth Teegarden: their leader, their pastor, their mentor, their friend. They were silent in their homage, quiet in their remembrances.

They had come from all quarters of the United States. Students, who sat in his classes in the Moore Building of Brite

Divinity School, who sought his counsel over a private morning coffee in Weatherly Hall, and who prayed beside him in Robert Carr Chapel. General unit executives of the Christian Church (Disciples of Christ), who served by his side throughout his twelve years as general minister and president of the Christian Church (Disciples of Christ). Regional ministers, who were his colleagues in ministry during the implementation of the Design and the living into covenant. Scores of pastors, whom he had mentored, nurtured, and befriended. Parishioners, who had received his pastoral care in times of crises and listened to the wisdom of his sermons during those years of his congregational ministry. Legions of friends, formed out of his enormous capacity for friendship and his deep sense of human caring. And his cherished family, two sons, two daughters-in-law, four grandsons, and his beloved wife Wanda, companion in life, partner in faith. All of them were there that day, a testimony to the reach and profundity of his life.

Disciples had depended heavily upon Kenneth Teegarden, and many questioned what their church might become without him. As administrative secretary of the Commission on Brotherhood Restructure, he had been the guiding architect of the new design for church, and he, better than anyone else, could explain its meaning. He became the foremost teacher of church and covenant. He had been the driving force for Christian unity in the growing relationship with the United Church of Christ, helping organize joint general assemblies, a joint overseas ministries board, and the mutual recognition of ministers. As the only person to date to serve two complete terms as general minister and president, he had successfully demonstrated the proper balance between the ecclesial roles of minister and president. Under his leadership, the general cabinet, for the first time, bonded in mutual respect for their covenanted ministry. For the whole church he had been a powerful and constant advocate of "peace with justice"—arranging the preparation and publication of *Seeking God's Peace in a Nuclear Age,* and urging the passage of sixteen peace resolutions by the general assembly during his two terms, more than twice as many as in the twenty years since. And his leadership in Civil Rights, creating models of bi-racial community cooperation in Little Rock and Fort Smith, and bringing African American Disciples into institutional relationship with the restructured church.

In silence, they remembered these things. All knew that he was not perfect, not without his flaws, not indispensable. Nonetheless, they tried to grasp the impact of his absence, and they wondered about a future without the persuasiveness of his voice, the clarity of his pen, and the wisdom of his thought. Against the stillness, a friend stood in the distant pulpit and spoke words of remembrance . . . . [1]

Genealogy: *1650–1921*

Nobel Laureate V.S. Naipaul once observed, "Most of us know the parents or grandparents we come from, but we go back and back—in our blood and bone and brain we carry the memories of thousands of beings." Kenneth's lineage was crowded with pioneer farmers, tradesmen, artisans, and small country town residents who were shaped by the values of rural America and who followed the westward movement of the frontier, from the eastern Appalachia to the Osage plains in Oklahoma. The Teegarden bloodline connected Kenneth to history and determined how he fitted into society. It helped sculpt the features of his character and informed him of who he was. This legacy flowed from a people widely regarded as industrious, independent, forward looking in their religion, and described as persons of solid integrity, determination, devotion, fierce loyalty, compassion and extraordinary hospitality. These traits were etched into the character of Kenneth L. Teegarden, who though a descendant of a Solingen sword maker, was destined to be a proclaimer of the Isaiac wisdom of "turning swords into plowshares."

The name had many spellings—theegarten, tigarden, thiegarden, thegarden, tegarden—all translated from North German to mean "The Garden." In America, the name was corrupted to tee-garden. The Theegarten (*sic*) farm that gave the family its name, was one of five "gardens" or "farms" of the Franconian kings court at Solingen, Germany. In time, the five farms grew into suburbs. Centuries later, they were joined to form present-day Solingen and are represented today by the five points on the crowned crest of the town. [2]

Kenneth's genealogical line traces directly to Christian Tegarden (sic), born 1650, in the tiny community of Meigen, Germany. He was married to Maria Tilmans, the Tilmans being one of only ten families who resided in the little village of Meigen. Christian was a sword-smith—a toolmaker, or reider, who put together blades and handles, a craft he performed in the workshop of his black and white half-timber farmhouse. [3]

He was a member of the Reformed Church with which the Teegardens affiliated at the time of the Reformation after its separation from Martin Luther. Following the precepts of Calvin and Zwingli, the Reformed Church developed a more intense moral vigor along with more democratic forms of church life than the bishop-directed Lutheran Church. From these earliest times, therefore, the Teegardens identified with the democratic trends in the church.

The seventh and youngest child of Christian and Maria was a son named Abraham, born near Solingen in 1688. He too, was a sword-smith and a member of the Reformed Church who believed strongly in representative forms of government, both church and civil. He married Anna Margaretha Albrecht. Abraham, at age forty-eight, was the first of the line to leave Solingen and dare to cross the daunting north Atlantic to the new world. He and his family were among the 388 passengers who sailed from Rotterdam on the *Harle of London* in 1736, arriving in Philadelphia seven weeks later on September 1, nearly two centuries before Kenneth Teegarden was born. As part of a large German migration, they had left their homeland to free themselves from exorbitant taxation, conscription into the endless wars of their principality, imposed religious conformity, and a growing population that strained the limits of German rural economy.

Literate and free, the Teegardens moved a short distance south of Philadelphia, about ten miles beyond present-day Frederick, Maryland. Following Indian pathways they found their way to Conocoheage Creek, not far from what would become known as Hagerstown. Jonathan Hager was said to have accompanied the Teegardens on their trip from Philadelphia, a fact that prompted Kenneth in later years to jokingly inquire, "I've always wondered why they named it Hagerstown instead of Teegardenstown." [4]

Abraham acquired a piece of land there, extending "from a white oak standing on the side of a hill to within one and a half miles of the Conegochiege (sic) creek and close by the wagon road. . . ." He called it "Tecart's Delight." Here the family settled for seventeen years. Abraham farmed, trapped, and managed a small implement workshop while Anna saw that the family kept their German traditions and customs. His older son, Abraham Jr., became closely associated with the Ohio Company, working as a land speculator in the West. He is mentioned more than once in the correspondence of George Washington. However, at age sixty-five, shortly before his death in 1753, the elder Abraham transferred the Maryland land to his younger son, William. [5]

William, too, had been born in Solingen and was just sixteen when the family embarked on their voyage to the unknown American wilderness. He and his wife Ann eventually sold Tecart's Delight and settled in Westmoreland County, Pennsylvania, where he died in 1778. As his father before him, William put his plow to the ground and achieved success as a farmer. Two of his sons served in the Continental Army during the American Revolution.[6]

Moses Teegarden (1759–1844), born in Frederick County, Maryland, was the youngest of William and Ann's nine children. Following the Teegarden custom, he and his wife, Mary Huston, parented a large family of eleven children. Moses, recorded in the nation's first census of 1790, was the first in the lineage to leave the eastern piedmont and move overland to the region of Southern Ohio in the Northwest Territory. During 1795 western settlement was encouraged, first by the opening of the Wilderness Road for wagon traffic into the Ohio country, and second, in early August, by the Treaty of Greenville that forced twelve Indian tribes in Ohio to cede their lands and secure their boundaries. In the late summer of 1795 Moses Teegarden drove his wagons across Braddock's Road to Pittsburgh, then on to Columbia Station, near Cleveland, later moving south to Darrtown in Butler County, Ohio, where family records say he was "ruined." [7]

William, the third of Moses' eleven children, was born in Westmoreland County, Pennsylvania, February 1793. When the War of 1812 broke out, he enlisted and served until the war ended. For his services he was granted the title of colonel. While bivouacking during the war years he discovered a beautiful spring on the old St. Clair Trail, Darke County, Ohio. After the war he returned to that spot, purchased the land, and built a home. In 1815 William took for his wife Catherine Watt, who bore him ten children. He farmed, raised stock, and, by the time of his death, owned 1,400 acres of land along with a large brick home. Founder of the historic Teegarden Settlement in Darke County, Ohio, he was the first Teegarden converted to the Disciples Movement by early followers of Alexander Campbell. William donated the land for the Christian church that became identified as the *Teegarden Congregational Christian Church* or the *Church at Teegarden's.* [8] They were widely known and respected for their devotion to the church as well as the warmth of their hospitality.

After the Civil War, one of William's sons left Southern Ohio and trekked westward with his family to farm a piece of land near Tryon, Oklahoma. His eldest surviving son, Marshall Chester Teegarden, born in Darke County, Ohio, in 1857, became the grandfather of Kenneth and his name would be handed on to one of Kenneth's sons. He married Ida South who was born in Appanoose County, Iowa, during the Civil War and lived to the age of ninety-seven, dying in 1960. Chester and Ida were married in 1881 at Goff, Kansas, where they lived and farmed for twenty-two years. They had four children. The youngest was Roy A. Teegarden, the father of Kenneth, born March 11, 1894, at Goff.

In 1903, during the presidency of Theodore Roosevelt, Chester and his wife packed their belongings and with their three youngest children—Ivan, Roy and Hazel—joined a group of settlers on their way to homestead in Lincoln County, Oklahoma Territory. They came by rail to Chandler, bringing stock, machinery, and household furnishings. By wagon they took their belongings to the Valley Queen settlement where they homesteaded. Five years later, after granting a right of way through his farm for the railroad, they built a new house south of Tryon and lived there for the remainder of their lives. Chester was a farmer—plain spoken, plain mannered, with little formal education—who made his way with his Bible and his farm tools. Ida was an active member of the little Christian church on the corner of Birch and Main in Tryon for fifty-three years. [9]

Roy, only nine when his parents moved to Oklahoma in 1903, was reared in Tryon, where he became a state champion high hurdler and a first stringer on the town baseball team. Chester, known as "M.C." by many, always maintained a pasture-stadium with homemade bleachers on his farm and the young men of Tryon came there to play baseball. Roy would one day briefly manage a minor league team on which the future hall-of-fame pitcher, Carl Hubbell, from Carthage, Missouri, was a star, and Hubbell once played a game on that Teegarden pasture-field.

Meanwhile, the James and Anna Belle Swiggart family had moved from Hickman, Nebraska, to the Liberty District just north of Tryon, Oklahoma, in 1899. Their daughter Eva Belle, an attractive brunette, caught the eye of the young, athletic, and handsome Roy Teegarden. The two were married in Eva's home just northeast of Tryon, on September 15, 1912: Roy was eighteen, Eva seventeen. Shortly, they moved to El Reno where Roy worked for the railroad, then returned to Tryon where Roy was employed at the cotton mill until he was injured. Upon his recovery they opened a café with Eva as cook. A daughter, Leonora Lynetta, was born to the couple in 1913. Lured by the oil boom, Roy and Eva decided in October 1919 to leave Tryon and move farther up the Cimarron to Cushing, Oklahoma, convinced it offered a much wider range of prospects. It was there, on December 22, 1921, a son was born to Roy and Eva. They named him Kenneth Leroy Teegarden—a fourth generation Oklahoman and a sixth generation Disciple. No mention of his birth appeared in the local paper. [10]

Childhood Environment: *Nation, State, City, Church, Home*

The 1920s—with World War I on one side and the Great Depression on the other, the years between the Armistice and the Crash—was one of the most sharply defined decades in American history. Like the Teegarden name with its several spellings, the decade had many labels applied to it—Golden Decade, Dollar Decade, The Jazz Age, Age of Ballyhoo, Age of Excess, and The Roaring Twenties. It was a frenzied, enchanted time that saw the introduction of the automobile, the radio, the movies, and the speakeasies, all of which disrupted social conventions—particularly Protestant morality. While the post-Civil War period looked backward with a nostalgic eye toward ante-bellum days, the 1920s looked backward toward the lost Arcadia of the 1890s. And like the decade after the Civil War, the decade after the first world war was a time of emergent conservatism in politics and social philosophy. In both eras the Republican party held an iron grip on national affairs, and government resembled an extension of large corporations, enacting high tariffs, providing laissez-faire oversight, and tax reductions for the well to do. Both eras were marked by a patriotic nationalism. Liberal thought weakened; no one in any political camp seemed capable of mustering an effective alternative to the forces of reaction. By 1920 the populace had become disillusioned with the high ideals of "progressivism" and, according to H. L. Mencken, turned to purely personal ambitions. [11]

The end of the world war brought international and domestic dislocation setting in motion a broad range of social tensions in America: labor disputes, race riots, a Red Scare, anti-immigrant reactions and the fateful internal schism of modernist vs. fundamentalist religious controversies, the best known of which was the Scopes Trial of 1925 on the issue of evolution. It was a time of shameful persecution of minorities, an action growing out of the strong nationalist impulse to preserve the values of an older America in the face of an ascending and powerful new urban culture. Even the fight over the prohibition amendment, wrote Walter Lippmann, "was a test of strength between social orders." The 1920 census revealed for the first time that the majority of persons (51.4 percent) in the United States lived in the city, rather than in rural America. The supremacy of rural, small-town, Protestant America was being challenged by the rise of the city. And when prohibition was repealed, the old order gave way to the new. A long dominant rural culture was superseded by urban culture; skyscrapers and subways displaced the general store and Main Street. [12]

The church in America experienced a post-war (1918–1924) resurgence of denominational loyalty, attendance, and giving. By 1924, according to the *Yearbook of the Churches*, one hundred million persons professed membership in 200,000 congregations. Even the Disciples were described as reaching their peak strength during those years. However, emerging social conditions of the twenties halted a century of Disciples advance as it also halted the century of American evangelicalism. And in 1927, during Kenneth Teegarden's first year in elementary school, the North American Christian Convention was formed, creating two distinct fellowships among Disciples. The division, later manifested institutionally, was born of the controversy over liberal theology and biblical criticism.

Then came the repeal of prohibition in 1933, a severe blow to Protestantism, resulting in a loss of influence over the culture and a diminished hold on American intellectual and literary leadership.

A distinct decline in the moral force of churches became apparent during the late interwar period, causing a partial relinquishment of Protestant leadership in defining values. Simultaneously, a new challenge to the church, religious neo-orthodoxy, made its appearance during the late twenties and early thirties, led by such theological giants as Karl Barth, Paul Tillich, Reinhold and Richard Neibuhr. Angered by the obscurantism and superficiality of the fundamentalists, they launched an intellectual movement advocating the church fulfill its mission by separating itself from the world, rediscovering the gospel, becoming a confessing community, and restoring the preaching office. Individuals, they believed, were capable of altruistic behavior, but not institutions; therefore, the church should stand apart from the world. [13]

Teegardens in Cushing, Oklahoma

For 100 years, reaching back to the decades before the land runs and statehood and extending forward well into the 1970s, families named Teegarden played modest roles in the development of Oklahoma—cultivating the soil and working in the oil fields of the Cimarron Valley. At the time of Kenneth Teegarden's birth, December 22, 1921, Oklahoma was still a raw and clumsy young state, just fourteen years removed from its territorial days. The state capital building in Oklahoma City was completed only three years before. [14]

One Oklahoma historian described the cultural setting surrounding the 1921 birth of Kenneth Teegarden, as "a time of turmoil and disorder." Seven months before his birth, the Tulsa race riot took more than 100 African American lives in two days of white rioting, and fifty-one lynchings of blacks were reported across the nation in 1922. On a global scale, racial identity had become the justifier of power, privilege, and property. During the course of that same year both the eighteenth (prohibition) and nineteenth (women's suffrage) amendments to the United States Constitution were approved by the Oklahoma legislature bringing much social disruption to the new state. Through the first nine years of Kenneth's life, four Oklahoma governors were impeached and two removed from office. The most prominent political group in the state at the time of the 1920 election was the resurgent Ku Klux Klan, an organization driven by its exploitation of human prejudices and fears. [15]

In Kenneth's youth, old-timers found much pleasure in recounting stories of their days in the quiet little village of early Cushing. They spoke of the Johnson Brothers saloon, Doc Hayes Drugstore, and of old Tom Symes, a one-legged blacksmith with a metal cap on the end of his peg leg, whose shop was under a black-jack tree on the northeast corner of Walnut and Noble. And they talked of the livery stable located near the mud puddle at the intersection of Harrison and Main. Marion Eaton, the first barber in Cushing, was the subject of many colorful stories because he "fought and shot a lot" and was a member of the town posse. Kenneth and his young friends were especially taken with the legends of Bitter Creek Newcomb, the Bill Doolan gang, and the daring bank robberies of the infamous Dalton brothers. Tales of the Sac and Fox Indians, removed to North Central Oklahoma during the last half of the nineteenth century, were often retold, but by the time Kenneth left Cushing in the mid-1930s, a full blooded Sac and Fox was a rarity. The town in which Kenneth was born consisted of streets, houses, and shops, none of which was more than thirty years old. This was the world he would make his own. [16]

The first decade of Kenneth's life saw the character of the town transform into a materialistic Eden. Oil was discovered on the Frank Wheeler farm near Cushing, March 17, 1912, a discovery that became world famous under the name of the Drumright Field. Cushing evolved from a wild and unruly oil boomtown to a sophisticated small city, causing one national magazine to portray the community as "Cushing—The Wonder City." From 1914 to 1927 the number of producing wells grew from 786 to 2,375, generating more than eight million barrels per month at its peak.

Twenty-three oil company installations and five supply houses appeared, triggering a population boom from approximately 1,000 in 1910 to 10,000 in 1930. [17]

The business district became a showplace and trading center for the counties of Payne, Lincoln, and Creek. The $200,000 new Dunkin theater opened on Broadway in 1926; the *Cushing Citizen* was established in 1925. In 1922 C.R. Anthony opened the first of his national chain of stores in Cushing; 1924 saw J.C. Penney place a store in the 100 block of East Broadway. Two rail lines were competing fiercely for Cushing's commerce—the Santa Fe and the famed Katy. The Long Bell Lumber Company, Safeway, Piggly Wiggly, and F.W. Woolworth were businesses that started during the decade; and in 1929 Montgomery Ward and Co. opened a store on the southwest corner of Broadway and Harrison streets. Kenneth's sister, Leonora, began working at Wards the year it opened and retired there forty years later in 1970. Kenneth and the city grew together. It was a memorable era for Cushing—alive, exciting, bustling—boyhood poetry for a lad under the age of ten. [18]

Following a brief employment at the Cushing post office, Roy became, for many years thereafter, an equipment manager and salesman in the Cushing oil fields. Eva had attended Tryon schools through the tenth grade and then spent two years at Teachers Normal in Chandler, 1911–1912. Her mother, Anna Belle Swiggart had been an early campaigner for women's suffrage, an active WCTU member, and an author who wrote poetry for the campaign of William Jennings Bryan. "When I was a little boy, three or four years old," recalled Kenneth, "I remember sitting on my grandmother's lap and hearing her quote a poem she had written, 'Hurrah for Billy Bryan!'; and one of the first speeches I learned when I was ten or twelve was William Jennings Bryan's oration on labor, in which he said, 'You shall not press down upon the brow of labor this crown of thorns! You shall not crucify mankind on a cross of gold!'" [19]

After her marriage to Roy, Eva supplemented their uncertain family income by taking in boarders and with intermittent teaching assignments. Their home, 215 East Moses, was a modest white clapboard house. Eva, stricken with severe asthma, was in and out of the hospital a good bit of the time and, due to the extensive travel demands on his father, Kenneth was often shuttled back and forth between the house on Moses Street and the homes of nearby relatives, particularly the farm of his grandmother Teegarden and fun-loving aunt Hazel—remembered as a "real character." Kenneth spent most of his summers on aunt Hazel's farm, where he raised Spangled Hamburg chickens, successfully competing with them at the state fair, winning eight blue ribbons. His sister, Leonora, who never married, became something of a surrogate mother, caring for Kenneth through those early years. Fifty-five years later, Kenneth observed, "I've always felt Leonora made a lot of sacrifices for me." A glimpse into his young life is found in an old letter surviving Kenneth's childhood, a letter he wrote to his mother during one of her absences when he was staying with uncle Edgar and aunt Nettie Swiggart. In a child's scrawl, but with correct spelling and an articulate ability beyond his years, he wrote:

> *Cushing, Oklahoma*
> *Wed. afternoon*

> *Dear Mother:*
> *How are you? I am fine. Gerald and Forrest (cousins) made a snow house. I play in it every day. It is fun.*
> *I made 70 in my arithmetic test and 95 in my spelling test.*
> *Aunt Nettie made some doughnuts, and Florine (cousin) and I a gingerbread boy. They were good too.*
> *I don't think I have to go to school Friday but just to get my grade card.*
> *I went to Aunt Nettie's house two times for dinner and took my lunch today.*
> *I went with Leonora to a basketball game Saturday night and to a wrestling match Monday night, and going to another basketball game Thursday night and wrestling Friday night.*
> *So I must close,*
> *Kenneth Teegarden*

Eva, a gifted conversationalist, was head of the family, the one who set the example and explained expectations to the children. Her devotion to them was never in doubt. Roy, a quiet but caring man, a listener, stood mostly in the background of his son's life, a distant figure due to the demands on him for frequent travel, and to a partial obscurity created by the dominant and nurturing presence of Kenneth's mother and sister. Seeing his father only rarely, Kenneth knew him as someone other than an authoritarian, omniscient figure. [20]

The centerpiece of the Teegarden family during the 1920s was First Christian Church, founded in 1903, in Cushing, Indian Territory. When Kenneth was four years old plans were laid to construct a new brick church building on the corner of Moses and Noble. It was dedicated February 20, 1927, with more than 1,300 persons in attendance. Commenting on his childhood experience there in later years, Kenneth said, "the church was all I knew." In spite of her illnesses and her work, Eva was scrupulously faithful to her perfect attendance at Sunday school, compiling an unbroken record of twenty years. It was amusingly said that she resented Kenneth's birth because she had to miss one Sunday. Perfect attendance at Sunday school became a practice Kenneth began when he was three-weeks old, and which he maintained for a remarkable twenty-nine years, filling his lapel with medals. He was zestfully active in the Cushing Church, pastored by Clyde Sherman, Ivan Young, and Shelvy Anglemyer. In Anglemyer, especially, Kenneth found a kindred spirit, an influence that eventually drew Kenneth into ministry. Anglemyer was a man of medium stature, sandy hair, who wore round, horn rimmed glasses, and who ingratiated himself to people with his gentle, scholarly demeanor, his erudite sermons, and the quiet wisdom of his counsel. He was particularly good with youth. It was said of him—in the tradition of Plato's academy, "he held before the young a vision of greatness." Kenneth's spiritual journey began here. Late in life Kenneth was asked about those persons he considered mentors, the shapers of his life and thought. He named three persons, one of whom was Shelvy Anglemeyer. "As a young boy and teenager," recalled Kenneth, "I had local pastors who believed they had a responsibility to encourage young people to go into ministry. They laid out the ministry as a viable professional choice. A man by the name of Shelvy Anglemeyer did that for me . . . and he made arrangements for me to receive a scholarship at Phillips University." Early in his second term as general minister and president, Kenneth received a letter from Reverend Anglemyer: "I remember your decision to dedicate your life to the Christian ministry . . . congratulations upon your fine leadership. I think often of your advance through the years to the position you now hold in our Brotherhood." In his lengthy response, Kenneth commented, "I am deeply indebted to you for your influence early in my life. Your model and example have been important to me." [21] First Christian Church in Cushing was the birthplace of Kenneth's faith, a fact it would never forget. And Kenneth never forgot his humble beginnings.

Modern Cushing—known as the "Pipelines Crossroads of the World," has grown eastward toward an expansive new high school campus and stadium. The former business district exists mostly in memory and is no longer a showplace. Kenneth's schools—his old high school now a practice field—have been demolished. So has his church, and also one of the houses in which he lived. But the stately new First Christian Church has an elegant foyer with a tastefully appointed welcoming parlor. And on the east wall of that parlor is a large, color portrait of Kenneth. On the frame is a small gold plate proudly announcing to the viewer—*Kenneth L. Teegarden, General Minister and President of the Christian Church (Disciples of Christ), 1973–1985—Timothy, of First Christian Church, Cushing.* [22]

TEEGARDEN GENEALOGICAL CHART

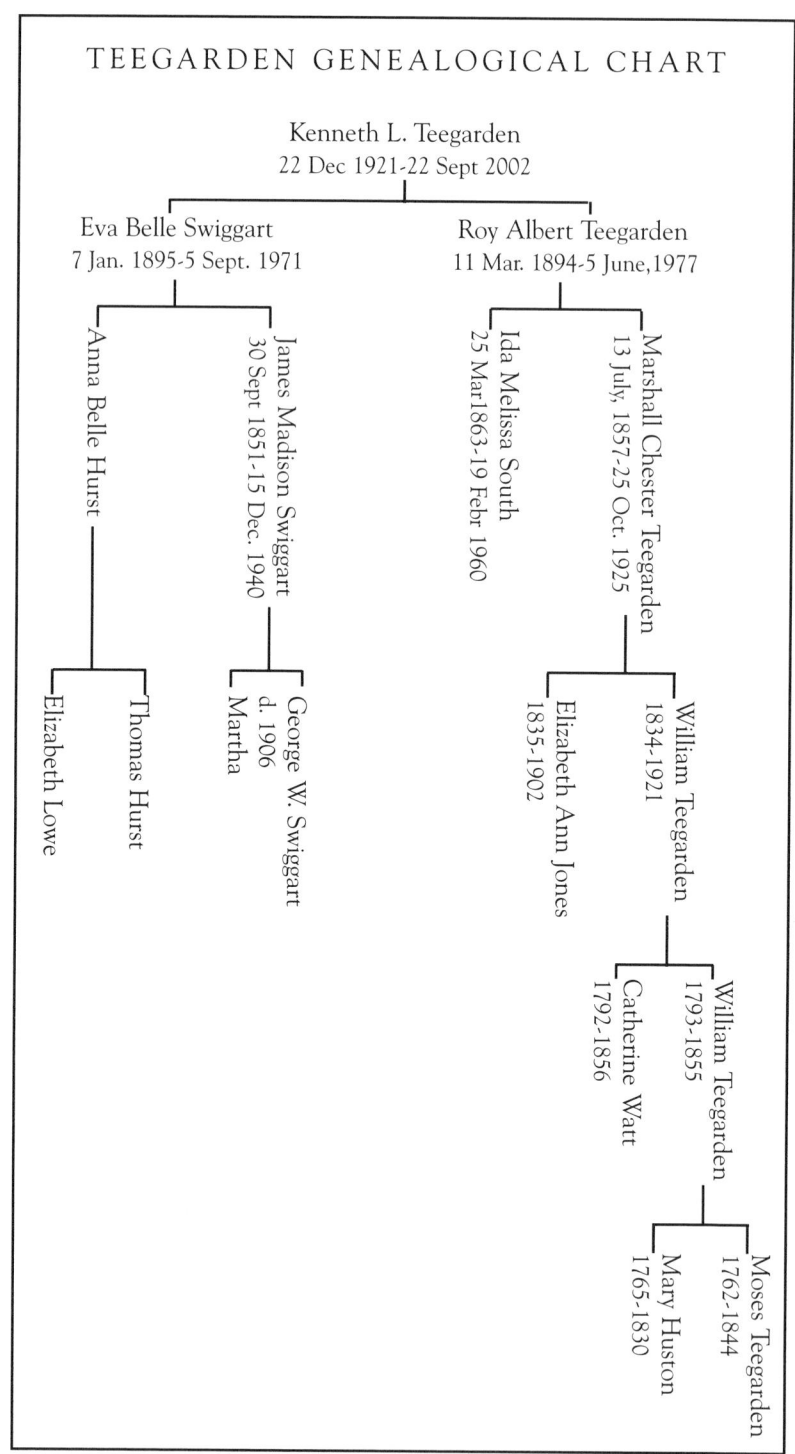

Kenneth L. Teegarden
22 Dec 1921-22 Sept 2002

Eva Belle Swiggart
7 Jan. 1895-5 Sept. 1971

Roy Albert Teegarden
11 Mar. 1894-5 June,1977

Anna Belle Hurst

James Madison Swiggart
30 Sept 1851-15 Dec. 1940

Ida Melissa South
25 Mar1863-19 Febr 1960

Marshall Chester Teegarden
13 July, 1857-25 Oct. 1925

Elizabeth Lowe

Thomas Hurst

George W. Swiggart
d. 1906

Martha

Elizabeth Ann Jones
1835-1902

William Teegarden
1834-1921

Catherine Watt
1792-1856

William Teegarden
1793-1855

Mary Huston
1765-1830

Moses Teegarden
1762-1844

NOTES

1. *Dr. Kenneth L. Teegarden, A Service of Remembrance,* University Christian Church, Fort Worth, Texas, September 26, 2002, 1.

2. Helen Elizabeth Vogt, *Descendants of Abraham Teegarden* (Willowick, Ohio: George and Shirley Teegarden, 1988), 11.

3. Ibid., 13–14; Genforum: http://genforum.genealogy.com/teegarden/ [Accessed November 5, 2005].

4. Alan Taylor, *American Colonies,* (New York: Penguin, 2001), 318–319; Vogt, Descendants, 23–30; Lani Johnson. "Friendship and Trust," The Disciple. (June 1, 1980): 4.

5. Vogt, *Descendants of Abraham Teegarden,* 23–30.

6. Ibid., 631–632.

7. Ibid., 730–731.

8. Ibid., 745; Newspaper interview with William Teegarden (1834–1921). About 1905. Undated clipping. Wanda Teegarden Collection.

9. Lincoln County Historical Society. *History of Lincoln County Oklahoma,* 1988, p. 1334; Vogt, *Descendants,* 758; *Cushing Citizen.* Obituary, Ida Teegarden, February 21, 1960.

10. Interview with Wanda Teegarden, February 24, 2005; *History of Lincoln County Oklahoma,* p. 1334; *Cushing Weekly Citizen.* Obituary, Roy Teegarden, June 6, 1977; *Cushing Weekly Citizen. Obituary,* Eva Teegarden, September 6, 1971; *Cushing Weekly Citizen.* December 22 and 29, 1921.

11. Samuel Eliot Morison, Henry Steele Commager, and William E. Leuchtenburg, *The Growth of the American Republic,* Vol. II (New York: Oxford University Press, 1980), 418–419, 427; James MacGregor Burns, *The American Experiment,* Vol. II (New York: Alfred Knopf & Co., 1985), 508–509; David Traxel, *The United States in Peace and the Great War: 1898–1920* (New York: Alfred Knopf & Co., 2006), 354.

12. Andrew Sinclair, *Era of Excess* (New York: Little, Brown & Co., 1962), 5, 220–221; William Leuchtenburg, *The Perils of*

Prosperity (Chicago: University of Chicago Press, 1958), 7; Edward Larson, *The Scopes Trial* (New York: Basic Books, 1997), 68–78.

13. Lester G. McAllister and William Eldon Tucker, *Journey in Faith: A History of the Christian Church (Disciples of Christ)* (St. Louis: Bethany Press, 1975), 359; Sydney Ahlstrom, *A Religious History of the American People* (New Haven: Yale University Press, 1972), 895–941; Martin Marty, *Modern American Religion: 1919–1941*, Vol. II (Chicago: University of Chicago Press, 1991), 10–23.

14. Arrell Morgan Gibson, *Oklahoma* (Norman: University of Oklahoma Press, 1981), 209.

15. Ibid., 212–220; Kevin Boyle, *Arc of Justice* (New York: Henry Holt & Co., 2004), 123.

16. Laura Lou Wells, *Young Cushing in Oklahoma Territory* (Perkins, OK: Evans Publications, 1985), 16–17, 31, 35–36, 108; Earl D. Newsom, *The Story of Payne County* (Stillwater, Okla.: New Forums Press, 1997), 91–97; William Hagan, *The Sac and Fox Indians* (Norman, OK: University of Oklahoma Press, 1958), 245–265.

17. *Harlow Weekly Magazine.* Vol. 8, No. 24. June 5, 1915. (as quoted in Wells, Young Cushing.)

18. Newsom, *Payne County*, 43, 81–83; V.V. Masterson, *The Katy Railroad* (Norman: University of Oklahoma Press, 1952), 273.

19. *History of Lincoln County, Oklahoma*, 1326; Johnson, "Friendship and Trust," 4.

20. Interview with Wanda Teegarden. February 24, 2005; Telephone interview with Wanda Teegarden, November 3, 2005; Interview with Wanda Teegarden, November 17, 2005; Kenneth Teegarden to Eva Teegarden, about 1927. Wanda Teegarden Collection; Mazie Cox Read, "Disciples of Christ leader recalls Cushing boyhood," *Cushing Tribune.* 1977. p. 1; Blue Ribbon collection 1934–1935 for poultry. Wanda Teegarden Collection.

21. Interview with Wanda Teegarden. February 24, 2005; David A. Roozen Interview with Kenneth L. Teegarden. Nd. 311.

Wanda Teegarden Collection; Johnson, "Friendship and Trust," 4; Author unknown. "History of First Christian Church, Cushing, Okla." Unpublished. Ten pages. October 2004. 1–2; Shelvy Anglemyer to Kenneth L. Teegarden, March 5, 1980. General Minister and President files, Disciples of Christ Historical Society, Nashvhille, TN. Correspondence A, 1; Kenneth L. Teegarden to Shelvy Anglemyer, March 13, 1980, GMP files, DCHS. Correspondence A, 1.

22. Visit by author to Cushing, Chandler, and Tryon, Oklahoma, February 15, 2006.

The Education of an Oklahoma Pastor

I have made an important decision for my life.
A week ago Sunday, I dedicated my life to Christian
service, and have decided to go to Phillips next year
and study for the ministry.
Kenneth L. Teegarden

Early Schooling

"My mother served meals to schoolteachers," Kenneth remembered, "to keep the family going . . . as many as ten or twelve schoolteachers would come for lunch and dinner in our home every day . . . the presence of schoolteachers had a very positive influence on me." In 1926, Kenneth Teegarden began his first grade year at Highland Elementary School in Cushing. Although each school year contained 160 days, on average, a student in Oklahoma during that era attended 136 of those days. Kenneth's attendance record, however, was near perfect and his grades were all As and Bs. He enjoyed every aspect of school: his subjects, his friends, and especially his teachers with whom he tended to develop long-term relationships. Among the Highland elementary teachers with whom Kenneth studied in a mutually supportive relationship were Mrs. Lobingier, Miss Smith, Miss Ruth Hinchcliffe, and Mr. Nichols. [1]

By the 1920s the high school had become a flourishing new American institution. Enrollment doubled from 2.2 million in 1920 to 4.4 million in 1930; and the progressive educational philosophy of John Dewey—America's premier educational philosopher—received wide experimentation and exposure. Health, vocational studies, industrial/manual arts, homemaking, music, and social science learning techniques were included within the traditional curriculum as well as instruction tailored to students at different academic levels. [2]

Despite those progressive trends, Kenneth's educational experience was largely traditional. When he enrolled at Cushing Senior High School in 1934, the curriculum he found and in which he excelled over the following four years would best be characterized in today's vocabulary as "college prep." His four-year academic portfolio contained three units of English, four units of American and world history, two units of math, two units of Spanish, two units of public speaking/debate, and one unit of chemistry. The full eighteen-unit requirement for graduation was satisfied with one unit each of typing, journalism and bookkeeping; and one-half credit each in commercial law and business English. Absent from his transcript were John Dewey's suggestions of music, psychology, manual training, vocational studies, and domestic arts, although on his own he learned to play the trumpet and base viol. [3]

Hurst Swiggart, Kenneth's high school speech and debate teacher, was also Kenneth's uncle, brother to his mother Eva. Kenneth possessed outstanding talent for debate, competing in and winning many state, regional, and national contests. A case full of trophies at the school attested to his successes, as well as being named two successive years by the University of Oklahoma as one of the eleven superior high school debaters in the state. While still a student he assisted his uncle in teaching the class. Kenneth emerged from his debating experience an accomplished public speaker, who could construct a convincing argument, convey the sincerity of his feelings, and for whom words came with ease. Above all, debate taught him to express himself. Every turn of phrase was significant to him and he, therefore, learned to weigh the meaning of his words thoughtfully and carefully.

Another teacher with whom he remained in contact through the years was Thelma Zellars, who taught his high school typing class. Kenneth could easily type 100 wpm and was a typist superior to any secretary who ever worked for him. After becoming general minister and president he learned of Miss Zellars address and wrote to her: "I probably profited from that class (typing) as much as any other I had. As a matter of fact, I virtually paid my way through college as a typist, serving for a couple of years as a clerk typist to the dean of arts and sciences at then Oklahoma A & M and then for a couple of years as a secretary to the president of Phillips University. Of course, even more important than the typing skills you taught me was the evident interest you took in me as a person. I will always be grateful to you for your influence." [4]

Evidence of his talent for leadership began to appear during his high school years. He was elected president of his junior class, president of the Spanish club, captain of the debate team, president of the Oilers, and in his senior year Kenneth was elected president of the Cushing High School 20-member student council for 1937–38. He was also named "outstanding senior"—from a class of 124—by student peers and the faculty. In all four of his high school years, 1934–1938, he was named to the Oklahoma High School Honor Society for his academic achievement.

Kenneth's schooling occurred during the very heart of the Great Depression. According to the city librarian, and confirmed by one of Kenneth's classmates, the high school could not afford to produce a yearbook when he graduated. In Oklahoma, especially, there was mass unemployment resulting in mortgage foreclosures, bank failures, and large dislocation of families. The western part of the state, hub of the Dust Bowl, was tragically devastated. Governor William H. "Alfalfa Bill" Murray faced an Oklahoma state treasury with a $5 million deficit, but he made certain that free textbooks were provided to the Oklahoma schools. Many churches couldn't pay ministers and some simply discontinued preaching as part of their worship. The Disciples saw all of their institutions and agencies damaged by the Depression. The United Christian Missionary Society, for example, received $2.9 million in income in 1929, but only $1.4 million in 1935. Kenneth's school, his home, and his congregation in Cushing were battered by the austerity of the Great Depression. It put strain on an already lean Teegarden family budget, but each member knew the value of a dollar and lived modestly. Roy scrambled to find work and took it wherever he could get it. [5]

College Years

Following graduation from high school in 1938, at age sixteen, Kenneth enrolled at Oklahoma A & M College in Stillwater, "to become a lawyer." "I completed ninety hours of pre-law," he reported, "and had been admitted to law school." His plan was to practice law with the intent of entering politics. Uncle Hurst had encouraged him to study American history and speech in high school as preparation for this career path. With that ambition, the lanky sixteen-year-old took on the A & M academic program in September. By May of 1940 he had completed ninety hours of course work on the quarter system, highlighted by eighteen hours of American history and government, sixteen hours of European history, nine hours of state and municipal government and political parties, and nine hours of speech and debate. It was a challenging regimen, clearly designed for law school entry. In those subjects Kenneth made nearly all As and Bs.[6] And what he learned from these studies would serve as a rich constitutional and organizational resource two decades later when he led the restructure of the Association of Christian Churches in Arkansas and then became administrative secretary of the Commission on Brotherhood Restructure, charged with designing a governance model for the whole Disciples church.

His passion for debate continued in college and, once again, he participated in national competitions. It was on a 1940 debate trip to the University of Tennessee in March that Kenneth experienced a change of heart about his chosen career. To his mother, he wrote only of the events of the trip.

March 27

Dear Mother

I'm getting along just fine. We've already had six of the eight debates. We don't debate today because we are going on this tour of a hundred miles. We debated against Colorado State, William Penn, Augustana College, Ouachita College, Macalester College, and Illinois Wesleyan. We have found out the first five decisions. We won two and lost three and think maybe we won the sixth.

We are really having a good time. I think there are about 635 students here . . . Our rooms are costing us $1.50 apiece per day [Andrew Johnson Hotel, Knoxville] and meals, noon & evening, an average of 50 cents.

We don't have a chance to win since we have already lost three, but if we won the one last night we have a chance of breaking even, or winning five and losing three. There are schools here from the Atlantic to the Pacific, and from Maine to Texas.

I'll probably see you on Sunday.

Love,
Kenneth [7]

Within days of writing that letter, religious thought awakened in Kenneth and he made the profound decision not to continue his pursuit of a career in law, but to use his life, instead, for

Christian ministry. One evening, upon his return from Tennessee, he consulted at length with his pastor Shelvy Anglemyer about this interior transformation. Recognizing that Kenneth was struggling with a crucial decision, Anglemyer provided support and encouragement, including the arrangement for a scholarship to attend Phillips University to prepare for ministry. Later that same evening, after counseling with Kenneth, Reverend Anglemyer conducted an ordination service for Harold Abraham, a math teacher at Cushing high school, who subsequently performed solid ministries in Tulsa, Kansas City, and New Orleans. Kenneth attended the ordination service, and years later, was called upon by Harold to be a reference.

Within a few days, Kenneth shared the news of his decision to enter ministry with his father whose work had again taken him away from Cushing.

April 22, 1940

Dear Dad

It has been a long time since I have seen you. I hope you are getting along o.k. and will get to come home soon. I am doing some speaking now. Two weeks ago Frank Martin asked me to go to Bristow and speak at the Rotary Club. Wednesday I am going to Crescent and speak in the high school. While you have been gone I have made an important decision for my life. A week ago Sunday I dedicated my life to Christian service and have decided to go to Phillips next year and study for the ministry. I am making arrangements for work and I will get a scholarship so it will make it so I won't have to have much money from home. Reverend Anglemyer is seeing that I get a good deal. I hope that this decision will agree with you. I would have written to you from Tennessee but I did not know where you were. Come home as soon as you can.

Your Son,
Kenneth [8]

Roy Teegarden was somewhere in Illinois when he received this letter; but it is not known if he responded. What is known, however, is that he kept the letter and many years later returned it to Kenneth, who cherished it as a prized possession for the remainder of his life.

Kenneth's own account of what triggered this life changing decision was simple and straight forward: "I was a college debater and went to the national college debate tournament at the University of Tennessee. While I was there, I decided I didn't really want to be a lawyer. I wanted to be a preacher. I seriously reflected on where I felt I could make myself count for the most. My experience in the church and my appreciation for those who had been my pastors led me to think that a career as a pastor and preacher would be more fruitful. In terms of relating to people and their welfare and making a positive contribution to society, I believed I could do more in ministry than in law. I was interested in a more personal way of working with people, and at a deeper level of existence, than their defense."[9] Kenneth had gained the insight that political and cultural preoccupations of the day are secondary to the problems of the human heart.

Phillips University, founded in 1907, was a Bible college and liberal arts institution related to the Disciples. It consisted of eight buildings, forty-three faculty and 867 students. Of those students, 219 were enrolled in the College of the Bible, 156 men and sixty-three women. Overwhelmingly, the students in the College of the Bible came from Oklahoma (seventy-five) and Kansas (fifty-three), giving the campus a provincial bearing. The next largest group came from the perimeter states of Arkansas, Texas, Colorado, New Mexico, and Nebraska. Only about a dozen students came from geography beyond that rim, and only one of those was an international student. Most of the students were from small town backgrounds. Their fathers were farmers, ministers, tradesmen or owners of small businesses, a typical profile of students preparing for ministry during the middle decades of the century.[10]

In the fall of 1940, Kenneth arrived on campus exhibiting a virtually inexhaustible store of energy, a trait indelibly fixed in his character. In less than twenty-one months he completed sixty-two hours of course work and a Bachelor of Arts degree, graduating in May 1942. Simultaneously he was editor of the student newspaper, *The Haymaker;* was president of the The Harvesters social service club; performed the lead in a school play, Adolph Caesar; and was elected to Blue Key, the men's highest academic recognition at Phillips University. He earned most of his way through Phillips as typist for the president, a radio disc jockey, and a short order cook, while receiving modest help from his parents and his sister Leonora. On weekends he earned some additional income as student pastor at First Christian Church in Kaw City, Oklahoma. [11]

During November of his first semester at Phillips in 1940, he learned that the Christian Church at Kaw City was without a pastor. The community, with a population of approximately 350, was located on the Arkansas River in the northeastern part of Oklahoma, about sixty-five miles from Enid. It was a small congregation of 110 members and had a budget of slightly less than $900 per year. Without forewarning the congregation or the university, Kenneth took a train from Enid to a point as near Kaw City as he could and then walked the final few miles. Upon his arrival at the church he boldly announced, "I understand you do not have a pastor. I am Kenneth Teegarden, a ministerial student at Phillips University, and I am here to preach for you." After the service, he was asked if he could preach every Sunday. A suitable agreement was thereupon negotiated and Kenneth became their minister, November 10, 1940, and remained at the church until January 24,1943. [12]

At Thanksgiving, when Kenneth returned home to Cushing for vacation break, the Reverend Shelvy Anglemyer suggested that, since he had a church, perhaps he should think about becoming ordained. Kenneth agreed, and they planned an ordination for the Christmas holiday. At a special called meeting of the Official Congregational Board on Sunday, December 15th, the Reverend Mr. Anglemyer recommended Kenneth as a candidate for ministry. Dr. Claude R. Swander, elder, Sunday-school superintendent and local dentist, moved that Kenneth be ordained. The motion received a second from deacon E. O. Derrick and passed unanimously. At age eighteen, just three days short of his nineteenth birthday, Kenneth was duly ordained on Wednesday, December 18, 1940, at First Christian Church, Cushing, Oklahoma. Thirty-one years later the Disciples general assembly would approve a formal "Policies and Criteria for the Order of Ministry in the Christian Church (Disciples of Christ)," setting forth a complex procedure for ordination and standing that required the oversight of regional commissions on ministry. By comparison, Kenneth's ordination experience was purely congregational and distinctively nineteenth century in its features. Reflecting on his ordination fifty years later, Kenneth observed, "We have moved a long way from that. Now we have policies and criteria for the order of ministry that function very respectably. These have been helpful in stabilizing the ministry and furthering our ecumenical relationships. I am not sure, however, it has improved the quality of ministry." [13]

At age nineteen, Kenneth performed his first funeral at Kaw City. The man had died in prison, a victim of cancer, and it was decided the wake would be held in a private home in the countryside. But the doors in the home were too narrow for the casket to pass. Window frames in the side of the house were removed and the casket lifted in through those openings. Kenneth conducted the memorial service in the living room, after which the group moved to the cemetery for the graveside rites. The deceased's sister arrived late, missed the service in the home, but appeared in time for the graveside ceremony. She asked if the casket could be opened since she had not seen her brother in several years. So Kenneth had the casket opened. And the sister exclaimed, "This is not my brother!" People were stunned. Kenneth had the presence of mind to quickly arrange for the corpse to be fingerprinted and compared with those on file in the sheriff's office. They matched. Cancer had emaciated the woman's brother to such a condition that she simply did not recognize him. Such an unexpected experience might have caused Kenneth to have second thoughts about ministry. But he took it all in stride—although he remembered the experience at every funeral service he conducted thereafter.

Now that he had a church and was ordained, Kenneth applied himself to learning how to be a minister. During his first two terms at Phillips University, he enrolled in thirty hours of course work, twenty-two of which were taught by Professor Spencer Marion Smith, holder of M.A. and B.D. degrees from Phillips and nearing completion of his Ph.D. at the University of Chicago. Among the courses Kenneth studied with Professor Smith were The Science and Art of Preaching, Logic, The Development of the Sermon, Introduction to Philosophy, and two semesters of Elementary Greek. He took six hours in church doctrine from Dr. Claude Carson Taylor, a 1909 Phillips graduate, who later received his Ph.D. from Southern Baptist Theological Seminary, in Fort Worth. He capped his first year with the course, Great English Poetry, taught by Dr. Henry Grady Rooker, graduate of Vanderbilt and George Peabody, and professor of English at Phillips. [14]

In the summer term of 1941 Kenneth began studying with the acclaimed and celebrated legends of Phillips University. First among them was the old servant of God and honored academic pioneer, Dr. Frank Hamilton Marshall, dean of the graduate school of the College of the Bible. Marshall, born in 1868, was the holder of seven earned degrees: three from Butler, one from Phillips, one from TCU, one from the University of Chicago, and a Ph.D. from Yale. Everyone referred to him as "The Dean." He had produced through his teaching over 1000 Christian workers, including 781 ministerial graduates, twenty-four professors and twenty-seven missionaries. His fabled chapel sermons—dynamic, challenging, eloquent—were peerless and the scriptures he used were always quoted from memory. Chiseled features, a spare frame, a quick gait, clear-cut diction, a demanding but fair teacher, a taciturn expression that masked a warm sense of humor, all of these endeared him to his students. "The Dean," author of two books, was a commanding figure, universally beloved and a pillar of conservatism among Disciples. By 1941 he was one year from retirement, a veteran who had given himself wholly to the church as missionary, pastor, teacher and dean. [15]

Kenneth's first course with Dr. Marshall was the Epistle of Peter, taken in the summer of 1941. In subsequent semesters he chose four more courses taught by "The Dean:" Matthew and Mark, James and John, Acts of the Apostles, and Intermediate Greek. Dr. Marshall required his students to memorize scripture. On one occasion Kenneth had not found time to memorize his assignment. When "The Dean" called on him to recite, Kenneth thought the better part of wisdom was to be honest. So he stood and said forthrightly to Professor Marshall: "I am not prepared," then sat down. Dr. Marshall was silent for a moment before responding in a withering tone in front of the whole class: "Mr. Teegarden, people expect their lawyers to know a little law; they expect their doctors to know a little medicine; and they expect their ministers to know a little scripture!" Kenneth said he could not recall ever feeling so humiliated. He never again attended Marshall's class unprepared. [16]

During his second year, Kenneth began studying the Old Testament with Professor Robert Martin, chair of the undergraduate school of the College of the Bible, in his eighth year as a member of the university faculty. Martin had earned three degrees from Phillips University, the first in 1928, and was accumulating hours toward his Ph.D. at both the University of Chicago and Southern Baptist Theological Seminary. Kenneth selected three of Martin's courses: Old Testament Literature, Messianic Prophets, and Hebrew Prophets. To his Old Testament studies he added a single course on religious education entitled Education Work in the Church, taught by Dr. Wilford Powell, a 1919 graduate of Phillips and holder of a Ph.D. from Yale. [17]

Kenneth deepened his understanding of the New Testament and explored in greater breadth the history of the Disciples Movement by enrolling in a succession of five courses taught by the distinguished Dr. Stephen J. England. Professor of church history and patristic Greek, England was a 1924 graduate of Phillips, a 1940 Ph.D. recipient from Yale, a former parish minister, author of six books, and would later become founding dean of the Phillips Graduate Seminary and president of the International Convention of the Christian churches. Not as conservative as Marshall, and influenced by the neo-orthodox theology which sought to reclaim classic themes from the sixteenth century Protestant Reformation, England succeeded Frank Marshall as dean of the College of the Bible in 1942 and served in that position for the next twenty years. The renowned Dr. England taught Kenneth in these courses: Introduction to the New Testament, Introduction to New Testament Literature, The Life of Paul, The Church in the Modern World, and History of The Restoration Movement. [18]

But the person who had the most profound influence on Kenneth, the second of his three life's mentors, was Dr. Ralph Waldo Nelson, professor of philosophy and philosophy of religion. He was a 1915 Phillips graduate, recipient of a B.D. from Yale in 1918, and a Ph.D. from the University of Chicago in 1931. Nelson, who had been on the Phillips faculty since 1927, was the author of two books, *Experimental Christianity* and *Experimental Logic of Jesus,* as well as numerous pamphlets. It was the content of the *Experimental Logic of Jesus* that so impressed Kenneth, and helped him formulate the philosophical principles that guided him throughout his ministry. From the distant year of 1990, Kenneth reflected, "[Dr. Nelson] melded together the concepts of reason and emotion with Lockean philosophy. That under-girding principle in my religious faith influenced me strongly all during my life." He enrolled in eight courses under Dr. Nelson, totaling twenty-three hours, including the direction of his master's thesis. Among those courses were the Philosophy of Jesus, two courses in Applied Christianity, Philosophy of Religion, Christianity and War, Current Christian Philosophy, and two independent studies on Research Problems. Nelson was clearly Kenneth's favorite professor, the one who opened new intellectual landscapes and challenged his thought. [19]

The professors who prepared Kenneth for ministry were notable as scholars, as churchmen and for their Christian character. They were excellent teachers who for two generations arguably prepared more mid-twentieth century leaders for the Christian Church (Disciples of Christ) than any other college in the United States. They held more in common as well. All were born in the nineteenth century, all but Marshall earned their first degree from Phillips, all had been students of Frank Hamilton Marshall, and nearly all had a graduate degree from Yale, a divinity school that was pioneering a six track vocational approach to ministerial education. The stated purposes of the Phillips College of the Bible curriculum reflected the education of its professoriat, and sought

> 1. to provide three years of professional training for ministers;
> 2. to provide instruction that would enable the students to enter the divinity schools of the great universities; and
> 3. to offer courses of instruction as practical as is consistent with standardized work.

In a word, the tone and substance of the College of the Bible was conservative and was vocationally designed so students could go directly from undergraduate studies into the pastorate. Phillips was considered a citadel of conservatism within Discipledom—an image reinforced by the political and cultural values surrounding it in Oklahoma, the core geography for which the school supplied ministers. Kenneth disliked labels of any kind, and was, therefore, able to free himself from the conservatism of his environment, to learn what he thought he needed to learn without being ideologically indoctrinated. He emerged with his religious temperament blended with a growing intellectual rationalism. Kenneth was fortunate to be taught by seasoned, scholarly, accomplished, and congregationally oriented professors, and he absorbed the best they offered.

Near Christmas of 1942, a benchmark year in Kenneth's life, he received a letter from his father. It was one of only two letters from his father that are known to have been preserved by Kenneth. Roy wrote to Kenneth from Salem, Illinois, wishing him a happy twenty-first birthday and explaining why he could not come home for Christmas.

> *December 14, 1942*
>
> *Dear Son*
>
> *I am sending you $25 for your birthday . . . also for Christmas. Hope you are ok and that you have a big time on your 21st birthday. I can say I am mighty proud of you as a son. Keep up the good work and you will go places. . . . I wish I could be with you Christmas but it looks like I can't. Lots of work to do and a long trip to make. I am sending your Mother $75 so they can have a good Christmas. That extra work came in mighty handy. . . . Have a good time Christmas and write me when you have time. I will see you some time after the first of the year when I can get away. Here is hoping you have a nice happy birthday, Kenneth. You have done fine and I am proud of you.*
>
> *Your Dad*

The final phrase in that letter was not just an idle or passing comment. Thirty-two years later, after being elected general minister and president, Kenneth received a letter from an Oklahoma pastor who unknowingly revealed the enduring genuineness of his father's feeling, "I saw your dad the other day. . . . that is one proud man of his son! " [20]

Having completed all requirements, Kenneth was awarded a Bachelor of Arts in New Testament Language and Literature on May 25, 1942. That fall he returned to Phillips with a job as assistant public relations director and debate coach and with the intent of earning both masters of arts and bachelor of divinity degrees. After successfully completing two more semesters along with the summer session of 1943, and being named friendliest male graduate student on campus, Kenneth was discovered smoking a cigarette. The spartan and uncompromising rules of the university in those days forbade, among other things, smoking, dancing, drinking, and wearing certain types of clothing such as plaid trousers on campus. The penalty was suspension. For this infraction he was suspended but he gained readmission in the summer session of 1945 to resume his work. [21]

Husband, Father, and Pastor

A little growth had occurred in the measurable variables at the Kaw City church during Kenneth's student ministry. When he arrived the membership numbered 110 and the annual budget was a shade below $900. When he left the membership stood at 113 and the budget was $950. He led a large outdoor revival meeting there in, August 1941. But he is especially remembered in Kaw City for instigating a huge scrap metal drive during World War II. Kenneth was chairman of the local salvage committee in Kaw City and organized fifteen local merchants and the Boy Scout troop to initiate the drive. As result of an August "Junk Rally" day the drive brought in thirty-five tons of scrap material. In his remarks urging the community to participate, Kenneth said, "A number of young men from this community are already seeing action. We, on the home front, must see to it that industry shall not lack the materials needed for adequately arming and equipping them. As the war becomes more intensive on the various foreign fronts the need for scrap materials has steadily increased. Every pound of scrap we can collect will swell our national production of tanks, ships, planes, and guns." [22]

Following his temporary departure from Phillips, Kenneth resigned his student pastorate at Kaw City in order to accept an offer from First Christian Church in Yale, Oklahoma, January 24, 1943. The congregation at Yale, roughly ten miles north of Cushing, had only 100 members, but a budget of $1,800. Even with a pay raise, Kenneth still needed to supplement his depression era Yale income. Consequently, he accepted a teaching position at Norfolk Consolidated School containing grades one through twelve. The position paid him $130 per month. He preached on Sundays at Yale, then taught speech and English at both junior and senior high school levels, directed the junior and senior class plays and was assistant coach of the women's basketball team as well as basketball game official at Norfolk-where he met his life-long love and companion. [23]

Wanda Strong, a vivacious, multi-talented, strikingly beautiful woman with an adventurous spirit, was a student at the Norfolk school the year Kenneth arrived. She was a member of the women's basketball team for which Kenneth was assistant coach, played trombone in the school band, sang with her gifted voice in the girls quartet, performed several leads in school plays (directed by Kenneth), and was an avid student in Kenneth's speech class. It was his mentoring that helped her win first place in the state American Legion Oratory Contest with her oration entitled, "Democracy's Goals." She also played the piano at evening worship for Kenneth's church at Yale where she was very active in the youth program, attended prayer services and Bible study, and heard Kenneth preach twice every Sunday. Wanda was with Kenneth—as both her teacher and her minister—as much as she was with her own family. [24]

Her family lineage was rooted in Missouri. Henry and Sally Ann Strong, Wanda's grandparents, lived in Ozark County, Missouri, where Henry worked in a sawmill. He married Sally Ann Sanders in 1882 and across the next decade their family increased to include Homer, Artie, Addie, and in 1897 Hiram, Wanda's father. Hiram became a member of the Baptist Church, an active

Mason, and enlisted in the army during World War I. He was honorably discharged on November 22, 1918, following the Armistice. Soon thereafter, in August 1919, he married Caroline O. Shaw, known to her many friends as "Carrie." During the early months of their marriage, Hiram and Carrie moved to Glennpool, Oklahoma, where Hiram began work with Texaco as a painter of their famous logo, the red star. He remained with Texaco for forty-one years. A son, Marvin, was born to them in December of 1920; and two daughters were later added to their family, Lena, born in February 1924, and Wanda Jean, born January 25, 1927, in Tulsa, Oklahoma. [25]

Due to Hiram's work with Texaco, the family moved often. Wanda remembered living in Bristow and Drumright before moving to Norfolk, where she learned to drive her dad's new Pontiac. She recalled, too, the noise and smell of oil wells in her back yard at Drumright. Cushing, by comparison, was always a big city to Wanda, the place where they went to see the doctor, for special shopping trips or to buy groceries. The Strongs eventually joined the Christian church in Cushing, but it was at a church camp in Siloam Springs, Arkansas, where young Wanda, after hearing a powerful sermon by the Reverend Bill Alexander, a favorite camp speaker of Oklahoma church youth, made her confession of faith. [26]

Wanda and Kenneth soon recognized their affection for each other was more than a passing infatuation. A confident public speaker like Kenneth should have had little trouble proposing, but on the occasion of his proposal he was apparently stage struck and somewhat tongue-tied. He, therefore, eased into the proposal, asking Wanda a series of questions, "Do you mind ironing a white shirt now and then?" "Have you ever thought about being a minister's wife?" Finally he got to the main question, and she said yes. They set their wedding date for May 28, 1944. [27]

Kenneth wrote to his father, sharing the news of his engagement and impending marriage. It brought the second of the two letters from his father he would keep for a lifetime.

Salem, Ill. Wed. Noon

Dear Son

    I got your letter, also the one before, but I have been work-
ing night and day. We are building a new store. Most of the
work I am doing myself, and work the fields too . . . . . .

    Well, Kenneth, I was a little surprised to hear who you
was going to marry as I never did hear of you going with her.
I seen Fred Wagner who works for Texaco and he knows the
Strongs well. They say she is a very nice girl and you can't beat
old Hiram .. . . .

    I will be in a meeting at Tulsa on the 25th and 26th, then
on to Cushing. I want to be at your wedding.

    About the car payments, Kenneth, you can just forget
them. That can be your wedding present. . . . .

    I will see you the 27th.

Good Luck. So Long. As Ever,
Dad [28]

Kenneth then prepared himself to support a marriage by seeking a pastorate that could afford a full time minister and allow him
to devote himself to the career he had educated himself to fulfill.
He was offered the position of senior minister at the Manvel
Avenue Christian Church in Chandler, Oklahoma, twenty-six
miles south of Cushing. Founded in the 1880s, its new building
was only fifteen years old. Membership stood at 162 with a budget of $7,700. Manvel Avenue extended the full length of a high
ridge right through the center of Chandler. The red brick
Christian church occupied a prominent location on the far north
end of the avenue near the entry of the town. This would be
Kenneth's first total ministerial experience leading a congregation.
In his previous churches, Kenneth was expected to function more
like a chaplain—preaching on Sundays, taking care of the funerals and weddings—but remaining distant from the management of
congregational affairs. In Chandler he would carry the full responsibility of leadership. [29]

The wedding was held in the Christian church at Chandler at four P.M. on the twenty-eighth of May. Lena Strong, sister of the bride, was maid of honor, and Dr. C. G. Ewing, a physician from Yale and a good friend of Kenneth's, was the best man. Charles Malotte, Kenneth's closest friend from his Phillips student days and who would remain a lifelong confident sharing leadership in the church, conducted the ceremony. Kenneth and Wanda spent their wedding night at the Biltmore Hotel in Oklahoma City, where their car was vandalized and three of Kenneth's suits stolen, then honeymooned at Turner Falls. [30]

Following their honeymoon they moved into their first home at 220 West Eighth in Chandler, next door to the Presbyterian church, and soon acquired a black cocker spaniel named Inky. Kenneth also acquired a little black minister's book in 1940 and listed therein all the weddings, baptisms and funerals he conducted from 1940 to 1958. In 1944 he began listing in a black, three ring notebook the title and date of every sermon he preached from then until 1958, when he left congregational ministry. We know, therefore, that he launched his ministry in Chandler with a series of sermons under the theme, "A Faith to Live By." His first five sermons, all based on New Testament scriptures, were entitled "Finding Life's Meaning," "How We May Know Reality," "The Secret of Living," "Equal to Life's Demands," and "Living Creatively". In one year the congregation grew to 178 members and by the time he resigned in late 1946 to accept a pastorate in Texas, the budget had grown to nearly $10,500. More significantly, $3,340 of that budget was earmarked for outreach, compared to $780 when he began his Chandler ministry. Remarkably, the building indebtedness was paid off in full and a new Kilgen pipe organ was purchased and installed. Other sermons preached during his final year at Chandler included "Low Flames on the Altar of God," "The Church Builds Anew through People," "The Church Builds Anew through Possessions," and "An Angel in the Sun." The articulate titles and substantive content often moved people to request Kenneth to preach them a second time. [31]

Always active in civic affairs and community life, he was chairman of the Chandler U.S.O. drive, wrote a regular column in the Chandler News Publicist entitled the "Newsy-Pub," and founded and was charter president of the Chandler Lions Club. He preached a Children's Day sermon under the title "These Are Our Children," subsequently published in the newspaper, that resulted in galvanizing the whole community to develop wholesome recreation programs for its youth.

The dominant event in the nation's life during the Teegardens' Chandler ministry was World War II. In 1945, for example, major events occurred almost monthly: the Yalta Conference and Iwo Jima in February; the death of President Roosevelt in April; V-E day in May; the Postsdam Conference and Winston Churchill voted out of office in July; Hiroshima, Nagasaki and V-J day in August; and the formation of the United Nations in October. Like everyone else Kenneth and Wanda lived under the restrictions of war rationing. To supplement their income he officiated basketball games in the gym behind the old rock high school, two blocks from the church. Wanda occasionally substituted as a first grade teacher. From these meager earnings they did manage a memorable trip to St. Louis to visit Kenneth's father. He took Kenneth and Wanda to a Cardinals baseball game after which he surprised Wanda by purchasing for her a new green wool suit with shoes to match. It was Roy's way of demonstrating his love and support.

The most exciting and important event of the Chandler years for the Teegardens was the arrival of their first child, an 8-pound, 8-ounce boy whom they named David Kent. David was born April 15, 1946, to the wholehearted joy of the Chandler membership. When Wanda announced to Kenneth that the time of delivery was at hand, he immediately drove her to Rahbe's drugstore near the south end of Manvel Avenue. The drugstore was on the first floor; Dr. Robertson's office was on the second; and a two-room hospital was on the third floor. Wanda, in labor, climbed three flights of stairs to reach the hospital. At the news of the birth of his son, Kenneth raced downstairs to the drugstore, bought a box of cigars, went out onto the sidewalk, and began distributing them to friends. Sighting a friend on the opposite side of the street, Kenneth called to him and, in his excitement, started to cross the intersection, and was narrowly missed by an oncoming car. [32]

Another consequential happening during those years was Kenneth's readmission to Phillips and the completion of his Master of Arts in theology and philosophy. Wanda enrolled along with Kenneth, completing a year of course work while Kenneth chipped away at his degree requirements. He enrolled in eight hours during the summer term of 1945, another thirteen hours in the fall term of 1946, and finished the writing of his 165-page thesis, *Religion in the White House*. In his thesis, Kenneth detailed the ways in which religious principles influenced decision-making of the sixteen presidents from George Washington through Abraham Lincoln. All requirements for the degree were met by January of 1947 and it was awarded at the May graduation ceremonies. [33]

In addition to being a minister, he was now a husband and a father. He had acquired the finest education Oklahoma could offer an aspiring Disciples clergyman; and he had accumulated valuable experience in three congregations. An educational milestone had been reached with the awarding of his Master of Arts degree. And at age twenty-six, with an attractive family, pastoral experience, and academic credentials, he was ready to sever ties and venture beyond what he considered home. An offer came to Kenneth from the congregation in Texas City, Texas.

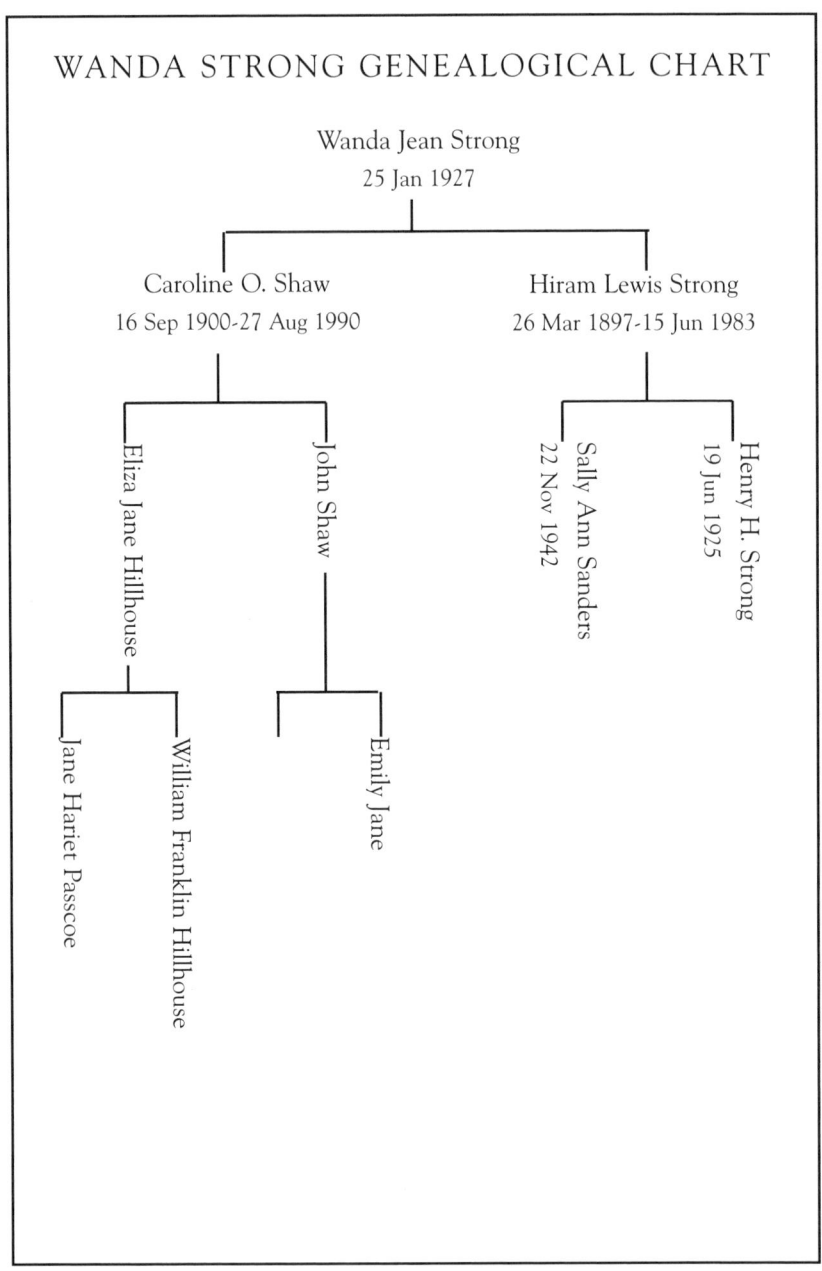

WANDA STRONG GENEALOGICAL CHART

Wanda Jean Strong
25 Jan 1927

Caroline O. Shaw
16 Sep 1900-27 Aug 1990

Hiram Lewis Strong
26 Mar 1897-15 Jun 1983

Eliza Jane Hillhouse

John Shaw

Sally Ann Sanders
22 Nov 1942

Henry H. Strong
19 Jun 1925

Jane Hariet Passcoe

William Franklin Hillhouse

Emily Jane

NOTES

1. Conversation with Roy Kemp, ninety-year-old citizen of Cushing, Okla. December 2, 2005; Lani Johnson, "Friendship and Trust," *The Disciple,* June 1, 1980: 5; *Highland Elementary School Report Cards.* Kenneth L. Teegarden. 1926–1934. Wanda Teegarden Collection.

2. Jay Martin, *The Education of John Dewey* (New York: Columbia University Press, 2002), 452.

3. Arthur Schlesinger and Dixon Ryan Fox, *A History of American Life* (New York: Scribner, 1927–1944. Repr. 1996, Mark C. Carnes, ed.,), 1022–1023; Arrell Gibson, *Oklahoma: A History of Five Centuries* (Norman: University of Oklahoma Press, 1981), 204; *Cushing High School Transcript.* Kenneth L. Teegarden. 1938, 1.

4. Kenneth L. Teegarden to Thelma Zellars, December 20, 1979, Quoted in *Guymon Daily Herald,* Saturday, November 28, 1987, p. 10.

5. Gibson. *Oklahoma,* 221–222; Lester G. McAllister and William Eldon Tucker, *Journey in Faith: A History of the Christian Church* (Disciples of Christ) (St. Louis: Bethany Press, 1975), 389–390.

6. David Roozen interview with Kenneth Teegarden, 1990, 312; *Oklahoma A&M College Transcript.* Kenneth L. Teegarden. 1940, 1.

7. Kenneth L. Teegarden to Eva Teegarden, March 27, 1940, 1–3. Wanda Teegarden Collection.

8. Kenneth L. Teegarden to Roy Teegarden, April 22, 1940. Wanda Teegarden Collection.

9. Roozen interview, 1990, 312; Johnson, "Friendship and Trust," 5; Lillian Moir, "Portrait of a Nominee," *World Call* (October 1973): 13.

10. *Phillips University Catalogue.* 1940, 161–164.

11. Ibid., 6–15, 18–19, 175; *Phillips University Transcript.* Kenneth L. Teegarden. 1947, 1–2; *Phillips University Yearbook.* 1942,1943. Multiple pages.

12. *Yearbook of the Christian Church* (Disciples of Christ). 1940, 534.

13. *Minutes of the Official Board,* First Christian Church, Cushing, Oklahoma, Sunday, December 15, 1940; Cheryl Wells, secretary, First Christian Church, Cushing, to D. Duane Cummins, Tuesday, March 15, 2005; "Policies and Criteria for the Order of Ministry in the Christian Church (Disciples of Christ)," Approved by the general assembly, 1971; Roozen interview, 323.

14. *Phillips University Catalogue.* 1940, 6–15; *Phillips University Transcript.* Kenneth L. Teegarden. 1947, 1–2;

15. *Phillips Transcript.* Ibid.; Oma Lou Myers, *This One Thing I Do: A Biography of Frank Hamilton Marshall* (Portland, OR: Metropolitan Press, 1942), 121.

16. *Phillips Transcript.* 1-2; Conversation with Kenneth Teegarden by D. Duane Cummins. July 1980.

17. *Phillips Transcript.* 1-2; *Phillips Catalogue.* 6-15.

18. *Phillips Catalogue.* Ibid.; *Phillips Transcript.* 1-2; Douglas A. Foster, Paul M. Blowers, Anthony L. Dunnavant, D. Newell Williams, eds. *Encyclopedia of the Stone-Campbell Movement* (Grand Rapids, ND: Erdman's Press, 2005), 300–301; George England, *In A Tall Shadow: Biography of Stephen J. England.* (Privately published, Midwest City, OK, 1990), 177-207.

19. *Phillips Transcript.* 1-2; Ralph W. Nelson, *The Experimental Logic of Jesus* (New York: Fleming H. Revell Co., 1936), 81–82, 87–93; Roozen interview, 311; Ralph Waldo Nelson. Biographical file. Disciples of Christ Historical Society. Nashville.

20. Roy Teegarden to Kenneth L. Teegarden. December 14, 1942. Wanda Teegarden Collection; David Haun to Kenneth Teegarden. June 14, 1974. GMP files, DCHS. Box 3, Correspondence H.

21. *Phillips Transcript.* 1-2.

22. *Yearbook of the Christian Church,* 534; *Kaw City Democrat,* July 24 and August 22, 1942.

23. *Yearbook of the Christian Church.* 1943. 493; One Year Teaching Contract, Norfolk School, 1943, Kenneth Teegarden, Wanda Teegarden Collection.

24 Interview with Wanda Teegarden, February 24, 2005; Interview with Wanda Teegarden, November 13, 2005.

25. Interview with Wanda Teegarden, February 24, 2005; Interview with Wanda Teegarden, December 10, 2005.

26. Ibid.

27. Ibid.

28. Roy Teegarden to Kenneth Teegarden, May 1944, 1–2, Wanda Teegarden Collection.

29. *Yearbook of the Christian Church.* 1944, 494; Visit by Author to Cushing, Chandler, and Tyron, Oklahoma, February 15, 2006.

30. "Miss Strong is Bride of Rev. Teegarden in Chandler." *Cushing Democrat.* May 29, 1944; Interview with Wanda Teegarden, February 24, 2005.

31. Kenneth L. Teegarden. "Sermon Chronicles: 1945–1958," 1, 5; *Yearbook of the Christian Church.* 1945, 498 and 1946, 553; *Ministers Manual.* Kenneth L. Teegarden, 1940–1958.

32. Interview with Wanda Teegarden, March 2, 2006.

33. *David Kent Teegarden Birth Announcement.* 1946; Phillips University Transcript, 1947, 2; Kenneth L. Teegarden, *Religion in the White House: 1789–1865,* Unpublished Masters Thesis. Phillips University, January 1947, vi.

✠

The Formation of a Leader

My purpose in life is to promote
Christian cooperation on all levels.
Kenneth L. Teegarden

Texas City, Texas

Inky, the Teegarden's little black cocker spaniel thrived on barking at the postman. When the family moved to Texas early in 1947, Inky was left behind in Chandler. Inky, however was faithful to Kenneth. One summer Sunday evening in Chandler, Kenneth was guest preacher at the Methodist church. During the sermon, Inky, having walked across Chandler, came through the open door and trotted down the center isle toward the pulpit. Kenneth remarked, " Well, the whole family is here now. We have a Disciples dog in a Methodist church." When they moved to Texas, they gave Inky to a Chandler friend, Bob Wynd. But the little dog continually wandered back to his former home. Another family with children tried their luck, but Inky still ran back home. Then, grieving for his vanished master, he started refusing to eat and began wasting away. Jack Prichard, the Presbyterian minister in Chandler, contacted Kenneth, and with his permission arranged for friends to build a huge crate, vaccinate the dog and ship him by train and truck to Texas City. The truck arrived at the Teegarden home and the driver placed Inky's crate in front of the house. Kenneth came out of the house to retrieve him, but Inky, seeing Kenneth approaching, demolished the side of his crate, jumped out, ran to Kenneth, and leaped into his arms. Soon, Inky was back on full feed and barking at a new postman. [1]

Kenneth's ministry at First Christian Church in Texas City, Texas, began February 5, 1947. Texas City, a community of 20,000 people, was a defense-industry town during World War II, run by the military and oil, metal, and chemical companies. Called "Texas City: Port of Opportunity," it was a working-class coastal town—pipe-welders, trench diggers, heavy construction crews, pipe fitters, boiler makers, furnace operators, wharf crews, turbine operators—one of the fastest growing in the United States. It was the fourth largest port on the Gulf and it was said the waterfront looked like "Oz" with its gun-metal fortress of towering pipes, catalytic cracking furnaces, steam super-heaters, domed oil storage tanks, catwalks, condensers, and tin-roofed warehouses. It was a billion-dollar stretch of oil refineries, oil tank farms, and chemical plants along the coastline of the pewter colored waters of Galveston Bay, one of the most lucrative petrochemical centers in the world, owned by the Rockefellers, Howard Hughes, and members of the Bush family. Early in April, merely two months after the Teegardens arrived, *Time* ran an article proclaiming that "Texas was becoming the chemical capital of the world!" [2]

Kenneth, Wanda and David settled into their new home at 305 19th Avenue North, and were subsequently joined by Inky. First Christian Church. a membership of 108 and a budget of

$5,800, was barely three years old, and Kenneth was their first full time minister. Seven people had established the congregation in January 1944. They invited Lloyd Thompson, of the Texas State Missionary Society, to hold an evangelistic campaign, and in March 1944 a charter was signed by sixty-four members to organize the church. In the beginning, the congregation was pastored by ministers who served congregations in addition to Texas City. Initially, the minister of Central Christian in Galveston added Texas City to his responsibilities; and later, the minister of the Christian Church in LaMarque preached during 1945 and 1946. For a time they met in the music room of Danforth Elementary School on Sunday afternoons, but soon plans were in place to build a new sanctuary on 4th Street and 8th Avenue. The first section of the building was dedicated in April 1945.³

A long time member of the congregation, Willie-Dee Criss, remembered the Teegarden's arrival and that Kenneth was "a very young man with a wife and baby . . . He was full of energy with a 'gung-ho' personality! He had very good sermons and presented those messages to our appreciative congregation." Among his first sermons in Texas City were "The Lost Word," "Disciples Jesus Doesn't Want," "The Open Road," and later for Easter Sunday, "The Triumphant Christ." Willie-Dee, teacher of the nursery class at that time, remembered too that he was very interested in promoting attendance and "wanted to send congratulatory messages to all the new mothers at the local hospital and invite them to bring their little children to our church, giving them a good foundation for a Christian life." And of course she remembered that on April 6, 1947, Kenneth baptized her thirty-year-old husband, Henry. He was muscular, athletic, and over six feet tall, and, according to her, "Kenneth had his hands full immersing Henry."⁴

Just ten days later, Wednesday, April 16, dawned with a brisk breeze, a clear sky and a temperature of fifty-three degrees in Texas City. Kenneth and Wanda were sitting at the breakfast table, still in their pajamas, feeding David in his high chair. Hearing a deep rumble, Kenneth put on a pair of trousers over his pajamas, and the three stepped outside their front door to determine what it was. As they emerged from their doorway, an enormous explosion occurred a mile-and-a-half away, knocking the Teegardens to the ground. Upon reentering the house they discovered the windows had been blown out of their frames and shards of glass were driven completely through the refrigerator door as well as scattered across the floor and embedded in the walls. If they had stayed in the house, someone would likely have been seriously injured or even killed. [5]

A 7,200-ton freighter, the *Grandcamp*, loaded with 2,300 tons of ammonium nitrate fertilizer had exploded in the harbor. It was a prodigious blast, 300 times more powerful than the 1995 explosion of ammonium nitrate unleashed by Timothy McVeigh in Oklahoma City. A twenty-ton section of the *Grandcamp* was thrown 2,500 feet; and its one-and-one-half ton anchor was found two miles away, embedded ten feet in the earth. The blast was heard 150 miles away, broke windows in Houston forty miles distant, and knocked people to their knees in Galveston, ten miles up the coastline. The blast created a twenty-foot tidal wave of oil-covered, flaming and scalding water that hit the waterfront ghettos known as "The Bottom" and "El Barrio." Two light planes passing overhead were blown out of the sky. And twenty crude oil and gasoline tanks shot up like rockets. Two miles of waterfront were suddenly ablaze. Then in a series of smaller explosions, the Monsanto plant and other parts of the waterfront blew up. The big clock atop the Magnolia garage was stopped at 9:13. [6]

Word came from the police almost immediately that the city had to be evacuated for fear of another explosion and poison gases in the air. About 40 percent of the remaining inhabitants left the city that day, by truck, car, train, bus, or on foot. Kenneth drove Wanda, David, and their neighbor's four year-old daughter some thirty miles to Goose Creek, where they stayed in safety with a clergy friend, Lee Pierce. Kenneth returned to Texas City to assist with rescue efforts. The previous day was David's first birthday, and Kenneth's mother had come to visit. Late on the evening of the fifteenth Kenneth had taken her to Houston for the train to Guthrie, Oklahoma, to return home to Cushing. The following morning the conductor came through the train telling of the explosion in Texas City and that it may have taken the lives of the entire population of the city. Eva Teegarden collapsed in a faint on the train. It was evening of that day before Eva and Roy along with Hiram and Carrie learned that their children were safe.

At 1:10 A.M. on the morning of the seventeenth, a second explosion, greater than the first, sent a 3,000-foot tower of fire into the air when a sister ship in the same harbor, the *High Flyer,* exploded. Remains of "The Bottom" and "El Barrio" were virtually splinters and boards. Oil tanks were exploding in all the refineries. But by the seventeenth there was no local fire department to help Texas City put out its many fires. On the sixteenth the Grandcamp had caught fire below deck before exploding and twenty-seven members of the fire department had entered the ship to extinguish the flames. Twelve minutes later the ship exploded and the entire fire department had been killed—the worst fire department tragedy in the nation's history until 9/11. The next day, following the second explosion, the roads were jammed with people leaving Texas City. Kenneth drove back to Goose Creek to take Wanda and David to Galveston, where they boarded a plane to fly to safety in Oklahoma where they stayed with relatives over the next several weeks. Kenneth once more returned to assist Texas City. [7]

The scene he found was catastrophic. It is known that 5,000 were injured, that over 2,000 were homeless, and that property damage was near $5 billion. So many persons were simply vaporized by the blasts that it was difficult to determine the exact number of dead, but estimates reached at least 800. It claimed more lives on American soil than any other man-made disaster in America until 9/11, and is still considered the worst industrial disaster in the history of the United States.

After little more than two months in Texas City, Kenneth held two community leadership positions: president of the Texas City

Ministerial Alliance and member of the Community Relief
Committee of the Lions Club. These positions suddenly thrust
him into the midst of dealing with the city's trauma and relief.
Texas City had no disaster plan and depended heavily on individual volunteers. The Salvation Army and Red Cross provided coffee and sandwiches for the volunteers, while the National Guard,
under the command of General Jonathan Wainwright—a veteran
of Bataan and Corrigidor—arrived to maintain order. The high
school gymnasium was used as a temporary morgue where blan-
ket-covered bodies were toe tagged and placed in lines after
embalming at the McGar garage, where it was said 150
embalmers, mainly from Fort Worth and Houston, stood in a foot
of blood. Kenneth, carrying a list of the dead, was at the gymnasium every day helping long lines of citizens—escorting ten people
at a time into the gym—find and identify the remains of their
loved ones, then attempting to console them after their often
ghastly discoveries. He was responsible, too, for organizing and
leading the mass memorial service on the nineteenth attended by
1500 persons at the high school football field. In his opening sentences, Kenneth spoke words of assurance to all of those assembled, "The whole country is grieved by this disaster. People from
all over the United States have come to help." On the twentieth
there were thirty-eight individual funeral processions. And there
was the matter of dealing with the hundreds of homeless, a situation Kenneth helped address through the Lions' community relief
committee by distributing $27,000 in funds to the stricken and
organizing the committee to help locate temporary shelter, food,
and clothing for the victims. [8]

The community was hit hard, and so was Kenneth's First
Christian Church. Warren Mays, superintendent of the Sunday
school and member of the board was killed. So was John
Shoemaker, a beloved member of the congregation. Many others
were injured. Henry Criss had survived because a late shipment of
pipe had not arrived the day before at Monsanto Chemical where
he was employed. He was home with his wife and two children

when the explosion destroyed Monsanto. The windows in the church building were blown in, splinters of glass penetrated the pews and the walls, and the rear of the church had collapsed. The estimated cost of repair was over $2,000.

Kenneth and Wanda corresponded almost every day during her absence from Texas City. The sizeable cache of letters she saved from that time reveal Kenneth's inner thoughts. Excerpts from only three of those letters tell a touching story.

> *Dear Wanda. . . . I got your letter this morning. I was glad to get it because they sure break the [loneliness]. . . . .All the fire is out now and they are sure there is nothing more that can occur. It is raining here this morning and it is awfully dismal. . . . All the things about David make me wish I could see him. He will probably be walking all over the place [soon] . . . I'm very well satisfied here but I surely wish I hadn't made the change because it is going to be so difficult to accomplish anything now. But I would hate to desert the church when I'm needed. . . ."*

> *Dear Wanda. . . . I've been real busy since you left [doing] much the same things . . . We still haven't found Warren or John so it looks as if there isn't any hope . . . I got checks today from several . . . that makes $301, so we're planning to go ahead with the new building . . . The bodies have been moved to Camp Wallace and things are beginning to settle down. They sprayed the city with D.D.T. today from airplanes . . . It gets pretty lonesome without you and David . . . Is David walking? Wish I could hold him. Good Night, Honey.*

> *Dear Wanda . . . They found John Shoemaker's body at the morgue last Thursday night. His body had been in the morgue for a long time but his face was disfigured so we couldn't recognize him. They identified him by his fingerprints. Maybe you remember me telling you about a ring that said 'To*

the one I love." That was his and Aline had given us the wrong inscription or we could have identified him two weeks ago. I was sure glad they found him. They still haven't located Warren. . . . We had about 60 in church this morning and the service went pretty well. We still aren't having Sunday school because the back of the church is just like it was. I had one addition by confession this morning. . . . Kiss David for me. I'm getting anxious to see you. . . . Love, Kenneth. [9]

Although Kenneth confessed in another of his letters to be emotionally exhausted, his ministry to the community and to the church remained strong. Attendance dropped to an average of sixty for a few months after the explosion, but he provided an inspiring series of sermons, like a coda to the emotional maelstrom the congregation had experienced: "Why Human Suffering?," "When Faith Falters," "In Life's Storms," and "The Light That Has Never Failed." These were intended to uplift their spirits and to help them understand that this horrific event should not undermine their faith. To that end, he urged the congregation toward a vision, leading them forward into a building campaign to add a masonry and stucco structure to their original building. The campaign proved quite successful. These things were being accomplished while Kenneth was living in a windowless house, clearly experiencing personal loneliness for his family, undergoing an appendectomy, and, in his fatigue, expressing doubts about his decision to move to Texas City. In later years members of the Texas City congregation gratefully recalled Kenneth's steadfast leadership. Mrs. J. C. Jones recorded in the history of the congregation, "Reverend Teegarden was a light in the darkness, guiding, comforting, and working with a stricken people." [10]

Five days after the Texas City disaster, Kenneth was asked to write an eyewitness account for the Lincoln County News in Chandler. It was a fortuitous request because it preserved an account of the tragedy in Kenneth's own words "Five days ago began the most harrowing experience of my life. Since that time we have been in the midst of a virtual hell." So began his article.

It continued with a description and cause of the explosion, the damage to his home, and his work in the high school gymnasium. "When I first went to the morgue there were 191 bodies and parts of bodies covered with army blankets, lining the floor. Tonight when I left there were still seventy-five or eighty unidentified and over 100 missing." He told of taking Wanda and David to Goose Creek and what he saw on his return.

> On my return I saw sights which many have termed more terrifying and ghastly than Nagasaki and Hiroshima . . . For the first two days and nights sirens screamed as the dead and dying were brought in by truckloads. Help came from all over the country . . . There were nearly as many volunteer workers in the city as residents . . . I have lost two men from my church and many more are seriously injured. We have found the billfold of one of my men— nothing more. . . . At the morgue, I went with one woman who identified a decapitated body as her husband. The night before she had playfully put red nail polish on his big toe. . . . Tonight the search is continuing in the scorched and battered waterfront. More bodies are being found along the fire-seared beaches and in oily harbor waters . . . Even in disaster there is an inspiring note. People all over the world have come to our assistance. [11]

On June 22nd, some closure came to the event when the ministerial alliance organized a service for the community to bury its un-named dead. A one-acre memorial park was designed with a monument and mirror-lake near the graves of sixty-three unidentified victims of the disaster. Five clergy presided: one rabbi, one Catholic priest, three Protestant ministers. Kenneth led the ceremony and fashioned his remarks around Romans 8:14–17: "be led by the spirit, . . . we suffer with him in order that we may also be glorified with him." More than 2,200 attended the service. At last the grieving and heartbroken community could begin the process of moving forward in the struggle to restore their families, their homes, their lives, eloquent testimony to the ability of the human spirit to prevail in the most unjust circumstances. The experience of Texas City brought national legal standards for determining if elected officials have been negligent in their duties to protect the American people. It redefined the way federal, state, and municipal officials respond to most massive emergencies. And lawsuits stemming from the disaster remained in the United States court system until 1955. [12]

For the twenty-five-year old Kenneth, moving forward was fraught with considerable uncertainty. The whole experience had seared his soul. He wondered if he was properly prepared to deal with the anguish, the grief, the unspeakable hurt that had come to so many people. He was unsure that his education had equipped him to lead a church out of such circumstances. And he and Wanda harbored concern for the future safety of their family in Texas City. Kenneth ultimately concluded he needed additional education for his ministry. He resigned from Texas City First Christian Church on June 6, 1948, to continue his studies at Brite College of the Bible in Fort Worth, where he had enrolled the previous January. Despite the disaster the church at Texas City had grown under Kenneth's leadership. At the time of his departure the membership stood at 122 with a budget of $6,300. Quite significantly, $635 was given to outreach, a three-fold increase to outreach over what it had been when he arrived. The new addition to the church building was completed late that summer, and Kenneth was invited back to lead the dedication ceremony on October 3rd. [13]

Brite College of the Bible

Lee Pierce, the minister at Goose Creek who provided safe haven for Kenneth's family during the early hours of the Texas City disaster, received a freshly minted Bachelor of Divinity degree from Brite College of the Bible in May of 1947. In light of his friendship with Kenneth, he may well have been an influential voice encouraging Kenneth to choose Brite as the place where he could fulfill his desire to advance and deepen his preparation for ministry. Whatever the influences, Kenneth chose Brite. He began his second academic term there in the summer of 1948. [14]

Brite College of the Bible, originally a department of religion at Texas Christian University, was legally incorporated in 1914 due to the urging of its most generous benefactor, Lucas Brite. The American Association of Theological Schools accredited Brite in 1941. By 1948 the school had a faculty of ten. Two held Ph.D. degrees, six held B.D. degrees from Brite, and one, Clinton Lockhart, was an emeritus who did not teach. Dr. D. Ray Lindley had just become dean in the fall of 1947. Senior, middler, and junior students totaled eighty-eight, nearly double the enrollment for the previous year; Masters degree candidates added another eight students. Of this total forty-eight were from Texas, and fourteen of those who listed a B.A. degree were known to be graduates of Phillips University, including Dean Lindley, class of 1926. There were no women among the seniors, middlers, or juniors, but six of the eight masters students were female. Among Kenneth's middler classmates were James Moudy, who later became chancellor of TCU, and Jack Suggs, who became dean of Brite Divinity School. [15]

By comparison, Brite was more conservative, more provincial, with a pre-ministerial population of less than half the size, and a smaller faculty holding fewer credentials and publications, than the College of the Bible at Phillips University where Kenneth had received his Bachelor of Arts in New Testament Language and Literature and Master of Arts degree in Theology and Philosophy. But the smaller-sized school engendered a closer fraternal affinity among the students. Within the confines of the Bachelor of Divinity degree requirements and limited range of courses, Kenneth selected his subjects with care, generally basing his choices upon the reputation and education of the faculty member as well as his assessment of his own professional needs. In those days Brite requirements for a B.D. included nine hours of Old Testament, fifteen hours of New Testament, twelve hours of church history, twelve hours of Christian ministries, six hours of religious education and six hours of Christian doctrine. Kenneth chose to concentrate in Christian ministries, or the "practical field" as it was commonly known. He enrolled in seven courses in this field, five of them taught by Dr. D. Ray Lindley, a 1947 Yale Ph.D.: Introduction to Christian Ministry, Contemporary Preaching, Pastoral Ministry, Church Organization and Administration, and Use of the New Testament in Preaching. The other two courses in Christian Ministries in which he enrolled were Effective Evangelism, taught by a visiting, nationally known evangelism specialist, Bayne Driskill, and Effective Stewardship Programs, taught by visiting professor L.N.D. Wells. He took a sixth course from Dr. Lindley, Psychology of the Religious Experience. [16]

Kenneth's second major concentration at Brite was Old Testament, taught by William L. Reed, the other faculty member who had a Ph.D. awarded by Yale. Having joined the faculty at Brite in 1946 he was still considered a new mind when Kenneth arrived. Kenneth enrolled in four courses taught by Dr. Reed: Old Testament History and Literature parts one and two, Pre-Exilic Prophets, and The Apocrypha. He also took New Testament History from Dr. Reed. The other professor with whom Kenneth studied multiple courses was Glenn Routt, who received his B.D. from Brite in 1945 and his S.T.M. from Union Theological Seminary in New York in 1947. The spring of 1948 was Routt's first professorial term at Brite College of the Bible. Kenneth took three courses from Professor Routt: Ethics and Eschatology of Jesus, Christology of Paul, and Christian Doctrine of Man. [17]

Of the twenty-one courses Kenneth took at Brite, thirteen, well over half, were taught by these three professors. One professor of note from whom he took a single course, New Testament History part two, was W.A. Welsh, a 1941 Brite B.D., who would later become pastor of East Dallas Christian Church and president of Lexington Seminary, and who would work with Kenneth on restructure and then, serve as one of Kenneth's cabinet members in the capacity of president of the Christian Board of Publication. In the twenty-one courses, Kenneth received twenty As and one

B, the B in Effective Stewardship Programs. The degree, Bachelor of Divinity, later changed to Master of Divinity in 1972, was awarded to Kenneth on May 29, 1949. In his retirement years Kenneth recalled those long ago days at Brite, "Classes were held in a small, un-air conditioned building. It was a time of [financial] sacrifice for all of us, but there was a great sense of community."18

One part of the B.D. program requirements was a student pastorate. On June 20, 1948, Kenneth began his student ministry in Healdton, Oklahoma, about an hour's drive north of Fort Worth. It was a community of approximately 3,000 with a Christian church founded in 1920. By the time of Kenneth's arrival it had a membership of 123 and a budget of $6,750. Although considered a small congregation in a modest-sized rural community, it made a critical contribution to Kenneth's development because it was a testing ground for many of his new learnings from Brite. More importantly, through its keen sensitivity and abundant care for others, that little congregation helped restore Kenneth's inner resolve for ministry. He described his time at Healdton as " . . . one of the most important years of my ministry. I had returned to Brite to finish my last year of seminary and was able to do only a part-time ministry at Healdton. We lived across the street from the church and my wife, Wanda, was able to be there full-time with our two-year old son, David. . . . I remember the loving care I received from the congregation and the strong influence First Christian Church had in the community." [19]

A recent history of the congregation notes that "outreach is one of the prime concerns" of First Christian Church. The congregation practiced an open door policy and was a very positive influence throughout the community, serving it in many ways. From its beginnings it had a reputation of being one of the most loving and caring churches in Healdton. Kenneth's first sermon was preached on June 20, entitled "Three Fundamentals of a Crusading Church," delivered at a time when Disciples, nationally, were involved in "A Crusade for a Christian World." The three fundamentals identified by Kenneth were: "an unwavering faith in God, a ministry of evangelism and outreach, and a commitment of ourselves through service and stewardship." During the late summer Kenneth experimented with techniques he had learned from Bayne Driskell regarding evangelism. At the close of their brief evangelistic campaign, Sunday, September 12, twenty-three people joined the Healdton congregation, the largest number ever to join that church on a single day. During the year at Healdton, Kenneth baptized eighteen persons, officiated at two weddings and one funeral, and nurtured a Timothy, Donald Jones, into ministry. When he left Healdton in June 1949, the congregation had grown to 141 members and was operating with a substantially increased budget, particularly in outreach. His series of four sermons during their successful stewardship campaign were: "Stewardship of Talents," "Stewardship of Time," "Stewardship of Possessions," and "Stewardship of Life." Kenneth was invited back in 1955 to speak at the dedication of the church's new building, and again in 1985 to speak at the sixty-fifth anniversary of its founding. [20]

The Post-War Environment

Kenneth's ministerial service and academic studies, during the period from 1947 to 1957, occurred in the social, political, and economic milieu of post-World War II America. Following the devastating experiences of the Great Depression and World War II, the late 1940s and early 1950s, by contrast, were more orderly. Pulitzer Prize-winning journalist David Halberstam assessed these years as exhibiting an abiding respect for the "social covenants of the nation." The federal government had helped deliver the citizenry from economic collapse and had achieved victory in World War II. Few, therefore, in those post-war years doubted the good intent of government. A liberal ideology, appreciative of the growing role of government in the life of the society, prevailed. The traditional system of authority also prevailed. Men presided in politics and business as well as the family, and nearly all had been born in the previous century. The nation's youth were given the sobriquet "the silent generation," but their children were called "baby-boomers," a potential source of energy and talent for the nation's future. [21]

The nation grew from 144 million in 1947 to 172 million in 1957. By 1950 two-thirds of the country lived in metropolitan areas. In 1956 white collar workers outnumbered blue collar workers for the first time, and by 1960 the spread had reached fifty-five million to thirty-two million. Old rural patterns—in which Protestantism was rooted—were vanishing. With the advent of television, emergence of air travel, rapidly expanding ownership of automobiles, and the construction of a national highway system, even rural America was becoming quasi-suburban. State agricultural colleges dropped "agriculture" from their names, reflecting the socio-cultural shift across the land . [22]

Mobility and television along with economic abundance and technological developments contributed to a strong 'national unity.' A social and cultural conformity emerged, called by many analysts a "mass culture," by others a "homogenized society." It was marked by a growing bureaucratization in all organizations and a standardization of life and culture among the people symbolized by the appearance of Levittown, MacDonalds, and Holiday Inn. Distinguished American historian Daniel Boorstin interpreted the post-war civilization in America as a people held together in national unity, less by hopes, belief, tradition, or place, and more by common experience, by their wants, what they made, how they learned, the things they owned, and the ways they thought about themselves. These trends were reflected in the popular literature of the time: *Organization Man, The Status Seekers, Man in the Gray Flannel Suit,* and especially in David Riesman's *The Lonely Crowd,* which claimed individuals had become "other directed" rather than "inner directed." [23]

But underneath the thin veneer of national unity was a growing awareness of perhaps the most powerful force of all—*pluralism.* Many ethnic minorities were discovering power within their own separate identities; many new religious faiths had grown strong enough to challenge Protestantism's grip on the culture. A generational separation was born in the increasing numbers of young who began to question the establishment. An economic gap was widening between the rich and the poor. A gender strain separated men from the emerging liberation of women. And all were exacerbated by the stubborn, old tensions between urban and rural America. This growing pluralism, later called "multi-culturalism," was creating deep fissures beneath the placid surface of national unity in the 1950s. Nowhere were the implications of pluralism more vivid than the Civil Rights Movement that began in this decade.

For the church, national unity spawned a religious cohesion, bringing a new empowerment to ecumenical and interfaith efforts. Among other organizations, the period gave birth to the National Council of Churches, the World Council of Churches, and the National Conference of Christians and Jews. The world war had given evidence of the need for Christian unity; the cold war that followed, with its threat of atheistic communism, provided additional impetus for inter-faith collaboration; and the force of consensus and conformity in the fifties brought ecumenism into high profile. [24]

The United States, alone among western nations, experienced a religious resurgence during the post World-War II years, a religious revival that Sydney Ahlstrom analyzed as taking several forms. Religion allied with patriotism when "under God" was added to the Pledge of Allegiance to the American Flag in 1954, making people believe that personal religious faith was an element of patriotic commitment. The revival generated a popular interest in religion as a counterpoint to the "age of anxiety," especially through such publications as Norman Vincent Peale's *The Power of Positive Thinking*, Fulton J. Sheen's *Peace of Soul*, Joshua Liebman's *Peace of Mind*, Billy Graham's *Peace with God*, and Anne Morrow Lindbergh's *Gift from the Sea*. The religious revival of the 1950s also manifested itself in a "new conservative evangelicalism" that became a growing force in American Christianity. The worshiping congregation and advances in the use of liturgy, along with religious educational reform and revitalization of the preaching office, also grew out of the fifties revival in a movement identified as "parish renewal." And finally, leaders of the old "Neo-orthodox" theology, although waning in their influence, published some of their most important works during this period. Among them is H. Richard Niebuhr's *Christ and Culture* that identified options for relating the church to the world. The revival of the fifties was a genuine time of growth and reinvigoration for the church and it took many forms; however, by the end of the decade, it was spoken of in the past tense, an Indian summer of religious interest. [25]

Disciples, during this decade, prepared the way for restructure. Emulating the culture at large, they added a degree of standardization to their highly individualized congregational life. In 1946, Orman L. Shelton published a little book entitled *The Church Functioning Effectively* that offered a congregational governance design consisting of seven functional committees:—membership, worship, education, outreach, stewardship, evangelism and property—reporting to a reorganized local church board. The plan was broadly adopted, as was the content of G. Edwin Osborn's *Christian Worship: A Service Book,* published in 1953. The combination of these two works coupled with the three-year [1947–1950] national program "A Crusade for a Christian World," brought an element of common ground to the diverse Disciples congregations. As a result of the lessons learned about coordination of state, national and local leadership during the crusade, program coordination and long term planning became more effective at all levels. Especially effective was the Council of Agencies that first convened in 1950. The strength of the "cooperative tradition" among Disciples increased during these years. Cooperatives were encouraged by the election of Gaines Cook in 1946 as the first full-time executive secretary of the international convention. Added to this was the selection of A. Dale Fiers as president of the United Christian Missionary Society in 1953. A few key players were beginning to emerge, program coordination was improving, momentum for cooperation was increasing, and the stage was set for a structural reorganization. [26]

Vernon, Texas

"It might be well for us to consider at the very beginning of this new ministry what our real task is!" These words opened Kenneth's third sermon, "What is the Church Supposed to Do?," at his new congregation, the Central Christian Church, Vernon, Texas, July, 24, 1949. He continued:

> Those who claim that the church has failed, often reveal their assumption that the church ought to create a perfect world, or more immediately, to create perfect people. Didn't Jesus say, 'Be ye perfect, even as your heavenly Father is perfect?' Yes, but to see this as a simple moralism does violence to its meaning. It was a corrective to a common problem in religion, persons concluding that they were as good as their neighbors and so settling into complacency. It is a standard, not a promise.

Then, Kenneth lifted up four ways in which Jesus spoke of the church:

> First, Jesus spoke of the church as a shepherd. In ways that never get into the news, countless thousands of persons today are bearing up under bereavement, enduring acute physical illness, maturing under relentless frustration—and doing it because the Christian Faith—the church— has given them a meaning and hope that makes it possible. In a world of tremendous odds and infinite possibilities the church does not promise perfection to people. It offers power—to do more than you could alone. Thus has the church been a shepherd in countless lives

where the drama has run deep. It has not brought them to perfection—but it has enabled them to endure." [27]

Using vivid illustrations enhanced with his unique eloquence, Kenneth expounded on three additional ways in which Jesus described the church. In summary he said to his new congregation that Jesus also spoke of the church as: *salt,* a preservative, since the church has preserved for us the essentials of human life. It has been the guardian, the custodian of the best achievements of humanity. As *leaven*, Christianity can lose its identity and be known only by the influence it has on something else. Many of the great social advances in history were produced through the influence and ideas of Christianity, a leaven without which many of those advances would not have occurred. As *light* Christianity gives us understanding of the depth of our darkness. Because Christ is in the world, we know what is anti-Christ, we know that darkness is darkness, and we shall seek to do something about it. Then he concluded, "To be shepherd, and salt, and leaven, and light—let us 'be about our Father's business.'" [28]

With this sermon, Kenneth entered a six-year ministry that he would later claim to be the favorite period of his entire career, the ministry he always held closest to his heart. Central Christian Church was barely sixty years old, located in Vernon, Texas, a community of about 12,000, approximately 100 miles northwest of Fort Worth near the Oklahoma border on the Pease River, a fork of the mighty Red. When Kenneth and Wanda arrived, July 1, 1949, the congregation had a membership of 378 and a budget of $10,800 with $1,200 designated for outreach. The publications of the congregation all carried the phrase, "A friendly church in a friendly community with a warm welcome for you." [29]

Kenneth immediately set to work on the issues of membership and stewardship. Again, using the popular Bayne Driskill method of the time, he organized an evangelism campaign during the early spring of 1950. On Sunday, March 26, 102 new members joined Central Christian Church, the largest ever to join on a single day. By the end of 1950 the church had grown to 430 participating members with a budget of $17,600. It was a spectacular beginning—made more so by the birth of Kenneth and Wanda's second son, Marshall Kirk on May 31, 1950. Prior to Kirk's arrival, the ladies of the congregation sent an affectionate and affirming note to Wanda.

> *We, the ladies of the church, extend our warmest congratulations on two counts. First, we know that you and Kenneth have wanted a baby since you moved to Vernon. Second, all the mothers in the church think it is so fortunate that the baby is to be a Central Christian baby—since we all know that the finest, the smartest, the most beautiful, and in fact the most perfect children in the whole world either have been, or now are Central Christian babies.*
>
> *We want you to know we love you, and we hope you are happy here. We have read that in olden times each man was required to build and maintain a room in his home in which to care for the preacher. Nothing was said about caring for the minister's wife. Tonight, Wanda, we want you to know that each of us has a place in our heart just for you.*
>
> The Ladies of Central Christian Church

As in every congregation they served, Wanda endeared herself to the Vernon members as a loyal participant and soloist in the choir, Christian Women's Fellowship (CWF), church dinner preparations, and Sunday School. In Vernon, she was also an active member of the community Altrusa Club. [30]

In March 1951, Kenneth organized another ten-day Crusade for Central Christian, this time using the L.O. Leet Stewardship-Evangelism team from Dallas. It was a team sponsored by such notables as Theodore Beasley, Chair, L.N.D. Wells, Edgar DeWitt Jones, and Harry Hines, all of whom were members of the sponsoring committee. At the conclusion of the ten days in Vernon, the Leet group invited Wanda to join them on their next tour as a vocalist. She and Kenneth agreed. Wanda traveled with the team for approximately a month, as far west as Yakima, Washington. Her solos and duets were warmly received at every stop on the tour, but due to her loneliness for Kenneth and the boys, she left the tour early. In a letter to Kenneth, she confided, " I have really missed you, and I am just counting the days to see the boys." [31]

On December 15, 1951, Kenneth led the church to make a major decision to launch a $200,000 building program. Under the leadership of Hollis Miller, building advisory chairman, a kickoff fundraising dinner was held in February 1952. A three-acre site was purchased on South Hillcrest Drive and the sale of the old property was completed. Construction required a full two years. The dedication of the new facility was planned for January 3–8, 1954, consuming a full week. The congregation met at the old church on Wilbarger and Mesquite on the morning of the third, and moved as a caravan to their new building. The four great pillars at the front entrance offered an imposing welcome of strength and support. It was an edifice of contemporary architecture, designed to achieve dignity and beauty through clean, simple lines. The graceful, freestanding arches of steel not only supported the structure, they created the illusion of height and spaciousness. The pattern formed by the ceiling beams focused attention on the chancel, baptistery, communion table, and the towering oak cross reaching from floor to ceiling. The placement of the pulpit and lectern gave emphasis to the church's ordinances of baptism and the Lord's Supper. [32]

"The Beauty of Holiness" was the title of Kenneth's first sermon in the new sanctuary, delivered the morning of January 3rd. During the week that followed, beginning on Sunday afternoon and continuing each evening thereafter, a who's who of Texas Disciples dedicated parts of the new facility. Dr. Roy Snodgrass, dean of Brite College of the Bible gave the dedicatory address for the building; Dr. George Davis dedicated the pulpit; W.A. Welsh dedicated the communion table; Dr. L.N.D. Wells dedicated the baptistery; and Dr. D. Ray Lindley dedicated the hymnals and offering trays. In his remarks, Dr. Snodgrass singled out Kenneth for making "this ambitious program a reality;" and he commended the whole congregation for their "example of Christian faith and Christian work." [33]

In addition to totally immersing himself in the ministry of the congregation, Kenneth was extensively engaged in the life of the community and the ministry of the larger church. The name of Kenneth Teegarden could be found on the membership list of practically all civic and charitable organizations in Vernon. And he didn't just lend his name to these organizations; he served them fully. Kenneth was a 32nd º Scottish Rite Mason, member of the Maska Shrine Temple of the Shrine in Wichita Falls, prelate of the Vernon Commandery of the Dallas Scottish Rite, and grand chaplain of the Grand Lodge of Texas consisting of 225,000 members. He was advancement chairman for the Central District of Boy Scouts of America in Texas, institutional representative for Pack 46, Troop 46 and Post 46 of Vernon, and member of the Executive Board for Boy Scouts of America in Northwest Texas. Kenneth was secretary-treasurer of the board of directors of the Wilbarger County Chest; member of the service unit of the Salvation Army; founder and director of the Vernon youth center called Lions Den as well as chaplain of the Lion's club all his years in Vernon. During 1953 and 1954 he gave either the baccalaureate or commencement address at every high school in Wilbarger County. He spoke to or served on committees of every P.T.A. organization in Vernon; and found time to coach a Pee-Wee League baseball team that won the city championship. The high school football team requested he be their toastmaster and speaker at their banquet; and high school students asked that he direct several of their activities, including the annual Christmas program. Kenneth organized conferences involving nurses and ministers at the local hospital to enhance mutual cooperation between nurses and ministers. And for the larger church, he served as a member of the State Board of Religious Education, chairman of the state youth committee for Disciples, member of the Texas

Board of Christian churches, representative of Texas Disciples at the International Convention of Christian Youth Fellowship (CYF), and the person who brought members of Vernon churches together to work with the Texas Council of churches. Finally, he served as a member of the board of directors of the Texas Tech Foundation that planned religious activities for students. Kenneth was highly regarded by the young people of Vernon, and he was beloved by their parents because of the enormous investment of his time and skill in organizing activities for and counseling their sons and daughters. [34]

It was not a great surprise, therefore, when the Chamber of Commerce in 1954 named the thirty-three-year-old Kenneth Teegarden the "Most Outstanding Citizen of Vernon," and presented to him the Distinguished Service Award. The president of the Chamber noted in his presentation before several hundred guests, "Reverend Teegarden is totally dedicated to assisting youth, and has devoted many hours to civic enterprises. He has made a great investment in our youth, and has won the respect of every Vernon citizen by his efforts for boys and girls." Responding to the recognition Kenneth affirmed his faith in youth, by observing, "For the thousands [of youth] who appear in courts all over the United States, there are thousands more who do things the right way." He added that he believed his "purpose in life is to promote Christian cooperation on all levels." [35]

Kenneth was an unusually gifted and popular public speaker. On average, he received ten invitations each month to speak somewhere outside Vernon; however, he accepted only about one per week. Aware of his love for debate and his talent for speaking, Vernon's local Toastmasters club entered Kenneth in the 1952 National Toastmasters competition as their representative. At that time there were 1,200 Toastmasters clubs in America with 35,000 members. Kenneth won both the district and bi-district contests and then the Texas-Louisiana state competition. In the zone competition the participants were the winners from Colorado-Wyoming, Oklahoma, Kansas-Missouri, and Alabama-

Florida. In the final round it was Kenneth versus the Oklahoma champion who turned out to be an old Cushing boyhood friend, Darrell Minnix, a teammate with Kenneth on the Cushing championship debate team from high school days. Kenneth finished first and Darrell finished second. Kenneth proceeded to the national finals competition, held at the Palmer House in Chicago, August 16, 1952. His address was entitled "The Imitation of Christ." He finished second in the nation! The Vernon Toastmaster's club hosted a "Teegarden Night" to honor Kenneth's achievement. Newspaper columnist for the *Vernon Daily Record,* Orlin Brewer, noted in his column many years later, "Kenneth Teegarden was probably the best and most eloquent speaker this community has ever produced." [36]

Those who knew Kenneth were quite aware of his penchant for a practical joke. According to Orlin Brewer, while having a cup of coffee in Jack Eure's coffee shop (a sort of Lake Woebegone Chatterbox café), Kenneth, a frequent coffee consumer and friend, overheard a customer ask Jack if he had flashlights for sale. Jack said he had once carried them, but no longer had them in stock. Kenneth left the shop, persuaded some of his friends to visit Jack and ask to purchase a flashlight. Finally Jack ordered a supply of flashlights and put them on display. He did not sell a single one, much to the humorous satisfaction of Kenneth and his friends. [37]

At age thirty-four, and comfortable in the Vernon congregation, Kenneth received a telephone invitation to consider a move to one of the Disciples' oldest and most prestigious congregations, the century-old First Christian Church in Fort Smith, Arkansas. It had a membership of 935, a budget of $36,000 and outreach giving of $11,000. Several well-known Disciples ministers had served the congregation. The position of senior minister was widely coveted. But Kenneth told them he was not interested. The search committee, however, wanted to hear Kenneth preach and, unannounced, made a trip to Vernon to worship at Central Christian. On Saturday, a close friend of the Teegardens and member of

Central Christian, Jim Geer, a Texas Ranger, had died during surgery in Dallas. Kenneth quickly arranged for a substitute preacher on Sunday and had gone to Dallas to be with Jim's wife Velma and their family. The search committee worshipped at Central Christian without hearing Kenneth. Impressed with the spirit of the congregation and the content of their worship, the committee decided to return, but this time announced their coming. They were moved by Kenneth's sermon and pressed him to reconsider his initial response to their invitation. Kenneth ultimately agreed to accept their offer. But his letter of resignation from Central Christian at Vernon was tinged with pathos as well as appreciation.

> *Dear Friends*
>
> *Since June 27, 1949, I have served as pastor of Central Christian Church. It has been a happy and profitable six years for me as minister. . . I have grown considerably while serving in Vernon . . . During that time we have seen 299 people unite with the church by baptism and transfer. . . Stewardship has grown tremendously . . . Total giving in 1948 was about $8,500. Now our current expense budget alone is over $20,000. We have added a Link Missionary plus other benevolent and missionary enterprises; and we have built a new parsonage and the greater portion of a new church building . . . We have developed a functional program within the framework of a constitution, and there is a general spirit of unity and harmony in the church, which makes Central Christian one of the finest in the state.*
>
> *It is with regret, therefore, that I tender my resignation as the pastor of this fine church. I have been extended the call to become the pastor of the historic First Christian Church of Fort Smith, Arkansas. I have notified the Fort Smith church of my acceptance.*
>
> *Let me say again that it is with reluctance that I take this step . . . We are grateful for our many friends in Vernon and for the six years of happiness which we have enjoyed. We have*

*come to regard Vernon as "home" and as we make preparation
to leave I know we will experience a great feeling of loss. We
earnestly covet [your] best wishes and prayers. . . We shall
always remember this church and its members. . . . Sincerely,
Kenneth L. Teegarden* [38]

During a ministerial career, most every pastor serves one congregation with which there is an abiding affinity. When reflecting
upon a career as a whole, that one place always tugs at a minister's
heart. So it was with Kenneth and Wanda when they remembered
their ministry at Central Christian in Vernon. And the congregation held a similar affection. Kenneth was invited back in 1977 as
the featured speaker for the mortgage burning of the church he
helped build; and he was invited again as the featured speaker in
1988 for the centennial celebration of Central Christian in
Vernon. Nearly forty-five years after Kenneth left, his grandson
Grant came to Vernon to visit the church his grandfather had
served as minister. Upon entering the church a few people were
standing nearby and observed Grant viewing the photo gallery of
former ministers. They asked his name and he responded, "Grant
Teegarden. I am the grandson of Kenneth Teegarden." Grant was
absolutely astounded by the reception and reaction of the people—after four decades—and by the outpouring of their high
regard and respect for Kenneth, for Wanda and for their years of
ministry in Vernon.

Fort Smith, Arkansas

First Christian Church in Fort Smith voted unanimously in a
congregational meeting, July 10, 1955, to extend a call to Kenneth
and Wanda. The proposed compensation included a $6,000 salary,
parsonage, pension, moving expenses, auto expenses, convention
expenses, redecoration of the parsonage along with some new furniture, a two-month sabbatical after six years service, and a thir-
ty-day annual vacation. It was the most generous package

Kenneth had ever received. The moving van loaded their belongings in Vernon on August 30th, and the following day the Teegardens arrived in Fort Smith to begin settling into their new home at 2003 South Greenwood. His installation service, the first ever for both Kenneth and for First Christian, was held September 4th, with Ira Crewdson, secretary of the Arkansas Christian Missionary Society officiating and preaching. The next Sunday Kenneth delivered his first sermon, "Whose Affair is It?," based on Matthew 27:20–31. That evening a reception was held at the church welcoming the Teegardens. Their Arkansas ministry was under way. [39]

Kenneth chose to place emphasis on leadership training during his two and one-half year ministry in Fort Smith. Beginning in November of his first year, he taught a six-session course, the History of the Disciples, that drew an attendance so large the class had to be moved from the classroom into the sanctuary. This history course was followed with a study entitled, The Bible Book by Book, also taught by Kenneth. In May of 1956 he taught a training class for church-school teachers; and later in the year he offered a larger scale, four-week graded version with ninety persons enrolled. Again in the spring of 1957 he taught a six-session course entitled You Can Teach. He organized a young couples church school class with twenty-one charter members as well as a twenty-two-member junior fellowship during his first few months at First Christian. And in July 1956 he employed a director of music and youth activities, the first full-time staff position besides that of the pastor in the congregation's history. Building a strong educational program at First Christian became one of his major objectives and ultimately a significant legacy. [40]

In light of his previous successes with evangelism, Kenneth launched another huge effort in Fort Smith during the late summer of 1957. He set a goal of 117 new members to join on Decision Sunday, January 12, 1958. The campaign began in November, when fifty women from the CWF conducted a telephone census of new residents in Fort Smith. Two nights each week all members of the General Board made friendly cultivating calls on prospects, urging them to attend a church function. Starting in January, four divisions of evangelistic teams, each trained by Kenneth and led by a "major," began intensive calling on prospects. Each team had a goal, and each evening at 9:15 they reported back to the church the number of decision cards signed by prospects. A friendly rivalry developed among the teams that resulted in a dramatic climax on Sunday morning, January 12th, when 127 persons came forward to join during the invitation hymn! It was a thrilling success for the congregation—and like Vernon, it was the largest number ever to join on a single Sunday. This was the third congregation in succession where Kenneth had organized and led an extraordinarily productive evangelism campaign. Commenting years later about these successes, Kenneth noted, "The value of the program was organizing laypeople for their involvement in ministry and organizing them in a way they could do things they were capable of doing without fear of failure . . . We had four steps for encouraging people to come: want them, find them, love them, and win them. But then, we had twelve points for keeping them . . . It is three times as hard to keep someone as it is to get them. So we organized the church in ways that nurtured the people after they became members." [41]

Kenneth, true to his convictions about Christian cooperation, maintained an active involvement in the larger church. He was elected to the board of directors of the National Benevolent Association and appointed to the executive committee; elected to the seminary council of Phillips University; member of the Recommendations Committee of the International Convention; and in 1956 was elected president of the Board of Managers of the Arkansas Christian Missionary Society. Still there was time in 1956 for him to organize an effort to completely redecorate the sanctuary, repair and paint the exterior of the church, to host a meeting of men from across Fort Smith to develop and organize a citywide men's council, and to host the District 4 convention of Disciples at First Christian. [42]

But Kenneth's work during the late fifties civil rights crisis in the neighboring community of Little Rock is considered his most significant contribution to the city of Fort Smith. Little Rock had approved a gradual desegregation plan for Central High School by arranging for the admission, on September 4, 1957, of six black girls and three black boys from the Horace Mann School. On racial issues Arkansas was considered a moderate state, more Southwestern than Southern. Its medical and law schools had been integrated ten years earlier without incident, and most people thought the 1957 integration would progress the same way. But the governor, Orval Faubus, seeking an issue to help him win a third term, stirred racial feelings by calling out the National Guard on the pretext that the integration plan could not occur without violence. The guard, however, was not called out to protect the black students; it was called out to prevent their entry, a fact not widely known before September 4th. When the nine students arrived, they were barred from the building by the guard and by a growing mob of angry whites. In fact, they were not allowed to safely enter for nearly three weeks. Finally, President Eisenhower, after a snub by Governor Faubus, ordered federal troops to Little Rock, and on September 23rd the students entered the school with the protection of the 101st Airborne Division. [43]

Kenneth responded immediately to the Little Rock crisis in order to prevent something similar from happening in Fort Smith. He asked the Reverend Augustus Pearson, pastor of Ninth Street Baptist church, and Jerry Heilbron, president of the Sebastian County Bar Association, to join him in establishing a bi-racial organization to promote community unity, understanding, and communication among the races in Fort Smith. A pre-organization meeting, attended by twenty-six African Americans and whites (doctors, dentists, ministers, lawyers, laborers, and real estate executives) was held on September 19th at First Christian Church. "Listening to, understanding and appreciating the problems of others is our goal," stated Kenneth in his opening remarks.

"We must be thinking, and not just rearranging our prejudices. We have no drums to beat, no bill of goods to sell other than friendship and understanding, and no desire to be affiliated with any group—but to assist any and all groups." At the organizational meeting three weeks later, the group chose the name Community Relations Council of Fort Smith, and Kenneth was elected chairman. The council was a place where blacks and whites could meet together, present their problems, think together, and talk together sensibly in an effort to find solutions. Richard Smith, the chairman of the board of First Christian Church, observed of Kenneth's leadership in establishing the council, "Rev. Teegarden brings people together, brings out leadership in them, and inspires them to transcend themselves. He made it clear that he would not be dictated to on anything that affects his principles. People who criticized him went away with their arms around him." Nearly two decades later his leadership during the 1957 crisis was still remembered and appreciated, as one minister who wrote, recalled, "I am reminded of the early days of Little Rock and of the very generous and dynamic leadership you gave to the community during those horrendous days."[44]

In 1958, his pastoral and prophetic personality along with his reputation as a skilled administrator attracted a new call to leadership. Ira Crewdson was retiring as secretary of the Arkansas Christian Missionary Society and several Disciples leaders across the state encouraged Kenneth to take on this responsibility. On February 10th, he announced his resignation to the Fort Smith Congregation. "Let me say that I would not leave the Fort Smith church at this time to become the pastor of any other church in the country. I regard this congregation as a great people who have an unusual future . . . and I envy my successor in his opportunity to move forward with you." Kenneth, in a final report to the board, summarized his work at First Christian during nearly three years of ministry. By his accounting there had been 166 sermons, 171 outside addresses, 1,330 meetings attended, 2,358 personal calls, 805 conferences, twenty-three weddings, fifty-eight funerals,

292 additions to the church, 109 of those by baptism. He could have added that the budget had grown from $36,000 to $43,700 and outreach giving from $11,000 to $20,000; and that the membership had reached about 970. He would be invited back in the future to dedicate the new building in 1966, and again to assist with a stewardship campaign in 1990. His final sermon at First Christian Church in Fort Smith, "Taking Leave of the Brethren," was preached on April 27, 1958—and his days as a pastor of a local congregation were ended. The decades extending from the Texas City disaster through the civil rights crisis in Little Rock had contained hard earned lessons for Kenneth—lessons that shaped him for leadership in the larger causes of the church. Even so, being minister of a congregation was Kenneth's first love. More than a quarter century later he remarked, "If I have strengths as a minister, they are in my care for a congregation. People are the most important thing to me." [45]

NOTES

1. *Lincoln County News.* "The Smoking Room," and "A Preacher Proves a Dog's Best Friend," 1946. Two articles appearing in the press describing the incidents, along with a cartoon, n.d.; Interview with Wanda Teegarden, February 24, 2005.

2. Bill Minutaglio. *City on Fire* (New York: Harper-Collins Publishers, 2003), 4–5; "Texas Comes of Age," *Time,* (April 8, 1947): p. 27.

3. Mrs. J.C. Jones. *Unpublished History of First Christian Church, Texas City Texas.* (1960), 3.

4. Mrs. Henry (Willie-Dee) Criss to D. Duane Cummins, March 29, 2005, 1; Kenneth L. Teegarden. *Sermon Chronicles: 1945–1958,* 10–11; Mrs. Henry (Willie-Dee) Criss to Kenneth L. Teegarden, February 1, 2002; *Christian Church Yearbook.* (1947), 608.

5. Interview with Wanda Teegarden. February 24, 2005.

6. Hugh Stephens. *The Texas City Disaster,* 1947 (Austin: University of Texas Press, 1997), 1, 19, 48–55; "Pluperfect Hell," *Time* (April 28, 1947): 22–23; Newsweek (April 28. 1947): 29; Minutaglio. *City on Fire,* ix.

7. Interview with Wanda Teegarden, February 24, 2005; Minutaglio, *City on Fire,* 73–79, 172; *Time* (April 28, 1947): 22–23; *Newsweek* (April 28. 1947): 29.

8. Interview with Wanda Teegarden. February 24, 2005; Mintuaglio, *City on Fire,* x; Stephens, *The Texas City Disaster,* 4, 63, 70, 92–97; *Time* (April 28, 1947): 22–23; *Newsweek* (April 28, 1947): 29; *Houston Chronicle,* Friday, April 18, 1947, p. 16; *Houston Chronicle,* Saturday, April 19, 1947, p. 10; *Houston Post,* "Texas City Mourns Hundreds of Explosion Dead in Mass Ceremony on Athletic Field," April 19, 1947, p. 1.

9. Kenneth Teegarden to Wanda Teegarden. Sat. Morning, Undated, 1947; Kenneth Teegarden to Wanda Teegarden. Wed. Night, Undated, 1947; Kenneth Teegarden to Wanda Teegarden.

Sun. Afternoon, Undated, 1947, Wanda Teegarden Collection; Mrs. Henry Criss to D. Duane Cummins, March 29, 2005.

10. Kenneth L. Teegarden. *Sermon Chronicles: 1945–1958,* 12; Jones. *Unpublished History of First Christian Church, Texas City, Texas,* 2.

11. Kenneth L. Teegarden. "Eye Witness Account of Texas City Disaster Told by Kenneth Teegarden, Former Chandler Resident." *Lincoln County News,* April 21, 1947, p. 1.

12. *Houston Post,* "Throngs Pay Final Tribute to Blast Dead," June 23, 1947, p. 1,8; *Houston Chronicle,* "Texas City Bids Final Farewell to its Unknown Victims of April Disaster," June 23, 1947, p.1; Minutaglio. *City on Fire,* x, 204.

13. *Christian Church Yearbook,* 1948. 619; Interview with Wanda Teegarden, February 24, 2005.

14. Texas Christian University: *Official Transcript,* Kenneth L. Teegarden, 1948–1949.

15. *Brite College of the Bible Caller.* Vol. VIII, No. 1. (May 1948): 6, 9, 32–36; Texas Christian University: Official Transcript. Kenneth L. Teegarden. 1948–1949.

16. *Phillips University Catalogue:* 1940, 6–15; *Brite College of the Bible Caller.* May 1948, 6; *Brite College of the Bible Caller.* May 1949, 6; TCU: *Official Transcript, 1948–49;* D. Duane Cummins. *The Disciples Colleges: A History* (St. Louis: CBP Press, 1987), 109–115.

17. TCU: *Official Transcript,* 1948–49.

18. Ibid.; Karen Willoughby, "Brite Reunion Stirs Memories." *Fort Worth Star-Telegram,* February 15, 1989, p. 3.

19. *Christian Church Yearbook,* 1948, 570; Kenneth L. Teegarden to First Christian Church, Healdton, Oklahoma, December 1, 1996, 1.

20. *Christian Church Yearbook,* 1949, 576; Teegarden, *Sermon Chronicles: 1945–1958,* 23; Cleo LeVally. *History of Healdton First Christian Church* (Unpublished, 2000), 1–2; D. Duane Cummins interview with Cleo Le Vally, March 15, 2005; First Christian Church, Healdton Dedication Program, November 10, 1985.

21. Halbersam, David. *The Fifties.* (New York: Random House, 1993), x-xii; Eric Goldman. *The Crucial Decade: America 1945–1960.* (New York: Vintage, Random House, 1960), 49–50.

22. Goldman, *The Crucial Decade,* 266; Samuel Eliot Morison, Henry Steele Commager, and William E. Leuchtenburg. *The Growth of the American Republic.* Vol. II. (New York: Oxford University Press, 1980), 729.

23. Daniel Boorstin. *The Americans: The Democratic Experience.* Vol. 3 (New York: Vintage, 1973), 1; James MacGregor Burns. *The American Experiment.* Vol. II. (New York: Alfred Knopf & Co., 1985), 266, 279; Morison, Commager, and Leuchtenburg, *The Growth of the American Republic,* 730–731.

24. Martin Marty. *Modern American Religion: 1941–1960.* Vol. III. (Chicago: Univ. of Chicago Press, 1996), 3–5; Sydney Ahlstrom. *A Religious History of the American People* (New Haven: Yale University Press, 1972), 950.

25. Ahlstrom, *A Religious History of the American People,* 953–961; Marty, Modern American Religion, 277–312; Max Lerner. *America as a Civilization.* Vol. II. (New York: Simon & Schuster, 1957), 703–717.

26. Lester G. McAllister and William Eldon Tucker. *Journey in Faith: A History of the Christian Church (Disciples of Christ).* (St. Louis: Bethany Press, 1975), 411–416.

27. Kenneth L. Teegarden. *Sermon Chronicles, 1945-1958,* 72.

28. Ibid.

29. *Christian Church Yearbook,* 1949, 639.

30. *Christian Church Yearbook,* 1949, 639; *Christian Church Yearbook, 1950,* 667.

31. *Stewardship-Evangelism Crusade Program.* March 7–18, 1951, 1–4; Wanda Teegarden to Kenneth Teegarden, May 16, 1951, Wanda Teegarden collection..

32. *Central Christian Church Dedication Program,* January 3, 1954, 8; *Vernon Daily Record.* January 4, 1954, p. 1; *Vernon Times,* January 7, 1954, p. 9. Wanda Teegarden Collection.

33. Teegarden, *Sermon Chronicles, 1945-1958,* 72; *Central Christian Church Dedication Program,* January 3–8, 1954, 7.

34. Hershel A. McCarty to W. B. Smith. January 15, 1955; *Vernon Daily Record*, "Rev. Teegarden is Named Most Outstanding Citizen," January 28, 1955, p. 1; *Wichita Daily Times*, "Rev Teegarden One of Most Popular Men in North Texas," March 27, 1955, p. 7-D.

35. Ibid.

36. *Vernon Daily Record*, "Town Crier," by Orlin Brewer, July 19,1985, p. 12; *Vernon Daily Record*, July-August 1952.

37. Ibid.

38. Kenneth L. Teegarden to Central Christian Church Board Members, July 10, 1955, 1–2.

39. John Anthony to Kenneth L. Teegarden, July 12, 1955; First Christian Church, Fort Smith, Arkansas: *Minutes Congregational Meeting*, July 10, 1955; First Christian Church, Fort Smith, Arkansas: *Installation Program*, September 4, 1955; First Christian Church, Fort Smith, Arkansas: *Worship Bulletin*, September 11, 1955.

40. First Christian Church, Fort Smith, Arkansas: *Unpublished Church History*, Undated, 27–28; First Christian Church, Fort Smith, Arkansas: *Unpublished Historical Outline of FCC*, 1955–1958, 1.

41. FCC: *Unpublished History*, 28; FCC: *Board Minutes*, August 21, 1957, October 16, 1957; David A. Roozen Interview with Kenneth Teegarden, 1990, 311, 313. Wanda Teegarden Collection.

42. FCC: *Unpublished History*, 27–28; FCC: *Unpublished Historical Outline*, 1–4.

43. James Patterson. *Brown v. Board of Education: Its Legacy* (New York: Oxford University Press, 2001), 109–112; Taylor Branch. *Parting the Waters: American in the King Years: 1954–1963* (New York: Simon & Schuster, 1988), 222–224; David Halberstam. *The Fifties* (New York: Villard Books, 1993), 666–689.

44. *Fort Smith Times Record*, September 20, 1957, p. 1; FCC: *Meeting Agenda*, September 19, 1957; Lillian Moir. "Portrait of a Nominee," *World Call*. (October 1973): 12–13; Jon Regier to

Kenneth Teegarden, October 30, 1974, 1, GMP files, DCHS. Box 5, Correspondence R.

45. FCC: *Unpublished History,* 28; FCC: *Minister's Report to Official Board,* April 16, 1958; FCC: *First Christian Church Bulletin,* April 27, 1958.

CHAPTER IV

The Architect of Church

"Renewal is not just change. It is bringing the results of change into line with the continuity of our mission as the church. This is why we refer to restructure and renewal as a process. It is an endless Interweaving of continuity and change, conserving the meaningful aspects of a rich and enduring tradition, but realizing it must be a tradition facilitating its own continuous renewal."

Kenneth L. Teegarden

Executive Secretary: Arkansas
Christian Missionary Society
1958–1965

It was Friday afternoon in North Little Rock. The junior high school basketball team was playing a home game in the school field house. Seated in the stands, where he could be found every game day, was Kenneth Teegarden, executive minister of the Arkansas Christian Missionary Society. He and Wanda rarely missed a game, because their son David was a starter who would later be named to the all-city junior high school team. Kenneth was an avid sports fan, especially basketball, a sport he had both coached and officiated. And Wanda was a first-team starter on her high school basketball team. So the two of them held more than a passing interest in their son's games. Friends often accused Kenneth of organizing his work around his son's basketball schedule. And those friends further noted that Kenneth could become quite animated during a game, as he cheered the team on to victory. On occasion, they rumored, he even questioned the eyesight of officials!

Both Kenneth and Wanda had busy schedules. Wanda was taking classes at Little Rock University where she received her real estate certification and license. Kenneth was immersed in responsibilities in his new position with the state of Arkansas. But they somehow found time to be supportive of their children's activities—and to be a family.

The search committee announced its selection of the thirty-six-year old Kenneth in February; his installation occurred May 9th with Granville Walker presiding. After moving his family into their new home at 1323 Garland, he commenced his duties in Little Rock on July 1, 1958. Almost simultaneously with Kenneth's spring appointment in 1958, the Conference on Unification was held in Indianapolis to consult on the organization of states and areas. Through the years, state organizations had grown in topsy-turvy fashion with Christian Women's Fellowship and Christian Men's Fellowship groups developing separately from mass state conventions and from state missionary societies. The Indianapolis conference was called with the specific hopes of developing state delegate assemblies, thereby granting congregations a stronger voice in governance, and making the unification of state organizations a priority. By 1958 seven states had succeeded in unification, eleven had progressed to the use of committees on recommendations, but at least thirteen still functioned with mass conventions. Kenneth quickly saw state unification as a significant goal to be achieved in Arkansas. In 1959 and 1960 he traveled the state, visited congregations, met with various Disciples organizations and fellowships, and with task forces he had specifically appointed to address the matter of state restructure. With growing momentum from Kenneth's initiatives, the concept of a delegate assembly along with a change in the name to Arkansas Association of Christian Churches, were both approved at the April 1961 state convention in Little Rock. One year later the first delegate assembly convened in Harrison, with 1,450 registered and over 750 attending. It was the largest gathering of Arkansas Disciples in state convention history. The final draft of the new constitution for the Arkansas Association of Christian Churches was approved at this convention, combining the staff, assets, and program of the Arkansas Christian Missionary Society, the Arkansas State Convention of Christian Churches, the Arkansas Christian Women's Fellowship, and the Arkansas Christian Men's Fellowship. In less than four years Kenneth had accomplished the transformation of the organizational structure of the Christian church in Arkansas. The total number of states achieving unification by 1962 had reached fourteen, and the number relying on mass conventions was reduced to seven. Kenneth's success in Arkansas led to his appointment that same year as one of the 126 members of the Commission on Brotherhood Restructure. [1]

His ministry in Arkansas was one of much greater breadth than restructure. A reading of the seven regional assembly agendas prepared during his tenure as executive minister reveals that Kenneth designed each of those assemblies around four mission imperatives: (a) peace with justice, (b) Christian unity, (c) unified mission objectives of the brotherhood, and (d) mission of the Christian Church in Arkansas. In light of the predominant issue of race relations in Arkansas, the El Dorado convention of 1960 (already historic because Jane Furr of Fort Smith First Christian was the first woman in state history to serve as convention president) passed a peace with justice resolution that said in part that

Disciples in Arkansas would "seek all means available to make our witness felt and influence effective . . . in the present difficulties." Again in 1961 the Little Rock convention approved a resolution affirming that Arkansas Disciples would speak out "against all groups that attempt to limit freedom of speech and action of the individual under law," and expressed its support of "the church as a militant voice against oppression of all kinds," calling on every person opposed to tyranny "to live by the principles of Jesus Christ as the strongest force against oppression." [2]

These resolutions on peace with justice were not mere rhetoric for Kenneth. In 1960, along with a Catholic bishop and a Jewish rabbi, he co-founded the Little Rock Conference on Religion and Race. The Little Rock Conference on Religion and Race, which continues to exist, became a national model, an inspiring example of what a community can accomplish when its religious leaders work together in a common cause. Interviewed in 1980 on the success of the Conference, Kenneth responded, "The fact that today Little Rock has probably developed the most constructive race relations of any major city in the country, and the schools are more nearly integrated than any place I know, grew out of the fact that churches and synagogues joined together in leadership for the Christian ethical principles that were being confronted in those times." The experience reaffirmed Kenneth's long held belief that the church was a powerful force for social change. "I learned from that experience that of all human organizations— the church is the most effective in developing strong interpersonal relationships among different races . . ." He considered the creation of the Conference on Religion and Race in Little Rock "as probably one of the most significant aspects of my ministry." [3]

Regarding the imperative of Christian unity, Kenneth's address to the 1962 convention sounded his commitment: "The Disciples of Christ find their greatest relevancy in their conviction of the essential unity of the church." He was always careful to include in each Arkansas convention an ecumenical communion service. The speaker at that service in 1959 was Dr. Edwin

Dahlberg, president of the National Council of Churches; and the speaker in 1962 was Disciples layman, J. Irwin Miller, also president of the national council. The national council had recently come under severe attack, but the 1960 Arkansas gathering registered itself in strong support. The resolution said bluntly, "There are always apostles of discord present in society who seek to compound confusion for their own gain. The reputation and activities of the National Council of Churches are being unjustly impugned." In 1962, when the convention approved the creation of a Commission on Brotherhood Restructure, it did so by urging the commission to study "our place within the ecumenical movement with a view to accentuating the faith, traditions, and nomenclature which we hold in common with other communions of Christendom, so that restructure might narrow the divisions of church." Kenneth's strong ecumenical commitment was demonstrated through his leadership as president of the Arkansas Council of Churches from 1961 through 1963. His inaugural address stated it plainly: "This council must provide more than an occasional union service. It must extend and intensify the spiritual unity of Christians. Christians all over this country need to reconsider the use they are to make of their councils. The local council should be more than a shadow organization salving our bad conscience about unity through occasional fellowship meetings." [4]

Support of the unified causes of brotherhood mission was always a central issue in Kenneth's state convention plans. The Disciples' "Decade of Decision" proposal for the whole church was overwhelmingly approved by Arkansas in 1960, as was the formation of the Conference of State and Area Secretaries and Board Chairmen. Following the 1959 convention, Kenneth led a group of six teams of agency representatives in a four day swing across the state, visiting sixty-three congregations, in a successful effort to set financial goals for the Decade of Decision. Other examples were the aforementioned unanimous approval of the creation of the Commission on Brotherhood Restructure in 1962, and the ever increasing financial goal in Arkansas for unified promotion causes: $153,545 in 1960; $164, 349 in 1961; $170,000 in 1962; and $178,885 in 1964. As a further commitment to the wider church, Arkansas Disciples established a "Guidance and Recruitment" program in 1960 to bring qualified youth into church vocations. [5]

As could be expected careful attention to the mission of the Christian church in Arkansas was unfailingly a part of the convention agendas. In every convention from 1960 to 1963 attention was focused on the restructure of the region, with final approval coming at the Fayetteville Delegate Assembly in 1963. It was a huge step forward in structural efficiency to conduct the mission of Arkansas Disciples. For their own church growth, the region approved in 1960 an ambitious goal of 20,000 new members by 1970, evidence of Kenneth's firm belief in and personal success with evangelistic initiatives. And there were countless other initiatives taken on behalf of Arkansas youth, and women's and men's fellowships. The four priorities that clearly emerged through Kenneth's seven years of regional leadership in Arkansas—peace with justice; Christian Unity; unified mission of the brotherhood; and the mission of Arkansas Disciples—provided the template of his regional ministry, out of which came the plan of ministry underlying the mission of Arkansas Disciples during the Teegarden years. He maintained an even balance among the four and was able to advance Arkansas ministry in each of them. [6]

As was customary for Kenneth, his involvement in collaborative activities beyond his office became legendary. He served as a member of the Arkansas Council on Human Relations, co-founder of the Greater Little Rock Conference on Religion and Race, president of the Arkansas Council of Churches, chairman of the Board of Higher Education of the Christian Churches, member of the Board of Directors and Central Committee of Unified Promotion, member of the Agency Decade Program and Budget Evaluation Committee of the Council of Agencies, chair of the

Christian Service Committee of the Home and State Missions Planning Council, and trustee of Phillips University and the Drury School of Religion. He successfully combined these roles in providing creative ecumenical ministries to the religious leadership of the whole state. For example, he got the Arkansas Council on Human Relations, the Little Rock Conference on Religion and Race, and the Arkansas Council of Churches, to join in organizing a two-day Arkansas Ministers' Workshop, using the theme, "The Pastor's Role in Community Change." The workshop featured high profile religious leaders as speakers, along with consultants from the U.S. Office of Education and the U.S. Office of Economic Opportunity serving on panels to help pastors identify probable and possible changes that may come to their community and especially how to relate programmatically to the War on Poverty. The workshop was open to religious leaders of all faiths—Protestant, Catholic, and Jewish. It was the kind of collaborative effort that Kenneth believed best served all faiths and all people in Arkansas. He was forever active in community collaboration, integrating the life of the church with the needs of humanity.[7]

Arkansas was grateful for Kenneth's leadership. The 1960 state convention awarded him an all expense paid trip to the World Convention of Churches of Christ in Edinburgh, with a side trip to the Holy Land. It was the dream trip of a lifetime! Most days on the trip Kenneth wrote a postcard, addressed to David and Kirk, telling them something of what was pictured on the card, "Saw this castle today on the boat trip," or "I am flying by jet. We are really going fast, 570 mph, and at 24,000 feet in the air!" They were signed, "Love, Dad." He also wrote regularly to Wanda. On July 24 he commented, "Two weeks from tonight I will be back in New York and ready to start home! I can hardly wait because it seems such a long time that I have been gone. . . . .guess what! I ate SNAILS—six of them. I never thought I would be doing that. They weren't bad," he said, but he thought he could exist without "a steady diet of them." From London on July 29, he wrote "The days are going fast, but still too slowly. I am so anxious [to be home] I can't stand it. . . . I'll be home before long. It will be strange for you to set four places at the table again. Love you, Kenneth." [8]

Early in 1965, Dale Fiers and Jesse Trout made a special trip to Little Rock to persuade Kenneth to accept the position of administrative secretary of the Commission on Brotherhood Restructure, succeeding Dr. Fiers. Kenneth had impressed the commission with his leadership in the writing of a constitution for the unification of the church in Arkansas. Kenneth, however, turned them down, indicating that there was too much work remaining to be completed in Arkansas. But Dale made a second trip to visit Kenneth, this time making the compelling case that there "was no more important work in the church at that moment than restructure!" Out of his great respect and admiration for Dr. Fiers, Kenneth agreed to set aside his ministry in Arkansas and shoulder the ministry of administrative secretary of the Commission on Brotherhood Restructure, beginning July 1, 1965. [9]

The distinguished quality of his Arkansas regional ministry was acknowledged beyond the borders of Arkansas. In 1963, Phillips University awarded Kenneth an honorary Doctor of Divinity degree. And when he left his position in Arkansas, the Conference of State and Area Secretaries and Board Chairmen presented Kenneth with a Resolution of Appreciation, authored by Loren Lair, the powerful state secretary of Iowa.

RESOLUTION OF APPRECIATION
for
KENNETH TEEGARDEN

As a member of our fellowship he has served as Secretary-Treasurer and has represented us on the board of Directors of Unified Promotion. We have admired his commitment and trusted his judgment and counsel. He has endeared himself to all of us by his character, his wit, and his friendly spirit. Our fellowship has been made stronger because of his membership in the Conference.

As the executive of the Christian churches of Arkansas, Dr. Teegarden led this state in growth in stewardship, in world outreach, in social concern, and in organizational unity. His leadership at all times has been effective and positive. All of us have benefited by his example. The Conference wishes Kenneth well in his new work and we believe he will lead the commission on restructure wisely and in a statesmanlike way. We pledge to him our support as the brotherhood moves forward on this important task.

Loren E. Lair [10]

Administrative Secretary: Commission on Brotherhood Restructure 1965–1968

In June 1965, after resettling his family and their little mixed-breed dachshund Snitzie in Indianapolis on University Drive across the street from Dale and Betty Fiers, Kenneth officially began his ministry as administrative secretary of the Commission on Brotherhood Restructure. Wanda found employment at Community Hospital in Irvington as an administrative hostess, helping to prepare patients and families for surgery.

"Kenneth Teegarden—the office of leadership . . . to which you have been called, is of unusual historical significance in our Brotherhood's life." Disciples had long used the euphemism "brotherhood" in place of the term "denomination," a term that conveyed disunity and separateness. Granville Walker, chair of the commission, presided at Kenneth's installation. Following the opening words of his charge, Walker pledged that the commission would look to Kenneth for leadership and that he would not walk alone, but would be surrounded by dedicated leaders who shared the dream and were prepared to sacrifice. He spoke of the satisfaction that would come to Kenneth: " . . . you will have the singular privilege of watching a plan . . . prayed over reverently, thought through carefully, wrought out wisely . . . come to its full harvest."

Walker also warned Kenneth of danger: " . . . you will in this place of leadership also be the object of the 'slings and arrows of outrageous fortune' fired by opponents whose motives will vary from honest, though misinformed unwariness to unscrupulous ill will. It has ever been thus for those who march to the rhythm of a distant drum." "Be longsuffering," Walker advised Kenneth, "in dealing both with us who are your friends and with those who elect to be unfriendly." [11]

It was an important moment in Kenneth's ministry. He had become an acknowledged leader of the whole church, undertaking a leadership role that transcended agencies, societies, regions, and congregations. He opened his response on a light note, acknowledging that many who were present had expressed concern to him about his sanity and his judgment for accepting the position. But the compelling factor in his decision to accept, he attested, was his belief that there was widespread general acceptance of the need for this process of reorganization and reform. Then he proceeded to define the nature of the restructure process as well as anyone ever has before or since.

> Renewal is not just change. It is bringing the results of change into line with the continuity of our mission as the church. This is why we refer to restructure and renewal as a process. It is an endless interweaving of continuity and change, conserving the meaningful aspects of a rich and enduring tradition, but realizing it must be a tradition facilitating its own continuous renewal.

Kenneth said flatly that he did not underestimate the problems ahead, nor was he naïve about the outright attacks being made on restructure and its process. Fully aware of the universal tension between creators and consumers, he spoke of the restructure critics and their methods.

> A common stratagem of those wishing to avoid the swirling currents of change, or to thwart or impede the

process, is to stand on 'high moral ground' and view with alarm. They assert that the old way is intimately bound up in moral and spiritual considerations that will be threatened by any change. The new thing will look barbarous compared to the old. That which is being born is less spiritual and lacks the deeper values of the old . . . [But] our people will not let such impressions distort their judgment. They will reject the notion that the brotherhood has fallen victim to some nefarious plot to deprive freedom. Restructure will not diminish freedom—it will enlarge it! Growth and maturity in responsible structures enrich freedom.

Kenneth concluded his response with an acceptance of Walker's charge, and by quoting the words of his old professor and president of the international convention, Stephen J. England, "Now is the time to let the light of truth shine into the darkness of misunderstanding and misrepresentation. Let us move forward with increased determination to serve the will of Christ, the head of the church." [12]

Kenneth was neither new to the restructure commission nor its first administrative secretary. He had been an original appointee to the 126-member Commission on Brotherhood Restructure in 1962 and had participated in all of its meetings. The first administrative secretary, a part-time appointment, was George Earle Owen, who, due to an absence of funds to underwrite the position, was on short-term loan from the United Christian Missionary Society. One year later, 1962, A. Dale Fiers, president of the UCMS, succeeded Owen as administrative secretary. Then, in 1964, Dr. Fiers was installed as executive secretary of the international convention, while continuing to serve as president of the UCMS and administrative secretary of the Commission on Brotherhood Restructure. The workload was enormous. Less than a year later relief came when Kenneth accepted appointment as the first full-time administrative secretary of the Commission on Brotherhood Restructure. The position had finally received compensation, an adequate operational budget, and full funding. Kenneth commenced his duties as administrative secretary about mid-point in the commission's history. [13]

TIME LINE

Prelude to the commission

1956 *Panel of Scholars* founded and funded by the Board of Higher Education and the Division of Homeland Ministries. Panel met until 1962 when their work was published in three volumes.

1956 *Committee on Brotherhood Organization and Interagency Relationships* appointed by Dale Fiers at the Council of Agencies meeting held at Bethany College. Wilbur Cramblet appointed chair.

1958 Spring. *Conference on Unification* held in Indianapolis. Unification of state and area boards became a priority.

1958 July. Council of Agencies meeting at Canton, Missouri. Pivotal address by Williard M. Wickizer, "Ideas for Brotherhood Restructure."

1958 October. *Study Committee on Brotherhood Structure* composed of eleven members appointed at the International Convention in St. Louis with Williard Wickizer as chair.

1959 August. International Convention at Denver approved the recommendation to create a representative *Commission on Brotherhood Restructure.*

1960 October. Louisville International Convention approved the appointment of a *Commission on Brotherhood Restructure* constituted with 120 to 130 persons.

1961 February. *Office of the Commission on Brotherhood Restructure* established. Funding provided from Unified Promotion; International Convention; Christian Board of Publication, and National Benevolent Association.

1962 October. Los Angeles International Convention ratified the appointment of 126 members to the commission. All state societies represented. Kenneth Teegarden was one of the 126 members. Granville Walker was selected to chair the commission.

Commission History

1962 October. First meeting of the commission held in St. Louis.

1963 July. Second meeting of the commission held in Chicago.

1963 October. Miami International Convention approved the commission report and called for brotherhood-wide discussion of the document, "The Nature of the Structure our Brotherhood Seeks."

1964 June. Third meeting of the commission in Louisville. Three powerful lectures by Ronald Osborn proved highly influential on the nature of restructure.

1964 October. Detroit International Convention approved the revised document, "The Nature of the Structure our Brotherhood Seeks."

1964-65 Restructure Participation Meetings (RPMs).

1965 June. Fourth meeting of the commission held in Chicago. Kenneth Teegarden was installed as administrative secretary of the Commission on Brotherhood Restructure.

1965 October. Study documents presented to thirteen regional assemblies of the international convention and in all states.

1966 July. Fifth meeting of the commission held in Cincinnati.

1966 September. Sixth meeting of the commission held in Dallas.

1966 October. The Dallas International Convention received the proposed document "The Provisional Design," and approved the call for a representative assembly in 1967 to consider the provisional design.

1967 July. Seventh meeting of the commission in St. Louis.

1967 October. The St. Louis representative assembly revised and approved the Provisional Design.

1967-68 All states and agencies were to review and approve The Design.

1968 September. Eighth meeting of the commission in Kansas City.

1968 September 28. The International Convention in Kansas City was reconstituted in accordance with "The Provisional Design" by near unanimous vote. Ronald Osborn was the first moderator of the new representative General Assembly.

1968 October. Kenneth Teegarden resigned as administrative secretary, effective July 1, 1969, to begin his new ministry as executive minister of the Texas Association of Churches.[14]

Restructure: Background and Context

To grasp the magnitude of a Disciples attempt at institutional restructure in the 1960s and to fully appreciate the importance of Kenneth's specific role, the whole restructure effort should be viewed against the historic backdrop of the failed cooperative attempts. Disciples began as a movement in the nineteenth century to restore the unity of the church, which Thomas Campbell called essentially, intentionally, and constitutionally one, on the basis of the New Testament. The Christian Association of Washington, Pennsylvania, was organized to promote this plea. As time passed the urgencies of mission on a national and world scale increased, and it became clear to Alexander Campbell that the "restored local congregations" were not sufficiently equipped to do alone what needed to be done to fulfill Christ's mission for the church in the district, nation, or world. Campbell's approach to church organization began within the fellowship of Scottish Independents during his student days at the University of Glasgow. Nearly all of the essential elements of his early thinking on church order were supplied by the Independents. He emerged an advocate of the independence of each congregation free of any ecclesiastical organization beyond its own doors. In the thought of his younger days, not even unity could have a structural expression. But by 1841 his mind had turned, and he was writing, " . . . our organization and discipline are greatly defective, and essentially inadequate." Christ's institution is a kingdom, he said, "not a mob, not a lawless democracy. . . ." It was Campbell's view, by then, that "church" was a comprehensive term embracing nothing less than Christ's church universal. It was this basic fact, he claimed, that had to be considered in any plan of church organization. Campbell had grown to believe cooperation was a necessity, and was one of the first to call for a new look at organization structure. He became an advocate for correctional structure and wrote persistently in the *Millenial Harbinger* for what he plainly called church organization. In an article entitled "The Nature of Church Organization" he laid before the movement seven principles of church cooperation. [15]

The twenty-fourth chapter entitled "The Body of Christ," in his 1840 edition of the *Christian System* presented Campbell's whole plan of church organization; however, his most imaginative work on cooperative structure appeared in the *Millennial Harbinger,* 1843, under the title, "Church Organization," in which he described the planting of several congregations on the island of Guernsey and told of their natural progression into a cooperative structure. Kenneth Teegarden was particularly attracted to this writing by Campbell and often referred to it during his work on restructure. By 1849 Campbell was advocating a delegate assembly for the impending national meeting in Cincinnati, but the meeting turned into a convention and Campbell's attempt at cooperative structure failed. Instead, D.S. Burnett led the convention toward a "society" concept, and the American Christian Missionary Society was formed to assist in carrying out the mission of the congregations at home and abroad. "Society" was not thought of as a church organization, but an association of individuals. This "voluntary society" concept took root, allowing acceptance of organization in practice but repudiation of ecclesiastical structure in principle—which resulted in a long-term delay for new cooperative initiatives. Campbell continued to publish articles in the 1840s and 1850s on the need for church organization and cooperation, but to no avail.

Another attempt at unification occurred at Louisville in 1869 when Moses Lard, William K. Pendleton, Ben Franklin, and William T. Moore proposed the "Louisville Plan," a representation strategy consisting of delegates from congregations, counties, states, and the national convention. The attempt failed. Again in 1909 a Committee on Reconstruction and Unification was appointed to develop a proposal for a delegate assembly to which all agencies would be organically related. It too failed. But a compromise grew out of it; and thus the non-delegate International Convention of Christian churches was established in 1917 at Kansas City. Shortly thereafter came another attempt when a Committee on Cooperation and Unification was created to propose a constitution for the United Christian Missionary Society in 1919 that would bring all the general societies and boards, temporarily, into a single administrative unit. It was intended that state societies would follow by establishing an administrative linkage with the UCMS. But it did not happen. In fact the attempt at cooperation through a constituted UCMS sparked the calling of a "Restoration Congress." Less than a decade later the congress evolved into the North American Christian Convention and ultimately into a major schism in the movement.[16]

The Great Depression, World War II, and the post-war era generated a welcoming social environment for interagency cooperation. First to appear was Unified Promotion in 1935; then the Home and State Missions Planning Council in 1938; the Emergency Million campaign in the late 1940s; the church-wide Crusade for a Christian World in 1946 ; the national fellowship movement [Christian Women's Fellowship, Christian Men's Fellowship, Christian Youth Fellowship] in the late forties; the National Church Program Coordinating Council in 1950; the Council of Agencies in 1950; the Curriculum and Program Council in 1953; and the brotherhood-wide long-range plan for the 1960s Decade of Decision! The flow of these events activated the cooperative tradition and spirit within Disciples, demonstrating to the brotherhood that it was something more than disconnected clusters of independent congregations, and provided concrete beginnings for a major cooperative venture. [17]

Inspired by the success of this series of cooperative initiatives, and prompted by the fact that several state societies had begun to reorganize themselves into unified entities with delegate assemblies, the Council of Agencies appointed several ad hoc committees in the early 1950s to study interagency relationships and unification. In 1958, Williard Wickizer, chair of the UCMS Division of Home Missions and credited with being the "Father of Restructure," delivered to the Council of Agencies an address entitled, "Ideas for Brotherhood Restructure." It was a stimulating and insightful set of remarks that galvanized the Council into action. Four brief excerpts, reflecting the flavor of the nine-page, single-spaced address, appear in the sidebar.

With a century-long genealogy of failed attempts, what in the world prompted the leadership during the 1950s and 1960s to believe they could succeed in a restructure effort where so many before them had met defeat? The Disciples of Christ Historical Society conducted interviews with forty-seven leaders of restructure about twenty-five years after their work was finished. They were asked to state their reasons for attempting restructure at that time, and five general responses emerged.

First, it was noted by some that the World Council of Churches was urging all member denominations to study their structures in light of post-World War II social changes. Each denomination was to consider two questions: "Does your structure facilitate the fulfillment of the mission of the church?" and "Is the structure of your church responsive to the culture and to the world of the 1950s and the 1960s?" Several member denominations at that time began evaluating their structures and making some modifications. Sydney Ahlstrom, in his *Religious History of the American People,* noted "progressive organizational reform" in some of the denominations during that era and called it a sign of

[Only] in very recent days, has anyone dared to suggest that what the Disciples of Christ needs to do is to look at its total organizational structure and attempt a major restructuring that would result in more effective cooperation. Now it would seem that we have reached a degree of maturity as a religious body when such a restructuring might be faced with some hope of success.

We must come to appreciate the fact that freedom carries with it responsibility and that free persons in Christ must cooperate effectively with other free persons in Christ to accomplish those things we cannot do alone. In restructuring the brotherhood we must preserve the principle of voluntarism on the one hand, but must magnify the principle of responsibility on the other. That we have had too much of the former in the past and not enough of the latter goes without argument, but we must not be guilty of destroying the one to achieve the other. Responsible discipleship within the framework of freedom, should always be our organizational goal.

. . . . if [Disciples] were to get the idea that anybody was seeking to restructure the brotherhood in order to exercise greater control and to limit the autonomy of the local [congregation] the reaction would be violent. We have been strongly congregational from the very first and the vast majority of our people are determined that we shall stay that way.

Too frequently in the past we have wanted to prove our freedom by refusing to cooperate when all the time we could have proven it just as well and far more constructively by cooperating together for the advancement of God's kingdom. Of this I am sure, it is high time our brotherhood take a look at its organized life in its totality and restructure it according to a basic plan. For too long we have been willing to add patch on patch, never moving according to a carefully worked out master plan. I believe the mood of our people would support such an undertaking at this time. [18]

promise. By this reckoning, the Disciples' initiative in restructure did not occur in isolation, but was part of a general religious undertaking. [19]

Second, from 1920 to 1950 the increased number of Disciples agencies, both state and national, had resulted in a complex, multilayered system with less than adequate coordination and accountability. Many congregations thought they were little more than happy hunting grounds for state and agency financial appeals. Others thought the congregations operated as if the meaning of church began and ended with them. Acute pleas from congregations and the Council of Agencies demanded that an alternative be found to the freewheeling way of carrying out the mission—some practical and efficient means of cooperation. The agencies and states needed an integral unity, a responsible mode of making decisions, some sense of accountability to replace the "mine is mine and yours is an afterthought" mentality. Seven states had already begun the process of unification and had developed delegate assemblies. By 1962 the number of states with delegate assemblies had doubled, which helped spur the national societies and boards to do likewise. Recent decades had birthed a growing hope for an efficient, connecting relationship among congregations, states, and agencies, a hope for some form of representative delegate assembly that could engender at least modest accountability. Frustration with the lack of coordination, and the desire for more efficient connecting relationships, was cited most often and by most people as the single most important reason for attempting restructure in the 1960s. [20]

Third, Disciples had no theology of church beyond the local congregation. But in the thirties, forties and fifties they were, in practice, maturing into church, into something more than a loosely knit collection of congregations with agencies that tended to materialize as a need arose. Through the early years of Disciples history, an inadequate understanding of church had produced an inadequate structure. But there was a growing sophistication among seminary-educated Disciples clergy in the twentieth century. They understood the nature of church, what it ought to be, what it could be. Despite the growing conviction that church was something more than the sum total of local congregations, Disciples did not have a way to speak as church. Yet there was a hunger for church, a hope that the Christian Church could become a reality, a hope for recognition that church existed in regions and in general agencies just as surely as in local congregations. The concept of church, well down the list of reasons at the outset of restructure, gained force as the process unfolded, and became its most compelling feature. [21]

Fourth, the growing strength of the ecumenical movement caused some to seek restructure as a prerequisite to full participation in the ecumenical movement, its councils, and its collaborative ventures. That belief was fueled by a virtual explosion of ecumenical activity, including the establishment of the World Council of Churches in 1948, the National Council of Churches in 1950, the Consultation on Church Union in 1960, and Vatican II beginning in 1962. The momentum of ecumenism roused the quest for restructure in the minds of a fair number of Disciples. [22]

Fifth, the United Christian Missionary Society was a powerful Disciples agency, often resented because it was so much larger, had so much more budget, so much more programmatic material, and exercised so much more authority and leadership than the other agencies or states. It was criticized as being too big. Restructure was sought by some, particularly states, to trim back, if not break up, the UCMS. [23]

There were likely other reasons. The voice of Dale Fiers, contemporary with restructure, provides helpful insight. In July1962, Dale addressed the first meeting of the commission on Brotherhood Restructure with remarks entitled, "An Apologetic for Restructure." He began with the declaration that "[restructure] involves a fundamental reordering of Brotherhood life with principles that arise out of a fuller understanding of church." Dale proceeded to identify, from his front line experience, the four reasons he believed led Disciples to restructure: (a) reaching a climactic point in the long cooperative history of growing together;

(b) discovering a dynamic "sense of church," the basic concept emerging in the brotherhood's midst; (c) taking the movement toward unification in the state societies; and (d) insisting that appropriate unification must be achieved at the national level or the whole process will be incomplete. Then he concluded, "church is more than a local congregation—and appropriate expression of its life must be developed at all levels structurally, functionally, and promotionally. Failure to achieve this objective for Disciples of Christ is to miss the challenge of restructure in our time." [24]

Each of these forces held its place in the baroque pantheon of motives for seeking restructure in the 1960s. Together, they made the possibility of success appear more probable than ever before, even in the face of a hostile anti-institutionalism in the country at large. Most persons who supported the restructure effort were motivated by multiple reasons, some by all of them. In the beginning, the primary impetus for restructure came from the practical need for coordinating efficiency. A more distant impetus, was the theology of church, yet in time it became the premier objective and the most telling force advancing restructure.

Kenneth and the Provisional Design

During the period 1962–1968, the Commission on Brotherhood Restructure, one of the great creative assemblages of modern Disciples history, met annually. Its central committee, initially composed of eighteen members, and later twenty, and later still twenty-seven, met three to four times annually, and the five-member executive committee met, on average, three times per year. (See commission membership analysis and profile in Appendix, pp. 219-224.) Kenneth's responsibilities, as administrative secretary, included overseeing the logistics for these meetings, planning the agendas, managing the commission's budget, preparing special documents for the meetings, traveling extensively to help interpret restructure to congregations-states-areas-associations-societies-boards, writing articles defining the substance and process of restructure, responding to criticisms of restructure, preparing the central committee's reports and minutes for the commission, and preparing the commission's minutes as well as reports for the annual meetings of the international convention. These duties, of course, were not carried alone. Kenneth was blessed with exceptionally gifted colleagues: Howard Dentler, James Suggs, Gertrude Dimke, and Robert Friedly, who functioned together as a single team with Kenneth to assure that these responsibilities were accomplished.

At the start of its work in 1962, the commission requested a budget of $52,000 for its ministry but was granted only $20,000, thereby creating an annual scramble for funds that always left it undersubscribed. Until Kenneth came to the post of administrative secretary, it was uncompensated. But with his arrival a budget of $64,000 was finally approved and funded to support the commission's work. Slightly more than $18,000 of that amount paid for travel expenses for the commission and its committees. Another $18,000 was budgeted for interpretation. A third budget component of $18,000 underwrote the salaries of Kenneth and his secretary, along with insurance, pension, taxes, and housing. The final $10,000 covered postage, equipment, office supplies, telephone, printing, rent, and cost sharing in missions building. At the end of his first year Kenneth reported total budget expenditures of $57,375, or a surplus of $6,625. [25]

In his opening remarks to the June 1965 commission meeting, Kenneth advised, "we must enjoin the task of interpretation in a more definitive way." True to his word, Kenneth, worked in collaboration with James Suggs, the highly skilled and professional director of interpretation for the commission, to help prepare and circulate a thirty-two-page study booklet, *The Direction of Brotherhood Restructure.* Copies of this piece were mailed to every congregation as well as distributed at thirteen regional assemblies. Three restructure leaflets were written and printed, of which 275,000 copies of each were distributed churchwide. The filmstrip, "Brotherhood Restructure: A Process of Growing Up," was produced with a copy placed in every state and area office.

Brochures describing the filmstrip sent to every congregation with copies of the strip made available for use upon request through the office of the commission. Kenneth also helped arrange a special edition of *The Christian* for January 1966, based on the study booklet with reprints available in quantity for congregational distribution. Further, a schedule of articles was negotiated to appear in *World Call* during 1966. This immense effort was driven by the desire to assure full and accurate information was being circulated to all publications, regions and congregations.

An International Convention was not held in 1965. In lieu of that convention thirteen regional assemblies, or mini-conventions, were organized, each of three days duration—four in the east, four in the south, and four in the west. Collectively, these mini-conventions attracted a total of 15,000 people. A team was selected for each geographic cluster. Dale Fiers was the team leader for the assemblies in the east; Howard Dentler for the assemblies in the west; and Kenneth Teegarden for the assemblies in the south. The thirteenth assembly was held in Hawaii, for which Willard Wickizer volunteered to be team leader. In each of the thirteen mini-conventions the thirty-two-page booklet, *The Direction of Brotherhood Restructure,* was reviewed in depth, generating excellent interaction between the teams and those who attended. Kenneth requested that after each assembly the teams critique their performance so their presentation could mature and become stronger.

Between June and November, in addition to the four regional mini-conventions, Kenneth made restructure presentations at eleven state, district, and area conventions, in addition to six local congregations. Between November and the following March he delivered explanatory addresses to an additional thirteen state, district and area gatherings as well as ten local congregations. From 1965 through 1968 it is estimated that Kenneth conducted restructure sessions before approximately 340 Disciples associations, boards, institutes, councils, states, areas, regions, and organizations; 150 local congregations, and three international conventions [Dallas, St. Louis and Kansas City]—reaching a total of at least 40,000 persons. But it was the massive effort in 1965 that succeeded in placing the purpose and work of restructure on the radar screen for large segments of the Disciples' membership. [26]

Also, in the June 1965 commission meeting, his first as administrative secretary, it became apparent that the work of the Nature, Design and Authority Task Force was lagging. The commission had been in existence three years and the board of directors of the international convention had voted in February of that year, to "request the Commission on Brotherhood Restructure to exert every effort to complete its basic work by the St. Louis Convention, October 1967." But two of the NDA sub-committees were unable to find times to meet and the report submitted to the commission during the meeting was essentially a series of general philosophical statements on what the eventual design should ultimately contain. Due to the generalized character of the report, the plenary critique of its content trailed off in a dozen directions: covenant, ordination, ministry, congregational autonomy, delegate assembly, bicameral assembly, etc. The most prominent theme in the discussion was whether there should be an intermediate manifestation of church: region, zone, diocese, state, area, district, or no intermediate body at all. Late in the plenary session it was proposed and voted that The Design should contain national, regional and congregational "manifestations." The word manifestation was used to prevent the membership from thinking in terms of "levels" of church life, and particularly to relieve congregations from thinking of themselves as the bottom level, without authority. Everyone was to be on an equal playing field, one church without top or bottom. [27]

Sensing an impatient tenor in the commission on the production of a pre-constitution or provisional design, Kenneth saw the need to energize the committees' work. None of the task committees were scheduled to meet between June and December. During that hiatus, Kenneth read everything Alexander Campbell had ever written on church structure, organization, order, and discipline. He would always claim those readings were the major influence on his thinking about restructure. In addition, he reviewed all the documents the central committee and the commission had considered, read, heard or proposed. When the Task Force on Nature, Design and Authority convened in December, only half of its membership was present. Kenneth, however, was prepared and he prodded them into action. The first decision was to disband the three NDA sub-committees and to operate as a committee of the whole. It was also decided that the committee needed to immediately prepare a "pre-constitutional document." To expedite the process, Kenneth, as administrative secretary, was assigned the responsibility of preparing the first draft, with the advice of the task force to do so "along the lines discussed up to that time."

When the NDA task force regrouped in Indianapolis on January 12, attendance was 100 percent. Kenneth presented his draft. Suggestions were abundant. He was then assigned the task of preparing a second draft in time for the March 24th meeting of the central committee of the Commission on Brotherhood Restructure. Kenneth's second draft, accompanied by an invitation for written comments, was circulated in late February to all central committee members. As scheduled, the "Pre-Constitution " or "Provisional Design" document—as yet unnamed—was presented to the central committee in March and the whole meeting was devoted to the discussion of its content. At the conclusion of the session two motions were presented and approved: First, that The Design document be completed in language suggestive of a constitution, and that it be presented to (a) the commission in July; (b) the Dallas International Convention in October; and (c) the St. Louis International Convention in 1967. The second motion instructed the executive committee of the Commission on Brotherhood Restructure to bring to the May 1966 meeting of the central committee a report on the steps that would need to be taken for the provisional establishment and implementation of the Christian Church's constituting assembly. [28]

On Tuesday, July 5, 1966, in Cincinnati, Ohio, "A Provisional Design for the Christian Church (Disciples of Christ)" was read aloud by Kenneth, assisted by Myron Cole, vice chair of the commission, before the 112 members attending the Commission on Brotherhood Restructure. Following a period of questions, clarification, and general comments, the commission divided into six small groups and spent all of Wednesday considering the document paragraph by paragraph, noting their suggested revisions, which a rewriting committee, led by Kenneth, incorporated into the document that evening. On Thursday, in plenary, the "Provisional Design" was reviewed once again, with approval coming paragraph by paragraph. The final motion was put forward by Dale Fiers, "That the final article be approved as amended. . . . [and] that the 'Design' be submitted to the Dallas assembly." A seven-word sentence appeared in the minutes recording one of the most important benchmarks in Disciples history: "The entire document, as revised, was approved." [29]

It was a joyous moment. For the commission it was a milestone, a step toward church. For the NDA task force it was the end of their work and they were soon dismissed. For Kenneth it was a singular achievement! In six months, from December to June, he had moved the process from having a series of philosophical generalizations about a pre-constitutional document to having a commission approved third draft of "A Provisional Design for the Christian Church (Disciples of Christ)." Suggestions, revisions and ideas had come from nearly every member of the commission. W. B. Blakemore, for example, contributed language for the preamble, yet six others—Ronald Osborn, Kenneth Teegarden, Granville Walker, Dale Fiers, W.A.Welsh, and Albert Pennybacker—had labored for weeks on the preamble along side Blakemore. The preamble, in reality the "Covenant" in preamble language, appears today in congregational bulletins and Disciples literature all over the country, and is considered by many the most important element of the "Design." Kenneth had been the principal drafting author of the "Design" in its totality, which earned him the title "Architect of Restructure." Two decades later, George Earle Owen affirmed Kenneth's contribution: "Kenneth Teegarden was undoubtedly the key person. He was the one who did all the substantive work on restructure. He wrote it up in a masterful way with warmth, understanding and tolerance." [30]

But the work was far from over. Two more years of labor remained and the next major test, requiring immediate attention, was less than three months away. At the Dallas International Convention of 1966, "The Provisional Design" received major consideration on Monday, September 26th under the theme for the day, "Fullness of Life—Through the Church Renewed." The report of the commission, presented at 10:45 A.M., was discussed until noon. During the 3:15 P.M. business session a panel of commissioners seated on the platform before the convention was peppered with questions about the proposal. At the end of the session a vote was taken to receive the "Provisional Design" and transmit it to congregations, agencies, regions, and institutions for study and response, with the goal of provisionally constituting the international manifestation of the church under The Design at the 1967 St. Louis International Convention. The Dallas vote of more than two-thirds in support of this action was a truly affirming moment for the commission, more importantly for the church. Significantly, the Dallas Assembly approved representative assemblies for the future, with each congregation represented by at least two voting representatives and an incremental increase if the membership was in excess of 750. A later modification set representation at two per congregation plus one for each additional 500 participating members over the first 500 or portion thereof. [31]

One year earlier, the commission had exhibited a touch of impatience with what they perceived as a protracted process, but that opinion was reversed when the commission convened immediately after the international convention in Dallas. Loren Lair, state secretary in Iowa, said he wanted "for us to move as rapidly as possible, but not so fast that we will make mistakes in the next year or so . . . some points in the section on Regions are not acceptable as they are now. We can move too fast and lose what we have accomplished." Earnest Gray countered, "There is a danger in undue haste, but there is danger in undue delay. The indication in this assembly seems to say that people are wanting 'to get on with the job.'" Loren Lair rebutted, "It took us ten or twelve years to make the Council of Agencies effective." Action was taken by the commission to establish a consultative process between the central committee and the state and area secretaries to help define the work of regions and regional ministers. A Task Committee on Regions, chaired by W.A. Welsh, was confirmed; and at the November meeting the commission voted to invite all state secretaries not on the commission to participate. During the remaining months of its existence much of the commission's effort was focused on the issue of regions. It also fell to Kenneth during these months to negotiate a merger between the African American Disciples and the international convention. Kenneth succeeded in the negotiation, and Raymond Brown remembered that there were real differences of opinion, but Kenneth "stayed right in there and worked until he found a solution agreeable to everybody." [32]

When the commission met on January 11, 1967, Kenneth reported that 225,000 copies of the "Provisional Design" were in circulation, with orders still being received at a steady pace, pushing the publication of The Design into its third printing. Of the 9,000 responses in hand on that date, only a small percentage were negative. He further reported that he had delivered a presentation on "The Role of State Ministers and State Organizations in Interpreting and Implementing Restructure" to the Conference of State and Area Secretaries and Board Chairmen. Following his address the conference passed a recommendation to the commission, asking that the schedule for restructure be relaxed and stating there was not enough preparation time for any action to be taken at the 1967 St. Louis International Convention. The commission, after considering the recommendation, thought otherwise. It made plans to move ahead with the St. Louis International Convention as planned, adding a resolution by which the assembly could affirm its readiness or un-readiness to vote on the revised "Provisional Design" for provisionally constituting the Christian Church (Disciples of Christ). [33]

As the drive toward approval of the provisional design gained momentum, and with St. Louis a short distance ahead, opposition groups intensified their campaigns of criticism. One group, Disciples for Mission and Renewal, was led by Charles Bayer, a Missouri pastor whose opposition was based on the belief the Disciples were addressing the wrong issue. "I really didn't think our problem was ecclesiology. I thought our problem was the loss of our sense of mission. . . . I referred to our problem as a heart problem, not as an orthopedic problem. Simply getting the bones right wasn't going to help." In the 1965 plenary of the commission he had commented, "I hope restructure will bring renewal at every level. We have been called primarily to minister to the world as a servant people, and not to be democratic." Bayer's position was debated vigorously and openly. This group did not really oppose restructure. They wanted it to go further. Kenneth described the Bayer group in a neighborly tone, as a "counter balancing influence that kept the process from focusing entirely on 'how will it function best organizationally.'"[34]

Another group, called The Committee for the Preservation of the Brotherhood, was headquartered in Canton, Ohio. They operated anonymously with a return address of Box 1471. Kenneth often referred to them as "our friends at Box 1471." This group, led by James DeForest Murch, represented the Independent Christian Churches' point of view that had been critical of Disciples cooperative organizations for half a century. They wrote and distributed letters to all the congregations. They also sent their newsletter, *Restructure Report,* along with printed pamphlets such as *Freedom or Restructure?* and *The Truth about Restructure.* These publications brimmed with false claims: That restructure, among other things, would cause congregations to lose their property, lose their right to choose a minister, and that the proposed General Board and Administrative Committee in the new structure were nothing more than ecclesiastical courts. The statements were willfully misleading, confusing to some congregations, causing a few to withdraw: But they had almost no effect on cooperative congregations. It was estimated that of the 8,000 Disciples congregations, 4,000 to 5,000 of them were cooperative, and 3,000 to 4,000 were already of an independent cast and had not supported the current Disciples structure financially or any other way. In a long letter of response to Lesley L. Walker on this subject, Granville Walker had pointedly noted of this latter group," . . . [they] might be rallied to almost anything of a negative character. Many of these churches are already identified with the independent movement and could care less either about what is proposed in restructure or how we are currently organized. . . . [they] do not believe in what we have been doing in the past, and have not supported it." He ended his letter with the admonition that any congregation listed in the *Year Book of Christian Churches* that cares enough to go to the trouble to send voting delegates to the assembly can vote on this or any other issue, but each congregation must at least first care enough about the brotherhood's life to take this one step. [35]

The third group was the Atlanta Declaration Committee, led by Robert Burns and Robert Shaw. Burns was a member of the Commission on Brotherhood Restructure as well as a member of its central committee from 1963 onward. His deep concern was the protection of rights of congregational autonomy. On May 4, 1967, as support was clearly building for the provisional design, the Atlanta declaration committee circulated a document throughout Discipledom entitled "Atlanta Declaration of Convictions and Concerns." It contained inflammatory accusations, warning that restructure was an authoritarian, connectional system that would endanger congregational freedom; that it controlled from the top down; that the right of congregational voting delegates was taken away; that congregations would have no voice in the selection of the general minister and president; and that regions could prevent congregations from calling a minister of choice or from withdrawing. The statements were patently false and had been countered repeatedly by the commission, but to little affect. Kenneth said of the Atlanta group, "It was the one

Above: *The Teegarden church.*
Above R.: *Great-great grandparents: William Teegarden, 1793-1855; Catherine (Watt) Teegarden, 1792-1856; William Teegarden, 1834-1921.*
Right: *Grandfather Marshall Chester Teegarden, 1854-1925; Ida (South) Teegarden, 1863-1960; Kenneth's father Roy Teegarden, 1894-1977; Hazel Ann Teegarden, 1899-1984.*

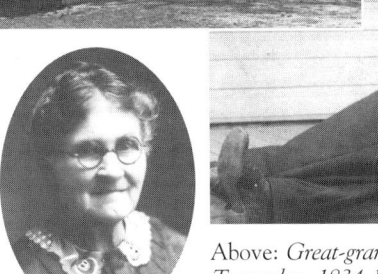

Above: *Maternal grandparents: James Swiggart, 1851-1940, Anna Belle (Hurst), Kenneth's mother Eva Belle Teegarden, 1895-1971; playmate, Hazel.*

Above: *Great-grandfather William Teegarden, 1834-1921.* Left: Kenneth's paternal grandmother Ida (South) Teegarden, 1863-1960.

Left: *Kenneth's boyhood home, 508 E. Broadway.*
Below: *Roy and Eva Teegarden, wedding photograph, 1912.*

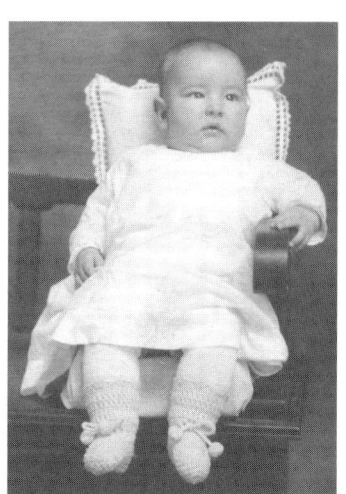

Above: *Kenneth Teegarden, 1922.*
Right: *Highland Elementary School.*
Below: *Kenneth Teegarden, second row, third from left. First grade, 1926-1927, Highland Elementary School, teacher, Miss Smith.*

Cushing, Oklahoma, 1921.

Sister Lenora, 1918.

Above: *Roy Teegarden, 1935 to 1940.* Below: *Kenneth, 1935.*

Kenneth, 1925.

Left: *Uncle Hurst Swiggart,
Kenneth's speech and debate teacher.*
Right: *Kenneth, high school gradua-
tion, 1938. Age 16.*

Kenneth, editor of school newspaper, Phillips University, 1942.

*Kenneth, president of Harvesters Service Club, Phillips University, 1942.
First row 3rd from right*

Kenneth, Blue Key, men's academic honor society, 1943. Second row 3rd from left

Above Left: Hiram and Carrie Strong, parents of Wanda Strong. Right: Henry and Sally Strong, grandparents of Wanda Strong; Hiram Strong (far right), father of Wanda Strong; Homer and Addie, brother and sister to Hiram.

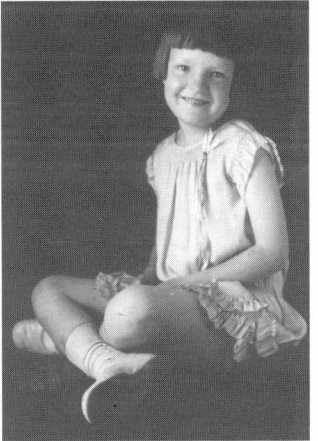

Above Left: Wanda, middle row, second from right, high school basketball team.
Above Right: Wanda Strong, age 6

Left: *Photo of First Christian Church, Kaw City, Oklahoma.* Right: *Kenneth · preaching at Kaw City, First Christian Church, his first student pastorate, 1940-1943.*

Right: *First Christian Church at Yale, Oklahoma, Kenneth's second pastorate, 1943-1944.*

Left: *Manvel Avenue Christian Church, Chandler, Oklahoma, Kenneth's first full-time pastorate, 1944-1947.*

Payne County Champions, 1944. Kenneth, assistant basketball coach, top left.

Above: *Kenneth Teegarden and Wanda Strong wedding photograph, May 28, 1944. Presiding minister and close friend from college, Charles Malotte.*
Left: *Kenneth and Wanda, 1944.*

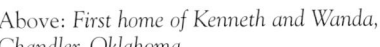

Above: *First home of Kenneth and Wanda, Chandler, Oklahoma.*
Right: *Kenneth, Wanda, and David in Texas City, 1947.*

Texas City, Texas, explosion, April 16, 1947.

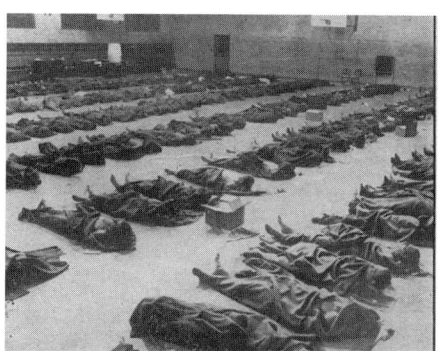

Left: *High school gymnasium, the temporary morgue.*
Below: *Kenneth, second from left, preparing to conduct mass memorial service,*
June 22, 1947.

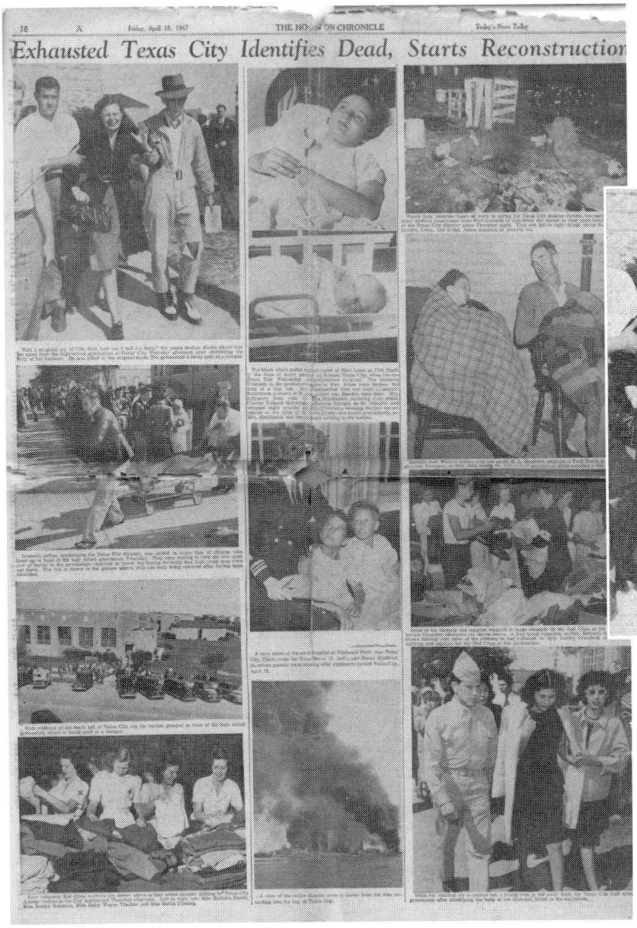

Friday, April 18, 1947

Exhausted Texas City Identifies Dead, Starts Reconstruction

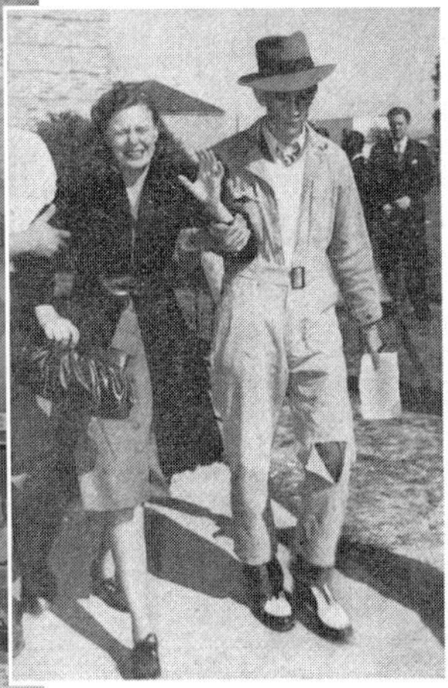

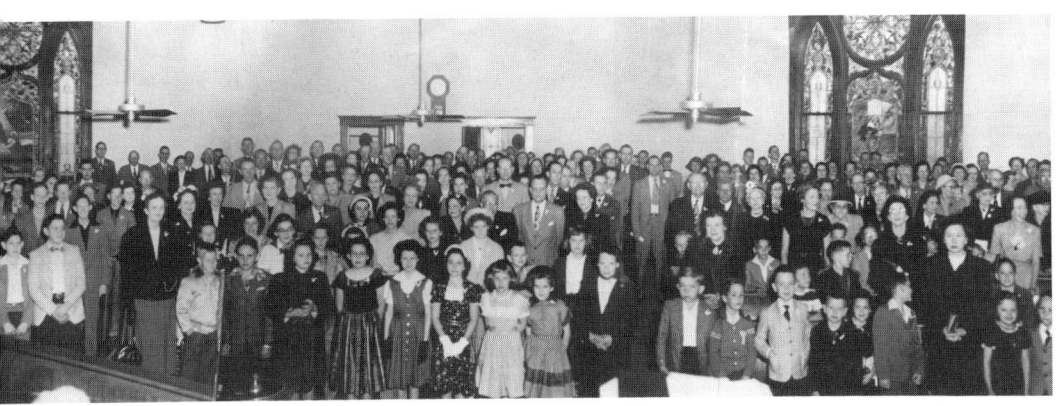

Kenneth (on right) assisting survivors in identifying the dead.

A record 101 joined First Christian Church on a single Sunday, March 18, 1951, Vernon, Texas.

The new First Christian Church at Vernon, Texas.

Left: *David Nowlen, Chairman of the Board, Vernon First Christian Church;* Center: *Kenneth Teegarden, Minister of Vernon First Christian Church;* Right: *Hollis Miller, Chairman of the Building Committee, Vernon First Christian Church, celebration of construction completion.*

Kenneth at construction site of new church.

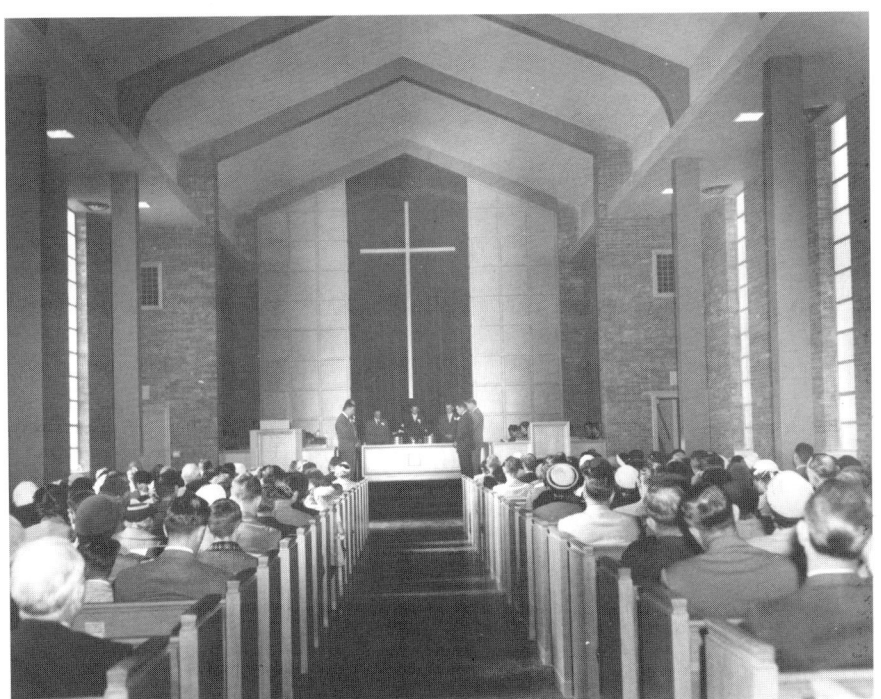

Above: First Sunday at worship in the new sanctuary, Vernon First Christian Church.
Left: Kenneth Teegarden preaching at First Christian Church, Vernon, Texas.

Kenneth (in back), coach of the city champion Vernon Buffaloes.

Top: *Kenneth, Wanda, and David, graduation from Brite College of the Bible, 1949.*

Above right: *Wanda Teegarden, mid-1950s.*

Above: *Kenneth, David, Kirk, and Wanda, Vernon, Texas, about 1953.*

Right: *First Christian Church, Fort Smith, Arkansas. Kenneth was senior pastor from 1955-1958.*

*Kenneth receiving Distinguished Citizen award from
Vernon Chamber of Commerce.*

Kenneth, Grand Chaplain of the Texas Masonic Lodge, 225,000 members.

From left: Hiram and Carrie Strong; Right: Eva and Roy Teegarden, 1967.

Kenneth: regional minister in Texas, 1969.

Kenneth and Wanda Teegarden with sons David and Kirk and daughter-in-law Susan Harris.

The Nature, Design, and Authority Task Force in session working on a draft of The Provisional Design. On the chalk board in back appears a hand drawn structure chart of the restructured church. Pictured from left to right are: Virgil Sly; chair, W.A. Welsh; and administrative secretary of the Commission on Restructure, Kenneth L. Teegarden. The man with his back to the camera is unknown.

Kenneth and Wanda Teegarden, 1971.

Fraternal visit to Asia, 1972, Ken & Wanda, tenth and eleventh persons from left, middle and back row.

Above: *Kenneth Teegarden, General Minister and President, 1973.*
Right: *Kenneth speaking at Sam Yek church in Thailand, 1972.*

Left: Kenneth speaking in Fayetteville, AK.

Above: *Kenneth and Dale Fiers in consultation, 1974.*
Left: *Kenneth with Bob Thomas, President of Division of Overseas Ministries General Assembly.*

Left: *Wanda and Kenneth Teegarden; Right: Dale and Betty Fiers.*
Photo taken at the time of Kenneth's election and Dale Fiers' retirement.

Above: *Kenneth in his Indianapolis office of General Minister and President.*
Left: *Kenneth in prayer at the 1977 Kansas City assembly.*

Wanda Teegarden, General Assembly, San Antonio, 1975.

Wanda Teegarden, 1978.

Above: *Kenneth and Avery Post, President of the United Church of Christ.*
Left: *Kenneth in Russia, 1974.*

Kenneth in Africa, 1976.

Kenneth addressing Disciples gathering.

Above: *Denomina-tional executives in consultation with President Carter. (Kenneth seated on President's right.)*
Left: *Kenneth Teegarden and President Jimmy Carter, 1978.*
Right: *Letter from Governor Jimmy Carter to Kenneth Teegarden, 1974.*

Office of the Governor

Atlanta

from the desk of
Jimmy Carter

11-15-74

To Kenneth Teegarden

Thank you for your expression of confidence & support. We'll keep you informed as my plans develop. I'll do my best never to disappoint you.

Your new friend,

Jimmy

THE WHITE HOUSE

WASHINGTON

November 13, 1980

To Reverend Kenneth Teegarden

I deeply appreciate your message of support following the election. Your friendship is very valuable to me.

As you know, my love for this country has guided my actions throughout my Administration, and I am proud of the progress we have made on a number of difficult issues. I have faith that as a people we will continue to meet the challenges of the future in a manner which reflects our highest principles of freedom, justice and human rights for all.

With my thanks for the encouragement you have given me and with best wishes,

Sincerely,

Jimmy

The Reverend Kenneth L. Teegarden
General Minister and President
Christian Church (Disciples of Christ)
Post Office Box 1986
Indianapolis, Indiana 46206

Left: *Denominational executives in consultation with President Ford, 1975.*
Below Left: *Letter from Jimmy Carter to Kenneth Teegarden, 1980.*
Below: *Kenneth Teegarden and President Gerald Ford, 1975.*

Above: *Teegarden family: Kenneth receiving honorary doctorate from TCU Chancellor and former classmate James Moudy, 1976.* Below: *Kenneth L. Teegarden and his two initial deputy general ministers, Howard Dentler and William Howland. This photo was taken in Kenneth's office in Missions Building in 1974.*

Kenneth Teegarden, John Humbert, and Duane Cummins. The Closing of Missions Building, 1995.

Above: *Kenneth preparing for chapel, Brite Divinity School, 1988.*
Left: *Kenneth visiting the historic site of "Brush Run" near Bethany in 1988.*

Kenneth and Wanda, taken near their Fiftieth Wedding Anniversary, 1994.

Above: *In retirement: Working a cross-word puzzle in six minutes.*
Right: *In retirement: Cutting out a cross-word puzzle.*

In retirement: With sons David and Kirk.

Above: *Kenneth's eightieth birthday party at Joe T. Garcia's, Fort Worth, Texas, December 22, 2001; four months prior to his stroke, nine months prior to his death.* Left: *In retirement: With son David*

The Teegarden Family, 2002, in the courtyard by University Christian Church. From left: Matthew, Grant, David, Wanda, a vacant place for Kenneth, Kirk, Sloan, and Blake.

that was primarily responsible for keeping on the [table] all the time the local autonomy issue." [36]

In the early summer of 1967 the Atlanta group demanded a meeting with members of the commission. The date of August 3rd was selected and seven commissioners (Granville Walker, Myron Cole, Ronald Osborn, Dale Fiers, Harrell Rea, Forrest Richeson, and Kenneth) traveled to Atlanta. Most of the meeting was an interrogation, with the Atlanta group raising its standard store of questions and the commissioners responding. At one point, Frank Drowota of Nashville raised a question about Winfred E. Garrison's widely referenced and circulated "Fork in the Road" address delivered at the Pension Fund breakfast during the 1964 Detroit International Convention. Drowota asked the commissioners if Disciples were taking the wrong fork. Kenneth responded sharply, "I could not and will not accept the concept that we have come to a 'fork in the road.' The choice of participation under the Provisional Design lies with the individual and the congregation. They always have the right to withdraw." This brought an attempted refutation, "I am not certain there is the right of withdrawal," whereupon Kenneth quoted the Provisional Design on the right of congregational withdrawal, and the issue was abruptly dropped. It was said of Kenneth that he was so knowledgeable and articulate about the content and meaning of the restructure text that he often intimidated people, even causing hesitancy on the part of some to raise questions. In his report to the commission regarding the Atlanta meeting, Kenneth wrote simply, "Your commission members made a serious effort to listen sympathetically and in a conciliatory spirit to the concerns expressed by the group and to interpret faithfully the revised provisional design." Robert Burns followed with his own letter to the commission reporting his opinion that questions and concerns were not satisfactorily answered. [37]

Kenneth interrupted his work in mid-August of 1967. He and Wanda flew to Dallas for the wedding of their son David. Kenneth officiated at the Central Christian Church ceremony. Then came the St. Louis Convention that gave triumphant approval to the provisional design in October. This was the first representative assembly—a long thwarted Disciples aspiration to strengthen the congregational voice in governance that had at last become a reality! Howard Dentler, a member of Dale Fiers' professional staff, reported 5,093 registered voting representatives from 1,967 congregations. In addition, there were 4,482 non-voting members who brought the total of local congregations present to 2,133—only 166 of whom, by their own choosing, did not have a registered representative. Of the 5,093 voting representatives, 1,750 were ministers. Even more important, the business sessions, rated excellent by 91 percent of the participants, had an average attendance ranging from 4,000 to 4,700. The convention majority vote by congregational representatives in favor was overwhelming, well beyond the two-thirds requirement with fewer than seventy-five votes in opposition. Following this congregational approval came the two-thirds majority approval from states, areas and agencies—achieved prior to the September 1968 assembly in Kansas City. At the February 1968 meeting of the central committee, Kenneth reported that since October he had spoken on restructure in forty-seven Disciples associations, boards, and conventions as well as twelve congregations. Other commissioners had been on the road as well, but not to so many places. By April, Kenneth could report that eleven national agencies had approved The Design, more than the two-thirds requirement, and that five states had approved, Georgia being the first by a delegate vote of 155 to ten. [38]

After six years of arduous labor, the Commission on Brotherhood Restructure presented the *Provisional Design for the Christian Church (Disciples of Christ)* to the convention in Kansas City on Saturday afternoon, September 28th. It was 3:35 P.M. when the moderator, Ronald Osborn called for a vote on Resolution # 55. It seemed like the entire auditorium stood to vote yes. The assembly, at the invitation of Dr. Osborn, broke into the doxology. In the long history of Disciples, this was one of its most storied moments—one of the rare cooperative triumphs in

Outline of the Provisional Design

I. Name
II. Membership and Participation
III. Christian Church in the United States and Canada
    A. The General Assembly
    B. The General Board
    C. The Administrative Committee
    D. Officers
    E. Administrative Units
    F. Nominations and Elections
IV Christian Church in Regions
    A. Nature and Purpose
    B. Membership and Participation
    C. Functions
    D. Shape and Boundaries
    E. Structure and Staff
V. Christian Church in Congregations
    A. Recognized Congregations
    B. Rights and Responsibilities
    C. Representation
VI. Ministry
VII. Revisions and Amendments

The Christian, December 10, 1967

structural politics. Near the back of the platform, Kenneth Teegarden rose from his chair and joined in the singing. Exactly one month later, Dale Fiers wrote a letter to the Commission on Brotherhood Restructure, stating, "It is with deep regret that I share with you the news of Dr. Teegarden's resignation as administrative secretary . . . to accept the call of the Texas Association of Christian Churches as executive minister. . . . Dr. Teegarden's contribution to the restructure of our Brotherhood is outstanding in every way. He will be greatly missed." [39]

Kenneth's Reflections on Restructure

Measured in time alone, Kenneth's ministry as administrative secretary was only four years. Measured by the intensity of the work and the magnitude of the achievement, it was one of the longest and most accomplished ministries of his life. Granville Walker had prophesied that Kenneth would enjoy the deep satisfaction of watching a plan "thought through carefully, wrought out wisely." Much of what had to be "wrought out wisely" was Kenneth's own doing. Walker also prophesied that Kenneth would be the subject of "slings and arrows." He was, indeed. But it was ever the case, before, during and after his ministry on restructure, that in the teeth of opposition, Kenneth's qualities were at their highest. Nothing seemed to daunt or weary him. Making hazardous decisions seemed a natural part of his ministry.

During subsequent decades, Kenneth was frequently interviewed about his role in restructure, about how effective or ineffective he thought restructure had become, and about several important issues dealt with during the course of developing the "Design." One of those interviews occurred in the spring of 1990, a little more than two decades after the fabled Kansas City Assembly and five years after retiring from the office of general minister and president, Kenneth sat for the recorded interview with James M. Seale, president of the Disciples of Christ Historical Society. The subject was restructure. This oral interview with Kenneth is one of the great treasures in the Disciples historical archives because it focused on the salient issues of the restructure journey: church, congregational autonomy, Christian unity, covenant, and the role of regions.

The first question to Kenneth was on the concept of "church" as the root of restructure. Kenneth accurately responded, "There was a maturing of thought with most of us throughout the beginning of the process. . . . we were about half way through the process when we began to see an ecclesiological concept emerge that said, we are not churches—we are 'church.'" What was the meaning of church to the twentieth-century design makers? In essence, they believed God, through covenant, called us to be a servant church, to be set apart from the world and to work for peace and justice among the peoples of all nations. Christ prayed fervently that we may all be one in him—one body, one spirit, one hope, one faith. Paul taught that we should build this oneness upon the cornerstone of Christ, and we would then be built "together" into a household, into a dwelling place for God, to perform Christ's ministry of seeking peace and justice. Nineteenth-century Disciples sought this oneness through the Body of Christ. They referred to it as a "community of communities." Twentieth-century Disciples leaders were inspired by a "sense of church" or oneness that led to an edification (restructure) or building up of the disciples as more than an association, a society, an assembly, a policy of cooperation; but a church, a whole church—congregations, regions, general units cooperating together as a single entity, Disciples becoming one with the whole Body of Christ, Christ's Church Universal. "Whole church in covenant is the very heart of Christ's great prayer for the church to be one (John 17:20-24); Paul's blueprint for building a household of God (Ephesians 2:19-22); Campbell's premise for church organization (*Christian System*); and the driving force for the twentieth-century edification (restructure) of Disciples into the Christian Church (Disciples of Christ) [The Design].

The documents of restructure reveal that Dale Fiers first introduced the concept at the second central committee meeting in January 1962. In that session Fiers spoke extemporaneously when the question "Why Restructure?" was raised, and the secretary recorded his remarks.

> "[Restructure] came as the logical consequence of far reaching program development and cooperative work, the critical focus of which was to develop the local church

in its life, in its outreach, in its mission, in its community, nation and world. You set in motion the forces that [brought] cooperative planning. You set in motion the forces that called for [the] bringing together of all the interests of the church. When you shift from the society concept . . . to the development of church you set the stage for a churchly base that gives life and vitality and direction to the whole community. Here is the dynamic base for all of this."

So impressed was the committee with Dr. Fiers' succinct comment that they asked him to develop a full address on the subject, which resulted in "An Apologetic for Restructure," delivered to the full commission six months later, and quoted earlier in this writing. Dale's 1962 statements came more than two full years prior to the famous set of three lectures presented by veteran scholar Ronald Osborn in Louisville, July 1, 1964. In his first lecture, "The Calling of the Church," Osborn turned to the servant poems and songs of Second Isaiah: "Behold my servant . . . in whom my soul delights. . . . bring forth justice to the nations". In the second lecture, "The Nature of the Church," he asserted, "The church properly understood is both institution and event, both organization and community, both form and spirit, it is both catholic and body. Its divine character inheres in both sides of each affirmation." Life must have structure, he proclaimed, "Spirit requires a body to give it a place to function." The third lecture, "Building the Church," contained his oft-quoted characterization of church corporate life, "It is something far more than a convention, far more than a policy of cooperation, far more than an association of churches. It is the church— as surely as any congregation is the church. It is not yet the whole church—but it is the church." [40]

The lectures were powerful, providing—according to many— the most dynamic moment in the work of the commission: a seismic change in Disciples ecclesiological self-understanding. They crystallized the commission's thinking around the concept of church and from that moment it became the driving force behind their work. So powerful were these lectures that they were quickly published in booklet form, *Toward the Christian Church,* and distributed as widely as possible throughout Disciples congregations and regions—selling for twenty-five cents per copy. Because of the wide circulation, many Disciples were under the impression the concept of church had been Osborn's. The concept, of course, can be found in Campbell's writings; but Dale Fiers reintroduced it to Disciples during the restructure discussions. Ronald Osborn performed the invaluable ministry of imbedding this guiding principle in the heart of the commission and expanding their grasp of its meaning through the force of his pen and rhetoric. Kenneth was quite accurate in saying the thought of the commission on the concept of church matured with the process.

Kenneth was regularly asked to comment on the question of "congregational autonomy." Aware that the question of autonomy had derailed all previous attempts to develop cooperative structure, he responded, "From the beginning there were fears that restructure was going to interfere with the autonomy of congregations. I don't think there was any inclination . . . to assault in any way the concept of autonomy of the congregation. We did not try to attack autonomy; we conscientiously and consciously did not use the word in the "Design," but recognized the church in all its manifestations. The concept of local determination was so inherent to the Disciples' understanding of church that we were not about to try to displace that concept, but to make it a more mature concept." Reference was made to the Atlanta Declaration group. Kenneth noted their catalogue of accusations: "it kept the process from being one of full enthusiasm to move forward to the fullest kind of covenantal concept. Instead of being able to begin with what is the most fruitful possibility, we had to say what is the most fruitful possibility that is favorable to [all elements]." The commission wanted to make the point that the work and witness of the local congregation did not end with the congregation; it was a unit of the body; but not the whole body. But in the final draft, congregational rights were detailed in the Design; responsibilities less so. Restructure was so intent on reassuring congregations of their autonomy that it fell short on knitting them together as a manifestation of "church." This deeply aggrieved Kenneth, yet it was the only way the "Provisional Design" could be approved. When one-half the congregations were planning to leave after restructure, Kenneth tried to prevent it. It was not the minor loss of funds that troubled him; it was the loss of half the membership he believed was needless! [41]

At the beginning of restructure, many opponents believed the only reason it was being attempted was to allow the Disciples to become a more prominent part of the ecumenical movement through the Consultation on Church Union or to merge with another religious body. Kenneth answered the accusation, "We did not restructure in order to unite, but we restructured in a way that will not deter our historic commitment to Christian unity." One of the negative restructure outcomes, Kenneth believed, was to delay church union. In 1974 the general assembly passed a resolution adopting a procedure for uniting with any religious body. "The requirements of that procedure are so rigid," declared Kenneth, "that we will not in the lifetime of most of us see any church union. It must be approved by two-thirds of the general assembly voting representatives; it requires approval by a majority of the regions representing two-thirds of the total membership; then it must go to the congregations, again representing two-thirds of the membership; then it returns to the general assembly for another two-thirds affirmative vote. Finally it provides that regions and congregations not wanting to participate may remain outside. We would not be able to come up with a plan that would meet all of those requirements satisfactorily." To date the procedure has not been tested. The work of the Consultation on Church Union collapsed before reaching Disciples for a vote. [42]

"Covenant," Kenneth emphatically and repeatedly proclaimed, "is the most significant accomplishment of restructure." According to Howard Dentler, Kenneth believed in it strongly; he lived the covenant; and he saw it as ever so much more than an agreement; much stronger than a legal contract. For Disciples, the authority of the church is understood through covenant: a call for trust, compassion and forgiveness. To Kenneth it was the heart of restructure; it was the heart of Biblical faith, God and God's people bound together in a solemn promise. The Bible overflows with covenants: the one with Noah, the one with Abraham, the one with the children of Israel at Sinai, the covenant written on the hearts of people as described by Jeremiah, the news of the Gospels as a new covenant, and the new covenant in Jesus' blood. It was clearly a biblical concept and therefore not at all unexpected for Disciples to express their restructure in covenantal relationships. One of the important intentions of restructure was to replace "autonomy" with "covenant." Kenneth described the essence of covenant as:

> . . . the very beginning of the nature of the church of which we are a part. We are a community bound by covenant. . . . our relationships are not hierarchical, they are not constitutional; they are covenantal! In our theological understanding of the word, we do not think of it as contractual. . . . 'I will be your God and you will be My people.' . . . we will be congregations together forming a region, we will be regions and congregations living together in covenant to form the Christian Church in a general manifestation. As a whole church we are bound in covenant to the whole church of Jesus Christ. We were not just establishing a structure; we were establishing a covenantal community.

Kenneth added: "I never preach a sermon, no matter the subject, no matter the text, that I don't slip in the point that we are a church bound by covenant, because I think it is the means by which we communicate something of the essence of a free church, a church that embraces diversity and encourages freedom and responsibility. Unfortunately, in the last ten years or so in orienting the post-restructure generation we have not done enough to communicate that we are a covenantal church." [43]

Finally, in regard to regions, from the beginning a controversial subject, Kenneth was firm in his view that, "The regional manifestation was spelled out as complete as was possible. It was left as an unfinished task." The commission spent more time and energy on this topic than most others, but was never able to pull it all together to everyone's satisfaction. In retrospect, Kenneth commented on the difficulty of finding common ground for regions, "You cannot have the same kind of regional expression in the Southwest as in the region of Utah. They are vastly different." As to the plan for fewer and larger regions, Kenneth wrote in 1975:

> The whole idea of fewer regions is based upon two primary principles: One, that all entities seeking to fulfill regional responsibilities should be viable operations from the numerical and financial standpoints; and secondly, that larger geography will require new understanding of administrative functions from a central location, with pastoral care and oversight dispersed. At the very heart of the concept of fewer regions is the proposition that administrative functions should be coordinated at fewer locations, [reducing] duplication of effort, and that pastoral care and concern should be operative at the nearest and most personal level possible. Unfortunately, the terminology of *larger regions* rather than *fewer regions* has been used and the implications have not been adequately discussed.

But his deeper concern was that structural development among regions was being determined more by economic circumstances than church planning within the context of covenant. When 2,700 congregations were announcing plans to leave the brotherhood if restructure was approved, Kenneth, who had been a state secretary, thought state secretaries should be doing more to educate and change the opinions of those congregations. He met with the state secretaries and pleaded with them to help congregations understand that the pamphlets coming from Atlanta and Canton were nothing but fear mongering. But he was unable to move the secretaries to action. He was profoundly affected by that failure. In the commission he continued to work hard analyzing numbers, developing diagrams without reference to state lines, [He once developed a model reducing the number or regions from thirty-nine to ten] trying to adjust boundaries in his quest to discover the most effective regional configuration, but it eluded him. New geography and new language were not readily acceptable to the state leadership of that generation, who tended more toward preserving rights and territory, than toward developing a new vision of region. [44]

Kenneth held a high opinion of regions and what they were capable of doing; he saw them as the key to successfully launching restructure through both education and leadership. He and Dale Fiers wanted desperately to redefine and strengthen the role of regions. Neither had envisioned regions clinging so tightly to their autonomy, boundaries and size of staff. But neither regions nor general units chose to take the lead in a teaching role to assist with the understanding of covenant, the understanding of church, or the general implementation of restructure. Consequently, the various manifestations all were initially unsure of the new structure, creating tentativeness in their early attempt to become "church." On the question of the initial implementation of restructure, Kenneth was disappointed. For example, regional leadership did not help local pastors catch the vision of sending informed members to general assembly. General assembly materials were always sent sixty days in advance with the thought that congregations and their voting representatives could research, study, and debate the issues thereby creating a better prepared constituency that could be brought together in assembly to debate from informed points of view. Kenneth stated repeatedly the general assembly was constituted as a representational assembly, not a delegate assembly. He always corrected anyone who referred to it as a delegate assembly. He argued that a representative is chosen and entrusted to act on behalf of those appointing the person and charged to decide based upon faith, reason, and conscience. A delegate, on the other hand, is elected to vote according to the dictates of those appointing the delegate. Representatives were not to arrive "instructed," but "informed." He believed it was a regional responsibility to see that this happened. He further envisioned that this process would be used to prepare for regional assemblies as well. Regions did not rise to the greatness Kenneth thought was in them. Yet Kenneth never failed to do or say all he could in support of regional leadership. In one of his last public interviews, in 1990, he was asked directly how he would rate the quality of regional leadership. He responded, "On balance, quite highly. If we were to examine the thirty-six regions we would find that at least thirty of them are very actively involved in state councils of churches, local ecumenical bodies, and frequently are among the leaders of those organizations." [45]

With restructure, Disciples had accomplished something quite extraordinary in the face of great historical odds! Some claimed that only the ecclesiological language changed, that the leadership of Disciples along with the general units, regions, and institutions remained visibly the same. But the change was in what could not be seen: "covenant" and "church." Disciples had found a new, vital, and creative means of linking everything in their structural life—including the promise that links one age to its successor. Previous generations of Disciples leadership had failed to accomplish this task.

Kenneth warned in 1965 that the new structure would look "barbarous" to some; to others it would seem "less spiritual and lacking the values of the old way." And in the years immediately following restructure it was fashionable and conventional to be critical: Restructure did not go far enough; or it was entirely too connectional; restructure developed too quickly; more time was needed; or the restructure process moved too slowly; if membership declined, it was the fault of restructure; if offerings sagged, it was the fault of restructure; if there was a planning glitch, it was the fault of restructure. People became particularly adept at tracing the roots of any controversy to a fault of restructure. Moving from autonomy to covenant was found to be complicated. Time was required to overcome the hardness of tradition.

But Kenneth had also assured, "our people will not let such impressions distort their judgment. They will reject the notion that the brotherhood has fallen victim to some nefarious plot. . . ." Through the peoples' judgment, expressed in representative forums, the provisional design within a decade became The Design of the Christian Church (Disciples of Christ) and by its own approved procedures it was successfully revised in 1984, 1994, and 2005! Understanding of "church" and "covenant" slowly took root in the hearts of the people, the regions, general units, and congregations; and it was determined unnecessary to have a constitution in addition to The Design! The covenantal structure among Disciples, at this writing, is approaching its fortieth birthday! This remarkable thing happened because, in Kenneth's words, "Growth and maturity in responsible structures enrich freedom."

Judged by most accomplishments in church history, the production of the provisional design was a monumental achievement. It was the product of the environment of the time as much as the minds of those who wrote it. And it was not conceived to be eternal. Kenneth made that plain when he told the commission that restructure was "an endless interweaving of continuity and change—a tradition facilitating its own continuous renewal." It was Kenneth who inserted into The Design the Committee on Structure and Function, later to become the Task Force on Renewal and Structural Reform, because of his absolute certainty about the continuous need for reform and renewal. He, more than anyone else knew The Design was neither immutable nor immaculate. It was a practical, workable document that has been successfully adapted by Disciples to the changing requirements of nearly four decades. Regarded by many as the most significant achievement in the modern history of Disciples, restructure will forever carry the imprint of Kenneth Teegarden, who is rightfully and deservedly identified as the "architect of restructure."

Executive Minister: The Region of Texas

Kenneth and Wanda labored over the decision to accept the Texas offer. He also talked to Dale Fiers at length about the matter. Dale told Kenneth he should make the decision in terms of what he felt "called" to do. He hoped Kenneth would stay, but assured him that he would fully support whatever decision he made. On August 9, 1968, Kenneth informed the Texas search committee he would accept their invitation. Nine months later, as the time for departure neared, Kenneth wrote to Dr. Fiers: "Now that the time for me to leave is about here, I really hate more than ever to leave. June 30th will make four years and one month with you and they have been the most meaningful ones to me. I am indebted to you personally for all I have learned from you, and especially for your friendship. I am most sincere when I say that my association with you and Howard has been the most rewarding experience of my life. We sincerely hate to leave." [46]

The Teegardens arrived in Fort Worth, Texas, during the month of June 1969, a bit ahead of the July 1st date scheduled for his new ministry to begin. Their son David had graduated from Texas Christian University five years earlier, was now married to TCU graduate Suzanne Harris, and completing his medical education in Galveston. Their son Kirk would commence his sophomore year at TCU in September. And Wanda found professional expression for her life in Fort Worth with a personnel placement firm, assisting individuals in their search for economic and employment stability. In addition, she settled the family into their Fort Worth home, managed the household, and created an atmosphere of home where all could continue to grow together as family.

They were a close family. They enjoyed each other and wanted to be near home. When the family learned of the impending 1969 move to Texas, David arranged a transfer from the medical school he was attending in Indiana in order to be in Texas near family. And Kirk who was attending his first year of college at Indiana State University, upon learning of his father's new appointment, joined in the move and transferred to TCU. Kirk in later years recalled of his father, "I 'heard' Dad's sermons throughout my early life, but didn't really 'listen' to them until later in years. My memory of Dad, was teaching more through actions than words. He preached sermons without opening his mouth. Dad was always approachable—although I was almost always aware of what his answers were going to be. He was a regular dad at home; he let me be myself—and not many knew I was a preacher's kid." David's recollections were quite similar, "He was soft spoken and easy going around the house. Religion was not prescriptive. Each of us understood our own faith on our own terms." David remembered too that his father "always championed the less privileged. He was not into possessions, he lived plainly and simply, drawing his strength from family, faith, and friends. He built a list of values and attributes that he believed best shaped life, and lived by them . . . he was without question the most influential person in my own life." [47]

A selection committee of eighteen members chaired by Dr. Travis White, president of Mid-West University at Wichita Falls, and including among its members Granville Walker, James Moudy, and William Howland, had unanimously agreed upon Kenneth Teegarden as the person to succeed Dr. Tilford Swearingen, under the new title of executive minister of the Christian Churches in Texas. Disciples' congregations in Texas at that time totaled 475. During the nine-month period between the announcement of his selection in October 1968 until their move in June 1969, Kenneth proceeded to build an extraordinarily strong staff to assist him with his regional responsibilities. Kenneth selected three associate executive ministers, Dr. Harrell Rea, Dr. Roy Holt, and Dr. James Suggs. Two of these, Rea and Suggs, would later succeed Kenneth as regional ministers of the Southwest. He also recruited James Oglesby to lead youth work in the region. And nearby, the Dallas County Joint Board of Christian Churches, originally established for oversight of new church establishment, was accumulating additional functions and transforming into "area" status. Warren Chrisman, who would later become regional minister of Mid-America, was head of that board and a member of Kenneth's original team. The High Plains area had just been formed by combining Districts 1 and 2, encompassing Amarillo and Lubbock, and John Knowles was selected as the area minister just as Kenneth arrived. Kenneth built a capable and seasoned staff that served the church with distinction, both during Kenneth's tenure and beyond. [48]

When Kenneth arrived in Texas, Disciples nationally, were launching a drive to raise $4 million for reconciliation, the urban emergency program of the Christian Church. The Texas state goal for the campaign was $400,000, or 10 percent of the entire general goal. Kenneth immediately tackled the issue, recommending the organization of a reconciliation committee in each congregation and setting individual and family goals of $100 to be paid at a rate of $5.00 per month. At the August Texas Disciples youth convention attended by 875, a total of $6,300 was pledged for reconciliation. By December 1st, Texas Disciples had pledged $424,130. The state was allowed to keep fifty percent for use within its borders and in the months ahead the region distributed grants to establish diphtheria immunization centers in urban poverty pockets, to help fund pre-school opportunity for children of minority groups in impoverished areas, and to help fund bilingual staff for minority kindergartens in the inner-city. These are merely representative, but they graphically tell the story of a very successful campaign and the wise deployment of those funds for

Disciples outreach ministry to urban areas of Texas under Kenneth's guidance. [49]

Kenneth's service of installation came on November 3, 1969, more than a year after his selection, almost six months after his arrival, and well after he had created a collegial staff and launched the reconciliation campaign. It was held at University Christian Church in Fort Worth with Granville Walker presiding, James Moudy conducting the actual installation, and Ronald Osborn delivering the installation sermon. The charge to Kenneth was to be " Shepherd of the churches and Pastor to the Pastors!" [50]

The first regional convention during Kenneth's four years of service was held in Fort Worth. Among the many items it considered was the approval of a task force (a) to expand the concerns and ministry of The Association of Christian Churches in Texas beyond establishing new church buildings; (b) to help in combining new church development and community service in ministry; and (c) to declare a five year moratorium on new buildings except those planned ecumenically for both church and community use. A number of amendments to the by-laws were also approved, helping the region conform to the concept of church rather than Association. A resolution to approve "Project Equality," which asked churches to purchase from firms that do not discriminate in their employment practices, was approved by a vote of 301–190. This was a significant vote, representing a reversal from the previous assembly where it had been rejected. And finally, the assembly soundly defeated a resolution recommending the National Council of Churches tone down its social action rhetoric. In these actions, Kenneth's long-held convictions about mission were clearly evident: supporting ecumenical initiatives, particularly the National Council of Churches; manifesting peace with justice through support of project equality; helping the region grasp the meaning of church by enacting important by-laws changes moving it toward "church" and away from "association;" and conducting outreach ministry, by moving the attention of the region beyond brick and mortar projects and toward ministries of reconciliation and community service. Kenneth was in full possession of his ideals, and capable of conveying them to the larger church. [51]

During the fall of 1970 he framed a five year plan of ministry organized around six mission imperatives with fifty-five action targets. The six imperatives were identified as: leadership, reconciliation, evangelism and renewal, peace with justice, ecumenical involvement, and financing mission. Kenneth appointed task groups to work continuously on each of these imperatives and to develop action targets. Leadership, for example, was assigned the following action targets: a school for church board chairs; evangelism training for lay leadership and ministers alike; a scholarship program for blacks and Hispanics seeking to be licensed ministers; continuing education for all ministers; urging ministers to continue formal studies while in service through study leaves provided by congregations. This plan, with a similar strategy for each of the six imperatives, was designed to guide the ministry of the regional church through 1975. [52]

Kenneth invested enormous energy on a subject of profound interest to him: the most efficient organizational design for ministry in the vast expanse of Texas. He believed the central office of the region could not provide adequate pastoral care for all of its 475 congregations. To achieve better care and service, he built upon the idea of merging some of the twenty-one districts in Texas to reduce their number. He then planned for the creation of a small number of areas, perhaps five or six, not to be mini-regions and not to have program functions, but to be pastoral units serving clusters of districts. The programmatic responsibility was to be centralized and operate out of the Fort Worth office. Through the "area concept" he envisioned a closer regional pastoral relationship with congregations. He realized the process of incorporating areas into the structure of The Association of Christian Churches in Texas would demand several years. In fact, it required almost a decade. The Coastal Plains Area was constituted in September 1971, consolidating fifty-seven congregations in districts 11,12, and 13. The West Central Area was formed in January 1972, covering districts 5 and 6, with thirty-four congregations and 6,000 members. The plan continued on a gradual trajectory, but as the years passed beyond Kenneth's departure from Texas in 1973, the concept evolved into something quite different from what he had anticipated or intended. [53]

The state assembly for the Association of Christian Churches in Texas at Corpus Christi in April 1972 would be the last major event in the region where Kenneth would exercise influence as executive minister. The theme was "That All May Be One;" and the distinguished list of speakers included Dr. A. Dale Fiers, general minister and president, along with the Reverend Dr. Walter Bingham, first African-American moderator of the Christian Church (Disciples of Christ). Attendance surpassed 1,500, of whom 873 were voting representatives. The resolutions before the assembly reflected the most compelling issues of the day confronting American society. In Corpus Christi that April, Texas Disciples, addressed those issues as a church: A resolution was passed approving busing as a means to achieve integration; a resolution was approved to establish a program for the care of Vietnamese children; a resolution was passed supporting the abolition of capital punishment; a resolution was approved welcoming the National Council of Churches to Texas for its biennial general assembly; a resolution was adopted urging all congregations toward Christian unity; a resolution was passed urging greater involvement of both youth and women in the structures of the church; and a resolution calling for the immediate withdrawal from Vietnam was defeated 378 to 118. [54]

It was Kenneth's abiding religious conviction that by addressing the issues of the day forthrightly, he was helping Texas Disciples live out the gospel in their communities, helping them understand religion as a source of personal and public morality, critical to the health of democracy. Confronting the issues in assembly forum, in his view, not only deepened their understanding of recurrent themes in the biblical tradition—reconciliation, justice, redemption—but it assisted Disciples in finding ways to put them into practice. True to his installation charge, this was his way of being a "Shepherd of the Churches." It was a hallmark of his congregational pastorates, his regional ministries in both Arkansas and Texas, and of his ministry yet to come as general minister and president.

Throughout 1972, Kenneth was shadowed by a potential call to another ministry. Near the end of a six-year term, Dr. A. Dale Fiers announced his intention to retire in 1973 from the position of general minister and president of the Christian Church (Disciples of Christ). A screening committee composed of Walter Bingham, Chair; Harry Baker Adams; K. David Cole; James K. Hempstead; William C. Howland; Owen Hungerford; Mrs. James Hutcheson; Alvin O. Jackson; James Noe; Mrs. H.G. Wilkes; and Miss Jean Woolfolk had been appointed to recommend a candidate. It spent the entire year receiving recommendations and sifting through names. The committee received eighty-seven nominations. Many of the nominees had worked diligently through the process of restructure. The list contained the names of the best known and most accomplished and distinguished leaders of the church—an unusually strong pool of candidates. Kenneth was on that list, and he had received more letters of recommendation than any other person among the eighty-seven. [55]

The process of selection was long and complex. After reaching its decision, the screening committee would carry a recommendation of not less than two nor more than five names to the forty-five member administrative committee in November 1972 for the purpose of ranking, The administrative committee met for eight hours behind closed doors to choose between two exceptionally strong finalists, T. J. Liggett and Kenneth Teegarden. T.J. Liggett was functioning as deputy general minister and president to Dale Fiers. He was also president of the UCMS, secretary of the Renewal and Structural Reform Committee, and was a former missionary to Argentina, and president of a Puerto Rican seminary. Kenneth's nomination was approved with a two-thirds majority on the fourteenth ballot. Then the executive committee was required to present the number one ranked candidate to a duly called meeting of the administrative committee in February 1973 with a two-thirds majority approval required of the forty-five members. This vote was followed by a required two-thirds majority approval by the 222-member general board in July; and finally a two-thirds majority approval by the general assembly meeting in Cincinnati, in October 1973. By the end of 1972 it was widely known that Kenneth was the candidate to be recommended to the administrative committee in February, however, ten months still remained in the process. Because of the length of time required by the search and the uncertainty created in the future planning processes for the Texas region, Kenneth chose to resign from his Texas office as executive minister in April 1973, stating to the executive committee of the regional board, "All of this has made a somewhat awkward situation for me, the rest of the staff, and I am sure, for you as well. I am anxious that there be no unnecessary adverse effect on our work by a continuing uncertainty about the future." [56] The administrative committee had rendered its full approval the previous February; in July, the general board rendered its unanimous approval, sending the nomination forward to the October general assembly.

Back in Fort Worth, near the end of June 1973 the region held an appreciation dinner for Kenneth and Wanda at University Christian Church. There was a long procession of speakers thanking him for his "pastoral care;" and in his honor, the region presented a gift of $4,000 to the Ecumenical Southwest Career Development Center, an operation that had received Kenneth's unstinting support throughout his four years as executive minister. The region also gave Kenneth a beautiful pulpit robe to wear in his new ministry! And in their 1973 summer conference, the Texas Youth Fellowship passed a resolution making Kenneth an honorary life-time member of the CYF. His years as executive minister in Texas were pastoral, progressive and warmly respected. [57]

Excitement ran high in Cincinnati. Disciples had come to tell Dale and Betty Fiers goodbye—and they had come that October to participate in the historic election of a new general minister and president. On the first day of business, Kenneth's nomination was placed before the assembly. After a long series of seconding speeches from the floor, the vote was called, and over 4,000 voting representatives voted yes. Only one dissenting vote was heard. As the fifty-one-year old Kenneth Teegarden came to the platform and stepped to the microphone to accept his election, he jokingly remarked, "I sympathize with the opposition." Then he added, "I am deepliy grateful for the confidence and support of the assembly. With all the limitations that I have, I give my ministry wholeheartedly." [58]

NOTES

1. *The Christian,* May 20, 1962, p. 628; *The Arkansas Christian,* June, 1958, p. 3; The Arkansas Christian, March, 1958, p. 1; The Arkansas Christian, April, 1958, p. 1 McAllister, Lester. *Arkansas Disciples.* (Christian Church, Disciples of Christ, 1984), 213.

2. McAllister, *Arkansas Disciples,* 211; The Christian, May 14, 1961, p. 267.

3. Lani Johnson. "Teegarden Interview," *The Disciple.* June 1, 1980, p. 6; Veston Rowe. "A Christian Pastor Takes a Look Back," *This Month At Phillips.* Spring 1985, pp. 1, 5.

4. McAllister, *Arkansas Disciples,* 210, 213.

5. *The Christian,* April 10, 1960, p. 10; McAllister, *Arkansas Disciples,* 210–214.

6. *The Christian,* April 10, 1960, p. 10.

7. *The Arkansas Christian,* June 1965, p. 1.

8. David and Kirk Teegarden from Kenneth Teegarden. July 4, 1960; David and Kirk Teegarden from Kenneth Teegarden, July 19, 1960; Wanda Teegarden from Kenneth Teegarden. July 24, 1960, 1–2; Wanda Teegarden from Kenneth Teegarden, July 29, 1960, 1–2. Wanda Teegarden Collection.

9. Robert Friedly and D. Duane Cummins. *The Search for Identity* (St. Louis: CBP Press, 1987), 49–50.

10. Loren E. Lair. "Resolution of Appreciation for Kenneth Teegarden." 1965. Recently discovered document, courtesy of William L. Miller, Jr., former regional minister of the Upper Mid-West and author of the regional ministry history, *Vision with Passion,* 2004. Wanda Teegarden Collection.

11. *Arkansas Gazette,* April 1, 1965, p.10-A; Granville Walker. "Installation Charge to Kenneth Teegarden," *Installation Program for Kenneth Teegarden.* June 21, 1965, Disciples of Christ Historical Society, Restructure, Box 1.

12. Kenneth L. Teegarden. *Installation Address,* June 21, 1965, 1–2, D.C.H.S. Restructure, Box 1.

13. D. Duane Cummins. *Dale Fiers: Twentieth Century Disciple* (Fort Worth: TCU Press, 2003), 148–149.

14. *Minutes of the Commission on Brotherhood Restructure; Minutes of the Central Committee; Minutes of the Council of Agencies.* 1958 to 1968. D.C.H.S. Restructure, Box 1.

15. Dwight Stephenson. "Church Organization in the Thought of Alexander Campbell." Unpublished, undated paper. D.C.H.S. Restructure, Box 1, 1–3; Alexander Campbell, "Nature of Church Organization." *Millennial Harbinger,* 1843, pp. 532–535; Cummins, *Dale Fiers,* 142–145.

16. Alexander Campbell. *Christian System,* 3rd ed. (Pittsbugh: Forrester and Campbell, 1840), 72–77; Alexander Campbell, "Church Organization," *Millennial Harbinger,* 1843, pp. 82–86; A. Dale Fiers, D.C.H.S. Interview, January 20, 1992, D.C.H.S. Fiers. Box 3; Cummins, *Dale Fiers,* 143; Anthony Dunnavant. Restructure (New York: Lang, 1993). 121–176; Mark Toulouse. *Joined in Discipleship* (St. Louis: Chalice, 1997), 219–241.

17. Lester McAllister and William Tucker. *Journey in Faith* (St. Louis: Bethany Press, 1975), 415–421.

18. Wickizer, Willard. "Ideas for Brotherhood Restructure." Unpublished paper, July 1958, 1–9 D.C.H.S. Restructure, Box 1; Friedly and Cummins, *Search for Identity,* 29–30.

19. Ahlstrom, Sydney. *A Religious History of the American People* (New Haven: Yale University Press, 1972), 1015; Cummins, *Dale Fiers,* 139. (This is an updated rewrite, with new research of four paragraphs originally appearing in my biography of Fiers); T. J. Ligget, D.C.H.S. Interview, November 29, 1990, 1.

20. Granville Walker, D.C.H.S. Interview, March 10, 1990, 1; Ronald Osborn, D.C.H.S. Interview, May 20, 1990, 1; Kenneth Teegarden, D.C.H.S. Interview, March 9, 1990, 1; Howard Dentler, D.C.H.S. interview, November 19, 1993, 1; James Moak, D.C.H.S. interview, December 12, 1989, 1.

21. Kenneth Teegarden, D.C.H.S. Interview, March 9, 1990; Ronald Osborn, D.C.H.S. Interview, May 20, 1990; Robert Thomas, D.C.H.S. Interview, May 26, 1990, 1; Paul Stauffer,

D.C.H.S. Interview, May 8, 1992, 1; Charles Bayer, D.C.H.S. Interview, April 3, 1990, 1; Howard Short, D.C.H.S. Interview, July 23, 1990, 1.

22. Robert Thomas, D.C.H.S. Interview, May 26, 1990; Charles Bayer, D.C.H.S. Interview, April 3, 1990.

23. Spencer Austin, D.C.H.S. Interview, November 14, 1989, 1; Jean Woolfolk, March 14, 1990, 1.

24. Commission on Brotherhood Restructure, *Minutes.* July 6–7, 1962, Fort Worth, Texas. Attachment: "An Apologetic for Restructure," by A. Dale Fiers, 1–4. D.C.H.S. Restructure, Box 1.

25. Commission on Brotherhood Restructure, *Budget Reports.* D.C.H.S. Restructure, Box 1, File 2.

26. Kenneth L. Teegarden. *Report of the Administrative Secretary,* November 3, 1965, 1–5, D.C.H.S. Restructure, Box 1, Teegarden File; Kenneth L. Teegarden. Report of the Administrative Secretary, March 24, 1966, 1–4, D.C.H.S. Restructure, Box 1, Teegarden File; *The Christian.* January 30, 1966. D.C.H.S. Restructure, Box 1; *The Direction in Brotherhood Restructure,* 1966. D.C.H.S. Restructure, Box. 1; Kenneth L. Teegarden. *Administrative Secretary Reports.* 1965–1966. D.C.H.S. Restructure, Box 1, Teegarden File.

27. Commission on Brotherhood Restructure. Minutes, June 21–25, 1965, 2–7. D.C.H.S. Restructure, Box 1.

28. Kenneth L. Teegarden. *Report of the Administrative Secretary,* March 24,1966, 1–4. D.C.H.S. Restructure, Box 1, Teegarden File; Central Committee. Minutes, March 24–25, 1966. 3. D.C.H.S. Restructure, Box 1; *A Possible Constitution.* Working Paper with Kenneth L. Teegarden's notes, March 24, 1966, 1–22. D.C.H.S. Restructure, Box 1, Kenneth L. Teegarden File.

29. Commission on Brotherhood Restructure. *Minutes,* July 5–8, 1966, Cincinnati, Ohio, 1–3. D.C.H.S. Restructure, Box 1.

30. Central Committee. *Minutes,* January 11–12, 1967, 5. D.C.H.S. Restructure, Box 1; George Earle Owen, D.C.H.S. Interview, January 21, 1992, 2.

31. Kenneth L. Teegarden. *Report of the Administrative Secretary,* July 5–8,1966, 3. D.C.H.S. Restructure, Box 1, Teegarden File; Commission on Brotherhood Restructure. *Minutes,* September 29, 1966, Dallas, Texas, 1. D.C.H.S. Restructure, Box 1.

32. Ibid., 2–4; Central Committee. *Minutes,* November 2–3, 1966, 7. D.C.H.S. Restructure, Box 1; Lillian Moir, "Portrait of a Nominee," *World Call,* October 1973, p. 13.

33. Kenneth L. Teegarden. *Report of the Administrative Secretary,* January 11, 1966, 1–2. D.C.H.S. Restructure, Box 1, Teegarden File.

34. Commission on Brotherhood Restructure. *Minutes,* June 21–25, 1965, 2–3. D.C.H.S. Restructure, Box 1; Charles Bayer, D.C.H.S. Interview, April 3, 1990, 3; Cummins, *Dale Fiers,* 152 [updated writing with new research of three paragraphs originally appearing in biography of Dale Fiers]; Kenneth L. Teegarden, D.C.H.S. Interview, March 9, 1990, 4–5.

35. Cummins, *Dale Fiers,*152; *Restructure Report,* September 1965; September 1966. D.C.H.S. Restructure, Box 2, Commission On President Of Brotherhood file; Pamphlet. *Freedom or Restructure?* D.C.H.S. Restructure, Box 2, CPB file; Granville Walker to Lesley L. Walker, November 9, 1967, 3. D.C.H.S., Restructure, Box 3. Black binder of correspondence.

36. Cummins, *Dale Fiers,* 153; Robert Burns, D.C.H.S. Interview, November 18, 1989, 1–6; Kenneth L. Teegarden. *Report of the Administrative Secretary,* March 8, 1967, 3. D.C.H.S. Restructure, Box 1, Teegarden File.

37. Atlanta Declaration Group Meeting. *Minutes by Robert Burns,* August 3, 1967, 7-10. D.C.H.S. Restructure. Box 2, Atlanta Declaration File; Kenneth L. Teegarden to Commission on Brotherhood Restructure, August 9, 1967, 1. D.C.H.S. Restructure, Box 1, Teegarden File; Robert Burns to Kenneth Teegarden and Commission on Brotherhood Restructure, August 23, 1967. D.C.H.S. Restructure, Box 2, Atlanta Declaration file; Bob Friedly to D. Duane Cummins, November 2005, 4.

38. Kenneth L. Teegarden to W. J. Sneed, January 16, 1968, 1. Restructure, D.C.H.S., Box 3. Black binder of correspondence; Howard Dentler. *Report to the Central Committee*, February, 1968, 1. D.C.H.S. Restructure, Box 1.

39. Commission on Brotherhood Restructure. Minutes, November 1–2, 1967; Howard Dentler. *Report to the Central Committee*, February 1968, 1. D.C.H.S. Restructure, Box 1; Friedly and Cummins, *Search for Identity*, 9; Kenneth L. Teegarden to Commission on Brotherhood Restructure, April 10,1968, 1; Kenneth L. Teegarden. *Report of Administrative Secretary*, February 1968, 1–2. D.C.H.S. Restructure, Box 1, Teegarden file; Dale Fiers to Commission on Brotherhood Restructure October 29, 1967.

40. Kenneth L. Teegarden, D.C.H.S. Interview, March 9, 1990, 1; Central Committee. *Minutes*, January 1962, 3. D.C.H.S. Restructure, Box 1; Commission on Brotherhood Restructure. Minutes, July 6–7, 1962, Attachment, "An Apologetic for Restructure." By Dale Fiers; Ronald Osborn, "The Calling of the Church," June 29, 1964, D.C.H.S., Box 2; Ronald Osborn, "The Nature of the Church," June 30, 1964, D.C.H.S., Box 2; Ronald Osborn, "The Building of the Church," July 1, 1964, D.C.H.S., Box 2; Ronald Osborn. *Toward the Christian Church* (St. Louis: CBP, 1964), 11, 26, 54. D.C.H.S. Restructure, Box 2.

41. Kenneth L. Teegarden, D.C.H.S. Interview, March 9, 1990, 3.

42. Ibid., 8.

43. Ibid., 9; Kenneth L. Teegarden Interview with David Roozen. Undated, 311; Howard Dentler Interview with D. Duane Cummins, February 26, 2005.

44. Dentler. Ibid.; Kenneth L. Teegarden to Howard C. Cole, March 18, 1975, 1, GMP files, D.C.H.S. Box 1, Correspondence C.

45. Dentler. Ibid.; Kenneth L. Teegarden Interview with David Roozen. Undated, 319.

46. Kenneth L. Teegarden to Travis A. White, August 9, 1968, Wanda Teegarden Collection; Kenneth L. Teegarden to A. Dale Fiers, May 5, 1969, Wanda Teegarden Collection.

47. Interview with Kirk Teegarden. November 17, 2005; Interview with David Teegarden, April 11, 2006; *Christian Courier*, Vol. 81, No. 7 (July-August 1969), p. 1.

48. *Christian Courier*, Vol. 80, No. 10 (November 1968), p. 1–4; *Christian Courier*, Vol. 81, No. 5. (May 1969), p. 1.

49. *Christian Courier*, Vol. 81, No. 11 (December 1969), p. 1; *Christian Courier*, Vol. 82, No. 2 (February 1970), p. 1; *Christian Courier*, Vol. 82, No. 4 (April 1970), p. 1; *Christian Courier*, Vol. 82, No. 8. (September 1970), p. 4.

50. *Christian Courier*, Vol. 81, No. 11 (December 1969), p. 5.

51. *Christian Courier*, Vol. 82, No. 3 (March 1970), p. 1; *Christian Courier*, Vol., 82, No. 5 (May 1970), p. 1.

52. *Christian Courier*, Vol. 82, No. 10 (November 1970), p. 1; *Christian Courier*, Vol. 82, No. 11 (December 1970), p. 1.

53. Interview with James C. Suggs, February 11, 2006; *Christian Courier*, Vol. 84, No. 2 (February 1972), p. 1; *Christian Courier*, Vol. 83, No. 9 (October 1971), p. 1.

54. *Christian Courier*, Vol. 84, No. 5 (May 1972), p. 1; *Christian Courier*, Vol. 83, No. 11 (December 1971), p. 1.

55. *Christian Courier*, Vol. 84, No. 11 (December 1972), p. 1; Walter Bingham to All Ministers of Disciples Congregations, May 12, 1972, D.C.H.S., Teegarden GMP Files, Box 1.

56. *Christian Courier*, Vol. 85, No. 4 (April 1973), p. 1.

57. *Christian Courier*, Vol. 85, No. 7 (July 1973), p. 3; Kenneth L. Teegarden to James Oglesby, November 16, 1973, 1, GMP files, D.C.H.S. Box 4, Correspondence O.

58. *Arkansas Gazette.* October 28, 1973, p. 15-A; *Christian Church News*, October 27, 1973.

CHAPTER V

The General Minister and President

*It is the responsibility of leaders of the congregation to give
people an opportunity to deepen their faith by confronting the
knotty moral and theological questions. That is as much a
ministry to them as calling on them when they are sick. There
is no question that social action and social issues have caused
some problems in congregations in the past decade. But the
agonies and ectasies of arriving at decisions of faith should be
what the gospel is all about.*

Kenneth L. Teegarden

Respite and Election

There were twenty-four persons on the trip. It was a fraternal visit to Asia from October 5 to November 2, 1972, under the sponsorship of the Division of Overseas Ministries. The visit, designed to place leaders in touch with their cognate counterparts in other churches around the world, included stops in Japan, Hong Kong,

Thailand, India, and the headquarters of the World Council of Churches in Geneva, Switzerland. Among the distinguished group of travelers were Walter and Becky Bingham, Robert Thomas, Harold Johnson, Margaret Wilkes, Fran and Jim Craddock, Jim and Lucy Reed, Joseph Smith, William Fox, John Updegrafe, Kenneth and Ruth Kuntz, Robert Friedly, T.J and Virginia Liggett, and Kenneth and Wanda Teegarden.

While in Japan, Joseph Smith arranged to meet the Japanese commanding officer of the Philippines' POW compound where Joseph had been held captive for three years during World War II. But now, decades later, in 1972 Kyoto, the former commandant and prisoner sat facing each other, cross-legged on a porch, remembering, forgiving, weeping, exchanging gifts. It was a moment that generated considerable emotion and inspiration within this little band of Disciples travelers. Joseph later wrote a book about his imprisonment, entitled *Three Years in the Belly of a Whale.* [1]

After Robert Friedly recovered his misplaced camera equipment and Harold Johnson learned to pronounce his name in Japanese, the group traveled on to Hong Kong. Memories differ on just when it happened, but at some point early in the trip word came informing Kenneth and T.J. that they had been recommended by the screening committee as the two finalists for the office of general minister and president. Upon their return in November, they were to appear before the administrative committee for formal interviews. The news sparked much private discussion among the traveling Disciples. The group, it was said, gave considerably more attention to the Liggett-Teegarden election than to the presidential campaign in the United States that month between McGovern and Nixon. [2]

From Hong Kong the group continued on to Thailand. They were strapped in their seats preparing for a landing in Bangkok when suddenly the plane hit an air pocket and dropped about 500 feet. Because they were at that moment over Cambodia in wartime, some thought they had been shot down. They landed safely, without injuries, in Bangkok. Here the group divided in order to attend several different churches. Kenneth was with the party that traveled into the wilderness west of Bangkok to the Sam Yek church, only a few miles from the River Kwai. He was to preach in this sharply arched church located in a forest clearing. In Buddhist culture every living thing has value. Robert Friedly, seated on the front row of the church, saw an ant climbing up the right side of the pulpit. It reached the top of the pulpit and wandered across. Kenneth, having read the scripture, held a closed Bible in his hand. He caught sight of the ant and, in simple reflex, popped the ant with the Bible without missing a word of his sermon. Friedly did not know whether to laugh or panic. Fortunately nothing happened. But the incident provided much good cheer on the remainder of the world journey as they told and retold the story of Kenneth in Buddhist Thailand, beating a poor creature to death on top of the pulpit—with his Bible no less. [3]

Traveling onward to India, the delegation stopped in Bombay and Delhi where, in addition to several churches, they visited the tomb of Mahatma Gandhi. Their final stop was at the World Council headquarters in Geneva, followed by the long flight home; thereby completing their trip around the world. October of 1972 was a respite, an untroubled and relaxed time, something Kenneth would rarely know for the following thirteen years. [4]

Once home, preparation began for the administrative committee interviews. Kenneth and T.J., both giants in the life of the Disciples church, held each other in highest regard. During their separate interviews, each lifted up the leadership virtues of the other! It required eight hours and fourteen ballots, but the administrative committee ultimately determined at their November meeting to send the name of Kenneth Teegarden forward as the nominee. After receiving unanimous approval by the administrative committee in February 1973, Kenneth resigned in April as executive minister of the southwest region. General board approval came in July, and he was officially elected to the office in October at the Cincinnati general assembly.

The procedures for nomination and election, approved by the administrative committee in 1972, called for an installation. But no one interviewed for this writing, including many of his close colleagues and his wife Wanda, could recall that such an installation ever occurred. And there is no documentation of such an event in the general assembly program or files. Wanda surmised, that given Kenneth's aversion to such ceremonies, he may have requested there be no installation. He gave a brief acceptance speech following the vote. On November 1, 1973, he simply went to the office and began work.

Kenneth, Wanda and—on a return stay—their little dachshund, Snitzie, moved into an apartment on Shadeland Avenue on a one year lease. Wanda, believing that selling real estate might be interpreted as a conflict of interest, began managing a 1,500-unit apartment complex. She later transferred to a high-rise facility in downtown Indianapolis. The children remained in Texas, and the distance seemed long. At the end of the year's lease they purchased a home at 7232 Highbury Drive, where they lived during their remaining years in Indianapolis, and where Wanda once again created a comfortable environment for the two of them and their faithful companion Snitzie. [5]

The way in which the press covered his election was always a matter of amusement to Kenneth. *The New York Times* ran an unfortunate headline, "Disciples of Christ Choose New Leader." *Playboy* picked up on it, and noted in their next issue, "We were afraid it would come to this one day."

Kenneth often referred to his title, *General Minister and President of the Christian Church (Disciples of Christ) in the United States and Canada,* as the longest title in Protestantism. But during the restructure process, the title, according to Kenneth, "was selected very intentionally. It was to be ministerial and administrative. The first part of the title was 'general minister' defining the responsibility for spiritual oversight and nurture of the whole church; and 'president'—not in the sense of having very much authority—defined the duty of administration." In response to one formal inquiry about the nature of his office, Kenneth explained that "president" meant chief executive officer, presiding over meetings and representing the church in interchurch relations and ecumenical circles. "The office," he wrote, "is both pastoral and administrative. It is not unlike the relationship the local pastor bears to the congregation or the regional minister carries for the region." Frequently, when asked about his concept of the office of general minister and president, Kenneth replied simply, "A. Dale Fiers." He held the deepest admiration and affection for Dr. Fiers—the first general minister and president—and the third of the three mentors who most influenced his life. Soon after it became known that Kenneth was the candidate to be recommended for election, Dr. Fiers wrote to him, "I feel a deep sense of inner peace. I know the church will be in good hands. I hear only comments of warm approval everywhere I go." [6]

The administrative committee had created its list of responsibilities that included:

To give the vision of what the church is to be and to do;
To speak to and for the church;
To lead the church in expressing its ministry as the body
    of Christ;
To serve as the chief executive officer of the church.

The long list of qualifications sought in a person by the administrative committee to perform those responsibilities, included: "Involvement in a local parish, in the regional manifestation of the church, in the work of the church through its national bodies, in the ecumenical structures of the contemporary church, [and] in the educational institutions related to the church." The qualifications also called for informed theological convictions, compassion for the needy and outcast, the courage to bear witness to God's will, and administratively, the ability to set objectives, to develop strategy, to delegate responsibility, to make decisions, to evaluate performance, to work with others, and to inspire confidence. The expectations were demanding but Kenneth was not dissuaded by the challenge. Soon after commencing his work he cheerfully responded to a friend's inquiry, " I have been in my position for five weeks now and find it quite exhilarating." [7]

The Social, Political and Religious Context

The year Kenneth became general minister and president— 1973—America's military participation in the Vietnam war ended, the Watergate investigations were well under way, the landmark case Roe vs. Wade became law, The Godfather won most of the academy awards, and media evangelists gained popularity with the founding of the Trinity Broadcasting Network. On August 9 of the following year, Richard Nixon resigned as president of the United States. It was the worst political scandal in American history and the signature political event of the early 1970s. Vice President Gerald Ford was elevated to the presidency, assuring the nation that "our long national nightmare is over." But his prompt pardon of Richard Nixon, intended to reduce public attention on the issue, actually increased attention. The country developed a sour taste for political leadership in particular and for leadership in general. Writing his regular column for The Disciple, Kenneth professed this negative trend: "It has been my lot to be called to be a 'leader' in the Christian Church (Disciples of Christ) at a time when nobody wants leaders. Leadership has fallen into disrepute. People's spirits have been dashed in the last decade by a succession of failures. . . . [Nevertheless] Disciples have listed leadership as one of their mission imperatives." [8]

The most important development of the decade was the socio-cultural shift occurring beneath the garish surface of Watergate, a shift that would transform American economic, religious, cultural, and political life. Many people thought of the 1970s, sandwiched as they were between the high octane sixties and the conservative eighties, as the time of bell-bottoms, punk, disco, *Jonathan Livingston Seagull* , tax revolts, Evel Knievel, stagflation, *Saturday Night Fever,* and Iran hostages. It was not generally considered an important era by lay observers; in fact it was thought of in unflattering terms. Thoughtful analysts, however, labeled it a decisive decade, perhaps the most significant in the postwar twentieth century. The "sunbelt," known as the continental underbelly, extending from "Orange County, North Carolina, to Orange County, California," experienced a huge economic boom in the 1970s while the "frost belt," the old northern industrial heartland, suffered serious economic and political decline. Between 1970 and 1990 the population of the sunbelt grew 40 percent! People, jobs, money and political power shifted from the northern to the southern states. Since the election of John F. Kennedy from Massachusetts to the presidency in 1960, all subsequent "elected" presidents from Lyndon Johnson in 1964 to George W. Bush in 2004, irrespective of party affiliation, have come from the sunbelt. So have most of the speakers of the house and majority leaders of the senate. Historical analyst Bruce Schulman asserts that this huge shift during the seventies "changed the nation's economic outlook, political ideology, cultural assumptions, and social arrangements." [9]

The affects of this shift were particularly acute on American religious life. The seventies were the twilight years of mainline protestant activism. Activists enjoyed significant success in the sixties Civil Rights Movement, then moved on to anti-Vietnam war protests (U.S. forces withdrew in March 1973; women's rights (an Equal Rights Amendment was passed by the U.S. Senate in March 1972, but was never ratified by the states); environmental issues (the first Earth Day celebration was held April 22, 1970); and finally nuclear disarmament. But the overriding religious story of the seventies and early eighties was the rise of the Christian right, a resurgence of evangelical Protestantism, and their agenda of defending traditional values against secular humanism. Membership in the evangelical churches literally exploded, claiming a quarter of the nation, according to a 1978 analysis cited by Bruce Schulman, while membership in mainstream Portestant denominations was plummeting by 8 to 15 percent per denomination. The political force of mainline Protestantism, as measured by

Robert Wuthnow from National Election Data studies, declined from 46 percent of the non-black electorate in 1960 to 30 percent in 1996, a decline of 16 percent.

The year 1977 saw the founding of "Focus on the Family" by James Dobson; and in 1979, the "Moral Majority" appeared under the leadership of Jerry Falwell. Also organized that year were the "Christian Voice" and the "Religious Roundtable," and, along with Falwell and Dobson, these organizations all supported a common agenda of promoting prayer in public schools, opposing abortion, condemning homosexuality, teaching creationism, opposing the Equal Rights Amendment, opposing nuclear test ban treaties, opposing school busing, promoting conservative judges for the U.S. court system, opposing gays in the military, and opposing secular humanism. [10]

During the seventies political and media attention shifted dramatically from the religious center to the religious right. The Christian right linked its voice with the conservative wing of the Republican party, blurring the line separating church and state. The Republican party grew strong in the burgeoning sunbelt, in part due to the Civil Rights legislation of the 1960s, proposed and enacted by the leadership of the Democratic party, that had alienated the South from Democrats and would transform the region into a solid Republican stronghold. Throughout the 1980s, President Ronald Reagan, a conservative Republican, played to the support of the Christian right by repudiating, during the presidential campaign, his earlier support of the ERA and liberalization of abortion rights, declaring 1983 the year of the Bible, proposing in 1982 a constitutional amendment for prayer in public schools, and designating a "human life" day in 1984. By 1989, Pat Robertson had created the formidable Christian Coalition, and later became a candidate for president. Added to this was an expanding pluralism brought on by immigration patterns that attracted many Muslims, Buddhists, Hindus, and other religious faiths, all entering the social and political mainstream. The non-Protestant religious identity grew large in its numbers and became

increasingly pluralized. All of this contributed to a significant erosion of mainline Protestant influence in social, cultural, religious
and political matters. With the growing strength of the Christian
right, political campaigns, complained many, took on the tone of
religious crusades. Others were annoyed that policy debates
sounded, on occasion, more like theological disputes. [11]

When Kenneth assumed the office of general minister and
president in 1973, the national environment was becoming less
supportive of mainline Protestantism, less dependent on it as a
political force, and less needful of it as a cultural support system.
The decline in influence of mainline Protestantism in America
had begun almost from the year of Kenneth's birth in 1921 when
its rural tradition was overpowered by the urbanization of society.
Now, at the peak of his career in 1973, he would find himself presiding over a denomination at a time when mainline Protestantism in general was being conflicted and overshadowed by a new
and virulent strain of the Christian right and by a growing religious pluralism within the nation. The crosscurrents of religion,
politics, history, and culture were whipsawing our world.

Renewal and Structural Reform

Kenneth was immediately faced with continuing the implementation of the provisional design. It would be a constant theme
of his twelve years in office, particularly his first term. Reading
about it today may leave the impression that it was the only subject receiving attention, but this was far from the case. Six years
had passed since the provisional design was approved in Kansas
City. Restructure had unleashed a broad range of competing emotions throughout the church: hope and fear, joy and sorrow, commitment and confusion, resentment and gratitude, and many
parts of the church were still trying to find their way into the new
covenantal community. When Virgil Sly sent his letter of congratulations to Kenneth in 1973, he shared a personal apprehension:
"I have one major concern—the concern is this—The Disciples of

Christ still do not know what church means." Understanding Virgil Sly's insight, Kenneth replied: "I also have felt the spirit of restructure has not caught hold in some places. I experience it frequently among the congregations. Some of my regional colleagues still think in somewhat sectional terms and I have observed evidences of an unwillingness to go too far among a few of the national agencies. I am hopeful that this attitude will diminish." [12]

In the fall of 1973 a five-year survey of the progress of restructure was conducted among general units and regions. This report, submitted to the Committee on Structure and Function, awaited Kenneth's arrival for action and response. The committee, sensing a special empowerment through the provisional design, exercised substantial initiative and functioned like a mini-commission on restructure. Chaired by Jean Woolfolk, it contained a powerful membership of nineteen: Spencer Austin, William Howland, James Moak, Albert Pennybacker, Robert Stewart, Kenneth Teegarden, Robert Thomas, Orville Wake, W.A. Welsh, Art Wenger, Charles Dietze, John Wolfersberger, T.J. Liggett, Dale Fiers, Gertrude Dimke, Sam Hylton, and Jay Calhoun. It may have been the strongest structure and function committee of the post-1968 era. Many of them had served on the restructure commission, and some had been key leaders in shaping the provisional design that stated, "The general assembly, upon recommendation of the general board, shall establish or recognize by constitution or contract administrative units . . ." [13]

Nearly all the provisional general units in the 1973 survey reported revisions in their by-laws in compliance with the new provisional design. The Board of Church Extension, however, said its relationship would be a contractual one, and consequently made no by-laws change. The 1972 provisional design stated specifically that administrative units " . . . shall be called divisions" and the Committee on Structure and Function urged consideration of a divisional concept upon general units. Two new divisions were incorporated in 1972: the Division of Overseas Ministries and the Division of Homeland Ministries. Their charters and by-laws were subsequently approved by the committee, by the general board, and finally by the Cincinnati general assembly in 1973. The National Benevolent Association, in 1973, approved the name Division of Social and Health Services, but kept NBA as its programmatic title. And that same year the Board of Higher Education launched a self-study that over the next five years led to the creation of the Division of Higher Education in 1977, converting itself from an association of dues paying institutions to a division of the church. The Pension Fund decided to take a "watch and wait" position on the matter of division status. [14]

Some of the ministries of the general manifestation, such as finance and ecumenism, involved all of the programmatic units and were identified as central "councils." Unified promotion responded, under the leadership of Spencer Austin, by reconstituting itself as the Church Finance Council in 1973. And the ecumenical arm of the church was of course already named the Council on Christian Unity. The Disciples of Christ Historical Society chose to keep their society status because the society concept was acceptable to all three branches of the Stone-Campbell Movement in the nineteenth century. Since the DCHS served all three, a concept change might somehow alienate one or both sister branches, even though they shared a common heritage. The Christian Church Foundation came into existence in 1969, one year after restructure and had designed its charter and by-laws in concert with the provisional design. One other new general unit, Christian Church Services, emerged during the dismantling of the United Christian Missionary Society for the purpose of placing all the overhead costs and functions in one place: technical services, office of communications, financial services, and managing the Missions Building in Indianapolis.

The eclectic group of general units greeting Kenneth as the new general minister in 1973 included three boards, three divisions, two councils, a society, a foundation, a services unit, and the pension fund. Five years later one board had converted to a division; and the services unit was reconstituted and deployed. [15]

The Committee on Structure and Function struggled to determine the most effective means to realign units: model comparable units on the basis of "audience" or create a gradual process of development. It studied carefully the progress of restructure efforts in five similar denominations at that time as well as producing numerous study documents of their own. They considered it axiomatic that structure flows from the functional requirements of mission. They were equally convinced that structure informs and shifts the character of mission. They also assumed that the church was free to preserve, delete, reorder, and form new structures appropriate at any point in its history. And they believed their committee was empowered to effect such change through the general board and general assembly. Structures, they asserted, were to be used like tools so long as they are useful, then adapt them or dispose of them as demands and opportunities require. After several meetings the committee concluded that the "gradual process of development" may be the most effective approach to general units. They recommended five guiding principles for the development of the general manifestation:

- The Principle of Creative Evolution;
- The Principle of Inter-relatedness;
- The Principle of Ecumenicity;
- The Principle of Parsimony [Maximizing Stewardship];
- The Pastoral Principle.

As hard as the Committee on Structure and Function labored, general unit structural changes turned out to be quite modest during the time that Kenneth was general minister and president. In spite of complaints, (e.g., CCU thought the concept of comparable units very disturbing, NBA warned of the church becoming more authoritarian, DHM thought administrative costs were greater than they were under the UCMS, Unified Promotion worried that too much power had been placed in the hands of congregations) the predominant response of general units to restructure was favorable. All claimed to be motivated by a greater understanding of the wholeness of "church," a spirit cultivated by regular meetings of the cabinet, the council of ministers, the administrative committee, and the general board that brought units, regions and congregational representatives into regular interaction with each other. Most general units claimed the new identity that came to them through restructure resulted in stronger ecumenical relationships with their counterparts in other religious bodies. And one of the important contributions Kenneth brought to general units, and therefore to the church, was his unceasing nurture of collegiality and their mutual support of a single mission. Inter-relatedness and common sharing became a more natural part of general unit life during Kenneth's years. There were of course disagreements, but in general the cabinet bonded, grew in confidence, collegiality, and churchliness that diminished turf protection and competition. By 1976 the Committee on Structure and Function had given up on realignment of general units. Minutes of their meetings in the early seventies were dominated by the subject, but in the February 1976 minutes, there was merely a single sentence: "As for general administrative units, the administrative committee and the general board are the appropriate place for continual prodding of the general manifestation for more effective structures for mission." [16]

Simultaneously, the committee, efficiently divided into several sub-committees, was working on regional realignment. In the 1973 progress report fifteen provisional regions had adopted new constitutions and by- laws in compliance with the provisional design. Many had formally changed their name from association or missionary society to "The Christian Church (Disciples of Christ) in [State name]." Several had developed regional structures variously called districts, clusters, areas, or consultations. Most of the regions had formal ecumenical relationships with councils of churches and many had working relationships with judicatories of other communions. Several claimed that restructure helped in clarifying and improving relationships with institutions and with area or city associations. And several joint staff meetings were being held involving at least a dozen regions. Ten regions gave very favorable evaluations for the over-all effects of restructure, emphasizing particularly the growing sense of church. On the other hand, some regions thought it was too early to determine the effects of restructure. Others believed the new demands on regions were too costly in both time and money. Some expressed fear about what they called a growing centralization of power in the church; three called attention to the loss of congregations as too high a price for restructure; one noted that wholeness of church was felt only by the clergy, not by the laity. But the largest and most pervasive complaint by many regions was their dislike of the model "fewer but comparable" regions suggested by the Committee on Structure and Function. [17]

The committee was operating on the understanding, as stated in the provisional design, that all general units and state organizations were provisional and it read the Provisional Design with a serious eye, especially during the seminal years of implementation in the early seventies. And the provisional design stated clearly in the case of regions: "The general board shall initiate procedures for reorganization of existing state and area organizations as regions of the Christian Church." [19] Viewing this statement as an empowerment, the Committee on Structure and Function with its formidable membership, set to work on the task, just as it had on general Units. The committee chair, Jean Woolfolk, sent a letter in October 1972 to all regional ministers with a list of eleven suggested guidelines for initiating regional realignment. The second guideline articulated the committee intent, "with responsibility to the general board, the Committee on Structure and Function may properly take initiative in suggesting consultation between two or more present provisional regions:" and the ninth guideline declared, "Regions should be established so that their strategy, resources, program and administration may be more effective and efficient in the accomplishment of mission." [18]

The committee soon proposed the concept of "fewer and more comparable regions." John Wolfersberger produced for the committee a thoroughly researched and thoughtful paper on the concept, in which he proposed as a model for beginning discussion, nineteen regions with a minimum of fifty-five areas, each area containing approximately sixty-eight congregations. The study noted that in 1972 Disciples experienced a decline in every single category of membership—number of participating congregations, total congregations, participating members, total members, church school enrollment, total baptisms, total transfers, and worship attendance. Wolfersberger said these facts pointed to the Disciples' failure to come to grips with the phenomenon of urbanization and that the church needed to restructure accordingly. He noted that in the 1970 census there were 243 metropolitan centers with 50,000 or more persons, a growth of 103 since 1940. Furthermore, 68 percent of the nation's population lived in those centers. Wolfersberger also noted that most Disciples lived, at that time, in the eastern half of the United States and below the forty-third parallel, or the northern boundary of Iowa. Within that geography were twenty-seven states and twenty-five Disciples regions, containing 3,297 of the 3,782 participating congregations, and 761,606 of the 881,467 participating members. In addition, $14 million of the $16 million given to outreach came from that geography. The density of Disciples in eastern United States, he surmised, offered a manageable geographic configuration. The western part of the United States provided a different picture with only three territories of relative density, Colorado, California, and the Northwest. Wolfersberger's study considered the placement of the interstate highway system, areas of major newspaper circulation and trade centers. He pointed out as well that, at that time, Disciples had twelve regions with 100 or more congregations, nine regions with sixty to 100 congregations, and fifteen regions with fewer than fifty congregations—one region with as few as three congregations. He concluded his study with the assurance that the suggestion of "fewer but more comparable regions" did not mean that small regions would be absorbed by large regions, but that new regions could be formed along new demographic and cultural lines, rather than state lines. Areas, he suggested, should be identified first. The boundaries of the region around them would be determined later. Regions, therefore, would be developed from the center outward, rather than the reverse. Disciples' attachment to state lines in an urban age, he warned, would divide Disciples, diminish efficiency, and increase cost. The study contained several maps documenting his research and illustrating the concept. And it claimed to be only a study, and was not to be presented as "a solution." [20]

In October 1973, Kenneth reviewed the progress report on general units and regions along with the Wolfersberger study, and proceeded to prepare a six-page paper reviewing the concept of "fewer and more comparable" regions to help engage regions in study and reflection. His review spoke of a model of ten regions, describing the central office of the region as a "regional resource center," and the areas as "pastoral and nurturing entities." The area, containing fifty to seventy-five congregations, was not to be a fourth manifestation of church in the sense the term was used in the provisional design, but was to be a legitimate churchly structure finding its integrity within the organizational life of a region and in its proximity to the congregations within its boundaries. The region, with its component areas, was conceived as one manifestation of the church. Kenneth suggested eleven functions for a region, eight functions for an area, and fourteen advantages of fewer and more comparable regions. Among the advantages were: (a) being more nearly equal in size and strength would enable a more efficient fulfillment of mission and purpose; (b) the church could more easily decentralize some functions of general units; (c) a greater ethnic and gender diversity would become possible for regional staff; (d) excessive parochialism would be discouraged; (e) close pastoral care would be available through areas; (f) increased specialized skills and services would become available through a regional resource center, (g) a greater flexibility for renewal would be possible by allowing easier boundary adjustments of areas within regions in response to growing urbanization; (h) duplication of several administrative and programmatic func-

tions could be reduced; and (i) the cost of publishing both regional and area papers might be minimized by publishing one regional
paper with a section provided for area material. [21]

Although there were positive reactions from several quarters
of the church to both the Wolfersberger and Teegarden papers,
discussion of the concept of "fewer and more comparable" regions
over the next several years became protracted, then negative.
Several regional and area leaders advocated a preference for
diversity in size, shape, and structure as the better way to serve
congregations and church mission, rather than "fewer and comparable." Others were concerned about property holdings. Some
thought the latitude of fifty to seventy-five congregations was too
great to identify an area, while others thought the range was too
constrictive and should be open to a wider variety of areas, and a
few claimed they could not relate to such figures. It was stated by
some that close pastoral care did not come from proximity, but
from working relationships. Like the Commission on Restructure,
the Committee on Structure and Function invested an enormous
amount of time and energy in research and in consultation with
regional leadership on the subject of regional realignment. But
across the twelve years that Kenneth was general minister and
president, only two regional realignments occurred. New Mexico
and Texas merged into the Southwest Region; and Utah and the
Central Rocky Mountain Regions agreed to share the same
regional minister, although when Kenneth retired in 1985, Utah
was still listed in the Year Book and Directory as a separate region.
In the twenty years since his retirement there have been only two
other regional realignments: the Great River Region, consolidating Louisiana, Mississippi, and Arkansas; and the Greater Kansas
City Region, created out of a metropolitan trade center.
Significantly, in recent years, the provision for the "general board
to initiate procedures for reorganization of existing state and area
organizations as regions," has been deleted from The Design and
replaced with the phrase, "The process of reshaping regional
boundaries (even if only one congregation is affected) includes

the participation and approval of the parties involved." In the final analysis, the Committee on Structure and Function during the time Kenneth was general minister and president experienced only limited success in its repeated attempts to realign both the general and regional manifestations of the church. [22]

The congregational manifestation of the Disciples' new covenantal community discovered that restructure had neither abolished nor diluted their freedom. They still owned all of their property; they continued to select their own ministers; their autonomy was not impaired; and they held representation and voting privileges on all general assembly issues. Their fears had been unfounded. For the most part they settled into the new restructure with comfort. In fact, Kenneth was confident enough about the congregational comfort level, that, six months after his election, he wrote an article for The Disciple about congregations entitled, "The Flip Side of Freedom." He noted that, "Some Disciples were fearful of an erosion of congregational integrity, but events since the approval of the Design have proved that the fears were groundless. We have come to realize that a congregation of the Christian Church . . . is safeguarded in the Design." Then, he adroitly proclaimed, "the flip side of freedom is responsibility," and reviewed, in the bulk of his article, the seven major responsibilities of congregations recorded in The Design. Kenneth estimated that across the twelve years he was general minister and president he preached in approximately five hundred local Disciples congregations. This was deliberate. "I took every opportunity I could," he said, " to be in local congregations and let them see me as a preacher [rather than a bureaucrat] . . . I organize my work in such a way that I'm out there." Kenneth was frequently accused of being a centrist. But the truth was precisely the opposite. He was pastoral. [23]

The colleges and universities had also raised questions about how they were to be related to the restructured church and were particularly unhappy with the inequity of mission fund distribution they received. In 1975 Kenneth appointed a Higher Education Evaluation Task Force, chaired by Dr. C.C. Nolen, president of North Texas State College. The task force reviewed a large quantity of material from each institution, conducted on-site visits, and held two concentrated review sessions sifting through their data. From this they identified the things that determined church-relatedness and recommended a covenantal relationship between the institutions and the church. Further, they recommended a four-part funding formula: (a) $30,000 as a base or historic figure; (b) $10 for every full-time student; (c) $100 for every student who was a member of the Christian Church (Disciples of Christ); and (d) $500 for each graduating student who enrolled in an accredited seminary. The formula was supplemented with ten recommendations on the process of implementation. The task force report was approved at the 1976 meeting of the general board. Implementation occurred in 1977 when the board of trustees of each institution approved and each president signed the covenant and accepted the formula. At this writing the covenant and formula are still in operation. [24]

Rewriting the preamble became a necessity in order to remove sexist language. Kenneth wrote to Ronald Osborn, indicating that the matter needed to be addressed: "I would appreciate it if you would take a look at the affirmation . . . to revise the statement in light of current attitudes toward language." Later, Kenneth and the Committee on Structure and Function requested a chopping block draft by January 7, 1977, adding, "[we] know you can help keep its theological authenticity and preserve the beauty of the cadence in the original." Osborn was reluctant, but recognized it had to be done.

> We are under necessity of revising our language to eliminate sexism . . . But it will involve some losses I hate to see. "Our Brotherhood" has had so much meaning for Disciples that we deliberately put the word in the statement. But the women at School of Theology at Claremont practically spit at that point when we use it in our chapel . . . Many at STC will not use Father, some will not speak of Christ as son. They blithely throw out all the

Trinitarian language (which might please some Disciples, but not me) . . . I think we lose something of great value when we abandon the central image in Jesus' gospel. I (admittedly male) resist making changes in the covenantal statement. I'd rather follow Barnett Blakemore and put a date on it. Nevertheless, I think we will have to change it.

Despite his misgivings, Osborn met the January deadline, and the draft was gratefully received and approved. Osborn wrote that he had been hesitant to "tamper with the wording, for it was intensely discussed by many people and . . . every word was carefully chosen (though without regard to this issue) and represents a careful balancing of many concerns. To change one word may easily change the balance of ideas. I hope we can respond with full sensitivity to the concerns the feminists are raising, without losing elements of great importance in the gospel." Then he jokingly concluded his correspondence on the subject by noting if someone "suggests that the final Amen is sexist, try Selah!" [25]

Proposals to amend The Design appeared at nearly every general assembly during Kenneth's tenure. The provisional design had been amended in both 1969 and 1971. Five resolutions to amend were considered at the general assembly in 1973. Four resolutions to amend came in 1975, only one of which was approved. And in 1977, the Kansas City assembly voted to drop the word "Provisional" and simply call the document The Design. It was further determined at the 1977 assembly that an additional constitution was unnecessary. Amendments regarding the setting of priorities and general board representation were presented in 1979. No amendments were proposed in 1981. In 1983 the general assembly amended The Design by allowing four ecumenical representatives to be elected to the general board. And there was a 1975 request, referred to the Committee on Structure and Function, to reduce the size of the general board. The proposal was to modify the formula for regions by raising the representative allowance from one per 10,000 members or less to one per 15,000 members or less, but twenty regions had less than 20,000 members, and adjusting the ratio would only have penalized the larger regions. The request to downsize the board was rejected by the committee. All in all, the yet malleable Design, so thoughtfully crafted by Kenneth and the Commission on Restructure two decades earlier and now being so carefully molded by Kenneth and the Committee on Structure and Function into a living instrument of covenant, stood the test of time quite well. During the seventies and early eighties, Kenneth coached Disciples in their successful quest to learn its meaning and how to use it constructively for effective self-governance, notwithstanding a few cases of clever manipulation. In his state of the church address to the 1977 Kansas City assembly where it was voted to drop the word provisional, Kenneth proclaimed to the 11,000 Disciples in the great hall: "When [the Christian Church (Disciples of Christ] is gathered as we are now, it is not just a collection of individuals who come to a convention, not even a collection of local churches, but a church—a distinctive, recognizable, working part of the church universal. And we have life, and hope, and responsibility for each other to prove it . . . A Provisional Design has worked well. It is a flexible document befitting a pilgrim people. It has protected our freedoms while underscoring our responsibilities. It has bound us together, not by law, but by covenant." [26]

Ordination of Gays and Lesbians

Pharisaical Sir:

So you have to appoint a committee. . . . The very idea would turn the stomach of a decent buzzard! When Christ was asked a question he did not turn it over to a committee. Don't your instincts tell you anything? The bible tells you that homosexuality is wrong. . . . . You have the nerve, apparently, to say that you are a Christian. Your actions place you among the people of whom Jesus said,

163

"Depart from me. I never knew you." If the world cannot tell the difference between a church and a den of iniquity, the church has no claim to an exempt status. You take the same stands on moral issues as Joe The Bartender.

And the indecent parts have been deleted! The letter, addressed to Kenneth just ten days after the 1977 Kansas City assembly, was one of hundreds received by him during the following months, excoriating with sarcastic jibes and tart comments both his leadership and the actions of the assembly on the issue of homosexuality. One publication, called the *Frying Pan,* carried a scorching article about him and the Disciples' actions at their assembly. A copy reached him through a friend, to whom Kenneth responded, "I felt sufficiently 'fried' from the comments in the article." [27]

With the rise of the gay liberation movement in the 1960s, homosexuals asserted their right to bring their sexual orientation into the open and demanded that this disclosure not be treated with discrimination. It forced churches to confront the problem of human rights, as it affected gays, both in and out of the ministry. Many church groups in 1977–1978, including Episcopalians, Presbyterians, and Disciples, launched studies of the subject in response to changing moral values and the findings of modern scientific and biblical research on sexuality. Episcopalians released their twenty-two-page report in August 1977, and the Presbyterians' report, accompanied by a 150-page background paper and a twenty-page minority report, was released in January 1978. Both caused major debates and controversy within their respective assemblies and denominations. [28]

The Disciples controversy erupted at the Kansas City general assembly, October 21–26, 1977. There were four resolutions before the assembly dealing with the issue of homosexuality. One, submitted by a congregation in Kokomo, Indiana, asked the assembly to oppose homosexuality as a lifestyle for Christians. It was rejected by a majority vote of 60 percent (2,304 to 1,538). The second resolution, submitted by the Division of Homeland Ministries, while neither approving nor condemning homosexuality, urged the passage of legislation from the local to the national levels of government that would end the denial of civil rights for reason of sexual orientation. The debate that followed was marked by Carol Blakely's dramatic and tearful reading of a personal letter from her gay son. The resolution was approved by a two-thirds majority vote (2,541 to 1,312). The third resolution was actually an eleven-page study document prepared by the Task Force on Family Life and Human Sexuality, a group appointed under the aegis of the Division of Homeland Ministries. It was submitted for use by the whole church in research and reflection on the issue. It was the resolution that generated so much ferocity and rancor. The document was not an endorsement of homosexuality, although some thought it slanted toward accepting homosexuality as a natural part of human sexuality, not condemned by the Bible, thereby becoming an apologetic for a homosexual lifestyle. It set off a firestorm in the assembly, with abuse of parliamentary procedures, emotional tirades, and threats of withdrawal from the denomination. At length, however, the study document was approved. [29]

The fourth resolution (No. 7744), submitted by a congregation in Santa Maria, California, asked the general assembly "to deny ordination status to any candidate who declares that he or she practices or prefers homosexuality as a lifestyle; that such candidates be screened out; that counseling resources be offered to such candidates; and that the church remain open to the candidates' change in lifestyle." As the heat of discussion drained the energy from the representatives, they voted to refer the resolution to the Task Force on Ministry for further "investigation and study" and to prepare a report for the 1979 general assembly in St. Louis.

Even before the resolutions on homosexuality came to the floor, observers could see the conflict taking shape. When discussion of the relationship with the United Church of Christ was being considered, individuals called for a point of order, asking if "the United Church of Christ ordained homosexuals." And when the resolution condemning violence on television was before the representatives, amendments were proposed to include homosexuality. They were defeated, but it was clear that the coming debates would be intense. [30]

In the course of the five and one-half hour-debate on homosexuality, one representative came to the microphone and asked: "Dr. Teegarden, will you please tell us how a congregation may withdraw from the Year Book?" Kenneth came to the podium and said simply, "It is my hope that this kind of action would be unnecessary in a fellowship that values diversity." He then stepped away from the podium and started down the stairway behind the platform. Halfway down the stair he stopped, sat down on a step, bowed his head with chin in hand, and prayed. Then Kenneth arose and walked directly to the representative in the audience who had raised the question and engaged him in discussion on the meaning of covenant community. "It was a moment," said James Merrell, editor of *The Disciple,* "when Kenneth learned again that one who serves Christ must often walk the way of the cross and experience its pain in order to be a channel of reconciliation." A pastor later wrote to Kenneth, "I want to express my belated heart-felt appreciation for your ministry to the general assembly around this emotionally-laden issue. Before Kansas City I would not have thought it possible to be a 'pastor' to a 'congregation' so large and short-lived, but the representatives from my congregation and I *all* felt nurtured by you during those days." Perhaps the inimitable Raphael "Rafe" Miller, Jr., stated it best to Kenneth, "I think everyone at the assembly felt your pastoral concern for the whole church and I hope that some measure of this has been conveyed to people in the churches through their representatives." And it was. A newsletter from a congregation in Chicago printed the following lines: "Ken Teegarden, General Minister of the Church, demonstrated his administrative skill in making it possible for so many people to be together, participate in worship, deliberate with an amazing amount of democratic participation on *so many* highly controversial issues. His State of the Church address was marked by excellence of preparation, grace of style and cosmopolitan spirit. His stance for depth in evangelism and commitment to social justice came through clearly."[31]

The final gavel had barely sounded on Wednesday, the twenty-sixth of October, 1977, when bundles of unfriendly mail and irate telephone calls began to arrive in Kenneth's office. Even before the assembly he had received a letter signed by four Indianapolis pastors requesting that he remove the four resolutions from the business docket. He responded with a question, "Do you really want the general minister and president to have the power to stop resolutions from congregations reaching the general assembly?" He heard no more from them. Three months after the assembly he confided to the new moderator, James Noe, it " has been an unbelievable period. The mail continues unabated and I am spending two and three hours a day responding to the letters . . . about the general assembly. Some of it is quite disconcerting and troublesome . . . I have decided to send you by United Parcel a big package of the correspondence . . . I thought by thumbing through . . . and sensing something of the scope and contents, you would have a flavor of what people have been writing to me and how I have been responding . . . I am going to make arrangements to have it analyzed in some fashion." Many of the letters threatened withdrawal from the denomination; others threatened to cut off their financial support; still others said they were going to designate or restrict their giving. A number of writers requested the elimination of controversial issues from the general assembly agenda. Some indicated they were not going to attend any more assemblies. And several were outright personal attacks on Kenneth. [32]

Kenneth answered nearly all the letters. His responses were measured, factual, gracious, and firm.

> I am glad you wrote me about your concerns. I hope you will have occasion to reconsider and come to the St. Louis assembly. I believe it is going to be a great one.

I don't operate in an ivory tower. I spend at least half my time among the churches and probably know as well as anyone in our church what people are saying and thinking. I also receive much correspondence from persons in the churches like yourself. I take what is said seriously and I always respond, frankly and candidly, because I believe such communication is essential to our understanding of our mutual involvement in our mission of witness and service.

You are certainly entitled to criticize the leadership—especially me. I cannot agree with you that the leadership of Dr. Cook and Dr. Fiers was weak. I think it was among the strongest of any church in America.

Your statistics are not accurate. We never had two million members. The most we ever had in this country was a million and a half, and we still count a million and a third. It is quite true that our church, like all other so-called Mainline churches, has remained almost the same size for the last Decade. I deplore that fact as you do.

Furthermore, Kenneth did not believe engaging the social issues was the cause of decreasing membership. He had stated forthrightly in his state of the church address in Kansas City:

> Occasionally we hear the claim that the involvement of the church in social issues is causing people to drop away. It is my personal belief that that is a myth we have concocted to cover our failures in evangelism . . . lay people have fewer misgivings than clergy about social involvement. What really is stunting our growth is the failure of the church to be challenging enough . . .

And his answer to those who sought to eliminate controversial issues from the business agenda of the general assembly and deal only with budget, officers, time, and place, was rooted in the conviction he held throughout his ministry. In November 1977 he wrote:

> I am glad to affirm the significant contribution our church is making in the life of the world. . . . what the church is doing far outweighs the negative impact of grappling with social and moral problems that people confront every day in today's world.

Despite all the criticism, Kenneth never wavered from his belief that by helping the church to deliberate issues of the day candidly in open assembly, he was helping Disciples live out the gospel in their communities, and helping them understand religion as a source of personal and public morality. Freedom, he declared, was safe only when diverse views can be debated openly, and the arrival of controversy should not force abandonment of a system. Above all, he thought, religious discussion of the public issues should not be left exclusively to the Christian right. It was a theme he reiterated again in a pastoral letter to the entire church shortly after the close of the Kansas City assembly, a letter that is now considered a classic. A brief excerpt reveals the depth of his conviction:

> The issue of Christian attitudes toward homosexuality could not be avoided by the general assembly. It came as business items from both congregational and general church sources. Actually, this issue, the same as others almost as bothersome, came from the troubled world in which we are called to minister and witness. The business docket reflected the true insight that the general assembly had a responsibility to inject Christian perspectives

into the mix of thoughts, emotions and actions affecting human life in our time.

We Disciples cherish and protect our right to differ. We consider our oneness in Christ equally precious. As the general assembly considered business items on homosexuality . . . differences of opinion among us were obvious. I earnestly hope that if your particular viewpoint did not prevail in the voting, you do not have a feeling of rejection. It would be contrary to our tradition for us to allow differences over such issues to damage our fellowship. The Design for the Christian Church (Disciples of Christ) encourages us to express any dissent from assembly actions "in love."

May our love of God and fellow human beings help all of us to continue to deal with difficult questions in a spirit of prayer and earnest searching for God's truth. God bless you.

Kenneth L. Teegarden [33]

For the next two years, resolution 7744 was the consuming subject of the Task Force on Ministry, chaired by Lester Palmer and staffed by William Howland and Kenneth Teegarden. Over Kenneth's signature a survey instrument was sent to the chairs of all regional commissions on ministry. The survey results revealed that none of the regions had knowingly ordained a candidate who was an avowed homosexual and that they did not confront candidates about their lifestyle. The question of sexual orientation had not arisen. All said they had not and did not intend to ordain a homosexual person. And there was strong unanimity among the regions, stating they did not want the general assembly establishing content definitions for personal fitness, emotional stability and maturity, or standards of morality. That was clearly viewed as a regional and congregational responsibility. None had studied the issue of homosexuality, and few had in place a process for counseling and guidance. [34]

As the year of 1978 progressed, several regions, Kentucky, South Idaho, Tennessee, Florida, began to consider resolutions not to ordain homosexual candidates. In March, the Division of Homeland Ministries produced a study packet to supplement the study document approved at Kansas City for congregational use. That summer, a judge ruled that Lexington Theological Seminary must award a degree to a homosexual student who had completed all the academic requirements. The judge stated the catalog phrases describing requirements were inadequate. The seminary appealed the ruling. [35]

In this environment, the Task Force on Ministry conducted and completed its work of preparing a report for the 1979 general assembly in St. Louis. The report was widely reviewed, including all regions, prior to final submission to the general board and general assembly. The task force noted that in sharp contrast with traditional consensus, some in the church now affirm that homosexual practices can be an appropriate way of life for consenting adult Christians. For Disciples, the report stated, the broader topic of homosexuality and ordination is intertwined with the procedure whereby Disciples nurture and authorize its ministry. Within Disciples ecclesiology, the nurture, certification, and ordination of candidates for ministry is the responsibility of the regions in collaboration with their congregations. The task force, therefore, developed a two-fold conclusion: "(a) Recent studies have not convinced us nor the church at large that the ordaining of persons who engage in homosexual practices is in accord with God's will for the church; and (b) The Christian Church (Disciples of Christ) intends to continue the current pattern of assigning responsibility to the regions with respect to the nurture, certification, and ordination of ministers. Throughout our church there is a general reluctance to have the general assembly establish doctrinal or moral standards for ministers." The report implied that at that moment the church would probably not ordain homosexuals, but it did not say that the church should not or could not ordain homosexuals. While neither the task force nor the church was convinced that such ordination was in accordance with God's will, it was not within the spirit of The Design to forbid regions from exercising their best judgment in each individual case. The importance of the report was that it recognized and affirmed the established procedures for examining candidates for the ministry. The assembly approved the report of the task force and the issue began to subside in light of other events such as Jonestown that temporarily overshadowed it. The issue, however, did not vanish, and Kenneth continued to receive ugly correspondence on the issue for several years. But the episode demonstrated irrefutably that the new structure—a community in covenant under The Design—could cope with a diversity of intense, passionate, and powerful points of view, and not collapse. [36]

Jonestown

The preoccupation of the church with the issue of ordaining homosexuals was suddenly eclipsed on November 19, 1978, when news was received of an unspeakable tragedy that had occurred in Guyana, South America. It was a murder-suicide that took the lives of 913 people, including the life of a California congressman, Leo Ryan. The shocking news was that the pastor, James W. Jones, claimed ordination as a Disciples minister, and the more than 900 dead were members of a congregation affiliated with the Christian Church (Disciples of Christ)! A sizeable volume of communications immediately arrived at Kenneth's office, nearly all of them angry that the church could allow such a congregation to exist in its midst, that the oversight of congregational life was so negligent, and that Disciples did not have a means to disassociate from such a group. Later the tone of the calls softened as the membership began to remember the sacredness of congregational autonomy within Disciples polity and realized it did not want the general assembly or anyone in Indianapolis to exercise any control over their congregation. The membership was somewhat bewildered by how it should respond to such a bizarre situation as the Jonestown massacre. [37]

Jim Jones, born during the Great Depression was a native of Lynn, Indiana, approximately fifty miles east of Indianapolis. He married at age eighteen, and then attended Indiana University from 1950 to 1951. He enrolled at Butler University in 1951, finally graduating with a Bachelor of Science degree in secondary education in 1961. According to his minister's information schedule, he completed the admission training course for ministerial licensing offered by the Methodist Conference in Indiana. On February 16, 1964 (he recorded June 1964 on his crudely written information schedule), he was ordained at Peoples Temple Christian Church (Broadway Christian Center) with his own minister Edward Malmin presiding, and John Harms, executive secretary of the Association of Christian Churches in Indiana giving the charge. Jones' interracial congregation of approximately 230 members, founded by him in 1953, was located in downtown Indianapolis, where he ministered to impoverished blacks. Impressed with his ministry, the city named Jones a member of its Civil Rights commission. [38]

In 1966, Jones, along with seventy families of the congregation, moved from Indiana to California, settling in Redwood Valley on the edge of the Mendocino National Forest a little more than 100 miles north of San Francisco. The membership, predominantly black, grew from approximately 100 the first year to 6,000 in the mid-seventies. There was a People's Temple in San Francisco with slightly more than 3,000 members, and a branch called the New People's Temple in Los Angeles, with slightly less than 3,000 members, all served by Jim Jones. Then Jones radicalized his evangelistic ministry. He created an autocratic theocracy in which he managed to take members' personal resources to support the church, threaten them with severe discipline and sexual abuse, asking his followers to call him father, and claiming to perform miracles and to be a faith healer. [39]

In August of 1977, *New West* magazine published an article critical of People's Temple and its legendary wealth. Jones' extreme paranoia about the article spurred him to relocate his congregation to a Marxist agricultural community that he had established in Guyana in 1974. Once there, he began to exercise even more control over the members, Beginning in early 1978 there were almost monthly signals of an impending mass suicide, with Jones making repeated statements such as, "it is better to die than to be harassed," and "we must develop the courage to die for a cause." San Francisco relatives of the members prevailed upon Congressman Leo Ryan to investigate. It was his visit and subsequent murder that precipitated the mass suicide. [40]

Disciples had no background in disciplining or defrocking ministers. Restructure, seemingly, had not provided the means to deal with a charlatan. A minister or congregation could leave easily, but it was nearly impossible to "throw" somebody out. The regional commission on ministry in Northern California had decided in 1977 to confront Jones with charges and review his standing, but he was in Guyana and wouldn't return, so they let the matter rest. Then the news broke. Kenneth caught the brunt of the news media questions. Within forty-eight hours after the tragedy he issued a statement of concern for the families of the victims and for survivors. He also acknowledged the relationship of both the congregation and its pastor to the Disciples of Christ. Furthermore, he took what he felt to be an appropriate step of getting the question of denominational follow-up out of the hands of staff and into the hands of those who initiate and make policy. Questions were being raised about what the Disciples were planning to do about People's Temple. Kenneth indicated that he "would make an inquiry with the legislative bodies of the church as to whether there ought to be a procedure for disavowing congregations, a procedure we have never had." [41]

On March 12, 1979, Kenneth presented a four-page address to the forty-four-member administrative committee. A small portion appears below, revealing Kenneth's thoughtful response to the tragedy and its meaning for the Christian Church Disciples of Christ).

Does this church have an obligation to itself, to other Christians, and to society to institute a procedure of dissociation from congregations that run amuck?

If fanatical fringe groups can enhance their credibility by aligning themselves with major denominations, the ministry and mission and witness of all mainstream Protestantism suffers. The anti-religionists tried more than once on national television following Jonestown to make the point that People's Temple was not a cult but a part of the Christian mainstream.

There is the church-state issue involved as well. The government would like to close the tax loopholes which cults and pseudo- religious bodies can take advantage of. We have come to the point where government is beginning to define what constitutes a church, and what appropriate church activities are. We believe this to be an infringement on the First Amendment protection of religion.

So, I bring to you, as I indicated I would, the matter of whether we have a weakness in structure that endangers Christian witness and mission. Let me share with you my recommendations.

First: Let us act with the good of humanity in mind, and not the reputation of the church. We are concerned with people and ministry. We are concerned with love and compassion. We are here to save the world, not the institution. As great a tragedy as Jonestown was, we should not act precipitately with our self-protection as the motivation.

Second: Having a policy to disavow congregations could not have foretold or averted Jonestown. People's Temple, until near the end, behaved like many other congregations with a strong devotion to their pastor. It is unlikely that the church would have used a disavowal procedure. We have developed responsible policies and criteria for the order of ministry, and those policies were operative concerning the standing of Jones at the time of the tragedy.

Third: Just as we ask the individual prospective member only if she or he believes in Jesus Christ, we offer relationship to congregations on the same basis, and accept on faith the reply in each case.

Fourth: It is not so much a body of common beliefs that binds us together as Disciples of Christ but an understanding of the church as one. In tolerating and welcoming difference of opinion, we leave ourselves no measuring rod by which errancy can be determined.

Fifth: Social witness, which got Jim Jones interested in the Disciples in the first place, should not be lost by the church because opponents tie it to the aberrations of Jones.

Sixth: If we have shortcomings in connection with our congregations and ministry, it is at the point of shepherding, not policing. Perhaps the most significant decision we Disciples made in the restructure period of the sixties was to recognize ourselves as a covenant church. We are still learning what that means.

With Kenneth's six recommendations before them, the members of the administrative committee reaffirmed Disciples congregational freedom and vowed not to take steps "passing judgment on a congregation's ministry." The committee did recommend improvement in "shepherding" congregations by encouraging regions to establish an annual visit to every congregation and to request ministers to report annually on the ministry in which they are involved. The administrative committee had been inspired by Kenneth's address, concurred in its content, and expressed appreciation to him for his pastoral care and his clear statement of the issues. [42]

The United Church of Christ

> *"How does the church confront a divided*
> *world with all of the hostilities that separate*
> *humanity? For a church to be separated and*
> *to present a divided witness is incongruous."* [43]

Kenneth spoke these words during an ABC television interview with Herb Kaplow in 1978. The words bespoke an abiding
conviction. Christian unity was an article of faith he had
expressed and acted upon repeatedly throughout his ministry. At
the time he spoke those words, dialogue had been reactivated
with the United Church of Christ and potential union between
them and the Christian Church (Disciples of Christ) would
remain a pro-active issue for Kenneth until his retirement in 1985.

Conversation between the two churches dated to 1912. Their
mutual history extended back to James O'Kelly and Elias Smith.
Two unions occurred to form the United Church of Christ
(1949–1957); the evangelical and reformed churches became one,
and the Congregational Church and the Christian Church also
became one. Disciples held their 1912 conversations with the
Congregational Church and participated as a consultant when the
UCC constitution was developed in the late 1950s. In 1961 the
general synod voted to begin union conversations with Disciples
"at the earliest mutually convenient time." Official conversations
began immediately and continued until 1966, when it was decided to delay bilateral discussion in favor of energetic participation
in the consultation on church union that envisioned a wider
union based upon an emerging theological consensus. In 1971,
the general assembly of the Christian Church (Disciples of
Christ), meeting in Louisville, received a resolution calling for an
"acceleration of conversations with the United Church of Christ,
looking toward early union." It was referred to the Council on
Christian Unity. Concluding that the work of COCU was a

longer-range process than originally thought, Kenneth Teegarden and Robert Moss, presidents of their respective church bodies, jointly proposed a resumption of union talks in 1975.

In 1977 the general synod and general assembly approved a joint resolution authorizing a two-year period of exploration at all levels of church life regarding union. At the end of two years, a six-year (1979–1985) study of baptism, the Lord's Supper, mission, and ministry was authorized and a joint steering committee was appointed with Kenneth Teegarden and Avery Post (successor to Robert Moss as president of the United Church of Christ) as co-chairs. "Progress," reported Kenneth in 1980, "is both good and slow." It is slow, he continued, because "everybody realizes that church union is not going to occur because of some legislative acts at denominational headquarters from the top down." Covenant study packets were prepared by the joint steering committee and 11,000 were sold during 1981 and 1982 alone. In partnership, regional and conference ministers invited 700 congregations to participate in a special study process and over 625 accepted. Disciples and UCC congregations were paired to share in the study together. A joint meeting of the Disciples Council of Ministers and the United Church of Christ executives was held in February 1983 to involve the leadership in the covenantal process. In fitting closure to Kenneth's last general assembly as general minister and president, the 1985 Des Moines general assembly approved the establishment of an "ecumenical partnership" between Disciples and the UCC, thereby making a firm commitment to become one church, but leaving any actual union to be worked out gradually and naturally through a "shared life." The general synod approved the same resolution. [44]

Not all Disciples were supportive of union conversations. Kenneth's correspondence contains a sprinkling of letters opposed to the talks, usually stating they did not want Disciples to "join" the United Church of Christ. As was his custom, Kenneth answered them courteously, but firmly. "I am glad you feel free to express any dissent you may have. This characterizes the kind of church we are—one that has unity with diversity . . . What is being explored is whether or not our two churches, which have so much in common from the beginning, should seek to discover whether God wills for us to be one church. It certainly would not be a matter of either joining the other. If it ever comes about it will be because of our faithfulness to the Bible which records Jesus prayer that all his followers should be one." By way of epilogue, in 1989 both the synod and the assembly passed a resolution declaring that "a relationship of 'full communion' now exists between our churches." And in 1995 the general synod and the general assembly both affirmed a common Global Ministries Board of the Christian Church (Disciples of Christ) and the United Church of Christ. [45]

Peace with Justice

Of all his religious convictions, the one Kenneth felt most deeply was "peace with justice." The church, he believed, needed to stand with the poor and the outcasts and defend them. In his view, the church needed to be an advocate of human rights, an instrument to alleviate world hunger and a maker of peace. When he made his decision to enter ministry, he had done so in the earnest belief that ministry could make a more positive contribution to the welfare of people than the law. Early in his tenure as general minister he wrote of the tension between church and state,

> More and more around the world, the church is finding itself coming in conflict with the state . . . the church teaches the people about individual worth and freedom—When human freedoms are curtailed the church-state conflict becomes inevitable, unless the church is a tool of the state. The Christian cannot blindly follow his or her nation's leading . . . Governments deal in friends and enemies; Christians must deal in rights and wrongs.

In separate media interviews two years later he addressed the subject again, "For the church not to be actively involved in seeking to secure basic human rights for people everywhere is really a denial of the fundamental precepts of Christianity." And then he added, "Separation of Christianity and humanism is unscriptural. It diverts us from the ministry of servant-hood." [46]

On five occasions between 1973 and 1980 Kenneth accepted invitations, along with his mainline protestant counterparts, to meet with presidents Gerald Ford and Jimmy Carter for the purpose of responding to briefings on human rights issues at home and around the world. Kenneth considered these sessions quite valuable and believed the voice of the church was taken seriously. Through those meetings and the correspondence regularly mandated by general assembly action, Kenneth developed a cordial friendship with President Carter. In 1980, following the election of President Reagan, these meetings were abruptly discontinued. Between 1980 and 1985, one session (September 1984—an election year) was convened, but with a Reagan staff person and not the president. Presidential briefings, however, were scheduled with conservative evangelical leadership. The practice of the president meeting with mainline Protestant leadership was briefly restored twelve years later during the administration of President Clinton with a single breakfast meeting of denominational executives attended by Richard Hamm—general minister and president of the Christian Church (Disciples of Christ). The practice was discontinued again with the election of George Bush in 2000 and has not resumed since. [47]

In 1975, Kenneth's first general assembly, four resolutions were approved asking the church and the nation to address the issue of world hunger. All but one originated in the general offices through the Division of Overseas Ministry and the Division of Homeland Ministries. In addition there were resolutions urging protection for civil liberties, support of farm workers, an interactive relationship with third world peoples, reconciliation with the people of Indochina, and support of human rights in the Philippines. All of these were approved by the general assembly, and Kenneth was one of their strongest proponents. Even in the explosive 1977 assembly two resolutions were approved on the support of human rights, one submitted by DHM; another submitted by DOM seeking peace and full franchise for voters in South Africa was also approved; and a resolution supporting farm workers was approved as well. [48]

In all five general assemblies held during Kenneth's years as general minister, resolutions regarding human rights and peace with justice appeared on the docket. At the 1979 gathering two lengthy reports on world hunger and human rights were received from DOM and approved, and there were resolutions to end the arms race, support the equal rights amendment, and urge the church to be a witness for world peace. In 1981 the assembly approved the designation of a "Peace Sunday;" a resolution supporting the establishment of a "Peace Academy;" and a resolution advocating a nuclear arms freeze. The 1983 general assembly debated and approved resolutions opposing apartheid in South Africa by use of divestment; opposing the mid-east arms race; supporting human rights in Iran; assuring asylum in the United States as required by law; and expressing appreciation to the Catholic bishops for their statement on world peace. The Disciples Peace Fellowship submitted the last resolution while the others originated with either DOM or DHM. [49]

Kenneth especially prized the 1985 publication of *Seeking God's Peace in a Nuclear Age.* In the preface, he explained his rationale for originating the project: "Believing," he said, "that the church has a responsibility to provide its members guidance for their ethical thinking, I appointed a Panel on Christian Ethics in a Nuclear Age . . . to reflect upon those issues and to share with the membership the results of that reflection." The panel, chaired by T.J. Liggett, was appointed in 1983 and worked two years on the subject, publishing their result in May 1985 to coincide with the International Year of Peace. Kenneth thought that *Seeking God's Peace in a Nuclear Age* may be the most significant thing to come out of the Disciples' "peace with justice" priority. The work proclaimed in part:

Every Christian heart is summoned to be a maker of
peace. Our faith demands that we respond. The threat of
war will continue to overshadow the planet until humanity is able to see that above all the tribes and all the
nations is the human family, the sisterhood and brotherhood of all people; until we are able to see our wholeness
with more clarity than we see our divisions and differences . . . recognizing that we are all "members one of
another" (Ep. 4:25) . . . Dare to set your course toward
the wholeness of the human family at peace!

The little eighty-five-page volume was circulated widely to
boards, committees, units and regions of the Christian Church
(Disciples of Christ). Ronald Osborn called this work the "high
water mark" of Kenneth's years as general minister and president.
And T.J. Liggett, who chaired the panel, wrote to Kenneth, "the
coming generation of Disciples will recognize your emphasis on a
Christian witness for peace as the most enduring contribution of
your leadership." [50]

The period of Kenneth's ministry as head of the denomination
saw more than thirty resolutions come before the general assembly regarding civil liberties, human rights, hunger, and peace with
justice. Sixteen of those were resolutions regarding peace with justice, twice as many as would appear during the twenty years that
followed. Kenneth did not personally sponsor them, but a sizeable
portion came from general units with whom he was in regular
communication. Disciples were well aware of his position on such
matters and knew they could count on his support. He had written openly to the membership:

It seems to me that it is the responsibility of leaders of
the congregation to give people an opportunity to deepen
their faith by confronting the knotty moral and theological questions. That is as much a ministry to them as calling on them when they are sick. There is no question that
social action and social issues have caused some problems

in congregations in the past decade. But the agonies and ecstasies of arriving at decisions of faith should be what the gospel is all about.

Two-thirds of the sixty resolutions on international relations considered by the general assembly between 1971 and 2003 came before the assembly during Kenneth's tenure. His theological conviction about the role of the church in society and his determination that the church should witness on the subject is clearly manifested in the high volume of resolutions addressing peace, justice, and social issues during his presidency. [51]

Examples of his sense of commitment to social action abound. In the year of Kenneth's election, the Cincinnati assembly passed a resolution supporting the principle of amnesty, in the belief that such an act was most likely to achieve the national goal of reconciliation after the Vietnam War. Eight months later Kenneth wrote to his Holiness Pope Paul VI, "Your Ascension Day Bull proclaiming 1975 a holy year and appealing to all nations to grant amnesty to political and other prisoners and urging works of charity and help for poorer nations is received by me with great appreciation and I write to communicate my support." In December he again recorded his support in his Disciple monthly column to the membership, "Amnesty—amnesia—means to forget, not forgive. No judgment is passed, either on those who went and fought and died for their country or on those who refused to go . . . Not all of those who went were motivated by patriotism, any more than all those who refused to were motivated by reasons of conscience. But to label either as 'killers' or 'cowards' is the cruelest of judgments . . . reconciliation calls for an act of mercy." President Carter pardoned the war resisters in January 1977 and almost immediately Kenneth issued a statement supporting the president "for his quick action to pardon persons identified with resistance to the war in Vietnam." Within a week letters began to arrive at 222 South Downey charging that Kenneth's public statement of support was "indefensible and contributing to the Disciples membership decline." Kenneth, refusing to be provoked, diplomatically responded, "While you do not agree with the statement I made when asked for a response to President Carter's pardon, I am sure you would want me to be honest and to report the position previously taken by our general assembly. One of the great things about our church is the room it has for people of widely divergent viewpoints. . . . My major concern in this present instance is to seek the reconciliation of our people as we put behind us the unfortunate past." [52]

His stand on corporate social responsibility was also well known. The issue surfaced repeatedly during the seventies and eighties. By action of the 1971 general assembly a task force was appointed to develop ethical and socially responsible investment guidelines for the church and its many agencies and institutions. The guidelines suggested that investors seek change by voting rather than divesting. The Disciples task force was a member of and advised by the Interfaith Center on Corporate Responsibility related to the National Council of Churches. Questions about the church and its investments filled many pages. Two will illustrate: Should the church support resolutions for peace while at the same time investing in companies that are defense contractors manufacturing weapons of war? Should the church send missionaries to foreign countries to help the poor and oppressed while investing money in companies that exploit the third world poor and ensure continued poverty?

Kenneth's correspondence with the chairman of the board at IBM clearly reveals his conviction. It was known that 50 percent of the computers shipped to South Africa came from IBM and were being used by the South African government to enforce the system of apartheid. In response to a shareholder resolution submitted by the church, the chairman wrote sternly to Kenneth: "In the conduct of its business overseas, IBM looks to the U.S. government for guidance. In this case, we follow the guidelines set forth by the U.S. government, which forbids the shipment of arms to South Africa. For IBM to go beyond the government's guidelines and act as if it were its own state department would be to take political action inappropriate for a corporation." Much of Kenneth's force came from his ability to shape debates in moral terms, appealing to the conscience. His response to the IBM chairman, after a gracious opening, came directly to the point. "Involved as we are in an effort to bring justice and equity to all people of South Africa, it would be inconsistent for us not to urge those actions which we believe would create a climate for reform. We realize that the guidelines set by the United States government for business involvement in South Africa are followed by IBM . . . We feel [those guidelines] do not speak for us regarding the moral and ethical issues involved. We want to feel that IBM will also be sensitive to these concerns and will work for a solution of the problems which will help to bring justice and peace to the people of the sub-continent." [53]

Again in 1980 Kenneth spoke directly to the subject. He was addressing the International Management Council at the Omni Hotel in Norfolk, Virginia, an audience of four hundred middle managers who had previously heard economist Milton Friedman. Kenneth said to the council, "Milton Friedman's comment that the only social responsibility of business is to earn profits is simply not true. History gives the lie to such a philosophy. We can no more escape the penalty of greed, individually or corporately, than we can escape the penalty for jumping off a cliff, individually or corporately. Nations have not escaped the penalty of national greed; corporations didn't escape it a half century ago; unions did not escape it after World War II." He concluded his May 29 address by stating, "The ultimate question in business ethics is whether there can be a distinction between 'self-interest' and 'selfish-interest.'" He believed that human relations were regularly degraded to a cash-nexus, often forfeiting their humanity, and that people had to be reminded of their Christian duty to others, especially the poor. During this period the church, under Kenneth's leadership, was quite attentive to the investment policies of its affiliated units, colleges, and seminaries, offending some, but bringing at least a tiny bit of hope and perhaps some small relief to the oppressed in far off corners of the world. [54]

Describing the issue of "peace with justice" during Kenneth's years would be incomplete without mention of the major policy transformation of the Division of Overseas Ministry. Robert Thomas, the president of DOM and a good friend of Kenneth, thought the proper description of the modern missionary era should be the "servant stage" of the Disciples' long heritage on the mission field. Disciples had originated the concept of self-administration under Dale Fiers' leadership of the United Christian Missionary Society. Robert Thomas now sought to construct a theological and philosophical framework for this new "servant stage." Thomas was an insightful and enlightened leader who understood and was thoroughly committed to the wholeness of the church. The policy he sought and of which he was the predominant author could easily have been developed by staff and approved by the DOM board with no further involvement from the general board or general assembly. But after a four year period of crafting the new policy statement, Thomas demanded that it be sent forward to the general board and finally to the general assembly at Anaheim in 1981. The policy was overwhelmingly approved, and consequently owned by the whole church. Following an extensive historical overview the document articulated twelve theological principles for overseas ministry, heavily abbreviated here simply to introduce the flavor of the theological underpinnings of the policy:

1. Mission is rooted in the scriptures.

2. Missionary commitment is grounded in God's love for all humankind and Christ's liberating resurrection, expressing itself by engaging in the struggle for a new and just community.

3. God has never, in any time or place, been without witness.

4. The church is one and exists for the sake of the world, not itself.

5. Accepting God's grace, calls forth a faith commitment.

6. Discipleship makes Christians aware they belong inescapably together.

7. The good news, by its nature, must be communicated.

8. The Gospel always includes the obligation to denounce all that hinders wholeness.

9. Christ calls the church to identify with the oppressed, the poor, the prisoners, and the sick.

10. Social action and evangelism are one.

11. Christ calls the church to stand against that which oppresses and destroys people.

12. Christ calls the church to support people who suffer on behalf of justice and freedom. [55]

Kenneth called these principles "thoroughly biblical, evangelical, radical, and recognizing the Christian as servant, not master; the mission as losing one's self, not gaining." The approval of the policy represented a major achievement for Disciples' world mission, and also for the polity of restructure that proclaimed the "wholeness of church." Kenneth found deep personal fulfillment in this significantly collaborative action by the whole church in covenant, and especially an action designed to address through mission one of his abiding religious convictions, "peace with justice."

Toward Retirement

The many achievements that grew from those twelve years of service were not Kenneth's alone. There was a support staff of the highest quality, including deputy general ministers Howard Dentler, Bill Howland, William Fox, and later John Humbert. Included also was Robert Friedly, the chief communications officer. They shared so much together, triumphs, failures, tears, laughter, scores of meals (Kenneth always ordered fried chicken, no matter how fine the restaurant); an uncountable number of meetings that Kenneth presided over with poise, calm and an unflagging command of procedures and structure; a thousand coffee breaks, each one highlighted with Kenneth showing photographs of his grandsons; agony over general assembly resolutions; and shared family evenings together. Kenneth's loyalty to them was almost boundless. Staff recalled that Kenneth was very meticulous in preparing the business docket for administrative committee, general board and general assembly, and that he often assisted his secretary in the typing of the material. They also recalled that when an attempt was made to raise Kenneth's salary to $34,000 per year, he refused the increase, saying that he "could not possibly accept a salary at that level. There are congregations that don't have a budget that large!"

The story is told of Kenneth and John Humbert having a watermelon seed-spitting contest in the hallway of Missions Building. John announced he was eastern seaboard champion, and Kenneth challenged him. Up and down the hallway, staff emerged from their offices to observe. A tour group arrived in the middle of the contest, much to everyone's embarrassment. And they tell of the 1978 Super Bowl party when several families gathered to watch the game. One of the teams was Kenneth's beloved Dallas Cowboys. During the course of the game Roger Staubach threw a long pass to Drew Pearson. Kenneth, following the flight of the ball, instinctively rose from his chair, totally caught up in the action, took two steps, his feet became entangled in a throw rug, and he fell to the floor. It was remembered at general assemblies that support staff sometimes worked all night long at the copy machines preparing materials for the following day or for special called meetings of the administrative committee. Kenneth would appear at three or four in the morning and offer encouragement. It was important to him to show he was aware, and it meant a lot to the staff. John Humbert remembered, "he reached out to those working with him . . . giving trust and loyalty." [56]

The moderators of the six general assemblies were among the finest to ever hold the position: Jean Woolfolk, James Moak, James Noe, Thomas Youngblood, Joy Greer and William Tucker. Time and again they helped guide the general board and general assembly through their early growing pains and unusually difficult deliberations. When Kenneth took office in 1973 the general cabinet was composed of veterans of restructure: W.A. Welsh, Robert Thomas, Kenneth Kuntz, William Gibble, William Martin Smith, Rolland Sheafor, William Miller, James Suggs, Spencer Austin, James Reed, Roland Huff, and George Beazley. In 1973 George Beazley unexpectedly died on a trip to Moscow and was succeeded by Paul Crow. Spencer Austin retired in the mid-seventies and was succeeded by Jean Woolfolk.

The veterans, however, were beginning to retire. The first arrival of the post-restructure generation was Duane Cummins in January of 1978, succeeding William Miller as president of the Division of Higher Education. By the time Kenneth left office, of the original cabinet leaders mentioned above only James Reed remained, (along with deputy general minister Howard Dentler), A whole new generation sat at the table, learning from Kenneth Teegarden. The same pattern was true of regional ministers. By 1985 a majority of the restructure generation had retired, and Kenneth was working with a substantially new group of leaders. In his final state of the church address at Des Moines in 1985, Kenneth made note of this circumstance: "Of the 128 people who made up the Commission on Restructure . . . one of five of them is now deceased. More than half the rest are retired. In the regions, 91 percent of the regional ministers who were serving at the time of the adoption of our new covenantal relationship are gone from their posts. Ten of the eleven presidents of the church's general administrative units have also changed." The meaning of this was not lost on Kenneth. "We come to Des Moines with the responsibility to end one era and initiate another. For the last twenty-five years we have been 'becoming church.' It is time to close one era and enter a new one. Now we put aside becoming and begin to be." [57]

During those twelve years Kenneth had communicated widely and frequently. One of his great strengths was the spoken and written word. He enjoyed writing. Noting that sentences should not end in prepositions, he said he knew one that ended in five prepositions: A mother selected a book on her way upstairs to read her small son a bedtime story. The little boy exclaimed, "Why did you bring that book I did not want to be read to out of up for?" His *Disciple* articles alone numbered 132, containing 79,000 words. His correspondence was legion and covered almost every subject imaginable: abortion, charismatics, ordination of homosexuals, criticisms of the general board and the general assembly, Jonestown, women in ministry, gender and ethnic equity, corporate responsibility, peace issues, communicating to United States presidents, popes, senators, religious leaders around the world, ministers seeking a reference, and junior high students who were writing research papers on the Christian Church (Disciples of Christ). In addition, Kenneth often wrote letters at random, as he once confided in a letter to a friend, "I am always anxious for a congregation to know that they are important to the whole church no matter how small in number they might be. I make it a regular practice to write an average of six to ten letters a month to random individuals in congregations about events I read about in local church newsletters. It helps me to keep in touch with them and I hope serves to emphasize their significance to the church." [58]

He also communicated his thoughts through a little book he wrote in 1975 entitled *We Call Ourselves Disciples*. It was and remains popular because it expresses as well as any publication available the nature of our covenant community. At some point in 1985 Kenneth was bombarded with letters complaining that Disciples had no identity. Being a wordsmith (it was frequently said that Kenneth could work a New York Times crossword puzzle, his favorite hobby, in six minutes) he decided to write a statement of exactly 100 words identifying Disciples. The result follows:

> The Christian Church (Disciples of Christ) is a community of believers who through baptism into Jesus Christ are bound by covenant to God and one another. Disciples draw their inspiration from Scripture and the Holy Spirit,

celebrating around the Lord's Table the life, death, and resurrection, and continuing presence of Christ. They proclaim the Good News of salvation and claim as their particular mission the quest for Christian unity. While stressing freedom and diversity under God, they believe unity and mission are inseparable, and witness and serve among the whole human family in the interest of peace, justice, mercy and kindness.

It is a statement, he said, for which he would like to be remembered. [59]

It often seemed that the ordination of homosexuals, amending The Design, Jonestown, peace with justice issues, and conversations with the United Church of Christ were all-embracing issues, leaving time for no other. But such was not the case. Kenneth was closely identified with the issue of "women in ministry." Throughout the seventies he deployed staff to help states in their effort to pass the Equal Rights Amendment. The three-fourths requirement was never achieved, but not because of any lack of support from Kenneth. Again, nearly every general assembly found the issue on the docket, urging equitable pay and consideration and support of women pastors. He was careful to appoint women to task forces and committees, and to recommend them for unit presidencies and regional minister positions. It was one of the themes of his full twelve years.

Another issue that reappeared from time to time was abortion. In his customary fashion, Kenneth quoted to his correspondents the resolution passed at the San Antonio assembly in 1975: "(a) affirming the principle of individual liberty, freedom of individual conscience, and sacredness of life for all persons; and (b) respecting differences in religious beliefs concerning abortion and opposing, in accord with the principle of religious liberty, any attempt to legislate a specific religious opinion or belief concerning abortion upon all Americans." [60]

He responded in much the same way to the charismatic phenomena. After the successful workshop on charismatics at the

Kansas City assembly, many wanted to create an office or formal structure in Indianapolis. Kenneth, believing such an office inappropriate, said to them, "I think it is fair to say that the general structures of the church have sought to be open to the charismatics. Several of the units have provided counseling and supportive events over the past two or three years. I am impressed that there seems to be less divisiveness than . . . previously. I support the position that an organization of charismatics might be more divisive than helpful." [61]

Among other developments was the establishment of the Committee on Black and Hispanic Concerns in 1976. For many years there had been a Committee on Black Church Work, but it was succeeded by this new and expanded committee that Kenneth called "a point of new beginning in the life of the church." He added that he was grateful we did away with "minority and ethnic minority titles," and expressed the hope that the designations of "black" and "Hispanic" would disappear as well. The meetings of this new committee were at times highly animated, but the voices of blacks and Hispanics were being sounded across the church with a new vigor. [62]

The polar star of Christian unity always shone bright for Kenneth. He once said "Even our name, Christian Church (Disciples of Christ) suggests the desire for unity. The first part of our name, Christian Church, recognizes the universality of the church. The part in parentheses, (Disciples of Christ)," he added, "shows the denomination is part of the division of the church." He worked tirelessly for the ideal of unity as a member of the boards or committees of nearly every major ecumenical body in the world: Consultation on Church Union, and the National and World Councils of Churches. He was thrilled with the 1982 publication of *Baptism, Eucharist, and Ministry* by the Faith and Order Commission of the World Council of Churches, believing it broke down dividing walls and theological barriers. Kenneth was described by many as an "ecumenists' ecumenist!" [63]

The twelve years in Indianapolis contained moments of personal exhilaration and moments of sadness. Near the end of September 1973, just prior to his election as general minister and president, Kenneth and Wanda traveled to Weatherford, Texas, for the wedding of their son Kirk. Kenneth assisted Father O'Brien in performing the ceremony. Breaks in the regimen came to Kenneth during fraternal visits, including a visit to Russia in 1974 and one to Africa in 1975, where he wrote home to Wanda, "It's going to be a long, lonesome three weeks!," and the World Council of Churches meetings in Nairobi, Kenya, 1973 and in Vancouver, 1983. There was the birth of their first grandson, Grant, on November 29, 1972, which generated celebration and delight even though it was right in the midst of the GMP interview process and the debriefing from the Asia fraternal visit. Two more grandsons were born during their Indianapolis years, Sloan in January of 1976, and Matthew in February of 1976. Sadness also visited their lives. Kenneth's father, Roy, died on June 5, 1977, a short time before the Kansas City assembly. Kenneth's mother had passed away September 5, 1971, never knowing that her son would become general minister and president. Wanda's father, Hiram Strong, died on June 15, 1983, three months before the San Antonio general assembly. Kenneth presided at the funeral service for Wanda's father, and later at the service for Wanda's mother in 1990. [64]

Moments of rich humor also enriched their Indianapolis years. A news column written by the famed University of Chicago religious history scholar Martin Marty became one of the best remembered of those moments. In the column Marty listed six names, one of whom was the Disciples' Kenneth L. Teegarden, and he asked the readers, "Do you know who these people are?" Confident that most people didn't, Marty explained that they were the heads of major denominations, and that the days of recognizable "giants" were gone. Kenneth carried the article home and showed it to his wife, Wanda, who innocently asked, "Who's Martin Marty?" Even Marty enjoyed telling the story.

As the Des Moines general assembly approached in 1985, Kenneth could reflect across his twelve years and see clearly that he had set the course. The design was implemented and working. The concept of a representative general assembly was accepted and functioning. The colleges and universities were in covenant. The church was learning to confront moral and ethical issues in the society around it. Both female and ethnic leadership had become formidable. The ordination of gays and lesbians had been addressed. The covenantal partnership with the United Church of Christ was ready to move toward "full communion." And the first wave of post-restructure leaders of regions and general units had been oriented and assimilated into their positions. Yet when asked to name the highlights of his time as general minister and president, he said, "Simple and homely things—experiencing the friendship and trust that people sharred with me." [65]

Hundreds of letters came to thank him for his leadership. Dale Fiers wrote, "It hardly seems possible that you have been at the helm for twelve years. That is, until one begins to add up the score of your achievements. I marvel at all you have done in so short a time. You have been a great general minister and president and have made a lasting and unreproducible contribution to the maturing of the Christian Church (Disciples of Christ). In concert with the whole church, we express our profound admiration and affection for you both." And from Ronald Osborn, whom Kenneth had known since their student days at Phillips University, came the words, "Kenneth, old friend . . . . . . you have made an inestimable contribution in giving substance to our dreams. I cannot recall a time when your heart has not been in the right place nor your counsel wise." Kenneth had been a wise and faithful servant, giving himself completely to the general ministry. He spoke to the church with clarity and conviction. This talent, coupled with his steady hand and gracious spirit were applauded and appreciated by a grateful church. The journey from Cushing to Des Moines had been both long and demanding. He looked older now. His 155 pound, 5' 10" frame was less sturdy. His jet-black hair had turned gray. Kenneth closed his final address at the Des Moines assembly as general minister and president with the words:

> Finally, I would like to recall for you the Apostle Paul's farewell speech to the elders in Ephesus found in Acts 20. He had five things to say: One, 'I have given the task my very best.' Two, 'I'm not ending my service but going to new service.' Three, 'Take care of yourself and the people of the flock.' Four, 'God will look after you.' And five, 'Remember, it is more blessed to give than to receive.' I've given the task of general minister and president my best. . . . I will continue my service on the faculty of Brite Divinity School . . . I urge you to be shepherds of God's church . . . I commend you to God . . . and remember, there is great joy in that which you give in the service of Jesus Christ. [66]

At the Des Moines banquet in his honor, he was given a pair of western boots and a Stetson hat to take with him into Texas retirement. Three persons spoke at the banquet. All took time for a playful roast of Kenneth, after which the first speaker, Avery Post, concluded:

> He is delightfully human with genuine pastoral warmth.
> He has deep and faithful care for all of the churches.
> He is an ecumenist's ecumenist.
> He is a Disciple in whom there is no guile.
> He is a loving husband and a proud father and grandfather.
> He has eyes and ears like radar and a mind like a steel trap.
> He is a prophet of the Lord who has not ducked the hard issues.

The second speaker, William Gibble, praised Kenneth's remarkable capacity for friendship.

And the third speaker added:

When historians of the future look back upon this era to write of the maturing of our church and the contribution of Kenneth Teegarden—they will identify him as the key architect of restructure, an author of the concept of covenant, the key craftsman of *The Design,* the general minister and president who implemented *The Design,* and one of the leading ecumenical statesmen of his day—and these historians will record for all generations to know, that Kenneth Teegarden was a just and humble man whose pastoral voice and pen taught us all how to join hands and become a church. [67]

NOTES

1. Interview with T.J. Liggett, March 4, 2006; Interview with Harold Johnson, March 4, 2006.

2. Interview with Wanda Teegarden, March 1, 2006; Interview with T. J. Liggett, March 4, 2006; Interview with Harold Johnson, March 4, 2006.

3. Robert Friedly to D. Duane Cummins, November 5, 2005, 1–2; Robert Friedly to Kenneth L. Teegarden, August 25, 2002; Robert Friedly to Kenneth L. Teegarden, July 15, 2002. Wanda Teegarden Collection.

4. Robert Friedly to Kenneth L. Teegarden, August 28, 2002. Wanda Teegarden Collection; *Christian Church News,* February 13, 1973; Christian Church News, July 28, 1973.

5. *Procedures for the Nomination and Election of a General Minister and President.* Approved by the Administrative Committee, March 1972, 4.

6. David A. Roozen Interview with Kenneth Teegarden, 1990, 311; Kenneth L. Teegarden to Mrs. Billy Dunn, September 20, 1977, Disciples of Christ Historical Society, Teegarden GMP files. Box 2, File D; Dale Fiers to Kenneth L. Teegarde, December 18, 1972. Wanda Teegarden Collection.

7. *Qualifications of the General Minister and President.* Prepared by Admistrative Committee, 1972. DCHS, Teegarden GMP files, Box 1; Kenneth L. Teegarden to Jane Mendel, December 10, 1973, DCHS Teegarden GMP files, Box 4, File M.

8. Bruce Schulman, *The Seventies* (New York: The Free Press, 2001), xi-xvii; 78–101; Jimmy Carter, *Memoirs of a President* (New York: Bantam, 1982), ix-xii; Gerald Ford, *A Time to Heal* (New York: Harper, 1979), 1–41; Kenneth L. Teegarden, "Take Me to Your Leader," *The Disciple* October 3, 1976, 15.

9. Schulman, *The Seventies,* 102–117; Earl Black and Merle Black, *The Rise of Southern Republicans* (Cambridge: Harvard University Press, 2002), 1–39.

10. Edwin Gaustad and Leigh Schmidt, *The Religious History of America* (San Francisco: HarperSan Francisco, 2002), 398–404; Robert Wuthnow and John Evans, *The Quiet Hand of God* (Berkley: University of California Press, 2002), 159–166; Schulman, The Seventies, 92.

11. Wuthnow and Evans, *The Quiet Hand of God,* 159-166; Robert Wuthnow, *The Restructuring of American Religion* (Princeton: Princeton University Press, 1988), 173–214; James T. Patterson, *Restless Giant* (New York: Oxford University Press, 2005), 145.

12.Virgil Sly to Kenneth L. Teegarden, January 23, 1973; Kenneth L. Teegarden to Virgil Sly, January 30, 19973. Wanda Teegarden Collection.

13. *Minutes.* Committee on Structure and Function. September 5–6, 1972, 1. DCHS, Teegarden GMP files, Box 5, File Structure; *The Provisional Design.* June 1972, Paragraph 43, 11.

14. *The Provisional Design.* Paragraph 44, 11; Committee on Structure & Function. *Progress Report.* October 1973, 1–14. DCHS, GMP, Box 5, File Structure; D. Duane Cummins, "The First Decade of D.H.E." *Disciples Theological Digest.* Vol. 9, No. 1, 1994, 35–51; *The Design.* July 2005, Paragraph 68, 14.

15. Spencer Austin and Albert Pennybacker, *Report of the Sub-Committee on the Function of General Units.* January 8, 1973, 7 DCHS. Ibid.

16. *Minutes.* Committee on Structure & Function. May 9–11, 1972, 1–7. DCHS, Teegarden GMP years. Box 5. File Structure; *Minutes,* Committee on Structure & Function. September 5–6, 1972, 1–5. DCHS, Teegarden GMP files, Box 2, File Structure; Committee on Structure & Function. *Progress Report.* October 1973, 1–14. DCHS, Ibid; Committee on Structure & Function. *Guiding Principles for use in Further Development of the General Manifestation.* May 30, 1973, 2–5. DCHS, Ibid; Minutes, Committee on Structure & Function. February 5–7, 1976, 2. DCHS, Teegarden GMP files, Box 5 File Structure.

17. Committee on Structure & Function. *Progress Report.* October 1973, 1–14. DCHS, Ibid.

18. *The Provisional Design.* June 1972. Paragraph 75, 14.

19. Jean Woolfolk, to Regional Ministers, October 17, 1972, 2. DCHS, Teegarden GMP files. Box 5, File Structure.

20. John D. Wolfersberger, *Toward Regionalization of the Christian Church.* Committee on Structure and Function, May 1, 1973, 1–15. DCHS, Teegarden GMP files, Box 5, File Structure

21. Kenneth L.Teegarden, *A Review of the Area Concept with Fewer and Comparable Regions.* Committee on Structure and Function October 2, 1973, DCHS, Teegarden GMP files. Box 5, File Structure.

22. Robert Stewart, *An Evaluation of Fewer and Comparable Regions,* October 1976. DCHS, Teegarden GMP files. Box 5, File Structure; *The Design.* July 2005, Paragraph 29, 6.

23. Kenneth L.Teegarden, "The Flip Side of Freedom." *The Disciple.* April 28, 1974, 22; Roozen interview, 324.

24. C.C. Nolen, Duane Cummins, Ann Dickerson, Jim Spainhower, Bill Howland, Kenneth Teegarden, and Robbie Chisholm, *Higher Education Evaluation Task Force Report.* June 12–15, 1976, 1–22 of 150 pages. In possession of the Author.

25. Kenneth L. Teegarden, to Ronald Osborn, September 12, 1975, DCHS. Teegarden GMP files. Box 5, Structure; Ronald Osborn to Kenneth L.Teegarden, June 25, 1976. DCHS. Teegarden GMP files. Box 5, Structure; Kenneth L.Teegarden to Ronald Osborn, November 19, 1976. DCHS. Teegarden GMP files. Box 5, Structure; Ronald Osborn to Kenneth L.Teegarden, January 4, 1977. DCHS. Teegarden GMP files. Box 5, Structure.

26. *Business Dockets of the General Board:* 1973, 1975, 1977, 1979, 1983 and 1985. DCHS files. General Board Dockets; Howard Dentler to William Howland. December 11, 1975, 1–4. DCHS. Teegarden GMP files. Box 5, Structure; Kenneth L.Teegarden, *State of the Church,* Kansas City General Assembly. October 22, 1977. Wanda Teegarden Collection.

27. N_____ to Kenneth L. Teegarden, November 5, 1977. DCHS, Teegarden GMP files, Box 3, File Homosexuality; Ruby Takanishi and Louis Knowles, "The Disciples of Christ," *Frying Pan.* December 1977. [quoted in *In Unity,* August-September, 1978, 9–10, 23].

28. *The Cleveland Press,* Saturday, January 31, 1978. p. 7; The New York Times, Friday, January 23, 1978, p. 12.

29. *Business Dockets of the General Board:* 1977. Resolution 7760, p. 211, Resolution 7747, p. 188; Resolution 7750, p. 191.

30. *Business Dockets of the General Board:* 1977. Resolution 7744, p. 184; Takanishi and Knowles, "The Disciples of Christ."

31. James Merrell, "Viewpoint." *The Disciple.* June 1985, 5; Takanishi and Knowles, "The Disciples of Christ;" J. Marshall Dunn to Kenneth L. Teegarden, April 13, 1978, 1. DCHS, Teegarden GMP files, Box 3, File, Homosexuality; Raphael Miller to Kenneth L. Teegarden, November 23, 1977. DCHS, Teegarden GMP files, Box 4, File M; Harvey Lord, "Controversy Attracts Largest Assembly," *The Messenger.* University Christian Church, Chicago. November 21, 1977, 1–2.

32. Kenneth L. Teegarden to James A. Noe, January 30, 1978, 1. DCHS, Teegarden GMP files, Box 3, File, Homosexuality.

33. Kenneth L. Teegarden to Eli McRorey, November 21, 1977, 1–2; Kenneth L. Teegarden to Maxine Miller, June 7, 1979, 1. DCHS, Teegarden GMP files, Box 4, File M; *Year Book and Directory,* 1978. Pastoral Letter, 288; Kenneth L. Teegarden "State of the Church." Kansas City General Assembly. October 22, 1977. Wanda Teegarden Collection.

34. Packet of regional ministers' letters to Kenneth L Teegarden, April 1978, responding to seven questions. Kenneth summarized the results in a letter to Jack Naff, March 19, 1979.DCHS, Teegarden GMP files, Box 3, Task Force on Ministry.

35. *Religious News Service,* July 10, 1978; Christian Church News, July 18, 1978. DCHS. Teegarden GMP files, Box 3, Task Force on Ministry; Christian Church News, March 1, 1978, Study Packet.

36. *Year Book and Directory,* 1980, 296–298. (Membership of the Task Force on Ministry included: Lester Palmer-Chair, Fred Craddock, Duane Cummins, David Darnell, Claudia Grant, William Fox, Gilford Olmsted, Harry Smith, Keith Watkins, and Tom Wood; It was staffed by Kenneth Teegarden and Bill Howland).

37. *New York Times,* November 26, 1978, p. 1; Christian Church News, November 22, 1978, p. 1–4, News Release.

38. *Minister's Information Schedule.* James Jones. November 3, 1969. DCHS. Jonestown File: *Program: Service of Ordination.* James Jones. February 16, 1964. DCHS. Jonestown File; Robert Friedly and D. Duane Cummins, *The Search for Identity,* (St. Louis: Christian Board of Publication, 1987), 141–149.

39. *New York Times,* November 26, 1978, p. 20; Friedly and Cummins, *The Search for Identity,* 141–149.

40. Ibid.

41. Kenneth L. Teegarden, *Statement of the General Minister and President.* Administrative Committee, March 12, 1979, 1–4. DCHS. Jonestown file.

42. Ibid.

43. Herbert Kaplow, ABC television network, "From Ecumenism to Union: The Long Courtship." (Interview with Kenneth L. Teegarden and Avery Post), December 5, 1982, 3. Wanda Teegarden Collection.

44. Ray Ruppert, "Church President Wary of Politics." *The Seattle Times.* October 18, 1980, p. A-10 [Interview with KLT]; George Beazley, "Conversations toward Union. General Board Business Docket, 1973, 133–136. DCHS; Paul Crow, "Report of Joint Working Group." General Board Business Docket, 1979, 207–209. DCHS; Steering Committee, *Report of Steering Committee.* General Board Business Docket, 1983, 186–188. DCHS.

45. Kenneth L. Teegarden to J. S. McKenney. March 5, 1979; J. S. McKenney to Kenneth L. Teegarden, February 26, 1979. DCHS, Teegarden GMP files. Box 4, File M.

46. Kenneth L. Teegarden, "Verdict Before Trial," The Disciple, August 1976, 15; Sylvia Hart, "Church Leader sees Need to Confront World Problems" *The Press Register*, 1978, p. 1; Kenneth L. Teegarden, "Church must not Sacrifice Human Concerns," *The Virginia Christian*, March 1978, p. 3.

47. Jimmy Carter to Kenneth L. Teegarden, November 13, 1980. Wanda Teegarden Collection; Photos of Kenneth with Presidents Carter and Ford. Wanda Teegarden Collection; *Christian Church News*. September 20, 1984.

48. Business Docket of the General Board, 1977, pp. 165–167, 204–207; *Year Book and Directory*, 1976, 204, 207, 215, 225, 241, 243

49. Business Docket of the General Board, 1979, pp. 226, 227, 215; Business Docket of the General Board, 1983, pp. 192–197, 202–205

50. Kenneth L. Teegarden, "Disciples Witness to Ethics in a Nuclear Age," *The Disciple*, May 1985, 52; [membership of the panel: Gene Brice, Duane Cummins, Newton Fowler, Kenneth Henry, Jane Hopkins, JoAnne Kagiwada, T. J. Liggett-chair, Ronald Osborn, Kenneth L. Teegarden]; T. J. Liggett, et.al., *Seeking God's Peace in a Nuclear Age* (St. Louis: CBP Press, 1985), 6, 85; D. Duane Cummins, *A Handbook for Today's Disciples*. (St. Louis: Chalice Press, 2003), 53; Ronald Osborn to Kenneth L. Teegarden, June 26, 1985; T.J. Liggett to Kenneth L. Teegarden, June 25, 1985.

51. Kenneth L. Teegarden, "Adult Pablum?" *The Disciple*. September 21, 1975, 17.

52. Kenneth L. Teegarden, to His Holiness Pope Paul VI, June 13, 1974. DCHS, Teegarden GMP files. Box 1, File Amnesty; Kenneth L. Teegarden, "1975—A Holy Year?" *The Disciple*, December 22, 1974, 28; *Christian Church News*, "Carter Pardon," January 21, 1977; Kenneth L. Teegarden, to Mrs. Glen Wampler, February 4, 1977. DCHS, Teegarden GMP files. Box 1, File Amnesty.

53. Frank Cary to Kenneth L. Teegarden, January 30, 1975, 1; Kenneth L. Teegarden to Frank Cary. February 17, 1975. DCHS, Teegarden GMP files, Box 1, File Amnesty.

54. Unidentified article. "Teegarden says Business Bears Responsibility For Effects of Action." May 29, 1980. Single page.

55. General Board Business Docket, 1981. *General Principles and Policies—DOM*, 165–176. DCHS; Friendly and Cummins. P. 153–160

56. Interview with Howard Dentler, February 26, 2005; John Humbert, "Kenneth L. Teegarden." September, 2002.

57. Kenneth L. Teegarden, "State of the Church," Des Moines General Assembly, August 3, 1985, 5.

58. Kenneth L. Teegarden to Martin Pike. August 18, 1977. DCHS, Teegarden GMP files. Box 5, file P.

59. Parchment copy of the 100 word statement. Wanda Teegarden Collection.

60. Kenneth L. Teegarden to R.B. Howard, June 27, 1979. DCHS, Teegarden GMP files, Box 1, file Abortion.

61. Kenneth L. Teegarden to B.O. Edwards, August 23, 1977.DCHS, Teegarden GMP files, Box 2, file Charismatics

62. *Christian Church News*, December 14, 1976. News Release. DCHS. Teegarden GMP files, Box 1, File Blacks and Hispanics.

63. Jim Jones, "Brite Graduate Returning to Join Faculty," *Fort Worth Star-Telegram*. (undated) 1985, p.3; Faith and Order Commission. *Baptism, Eucharist and Ministry.* World Council of Churches. Geneva. 1982.

64. Kenneth L. Teegarden to Wanda Teegarden, November 23, 1975, Wanda Teegarden collection.

65. Lani Johnson, "Friendship and Trust, *The Disciple,* June 1, 1980, p. 4.

66. Dale Fiers to Kenneth L. Teegarden, July 12, 1985; Ronald Osborn to Kenneth L. Teegarden, June 26, 1985; Kenneth L. Teegarden. "State of the Church," Des Moines General Assembly, August 3, 1985, 4–5. Wanda Teegarden Collection.

67. Avery Post, "Remarks for Kenneth Teegarden," August, 1985, 2; Duane Cummins, "Honoring Kenneth," August 6, 1985, 2. Wanda Teegarden Collection.

The Distinguished Minister in Residence

I spent more than sixteen years of my ministry in the tent that is Missions Building. I saw in this place a "brotherhood of disparate agencies and people become a "church" with divisions and councils and changed people. The halls and walls and Martin Rogers Conference room are not the altar, as dear as they are to us all. Not even Graham Chapel. My memories of wonderful and committed colleagues are many. But the ark and the altar move with us wherever we go; there are new offerings to be laid upon the altar. When it is time to fold the tent, we do so with loving care, but never do we worship the canvas. I am thrilled with the opportunities that lie ahead of us at 130 East Washington. A pilgrim people in a fresh pasture. God's mission confronts a very different world than it did eighty-six years ago, or even twenty-five years ago. We pitch our tent anew. And it too will mark holy ground

Kenneth L. Teegarden

Professor, Interim Minister and Board Chair

"They have given me the flamboyant title "Distinguished Minister in Residence." I teach a few classes and counsel with those preparing for the ministry." Through his own winsome humility, Kenneth described the new position at Brite Divinity School that awaited him following his retirement as general minister and president. The dean and the chancellor portrayed his impending presence in more ennobling terms. A former classmate and then dean of the school, M. Jack Suggs declared "Kenneth Teegarden brings to Brite immense knowledge of the church in its congregational, regional and general manifestations." And the chancellor, William E. Tucker noted, "As a distinguished Disciples leader and an ecumenical church statesman in our time, Dr. Teegarden will add an important dimension to the program of Brite Divinity School." [1]

A faculty colleague at Brite Divinity School remembered that Kenneth did not try to pass himself off as a scholar. He was not interested in the scholarly winds of the day. "He was a churchman. His concern was the students and the future of the church. The church meant everything to him and he encouraged the students to feel the same. He believed passionately in the church and remained optimistic about its future when others did not. When people spoke against the church, he would not do so—he was the mediator." To some he said in his unpretentious way he was the "Pooped Pope." Right up to the time of his final illness he was always in chapel, seated on the aisle of the pew about half way back on the north side near the window. For Kenneth, attending chapel was a life-long practice, a spiritual discipline, beginning with his twenty-nine years of perfect Sunday School attendance, continuing with twice weekly required chapel while a student at Phillips, and extending through his years as general minister and president in Missions Building. It was said that, "Kenneth, when he was in town, never missed chapel service no matter how light the attendance, or busy his schedule." Kenneth was highly supportive of student ministers, constantly telling them of a bright future in ministry. When he heard a student minister preach, "he just beamed." One student recalled, "Kenneth Teegarden was a preacher's preacher. In casual conversation with him over coffee or on a bench under a tree near the school—I learned how to be a minister to a congregation." Kenneth placed a very high value on these interpersonal relationships between himself and the students, and so did the school.[2]

Kenneth co-taught a course with Jack Suggs entitled "The Church's Mission and the Minister's Vocation." He also co-taught a course with Joey Jeter, "Foundations for Preaching," and was called upon to teach specific class sessions in many different courses throughout his years as a member of the Brite faculty. Kenneth also played a significant role in the candidacy process, interviewing each student who went through the procedure. Beyond teaching, he served as a mentor, friend and counselor to staff and faculty, as well as the students, on issues related to the state of the church. Kenneth taught an undergraduate course entitled The Christian Ministry, Religion 2703, in room 205, one day per week from 2:00 P.M. to 4:40 P.M. He established five themes or objectives for the course: (a) the purpose of the church and its ministry; (b) the role and function of the minister; (c) the call to ministry; (d) the preparation for ministry and ordination; and (e) the sermon in worship. Students were required to review two books, summarize two worship experiences in two different churches, practice daily spiritual devotions, prepare and deliver one sermon, and take the mid-term and final examinations. Kenneth provided a bibliography from which the students could select a title for their book reviews. One grouping was biography containing fourteen choices. Among those choices were *C.S. Lewis: A Biography* by Green and Hooper; *Confessions of Augustine; Here I Stand* by Roland Bainton; *Mother Teresa* by Desmond Doig; and *Albert Schweitzer* by George Seaver. The second grouping focused on ministry and included among the titles were *Creative Disarray* by Ronald Osborn; *Testing and Reclaiming Your Call to Ministry* by Robert Schnase; *Contemporary Images of Christian Ministry* by Donald Messer; and *Pastoral Theology* by Thomas Oden. [3]

For each class meeting Kenneth invited a special guest with whom he would interact on the subject of the day. On stewardship, for example, the guest was Gilbert Davis; on preparing the sermon Kenneth invited Eugene Brice; and on Disciples' history and structure the person sharing the session with Kenneth was Margaret Harrison, regional minister of the Southwest. The two-hour-and-forty-minute sessions were arranged for Kenneth to open the class with a forty-five- to fifty-minute lecture. This was followed with a thirty-minute dialogue between Kenneth and the guest specialist, a dialogue that always involved the students. After a brief class break, the guest would deliver a thirty- to forty-minute lecture on the subject, followed again by a twenty-minute dialogue between the two and the students. During the week between classes Kenneth would see the students regularly in the library or in Weatherly Hall where they would share a morning coffee and visit about the students' future plans or progress in the course. And he shared and prayed with them every Tuesday during chapel. At the end of his first year he received a thank-you card from the students that he kept among those private things that held deep meaning. It read:

> Dr. Teegarden
> Please accept our sincere appreciation for the life and warmth that you have added to the life of Brite Divinity School and to our lives individually.
> You are a blessing to us all.
> The Brite Student Community

As an expression of esteem for Kenneth's fifteen years (1985–2000) of service to Brite, the Divinity School established the Kenneth L. Teegarden award in his honor in 2003, The award is given annually during ministers' week at Texas Christian University to the local pastor who across his or her ministry has consistently supported the preparation of new ministers at Brite Divinity School. [4]

For some who retire it is a strange feeling to lay down the responsibility of office. A sense of psychological and physical relaxation comes upon them, a feeling of relief, and a feeling of diminished influence. This was not so for Kenneth because it was the power of his intelligence and moral distinction, his enlightened values and benevolent behavior that gave him his authority and influence, all of which carried uninterrupted into his retirement. Kenneth had given his entire adult life to the ministry, fighting for the mission imperatives in which he believed. It would have been thoroughly out of character for him to withdraw from the world of the church in his post-general minister and president years. In his last column for *The Disciple* he wrote: "I don't believe God gave us the Bible, closed it, and said, 'That's it! I'm retiring!'" Kenneth had more to say, more to do, and more to give on his long pilgrimage. [5]

He taught frequently and well at Brite, yet he also remained active in the structures of the church. In 1987 Kenneth was elected to serve a two-year term as chairman of the board of directors of the division of higher education. It was an important period for the division due to its search for a new president. Kenneth gave oversight to the selection of new leadership for the division in the person of James I. Spainhower. Kenneth also served as interim regional minister of the Southwest between the time of Margaret Harrison and James Suggs. And, despite the march of time, he continued to attend all the meetings of the general board of the Christian Church (Disciples of Christ) in addition to all the general assemblies. [6]

Congregations and regional assemblies called upon him regularly to speak and he was not hesitant to articulate his long held personal convictions. During his second year at Brite he spoke in Oklahoma on the subject of "peace with justice," contending "The major problem the church and civilization as a whole face is the nuclear threat and the hope for peace with justice. The church must continue to be in the vanguard of helping people develop ethical responses to the nuclear age and at the same time make our witness to the world about the principles of Jesus Christ." Speaking in Fort Worth's University Christian Church in January of 1986, Kenneth leveled his aim at the Christian right. "Religion in America is suffering from resurgent fundamentalism, sentimentality, successism, and downright foolishness. The world could use a new dose of rational religion." It was not the first time he had uttered sharp words about the fundamentalists. Six years earlier he had reflected on the Moral Majority, asserting "the issue is not whether churches should be involved in public issues, but whether anyone should bend Scriptures to fit one's own political ideas . . . there is a danger in equating the nation and its actions with Christianity . . . The history of civilization tells us that when well-intended, righteous people begin to band together under political motivations, very often oppression begins to emerge." Later in January he was the keynote speaker at the Dallas Area Association of Christian Churches meeting, the theme of which was "Characteristics of a Healthy Congregation." He was often invited to be a guest minister, and spent many of his weekends on the road traveling to Texas, Oklahoma, Arkansas, and New Mexico to deliver a sermon. [7]

His hometown always remembered Kenneth and expressed its pride in his achievements by bestowing upon him its highest honor in May 1986. He was a member of the first class of three to be inducted into the Cushing High School Hall of Fame. There were twenty nominees, subsequently narrowed to nine and then three. The other two inductees were Lloyd Haskins, secretary general of the International Federation of Petroleum and Chemical Workers; and Arthur Bartow, artistic director of the New Playwrights Theater in Washington, D.C. Four years later Kenneth was invited back to Cushing as the featured speaker for the Cushing High School Golden Circle. [8]

He was the keynote speaker at the Indiana regional assembly in 1988 choosing "peace with justice" as his subject. Several letters of appreciation were written to him following the address, including the associate regional minister who offered commendation, "I speak on behalf of the assembly program committee when I say, many, many thanks for your thoughtful, well presented address. It was absolutely what we had hoped for, and more! Our assembly evaluations plus letters coming in now, bear me out." He was grateful for the speaking engagements and appreciated the positive response. But each year that passed was marked by the sadness at the death of close friends and old colleagues: W.A. Welsh, Jean Woolfolk, Granville Walker, Ronald Osborn, William Gibble, Jack Suggs, Robert Thomas, Walter Bingham, James Moak, Virgil Sly, an ever lengthening list. [9]

Perhaps the most significant address he gave during his retirement years, was at the 1995 closing of the Missions Building at 222 South Downey in Indianapolis. His remarks helped the church understand the meaning of the relocation that was taking place. The building had been constructed eighty-six years earlier and was said to be "a great power house from which currents of spiritual influence will go forth to transform lives and hearts in the outermost parts of the earth." In the minds of those who worked there it had become a sacred place. It was called the "Vatican," "Mecca," or simply "Two Twenty-Two." "The Ghosts of Saints," it was said, "walked its hallways." But the old building had reached a point of deterioration and the cost of maintenance demanded either an enormous investment or sale. The decision was made to sell the building and relocate the Disciples' headquarters in downtown Indianapolis. So 300 people from across the nation gathered on a cold and snowy January morning to take part in the "Closing of Missions Building." Kenneth was asked to speak at this highly emotional event. His words helped everyone accept the change with understanding and grace.

> I have always liked the idea of a tent as a symbol of the dwelling place of God, and as a dwelling place for God's people. It is fitting for a God who is not confined. And it is equally fitting for pilgrims who always are on the march. Everywhere Abraham and Jacob went, they pitched their tents, sometimes before they set up an altar, sometimes after. Moses established a Tent of Meeting to house the Ark of the Covenant. But the tent never was the altar.

I spent more than sixteen years of my ministry in the tent that is Missions Building. I saw in this place a "brotherhood" of disparate agencies and people become a "church" with divisions and councils and changed people. The halls and walls and Martin Rogers Conference room are not the altar, as dear as they are to us all. Not even Graham Chapel. Folks gave much of their lives here. My memories of wonderful and committed colleagues are many. But the ark and the altar move with us wherever we go; there are new offerings to be laid upon the altar. When it is time to fold the tent, we do so with loving care, but never do we worship the canvas. I am thrilled with the opportunities that lie ahead of us at 130 East Washington. A pilgrim people in a fresh pasture. God's mission confronts a very different world than it did eighty-six years ago, or even twenty-five years ago. We pitch our tent anew. And it too will mark holy ground.

Kenneth L. Teegarden
January 29, 1995 [10]

The Joy of Family

These twilight years at 7013 Serrano Drive in Fort Worth were among the happiest for Kenneth and Wanda and their family. All four of their grandsons graduated from Texas Christian University: Grant '95, Matthew '98, Sloan '99, and Blake '01, and Kenneth was able to attend all their commencement exercises. Grant happened to receive his law degree from Texas Tech in 1999 on the same day that Sloan was graduating from TCU. Wanda attended Grant's ceremony and Kenneth attended Sloan's. They were intimately involved with the lives of their sons and their grandsons. In fact, Kenneth was one of the ministers who helped perform Grant's wedding in April of 2001 at University Christian Church, and Grant still feels moved by the meaning with which Kenneth read the scripture. Kenneth rarely missed a

TCU basketball game. From up in the student section, Sloan recalled seeing his grandparents sitting across the way, and walking over to sit with them. Blake was often at the games too, and particularly enjoyed going to Wendy's with Kenneth and Wanda after the game to get a frosty. Matthew remembered placing notes on the windshield of Kenneth's brown Honda Accord when he saw it parked on campus. He laughingly recalled being a small boy and not understanding what Kenneth really did in the church but knowing it was important. When his friends asked about his grandfather, Matt replied, "He is King of the Christian Church." All four grandsons recalled regularly finding their grandfather in the TCU library reading a book, conferring with a student, or walking through and especially seeing him in the periodical section reading the *New York Times* and the *Washington Post*. Grant remembered too that Kenneth was the only ardent Democrat in the family and he effectively challenged the other family members to defend their political position. The grandsons, who first came to know Kenneth well when they were teenagers after their grandparents returned to Fort Worth, especially remembered his sense of humor, his practical jokes, his quick and intelligent wit, that he "had it all together," that he was a caring man, always worried about the well-being of others, and that when he disciplined them as youngsters he would lean forward in his chair, draw a circle in the carpet with his finger, and say, "sit here."

When Kenneth and Wanda celebrated their fiftieth wedding anniversary in 1994, neither one desired a reception or special event. They preferred to be with their family, so the entire family, Kenneth, Wanda, sons, daughters-in-law, and grandsons, joined for a full Mexican dinner at Joe T. Garcia's in Fort Worth. It was a grand evening—family and treasured memories. And in 2001 Kenneth received a pleasant surprise on December 22, his eightieth birthday. Wanda suggested that the two of them should go to dinner at Joe T. Garcia's, their favorite restaurant. When they arrived, David, Kirk, and their families were there to greet them with a birthday cake! Many in the family believed this was the only time they had succeeded in surprising Kenneth. When he saw them he said simply, "Well, the whole tribe is here!" These years in Fort Worth allowed for substantially more family time than the years in Indianapolis. The result was a deep and joyful bonding. [11]

On the evening of May 7, 2002, Kenneth attended a meeting of the church board at University Christian Church. Upon returning home he mentioned to Wanda that he had felt a bit dizzy at the meeting. About one-thirty in the early morning of May 8, he got out of bed to get a glass of water. He dropped the glass of water and collapsed, which awakened Wanda. She heard him call, "Wanda, I need your help." He was quickly taken by ambulance to Harris Methodist Hospital in Fort Worth. It was determined that he had suffered a cerebral aneurysm and he was taken to Zale Lipshy Hospital in Dallas for surgery. The surgery appeared to be successful. Kenneth was without voice and unable to stand for a time, but he was mentally alert. On May 28, Wanda told Kenneth it was their 58th wedding anniversary, and if he still loved her, to move his toes. And he proclaimed his love for her by wiggling his toes. Kenneth progressed to the point that he was moved to Life-Care Hospital in Fort Worth where he was to recuperate over the next several months. But in the early fall he acquired a staph infection. He died at sunset on Sunday, September 22, 2002. The lonely hours of the night came, and the church grieved. [12]

Epilogue

The response to Kenneth's death was immediate. Monday morning an e-mail awaited the Brite faculty when they arrived for class. "It is my sad duty to inform you of the death of Kenneth Teegarden late yesterday afternoon. The birdsong may seem a little less eloquent to us today, our step not quite so light, our lives not so full as yesterday. But we will be sustained in all of our tomorrows by the warm memories of the friendship Kenneth gave to each of us: the friendly smile, the ready wit, the sharp insight, and his abiding love of the church." When Howard Dentler received the news he said, "I felt a sharp stab . . . and I wept. Kenneth was the closest friend I ever had in the ministry of the church. We respected and trusted each other like brothers." Charles Mallotte, a friend of sixty-one years—dating back to their freshman year at Phillips, a friendship that included performing Kenneth's wedding—wrote simply, " I have lost a very dear friend!" Avery Post, closely bonded to Kenneth as an ecumenical colleague, confessed: "Ken's death hit me very hard!" In an interview with the *Fort Worth Star Telegram*, Dr. Mark Toulouse, professor of church history, commented, "He was always able to portray patience and wisdom and had a commitment to justice, the church and society." Out of Indianapolis came word from the general minister and president, Richard L. Hamm, "Kenneth moved us from an association of congregations and agencies into a unified church. He is regarded as the primary architect of *The Design*." And it was reported in *The Christian Century*, "Ken Teegarden, more than any other human being, was the architect of the Christian Church (Disciples of Christ), bringing many traditions and organizations into one church. His contribution was enormous." Deeply meaningful to so many were the tender words of his wife Wanda, "He was a very gentle person. He was interested in the lowliest problem . . . He had time for anyone." [13]

Through his life and death he bequeathed to the Christian Church (Disciples of Christ) a church in covenant, a church governed by the democratic principles of *The Design*, a church in full communion with the United Church of Christ, a church sensitized to the importance of "peace with justice," a church that placed the highest value on wholeness, and a church committed to being a world ecumenical leader, achievements that will be enshrined forever in the hearts of Disciples. We must receive and care for this inheritance wisely. Future generations will make their assessment of Kenneth's towering ministry. As the years pass his actions will be studied in light of new social and political developments. But this generation knew him, stood shoulder to shoulder with him on the front lines, witnessed his courage, his faith, his readiness to serve. They worked with him, prayed with him, and can say unequivocally that they witnessed the depth of his belief in the church, his hope for humanity, his abiding desire for Christian unity, and they saw that nothing, absolutely nothing, could distract him from his rock-solid faith in the ennobling genius and regenerating power of religion.

His memorial service was held on Thursday, September 26, 2002.

Against the stillness, a friend stood in the distant pulpit and spoke words of remembrance.

> There is a line engraved high atop the war memorial in Edinburgh honoring the battle dead of Scotland. It reads: *At the going down of the sun, and in the morning, we shall remember them!* And so shall we remember Kenneth Teegarden—because his soul is deathless—it cannot and will not perish! [14]

fini

NOTES

1. "Dr. Teegarden: Special Guest Speaker," Guymon Daily Herald, November 28, 1987, p. 10; "Teegarden to Join Seminary Faculty," *Fort Worth Star-Telegram*, Undated, 1985, Religion Section, Clipped article.

2. Interview with Dr.. February 24, 2005; Joseph Jeter, "Ken Teegarden," September 24, 2002, Remarks in chapel in honor of Kenneth Teegarden; Interview with David Teegarden, April 11, 2006.

3. Kenneth L. Teegarden, *Course Syllabus for The Christian Ministry*. Brite Divinity School. 1986–1994. Wanda Teegarden Collection; Newell Williams to D. Duane Cummins, *E-mail*, April 10, 2006; Interview with Don Pittman, Dean of the Faculty, Phillips Theological Seminary, April 10, 2006.

4. Pittman Interview; Brite Student Community to Kenneth Teegarden. 1986. Wanda Teegarden Collection.

5. Kenneth L. Teegarden, "Share with others your own faith pilgrimage," *The Disciple*, August 1985, p. 84.

6. *Minutes*, Board of Directors, Division of Higher Education, April 10–11, 1987, 8

7. Jim Jones, "Church Leader decries religious foolishness," *Fort Worth Star-Telegram*, January 17, 1986, p. 18-A; Jim Jones, "Brite Graduate returning to join faculty." Fort Worth Star-Telegram. Undated, 1985, Clipped article; Ray Ruppert, "Church President wary of Politics," *The Seattle Times*, October 18, 1980, p. A-10; "Teegarden to lead Church Clinic," *The Christian Courier*, January 1986, p. 1.

8. "Hall Inductees Named," *The Cushing Daily Citizen*, May 18, 1986, p. 1; "CHS Golden Circle," *The Cushing Daily Citizen*, June 24, 1990, p.3.

9. Katherine Kinnamon to Kenneth L. Teegarden, August 25, 1988. Wanda Teegarden Collection

10. D. Duane Cummins, "A Dwelling Place for God," January 29, 1995, Address, Cummins private files: Lectures and Addresses; Kenneth L. Teegarden, "A Tent of Memories." January 29, 1995 Wanda Teegarden Collection.

11. Interview with Wanda Teegarden, March 26, 2006.

12. Interview with Wanda Teegarden, November 17, 2005.

13. D. Duane Cummins, "E-mail to Brite Faculty." September 23, 2002; John Gutierrez-Mier, "Kenneth Teegarden Obituary," *Fort Worth Star-Telegram*, September 25, 2002, Section T; Joe Simnacher, "Kenneth Teegarden Obituary," *The Dallas Morning News*, September 26, 2002, p. 33-A; Howard Dentler to Wanda Teegarden, September 25, 2002; Charles Mallotte to Wanda Teegarden, September 26, 2002; Avery Post to Wanda Teegarden, November 30, 2002. Collection of Wanda Teegarden.

14. D. Duane Cummins, "Kenneth." Funeral oration. September 26, 2002, Wanda Teegarden Collection.

APPENDIX

Membership of the Commission on Restructure
(*1962 Yearbook and Directory*, pages 100-105)

The Board of Directors of the International Convention appointed a Central Committee that served as a nominating committee, that in turn recommended 125-130 members for approval by the Board. It was a process of *selecting the most competent* rather than a broad based popular election guided by quotas.

Among the criteria or qualifications used in selecting those persons to serve on the Commission were the following: [1] ability to give the necessary time; [2] depth of interest and constructive attitude toward the Brotherhood; [3] capacity to approach problems objectively, with an open mind; [4] holds the respect of other people in their state; [5] ability to work with others; [6] competence in one or more of the following areas: churchmanship, biblical thought, theology, church history, organization and administration, current problems and issues of the social order, the church in modern culture, legal experience, ability to interpret.

The following categories were *kept in mind* [but neither proportionally defined nor slavishly followed] as all selections were made: geography, laymen, laywomen, ministers, theological professors, administrators, agency representatives, and members at large with exceptional experience. The initial group of 125 persons contained thirty-four lay-persons, ninety-one ministers; seventeen women, 108 men, thirty congregations classified as small [500 or fewer members] and ninety-five classified as large. The Commission membership carried a high proportional representation of ministers, large congregations and men.

The original eighteen-member Central Committee of the Commission was composed largely of religious professionals. Among the significant characteristics of the Central Committee were theological education, ecumenical participation and urban environment. A profile of the committee is provided below.

- Thirteen of the eighteen were ministers.
- Nine of the thirteen ministers received their theological education at non-Disciples institutions (Chicago, Yale and Union).
- Four of the thirteen ministers were local pastors, two were state secretaries, four were national agency staff, and three were educators.
- Four of the five lay members were members of national agency boards.
- Twelve of the eighteen were active in the National Council of Churches, four in the World Council of Churches, and fifteen in the Council on Christian Unity.
- Thirteen of the eighteen members were from cities with populations of more than 250,000; all eighteen were from cities of more than 25,000.
- The nine members of the executive committee were all clergy; seven had theological degrees from non-Disciples institutions (5 from Yale); seven were active in the National Council; and seven were from cities with populations over 250,000 (five from Indianapolis).

The average size congregation in 1962 was 219. While 50 percent of the congregations had memberships of 200 or less, the overwhelming majority of Disciples *membership* was in those congregations of 500 and above. The composition of the Commission and Central Committee has been a subject of criticism, but to have constituted the Commission otherwise—through some form of popular election—with a profile adverse to their recent successful, cooperative experience, accented with a predominantly rural, small congregation orientation, and with persons of passing interest in ecumenism would likely have resulted in adding still another failure to the long historic list of unsuccessful attempts to structure the Disciples. The original appointed membership of the Commission on Brotherhood Restructure is cited below.

Adams, Hampton
New York City, New York

*Austin, Spencer P.
Indianapolis, Indiana

Baird, William R.
Lexington, Kentucky

Barnes, Carnella
Los Angeles, Calif.

Barnett, Hubert L.
Wheeling, W.V.

Bayer, Charles
Alexandria, Virginia

Beazley, George G. Jr.
Indianapolis, Indiana

Becker, Edwin L.
Des Moines, Iowa

*Blakemore, W. B.
Chicago, Illinois

Borgaard, Kent
Sioux Falls, South Dakota

Bouchard, Tommie
St. Joseph, Missouri

Breeland, Mrs. S.W.
Holly Hill, South Carolina

Brooks, Mrs. Wm. Orien
Winchester, Kentucky

Brown, Harold Glen
Portland, Oregon

Buhler, Arthur E.
Albuquerque, New Mexico

Burns, Benjamin F.
Oak Park, Illinois

Burns, Robert W.
Atlanta, Georgia

Cloues, Richard W.
Pittsburgh, Pennsylvania

Coil, Cullen
Jefferson City, Missouri

Cole, Mrs. O. Ivan
Cincinnati, Ohio

Cole, Myron C.
Los Angeles, California

Coleman, C. Linwood
Raleigh N. Carolina

*Cook, Gaines M.
Indianapolis, Indiana

Cramblet, Wilbur H.
St. Louis, Missouri

*Dentler, Howard
Indianapolis, Indiana

DePew, Arthur M.
St. Petersburg, Florida

Dickson, Emmett J.
Indianapolis, Indiana

Doolen, D. Wayne
Great Falls, Montana

Ely, Lawrence O.
Des Moines, Iowa

England, Stephen J.
Enid, Oklahoma

Evans, Mrs. W. K.
Austin, Minnesota

*Fiers, A. Dale
Indianapolis, Indiana

Fitzgerald, Mrs. John T.
San Francissco, California

Ford, Wesley P.
Pasadena, California

Gantz, Hallie G.
Enid, Oklahoma

Garrison, Carlton D.
Ponca City, Oklahoma

Gray, Sidney L.
Lake Charles, Louisiana

Gresham, Perry E.
Bethany, West Virginia

Griffeth, Ross J.
Eugene, Oregon

Griffin, Thomas J.
Houston, Texas

Hooten, James L.
Savannah, Georgia

Hulan, Roy S.
Jackson, Mississippi

Jarman, William Jackson
Champaign, Illinois

Jones, Willis R.
Nashville, Tennessee

Kaufman, J. Kenneth
Murfreesboro, Tennessee

Kennedy, W.M.
St.Thomas, Ontario

Kerr, John
Austin, Minnesota

Knowles, John C.
Fort Worth, Texas

Gast, Mrs. Carl F.
St. Louis, Missouri

Gentry, Sloan
Tulsa, Oklahoma

Gibbs, Thomas J. Jr.
Los Angeles, California

Littrell, James A.
Springdale, Arkansas

Mabee, Frank C.
Enid, Oklahoma

McCully, Oliver W.
Toronto, Ontario

Miller, Raphael H. Jr.
Evansville, Indiana

Minck, Franklin H.
Akron, Ohio

*Moak, James A.
Lexington, Kentucky

Moffett, Robert
Tucson, Arizona

Monroe, Herald B.
Cleveland, Ohio

Moore, William J.
Lawrence, Kansas

Lair, Loren
Des Moines, Iowa

Lathrop, Scott
Sacramento, California

*Lemmon, Clarence E.
Columbia, Missouri

Osborn, Ronald E.
Indianapolis, Indiana

*Owen, George Earle
Indianapolis, Indiana

Pack, John Paul
Los Angeles, California

Parry, Willbur C.
New York, New York

Pearcy, William T.
Indianapolis, Indiana

Pennybacker, Albert M.
Youngstown, Ohio

Peterson, Orval
St. Louis, Missouri

Pugh, Samuel F.
Indianapolis, Indiana

*Putnam, Mrs. Russell C.
Cleveland, Ohio

*Moreland, Edward S.
Cincinnati, Ohio

Rea, Harrell A.
Kansas City, Missouri

Muir, Warner
Des Moines, Iowa

*Richeson, Mrs. Forrest L.
Minneapolis, Minnesota

Munson, K. Everett
Maywood, Illinois

*Rickman, Lester B.
Jefferson City, Missouri

Murray, William Elmo
Regina, Saskatchewan

Riley, Jo M.
Decatur, Illinois

Nutting, David W.
Kent, Washington

*Rogers, John
Tulsa, Oklahoma

Olmsted, Gilford E.
Kansas City, Kansas

Rowe, Mrs. F. W.
Omaha, Nebraska

Schoverling, Mrs. C.S.
Houston, Texas

Strain, Dudly
Lubbock, Texas

Seeley, Kenneth B.
Kalamazoo, Michigan

*Stoner, Richard B.
Columbus, Indiana

Sharp, Paul F.
Hiram, Ohio

Suggs, M. Jack
Fort Worth, Texas

Short, Howard E.
St. Louis, Missouri

Sutton, David Nelson
West Point, Virginia

Sikes, Walter W.
Indianapolis, Indiana

Swearingen, T. T.
Fort Worth, Texas

Sly, Virgil A.
Indianapolis Indiana

Teegarden, Kenneth L.
Little Rock, Arkansas

Smith, Mrs. C.C.
Spray, Oregon

*Smith, Harlie L.
Indianapolis, Indiana

*Smith, Joseph M.
Indianapolis, Indiana

*Smith, Leslie R.
Lexington, Kentucky

Snedaker, Lorence W.
Colorado Springs, Colorado

Spaulding, Helen F.
Indianapolis, Indiana

Stauffer, Paul S.
Louisville, Kentucky

Stevenson, Archie K.
Cheyenne, Wyoming

Stover, Mrs. Howard
Bountiful, Utah

Ward, Mrs. Mae Yoho
Indianapolis, Indiana

Welsh, W. A.
Dallas, Texas

Whitley, Oliver Reed
Denver, Colorado

Thomas, Mrs. O. G.
Birmingham, Alabama

Thomas, Robert A.
Seattle, Washington

Thompson, Rhodes Jr.
Daytona Beach, Florida

Turley, Hollis L.
Indianapolis, Indiana

Van Boskirk, Joseph J.
Washington, D.C.

*Van Doren, Earl H.
Seattle, Washington

Van Slyke, H. W.
Rupert, Idaho

*Wake, Orville W.
Lynchburg, Virginia

*Walker, Granville T.
Fort Worth, Texas

Webb, Mrs. Charles H.
Chicago, Illinois

Wenger, Arthur D.
Wilson, North Carolina

*Wickizer, Willard M.
Indianapolis, Indiana

Wilburn, Ralph G.
Lexington, Kentucky

Willis, Ross M.
East Orange, New Jersey

Wilson, George H.
New Orleans, Louisiana

Youngblood, Tom J.
Raleigh, North Carolina

Zimmerman, Clarence H.
Hoisington, Kansas

* An asterisk is used to identify members of the Central Committee of the Commission.

BIBLIOGRAPHY

Manuscript Collections

Disciples of Christ Historical Society. Teegarden Papers on Restructure. Boxes 1–2

Disciples of Christ Historical Society. Teegarden Papers on GMP Years. Boxes 1–7

Teegarden residence in Fort Worth, Texas. Personal Files. Cabinets 1–5

Disciples Headquarters. Indianapolis. Teegarden Papers. Box 1.

Interviews

Teegarden, Blake. Interview by the author, March 28, 2006.

Teegarden, David. Interview by the author April 11, 2006.

Teegarden, Grant. Interview by the author, March 28, 2006.

Teegarden, Kenneth L. Interview by the author, January 15, 1980.

Teegarden, Kirk. Interview by the author, November 17, 2005.

Teegarden, Matthew. Interview by the author, March 28, 2006.

Teegarden, Sloan. Interview by the author, March 27, 2006.

Teegarden, Wanda. Interview by the author. February 24, 2005.

————. Interview by the author. November 3, 2005.

————. Interview by the author. November 17, 2005.

————. Interview by the author, December 10, 2005.

————. Interview by the author, March 2, 2006.

————. Interview by the author, April 6, 2006.

Dentler, Howard. Interview by the author, February, 26, 2005.

Howland, William. Interview by the author, February 22, 2006.

Jeter, Joey. Interview by the author, February 24, 2005.

Johnson, Harold. Interview by the author, March 4, 2006.

Kemp, Roy. Interview by the author, December 2, 2005.

Le Vally, Cleo. Interview by the author, March 15, 2005.

Liggett, T. J. Interview by the author, March 4, 2006.
Pittman, Don. Interview by the author, April 10, 2006.
Suggs, Jim. Interview by the author, February 11, 2006.
Williams, Newell. Interview by the author, April 6, 2006.

Transcripts of the following interviews on restructure are in the archives of the Disciples of Christ Historical Society. All interviews were conducted at different locations.
by James Seale.
Spencer, Austin. November 14, 1989.
Bayer, Charles. April 3, 1990.
Burns, Robert. November 18, 1989.
Dentler, Howard. November 19, 1990.
Fiers, Dale. January 20, 1992.
Moak, James. December 12, 1989.
Osborn, Ronald. May 20, 1990.
Stauffer, Paul. May 8, 1992.
Teegarden, Kenneth L. March 9, 1990.
Thomas, Robert. May 26, 1990.
Walker, Granville. March 10, 1990.

Newspapers and Journals

Arkansas Christian.
Arkansas Gazette.
The Christian.
Christian Church News.
Christian Courier.
Cleveland Press.
Cushing Democrat.
Cushing Tribune.
Cushing Weekly Citizen.
The Disciple.
Fort Smith Times Record.
Fort Worth Star-Telegram.

Guymon Daily Herald.
Harlow Weekly Magazine.
Houston Chronicle.
Houston Post.
In Unity.
Kaw City Democrat.
Lincoln County News.
Millennial Harbinger.
Newsweek. April 28, 1947.
New York Times.
Press Register.
Seattle Times.
Time Magazine, April 8 and April 28, 1947.
Vernon Daily Record.
Vernon Times.
Virginia Christian.
Wichita Daily Times.
World Call.

Kenneth L. Teegarden Published Works

"Eyewitness Account of Texas City Disaster." *Lincoln County News.* 1947. P. 1

"Take me to Your Leader." *The Disciple.* October 1976.

We Call Ourselves Disciples. CBP Press. 1975.

"The Flip Side of Freedom." *The Disciple.* April 28, 1974.

"Verdict before Trial." *The Disciple.* August 1976.

"Disciples Witness to Ethics in a Nuclear Age." *The Disciple.* May, 1985.

"Adult Pablum?" *The Disciple.* September, 1975.

"1975—A Holy Year?" *The Disciple.* December 22, 1974.

"The 100 Word Statement." 1985.

"Share with others your own faith pilgrimage." *The Disciple.* August, 1985.

Kenneth L. Teegarden Unpublished Works

"Religion in the White House: 1789–1865." Unpublished Master's Thesis. 1947.

"Installation Address." June 21, 1965.

"A Possible constitution." March 24, 1966.

"A review of the Area Concept with Fewer and Comparable Regions." October 2, 1973.

"Statement on Jonestown." March 12, 1979.

"Pastoral Letter to the church on Ordination of Gays and Lesbians." November, 1977.

"Course Syllabus: The Christian Ministry." Brite. 1994.

"A Tent of Memories." January 29, 1995.

Unpublished Sources

History of First Christian Church, Cushing, Oklahoma. October, 2004.

Jones, J.C. *History of First Christian Church*, Texas City, Texas. 1960.

LeVally, Cleo. *History of Healdton First Christian Church.* 2000

Church History: First Christian Church, Fort Smith. Undated.

Historical Outline of First Christian Church, Fort Smith. 1955–1958.

Stephenson, Dwight. "Church Organization in the Thought of Alexander Campbell." Undated.

Wickizer, Willard. "Ideas for Brotherhood Restructure." July, 1958.

Fiers, A. Dale. "An Apologetic for Restructure." July 6, 1962.

Wolfersberger, John. "Toward Regionalization of the Christian Church." May 1, 1973.

Miscellaneous Sources

Brite College of the Bible Caller. Vol. VIII, No. I. May, 1948.

Business Dockets of the General Board. 1973 to 1985.

Blue Ribbon collection for Poultry: 1934–1935. Kenneth Teegarden

Central Christian Church Dedication Program. January 3, 1954.

Commission on Brotherhood Restructure Budget Reports. 1965.

Criss, Mrs. Henry [member of Texas City Christian Church] to D. Duane Cummins. March 29, 2005.

Cummins, D. Duane. "A Dwelling Place for God." January 29, 1995.

———. "Honoring Kenneth." August 1985.

———. "Tribute to Kenneth Teegarden." September 26, 2002.

Direction in Brotherhood Restructure. 1966.

Dr. Kenneth L. Teegarden: A Service of Remembrance. University Christian Church. September 26, 2002.

First Christian Church Healdton Dedication Program. November 10, 1985.

Friedly, Robert to D. Duane Cummins. November 10, 2005.

Highland Elementary School Report Cards: 1926–1934. Kenneth Teegarden.

Humbert, John. "Kenneth L. Teegarden." September, 2002.

Installation Program, First Christian Church, Fort Worth. September 4, 1955.

Installation Program for Restructure Position. June 21, 1965.

Jeter, Joseph. "Ken Teegarden." September 24, 2002.

Jim Jones Minister's Information Schedule. November 3, 1969.

Jim Jones Service of Ordination. February 16, 1964.

Kaplow, Herb. ABC-TV Interview with Kenneth Teegarden. December 5, 1982.

Minutes of the Atlanta Declaration Group. August 3, 1967.

Minutes Board of Directors, Division of Higher Education. April 10–11, 1987.

Minutes Congregational Meeting. First Christian Church, Fort Smith. July 10, 1955.

Minutes of the Official Board, First Christian Church, Fort Smith, August 21 and October 16, 1957.

Minutes of the Official Board. First Christian Church, Cushing, Okla. December 15, 1940.

Minutes of the Commission on Brotherhood Restructure: 1958–1968.

Minutes of the Central Committee. 1958–1968.

Minutes of the Council of Agencies. 1953–1959.

Minutes of the Committee on Structure and Function. 1972–1983.

Newspaper interview with William Teegarden (1834–1921) About 1905.

Norfolk School Teaching Contract: 1943.

Phillips University Catalogue. 1940.

Phillips University Yearbook. 1942, 1943.

Policies and Criteria for the Order of Ministry in the Christian Church (Disciples

of Christ) Approved by the General Assembly. 1971.

Post, Avery. "Remarks for Kenneth Teegarden." August, 1985.

Procedures for the Nomination and Election of a General Minister and President. Administrative Committee. March 1972.

Provisional Design. June 1972.

Qualifications of the General Minister and President. Adm. Com. March 1972.

Roozen, David A. Interview with Kenneth Teegarden. No date. Est. 1994.

Stewardship-Evangelism Crusade Program. March 7–18, 1951.

Teegarden, David Kent, Birth Announcement. 1946.

Teegarden, Kenneth L. Cushing High School Transcript. 1938.

Teegarden, Kenneth L. Oklahoma A & M College Transcript. 1940.

Teegarden, Kenneth L. Phillips University Transcript. 1947.

Teegarden, Kenneth L. Sermon Chronicles. 1945–1958.

Teegarden, Kenneth L. Texas Christian University Transcript. 1948–1949.

Teegarden, Kenneth L. Report of the Administrative Secretary. 1965, 1966, 1967, 1968.

Teegarden, Kenneth L. Report to Official Board. FCC Fort Smith. April 16, 1958.

The Design. 1978; 2005.

Visit by author to Cushing, Chandler & Tryon, Oklahoma. February 16, 2006.

Walker, Granville. Installation Charge to Kenneth Teegarden. June 21, 1965.

Wells, Cheryl [church secretary, Cushing] to D. Duane Cummins. March 15, 2005.

Yearbook and Directory of the Christian Church (Disciples of Christ). 1940, 1943, 1944, 1945, 1946, 1947, 1948, 1949, 1950 1973, 1974, 1975, 1976, 1977, 1978, 1979, 1980, 1981, 1982, 1983, 1984, 1985, 1986

Books

Ahlstrom, Sydney. *A Religious History of the American People.* New Haven: Yale University Press. 1972.

Black, Earl & Merle Black. *The Rise of Southern Republicans.* Cambridge: Harvard University Press. 2002.

Boorstin, Daniel. *The Americans: The Democratic Experience.* Vol. III, New York, Vintage. 1973.

Boyle, Kevin. *Arc of Justice.* New York City: Henry Holt & Co. 2004

Branch, Taylor. *Parting the Waters: American in the King Years: 1954–1963.* New York: Simon & Schuster. 1988.

Burns, James MacGregor. *The American Experiment.* Vol II. New York: Alfred Knopf & Co. 1985.

Carter, Jimmy. *Memoirs of a President.* New York: Bantam. 1982.

Campbell, Alexander. *Christian System.* 3rd ed. Pittsburgh: Forrester & Campbell. 1840.

Craddock, Fran. *In the Fullness of Time.* St. Louis: Chalice Press. 1999.

Cummins, D. Duane. A. *Dale Fiers: 20th Century Disciple.* Fort Worth: TCU Press. 2003.

―――. *Disciples Colleges: A Hisory.* St. Louis: CBP Press. 1987.

―――. *Handbook for Today's Disciples.* St. Louis: Chalice Press. 2003.

————., et. al. *Higher Education Evaluation Task Force Report.* June 12, 1976.

Dunnavant, Anthony. *Restructure.* New York: Lang. 1993.

England, George. *In A Tall Shadow: Biography of Stephen J. England.* Midwest City, Oklahoma. 1990.

Ford, Gerald. *A Time to Heal.* New York: Harper. 1979.

Foster, Douglas, Paul Blowers, Anthony Dunant, and Newell Williams. *Encyclopedia of the Stone-Campbell Movement.* Grand Rapids: Erdman's Press. 2005.

Friedly, Robert & D. Duane Cummins. *Search for Identity.* St. Louis: CBP Press. 1987

Gaustad, Edwin & Leigh Schmidt. *The Religious History of America.* New York: Harper. 2002

Gibson, Arrell M. *Oklahoma.* Norman: University of Oklahoma Press. 1981

Goldman, Eric. *The Crucial Decade: 1945–1960.* New York: Vintage. 1960

Hagan, William. *The Sac and Fox Indians.* Norman: University of Oklahoma Press. 1958.

Halberstam, David. *The Fifties.* New York: Random House. 1993

Larson, Edward. *The Scopes Trial.* New York: Basic Books. 1997.

Lerner, Max. *America as a Civilization.* Vol. II. New York: Simon & Schuster. 1957.

Leuchtenburg, William. *The Perils of Prosperity.* University of Chicago Press. 1958.

Liggett, T.J., Kenneth L. Teegarden, Ronald Osborn, D. Duane Cummins, et.al. *Seeking God's Peace in a Nuclear Age.* St. Louis: CBP Press. 1985.

Lincoln County Historical Society. *History of Lincoln County Oklahoma.* 1988.

Martin, Jay. *The Education of John Dewey.* New York: Columbia University Press. 2002

Marty, Martin. *Modern American Religion: 1919–1941.* Vol. II. University of Chicago Press. 1991.

————. *Modern American Religion: 1941–1960.* Vol. III. University of Chicago Press. 1996.

Masterson, V.V. *The Katy Railroad.* Norman: University of Oklahoma Press. 1952.

McAllister, Lester. *Arkansas Disciples.* Christian Church (Disciples of Christ) 1984.

McAllister, Lester & William Tucker. *Journey in Faith.* St. Louis: Bethany Press. 1975.

Minutaglio, Bill. *City on Fire.* New York: Harper-Collins. 2003.

Morrison, Commager & Leuchtenburg. *The Growth of the American Republic.* Vol. II. New York: Oxford University Press. 1980.

Myers, Oma Lou. *This One Thing I Do: Biography of Frank Hamilton Marshall.* Portland: Metropolitan Press. 1942.

Nelson, Ralph W. *The Experimental Logic of Jesus.* New York: Revell Co. 1936.

Newsom, Earl D. *The Story of Payne County.* Stillwater, OK: New Forums Press. 1997.

Osborn, Ronald. *Toward the Christian Church.* St. Louis: CBP. 1964

Patterson, James. *Brown v. Board of Education: Its Legacy.* New York: Oxford University Press. 2001

———. *Great Expectations: 1945–1974.* New York: Oxford University Press. 1997

———. *Restless Giant: 1974–2000.* New York: Oxford University Press. 2005

Schlesinger, Arthur & Dixon Ryan Fox. *A History of American Life.* New York: Scribner. 1927. [1996 edition].

Schulman, Bruce. *The Seventies.* New York: Free Press. 2001.

Sinclair, Andrew. *Era of Excess.* New York: Little, Brown & Co. 1962.

Stephens, Hugh. *The Texas City Disaster.* Austin: University of Texas Press. 1997.

Taylor, Alan. *American Colonies.* New York: Penguin. 2001.

Toulouse, Mark. *Joined in Discipleship.* St. Louis: Chalice Press. 1997.

Traxel, David. *The United States in Peace and the Great War: 1898–1920.* New York: Alfred Knopf & Co. 2006.

Vogt, Helen Elizabeth. *Descendants of Araham Teegarden.* Willowick, Ohio. 1988.

Wells, Laura Lou. *Young Cushing in Oklahoma Territory.* Perkins, OK: Evans Publications, 1985.

World Council of Churches. *Baptism, Eucharist and Ministry.* 1982.

Wuthnow, Robert & John Evans. *The Quiet Hand of God.* Berkley: University of California Press. 2002.

Articles

Cummins, D. Duane. "The First Decade of the Division of Higher Education," *Disciples Theological Digest,* Vol 9, No. 1. 1994.

Johnson, Lani. "Friendship and Trust," *The Disciple,* June 1, 1980.

Merrell, James. "Viewpoint," *The Disciple,* June 1985.

Moir, Lillian. "Portrait of a Nominee," *World Call,* October, 1973.

Rowe, Veston. "A Christian Pastor Takes a Look Back," *This Month at Phillips,* Spring, 1985.

World Wide Web

History of Cushing, Oklahoma: http://www.cushingchamber.org/history.shtml [Accessed July 27, 2006].

Teegarden Family Genealogy: http://genforum.genealogy.com/tee-garden/ [Accessed July 27, 2006].

INDEX

The Mystery in the Rye

Frank Petersen

The Mystery in the Rye

Ergot and LSD – A Cultural-Historical Quest

 Springer

Frank Petersen
Novartis
Basel, Switzerland

ISBN 978-3-662-69814-3 (Hardcopy)   ISBN 978-3-662-69811-2 (eBook)
ISBN 978-3-662-69813-6 (Softcopy)
https://doi.org/10.1007/978-3-662-69811-2

The contributions compiled in this book originally appeared in the journal Chemie in unserer Zeit and have been expanded and revised for this publication. Frank Petersen, Der Rote Keulenkopf. Copyright © 2023 Wiley-VCH GmbH Reproduced with permission of Wiley-VCH GmbH

This work was supported by Syngenta International, Novartis and Emilia-Guggenheim-Schnurr-Stiftung.

Translation from the German language edition: "Das Mysterium im Roggen" by Frank Petersen, © Springer Verlag GmbH, DE 2024. Published by Springer Berlin Heidelberg. All Rights Reserved.

Editor: Sarah Koch

Cover illustration: Martin Oeggerli (Micronaut) 2024, supported by FIBL and University Hospital Basel (Pathology)

This Springer imprint is published by the registered company Springer-Verlag GmbH, DE, part of Springer Nature.
The registered company address is: Heidelberger Platz 3, 14197 Berlin, Germany

If disposing of this product, please recycle the paper.

Foreword

Novartis would be unthinkable its current form without the efforts undertaken in natural products research and the early focus on the ergot fungus. These activities, which date back more than a century, not only established the scientific and economic basis of the pharmaceutical business of our predecessor company Sandoz but were instrumental in shaping the future course of Novartis, which was formed in 1996 to advance medical research.

At the beginning of the 20th century, the odds that the medical sciences would one day become the beacon of our business were small. A shed with a few chemists was all researcher Arthur Stoll had back in 1917 to kick-start pharmaceuticals research at Sandoz's headquarters in Basel and bring the company's first—self-developed—drug to market four years later.

What from today's vantage point may seem like a whirlwind development was anything but easy. Although Stoll had been hired from Zurich's prestigious ETH, where he had studied under Nobel Prize winner Richard Willstätter, his pharmaceutical research activities were initially a side show at Sandoz. At that time, the company was almost exclusively focused on chemicals and dyes.

When the first ergot derivative medicine, Gynergen, was launched for treating postpartum hemorrhage, sales proved disappointing. Management even discussed whether Sandoz's pharmaceutical efforts should be ditched for good. In 1921, the launch year, the company sold a mere 425 treatments, netting less than 1000 Swiss francs.

But Stoll did not give up. He improved the drug's dosing regimen, increased its efficacy, and won the trust of patients and doctors. His efforts helped Gynergen reach annual sales of more than 700,000 Swiss francs a few years later and his success allowed Stoll to expand his franchise, hire more chemists and start building modern laboratories.

One of the chemists employed by Stoll, Albert Hofmann, would later hit upon the ergot derivative LSD. It would become a problem child not only for Hofmann, but for Sandoz as well, which never commercialized the molecule and struggled with the fallout of the drug's role as the chemical beacon of the psychedelic counterculture of the 1960s and 1970s in the United States and in Europe.

The ergot derivative LSD was, nevertheless, a pivotal breakthrough for medical science. It opened a fresh research avenue that paved the way for the understanding of neurotransmitters and the treatment of neurodegenerative disorders and confirmed the potency of natural products research. To this day, LSD is inspiring scientists and clinicians to work on understanding the still mysterious mechanism of the molecule, which is once again being tested in clinics for the treatment of neurodegenerative diseases and mental disorders.

LSD and Gynergen are, however, only some of the highlights linked to the ergot fungus in a journey that goes back centuries and which Dr. Frank Petersen has diligently unearthed in his book, which illustrates the intricate interplay between science, culture, and society. By documenting the itinerary of this extraordinary natural product through the ages, Petersen has achieved a major feat which shows that our endeavor to understand the mystery of nature is a generational, open-ended project driven as much by the plight of human nature as it is by our innate curiosity.

Basel, June 2024   Joerg Reinhardt, Ph.D.
Switzerland   Chairman of the Board of Directors of Novartis

Foreword

In the intricate tapestry of medical history, the threads woven by our experience of the natural world hold a place of distinguished prominence. The study of substances from plants and fungi and their medicinal properties is not merely an academic pursuit but a narrative rich with discovery, innovation, and lifesaving breakthroughs.

From the willow bark that gave us aspirin to the extracts of sweet wormwood that provided artemisins for malaria, nature's pharmacopeia has been an invaluable ally in our quest to understand and combat disease. Among the myriad of botanical contributions, the story of ergot—a fungus that grows on rye and other grasses—stands out for its complex relationship with humanity. It has been both a scourge, as a source of deadly epidemics, and a boon, giving rise to lysergic acid diethylamide (LSD), a compound with profound implications for psychiatry and neurology.

The collective endeavors of remarkable scientists, transcending borders, disciplines and ages, underscore the collaborative spirit of scientific discovery and its profound impact on medicine. This narrative shines a light on the pivotal moments and trailblazers who have tapped into the potency of flora and fungi, navigating the rich and sometimes enigmatic domain of herbal remedies.

My own contributions as a British neuropharmacologist are woven into this tapestry, building upon the legacies of pioneers like Henry Dale, whose work on neurotransmitters laid the groundwork for modern pharmacology, and John Gaddum, who established mathematical principles vital to receptor pharmacology. Their insights continue to drive the development of new treatments, particularly in the realm of psychiatric disease.

The transformation of intriguing natural science into marketable medicines is an art in itself, one that Henry Wellcome, co-founder of Burroughs Wellcome & Co., mastered. His pursuit of pure alkaloids propelled ergot research and set a standard that still influences the pharmaceutical industry today.

As we turn the pages of this book, we honor the past and look to the future, inspired by the pioneers who have charted the course of therapeutic discovery. Their legacy fuels our ongoing quest to enhance human health through the wisdom of herbal medicine and microbial substances.

Cambridge, June 2024   Fiona Marshall, Ph.D.
USA   President of Biomedical Research of Novartis

Preliminary remarks

Dear readers, I am very pleased that you have indulged your curiosity and opened this biography or—perhaps more aptly—"chemography" of the purplish brown ergot fungus and its substances. To say it up front: You will encounter a peculiar fellow, a multi-faceted solitary figure in nature's rich cabinet of curiosities who flashes and twinkles. If we take a closer look at the fungus, also known as *Claviceps purpurea*, even its way of life is out of the ordinary.

Many phytopathogenic fungi penetrate their host plants via wounds or leaf openings, causing local infections or spreading throughout the entire organism. Their toxins and enzymes destroy the infected plant tissue on which the fungi feast. Unlike these killer microbes, the ergot fungus takes an almost "gentle" approach. It infects grasses—which it absolutely needs alive to reproduce—"minimally invasively". A tricky tightrope act that it masters perfectly. During ear ripening, the black-purple ergot, the horn-shaped surviving form of the fungus, forms in the infected flowers instead of a grass seed. Since the preferred grain to attack is rye, the highly active substances in ergot caused epidemic mass poisoning outbreaks in Europe from the early Middle Ages until the 20th century. In the course of the toxicoses, which were often fatal, those affected could lose entire limbs or suffer from severe psychoses and convulsions.

In the 19th century, attempts were made to isolate and pharmacologically investigate the ingredients of the ergot. It was a frustrating struggle. Early chemistry and pharmacy, with their limited knowledge of the properties of natural substances and the underdeveloped technological options of these young disciplines, were not yet prepared to unravel the mystery of the fungal substances. It was not until the beginning of the 20th century, when the research laboratories of the pharmaceutical industry began to tackle this scientific problem, that it became feasible to extract the active ingredients of the ergot in pure form. They were used to develop innovative drugs that are still used in medicine today. Thus. the evaluation of the therapeutic potential of lysergic acid diethylamide, LSD for short, which was synthesized from the active substances of ergot has also become the topic of recent studies in clinical psychiatry.

The traces of the fungus in history, biology, chemistry, medicine, and pharmacy can be pieced together into a cultural history of a plant-pathogenic microorganism that is peppered with drama, surprises, mysteries, happy twists, and scientific sensations. No other member of the universe of microbes can even come close to holding a candle to it.

But what do we actually mean by natural substances? First of all, they are substances that are produced by living organisms and fall into two biologically defined categories. The essential compounds form the material "basic equipment" of all living things, without which they cannot grow, develop or reproduce. They are referred to as *primary metabolites*. The situation in the other group of molecules, which includes the *ergot alkaloids*, is far more complicated and therefore much more exciting. These ingredients are not vital for their producers and are therefore called *secondary metabolites*. It seemed obvious that these could be waste products of their producers, and for a long time this viewpoint determined the hasty and rather unflattering view of their possible significance. The further the research penetrated into the world of these unusual compounds, which currently comprise about 280,000 known molecules, the more apparent their main properties became: They possess a high chemical diversity and cover a broad range of biological activities.

In his now famous *Playground Theory*, Swiss microbiologist Hans Zähner saw secondary metabolites as the random products of biochemical evolution. According to him, these molecules could be either advantageous, disadvantageous or biologically neutral for their producers. The compounds that improved the survival chances of living organisms in nature remained in the chemical repertoire of organisms, while others disappeared. These *fitness factors* became their molecular "special equipment", which is perhaps comparable to that of Ian Fleming's "double-zero hero", who only survives his missions in the hostile agent world thanks to Q's gadgets. In nature, secondary metabolites are not evenly distributed, but are mainly formed by plants, bacteria, fungi, insects or certain types of algae. In most cases, their exact biological functions are still a mystery. The deciphered functions of these molecules, on the other hand, paint a breathtaking picture of a form of communication between organisms and reveal the beauty of nature's "chemical language", the complexity of which is characterized by the diversity of its living beings.

Insects use natural products as substances that attract or repel, mark the way to a food source or control the behavior of their fellow species or other organisms with the help of alarm molecules. Natural substances help bees to navigate or are used by certain species of millipedes to anesthetize their predators. They indicate which flowers have already been pollinated, act as UV blockers or are sophisticated chemical props for the ingenious seduction techniques of some orchid species. As toxins, they create the conditions for symbiotic communities, help to hunt for food or simply prevent themselves from being eaten. Antibiotic-producing microbes use their "chemical clubs" to keep other microorganisms at bay. Certain leafcutter ants can in turn cultivate bacteria on their bodies, the active substances of which protect their fungal gardens from unwanted infections. The alkaloid cocktail of the ergot also protects grasses from insect pests.

The logic of why substances that act on plants, bees or fungi can be used to develop drugs against high blood pressure, psychiatric illnesses or hypercholesterolemia only becomes apparent at second glance. It results from the evolutionary relationship of all living organisms, which is expressed in the occurrence and high similarity of many macromolecules in different groups of organisms. Secondary natural substances in the human body therefore "recognize" nothing other than the target molecules whose activity they have been modulating in nature for hundreds of millions of years.

How did this book come about, given that there were originally two main arguments against it? Over the previous decades, numerous authors had published excellent scientific summaries of the chemical, pharmaceutical and microbiological literature on ergot fungi. Presumably everything worth discussing had already been said. It also seemed questionable to me whether a popular science story about a fungus could be of interest to a readership. So the spontaneous idea was shelved as soon as it was born. The risk of approaching this topic from a new and different angle was too great for me.

The fact that everything turned out differently in the end is due to Prof. em. Dr. Dieter Seebach, Laboratory of Organic Chemistry at ETH Zurich, and Dr. Peter Gölitz, Editor Emeritus of the journal "Angewandte Chemie" ("Applied Chemistry"), in Heidelberg. They swept my fickleness and reservations right off the table. "What is exciting for scientists also inspires others. You must write this book". Their encouragement and moral support had an effect, for which I thank them from the bottom of my heart, because for me it also marked the beginning of an "unexpected journey" full of fascinating encounters and connections.

The publication of this cultural history of the ergot would not have been possible without financial support. I would particularly like to thank Dr. Joerg Reinhardt, Chairman of the Board of Directors of Novartis AG, for his generous support of the project. I would also like to thank Syngenta Crop Protection AG and the Emilia Guggenheim-Schnurr Foundation of the Natural Research Society (Naturforschende Gesellschaft) in Basel.

In consultation with Dr. Doris Fischer-Henningsen, editor-in-chief of "Chemie in unserer Zeit" ("Chemistry in Our Time"), the idea was born to publish the ergot saga first as a serialized non-fiction novel and then in a book edition. However, neither of us had any experience with a serial form of publication, which is rather unusual for scientific work. Ms. Fischer-Henningsen nevertheless embarked on this adventure and accompanied me with professionalism and admirable patience when I had to rewrite individual chapters that had already been submitted or when a follow-up chapter was still being worked on for the next journal issue. In addition, her passion for archaeology became an incentive for me to embark on a search for an Assyrian clay tablet, which came to a happy end in the British Museum. I am very grateful to Ms. Fischer-Henningsen for all of this.

The task of assigning various subject areas of the book to a specific genre and the fact that it had been pre-published were underestimated obstacles on the way to finding a suitable publisher for a book edition. I would like to thank Renate Scheddin, Editorial Director for Medicine and Life Sciences Books, Dr. Sarah Koch, Senior Publishing Editor, Dr. Meike Barth, project manager, and the project coordinators Ms. Grit Kern and Ms. Kerstin Feindler-Koch, at Springer Nature for their immediate interest in the *ergot story* and for their willingness to make the book edition a reality. I would like to thank Ms. Bettina Loycke, Senior Rights Manager for Rights & Licenses, Wiley-VCH, Heidelberg, for her understanding and kindness, which ultimately made the publication of the book possible.

Without the following people I would have thrown in the towel on some of the tasks, sorting through the thicket of information of the last few centuries would have been illusory, and fact-checking on the basis of primary sources would have remained fragmentary.

My heartfelt thanks go to:

Drs. Martin Missbach, Philipp Krastel, Günter Engel, and Jean-Jacques Sanglier of Novartis AG, Basel, Prof. em. Dr. Karl-Heinz Altmann, Department of Chemistry and Applied Biosciences, Institute of Pharmaceutical Sciences, ETH Zurich, and Prof. Dr. Olivier Potterat, Institute of Pharmaceutical Biology, University of Basel, for their scientific comments.

Dr. Ralf Badur, Novartis AG, Basel, for his clarifying discussions on the dispute over the naming priority of ergometrine/ergobasine/ergotocine/ergostetrine.

Dr. Goran Mijuk for his editorial help in making some passages dealing with complex content more comprehensible. We had a lot of fun together puzzling and fiddling around with the material.

Jean-Jacques Sanglier and Günter Engel for important background information from the "ergot era" at Sandoz AG.

Maximilian Rein and Jean-Jacques Sanglier, Novartis AG, Basel, for their translation of Latin and Old French text passages.

Dr. Neil Press and Ms. Kathleen Kellog, Novartis AG, Basel, and Novartis US, for their corrections and linguistic improvements of the English manuscript.

Petra Hoffmann-Petersen and Moritz Petersen for their tireless, repeated proofreading. Even when I have tried their patience over almost four years now and was absent-minded from time to time, their curiosity about the growing manuscript was a motivating companion until the end of the ergot saga.

Prof. Dr. Mark Geller, Hebrew and Jewish Studies, University College London, Dr. Irving Finkel, Curator in the Department of Western Asiatic Antiquities of the British Museum, London, Dr. Troels Pank Arbøll, Institute for Assyriology, Oxford University, and Dr. Matthias Müller, Department of Classical Studies, University of Basel, for their classification, evaluation, and interpretation of Assyrian sources. The moment when Irving Finkel and Mark Geller confirmed that clay tablet BAM 510 in the British Museum was the one Henry Wellcome had referred to in 1908 will remain unforgettable for me.

Dr. Ulrike Unschuld, Berlin, and Prof. Dr. Paul U. Unschuld, Institute of Chinese Life Sciences, Charité Universitätsmedizin, Berlin, Prof. Dr. George Métailié, Membre honoraire du Centre National de la Recherche Scientifique, Paris, for their renewed search for traces of ergot in traditional Chinese medicine.

Prof. Dr. Philip G. Kreyenbroek, Institute for Iranian Studies at Georg-August University, Göttingen, and Prof. Dr. Almut Hintze, Zartoshty Brothers Professor of Zoroastrianism at SOAS, University of London, for their expertise in the evaluation of Avestan text passages.

Prof. Mark Hengerer, Department for the History of Western Europe in the Early Modern Period, LMU Munich, for his suggestions and corrections of the passages that shed light on the political background of Jansenism in France.

Dr. Hans-Wolfgang Bayer, Head of the Cultural Office of the City of Memmingen, and Dr. Adalbert Mischlewski (†) for their examination and clarification of culture-related historical facts about the Antonite Order.

Dr. Beat Stoll, Université de Genève, for reviewing the passages concerning his grandfather Prof. Dr. Arthur Stoll.

Pascal Goblot, Escalenta—Zadig productions—Manuel Cam, Paris, Stephanie Günther, Paris, and Martin Oeggerli (micronaut), Basel, for their cooperation leading to the splendid cover photo of a fruiting body of *Claviceps purpurea*.

Dr. Ryan Henry Gumpper and Prof. Dr. Bryan Roth, University of North Carolina, for their recalculation of the cryo-electron microscopic structure of the 5-HT_{2A} receptor with LSD as ligand, which they conducted especially for this work.

Prof. Dr. Matthias Liechti, Head of the Psychopharmacology Research Group of the Department of Biomedicine at University Hospital Basel, for his improvements to the autotoxin psychiatry section.

The following persons and institutions granted publication rights for the images shown or provided the necessary clarifications. I would like to thank them all for their kind support.

Douglas R. Atkins, U.S. National Library of Medicine, Bethesda, Maryland,
Anne-Catherine Biedermann and Florence Hemici, Louvre, Paris,
Daniela Blum, Diocesan Museum Rottenburg,
Elisabeth Bray, British Museum, London,
Dr. Pantxika de Paepe, former Director and Chief Curator of the Unterlinden Museum, Colmar,
Emilie Dreyfus, Service Patrimoine Médiathèque Jean-Jacques Rousseau, Chambéry,
Benedicta Erny, Basel University Library,
Baptiste Etienne, Bibliothèque patrimoniale d'Avranches (Manche),
Prof. Dr. Danielle Fauque, Société chimique de France, Paris,
Alrun Gutow and Olaf Teßmer, Vorderasiatisches Museum Berlin (Museum of the Ancient Near East),
Thomas Haggerty, Bridgeman Images, New York,
Michael Hoffmann,
Sophie Hosotte, EDP Sciences, Paris,
Ursula Korber, Augsburg State and City Library,
Moir family, England,

Gabi Protzmann, Luther Memorials Foundation in Saxony-Anhalt, Wittenberg,

C. Raman Schlemmer, Curator, The Oskar Schlemmer Theatre Archives, Switzerland,

Vera Schulz, Heidelberg University Library,

Corinne Sigrist, Museum Unterlinden, Colmar,

Prof. Patricia M. Whitaker-Azmitia, University of Toronto,

Janine Wiedel, London,

Tania Williams, Wellcome Trust, London,

American Cancer Society, Atlanta, Georgia,

Marine Biological Laboratory Archives, University of Chicago, Illinois,

National Portrait Gallery, London,

Oxfordshire Blue Plaques Board, Oxford,

Winterthur Museum, Greenville, Delaware.

* * *

I would like to pay special tribute to my two colleagues Walter Dettwiler, Head of the Corporate Archives of Novartis AG, Switzerland, and Roger Bennet for their uncompromising help and infinite patience during the numerous reviews of the image and document collections from the early days of our company. My unusual requests were archival challenges for both of them, which didn't diminish their enjoyment of the ergot project for a second. The images they uncovered in the process are real gems.

Weil am Rhein, Germany   Frank Petersen
October 2024

Contents

Fungi are fascinating all-rounders.
Some are among the most dangerous organisms in nature.
Fungi are not dissimilar to humans.

F.P.

1

A momentous ménage à trois of fungus, grass, and insect develops

Fungi are key organisms that keep the material and energy cycle of nature going. They can live in symbiotic or parasitic communities with plants and insects and are mainstays of the biotechnology industry. As pathogens, they infect plants, animals and humans, producing toxic substances as well as life-saving drugs. Their exploration as potential suppliers of future food, industrial materials or textiles underlines the fact that the process of making these organisms useful to humans is far from over; perhaps it has not even really begun.

Although fungi can form tissue-like growing cell filaments or even clearly visible fruiting bodies, like bacteria or microalgae, they belong to the group of microorganisms that can only be recognized as individual organisms with the aid of a microscope. To date, around 120,000 species of fungi have been scientifically classified, and yet they are among the least studied living organisms. According to the latest estimates, 99% of fungal species are still unknown, and the gene sequences of only 30% of the described species have been published [1]. Since knowledge of bacterial diversity is no better, the most extensive *terra incognita* of our planet is the domain of microbes. The following account is about one of the most extraordinary protagonists of this microcosm, the ergot fungus.

The ergot fungus specializes in infesting grasses

For centuries, scientists have observed this microorganism, which they gave the taxonomic name *Claviceps purpurea* (Fr.) Tul. (Fig. 1.1 and information box). In the systematics of fungi, it belongs to the order of *Hypocreales*, in

Fig. 1.1 Long-stalked fruiting bodies of *Claviceps purpurea* growing from a sclerotium. (© Michael Hoffmann)

which many of its relatives are associated with arthropods and plants as parasites or symbionts.

Genomic studies suggest that the evolutionary precursor of *Claviceps purpurea* was originally an animal pathogenic microorganism that probably attacked arthropods. Over time, this member of the taxonomic family *Clavicipitaceae* changed hosts in a singular event and jumped from the animal kingdom to that of plants. Here it transformed into an impressive plant parasitic specialist with a complex life cycle centered on the exclusive infection of the ovaries of grasses [2].

In the spring, the ergot fungus germinates from its survival form, the sclerotium—a densely packed, hard, resting mass of fungal hyphae. It forms small caps on its mycelial stalks, which contain the sexually formed ascospores (Fig. 1.1). Once they have matured, they are expelled and distributed by the wind. When a spore hits the stigma of an unfertilized grass flower, the primary infection phase of the fungus begins. Within 24 hours, fungal hyphae grow from the ascospore down into the ovary. As a rule, a plant produces defensive substances when it is attacked by pests. Although the grass plant recognizes the intruder as foreign and activates its defense mechanisms, the fungus overrides them. It makes itself invisible, so to speak [3]. When its hyphae reach the ovary, a complex interaction is established between the parasitic invader and its host plant. In the ovary of the flower, a new genera-

Fig. 1.2 Sclerotium of *Claviceps purpurea*. (© Roman, CC BY 4.0)

tion of fungal spores, the conidiospores, forms via asexual reproduction and stimulates production of the syrupy honeydew of the grass flower. The rising sugar sap pushes the spores out of the ovary and attracts flies and moths, to which the sticky conidial mass adheres. In the secondary infection phase that now begins, the flying insects spread the spores to other unfertilized grass flowers. While the wind distributed the spores randomly in the first wave of infection, now the contaminated insects infect the flowers in a targeted manner. This leads to an explosive spread of the infection. Instead of a seed, the blackish/dark-purple looking sclerotium of the parasite, the ergot kernel, now grows from an infected ovary (Figs. 1.2 and 1.3). Cool, damp springs favor the two infection phases of *Claviceps purpurea*, as both grass flowering and honeydew production lasts particularly long under these climatic conditions [4].

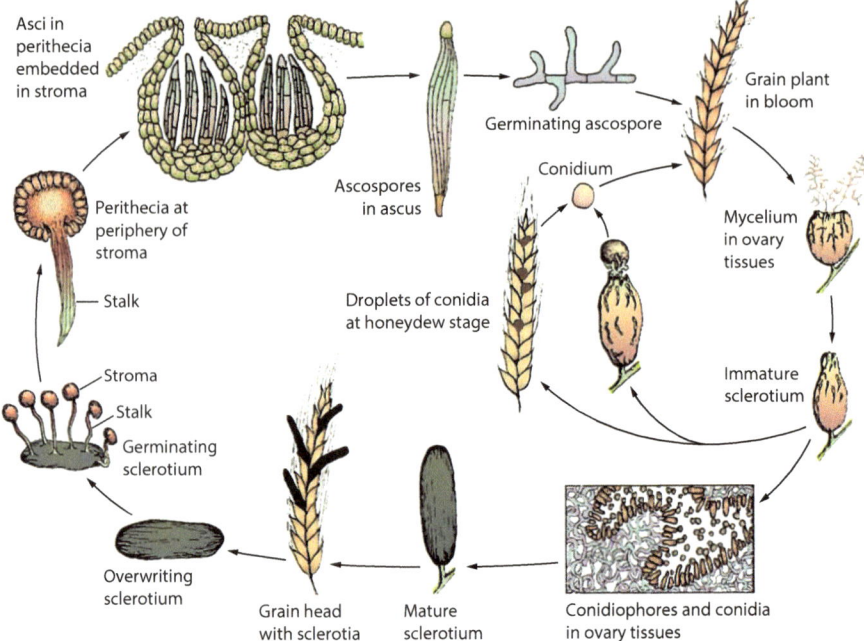

Fig. 1.3 Life cycle of *Claviceps purpurea* [5]. (Courtesy of Elsevier)

Taxonomic names

A taxonomic name is composed of the name of the genus followed by that of the species, both of which are written in italics. The complete binomial nomenclature includes an author abbreviation which is in normal typeface. The name *Claviceps purpurea* (Fr.) Tul. indicates that Elias Magnus Fries made an initial classification of the fungus, which Louis René Tulasne modified. The author abbreviation "L.", frequently used in the text stands for the Swedish naturalist Carl von Linné.

The ergot kernel was given its traditional German name *Mutterkorn* (literally "mother grain") after a spirit called the "Grain Mother". It is one of the grain spirits of Central and Northern European mythology, embodying the earth's powers as a protective demon of grain, and providing a good harvest [6]. People believed that they could see the Grain Mother walking in the waves of the cornfields and interpreted the sudden appearance of the ergot on the ears of corn as a sign of her appearance [7, 8]. In France, the fungus was called *ergot*, which is based on *ergot d'un coq* (English: cockspur) and signifies the growth form of its compact overwintering mycelium. Both names have been incorporated into the vocabulary of many European languages. Where the sclerotium of *Claviceps purpurea* occurred, it was given further regional names; 62 are recorded in the German language alone, 26 in French, 21 in Dutch, 13 in each of the Scandinavian languages and 13 in Italian [9]. The conspicuously high number of regional names is due to the frequent occurrence of ergot especially in Northern, Central and Eastern Europe. As we will show later, there was a very specific reason for this.

The rather unusual host change of the ergot fungus from arthropods to grasses would certainly have remained of purely academic interest to evolutionary biologists if it had not also affected cereals—so it was only a matter of time before the fungus had to cross paths with humans.

Claviceps purpurea, a true master of specialization, parasitizes wind-pollinated grass species and, among cultivated grasses, mainly attacks rye. Barley, wheat and oats are also at risk of infestation, however, as they have often self-pollinated before the flowers open, they are less likely to be affected by infection. Even if the fungus is classified as a plant parasite, this community is not completely parasitic. In contrast to other plant pathogenic fungi, which can infect all parts of the plant, this representative only infects individual ovaries. Its "microsurgical intervention" does not damage the host plant itself, as a seed is merely replaced by an ergot. This loss seems to have been bearable in evolutionary terms. The infection of the ovary is regarded by some plant physiologists as "pseudo-fertilization", in which the hyphae from the fungal spores penetrate the ovary instead of the pollen tube. But the plant does react to the fungal infection, albeit not with an effective defense. Rather, it appears to tolerate the intruder in order to achieve peaceful coexistence for the benefit of both sides: on the one hand, the fungus protects the host plant from pests with its highly potent cocktail of active ingredients, while, in return, attracted flying insects help to spread *Claviceps purpurea* after visiting the flowers [3].

The true victims of this complex *ménage à trois* of fungus, plant, and insect are human beings. They unknowingly began to chronically poison themselves with cereal products contaminated with the sclerotia substances, the ergot alkaloids. Like the seven plagues of Doomsday, the poisoning, which always occurred in waves, struck the people of the Middle Ages, who recognized the dreaded harbingers of the "plague" in the cool, damp spring seasons.

Ergot alkaloids are similar to signaling substances of the nervous system and hormones in humans

The characteristic, tetracyclic ergoline skeleton of the alkaloids of the ergopeptide, lysergic acid amide, and clavine groups contains an indole building block that is extended by an ethylamine moiety (blue). The compounds of the ergot fungus are thus similar to the signaling molecules serotonin, dopamine, adrenaline, and noradrenaline in the human body (Fig. 1.4).

Due to these structural similarities, ergot alkaloids interact with the receptors of these neurotransmitters and hormones and, depending on the amount and duration of intake, lead to acute or chronic poisoning. As will be discussed later, these highly potent fungal metabolites have been intensively studied in medicinal chemistry and pharmacology. Through synthetic and enzymatic structural modifications, their *in vivo* profiles and inhibitory or activating

natural ergot alkaloids of the ergopeptide group

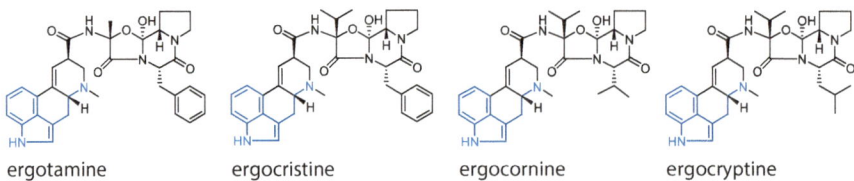

| ergotamine | ergocristine | ergocornine | ergocryptine |

ergot alkaloids of the lysergic acid amide group

ergot alkaloid of the clavine group

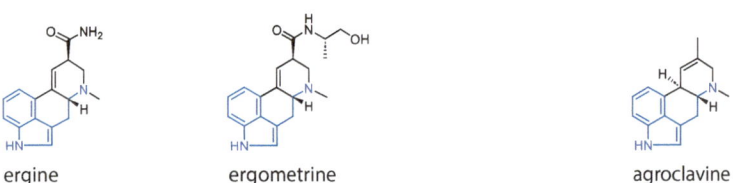

ergine   ergometrine   agroclavine

structures of neurotransmitters with whose receptors ergot alkaloids interact

dopamine   noradrenaline   adrenaline   serotonin

Fig. 1.4 Ergot alkaloids and neurotransmitters in comparison. Examples of naturally occurring ergot alkaloids and their structural similarity to neurotransmitters and hormones in the human body

effects were modulated in such a way that numerous drugs for the medical treatment of humans have emerged from ergot alkaloids.

Three forms of ergot alkaloid poisoning: acute ergotoxicosis, and gangrenous and convulsive ergotism

The ingestion of large amounts of ergot alkaloids leads to acute poisoning—causing diarrhea, miscarriages, unconsciousness, cardiovascular complications, cramps, and vomiting. Death then occurs due to respiratory arrest or circulatory failure.

The chronic ingestion of smaller amounts of alkaloids and the associated prolonged disruption of signal transmissions causes two characteristic forms of poisoning:

In gangrenous ergotism, the ergot alkaloids constrict blood vessels and reduce or cut off blood supply to the affected tissue. During the early phase of poisoning, cold and hot sensations occur simultaneously. The persistent lack of blood flow leads to extremely painful necrosis. Nose, hands, fingers, ears, toes, feet or entire extremities turn black, mummify, and can later fall off painlessly. Amputations in the Middle Ages were primarily performed on patients suffering from ergotism [10]. During the surgery, the dead limbs could often be cut off without bleeding. The characteristic burning pain has also given this form of ergotism the name *Ignis sacer*, "holy fire", "St. Anthony's fire" or "cold gangrene". In severe or advanced cases of poisoning, the mortality rate was around 90% [11, 12].

The symptoms of convulsive ergotism are different. A tingling of the skin—the dreaded "formication" (the feeling of having insects crawling on the skin)—is the first sign of poisoning. This is followed by severe tonic or tonic-clonic spasms of the flexor muscles. If the extensor muscles of the neck and back are severely affected, a "bridge-like" posture develops. The attacks, which can last for weeks and months, are accompanied by extreme sweating, a feeling of coldness, vomiting, psychosis, fits of raving and choking, unconsciousness, and loss of speech or hearing. Because of the initial tingling all over the body, this form of ergot poisoning was called in German literature *Kribbel-/Kriebelkrankeit* or Krampfseuche (literally "crawly disease" or "cramp disease"). The mortality rate for convulsive ergotism was significantly lower than for gangrenous ergotism, with a death rate of about 6–12% of patients [11–13].

Children were at risk of ergot alkaloid poisoning in different ways. If pregnant women suffered from acute or chronic poisoning, their children could die if premature births occurred. After surviving the embryonic and fetal periods, the children appear to have been protected from absorbing the ergot substances during the breastfeeding period. When their diets were switched to rye products during weaning, the risk of death increased significantly [14]. In contrast to adults, much lower quantities of alkaloids were sufficient for severe poisoning in children.

In an epidemic year, ergotism was typically rampant in the first four months after the rye harvest, which could contain up to 50% ergot, and would then quickly subside. The downturn in mass poisoning is due to the chemical instability of ergot alkaloids, which decompose during grain storage [11]. Tragically, the rural population, who lived from hand to mouth, could not wait for the crop harvest to become safe through storage. In this way, the ergot fungus transformed the areas it haunted into hell on earth. It poisoned, destroyed and threatened the lives of the people affected, their communities, and their financial existence for over 1000 years.

Unraveling the connections between the epidemic-like poisonings and understanding the effects of ergot compounds on the human body are outstanding achievements of scientific and medical research. At the end of this development, not only were the first pure substances of a microorganism introduced as drugs in the medical treatment of humans, but the ergot substances also served as molecular probes that enabled scientists to discover the biochemical processes of signal transmission between nerve cells, and from nerve to muscle cells. All these discoveries paved the way for new treatments in gynecology, obstetrics, hypertension, migraine, asthma, or psychiatric disorders.

Let's take a look over the shoulders of researchers and into the machinery of the scientific and medical works that finally solved the mystery of the janus-faced ergot fungus and its active ingredients.

Ergot in early cultures—a search for clues

Greece

Even Hippocrates could not make sense of it. The ancient Greek physician, who founded a medical school on the Mediterranean island of Kos in the 5th century BC, noticed that after warm, humid winters with prevailing southerly winds, miscarriages often occurred in a subsequent dry spring with cool winds from the north. How could that be? In his view, gods and demons were not the cause of illness, death or healing. He attributed it to the sensitive balance of the humors. It thus had to be this characteristic weather situation itself that upset the humoral equilibrium and ultimately caused the increase in premature births. This concurrence of both phenomena was so clearly recognizable that Hippocrates also included it in his *Meteorological Medicine*, which was taken up in the collection of writings of the medical school of Kos, the *Aphorisms* [15, 16]. The concise and briefly formulated doctrines became compulsory reading for subsequent generations of physicians, and the canon was also the first work of the literary genre of the same name.

> "Life is short, art long, opportunity fleeting, experience treacherous, judgment difficult."
> 1. Section, § 1 Aphorisms, Hippocrates

Around the same time, the holy books of Zoroastrianism mentioned plants that induce abortion. Zoroastrianism or Zarathustrism, is one of the oldest monotheistic religions, which developed from the 2nd millenium BC onwards in the Eastern Iranian cultural region, was subsequently adopted by the Achaemenid Empire, and assigns an important role to the struggle between good and evil forces. The followers of the ancient Iranian priest and prophet Zoroaster recorded these abortifacient plants in the *Vendidâd* 15.14 of the *Avesta*, which was written before the 6th century BC:

> "And the damsel goes to the old woman and applies to her for one of her drugs, that she may procure her miscarriage; and the old woman brings her some Banga, or Šaeta, or Ghnāna, or Fraspāta, a drug that kills in the womb or one that expels out of the womb, or some other of the drugs that produce miscarriage and [the man says], 'Cause thy fruit to perish!' and she causes her fruit to perish (…)" [17].

Were they grasses again? Unfortunately, so far it has not been possible to clarify which plants that are active as uterotonics are hidden behind the names in the Zoroastrian script (personal comment by Prof. Philip Kreyenbroek, 2022).

In contrast, a sweet grass that Hippocrates used as a birth medicine is well known: he applied barley (*Hordeum vulgare* L.) to stimulate labor pains. When the traveling physician and his students Polybos, Drakon, and Thessalos were called to a delivery where the contractions were slow to start or were not strong enough to give birth, great haste was required as well as reliable medication. The doctors' barley medicine was amazingly simple:

> "A means to promote delivery (is the following). Boil half a *choinix* [ancient Greek unit of dry capacity] of coarsely ground barley flour in four *heminas* of water, and when it has bubbled up, administer it two or three times as a sipping drink" [18].

After a short time, the medicine would begin to take effect—the contractions became more intense, and the child would soon be delivered.

In their extensive weather observations, the Greek doctors focused on wind directions, temperatures and rainfall, but unfortunately did not keep an eye on the grasses, although they recommended barley flour as a labor remedy and for the treatment of postpartum hemorrhages. They mixed it with blackberries and stirred it in with wine or added butter [18]. Pharmacologists of the 19th century read the compositions of barley medicine in disbelief. They were not aware of any pharmacological effect of barley.

In ancient Greece, barley was not only used for medicinal purposes. It also enjoyed cult status: it was the first type of grain to be cultivated before wheat, and Demeter, the goddess of grain and fertility, was believed to have brought it with her from Sicily. This divine gift was irreplaceable as sacrificial barley in various ceremonies. Barley grains were given as gifts to a host, and they were an important utensil in the frequently consulted chicken oracles (if, for example, the birds greedily picked at the presented seeds, it was understood as a sign that the gods were in support of a situation; ignoring the seeds was interpreted as divine disapproval).

The "Mysteries of Eleusis" were also unthinkable without barley flour [19]. The story of the goddess Demeter and her daughter Persephone, whom Hades, the god of the underworld, had abducted to his kingdom beneath the earth, was re-enacted in this official ceremony of Athens, which lasted nine days. Demeter searched desperately for her beloved daughter and could no longer fulfill her duties to nature, which was an unacceptable situation. The combatants agreed on a compromise. Persephone had to stay with her husband Hades in the realm of the dead for four months out of the year. She was allowed to return to her mother on earth for eight months each year, during which time Demeter brought nature back to life: thus, the ancient Greeks had their explanation for the seasonal change. At the end of the Mysteries, in which they celebrated the Persephone myth as an allegory of the immortality of the soul, the adepts were served a ritual drink in the temple of Eleusis. This *Kykeon* sent the assembled congregation into a frenzy of enlightenment and understanding of the world. Plato, Plutarch, Marcus Aurelius, and Cicero, who also belonged to this select circle, were overwhelmed by their "mysterious" experiences. According to tradition, this "mind-blowing" brew is said to have been made simply from barley flour, water and pennyroyal (*Mentha pulegium* L.) [20].

The natural product chemist Albert Hofmann, the ethnomycologist Gordon Wasson, and Carl Ruck, professor of classical studies, speculated in their 1978 book *The Road to Eleusis* that ergot could have formed on the processed ripe barley ears of the *Kykeon* (perhaps also on fruiting heads of representatives of the genus *Paspalum* L.). The centrally acting ingredients or their degradation products could have caused the hallucinations described. This working hypothesis would be scientifically supported twenty years later. In 1997, the Spanish ethnochemist Jordi Juan-Tresserras examined two archaeological finds that had been discovered at the excavation site of the temple of the goddesses Demeter and Persephone in Mas Castellar de Pontos in Spain. He identified the remains of ergot in several interdental spaces of a human lower jawbone, which he was also able to discover on a small goblet using microscopic images. To find sclerotia remains on one tooth could have been chance, but to find them between several teeth can be interpreted as a deliberate ingestion of ergot [21, 22].

Mesopotamia

The evidence from Zoroastrian and Greek sources can be supplemented by an Akkadian text from the 2nd century BC, which tells of an epidemic-like disease that led to premature births. The Assyrian clay tablet EAE XXI reads (Fig. 1.5):

> "(...) li-'-bu ina KUR u-la-'-ib SAL.PES$_4$.MEŠ sa SA-si-na NU SILIM.MEŠ"
> "(...), an epidemic of li'bu disease will break out in the country, pregnant women will not carry their pregnancies to term" [23–25].

Do the texts on inducing and supporting labor and premature births ultimately describe the contracting effect of ergot alkaloids on the uterus? Unfortunately, none of these reports describe the conspicuous persistent structures of the ergot fungus in the grass ears. However, the missing link could have been preserved in a Neo-Assyrian cuneiform script mentioned by Henry Wellcome, the co-founder of the English pharmaceutical company Burroughs Wellcome & Co, in his book *From Ergot to "Ernutin"* published in 1908 [26].

Around 660 BC, an Assyrian scribe pressed a text into a moist clay tablet with a stylus made from the giant reed. According to Wellcome, he reported a "noxious pustule in an ear of grain". Although Wellcome gave no further details about the source of the quotation, the Assyriologists Prof. Mark Geller (University College London), Dr. Irving Finkel (curator of the Mesopotamian

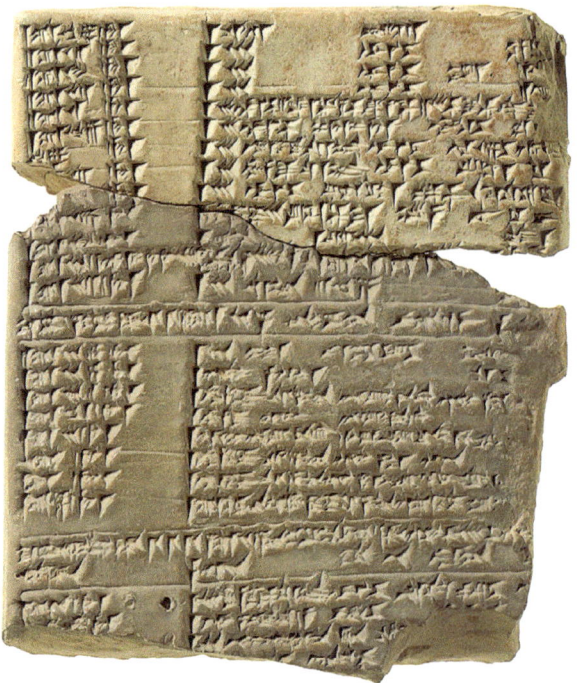

Fig. 1.5 Clay tablet EAE XXI from the Uruk catalog of Enūma Anu Enlil (EAE); (194 BC), Neo-Assyrian, Nineveh. (Upper fragment VAT7814. © Staatliche Museen zu Berlin, Vorderasiatisches Museum, photo: Olaf M. Teßmer; Lower fragment cast of AO6470. © RMN-Grand Palais (Musée du Louvre), photo: Franck Raux)

collection at the British Museum in London), and Dr. Troels Pank Arbøll (Oxford University) are certain which passage it must be. It belongs to a popular incantation used in Babylonian-Assyrian medicine at the time, which was deciphered on the clay tablet BAM 510 (Fig. 1.6):

196′ habburra kanna kannu kiṣra kiṣru šubulta šubultu
197′ merʾa Šamaš eṣṣid Sîn upahhar Šamaš ina eṣēdīšu Sîn ina puhhurīšu
198′ ana īn etli merhu īrub Šamaš u Sîn išizzānimma merhu lilâ [tê šipti]
199′ kaʾinimma merhu ša libbi īnī šūlî

196′ the sprout to the root-stock, the root-stock to the bud, the bud to the head-of-grain, (and) the head-of-grain to

197′ the merhu-kernel. The Sun-god was harvesting, the Moon-god was reaping. While the Sun-god was harvesting (and) the Moon-god was reaping,

198′ the merhu-kernel entered into the eye of the lad. O Sun-god and Moon-god stand by me, and let the merhu-kernel take off! [Incantation spell.]

199′ Invocation for removing the merhu from out of the eyes [26].

Fig. 1.6 Clay tablet BAM 510, "If a man's eyes are sick", Library of Aššurbanipal (c. 911–612 BC), Neo-Assyrian, Kouyunjik. (© The Trustees of the British Museum, London)

Wellcome used the English translation *noxious pustule* for the term *merḫu-kernel*, which had been held responsible for a disease of the eye and sees the particular excrescence "in the ear of grain" as a possible allusion to ergot. Fifty years later, Assyriologists discovered a much earlier version of the incantation text from the 2nd millennium BC. When they came across the ominous *merḫu* nucleus, they now officially translated it as ergot. However, the *merḫu* structure had nothing to do with ergotism. Assyrian doctors and conjurers probably used the ancient magic formula to treat an inflamed eyelid, a stye [26].

China

The traces of ergot in Greece were probably passed down in the pharmaceutical texts of the Hippocratic school of medicine and in the composition of the *Kykeon*. But can they also be found in the writings of traditional Chinese medicine, whose literary roots date back to the 4th century BC? Thanks to the valuable support of sinologist and pharmacist Dr. Ulrike Unschuld, Berlin, and ethnobiologist, sinologist and historian of science Prof. Georges Métailié from the *Centre National de la Recherche Scientifique, Paris*, an old question was re-examined that seems to have been answered long ago.

* * *

The Chinese lexicon *Erh ya* 爾雅 is considered the oldest source, according to which ergot is said to have been used as a medication in obstetrics as early as 1100 BC [27, 28]. On re-reading the original Chinese text, neither a direct reference to ergot nor to its pharmaceutical effect could be found (personal comment by Prof. George Métailié, 2022). This meant that the theory of a three-thousand-year-old history of ergot medication in Chinese medicine suddenly became obsolete. All subsequent literature searches always led to a famous article from 1849, written by the most important sinologist of his time, the Frenchman Stanislas Julien at the *Collège de France* in Paris. When ether and chloroform were introduced as anesthetics in surgery in 1846 and 1847, Julien was fascinated by the reports from the operating rooms. He then became interested in medical writings from ancient China as a way to discover new healing methods and began translating texts from a fifty-volume work that is still in the *Bibliotèque National de France* today. During his work on the *Gu jin yi tong da quan* 古今医统大全 (*The Complete Compendium of Ancient and Contemporary Medical Works*) by the physician Xu Chunfu, published in 1556, Julien came across the anesthetic *Ma fei san* 麻沸散 by the surgeon Hua To (2nd/3rd century AD). The composition has been lost, but he suspected a medication based on hemp (*Cannabis sativa* L.) and wine, which the physician had applied during major surgical procedures. Julien's publication on the Far Eastern method of anesthesia caused worldwide astonishment at how highly developed Chinese medicine already was 1500 years ago. In a subordinate clause of his introduction, the sinologist noted *en passant* that ergot was known in early Chinese medicine:

"J'ai vu, par exemple, que depuis bien longtemps, les Chinois font usage (…), du seigle ergoté pour hâter les accouchements laborieux, (…)" [29].

   "I have seen, for example, that for a long time the Chinese apply ergot to hasten difficult birth (…)."

Without further details, Julien's colleagues from the field of pharmacy had to make do with this somewhat meagre fare from the sinologist, but the short insertion on the use of ergot in Chinese obstetrics caused a sensation and was enough to be addressed again and again in subsequent encyclopedias and textbooks by renowned French, Swiss and German pharmacists of the 19th and early 20th centuries. The description "for a long time" in Julien's original article changed within a year to "since time immemorial" [27, 30–32]. The later readership of pharmacologists did not learn more than that.

   But what had Julien actually read about *seigle ergoté* in the *Gu jin yi tong da quan*, and can the beginnings of a possible ergot alkaloid-containing medicine in ancient China be traced? On close inspection of the gynecology chapter, in the section "If the birth is not smooth" under "What you need to know for a smooth birth", the recipe *Niu xi tang* 牛膝湯 is found (personal comment by Dr. Ulrike Unschuld, 2022). The decoction of this plant mixture was given to women to drink during a difficult birth. As before in Greek medicine, the medicinal plants of the *Niu xi tang* again included a sweet grass: *Que mai* 雀麦, the Japanese brome (*Bromus japonicus* Thunb.) [33]. *Que mai* was later included in the medicinal plant treasury of the most important Chinese pharmacopoeia recorded, the *Ben cao gang mu* 本草綱目 from 1593. The physician Li Shizhen (1518–1593) and his team had studied 800 medical books for almost 30 years and compiled 1900 pharmaceutical substances in their curated canon of *Materia Medica*. In the *opus summum* of China's medical and pharmaceutical literature, Li Shizhen mentioned Japanese brome as a therapeutic agent administered after the death of fetuses for the expulsion of the afterbirth [34]. He had taken the composition from the medical book *Xin xiu ben cao* 新修本草 from 659 AD, in which *Que mai* was written down as a medicinal plant for the treatment of tedious labor. Women in labor received the medicine as a decoction of *Miao* 苗, the sprouts or seedlings [35].

   Obviously, Julien saw the labor-promoting effect of *Niu xi tang* alone as infallible proof of the presence of *seigle ergoté* with its unmistakable pharmacological activity, even though the Chinese text does not mention ergot. It is unclear why the drug *Que mai*, which was listed in the catalog of Chinese pharmacopoeias for almost a thousand years, is no longer mentioned in any of the 41,000 compositions of Chinese healers of the 19th and 20th centuries (personal comment by Prof. Paul U. Unschuld, 2022; see also "Unschuld Collection", Staatsbibliothek Berlin).

In the mid-19th century, the British physician and missionary Frederick Porter Smith translated medicinal plant portraits from Li Shizhen's *Ben cao gang mu* into English and added further phytotherapeutics with obstetric and gynecological indications. In addition to the Japanese brome (Smith erroneously equated *Que mai* with wild oat (*Avena fatua* L.)), Smith also mentions common oat (*Avena sativa* L.), which was prescribed to stimulate labor and for placental retention [36, 37]. In his *Contributions Towards the Materia Medica & Natural History of China*, published in 1871, he added the drug *Mai mei* 麥霉 ("mold on wheat"), which refers to ergot-infected cereals such as maize and rice, as well as *Kuang mei* 穬霉 ("mold on barley")—a collective term for various cereals—which caused miscarriages [38].

While Hippocrates had treated labor weakness with barley (*Hordeum vulgare* L.), Li Shizhen recommended naked barley (*Hordeum vulgare var. nudum* L.) *Kuang mai* 穬麥 as a uterotonic (Fig. 1.7). After a short germination period and subsequent drying of the barley sprouts *Kuang mai nie* 穬麥蘖 in the sun, the shoots were removed and the grains ground. Doctors used the flour to prepare a medicine that was used for abortions. Li Shizhen took the preparation of the medication from the medical book *Wai tai bi yao* 外台秘要 from 752 AD, in which barley medicine had been recorded as an abortifacient [37, 39–41].

Based on the reliable premise that the sweet grasses mentioned in the Greek and Chinese compositions were contaminated with ergot alkaloids, they could have been applied from the 7th century BC. The priests of the Mysteries of Eleusis prepared the hallucinogenic *Kykeon* using infected barley or paspalum ears. Greek doctors of the 5th century BC, just like their Chinese counterparts from the 7th and 8th centuries AD, administered ergot alkaloids via barley for gynecological and obstetric indications. In Far Eastern medicine, the Japanese brome was later added as a further treatment option. But why did the doctors of the time not attribute the medicinal effects of the grasses to the sclerotia themselves? Was it perhaps not mentioned because they regarded ergot as part of these healing plants? The question of the nature of sclerotium was not a simple one, after all, and ignited the minds of scientists well into the 19th century.

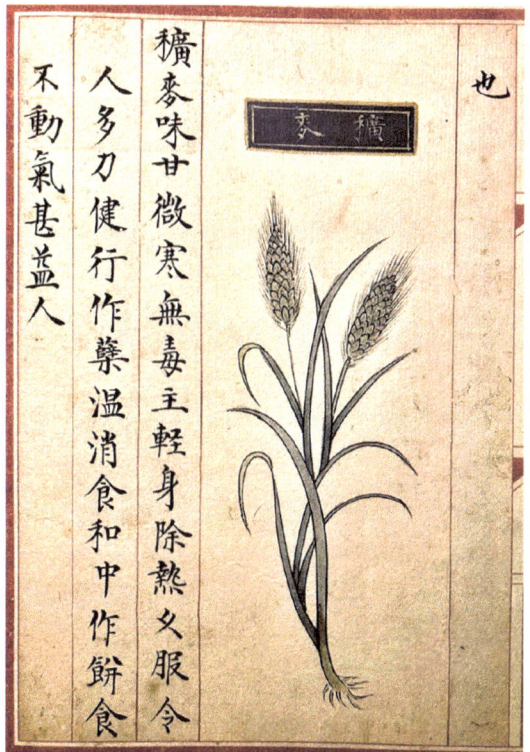

Fig. 1.7 *Kuang mai* 穬麥, *Shi wu bencao* (1571). (With permission by Dr. Ulrike Unschuld)

However, if the sclerotia of *Claviceps purpurea* were found in cereal fields and meadows, ergot poisoning would probably have already been known at that time, even if this is not clear from the old writings [23]. Mass ergot poisoning was first documented in Europe in the early Middle Ages. But how did this come about? It had to do with the spread of rye.

The ergot fungus in the rye's luggage

Barley, followed by einkorn, emmer and spelt, is the oldest type of grain in Europe. These mainly self-pollinating sweet grass species originated in the Middle East and southern Turkey and reached the European continent via a south-easterly route.

The cross-pollinating rye, whose regions of origin are traced to eastern Turkey, north-eastern Iran, and the Transcaucasus, took a completely different path. It reached the Iberian Peninsula via the Black Sea region, the Balkans, and along the western Mediterranean coast. On a second, more northerly route, it initially spread as far as Eastern Europe (c. 1800 BC). It was here that Slavic tribes began to cultivate rye, as it is extremely resistant to wet, dry, and cold conditions and produces good yields even in sandy soils. Independently from Slavic groups, Germanic tribes grew the rye, which became their preferred grain from 500 BC. Around 375 AD, when the Huns invaded Europe, they moved to western and southern Europe, carrying their sacks of rye with them. In their new settlement areas, the hardy rye displaced the more demanding wheat preferred by the Romans, so that the rye-growing regions eventually extended as far as northern Italy. Prof. Thomas Miedaner, head of the Rye and Biotic Stress Research Group at the State Plant Breeding Institute at the University of Hohenheim, states that in the 3rd to 6th centuries AD, rye had become the cultivated grain of central, northern, and eastern Europe [42, 43]. Naturally, the ergot fungus always traveled with the rye grains as a stowaway and was thus able to spread massively across almost the entire continent.

References

1. B. Wu, M. Hussain, W. Zhang, M. Stadler, X. Liu, M. Xiang, Current insights into fungal species diversity and perspective on naming the environmental DNA sequences of fungi. Mycology **10**, 127 (2019)
2. J.W. Spatafora, G.-H. Sung, J.-M. Sung, N.L. Hywel-Jones, J.F. White Jr, Phylogenetic evidence for an animal pathogen origin of ergot and the grass endophytes. Mol Ecol **16**, 1701 (2007)
3. B. Oeser, S. Kind, S. Schurack, Th Schmutzer, P. Tudzynski, J. Hinsch, Cross-talk of the biotrophic pathogen Claviceps purpurea and its host Secale cereale. BMC Genomics **18**, 273 (2017)
4. T. Miedaner, H. Geiger, Genetics, and management of ergot (Claviceps spp.) in rye, sorghum, and pearl millet. Toxins 7, 659 (2015)
5. G.N. Agrios, *Fruit and general diseases caused by Ascomycetes and Deuteromycetes (Mitosporic fungi): ergot of cereals and grasses*, 5th edn. Plant Pathology. (Elsevier Academic Press, Amsterdam, 2005), p. 503
6. A. Kledt, *Die Entführung Kores: Studien zur athenisch-eleusinischen Demeterreligion* (Franz Steiner Verlag, Stuttgart, 2004), pp. 16–25
7. W. Mannhardt, *Die Korndämonen: Beitrag zur germanischen Sittenkunde* (F. Dümmler's Verlagsbuchhandlung, Berlin, 1868), pp. 20–21

8. W. Mannhardt, Die nordeuropäische Kornmutter, in *Mythologische Forschungen aus dem Nachlassen von Wilhelm Mannhardt*, ed. by H. Patzig (Karl J. Trübner, Strasbourg London, 1884), pp. 296–315

9. F.J. Bové, The nomenclature of ergot, in *The story of ergot* (Karger, Basel, 1970), pp. 3–14

10. F. Messmer, *Karl Lang: Die Wissenschaftlichen Publikationen in ihrer medizingeschichtlichen Bedeutung; Bilder zur Geschichte der Chirurgie* (Allitera, München, 2008), p. 75

11. F. Eichholtz, *Lehrbuch der Pharmakologie – Im Rahmen einer allgemeinen Krankheitslehre für praktische Ärzte und Studierende*, 3, 4 edn. (Springer, Berlin Heidelberg, 1944), pp. 97–99

12. C. Kissel, Vergiftung durch Mutterkorn, in *Handbuch der speciellen Pathologie und Therapie* vol 1. (Ferdinand Enke, Erlangen, 1863), pp. 263–268

13. B. Hussa, E. Forssell, 630. Über Kriebelkrankheit u. Vergiftung mit Lolium temulentum, in *Schmidt's Jahrbücher der in- und ausländischen gesammten Medicin* vol 91., ed. by H.E. Richter, A. Winter (Otto Wigand, Leipzig, 1856), pp. 172–174

14. A.W.M. van Hasselt, Chronische Vergiftung mit Mutterkorn, in *Allgemeine Giftlehre und die Gifte des Pflanzenreichs*, 2nd edn. (Vieweg, Braunschweig, 1862), pp. 199–200. freely adapted from the Dutch by J.B. Henkel

15. Hippokrates: Aphorismen, III. Abschnitt, § 12, J. D. Hörling'sche Buchhandlung, Wien, 1791, p. 70

16. R. Kobert, *Zur Geschichte des Mutterkorns. – Historische Studien aus dem Pharmakologischen Institut der Kaiserlichen Universität Dorpat* vol. 1 (Tausch & Grosse, Halle, 1889), p. 20

17. F. Wolff: Avesta: *die heiligen Bücher der Parsen. Übersetzt auf der Grundlage von Chr. Bartholomae's Altiranisches Wörterbuch*, Verlag von Karl J. Trübner, Strassburg, 1910, p. 409; (translation by J. Darmesteter: The Zend-Avesta Part 1: The Vendidad, Sacred Book of the East (Vol. 4), Oxford University Press, 1880, p. 175)

18. R. Kobert, *Zur Geschichte des Mutterkorns. – Historische Studien aus dem Pharmakologischen Institut der Kaiserlichen Universität Dorpat* vol. 1 (Verlag v. Tausch & Grosse, Halle, 1889), pp. 21–22

19. K.G. Fiedler, *Reise durch alle Theile des Königreiches Griechenland in Auftrag der Königl. Griechischen Regierung in den Jahren 1834–1837 – Teil 1* (Friedrich Fleischer, Leipzig, 1840), pp. 662–663

20. F.M.K. Kähler, *Frauen und Mädchen im Kult. Priesterinnen und weibliches Kultpersonal in Athen und Attika von der archaischen Zeit bis zur Spätklassik* (University of Vienna, 2013), pp. 115–126. Dissertation

21. J. Juan-Tresserras, La arqueología de las drogas en la Península Ibérica. Una síntesis de las recientes investigaciones arqueobotánicas. Complutum **11**, 261 (2000)

22. J. Juan-Tresserras, Estudis dels residus organics per a la identificaci de possibles ritus i ofrenes, in *Mas Castellar de Pontós (Alt Empordà). Un complex arqueològic*

d'època ibèrica (Excavacions 1990–1998), ed. by E. Pons (Museu d'Arqueologia de Catalunya, Girona, 2002), pp. 548–556

23. R.D. Biggs, Ergotism and other Mycotoxicoses in Ancient Mesopotamia? AuOr **9**, 15 (1991)

24. M. Stol, F.A.M. Wiggermann, What is going to happen? Prognostics, in *Birth in Babylonia and the Bible—Its Mediterranean setting* Cuneiform Monographs 14. (Styx Publications, Groningen, 2000), p. 91

25. H. Hunger, Religion und Wissenschaft im Alten Orient, in *Uruk – 5000 Jahre Megacity*, ed. by N. Crüsemann, B. Salje (Michael Imhof, Petersberg, 2013), p. 301

26. H.S. Wellcome, *From Ergot to "Ernutin": An historical Sketch* (Burroughs Wellcome, London, 1908), p. 12

27. A. Tschirch, China, in *Handbuch der Pharmakognosie. Erster Band – Allgemeine Pharmakognosie* (Christian Hermann Tauchnitz, Leipzig, 1910), p. 520

28. F.J. Bové, The history of ergot, in *The story of ergot* (Karger, Basel, 1970), p. 136

29. S. Julien, *Chirurgie Chinoise—Substance anesthétique employée en Chine, etc* Comptes rendus hebdomadaires des Séances de l'Académie des Sciences (Séance du 2. Janvier) (1849), p. 195

30. F. Dorvault, *L'officine ou Répertoire général de pharmacie pratique*, 3rd edn. (Béchet Jeune & Labé, Paris, 1850), p. 515

31. H. Schelenz, China, in *Geschichte der Pharmazie*, 2nd edn. (Georg Olms, Hildesheim Zürich New York, 2005), p. 75

32. F.A. Flückiger, Secale cornutum, in *Lehrbuch der Pharmakognosie des Pflanzenreiches* (Rudolph Gaertner, Berlin, 1867), p. 136

33. Xu Chunfu: *Gu jin yi tong da quan* 古今医统大全, 1556, 10, p. 5444

34. S. Li, *Ben Cao Gang Mu* 本草綱目 *(BCGM): Chinese Historical Illness Terminology* vol. V (University of California Press, Oakland, 2015), ch 22-07, pp. 658–659. Eds.: Zhang Zhibin and Paul U. Unschuld

35. S. Li, *BCGM: Creeping herbs, water herbs, herbs growing on stones, mosses, cereals*, 1st edn. vol. V (University of California Press, Oakland, 2015), ch 22-07, pp. 658–659. Ed and transl.: P.U. Unschuld

36. F.P. Smith, *Contributions towards the materia medica & natural history of China: For the use of medical missionaries & native medical students* (American Presbyterian Mission Press, Trübner & Co, Shanghai, London, 1871), p. 157

37. G.A. Stuart, *Chinese materia medica: vegetable kingdom* (American Presbyterian Mission Press, Shanghai, 1911), p. 59. Extensively revised from F. Porter Smith's work

38. F.P. Smith, *Contributions Towards the Materia Medica & Natural History of China: For the Use of Medical Missionaries & Native Medical Students* (American Presbyterian Mission Press, Trübner, Shanghai London, 1871), p. 93

39. S. Li, *BCGM: Creeping herbs, water herbs, herbs growing on stones, mosses, cereals*, 1st edn. vol. V (University of California Press, Oakland, 2015), ch 25-18-03, pp. 891–893. Ed and transl.: P.U. Unschuld

40. G.A. Stuart, *Chinese materia medica: vegetable kingdom* (American Presbyterian Mission Press, Shanghai, 1911), p. 164. Extensively revised from F. Porter Smith's work

41. Ibid, p. 208

42. K.-E. Behre, The history of rye cultivation in Europe. Veget Hist Archaeobot **1**, 141 (1992)

43. T. Miedaner, *Roggen – Anspruchslos und hartnäckig. In, Kulturpflanzen Botanik – Geschichte – Perspektiven* (Springer, Berlin Heidelberg, 2014), pp. 70–74

2

The horror begins!

First evidence of rampant ergotism in the early Middle Ages

After the turmoil of the Migration Period and the collapse of the Western Roman Empire, diocesan and monastic chronicles were among the earliest historical sources in Europe, with the oldest writings dating back to the early 6th to 9th century. In them, monks recorded what they considered worth knowing, memorable, significant or curious. In addition to political events, military campaigns, divorces of emperors, trips to Rome by their abbots, rancor, weather phenomena, earthquakes, and burials, they documented the appearance of comets and also wrote down when nothing had happened in a year. In these uncertain times, this was also something extraordinary.

However, starting in 857, something completely inexplicable happened. None other than the court librarian of Emperor Louis the Pious, the monk Gerward (c. 794–c. 860), the first confirmed outbreak of ergotism in the *Annals of Xanten*. "Blisters and swellings" had formed on human bodies, and the tormented had been consumed by "a hideous putrefaction", in the course of which "filleted limbs detached themselves before death". This great affliction probably tormented the people in the area around Gerward's monastery in Ghent [1]. It was the beginning of horrific mass poisonings by ergot, which recurred at regular intervals for almost 1000 years. Initially, mainly the regions of present-day France and Flanders were affected; specifically, Aquitaine and the area around Paris in 944 and 945. The archivist of Reims Cathedral, Flodoard of Reims (c. 894 Epernay – 966 Reims), reported in the *Flodoardi*

Annales—one of the most important historical sources of the Frankish Empire—on the devastating plague that struck Paris in 945:

> "In the *pagus* (Latin for 'district'; editor's note) Paris and also in various other *pagi*, men were afflicted on various limbs with wounds from fire. Gradually they burned down until death ended their punishment. Some of those affected sought out the places of the saints and thus escaped the torture. Many were healed in Paris in the church of Mary, the Holy Mother of God (Notre-Dame de Paris). All those who came there were sure that they were saved from their suffering. Duke Hugo (the Great) gave them food in daily rations. Some wished to return home, but there the fire started again, and they returned to the church (Notre-Dame) and were again freed from their suffering" [2].

In his entry, the chronicler from Reims mentions for the first time the healing of gangrenous ergotism, which he unquestionably attributed to the merciful saint. Flodoard simply did not consider that the daily food rations from the Count of Paris' larders could have had a role in the healing process, and subsequent clergymen did not attach any importance to this note. It took another 600 years before a scientific report from the University of Marburg suggested that food was one of the causes of ergotism.

Meanwhile, the series of horrors continued: Paris was plagued again in 957; in 994 there were mass poisonings in Aquitaine and the Limousin. In 1039 the plague ravaged Metz, and in 1085 it broke out again in Lorraine. The monk doctors at the Benedictine Abbey in Tours now distinguished between the two forms of the plague, which were later referred to as gangrenous and convulsive ergotism. They drew on an old disease name from Roman antiquity, *Ignis sacer* (Latin for "holy fire"). The Roman poet Lucretius (c. 97–c. 55 BC) first used the term in his didactic poem *De Rerum Natura*, in which he compares the burning of limbs to the fire of the volcano Etna. Later, all reddened, inflammatory or ulcer-forming skin diseases were summarized under the collective term *Ignis sacer* [3].

In 1089, the Benedictine monk Sigebert of Gembloux (c. 1030 Gembloux – 1112 Gembloux), again reported a mass death in Lorraine (Fig. 2.1). He had already adopted the concept of *Ignis sacer* from his fellow brothers at the abbey in Tours, but what is truly remarkable is that Sigebert was the first to record the joint occurrence of the symptoms of gangrene and convulsions:

> "1089. It was an epidemic year, especially in the western part of Lorraine, where many whose insides were consumed by the holy fire rotted from their corroded limbs, which turned black as coal; they either died miserably or continued an even more miserable life after the rotten hands and feet were cut off. But many were tormented by nervous cramps" [4].

Fig. 2.1 *Sigebert de Gembloux dicte sa Chronique à un copiste; Détail: Initial D de Dicturi. Chronique de Robert de Torigni, Scriptorium du Mont-Saint-Michel, 2e moitié du XIIe siècle.* (© 01/2022, Avranches, Bibliothèque patrimoniale, ms 159, f° 70)

The "epidemic foci" of the year 1089 flared up again and again, and the suffering did not end. After the grain harvest in August, ergotism broke out in Orléans, and 14 days later the people of Flanders and Lorraine fell victim to it. Just one year later, the curse spread as far as the Dauphiné [5–7].

The people were helplessly at the mercy of the holy fire. They neither knew how to protect themselves from it nor how to alleviate its terrible symptoms. It had to be God's punishment for their sinful life, and only God alone could redeem them from it. A poor sinner was hardly in a position to enter into a wholesome dialog with the ruler of the world without an intercessor. For such special missions, saints were called upon as mediators who, at best, already had some successes to their name. This Herculean task was now entrusted to St. Anthony the Great, with unexpected side effects.

Two knights found the Brotherhood of St. Anthony

During the catastrophic epidemics of 1089 and 1090, the people of Dauphiné remembered that the bones of St. Anthony (c. 250 Koma – c. 356 Colzim mountain) were buried in the small church of Saint-Antoine en Viennois.

Fig. 2.2 Matthias Grünewald (Mathis Gothart Nithart) (Würzburg, between 1475/1480 Halle an der Saale, 1528): The Isenheim Altarpiece, St. Anthony's visit to St. Paul Eremita, detail. (© RMN-Grand Palais (Musée Unterlinden) / Stéphane Maréchalle / Mathieu Rabeau)

Legend has it that Emperor Romanus IV. Diogenes gifted them to Count Jocelin (Josselin or Geilin II) de Châteauneuf de l'Abenc in gratitude for his brotherhood in arms in the fight against the Seljuk Turks. In 1070, the brave knight transferred the relics from Constantinople to the village church in the Dauphiné, which thirteen years later was granted to the Benedictine Abbey of Saint-Pierre in Montmajour, along with the saint's relics. The order established a priory in the village, which took over the care of the remains of the "Desert Father" from Egypt [8–12].

Anthony (Fig. 2.2) was an early Christian monk who withdrew to the solitude of the Egyptian desert to lead an ascetic life. There, in his hermitage, he had to resist all demonic temptations and healed the sick who came to his cave. Thus, those who had fallen ill now from the holy fire made a pilgrimage to Saint-Antoine en Viennois so that the miracle-working hermit might also relieve them of their torment. Even though many succumbed to the disease, word of the cures spread all the more quickly. The numerous pilgrims to Santiago de Compostela who stopped off here reported on the miracles performed on their way through Europe, which is why the holy fire was also known as "St. Anthony's Fire" as early as in the 11th century.

In 1093, two noblemen arrived in the small town in the Dauphiné. Gaston de la Valloire, who had been healed here earlier of St. Anthony's fire, now brought his sick son Guérin to the pilgrims' church. After Guérin touched a relic of the saint, he too was healed. When they both went on pilgrimage to Saint-Antoine en Viennois again in 1095 to give thanks for their healings, they saw the misery and the almost unmanageable crowds of sick people. St. Anthony is said to have appeared to Gaston in a dream and instructed both men to dedicate their lives to caring for people who had fallen ill from the holy fire. On June 27, 1095, father and son founded a lay brotherhood exclusively for the care of ergotism patients. Six other companions soon joined the Hospital Brothers of St. Anthony, which was placed under the local Benedictine priory. The *Frères de l'Aumône*, who initially had to accommodate healthy pilgrims together with the sick, built the *Hôpital des Démembrés* in 1120 for the separate care of those suffering from ergotism [9, 12–14].

The lay brothers' reputation spread like wildfire. The fact that those afflicted by St. Anthony's fire were nursed and healed in the hospital caused the never-ending stream of people seeking help to swell. The additional care of the pilgrims on their way to the tomb of St. James the Apostle in Galicia made an extensive expansion of the supply facilities unavoidable. Supported by generous donations and fundraising, the initially small house of the Hospital Brothers grew steadily, becoming more prestigious and soon wealthier than the neighboring Benedictine priory. In 1289, the lay brothers bought the entire estate of their village and the noble *Frères de l'Aumône* thus became the lords of the priory to which they were subject. The legal confusion and the uncertainty about who was whose superior led to growing tensions between the Benedictine monks and the now powerful Hospital Brotherhood. The negotiated compromise to merge the two communities under the leadership of the *Frères de l'Aumône*, who had to pay an annual tribute to the Benedictines, did not solve the problem either. The disputes finally escalated when one of the lay brothers remembered his knightly and defensive past, took off his cowl, grabbed a sword and chased the Benedictines away with an armed troop [9]. The turmoil among the God-fearing men did not go unnoticed by the Holy Father in Rome. In 1297, Pope Boniface VIII ended the feud in the Dauphiné by elevating the Hospital Brothers of St. Anthony to the status of an independent order with the rank of an abbey. The Benedictines had to cede their priory to the new order and retreat to their mother abbey in Montmajour [12].

The independence gained by the Hospital Brothers was undoubtedly a great success, but ultimately, they had won something even more precious, which outshone everything else: the monks of the St. Anthony brotherhood were finally able to take the long-awaited St. Anthony relics into their care.

The holistic ergotism therapy of the Hospital Brothers of St. Anthony

St. Anthony's wine and balm

The founding of the St. Anthony order with the unique mission of exclusively caring for those suffering from ergotism was accompanied by extensive restructuring. The numerous hospitals of the Brotherhood, which were to be expanded into a European-wide network of over 370 facilities by the end of the 15th century, had previously been largely self-governing. The subordination of all local preceptors to the new abbot-general of the mother monastery in Saint-Antoine en Viennois ended their independence [12].

Patient care in the hospitals was increasingly standardized and followed a precise procedure and treatment scheme. Before patients were admitted, they had to undergo a series of preliminary examinations to clearly diagnose ergotism and to filter out any impostors. After confession, the patients were treated with medicinal herbs, which were administered to them in the form of St. Anthony's balm and St. Anthony's wine. On Ascension Day, when the preceptors of the Antonites gathered for the annual general chapter meeting in Saint-Antoine en Viennois, this *saint vinage* was brought into contact with the relics of St. Anthony in order that it become curative. The monks then carted it by the barrel to the hospitals of their order (personal comments by Dr. Hans-Wolfgang Bayer and Dr. Adalbert Mischlewski, 2022) [15, 16].

Medicinal plants

For a long time, it remained a puzzle as to which medicinal plants the monk doctors might have used, as they had kept the formulas for the herbal balm and St. Anthony's wine secret. Attempts to identify the plant species, which are depicted in striking detail on the winged altar of the Antonite monastery in Isenheim, gave botanists, art historians, and pharmacists a hot lead (Fig. 2.3). Of the fourteen plants presented, common vervain (*Verbena officinalis* L.), broadleaf plantain (*Plantago major* L.) and ribwort plantain (*Plantago lanceolata* L.) were particularly emphasized. The painter of the altarpieces, Matthias Grünewald, accentuated the three plants as a pictorial element by setting them apart from the other plants and positioning them together with the coat of

Fig. 2.3 Matthias Grünewald: The Isenheim Altarpiece, St. Anthony's visit to St. Paul Eremita, detail with three medicinal plants: *Right*: Broadleaf plantain (*Plantago major* L.), *center*: Common Vervain (*Verbena officinalis* L.), *left*: Ribwort plantain (*Plantago lanceolata* L.). (© RMN-Grand Palais (Musée Unterlinden) / Stéphane Maréchalle / Mathieu Rabeau)

arms of the Antonite preceptor of Isenheim, Guy Guers, at the feet of St. Anthony. Undoubtedly, the three plants must have had special meaning.

* * *

In fact, these medicinal plants were known as effective remedies for the treatment of inflammatory skin diseases. Secular doctors of the Middle Ages used

Fig. 2.4 Heinrich Füllmaurer (active c. 1530/40): Leonhart Fuchs (1501 Wemding – 1566 Tübingen), German physician and botanist. (Landesmuseum Württemberg, Hendrik Zwietasch, license: Public Domain Mark 1.0)

vervain to treat tumors, skin blemishes, and mouth sores. The Tübingen physician and botanist Leonhart Fuchs (1501 Wemding – 1566 Tübingen) (Fig. 2.4) treats vervain in detail in his *New Kreüterbuch* as a medicinal plant for the internal and external treatment of inflamed tumors:

> "They also heal the rotten and unclean damage / crushed and topically applied. In the same way also the fresh wounds / boiled in water / or crushed when green and topically applied / and the old ones are mixed with honey. (…) Boiled in water / or crushed when green and topically applied / they soothe hot swellings. They' clean and cleanse unclean wounds. The whole herb boiled in wine / heals mouth rot / and ulcers of the mouth that eat through it" [17].

But was vervain also one of the medicinal plants that were used not only to treat "hot swellings" but also for holy fire? Indeed, the physician, theologian, and botanist Otto Brunfels (1488 Mainz – 1534 Bern) wrote the following

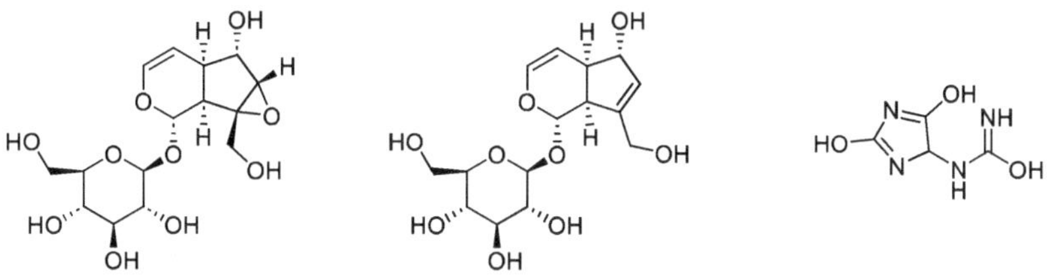

Fig. 2.5 Components of the medicinal plants used

application in his *Contrafayt Kreüterbuch* of 1532: "If said leaves are moistened with vinegar / and applied to St. Anthony's fever / they will cool it down" [18].

Later, natural product chemists isolated catalpol and aucubin (Fig. 2.5) from common vervain. The two substances belong to a class of compounds that are said to have spasmolytic, anti-inflammatory, and vasodilatory effects. Catalpol, aucubin, and allantoin, which relieves pain and supports wound healing, are also found in ribwort plantain and broadleaf plantain [19, 20]. Doctors of traditional medicine deliberately combined medicinal plants that had similar effects. Using this trick, they stabilized the often considerably varying pharmacological activities of the individual drugs. The pharmaceutical effects of the three substances address the main symptoms of the gangrenous ergotism in a remarkably precise manner. It could not have been a coincidence that the Antonites wanted to see these three plants depicted so prominently on their winged altar. But were they really the basis of their healing balm? Did Grünewald perhaps paint Mary Magdalene's ointment jar next to the Holy Rood in the crucifixion scene of the Isenheim Altarpiece in order to visualize the interrelationship between redemption, salvation, and healing from ergotism and *Christus medicus* and *apothecarius*?

Finally, in 1992, what no one had dared to hope for happened: during her research, the French historian Elisabeth Clémentz came across the instructions from 1726 for the production of the St. Anthony's balm at the Isenheim House (info box). The substance and quantity details had been almost completely preserved. Art historians and pharmacists must have been delighted, because the monastery doctors' composition also contained the suspected ribwort and broadleaf plantain plants [21]. Matthias Grünewald had shown us the right way with his paintbrush. The composition of St. Anthony's wine, on the other hand, seems to have been lost forever. Perhaps the monk doctors added common vervain to the *saint vinage* together with plants from the balsam composition? It is possible. Different compositions of the same active ingredients were already common practice at that time.

The formula for St. Anthony's balm

Take 4 pounds ... 4 pounds tallow – 4 pounds lard – 4 pounds spruce resin – 4 ounces yellow wax – 4 ounces turpentine – 2 ounces verdigris – cabbage leaves – nut leaves – leafy goosefoot – lettuce – plantain, both kinds – elder leaves – wound sanicle or *Pedis leonis* – coltsfoot – leaves or grains of "Satz" (?) growing on the walls – leaves of burning herb (nettle?) – blackberry and raspberry leaves and twig tips – Select 6 handfuls of these herbs, boil in a clean kettle and squeeze out the juice [21].

The white St. Anthony's bread

The local and systemic application of medicinal plant extracts, combined with numerous "Our Father" and "Hail Mary" prayers, formed the acute medical care for ergotism patients in the Antonine hospitals. This was supplemented by a strengthening diet to stabilize the weakened patients physically. The so-called St. Anthony's bread ensured long-term healing success and had a special property: the monks baked it with wheat flour. As a predominantly self-pollinating cereal, wheat was almost entirely clear of ergot. The change in diet from contaminated rye products, on which the sick mainly fed at home, to the monastery's white bread stopped the absorption of ergot alkaloids and prevented the holy fire from reappearing.

* * *

White wheat flour has always been surrounded by an aura of purity and exclusivity. The highest quality white bread of Roman antiquity, *panis candidus*, *siligineus* or *primarius*, was baked with precious, finely sieved wheat flour. This highest quality of wheat flour was also an expression of the prosperity and high social status of its consumers. The less well-off could afford the somewhat inferior white *panis secundarius*. For everyone else, they could only afford the *panis plebeius, rusticus* or *militaris*. The quality grades of the breads resulted from the decreasing degree of sieving of the flour and the increase in the husks and sand grains from the millstones [22, 23]. In the European Middle Ages, the *panis primarius* of the Romans became the "bread of nobility", church dignitaries, and the wealthy upper classes in the cities [24–26]. In their bakeries, the monasteries baked bread for their own use or for important visitors and used wheatmeal to brew wheat beer for lent. However, the finely sieved wheat flour was indispensable for the celebration of Holy Mass. Only this precious flour, which to this day may only be mixed with a little water, can be used to bake the blossom-white wafers, which must not crumble during communion.

For members of the urban lower class and the rural population, this expensive wheat flour was simply unaffordable. Their staple foods were coarse oatmeal, millet gruel, and bread baked with cheap, dark, contaminated rye flour. It is therefore not surprising that ergotism was also known as the "peasants' or poor people's disease".

Powerful altars—the Isenheim Altarpiece

The monk doctors integrated St. Anthony's wine, balm, bread, and restorative food into a comprehensive medical treatment concept, which centered around their altars. They were of outstanding therapeutic power for the Antonites, for it was through them that Christ acted as the one and only, the true *medicus*.

Fig. 2.6 Matthias Grünewald: The Isenheim Altarpiece, The Crucifixion. (© RMN-Grand Palais (Musée Unterlinden) / Stéphane Maréchalle / Mathieu Rabeau)

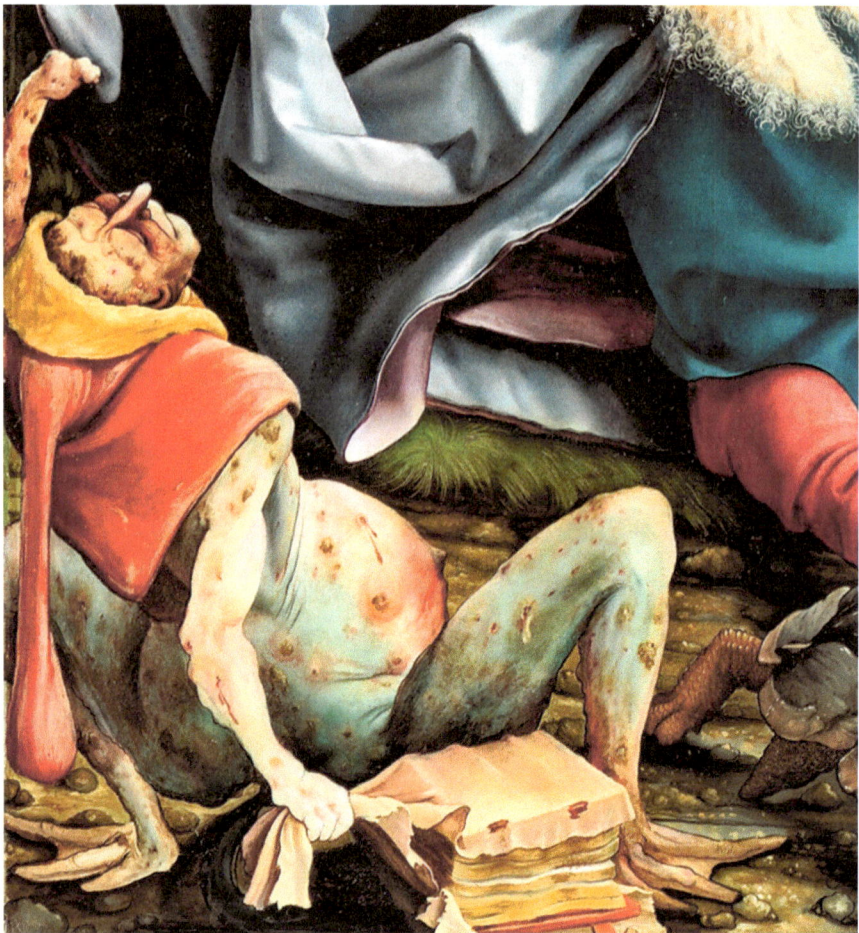

Fig. 2.7 Matthias Grünewald: The Isenheim Altarpiece, Temptation of Saint Anthony, detail depicting *ergotism gangraenosus* (crippling of the left arm, inflamed skin lesions, black coloration of the nostrils and incipient discoloration of the cheeks) and *ergotism convulsivus* (strong backward tilt of the head; sensation of coldness indicated by the blue coloration of the body and the fin-like feet). (© RMN-Grand Palais (Musée Unterlinden) / Stéphane Maréchalle / Mathieu Rabeau)

The preceptor of the Isenheim Antonite monastery, Guy Guers, commissioned the painter Matthias Grünewald and the carver Nikolaus von Hagenau (c. 1445 Hagenau – c. 1526 Strasbourg) to create a winged altar (Fig. 2.6), which they completed after four years in 1516. Guers' polyptych, on which the physical and mental torments of the ergotism patients are depicted in the most intense way (Fig. 2.7), was not created for pilgrims or lay people, and only to a limited extent for his fellow brothers. The healing power of the altar

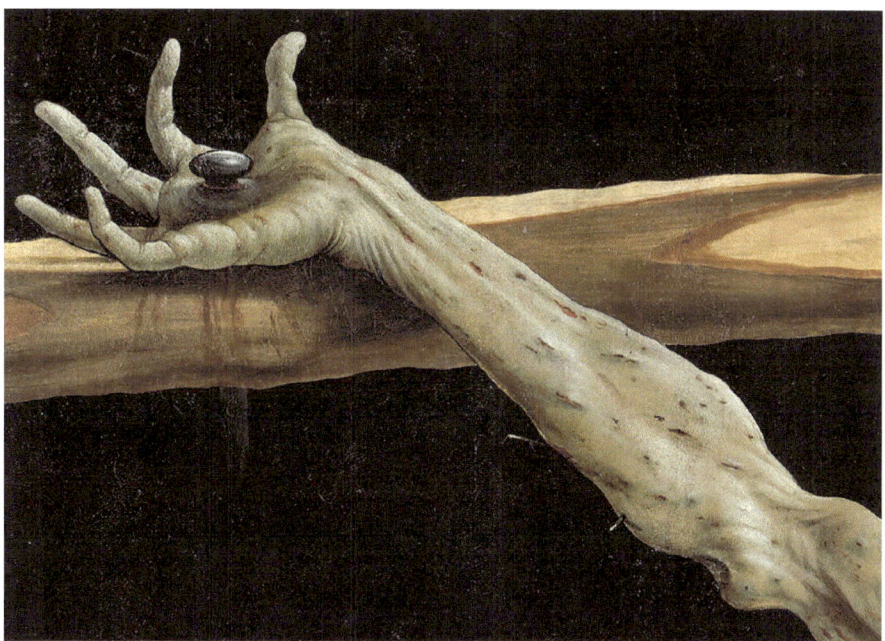

Fig. 2.8 Matthias Grünewald: The Isenheim Altarpiece, The Crucifixion, detail with presumed depiction of cramping of the hand in *ergotism convulsivus*. (© RMN-Grand Palais (Musée Unterlinden) / Stéphane Maréchalle / Mathieu Rabeau)

served solely those tormented by the holy fire who were housed in the hospital. Several times a day, they were taken from the infirmary to the choir room of the church to pray before the crucified one. Grünewald painted the dying Christ on the cross with features of the gangrenous and convulsive ergotism so that the sick could recognize that through their suffering, they were following Jesus on his way of the Cross and could hope for healing and the salvation of their sinful souls through him: "The spread fingers, the colors of the body that correspond to the contemporary description of the disease, the wounds that do not bleed, the blue lips that indicate the respiratory distress of ergotism" (Fig. 2.6, 2.7 and 2.8; [27, 28]).

The hospital order's triple therapy using medicinal plants, poison-free white bread, and prayers brought the desired success. The horrible cries of pain in the wards quieted and the symptoms of the illness slowly subsided. Nevertheless, 6–12% of those infected died of the convulsive form of the disease and only 10% survived St. Anthony's fire in the advanced stages of poisoning. Overall, about 50–75% survived both forms of the disease [29, 30]. Between the 9th and 19th centuries, around 130 ergot epidemics were recorded, during which millions of people were crippled, lost their limbs, died, became disfigured, stigmatized and unable to work, or fell into despair with their families. The Rhine formed a strikingly precise boundary separating the regions where the two forms of the disease predominated. Convulsive ergotism occurred mainly east of the Rhine River in Germany, Russia and in Sweden, whereas the gangrenous form was predominant west of it in France and Flanders [7, 31].

After recovering from the St. Anthony's fire, the patients would leave the hospitals. When they got home, the holy fire usually broke out again. They had obviously not kept the vows they had taken in the monastery and had resumed their sinful lives. The plague forced the poor sinners to repent and turn back. The godly nobles shook their heads uncomprehendingly, continued to enjoy their white noble bread, and stayed healthy.

The "social network" of the Order of St. Anthony

Despite the effective care in the Antonine hospitals, the holy fire had already progressed so far in many patients that their fingers, ears, noses, hands, arms or legs were affected by gangrene and had died off. In the Middle Ages, amputations were only performed in exceptional cases, but in the hospitals of the monasteries, the removal of gangrenous or mummified limbs was part of the everyday business of specially employed surgeons [32]. For those who survived these complicated operations but were unable to work afterwards, it was possible to transfer their assets to the order, for example, to receive care for life as oblates in the monasteries. Those able to work, on the other hand, took on jobs in the cloisters or were called upon to perform special tasks. One convalescent ran errands to Rome and another, whose leg had been removed, was even entrusted with secret missions on behalf of the Isenheim monastery. He organized the confidential correspondence between the preceptor and the city of Strasbourg and carried the secret letters in his hollow wooden leg [33].

Destitute people who could no longer work were forced to ask for alms and thus contributed to the order's provision for them. Beggars are depicted in the paintings of St. Martin as people who had lost their hands or feet due to the disease and could only move around with the help of walking aids: some as a warning against a sinful life, others as a reminder to be merciful (Fig. 2.9). Renaissance painters such as Hieronymus Bosch (c. 1450–1516) (The Temptation of St. Anthony, The Last Judgment) or Pieter Breughel the Elder (1525/30–1569) (The Fight between Carnival and Lent, The Cripples) adopted this imagery from Christian art and used the motif of maimed people as an allegory of earthly suffering [34].

Fig. 2.9 Master of the Rieden Altarpiece (1460/70): St. Martin dividing his cloak. (© Diözesanmuseum Rottenburg Inv. No. 2.1)

Ultimately, all those affected by ergotism, as well as those who were spared, contributed according to their means to supporting a social security system whose origins go back to the ancient Babylonian Empire and to Greek and Roman antiquity. In the City of Tiber, for example, there were death and health insurance funds, state institutions and "funds" that coordinated and financed the care of veterans, invalids, and the poor and sick. Systemically important occupational groups such as bakers and sailors were united in guilds that protected their members from the economic consequences of illness and accidents. With the fall of Western Rome, its differentiated social system also collapsed. In the course of Christianization, hospital orders such as the Brotherhood of St. Anthony re-established this system of care for the sick and disabled, which was supported by donations and public funds, and in which can be seen emerging the basic principles and ethics of later social insurance systems [35–38].

While the Antonites were fighting for the survival of their patients against an unknown enemy, European folk medicine was discovering the pharmaceutical effects of ergot: midwives administered it for womb pains, while doctors recommended it to stop bleeding. For a long time, none of them suspected that the useful horn-like formations in the ears of rye could also cause the terrible St. Anthony's fire. It was only when research by early scientists uncovered this connection that the ergot of midwifery medicine came under fire from conventional medicine. The horror of the recurring epidemic chilled its physicians to the bone. The initial likelihood of the horned rye, *Secale cornutum*, ever being included by medical professors in the pharmacopoeia of gynecology and obstetrics was extremely unfavorable [39, 40]. Nevertheless, that's exactly what was going to happen, though it took time.

References

1. Annales Xantenses. In, *Monumenta Germaniae Historia Tomus II (MGH SS, 2)* (Ed: G.H. Pertz), Impensis Bibliopolii Aulici Hahniani, Hannoverae, 1829, p. 230
2. Flodoardi annales a. 919–966. In, *Monumenta Germaniae Historia Tomus III (MGH SS, 3)* (Ed: G.H. Pertz), Impensis Bibliopolii Aulici Hahniani, Hannoverae, 1839, p. 393
3. E. Wickersheimer, *Ignis sacer* – Bedeutungswandel einer Krankheitsbezeichnung, in *CIBA Symposium* vol 8. 1960), pp. 160–169
4. Sigeberti Gemblacensis chronica cum continuationibus. In, *MGH Scriptores (in folio) 6: Chronica et annales aevi Salici* (Eds.: G.H. Pertz et al.), Hannover, 1844, p. 366
5. G. Barger, *Ergot and Ergotism—A monograph* (Gurney and Jackson, London Edinburgh, 1931), pp. 49–50
6. G. Barger, The Alkaloids of Ergot, in *Handbuch der Experimentellen Pharmakologie (Ergänzungswerk)*, 1st edn. vol 6., ed. by W. Heubner, J. Schüller (Springer, Berlin Heidelberg, 1938), p. 214
7. T.O. Heusinger, *Studien über den Ergotismus insbesondere sein Auftreten im neunzehnten Jahrhundert; aus Anlass einer Epidemie in Oberhessen im Winter 1855/56* (Joh. Aug. Koch, Marburg, 1856), pp. 11–15
8. L.-T. Dassy, *L'abbaye de Saint-Antoine en Dauphiné, Essai Historique et Descriptif* (Baratier Frères et Fils, Grenoble, 1844), pp. 13–21

9. L.-T. Dassy, Le trésor de l'église abbatiale de Saint-Antoine, in *L'Ami de la religion et du roi: journal ecclésiastique, politique et littéraire (01 Janvier)* vol 171. (De Soye et Bouchet, Paris, 1856), pp. 215–218

10. A. Borel d'Hauterive, *Revue historique de la Noblesse* vol. 1 (Bureau de la Publication, Paris, 1841), pp. 352–354

11. *Biographie universelle, ou Dictionnaire de tous les hommes… etc. Tome Premier.* Ed: A. A. F. Baron. (H. Ode, Bruxelles, 1843), p. 91

12. J. Rauch, Der Antoniterorden, in *AMrhKG Year 9*, ed. by L. Lenhart, A. Ph Brück (Druck und Verlag der Jaegerschen Buchdruckerei, Speyer, 1957), pp. 33–39

13. M.-L. Windemuth, *Das Hospital als Träger der Armenfürsorge im Mittelalter* Sundhoffs Archiv, supplement, vol. 36 (Franz Steiner, Stuttgart, 1995), pp. 53–65

14. G.J. Aillaud, L'ergot du seigle et le mal des Ardents, in *Herbes, drogues et épices en Méditerranée: histoire, anthropologie, économie du Moyen-Age à nos jours*, ed. by G.J. Aillaud et al. (Institut de recherches et d'études sur les mondes arabes et musulmans, Centre régional de publication de Marseille (CRNS Editions), Aix-en-Provence, 1990), pp. 57–65

15. K.P. Jankrift, Herren Kranke, arme Siechen: Medizin im spätmittelalterlichen Hospitalwesen, in *Sozialgeschichte mittelalterlicher Hospitäler*, ed. by N. Bulst, K.H. Spieß (Jan Thorbecke, Ostfildern, 2007), pp. 163–164

16. C. Hanebeck, *Der heilige Antonius der Große – Ein Beitrag zur Kulturgeschichte des Schweines unter besonderer Berücksichtigung der Mutterkornvergiftung* (Fachbereich Veterinärmedizin, Freien Universität, Berlin, 2011), p. 30. Diss. Journal no. 3485

17. L. Fuchs, Von Eisenkraut. In, *New Kreüterbuch*. Michael Isingrin, Basel, 1543, p. CCXXVI

18. O. Brunfels, Issenkraut. In, *Contrafayt Kreüterbuch.Nach rechter vollkommener Art/ vnud Beschreibungen der Alten/ besstberümpten Ärtzt/ vormals in Teütscher sprach/ der maßen nye gesehen/ noch im Truck außgangen. Sampt einer gemeynen Inleytung der Kreüter Urhab/ Erkantnüsß/ Brauch/ Lob/ und Herrlicheit.* (Hans Schott, Strasbourg, 1532), p. XLVIII

19. S. Büechi, T. Wegener, Spitzwegerich (Plantago lanceolata) – Neue Erkenntnisse zu einem alten Heilmittel. Schweiz Zschr Ganzheitsmedizin **17**, 167 (2005)

20. A.V.O. de Urbina, M.L. Martin, L. San Roman, L. Cubillo, In vitro antispasmodic activity of peracetylated penstemonoside, aucubin and catalpol. Planta Med **60**, 512 (1994)

21. E. Clémentz, Vom Balsam der Antoniter. Antoniter-Forum **2**, 14 (1994)

22. M. Voigt, Die verschiedenen Sorten von Triticum, Weizen-Mehl und Brod bei den Römern. Rheinisches Mus Philol Rhm **32**, 105 (1876)

23. E. Alberus, Brod. In, *Novum Dictionarii genus*, Chr. Egenolphus, Francoforti, 1540

24. H. Junius, *Nomenclator*. Ex officina Michaelis Mangeri, Augustae, 1592, p. 47

25. G. Imboden, Von Brot und Korn. Brotgetreide und Brotherstellung im Wallis. Ed: Geschichtsforschender Verein Oberwallis (Druckerei Mengis AG, Visp), Blätter aus Walliser Gesch **42**, 65 (2010)

26. H. v. Bruiningk, *Zur Geschichte des Anbaues von Feldfrüchten in Livland im Mittelalter*. In, *Sitzungsberichte der Gesellschaft für Geschichte und Altertumskunde der Ostsee Provinzen Russlands* 702.Versammlung am 10. Januar 1907. (W.F. Häcker, Riga, 1908), pp. 3–5

27. I. Karle, Die Passion Christi und menschliche Passionsgeschichten – Der Isenheimer Altar von Matthias Grünewald, in *Dem Schmerz begegnen: Theologische Deutungen* p, vol 244., ed. by K. Greschat, C. Jahnel (transcript, Bielefeld, 2021), pp. 244–247

28. C. Dietrichs, *Woran stirbt Christus? Und warum? – Die Kreuzigungstafel des Isenheimer Altars von Mathis Gothart Nithart, genannt Grünewald*, 2nd edn. (Books on Demand, Norderstedt, 2017), p. 90

29. F. Sidler, Das Mutterkorn in Vergangenheit und Gegenwart. Heimatkd des Wiggertales **15**, 14 (1954)

30. F. Eichholtz, *Lehrbuch der Pharmakologie – Im Rahmen einer allgemeinen Krankheitslehre für praktische Ärzte und Studierende*, 3.4. edn. (Springer, Berlin Heidelberg, 1944), pp. 97–99

31. A. Hirsch, *Handbook of Geographical and Historical Pathology* vol. 2 (The New Sydenham Society, London, 1885), pp. 203–216

32. F. Messmer, *Karl Lang: Die Wissenschaftlichen Publikationen in ihrer medizingeschichtlichen Bedeutung: Bilder zur Geschichte der Chirurgie* (Allitera, 2008), p. 75

33. E. Clémentz, Die Isenheimer Antoniter: Kontinuität vom Spätmittelalter bis in die Frühzeit, in *Funktions- und Strukturwandel Spätmittelalterlicher Hospitäler im Europäischen Vergleich*, ed. by M. Matheus (Franz Steiner, Stuttgart, 2005), p. 164

34. V.H. Bauer, *Das Antonius-Feuer in Kunst und Medizin* (Springer, 1973), pp. 76–112

35. M. Wagner-Braun, Die frühe historische Entwicklung der berufsständischen Krankenversicherung, in *Zur Bedeutung berufsständischer Krankenkassen innerhalb der privaten Krankenversicherung in Deutschland bis zum Zweiten Weltkrieg* (Franz Steiner, Stuttgart, 2002), pp. 26–28

36. M. Henkel, Historische Formen sozialer Politik bis zur Französischen Revolution, in *Sozialpolitik in Deutschland und Europa* (Druckerei Sömmerda, Erfurt, 2002), pp. 13–15

37. R. Waltermann, § 3 Geschichte der sozialen Sicherung in der industriellen Gesellschaft, in *Sozialrecht*, 10th edn. (C.F. Müller, Heidelberg, 2012), pp. 22–23

38. S.A. Moebus, *Die soziale Versorgung im badischen Heerwesen und ihre Politik 1771 bis 1848/53. Soziale Verpflichtung oder Staatspolitisches Kalkül?* (University of Heidelberg, 2011), pp. 3–27. Dissertation

39. Joh. Chr. T. Schlegel, *Disputationem de Metastasi In Morbis. Praefatio Docet Secale Cornutum Perperam A Nonnullis ab Infamia Liberari*, Ex Officina Straussii, Jenae, 1771

40. S.A.D. Tissot, *Nachricht von der Kriebelkrankheit und ihren wahrscheinlichen Ursachen, aus dem Genusse des Mutterkorns*, Johann Gottfried Müller, Leipzig, 1771

3

Unraveling the mystery of gangrenous and convulsive ergotism: a beacon for the Order of St. Anthony, a dilemma of the ergot remedy in medicine

Protestant doctors of the Renaissance investigate ergot

Traditional Chinese and Greek medical practitioners knew of a sweet grass medicine that was almost certainly based on the pharmacological effects of ergot alkaloids. But it was not until the 15th century, mentioned in a Nuremberg manuscript in 1474, that ergot appeared in European pharmacology as a specifically listed ingredient in prescriptions (Fig. 3.1): a powder made from laurel, (scented) Solomon's seal/dittany, and rye mother (= ergot), which was to be taken with warm wine to alleviate abdominal or uterine complaints:

> "Fur die helf muter.
> Item fur die heffmutter oder permutter. Nÿm lorper würcz vnd weÿdwurcz rocken muter gepuluert vnd yn wein getruncken warm" [1].

It was to be another hundred years, till the end of the 16th century, before this strange formation in the ears of rye became the subject of research for a new generation of physicians and botanists who had been trained at the European universities of the Renaissance. They all had one intriguing thing in common (and the Antonites may have been horrified by it): without exception, they had grown up in Protestant homes that belonged to the circle of reformers Martin Luther and Huldrych Zwingli. These early scientists investigated the medical effects of the sclerotium and began to publish their findings. One of the most renowned among them was the Frankfurt city doctor and publisher, Adam Lonicer (info box 1).

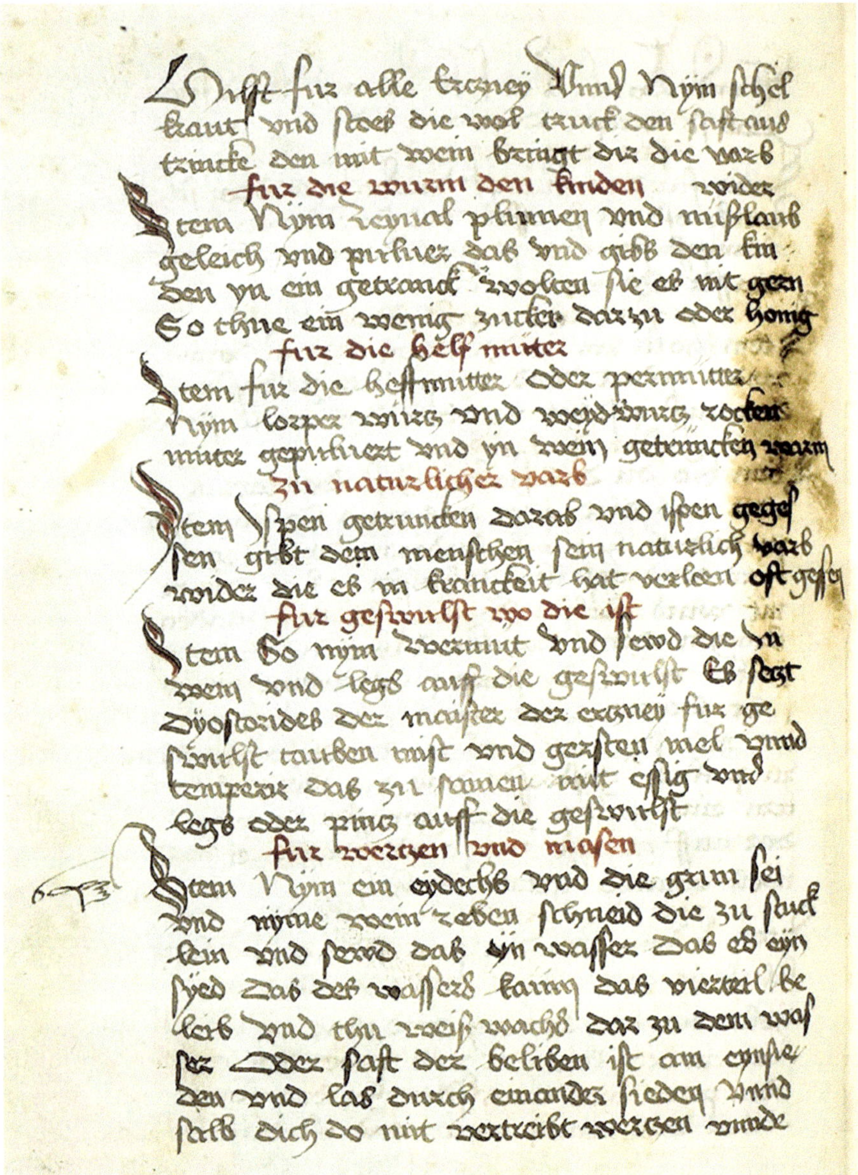

Fig. 3.1 Ergot as a component of a medicinal recipe in a Nuremberg manuscript from 1474. (Heidelberg University Library)

Info box 1: Adam Lonicer

In 1526, Landgrave Philipp I of Hesse introduced the Reformation into his dominion and dissolved the monasteries in his land for the "common good". In 1527, Philipp founded the oldest Protestant university, still in existence today in Marburg, and transferred to it the extensive estates of the expropriated Antonite Preceptory General in Grünberg. Adam Lonicer was born into a Protestant family of scholars near the river Lahn in 1528. His father, Johannes Lonicer, professor of Greek, Hebrew, and theology at the new university, was a confidant of the reformers Martin Luther and Philipp Melanchthon.

Adam studied medicine and botany in Marburg and Mainz. Upon being awarded his doctorate degree, he married Magdalena Egenolff, the daughter of the Frankfurt book printer Christian Egenolff, in 1554. In the same year, Lonicer was appointed successor to the Frankfurt city physician Eucharius Rösslin the Younger. After the death of his father-in-law, the bustling physician took over the management of the publishing house in 1555, where he began publishing his *Kreuterbuch* (Book of medical plants) in 1557. Together with the herbals that Egenolff had previously published, Lonicer's book of medicinal plants in 24 editions became one of the most popular botanical publications of the Renaissance in Germany [2].

Johann Theodor de Bry (1561–1623): Adam Lonicer (1528 Marburg – 1586 Frankfurt a. M.), German physician, botanist, and publisher. (Wellcome Collection. Public Domain Mark)

In the new edition of *Kreuterbuch* published in 1582, he added a new paragraph to the chapter *Rocken oder Korn/Siligo* (Rye or Grain) and described the occurrence and appearance, as well as the dosage, formulation, and gynecological indications of the *Kornzapffen* (= ergot) (Fig. 3.2):

"Nota: Von den Kornzapffen/ Latinè Claui Siliginis. Man findet offtmals an den ähren deß Rockens oder Korns lange schwartze harte schmale Zapffen/ so beneben vnd zwischen dem Korn/ so in den ähren ist/ herauß wachsen/ vn sich lang herauß thun/ wie lange Neglin anzusehen/ seind innwendig weiß/ wie das Korn/ vnd seind dem Korn gar vnschädlich. Solche Kornzapffen werden von den Weibern für ein sonderliche Hülffe vnd bewerte Artzney für das auffsteigen vnd wehethumb der Mutter gehalten/ so man derselbigen drey etlich mal einnimpt vnd isset" [3].

"Note: On the cone of rye/grain/ *Latinè Claui Siliginis*. One often finds on the ears of the rye or grain those long black hard narrow cones/ betwixt and between the grain/ that grow out of the ears long/ and look like long nails/ and are internally white/ like the grain/ and are not harmful to the grain. Such grain cones are regarded by women as a great aid and proven medicine for the pain and wandering of the womb, if one takes and ingests three of these several times."

This brief introduction to the *Kornzapffen* as a medication for painful uterine conditions (menstrual pain) marks the official introduction of the sclerotia of *Claviceps purpurea* into medicine, as well as the zero hour of ergot research with its active agents.

Only a few years later, the son of another member of Martin Luther's inner circle reported on his medical experiences with the long black grain(s) of rye ears. The Nuremberg city physician and botanist Joachim Camerarius the Younger (1534 Nuremberg – 1598 Nuremberg), whose father was a friend of Philipp Melanchthon, recommended in his 1586 *Kreutterbuch* that ergot be placed under the tongue to stop bleeding in the oral cavity [4].

The family of the botanist and personal physician to the Counts of Stolberg, Johannes Thalius the Younger (1542 Erfurt – 1583 Peseckendorf), was also acquainted with the German reformer. His father, Johannes Thalius the Elder, became the parish priest of Erfurt on Luther's recommendation, making him one of the first German Protestant pastors. During his time in Stolberg, Thalius the Younger compiled a list of the flora of the Harz Mountains and noted the hemostatic effect of the "rye mother". He dedicated the work to his friend Joachim Camerarius the Younger and, fortunately, sent the manuscript to him in Nuremberg as early as 1577. Thalius the Younger became the city physician in Nordhausen in 1581, but in 1583 he suffered a fatal accident with his cart while driving to a patient. In 1588, Camerarius published the treatise on the flora of the Harz Mountains, the *Sylva hercynia*, posthumously

Von Kreutern.   CCLXXXV

A   Die beste zeit ihrer distillierung ist im ende deß Mayen.
Gerstenkraut Wasser ist gut in die Augen gethan/für die bösen bresten der Augen/ dann es macht sie lauter vnd klar.

Speltz/   Zea.   Cap. ccclrir.

Spelts oder Dinckel/Einkorn/S. Peters Korn/ Græcis, zaa. Latinis, Zea, Semen, Vulgò Spelta. *Ital.Biada.Gall.Peaulte.Hispa.Biada.*
Spelts hat Körner gleich der Gerst/vnd speiset minder dann die Gerst/reucht wol/speiset gar wenig/hat viel Kleyen/ist vnverdäuwlich/ weychet den Bauch. Ist feucht vnd kalt. Seine Wurtzel stehen tieff in der Erden/ist allen Vögeln ein angeneme Speiß. Korn mit Gersten gemischet/gibt gut Brot.

¶ Krafft vnd wirckung.

Spelts ist gut der feuchten Lungen/harten Husten/ vnd weychet die Husten. Brust. Ist auch gut zu aller Geschwulst/in Wein vnd Essig gesotten/ Geschwulst, vnd darmit bestrichen oder vbergelegt. Ist auch dem Augengeschwer/der Augen geschwer, Wrner genandt/fast gut.

Rocken oder Korn/ Siligo. Cap. ccclrr.

Rocken oder Korn/darauß man das gemeine Brot machet/halten wir für das Siligo,oder Siligo frumentacea Columellæ,vnd Secale. *Ital.Segala.Gall.Seigle.* Ist jederman an vnsern orten wol bekandt/ wächßt auff eintzigen Halmen/obenauß mit ähern/hat ein dünne zaßlechte Blüet/so auß den ähern wie kleine fäßlin herauß henckt/vnd abfellt/in

Korn/Siligo,

ähern steckt die rund lange frucht/ in jren Hülßlin eintzig vnderschei den/offt in einer ähern sechtzig vnd auch mehr.
¶ Hamelkorn Columellæ Far candidum, Dioscoridi Tragus cerealis. Ist deß wilden Korns Geschlecht / gibt geringere Nahrung dañ Spelts/hat viel Spreuwer. In der speiß gebraucht/weychts den Bauch.

Hamelkorn,

Nota: Von den Kornzapffen/ Latinè, Claui Siliginis: Man findet offtmals an den ähern deß Rockens oder Korns lange schwartze harte schmale Zapffen/so beneben vnnd zwischen dem Korn/so in den ähern ist/herauß wachsen/vñ sich lang herauß thun/wie lange Neglin anzusehen/seind inn wendig weiß/wie das Korn/vnd seind dem Korn gar vnschädlich.

Solche Kornzapffen werden von den Weibern für ein sonderliche Hülffe vnd bewerte Artzney für das auffsteigen vnd wehethumb der Mutter gehalten/so man derselbigen drey etlich mal einnimpt vnd jsset.

Mutter,

¶ Krafft

Fig. 3.2 *Kreuterbuch*, CCLXXXV, *Rocken oder Korn*/Siligo, Adamum Lonicerum, 1582, Zu Franckfort/ bey Christian Egenolffs seligen Erben, 2 Nat 91, fol. 285r. (© Augsburg State and City Library)

under his friend's name. Thalius' *Florilegium* is considered the oldest botanical work of its kind [5–8].

Marburg medical professors develop a "therapy" for "Crawly Disease"

When massive waves of convulsive ergotism hit Hesse and southwest Germany in 1596 and 1597, the medical faculty of the University of Marburg was asked to clarify the causes of "Crawly Disease" (crawling sensations on the skin) and suggest possible treatments. In their 1597 report, the Marburg medical professors recognized the spreading plague as an "infectious poisoning" mainly caused by food, such as "badly baked and unclean bread, malnutrition, unripe fruit, but also by hunger and hardship among the poor" [9]. As treatment, the university physicians recommended, in addition to "a good diet and the necessary purging, a crawly disease electuary consisting of drastic purgatives, castoreum, saffron, (…) and roasted human skulls" [10]. Emetics and diaphoretic agents were just as much a part of the treatments as cat lard and earthworm oil. If the Antonites had ever studied the recommendations of the Protestant professors, they would undoubtedly have seen their reservations about the new doctrine and its academic protagonists confirmed. The Marburg treatment could only be seen as continuing the suffering of the patients by other means. Meanwhile, healthcare in the Antonine hospitals remained the gold standard.

A Swiss botanist tries his hand at the nature of ergot

At the time, the medical training curriculum specifically included the study of botany. Its elevated status in the canon of medicine was expressed by the fact that it was nothing other than a synonym for *materia medica* (lit. medical material). Even the first professorship of botany, which was established at the University of Padua in 1533, was not independent, but part of the Faculty of Medicine. In university medicinal gardens, students learned to identify medicinal plants according to their characteristic features and to use them correctly as phytotherapeutics. Doctors were also botanists. In summer, they studied the structure of plants, while for logical reasons in winter the anatomy of the human body was the subject of the curriculum.

While physicians had previously focused on the pharmaceutical effects of ergot, as botanists, they now took a closer look at this strange black-purple grain. First, it had to be grouped into the system of living organisms. The only problem was that nobody had the slightest idea what it was. The first person to attempt the taxonomic classification of this horn-like kernel on an ear of rye was the Swiss botanist and physician Caspar Bauhin (info box 2).

Info box 2: Caspar Bauhin

Caspar Bauhin was born in Basel in 1560. His father, Jean the Elder (1511 Amiens – 1582 Basel), was a loyal follower of Calvinism and the personal physician to the sister of King Francis I of France, Margaret of Angoulême. During the Huguenot persecutions, despite royal protection, Jean the Elder and his family only narrowly escaped the waves of arrests by leaving Paris via Antwerp to Basel in 1542, where he set up as a surgeon. Judging by the inscription on his gravestone, where he is honored as a *clinicus elegans, chirurgus felix*, he was also a highly respected doctor in Basel.

Like his older brother Jean the Younger (1541 Paris – 1613 Montbéliard), Caspar studied medicine and botany in Basel and undertook study trips to Bologna, Padua, Montpellier, and Tübingen. Caspar, Jean the Elder, and Jean the Younger had scholarly exchanges with the Swiss universal scholar Conrad Gessner, whose mentors had been the Swiss reformers Huldrych Zwingli and Heinrich Bullinger. In 1589, Caspar Bauhin became the first full professor of anatomy and botany at the University of Basel. He was subsequently appointed president of the university several times, and in 1614 became Basel's city physician. He introduced a binomial nomenclature (genus and species name) for the scientific naming of plants, which the Swedish taxonomist Carl von Linné later enforced and extended to zoology [11].

Peter Aubry (1596–1666): Caspar Bauhin (1560 Basel – 1624 Basel). (Wellcome Collection CC BY 4.0)

GASPARD BAUHIN.

433   LIBER PRIMVS SECTIO QVARTA CAP. XVII.   434

in linteo capiti circumligata. Oculis illacry-A
mantibus collyrium fit ex granis combu-
ftis, puluerifatis, & vino albo mixtis. Vlce-
ribus à frigore hyberno caufatis hic puluis
vtiliter afpergitur, vt & ad vlcera antiqua,
cum rutæ combuftæ pari dofi. Vulneribus
farina diligenter cribrata & infperfa icho-
rem (Bluttwaſſer vocant) fiftit. Ad aluum
follicitandam ex farinæ partibus duabus, fa-
lis vna, cum albumine oui in paftam mixtis,
fuppofitoria formantur. Oleum, etiam fit
fecalinum, hoc pacto : Ex granis, duabus B
laminis ferreis calidifsimis exprimunt: alij
craffe contundunt, bocciæ indunt, & ar-
te chymica oleum eliciunt: alij contufa, pa-
læ indunt, torrent, vino generofo irroran-
do, calidifsima torculari fubdunt & exprimunt. Cuius olei vfus ad maculas, afperi-
tates cutis, impetigines, fiffuras & achores
infantum. Manuum s pedumque rimis,
cinis culmorum aqua fubactus & illitus me-
detur. Apoftemata calida maturat farina, in
aqua in modum pultis decocta & impofita : C
nam emollit & pus mouet. Ad capillitium
pulchrum, lixiuium ex fpicis commenda-
tur: huius paleæ t & corticum arantiorum
decoctum, capillitium flauum & nitidum,
frequenti muliercularum experimento, ef-
ficit. Furfuribus Secales, pleraque quæ &
Triticeis (de quibus fupra) tribuuntur :
quod fi cum Rutæ fucco coquantur in modum cataplafmatis, mammis poft partum
dolentibus & induratis vtiles erunt. Cul-
mis lentis, flexilibus, aqua madefactis, viti-D
lium vice, maximè ad vites alligandas utun-
tur, & noftri Schaub vocant. Nunc pauca
de ipfius Secales luxuria afpergamus.

SECALE LVXVRIANS : In Secale fæpif-
fimè accidit, ut fpicæ quædam, poftquam
flores deciderunt, ac femina iam augmen-
ta fufcipere incipiunt, vitium aliquod in
granis contrahant : videmus quædam femina longiùs ex fuis vtriculis feu glumis
protendi, ac in mediocrem etiam crafsi-E
tiem excrefcere, quorum quædam in cor-
niculi modum recuruantur, quæ omnia ni-
grum colorem foris contrahunt, intus ve-
rò candida farina denfioris materiæ con-
ftant. Hoc contingit, vbi tempore quo flo-
ret copiofæ funt pluuiæ, & ijs calor folis
feruidior fuccedit : fortè quia maior fucci
copia, quàm ad grani iuftum alimentum

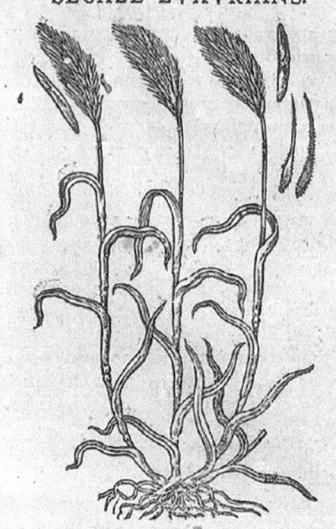

SECALE LVXVRIANS.

opus eft, attrahitur, ita vt corticem adhuc
tenerum rumpi & internam fubftantiam in
maiorem molem augeri neceffe fit. Re-
fert Plinius u inter vitia fegetum & luxuriam effe, cum onerata fertilitate pro-
cumbunt : quibus verbis Plinium hoc i-
pfum notare voluiffe, ftatuimus : etfi fint
qui velint eum id vitij innuere voluiffe,
quod Theophraftus x φυλλομανίας, feu infa-
nam foliorum luxuriam vocauit. Lonicero
Germanicè Kornzapffen, id eft, Claui fili-
ginis, dicuntur : at Thuringis, monente
Thalio y Rockenmütter, hoc eft, Secales mater, vulgò dicitur, quo ad fiftendum fangui-
nem vtuntur. Nouimus quendam qui in
frequenti gingiuarum hæmorrhagia, ho-
rum granorum fola in ore detentione, feli-
ci cum fucceffu, vfus eft. In vterinis dolo-
ribus mulierculæ, grana tria, iteratis vici-
bus affumta, commendant.

SECALE LATIFOLIA PEREGRINA : cul-
mis exfurgit candicantibus, rotundis, ftria-
tis, quibus fpica palmum longa, craffa, ari-
ftis longifsimis, & vt in vulgari, tenuifsi-
mis denticulis afperis armata, infidet : folia
habet cubitum longa, vnciam lata & per
marginem leuiter exafperata : grana non vi-
dimus : fpicam & folia ex horto Clarifsimi
Contareni, Senatoris Veneti habemus.

s Matth. Lobel.   t Aduerf.   u lib. 18. cap. 17.   x 8. hift. 7.   y in Hærcyniæ titulo de Gramine.

EE

Fig. 3.3 *Pinax Theatri Botanici*, Caspar Bauhin (1658) [13]: *Secale luxurians*. (Basel University Library, Lo I 21, p. 434)

In 1596 Bauhin concluded that ergot-bearing rye must be a new species. In accordance with his binomial nomenclature, he gave the new rye species the name *Secale luxurians* (i.e. Luxuriant Rye). He thus wrongly assigned ergot to the plant kingdom, where it was to remain for the next 250 years [12]. After Bauhin's death, his son Johann Caspar (1606 Basel – 1685 Basel) depicted the Luxuriant Rye for the first time in the botanical treatise *Pinax Theatri Botanici* (1658) (Fig. 3.3; [13]).

Doctors and botanists had done their utmost to get clarity about the nature and medicinal benefits of ergot, but before they would finally recognize that it was the cause of ergotism, certain challenges with personnel stood in the way. To overcome them, none other than the French statesman Jean-Baptiste Colbert himself had to appear before his king. At this point, he was not even remotely thinking about ergot.

The Sun King initially says *"Non!"*

In 1666, Jean-Baptiste Colbert, likely the most important minister of King Louis XIV, founded the *Académie Royale des Sciences*. The initial twenty-one academics appointed by Colbert were assigned to either *Sciences Mathématiques* (geometry, mechanics, astronomy) or *Sciences Physiques* (chemistry, anatomy, botany). One of the society's first projects was the publication of a *Histoire naturelle des plantes*. This encyclopedia was envisaged a grandiose work of the highest scientific standard, in which the plants were to be depicted in unprecedented detail. But by 1670, the mammoth French botany project had already stalled. With the appointment of the physician and botanist Denis Dodart to the Academy, it was hoped that the ambitious project would be brought to a successful conclusion with fresh impetus (info box 3) [14–16].

Info box 3: Denis Dodart

Denis Dodart grew up in a solid middle-class family in Paris. His father Jean worked here as a notary, and his mother Marie, née Dubois, was the daughter of a lawyer at the Supreme Court of the monarchy in Paris, the *Parlement*. His parents loved literature and were the proud owners of an impressive library. As members of two families of legal practitioners, they were related to a professional group that was one of the driving forces behind the *Fronde parlementaire*. This revolt of the French nobility, lawyers, and judges of the Paris *Parlement* in 1648 was sparked by the refusal of the Supreme Court to approve the Crown's new tax laws. At the same time, the movement was directed against the policies of Cardinal Mazarin and the mother of King Louis XIV, who was still a minor. The aim was to regain the former feudal rights and rights of objection of the Paris *Parlement*.

The Dodarts attached great importance to a comprehensive education, and Denis' curriculum ranged from Latin, Greek, and literature to learning various musical instruments. He began studying medicine at the Sorbonne, graduating as a *Docteur-Régent* in 1660. In 1666, he took up the chair of pharmacy and became personal physician to Anne Geneviève de Bourbon-Condé, the Duchess of Longueville, a major driving force behind the *Fronde des Princes*. In 1673, Dodart was admitted to the Royal Academy of Sciences. His publication *Mémoires pour servir à l'histoire des plantes*, which appeared in 1676, became a masterpiece of botanical illustrations [14, 16].

Charles-Nicolas Cochin the Elder (1688–1754): Denis Dodart (1634 Paris – 1707 Paris), French physician and botanist

Claude Perrault, one of Colbert's closest advisors during the planning phase of the academy, was a staunch supporter of Dodart's admission. He was instrumental in the appointment of members to the *Sciences Physiques* and initiated the compilation of the *Histoire naturelle des animaux et des plantes* in 1667. Perrault's praise of Dodart's personality and scientific brilliance was surprising in that the botanist had not yet attracted attention with significant publications or highly regarded research contributions. Nevertheless, Perrault was able to convince Jean-Baptiste Colbert that Dodart was the ideal person to elaborate the encyclopedia of plants. Appointments to the Academy required the approval of Louis XIV and, as a rule, this was a mere formality. The first scientists were appointed in 1666 following a consultation between the king and Colbert [17]. But this personnel matter turned out to be extremely tricky. Dodart came from a family of legal practitioners, was a convinced Jansenist, and was closely associated with the hotbed of this religious reform movement, the Abbaye de Port-Royal des Champs. He was thus certain to arouse the king's distrust in two respects.

"The Jansenists were a Catholic group with connections to influential aristocratic clans and families of the Parlement. It relativized the importance of free will for the attainment of salvation and instead emphasized the role of divine grace. From the point of view of Sorbonne and Jesuit theologians, this was an essentially reformist position. In addition, the founder of Jansenism (as well as parts of the Catholic elite) had criticized France's war against other Catholic states (Mars Gallicus, 1635). Against this multi-layered background of the formation of a politically and religiously oppositional and influential group, the Jesuit-influenced French court urged various popes to issue several formal condemnations (1653, 1656, 1705, 1713)" (pers. comm. by Prof. Mark Hengerer, 2023).

In 1648, the Jansenists supported the revolt of the French nobility and the legal practitioners of the Paris *Parlement* against the king and his government, which escalated into a civil war and became a traumatic experience for ten-year-old Louis. In 1649, he had to flee by night from Paris to Saint-Germain-en-Laye with his younger brother Philippe, his mother Anne of Austria, and the reigning minister of France, Cardinal Jules Mazarin, to be safe from the insurgents [18]. Influenced by these circumstances, the king later no longer trusted the nobility and sensed a smoldering danger of conspiracy among the Jansenists [19, 20]. It is therefore no wonder that he had grave misgivings about the appointment of a Jansenist scion of a legal practitioner's family to the Royal Academy of Sciences. Louis had previously shown how he was accustomed to dealing with such personnel issues. He had rejected the appointment of a nobleman out of hand who was suspected of being a Jansenist. However, when he was assured that the candidate was an atheist, the aspirant received his certificate of appointment without further ado [20].

Colbert must have pulled out all the stops to persuade him, because in 1673 the monarch finally gave his approval for Dodart's appointment. It is impressive that the king's first minister went through such trouble to appoint a suitable botanist for the *Histoire naturelle des plantes*. However, the ambitious project was never completed and did not go beyond Dodart's *Mémoires pour servir à l'histoire des plantes* (1676) with its lifelike plant illustrations, which required the use of a microscope and all the finesses of copperplate engraving [14].

An unusual triumvirate at the Académie Royale des Sciences gets to work

Colbert soon needed Dodart's medical expertise for a completely different mission: the minister was looking for ways to improve the health situation of the poorer sections of the country's population and entrusted three scientists from the Academy's *Sciences Physiques* with this task.

Dr. Dodart was to become the *spiritus rector* of this group. As an ascetic Jansenist, he preferred to dress modestly. Perhaps he exaggerated this humble trait somewhat, as the scientist, who had now become the doctor to the king and his daughter Marie Anne de Bourbon, walked around dressed so poorly that at one time the princess mistook him for a beggar on the street and wanted to give him alms. Dodart was a doctor who frequently treated noblemen, but throughout his life he took one day off a week to treat sick people—free of charge—who could not even have afforded the quacks at the fairs [21].

The second member of the group was the amateur architect, classical philologist and doctor, Claude Perrault. He played a key role in designing the colonnade façade of the Louvre, which is one of the architectural masterpieces of French classicism. In 1673, Perrault's French translation of *De Architectura* by the Roman architect Vitruvius, the only surviving work of architectural theory from antiquity, was published. The patient workload of his medical practice was manageable, as he only treated family members [21].

Claude Bourdelin completed the scientific triumvirate. Before he was appointed to the Academy, he was the court apothecary to Louis XIV's uncle Gaston de Bourbon, the *Duc d'Orléans*, and had looked after the duke's officers and horses. The original member of the Academy analyzed an impressive number of the kingdom's mineral waters. His preferred separation process was distillation. Once he had also begun to investigate plants chemically, he did not want to abandon his methodology and investigated over 500 representatives of the plant kingdom by extraction and distillation from 1670 until his death in 1699 [22–24].

This triad formed a task force whose main objective was to liaise with doctors in France to determine the nature and extent of the inadequate health care and nutritional situation of the lower echelons of society, and to suggest improvements. In 1674/75, the Paris project group received several letters from doctors in the regions of Sologne, Blois, and Montargis, which were among the main rye-growing areas in France. The Drs. Bellay, Dubé, Thuillier the Younger, and the surgeon Chatton stated in their letters that, in their opinion, ergot must be the cause of St. Anthony's fire. The working group agreed that Dodart should evaluate the various reports and Bourdelin should chemically analyze the "natural" and "spoiled" rye grains sent along (presumably using his beloved distillation process). The letter from Dr. Thuillier the Younger from the medical faculty of the University of Angers was of particular importance. In it, he reported that his father had been convinced that ergot had caused the 1630 epidemic in Sologne. To confirm his hypothesis, Dr. Thuillier the Elder had fed the suspicious grains to chickens, which soon died.

Dodart drew up his conclusions in an official investigation report to the Royal Academy: 1) The ergot of rye is the cause of gangrenous ergotism, 2) The toxins are absorbed via rye bread, 3) Poor people in particular fall ill with it, 4) People must be informed about these connections and instructed to sift out ergot, and 5) Millers are not allowed to grind the ergot grains, which are easily recognizable. In his explanations, he distinguished *bon seigle*, the "good rye", from *seigle cornu*, the "horned rye", from whose direct French Latin translation the official medicinal name *Secale cornutum* was later derived. Dodart's famous letter, published in 1676, was of the utmost urgency [21, 25, 26]. St. Anthony's fire could now be dealt with by simply sifting out the ergot grains, if not …

The personal physician to the Elector Palatine takes a closer look at a patient in the Harz Mountains

In France, the gangrenous ergotism predominated, but east of the Rhine, the convulsive ergotism prevailed. Even though it had long been known that some patients suffered from gangrene and convulsions at the same time, the question remained unanswered as to whether these were two different diseases or whether they could be two different forms of the same disease. Finally, the Swiss physician Johann Conrad Brunner (info box 4) revealed the secret of the second variant of ergotoxicosis, the crawly disease.

Info box 4: Johann Conrad Brunner

Johann Conrad Brunner had studied medicine in Strasbourg, Paris, London, Oxford and Leiden. Together with his father-in-law, the Schaffhausen town physicist Johann Jacob Wepfer, he was called to Heidelberg in March 1685 to provide medical care for the seriously ill Charles II, Elector Palatine. In addition to Wepfer and Brunner's excellent reputations, there was another good reason why these two physicians were given the honor of treating the sovereign: crowned heads could not be careful enough when appointing their personal physicians and therefore preferred doctors who adhered to the same faith as themselves. As the Palatinate was the first Calvinist principality on German soil and the Elector firmly supported Calvin's teachings, Charles II appointed two doctors, Wepfer and his son-in-law, who subscribed to the beliefs of the Swiss reformer Huldrych Zwingli.

When Brunner arrived in Heidelberg (Wepfer was unable to attend), Karl was already terminally ill and died a few months later. His successor, Elector Philipp Wilhelm, was a Catholic, and Brunner had to consider his resignation and loss of office. To Brunner's surprise, he was offered the professorship for physiology, anatomy, and botany at the University of Heidelberg, despite his different beliefs, and his medical services at court remained in demand. The Protestant personal physician to his Catholic sovereign rose to become one of the most respected physicians of his time and was elevated to nobility in 1711. Brunner is regarded as discovering the glands of the twelve-finger intestine (duodenum), which were named after him [27].

Johann Georg Seiler (1663–1740): Johann Conrad Brunner (1653 Diessenhofen – 1727 Mannheim), Swiss physician and physiologist. (Wellcome Collection; CC BY 4.0)

On a trip through the Harz Mountains, a wound doctor—according to Brunner, he was an experienced stone cutter—introduced him to a woman who showed symptoms of both forms of ergotism. Her fingers were "stiff, numb, and gangrenous", and the patient reported "eleven seizures a day". After further explanations from the doctor, there was no longer any doubt in Brunner's mind that the degenerated rye grains were causing both crawly disease and St. Anthony's fire. In 1695, Brunner had his report printed [28, 29].

In the 18th century, doctors were still divided in their assessment of Dodart's and Brunner's research results. While some were convinced of the harmfulness of ergot, others remained skeptical as to whether sclerotium could be the sole cause of crawly disease. They suspected a combination of things, with predisposing factors such as the hardship and poor nutrition of the rural population. A third group, on the other hand, believed that crawly disease was an effect of scurvy, and saw honeydew and mildew, the earth, the air, impure water, garden crops, earth sponges, shriveled dark brown rye grains, wild radish or a kind of "grain caterpillar" as additional causes of the evil [30–32].

While the experts argued, the rural population refused to pick the ergot kernels out of the harvest. Their hunger was too great to waste even the smallest crumbs of food. The sclerotia continued to be ground down and St. Anthony's fire, along with crawly disease, swept through the country as before. Following the devastating number of cases in 1770/71 in northern Germany, Sweden, and France, governments issued decrees to remove the sclerotia from the rye harvest [33, 34]. The scientific basis for this was provided somewhat belatedly in 1778, when the French physician and agronomist Henri-Alexandre Tessier (1741–1837) proved the toxicity of ergot by means of animal dissections [35].

The extinction of the Order of St. Anthony

These decrees led to a significant reduction in the number of ergotism cases but placed the Antonine hospital system under massive pressure. The Antonite monasteries had already been struggling with financial losses. Historically, the St. Anthony's pigs were a lucrative source of income (Fig. 3.4), where a piglet from a litter was donated to the Order. They were identified by little bells attached to their ears and roamed freely around the villages and towns, where they were fed or ate their fill of garbage and acorns found in the woods. The pigs were slaughtered on St. Anthony's Day (January 17) and provided the meat for the meals of the sick and the lard for medicinal herbal ointments in the monastery pharmacies. Even though the pigs were repeatedly involved in accidents (the tinkling of the bells provided little warning), and the cities of the late Middle Ages issued increasingly strict hygiene regulations, the wealthy Antonites were able to retain the privilege of fattening pigs free of charge. It was not until the Reformation that this custom was dealt a severe blow, when the number of St. Anthony's pigs was drastically reduced [36, 37].

In the wake of the rise of Protestantism and the Huguenot Wars in France, donations, endowments, and income from alms collections *the Quest*, had declined, raising red flags on the monasteries' balance sheets. Like all other mendicant orders, the subsequent "alms collection ban" had also hit the Antonites hard, as they had been true masters in organizing fundraising campaigns. This documented right to beg for goods and money in a certain area had been abolished by the decision of the Council of Trent (1545–1563).

Somehow the devil was at work, and everything seemed to be conspiring against the Antonites. The introduction of the potato in Europe brought further trouble to the hospital order. Although the tuber had been on the tables in Spain since the middle of the 16th century, farmers in France and Germany were suspicious of it and preferred to feed it to their pigs. The tireless efforts of the pharmacist and agronomist, Antoine-Augustin Parmentier (1737–1813), to promote potato cultivation in France could only modestly increase the acceptance of the new foodstuff. When the famine struck France in 1770, farmers had no choice but to include the foreign-inspired *pomme de terre* on their menus.

The growing popularity of the potato and the decreed ergot-culling accelerated the decline in bed occupancy rates at the Antonine hospitals. The Order should have freed itself from its economic downward spiral before this, but it was not able to do so. Its seven-hundred-year-old founding statutes of focusing on the care of ergotism sufferers, together with its patron saint, had been innovative and powerful. But now their mission had become insurmountable. As the Antonites did not open up the hospitals to treat other diseases, the number of empty hospitals dramatically increased. There were also internal disputes: monks brought lawsuits against their leadership, and weak preceptors were unable to remedy mismanagement, indiscipline, and financial inconsistencies. The Antonites had already experienced many challenges, such as the extensive expropriation of their land in the German territories at the beginning of the Reformation. These difficult times had come and gone, but now threatening cracks appeared in the mighty monastery walls, under which two groups of miners were driving their tunnels [38].

The Archbishop of Toulouse, Etienne-Charles de Loménie de Brienne, recommended to King Louis XV that the abuses in the monasteries and their profitability be investigated. The Prince of the Church's request was granted and the *Commission des Réguliers* was convened, with de Loménie de Brienne

Fig. 3.4 Lucas Cranach the Elder (1472 Kronach – 1553 Weimar): St. Anthony (1515/20) (© Land Sachsen-Anhalt)

conveniently appointed as its spokesman. The religious orders were caught in the crosshairs of politics, but also in the sights of the pioneers of Enlightenment. Their criticism of the monastic way of life was of a fundamental nature, in keeping with the spirit of the times. The question was openly raised as to what nuns and monks contributed to the common good. The Swiss philosopher Jean-Jacques Rousseau had already formulated the answer to this in his work *Du Contrat social* (1762), when he principally deduced from his concept of freedom: "To renounce liberty is to renounce being a man, to surrender the rights of humanity and even its duties" [39]. In addition to the clash of mutually exclusive intellectual movements, there was also something more profane. Monastery ownership meant secure benefices for the secular clergy and commendators while the kingdom was in a chronic financial crisis. This imbalance drew governmental interest.

The *Commission des Réguliers'* financial and profitability analysis came to a devastating conclusion. Many monasteries were understaffed and their financial situation was not sustainable. Their plight was partly out of their control, as the commendators had limited the number of monks in the monasteries to which they had been enfeoffed, in order to improve their income. The hammer of the Archbishop of Toulouse came down relentlessly on the religious orders, and Etienne-Charles de Loménie de Brienne listened neither to the pleas from within the country nor to the protests from Rome. As a result, 458 male monasteries alone fell victim to the ordered restructuring of monastic estates for purely economic reasons. Their property was secularized or assigned to the dioceses.

The Prince of the Church also rang the death knell for the Antonites. His commission presented them with three options: complete disintegration, secularization of their community, or unification with another order. On October 25, 1774, at eight o'clock in the evening, the Preceptors General of the Antonites gathered in Saint-Antoine en Viennois around their 35th Abbot General Jean-Marie Navarre de Lyon, stood before the relics of St. Anthony, and struck up the hymn *Veni Creator Spiritus*. The final meeting of the General Chapter then began at which it was unanimously decided to join the Order of Malta. Nine months later, the *Freytägige Münchnerzeitung* of July 21, 1775, informed its readership of the Order's decision and wrote: "Two hours later they sent their deliberation by courier to [the royal] court, which expressed its satisfaction with it in a letter of reply" [40]. After two years of accession negotiations, Pope Pius VI approved the unification treaty. The Order of the Knights of Malta took in the Antonites, who were no longer permitted to bear arms. Just in case … [38, 41–44].

The rocky road of turning *Secale cornutum* into conventional medicine

Midwives use ergot as a uterotonic, conventional doctors shake their heads

Dodart's and Brunner's reports had revealed one thing: ergot was both a terrible poison and a useful medicine. Its careful application belonged in the hands of trained physicians who had long been using ergot to stop nosebleeds and other hemorrhages [45, 46]. At the same time, conventional physicians were suspicious of the practice of midwives who administered the ergot medicine as an oxytocic agent. In 1709, the medical student Johann Andreas Planer completed his doctoral thesis under Rudolph Jacob Camerarius (info box 5), Professor of Medicine at the Eberhard Karls University of Tübingen. Planer praised the haemostatic properties of ergot and emphasized that it was the only aid in the treatment of lochiostasis. Midwives, however, would use ergot in obstetrics. The student and his teacher viewed this practice in obstetrics with great personal distrust as well as with conventional medical skepticism. Planer considered its administration as an oxytocic agent to be negligent humbug (*sub vano forte praetextu*; perhaps under a false pretext), Maximilian Rein, 2022 [47].

Info box 5: Rudolph Jacob Camerarius

Rudolph Jacob Camerarius came from a distinguished family of physicians and pharmacists in Tübingen. His father, Elias Rudolf, was the first Professor of Medicine at the University of Tübingen to be admitted to the *Academia Naturae Curiosorum*, today's Leopoldina (National Academy of Sciences), in 1668, being awarded the surname Hector I. Rudolph Jacob studied medicine and botany under his father and the botanist and anatomist Georg Balthasar Metzger, Director of the Medical Garden at the University of Tübingen. After completing his studies and a two-year study trip through Europe, Camerarius returned to his hometown on the Neckar River in 1687. In 1688, he succeeded Metzger as Director of the Botanical Garden and was appointed to the *Academia Naturae Curiosorum*—under the surname Hector II. In 1695 he took over his father's full professorship. In keeping with his motto *Herbis, non verbis!* (i.e. with plants, not with words), Camerarius undertook crossing experiments with the annual mercury and with spinach. He summarized the sexual reproduction he discovered in 1694 in a letter to the Giessen professor Michael Bernhard Valentini. Today, Camerarius is considered the founder of the sexual theory of plants [48].

Johann Christoph Dehne (16??–1742): Rudolph Jacob Camerarius, (1665 Tübingen – 1721 Tübingen), German botanist and physician. (Wellcome Collection CC BY 4.0)

This was followed in 1717 by Rudolph Jacob Camerarius' comprehensive treatise on ergot and its dangers. In the *Observatio* 82 of the *Ephemerides*, the publication organ of the *Academia Naturae Curiosorum*, the Swabian professor expressed his considerable reservations about the use of the *Rockenmutterle* by midwives who "administered it to poor women to induce labor; these practices are doubtful and unsafe" (Maximilian Rein, 2022) [49]. In the following decades, the university physicians' tenor regarding the folk medicines' labor remedy did not change. After the uterotonic had been administered with fatal consequences, for example, in transverse lies, it was banned in France in 1774, in the Kingdom of Hannover in 1778, and in the Electoral Palatinate in 1791, and almost completely disappeared from obstetrics [50]. *Secale cornutum* was at an impasse, and it was not to be the last.

Very slowly, almost imperceptibly, the tide began to turn in favor of ergot medicine. Around 1757, a Dutch obstetrician appeared in the small German town of Kirn on the Nahe River, who instructed midwives and doctors in the use of his *pulvis ad partum* ("birth powder"). There are some indications that it could have been the ophthalmologist and obstetrician, Jan Pieter Rathlauw, who claimed to have an excellent, labor-promoting secret medicine with which he had had the best results for over ten years, even with difficult births. It did not need to be administered more than twice before the job was done [51]. The Kirn midwives were unanimous in their assurances that "the fine powder stimulated labor more quickly and powerfully than any other remedy". The oxytocic agent that Rathlauw sold through the local town pharmacy also boosted the business of the capable Dutchman. The former Kirn town doctor, Heinrich Felix Paulitzky, had the therapeutic successes of *pulvis ad partum* published in 1787 under "Miscellaneous Remarks" in the journal *Neues Magazin für Ärzte* (New Magazine for Physicians). In it he communicates his conviction that "the [uterotonic] power of the ergot depends on the [same] one that produces spasms and convulsions" [51–54].

Paulitzky's article followed a communication from Antoine-Augustin Parmentier, the father of French potato cultivation and Inspector General of the Medical System in Paris, in which he had published a letter from a Madame Dupille from Chaumont-en-Vexin. According to this, the midwife and her mother before her had used the oxytocic agent with remarkable success [55]. Jean-Baptist Desgranges, head of the *Hospice de la Charité de Lyon*, confirmed that he had been successfully using his *Poudre obstétricale* for births since 1777. Local midwives, who crushed the ergot grains in coffee grinders, had referred him to their medicine. Unfortunately, Desgranges did not inform his colleagues about his excellent experiences with the uterotonic until 40 years later [56].

In Europe at the end of the 18th century, ergot remedy had a difficult time for three reasons: its use in obstetrics was associated with high risks, it was classified as folk medicine and, just as importantly, it was mainly administered by women. Conventional physicians viewed these circumstances with required caution, but also with traditional reservations. The ergot had to be taken up by conventional medicine so that the oxytocic agent could be examined in detail. This path was blocked for it in Europe. However, an unprejudiced view on folk and midwifery medicine was achieved in a country that had only had a medical faculty since 1765. At the beginning of the 19th century, American gynecologists and obstetricians began to take an interest in the pharmaceutical effects of the sclerotia of *Claviceps purpurea*.

US doctors recommend ergot for stopping postpartum hemorrhage
John Stearns, a physician from Waterford, Saratoga County, had heard of Scottish women in his neighborhood who used ergot in obstetrics. Curious, he examined the medication in his practice and summarized his experiences in 1808 in an extremely positive report. He emphasized the surprisingly fast effect of the drug and underlined the necessity to have everything one needs on

hand when starting the treatment. In 1822, Stearns communicated in a more critical article on when ergot administration may be indicated and under what circumstances it was dangerous for mother and child [57, 58].

It was thanks to the lecture given by the American physician Oliver Prescott Jr. to the Massachusetts Medical Society on June 2, 1813, that ergot medicine was finally recognized by European orthodox medicine, after his contribution was printed and translated into French and German. Prescott stated that if the medicine was administered correctly, "it must be esteemed an important and valuable acquisition to our *materia medica* and is unquestionably destined to hold a high rank among the means which Nature has provided for relieving the sufferings of her children" [59]. After careful consideration of all the medical preconditions that allowed the administration of *Secale cornutum*, the medication meant considerable relief for many women in labor—bloodletting or the intentional rupture of the amniotic sac had previously been the only procedures to speed up childbirth. Unfortunately, many doctors ignored Prescott's limitations and Stearns' list of contraindications to ergot medicine. In the USA, maternal mortality and perinatal deaths increased with the increasing administration of the medication. The situation could not continue without massive opposition. One of the harshest critics of *pulvis ad partum* was the New York doctor and botanist David Hosack (info box 6).

Info box 6: David Hosack

David Hosack was born in New York City, the son of a wealthy businessman, and studied medicine at Columbia University and Princeton. Convinced of the high quality of medical education in Europe, he continued his studies at the University of Edinburgh in 1792, where he often visited his Scottish relatives in Elgin, the birthplace of his father. After studying botany and Linnaeus' plant systematics in London, Hosack returned to New York in 1794. Here he joined the group practice of his former mentor Samuel Bard, whose patients included George Washington. In 1794, Hosack took over the chair of botany at Columbia University and in 1797 was appointed professor of *materia medica*. As a university lecturer, he contributed significantly to the reform of medical training and was regarded as the most renowned and influential physician in his country. As a doctor to the family of Alexander Hamilton, one of the fathers of the constitution and the first US Secretary of the Treasury, Hosack saved the life of his son Philip, who had fallen ill. In 1801 he was again called to Philipp Hamilton, who had been so badly injured in a duel that this time Hosack could no longer help him. In 1804, he was the dueling physician of two of his friends who had challenged each other: Alexander Hamilton (Philip's father) and Aaron Burr, the Vice President of the United States, fought this duel, which has gone down in US history and in which Hamilton succumbed to his gunshot wound.

Botany and horticulture were among Hosack's private passions. Financially well off, he bought an 8-hectare (2.5 acres) plot of land in New York in 1801 and had a botanical garden created with 1500 ornamental and medicinal plant species from all over the world, including the first physic garden in the USA. He named it after his father's Scottish hometown, Elgin Botanic Garden. After selling the garden to the State of New York, Hosack acquired the 250-hectare Hyde Park Estate in the Hudson Valley from the heirs of his former partner Samuel Bard in 1828. The Elgin Botanical Garden project and Hosack's decision to have the Belgian landscape architect André Parmentier design the park of his new country estate contributed significantly to the popularity of European garden architecture in the USA [60, 61].

Thomas Sully (1783–1872): David Hosack (1769 New York – 1835 New York), US-American physician and botanist (Portrait of David Hosack, M. D. painted by Thomas Sully (1783 Horncastle/UK – 1872 Philadelphia). Philadelphia, PA 1815. Oil paint and Canvas, 1977.0170. Gift of Mr. J. Hampton Barnes, Jr., Courtesy of Winterthur Museum, Greenville, DE)

While analyzing death notices in New York newspapers, Hosack realized that the stillbirth rate in the city had risen since the use of ergot. He attributed this to overdoses of ergot extracts and the resulting overstimulation of the uterine muscles. This would impair or even completely interrupt the blood and oxygen supply between mother and child. In his publication of 1822, the physician quickly renamed the *pulvis ad partum* as *pulvis ad mortem* ("death powder"). Hosack's risk assessment prompted the Medical Society of New York to limit *Secale cornutum* to the treatment of postpartum hemorrhage [62, 63].

The work of US and European physicians on the contraindications and the extremely delicate dosage of ergot medicine was apparently disregarded in

Berlin in 1859 [64, 65]. But a child was to be born here in January, who would subsequently rank third in the Prussian line of succession. The Crown Prince's palace was buzzing with anticipation, the chloroform bottle was ready—the eighteen-year-old Princess Victoria of Prussia had gone into labor.

References

1. Unknown, Codices Palatini germanici, Nuremberg (?), 1474, 545, 70v
2. F.M. Kirkemo, Adam Lonicer Physician and printer in Frankfurt am Main, in *Adam Lonicer's Kreuterbuch and 16th century distillation* (Norwegian University of Science and Technology, Trondheim, 2014), pp. 27–46
3. A. Lonicer, Rocken oder Korn/ Siligo. In, *Kreuterbuch: Kunstliche Conterfeytunge der Bäume, Stauden Hecken, Kräuter, Getreyde, Gewürtze. Samt künstlichem Bericht deß Distilierens. Item von fürnembsten Gethieren der Erde, Vögeln und Fischen. Deßgleichen von Metallen, Ertze, Edelgesteinen, Gummi und gestandenen Säfften*, Chr. Egenolphs Erben, Franckfort am Mayn, 1582, cap. CLXXXXV, p. 285
4. J. Camerarius, *Kreutterbuch Desz Hochgelehrten vnnd weitberühmten Herrn D. Petri Andreae Matthioli*, S. Feyerabend, P. Fischer and H. Dack, Franckfort am Mayn, 1586, p. 109v
5. J. Thalius, *Sylva Hercynia, sive Catalogus Plantarum Sponte Nascentium In Montibus, Et Locis Vicinis Hercyniae etc.*, S. Feyerabendii, H. Dackii et Petri Fischeri, Francofurti ad Moenum, 1588, p. 47
6. H.S. Murphy, *Reforming Medicine in Sixteenth Century Nuremberg* (California Digital Library, University of California, Berkeley, 2012), pp. 114–115. UC Berkeley Electronic Theses and Dissertations
7. R. Kobert, Ueber die Bestandtheile und Wirkungen des Mutterkorns. Arch exp Pathol 18, 343 (1884)
8. S. Wright, An experimental inquiry into the physiological action of ergot of rye. Edinb Med Surg J **52**, 293 (1839)
9. Ch.G. Gruner, *De convulsione cereali novo morbi genere*. Facultatis Medicae Marburgensis 1597, Jena, 1793, pp. 20–22
10. K. Sprengel, Kriebel-Krankheit, in *Versuch einer pragmatischen Geschichte der Arzneykunde*, 3rd edn. vol 3. (Gebauer'sche Buchhandlung, Halle, 1827), p. 271
11. H.P. Fuchs-Eckert, Die Familie BAUHIN in Basel Teil 1. Bauhinia **6**, 13 (1977)
12. C. Bauhin, *Phytopinax seu Enumeratio plantarum ab herbariis nostro seculo descriptarum: cum earum differentiis: cui plurimarum hactenus ab iisdem non descriptarum succinctae descriptiones & denominationes accessere: additis aliquot hactenus non sculptarum plantarum viuis iconibus*, Sebastianum Henricpetri, Basel, 1596, pp. 50–51
13. J.C. Bauhin, *Pinax Theatri Botanici. Liber Primus Sectio Quarta varta*, J. König, Basel, 1658, CAP. XVII, pp. 433–434

14. D.J. Sturdy, Two life scientists: Denis Dodart (1634–1707) and Joseph-Guichard du Verney (1648–1730), in *Science and Social Status: The Members of the Académie des Sciences 1666–1750* (Boydell & Brewer, Woodbridge Rochester, 1995), pp. 184–189

15. D.J. Sturdy, Two life scientists: Denis Dodart (1634–1707) and Joseph-Guichard du Verney (1648–1730), in *Science and Social Status: The Members of the Académie des Sciences 1666–1750* (Boydell & Brewer, Woodbridge Rochester, 1995), pp. 77–79

16. B. le Bouyet de Fontenelle, Eloge de Dodart, in *Œuvres de Fontenelle* vol 1. (Salmon-Peytieux, Paris, 1825), pp. 170–182

17. J.C. Rule, Louis XIV, Roi Bureaucrate, in *Louis XIV and the craft of Kingship* (Ohio State University Press, 1969), p. 37

18. J.C. Rule, Louis XIV, Roi Bureaucrate, in *Louis XIV and the craft of Kingship* (Ohio State University Press, 1969), pp. 15–18

19. J.C. Rule, Louis XIV, Roi Bureaucrate, in *Louis XIV and the craft of Kingship* (Ohio State University Press, 1969), pp. 23–24

20. J.C. Rule, Louis XIV, Roi Bureaucrate, in *Louis XIV and the craft of Kingship* (Ohio State University Press, 1969), p. 244

21. A. Stroup, Some assumptions behind medicine for the poor during the reign of Louis XIV, in *The Light of Nature: Essays in the History of Philosophy of Science presented to A. C. Crombie*, ed. by J.D. North, J.J. Roche (Martinus Nijhoff Publishers, 1985), pp. 35–56

22. A. Rees, Bourdelin, Claude, in *The Cyclopaedia; or, Universal Dictionary of Arts, Sciences, and Literature* vol 5., ed. by Longman, Hurst, Rees, Orme, Brown [etc.] London, 1819, Bou

23. P. Dorveaux, Les Grands Pharmaciens: Claude Bourdelin. Bull de La Société d'histoire De La Pharm **64**, 289 (1929)

24. M. Bycroft, Experiments on Collections at the Royal Society of London and the Paris Academy of Sciences, 1660–1740, in *The Institutionalization of Science in Early Modern Europe*, ed. by G. Giannini, M. Feingold (Brill Academic, Leiden Boston, 2019), pp. 236–265

25. A. Stroup, *A company of scientists: botany, patronage, and community at the seventeenth-century parisian royal academy of sciences* (University of California Press, Berkeley Los Angeles Oxford, 1990), pp. 169–179

26. D. Dodart, Lettre de M. Dodart de l'Académie Royale des Sciences, à l'Auteur du Journal contenant des choses fort remarquables touchant quelques-grains. *Le journal des Sçavans (6th Janvier)* , 69 (1676)

27. E. Küthmann, Johann Conrad Brunner in Heidelberg als Hochschullehrer und Therapeut. Gesnerus **14**, 119 (1957)

28. J.C. Brunner, The Granis secalis degeneribus venenatis. In, *Miscellanea Curiosa sive Ephemeridum Medico-Physicarum Germanicarum Academiae Caesareo-Leopoldinae Naturae-Curiosorum.Decuriae III. Annus Secundus, Anni MDCXCIV,*

Observatio 224, Th. Fritschius and J. Ph. Andreae, Lipsiae et Francofurti, 1695, pp. 348–352

29. J.F.C. Hecker, Ursachen der Kriebelkrankheit, in *Geschichte der neueren Heilkunde* vol 1. (Th. Ch. F. Enslin, Berlin, 1839), p. 322

30. J. Taube, Die Geschichte der Kriebel=Krankheit besonders derjenigen welche in den Jahren 1770 und 1771 in den Zellischen Gegenden gewütet hat, Johann Christian Dieterich, Göttingen, 1782, pp. 34–62

31. J.F.C. Hecker, Ursachen der Kriebelkrankheit, in *Geschichte der neueren Heilkunde* vol 1. (Verlag von Th. Ch. F. Enslin, Berlin, 1839), pp. 330–341

32. C. Meyer, Das Mutterkorn als Ursache der Kriebelkrankheit, in *Secale cornutum, Mutterkorn als Krankheitsursache im 18. und 19. Jahrhundert am Beispiel des Herzogtums Braunschweig-Wolfenbüttel* (Technische Universität Carolo-Wilhelmina zu Braunschweig, 2010), pp. 46–54. Dissertation

33. C. Meyer, Das Mutterkorn als Ursache der Kriebelkrankheit, in *Secale cornutum, Mutterkorn als Krankheitsursache im 18. und 19. Jahrhundert am Beispiel des Herzogtums Braunschweig-Wolfenbüttel* (Technische Universität Carolo-Wilhelmina zu Braunschweig, 2010), pp. 87–99. Dissertation

34. F.H. Walchner, Das Mehl, in *Die Nahrungsmittel des Menschen, ihre Verfälschungen und Verunreinigungen* (Springer, Berlin Heidelberg, 1875), pp. 100–103

35. Abbé Tessier, Mémoire sur les effets du seigle ergoté. In, *Histoire et mémoires de la Société Royale de Médecine*, 1778, p. 587

36. B. Schneidmüller, Städtische Umweltgesetzgebung im Spätmittelalter, in *Mensch und Umwelt in der Geschichte*, ed. by J. Calließ, J. Rüsen, M. Striegnitz (Centaurus, Pfaffenweiler Herbolzheim, 1989), p. 131

37. A. Mischlewski, Soziale Aspekte der spätmittelalterlichen Antoniusverehrung, in *Laienfrömmigkeit im späten Mittelalter, Formen, Funktionen, politisch-soziale Zusammenhänge* Schriften des Historischen Kollegs 20., ed. by K. Schreiner, E. Müller-Luckner (R. Oldenbourg Wissenschaftsverlag, Munich, 1992), pp. 144–149

38. R. Gatt, The Suppression of the Order of St. Antony of Vienne in 1775: The Consequent Interactions between the Order of the Hospital and the Order of St Lazarus, in *Acta Historiae Sancti Lazari Ordinis: Proceedings Sancti Lazari Ordinis Academia Internationalis*, ed. by Ch. Savona-Ventura, M. Ross (Malta, 2016), pp. 66–68

39. J.J. Rousseau, *Vom Gesellschaftsvertrag* (Reclam, Stuttgart, 1986), p. 11. Ed: H. Brockard

40. Lyon, 6. July *Freytägige Münchnerzeitung of 07/21/1775*. Number 116

41. P. Chevallier, *Loménie de Brienne et l'ordre monastique (1766–1789)* Bibliothèque de la Société d'Histoire Ecclésiastique de la France, vol. 1+2 (Librairie philosophique, J. Vrin, Paris, 1959)

42. J. Rauch, *Der Antoniterorden. AMrhKG Year 9* vol. 9. Eds.: L. Lenhart and A.Ph. Bruck (Verlag der Jaegerschen Buchdruckerei, Speyer, 1957), pp. 47–48

43. *Die neuesten Staatsbegebenheiten mit historischen und politischen Anmerkungen, Erstes Stück*, Varrentrappische Buchhandlungen, Frankfurt a. Mayn und Maynz, 1775 (1776), pp. 1007–1008

44. L.-T. Dassy, *L'abbaye de Saint-Antoine en Dauphiné: essai historique et descriptif* (Baratier Frères et Fils, Grenoble, 1844), pp. 343–351

45. J. Stockerus, The haemorrhagia narium. In, *Praxis aurea, ad corporis humani morbos omnes, tum internos, tum externos*, Ex Officina J. Maire. Lugduni Batavorum, 1657, p. 118

46. W. Hamburger, Geschichte des Mutterkorns als eines Heilmittels, in *Das Mutterkorn und seine außerordentlichen Heilwirkungen in Nervenkrankheiten: Nach eigenen zahlreichen Beobachtungen und Versuchen* (Arnoldische Buchhandlung,, Dresden Leipzig, 1848), pp. 16–17

47. J.A. Planer, *Disputatio botanica de Ustilagine Frumenti*, Joh. Cunradi Reisl, Tubingae, 1709, pp. 13–14

48. R.J. Camerarius, *Ad Mich. Berne. Valentini de sexu plantarum epistola*, Typis Viduae Rommeii, Tvbingae, 1694

49. R.J. Camerarius, Sphacelus pedis sponte terminatus. Acta Naturae Curiosor Centur VI Obs **82**, 346 (1717)

50. L. Lewin, Abortiva. Emmenagoga, in *Die Nebenwirkungen der Arzneimittel* (Springer, Berlin Heidelberg, 1899), p. 608. see also: Hecker: Ueber die Anwendung des Mutterkorns in der Geburtshülfe. Sitzung vom 11. November 1851. In, *Verhandlungen der Gesellschaft für Geburtshülfe in Berlin, Vol. 5*, Georg Reimer, Berlin, 1852, p. 54

51. A. Levret, *Observations sur les causes et les accidens de plusieurs accouchemens laborieux, Édition 2nd*, Delaguette, Imprimeur du Collége & de l'Académie Royale de Chirurgie, Paris, 1750, p. 213

52. F.J. Bové, The Clinical uses of Ergot, in *The story of ergot* (Karger, Basel, 1970), pp. 272–276

53. H.F. Paulitzky, Vermischte Bemerkungen: 4. *Pulvis ad partum* aus dem Mutterkorn. *Neues Magazin für Ärzte* 1787, 9, 44

54. H. Vezin, Ueber die Wirkungen des Mutterkorns als Heilmittel. Nach dem Holländischen. J Geburtshülfe Frauenzimmer- Kinderkrankheiten **16**, 310 (1837). Ed: E.C.J. von Siebold

55. A.A. Parmentier, Lettre de M. Parmentier, Apothicaire-Major de l'Hôtel Royal des Invalides. *Observations et Memoires sur la Physique, sur L'Histoire Naturelle et sur les Arts et Métiers Tome 4me, Août*, Ruault Libraire, Paris, 1774, pp. 144–145

56. J.-B. Desgranges, Sur la propriété qu'a le Seigle ergoté d'accélérer la marche de l'accouchement, et de hâter sa terminaison. Nouveau J de Médecine Chir Pharm Etc **1** (Migneret et Crochard, Paris, 1818) pp. 54–61

57. J. Stearns, Account of the *Pulvis parturiens*, a remedy for quickening child-birth, in *New York Medical Repository, Hexade II vol V*. (T. & J. Swords, New York, 1808), pp. 308–309

58. J. Stearns, Observations on the Secale Cornutum, Or Ergot; with Directions for Its Use in Parturition. Am Med Rec **5**, 666–673 (1822)

59. O. Prescott, A Dissertation on the Natural History of Medical Effects of the Secale Cornutum, or Ergot. Med Phys J **32**, 90 (1814)

60. V. Johnson, *American Eden: David Hosack, Botany, and Medicine in the Garden of the Early Republic* (Liveright Publishing, New York, 2018)

61. E.R. Jeffe, Hamilton's Physician: David Hosack, Renaissance Man of Early New York. N Y J Am Hist **3**, 54 (2004)

62. M. Saincher, From Deadly Plague to Life-Altering Prescriptions: The story of Ergot as a Case in Favor of Complementary and Alternative Medicine, in *The Proceedings of the 18th Annual History of Medicine Days Conference 2009*, ed. by L. Peterman, K. Sun, F.W. Stahnisch (Cambridge Scholars, 2009), p. 205

63. D. Hosack, Observations on Ergot: communicated in a letter to James Hamilton, M.D. Professor of Obstetrics in the University of Edinburgh, & c. By David Hosack, M.D.F.R.S. Professor of the Theory and Practice of Physic in the University of the State of New York (June 2nd, 1822). N Y Med Phys J **1**, 205 (1822)

64. C. Meyer, *Secale cornutum, Mutterkorn als Krankheitsursache im 18. und 19. Jahrhundert am Beispiel des Herzogtums Braunschweig-Wolfenbüttel* (Technische Universität Carolo-Wilhelmina zu Braunschweig, 2010), pp. 20–22. Dissertation

65. J.U. Rüsch, *Ueber das Secale Cornutum, als ein die Geburtsthätigkeit erhöhendes Mittel* (Meyer und Zuberbühler, Trogen, 1829), pp. 17–28. Eine Inaugural-Abhandlung, Universität Würzburg

4

A lawyer clarifies the nature of ergot, but it remains a tough nut for pharmacists to crack

An heir to the throne is born, or the risk of ergot as a labor remedy

Chloroform, the *dernier cri* of obstetrics at the time, was sent to Berlin from England especially for the new obstetric method of "intermittent narcosis". During short periods of anesthesia, the narcotic was administered to those giving birth to provide relief and gather new strength. It had helped Queen Victoria of England wonderfully during her births, and now it was also to assist her daughter "Vicky", Princess Victoria of Prussia, during the birth of her child. But things were to turn out differently. Victoria's personal physicians had diagnosed the baby's breech presentation too late, so that an external cephalic version was no longer possible. The director of the Maternity Hospital at the Charité, Prof. Eduard Arnold Martin, was hastily summoned to the Crown Prince's Palace. As Victoria was suffering from unusually severe pain, it was decided to anesthetize her continuously, for hours on end. However, the anesthesia reduced the strength of the contractions, so Martin administered ergot three times during the expulsion phase. The high dosage over-stimulated the uterus, causing the neck, head and umbilical cord to become clamped in the birth canal, and restricting the blood and oxygen supply; the boy's life was in acute danger. Martin and the assisting doctors only had a few minutes left to save the child. The infant, William, was dragged into the world "under the flannel skirt [of his mother] with all the strength that could be mustered" using the Mauriceau-Veit-Smellie maneuver for arm release and head delivery by neck flexion. In the process, his left brachial plexus was torn off [1, 2].

The arm of William, later to become Emperor William II, remained shortened and motionless—an embarrassment for the royal family, and a humiliation for Princess Victoria. In 1861 she wrote to her mother in London: "The arm spoils any joy and pride I should have in him". All the physical ordeals involving arm-stretching machines, electrifying baths and shoulder-pelvic fixation frames that the little prince had to endure over the years—several times a day—to get his arm back in shape and functional were in vain. According to the German historian Wolfgang Mommsen, William's childhood was characterized by "his mother's negative attitude, his parents' disappointed high expectations, and a lack of personal affection" [3].

Safe administration of *Secale cornutum* remained a challenge, and one not to be underestimated, even for experienced obstetricians. This could only be delivered with a standardized drug that contained the ergot active ingredient, either highly enriched or as a pure substance. The path to this opened at Cramer's Court Pharmacy in Paderborn.

Ergot becomes a research topic for 19th-century natural scientists

Joseph Bonjean from Chambéry commercializes his ergot medicine

Around 1804, the pharmacist's assistant, Friedrich Wilhelm Sertürner in Paderborn, succeeded in obtaining the active principle of a medicinal plant in its pure form for the first time: the morphine of the opium poppy [4]. His work triggered a veritable gold-rush atmosphere in early chemistry. More and more active plant ingredients were isolated using Sertürner's method, and from 1819 they were grouped into the newly defined substance class of "alkaloids". It was, therefore, only a matter of time before pharmacists and chemists turned their attention to the active agents of the ergot sclerotia. Entire generations of scientists found the problem a hard nut to crack.

The first person to try his hand at the ergot alkaloids was the French pharmacist and chemist Louis Nicolas Vauquelin (1763–1829), a well-versed, and extremely successful, expert in his field. He had previously discovered aspartic and hippuric acid, chromium, and urea, and was a pioneer of early isolation chemistry. However, Vauquelin stopped his experiments after the first taste tests and color descriptions of the extracts [5]. The work of the Göttingen pharmacologist and botanist, Heinrich Ludwig August Wiggers (1803–1880), went further. He generated two extracts in 1832: the first, a mixture of substances that was soluble in alcohol and insoluble in water, showed a toxic effect

Fig. 4.1 Joseph Bonjean (1810 Chambéry – 1896 Chambéry), Savoy chemist and pharmacist. (© Collection Bibliothèques municipales de Chambéry)

in chickens (since Dr. Thuillier the Elder's first ergot experiments in France, the chicken remained the preferred indicator organism for ergotoxicosis until the 20th century. To avoid having to kill any more animals, the alkaloid concentrations were gradually increased until a black coloration of the well-vascularized cockscomb indicated the onset of gangrene). Wiggers named this first fraction "Ergotin", and he called the water-soluble, bitter-tasting fraction, which in his opinion must contain the healing property of ergot, plant osmazome [6].

In 1842, Wigger's work was taken up by the Savoy pharmacist and chemist Joseph Bonjean (Fig. 4.1) from Chambéry. It is still unclear even today how the confusion arose, but Bonjean called his effective, water-soluble extract "Ergotine" and found Wigger's ergotin to be ineffective. The fact that there were now two ergotine extracts with different properties irritated pharmacists and chemists alike. They investigated the two preparations for thirty years with rarely observed tenacity, but without ever being able to satisfactorily clarify the contradiction [7–9].

Fig. 4.2 Bonjean knew how to market his ergotine

In the meantime, Bonjean had begun marketing ergotine as an *Extractum haemostaticum*, among other things (Fig. 4.2). The drug was prescribed not only to treat the dreaded postpartum hemorrhage, but also to stop any blood loss, whether it was menstrual or intestinal bleeding, as can occur with yellow fever. The catalog of applications also included the treatment of surgical wounds and arterial and venous bleeding from gunshot wounds. In 1851, Bonjean received the *Médaille d'Or de la Societé Pharmacie de Paris* for his ergotine or *Dragées d'Ergotine*. The enterprising pharmacist remained somewhat vague about the manufacturing method for his drug, so that forty years later there was still uncertainty about the exact ergotine production process [10–12].

The drug from Savoy was unrivaled for a long time and was even sold across the Atlantic as Ergotine (Bonjean) by US companies such as Eli Lilly, Wyeth, Merck, and Parke, Davis & Co. Even though Bonjean's ergot extract was now being produced on a larger scale, the nature of the excrescence in the rye ears was still a mystery. It was not the biologists who shed light on this conundrum, but a lawyer who became increasingly annoyed working his way through dusty piles of files. But until then, the experts were once again at each other's throats.

Info box 1: Osmazome

Osmazôme (gr. ὀσμή, smell; gr. ζωμός, meat broth): a term introduced into chemistry by the French chemist Louis Jacques Thénard in 1806 for a "meat extract". The osmazome is obtained by evaporating the aqueous extract of muscle meat to dryness, dissolving it in alcohol, and distilling off the clear organic phase. The residue contains, among other things, the aromas and flavors of the meat. Later, all animal and plant extracts were encompassed by the term "osmazome" [13].

Ergot is the persistent form of a fungus! A lawyer sorts out the confusion

For 200 years, ergot was regarded as the fruit of a new rye species, *Secale luxurians*, the luxuriant rye, whose seeds were significantly larger. At the beginning of the 19th century, more and more reports questioned this earlier classification in the plant kingdom by the Basel botanist and physician Caspar Bauhin. In 1815, the Geneva botanist Augustin Pyramus de Candolle (1778–1841) announced that this strange growth must be a fungus, judging by its smell, color, constant shape, harmfulness, components, and similarity to other sclerotia [14]. As late as in 1831, August Wiggers in Göttingen believed that "ergot should be regarded as a sporadic disease of plants, which is caused by the deviant assimilation of the general elementary substances of the bodies of the plant kingdom". The French physician and mycologist Joseph Henri Léveillé (1796–1870) saw it more as a malformed ovule caused by a fungus [15, 16]. For the British botanist John Smith, who, as stove boy, had been responsible for heating the greenhouses at the Royal Botanic Gardens in Kew and had since risen to the position of senior assistant to the gardeners, the ergot that contained spores was not a fungus but the result of a fungal effect [17]. The English botanist and physician Edwin John Quekett listened attentively to his report, which Smith presented to the Linnean Society in London in 1838. As a result, Quekett also began to examine ergot more closely and concluded that ergot was a mixture of components of diseased grain and a fungal mass [18]. Franz ("Francis") Bauer, who, according to his own account, had observed the ergot for twenty-five years, contradicted Smith's and Quekett's statements and described the *corpus delicti* ("concrete evidence of a crime") as the monstrous embryo of the rye grain, which emerged for unknown reasons, and furthermore, the ergot question was far from being settled [19]. Despite the Austrian plant illustrator and first artist-in-residence at the Royal Botanic Gardens being completely wrong with his giant seedling idea, Bauer has gone down in the history of botanical painting as one of the greatest artists of his profession.

Quekett published his findings in the medical journal *The Lancet*. A year later, he was subjected to a fierce attack by an anonymous "F.B.". According to the critic, Quekett had claimed the clarification of the origin of ergot for himself and swept Smith's important contributions under the carpet. Quekett responded with a meticulous counterstatement to refute the allegations made by "F.B." [20, 21]. All the excitement was gratuitous because all three were wrong in their conclusions. For the time being, however, earlier views that ergot was caused by the bite of the June beetle or by butterflies, for example, endured. Most botanists were also unimpressed by the fungal hypothesis and stuck to their conviction that ergot was "a pathological condition of the grain".

It took a lawyer to correct misinterpretations and erroneous taxonomic classifications of ergot once and for all. After studying law in Poitiers, Louis-René Tulasne (1815 Azay-le-Rideau – 1885 Hyères) initially worked as a lawyer until he became financially independent thanks to a large inheritance. The first thing he did was to hang up his profession and move in with his brother Charles (1816 Langeais – 1884 Hyères) in Paris, who could happily retire from his unbeloved medical profession. Here they worked side by side almost like the Grimm brothers and devoted themselves to their true passions: botany, mycology,—and extensive charitable activities.

It is not surprising that Louis-René and Charles also succumbed to the attraction of the strange *seigle cornu* (horned rye). Unraveling the taxonomic mystery was simply too tempting. In 1853, their precise observations and microscopic studies finally proved that the object of their research was the overwintering form of a parasitic fungus. The result of their joint scientific work did not only put an end to the decades-long dispute about the biology of ergot [22]. Louis-René's publication of the complete life cycle of the fungus, for which Charles made the microscopic drawings *en détail*, is also one of the most beautiful pioneering works and scientific highlights of early mycology (Fig. 4.3).

As the fruiting body of the ergot fungus resembles the shape of a club head, Louis-René composed the genus name *Claviceps* from the Latin *clava*, club, and the Greek *kephalē*, head. Because of the black-purple coloration of its sclerotia, he adopted the Latin name *purpurea* as the *specific epithet* and proposed the taxonomic species name *Claviceps purpurea* (lit. "Red Club Head") which is still valid today [23].

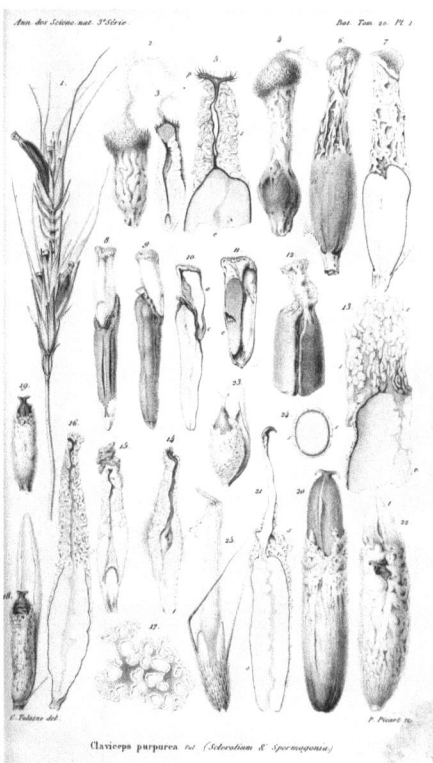

Fig. 4.3 Illustrations by Charles Tulasne on the infection cycle of the ergot fungus [23]

Preparative chemistry intervenes—Charles Tanret and the first ergot alkaloid crystals

The mycologists had made a big step forward, of which the chemists and pharmacists who were struggling with active ergot components could only dream. The French pharmacist Charles Tanret (Info box 2) came a good deal closer to this dream of isolating the pharmaceutical ingredient of the ergot fungus.

In the small laboratory of his pharmacy in Troyes, he extracted the substances of the ergot-kernels with high-proof alcohol and treated the resulting mixtures with chloroform and ether in the hope of obtaining the pure active component. In 1875, he produced a solid for the first time. Assuming that he had discovered the active principle of ergot, he wrote to the French Academy of Sciences on November 15:

"J'ai l'honneur d'annoncer à l'Académie que je viens de trouver, dans le seigle ergoté, un alcaloïde nouveau, solide et fixe. Comme divers produits mal définis portant déjà le nom d'ergotine, et que le donner à un nouveau corps serait encore augmenter la confusion, je propose de l'appeler ergotinine. (…)" (C.R. des séances de l'Acad. des sciences) [24].

"I have the honor to announce to the Academy that I have just found, in the ergot, a new, solid and stable alkaloid. As various poorly defined products already bear the name of ergotine, and thus to give it to a new compound would increase the confusion still further, I propose to call it ergotinine. (…)" (Report of the sessions of the Academy of Sciences).

In 1877, after preparing a crystallization experiment with ether and placing the glass vessel in a cold place overnight, Tanret discovered crystals had formed on the vessel wall and an amorphous powder had precipitated the next morning. He must have been overjoyed, as crystals had always been the unmistakable sign of the presence of a pure substance. To make his compound recognizable as a new alkaloid, but above all to distinguish it from Bonjean's commercial ergotine mixture, he called his substance *Ergotinine cristallisée* and *Ergotinine amorphe* according to its two solid states [25–27].

Info box 2: Charles Tanret

Charles Tanret was born in Joinville, Haute-Marne, the son of a knitwear merchant and hobby winemaker. To study pharmacy, he first had to complete a three-year internship. The local pharmacist offered Tanret an apprenticeship, and during this time he became enthusiastic about the ergot fungus and its unusual history. After studying at the *École supérieure de pharmacie* in Paris, he continued his training under Marcelin Berthelot at the *Collège de France*, where he would have liked to continue his laboratory work. However, to build a livelihood for himself, Tanret left Paris in 1872 and became a pharmacist in Troyes. He set up a small laboratory on the premises, where he began his preparative work on alkaloids from ergot and pomegranate bark. In 1879, he returned to Paris and bought a new pharmacy where he isolated and commercially distributed alkaloids. In 1897, Tanret became president of the *Société chimique de Paris* and was knighted with the *Légion d'honneur* [28].

Charles Tanret (1847 Joinville – 1917 Paris), French pharmacist and chemist. (© Société chimique de France, with kind permission)

Chemists and pharmacists are at their wits' end, but perhaps a pragmatic company director in London will find the solution to the ergot problem?
Tanret assumed that both fractions were the same substance and selected the *Ergotinine cristallisée* for his intended sales product. He no longer paid any attention to the amorphous residue. According to the textbook knowledge of his time, he had done everything right, but that was precisely why he chose the wrong fraction. The tragedy is that at that time, it was not yet known that very similar substances could crystallize together in a solution. And, bad luck is often accompanied by misfortune: in his experiment, only the practically inactive ergot alkaloids *ergocorninine*, *ergocryptinine*, and *ergocristinine* crystallized (Fig. 4.4a). Instead, he should have marketed the *Ergotinine amorphe*, which contained the much more active substances of the ergot [27, 29]. It was bound to happen: Tanret was subjected to fierce criticism and never-ending discussions by the international pharmacological community. Some said that *Ergotinine cristallisée* was ineffective, others came to the conclusion that it was toxic, its clinical use was sometimes effective, but at other times not. Scientists must have a thick skin. Tanret had grown one for himself, turned a deaf ear to the surging waves of criticism, and marketed his medicine with moderate

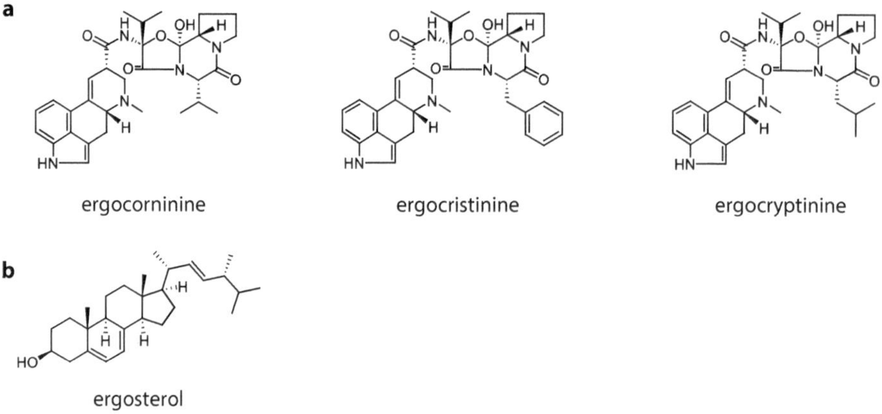

a

ergocorninine   ergocristinine   ergocryptinine

b

ergosterol

Fig. 4.4 Ergot alkaloids of the peptide group. **a** Structures of the epimeric ergot alkaloids of the peptide group in Tanret's *Ergotinine cristallisée*: Ergocorninine, ergocristinine, ergocryptinine; **b** Structure of ergosterol

success as *Ergotinine de Tanret* or *Sirop d'Ergotinine de Tanret* for the treatment of severe menstrual and postpartum bleeding, as well as uterine bleeding.

During his time in Paris, the tireless pharmacist devoted himself to the isolation and production of alkaloids without ever having obtained a pure ergot alkaloid [30]. In 1889, he achieved notable success when he extracted a substance from the sclerotia that Tanret called *Ergostérine* (ergosterol) [31]. Ergosterol (Fig. 4.4b) is an essential building block of the cell membrane of fungi. In the 20th century, the selective inhibition of its biosynthesis was used to develop new drugs for the targeted treatment of fungal infections. The German physician and chemist Adolf Windaus proved that vitamin D2 is formed from ergosterol in a photochemical reaction under the influence of UV-B radiation. His work proved that rickets, which was rampant at the time, was caused by a vitamin D deficiency and could be treated by administering vitamin D2/D3. In 1928, Windaus was awarded the Nobel Prize in Chemistry "for the services rendered through his research into the constitution of the sterols and their connection with the vitamins".

Charles Tanret's son Georges, who had observed his father experimenting in the laboratory, was infected by his passion for natural substances. After studying pharmacy and chemistry, he researched metabolites from medicinal plants. In 1914, Georges Tanret discovered *galégine*, the blood sugar-lowering active ingredient of goat's rue, *Galega officinalis* L. Years later, medicinal chemists developed the antidiabetic metformin from the natural substance. Today, it is the most frequently administered therapeutic agent in the treatment of Type 2 diabetes [32, 33].

Despite his failures, Charles Tanret's preparative work was a major step forward; after all, he was the first chemist to succeed in crystallizing ergot alkaloids. However, even he was unable to solve the real dilemma of ergot alkaloid research at the time. All the working groups assumed that they were dealing with pure substances and did not realize that they were working with mixtures. Their publications therefore shared the same fate, whether they dealt with ergotinine or the preparations of later 19th-century authors: they all remained contradictory. Research groups that sought to confirm published data always came to the same conclusions: ineffective, exclusively toxic or not reproducible, but other activities were found.

From today's perspective, this "linguistic confusion" is almost tragicomic, because everyone—chemists, pharmacologists and pharmacists—was right about their scientific findings. The crude extracts of the sclerotia were wild mixtures composed of various chemically labile ergot alkaloids and biologically active peripheral substances. Their fluctuating concentrations made reliable pharmacological studies impossible. Ultimately, the wrangling, interpretations and refutations were completely useless. What remained were increasingly perplexed scientists who were unable to solve the ergot enigma [34]. By the beginning of the 20th century, the paths had been trodden many times over and every stone had been overturned. Scientific art had reached its limits.

To finally solve the grueling *Secale cornutum* problem and put an end to the decades-long flitting about, a new beginning was needed: a new generation of scientists, new physiological test systems, and innovative separation methods, in order to leave the old "mixtureology" behind and start working with defined pure substances. All these conditions seemed to be fulfilled in London when, at the end of the 19th century, an American entrepreneur wanted to expand his company's product range with innovative medicines, which had previously ranged from shoe polish to animal gland extracts. The provision of the necessary capital investment for the establishment of modern research facilities also breathed new life into the work on ergot substances along the Thames.

Pharmaceutical industry research laboratories tackle ergot

Henry Wellcome has a vision

In 1879, Henry Wellcome (Info box 3) had opened a letter from Silas Mainville Burroughs in England. His friend from their student days had made a considerable fortune there as the sole sales representative of the US company John Wyeth & Brother, and also as an independent businessman. In his letter, he had suggested that Wellcome set up a company with him in London, which would, among other things, import goods from the USA into the market of the British Empire.

Info box 3: Henry Wellcome

Henry Solomon Wellcome was born in a log cabin in Almond, Wisconsin. His father, Solomon, was a farmer who, together with his wife Mary, traveled in a covered wagon through the tribal territories of the Menominee, Chippewa, and Dakota in Wisconsin and Minnesota, where Henry spent his early childhood. He later attributed his great interest in foreign cultures to this formative time. The family, living in poor circumstances, had to move to Garden City, MN, where Henry was able to work in the practice and pharmacy of his uncle Jacob Wellcome. Jacob was friends with the physician and chemist William Worrall Mayo, who in 1870 arranged for Henry to work in a pharmacy in Rochester, where Mayo ran his practice one floor above. The founder of the Mayo Clinic became Wellcome's most important mentor. He recognized Henry's scientific talent and encouraged the seventeen-year-old to study chemistry and pharmacy.

Wellcome graduated from Philadelphia College, where he became friends with Silas Mainville Burroughs. In 1880, the two founded their joint pharmaceutical company Burroughs, Wellcome & Company in London, which Henry continued to run alone after Silas' death. Wellcome was a passionate collector of medical history objects. Over the course of his life, he built up a collection of 1.5 million artifacts for his planned medical museum. He decreed that after his death, the company should be converted into a trust to promote research in order to improve human and animal health. The resulting Wellcome Trust had assets of around £ 29 billion in 2020 [35, 36].

Sir Henry Solomon Well-
come (1853 Almond,
Wisconsin – 1936 London),
British-American pharmacist
and entrepreneur (1890).
(Wellcome Collection CC
BY 4.0)

Wellcome had embraced the idea and moved to London. Initially, their company Burroughs, Wellcome & Company, founded in 1880, had done reasonable business with cod liver oil, malt and witch-hazel extracts, face cream, and soda water. Thanks to their entrepreneurial skills, they had sold pharmaceutical products early on, which had allowed the business of the two Americans in London to flourish. There, they had introduced a product from the USA that made taking and dosing medicines easier and safer: the tablet. In 1872, Wyeth & Brother had developed one of the first rotary tablet presses, which made industrial mass production of a pharmaceutical company's medicines possible. The rotary press revolutionized the production of active components in a solid dosage form and replaced the cumbersome weighing and filling process in pharmacies. Burroughs and Wellcome had initially marketed the tableted drugs on behalf of their former US client. After British doctors had overcome their reservations about the innovation from the United States, in 1883 the two entrepreneurs rented production premises in Wandsworth, London, in order to start manufacturing their own tablets [37]. In 1884, Henry Wellcome's marketing genius had come up with the brilliant idea of calling the drugs pressed into form "tabloids" (a contraction of tablet and alkaloid). The patented brand name made the drugs true best-sellers, which further boosted company sales.

From his company's modern office building, which was one of the first in London to be equipped with electric lighting, Henry Wellcome observed the new directions taken by the successful German pharmaceutical companies that had emerged from the tar dye industry. Wellcome and Burroughs wanted to expand their company in the same direction and invest their growing profits in their own drug research.

In the middle of the strategic decision-making process, Burroughs suddenly left London. He loved to travel and set off on an extensive bicycle tour with his sister Lena in the fall of 1894, which took them from England via the Black Forest to Tyrol. The two tourists must have been in very good physical condition—they once cycled a distance of 110 km in one day. After returning to England, Burroughs fell ill. His doctors advised him to spend the winter on the French Riviera, where his condition worsened. The initial cough developed into a fatal pneumonia. Silas Burroughs died in Monte Carlo in 1895, and Henry Wellcome became the sole owner of Burroughs, Wellcome & Co. He purposefully developed the company into a research-driven pharmaceutical company and founded a number of institutes that were to operate largely independently of the company: in 1896 the Wellcome Chemical Research Laboratories (Fig. 4.5) was created and in 1903 the Wellcome Tropical Research Laboratories in Khartoum.

In 1894, shortly before the passing of his business partner, Wellcome founded the Wellcome Physiological Research Laboratories (Fig. 4.6). The research institute, which consisted of horse stables and a small laboratory, produced the antitoxins against tetanus and diphtheria that had recently been discovered in Germany. Wellcome's industrial researchers also produced "animal substances" such as hormone gland extracts for the pharmaceutical market, which they obtained from the adrenal or thyroid glands of sheep. The thyroid tabloids, in particular, had an impressive effect on the widely acclaimed weight reduction of the Prince of Wales, who later became King Edward VII. In their newspaper columns, journalists also recommended the thyroid preparation to the King's mother Queen Victoria, who had become somewhat corpulent. The well-read comments in the gazettes were a real source of joy for the company's marketing department, from which Wellcome always demanded aggressive product advertising and a strong presence in the press [38, 39].

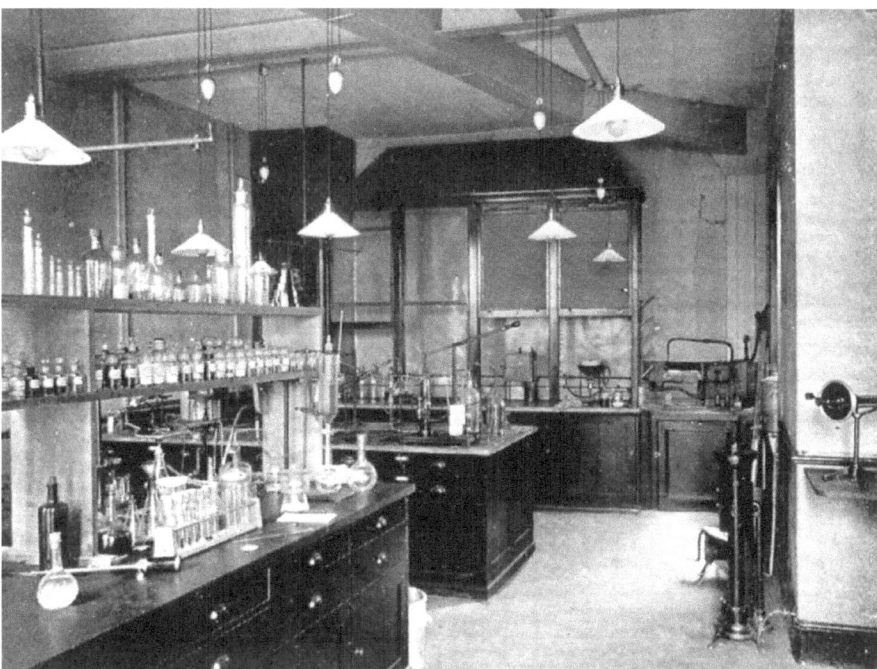

Fig. 4.5 Wellcome Chemical Research Laboratories, c. 1896. (Wellcome Collection. Public domain)

New crystals: Henry Dale, George Barger and Francis Carr isolate ergotoxine

In 1904, Wellcome was looking for a new scientist for his physiological research and contacted the British physiologist Ernest Starling at University College London to see if he could recommend a suitable candidate. Wellcome had precise ideas about what qualities the future employee needed to have:

> "(…) a man who is capable of broad and deep thinking, who has fertility of mind, originality and alertness, and patient persistence; a man who will concentrate his whole mind and energies on his work. I want the work in these laboratories to be done on the highest scientific lines and with such a thoroughness and precision that it will stand the test of time and keenest criticism" [40].

With this ambitious job profile, Starling could only recommend one candidate with a good conscience, the young London physician and physiologist Henry Dale (Info box 4).

1—Bacteriological and Pathological Laboratories   2—Laboratory for Physiological and Bacteriological Chemistry   3—One of the Stables   4—General View   5—Physiological Laboratory   6—Laboratory for preparing nutrient media   7—Secretary's Office   8—Serum Laboratory

WELLCOME PHYSIOLOGICAL RESEARCH LABORATORIES
HERNE HILL, LONDON (ENGLAND)
This PRIVATE INSTITUTION is absolutely separate from the business of BURROUGHS WELLCOME & CO., and is under separate and distinct direction, although in this Institution a large amount of important scientific work is carried out for the firm.

Fig. 4.6 Wellcome Physiological Research Laboratories, 1909. (Credit: From Ergot to "Ernutin": an historical sketch: lecture memoranda, Medical Congress, Bombay, 1909, Wellcome Collection. Attribution 4.0 International (CC BY 4.0))

Info box 4: Henry Dale

Henry Hallett Dale, son of the director of a London earthenware company, began studying medicine at Trinity College at the University of Cambridge, in 1894. From 1898 to 1900, he worked in the laboratory of the British physiologist John Newport Langley, who researched the structure and physiology of the autonomic nervous system. After a four-month research stay with Paul Ehrlich in Frankfurt, he returned to London in 1904 and completed his clinical training in the same year. A scholarship at University College secured him an annual income of £150, which was at best enough for a frugal bachelor's life. However, because he wanted to start a family, Dale tried to get a better-paid permanent position at the university ("This song of science is an old one, but again and again it resounds anew")—fortunately without success. When Henry Wellcome offered him a starting salary of £400, Dale accepted the offer, moved to Burroughs, Wellcome & Co. in 1904, and married his cousin "Nellie" after a long engagement. In 1906 he became director of the Wellcome Physiological Research Laboratories.

In 1914, after eight years of research on ergot alkaloids, acetylcholine, and histamine at Burroughs, Wellcome & Co., Dale became head of the Department of Biochemistry and Pharmacology at the Medical Research Committee in London. Here, he was instrumental in the transfer of insulin production from Canada to the UK and in the formulation of the active ingredient into standardized units. In 1928, Dale became director of the British National Institute for Medical Research. In 1936, he was awarded the Nobel Prize for Physiology or Medicine, was elected President of the Royal Society in 1940, and from 1942 was Chairman of the Secret Science Committee of Winston Churchill's War Cabinet. From 1938 to 1960, Dale was chairman of the Wellcome Trust [41].

Sir Henry Hallett Dale (1875 London – 1968 Cambridge), British physiologist and biochemist. (Wellcome Collection CC BY 4.0)

The interview at Wellcome was successful, and Dale received a job offer. But should he really make the switch from academic research to industry? Friends advised him not to do so, because that would mean nothing more than "selling [his] (my) scientific birthright for a mess of commercial pottage" [42]. On the other hand, his financial situation at the university was less than modest, and the prospects of a successful academic career were uncertain at best. The working conditions in Wellcome's research department were nothing short of heavenly in comparison: good laboratory equipment, laboratory staff, great scientific colleagues, the freedom to pursue his own research projects, and to occasionally perform physiological tests of production extracts. Dale accepted and was looking forward to continuing his scientific work at the Wellcome Physiological Research Laboratories.

He eagerly awaited the project that his new boss had planned for him. Henry Wellcome had crystal-clear ideas about this, which were less scientific than strategic in nature. Several US companies were very successful in selling ergot extracts for obstetrics and gynecology; the head of the company thus decided it was the right time to play his modern research laboratories as a trump card in order to penetrate this attractive market segment with the discovery of the pure active ingredient. Although Wellcome told Dale that he should take care of the "ergot substances when he had time", the priorities of his tasks were unequivocal and the disappointment of the newly married physiologist was significant. He had hoped for more attractive things for his first pharmacological work than having to deal with the "ergot morass", as he called it [39, 43]. Dale's research colleague in chemistry was George Barger (Info box 5), whom Wellcome had hired a year earlier.

Barger decided to continue the chemical-preparative ergot work at the point where Charles Tanret had taken a "wrong turn" 30 years earlier when he decided to work on the almost inactive *Ergotinine cristallisée*. The British chemist now tried to obtain the pharmaceutically relevant ergot compounds from the *Ergotinine amorphe* mother liquors. In 1906, George Barger and Francis Howard Carr, head of chemical production, isolated a new substance that crystallized when phosphoric acid was added (at the same time, the Swiss pharmacist Fritz Kraft from Brugg also succeeded in doing this) [44]. When it triggered the hoped-for contraction of the uterine muscles, the ergot problem was solved for the three scientists. The rejoicing in the Wellcome Physiological and Chemical Research Laboratories (Fig. 4.7) must have been exuberant, and Barger gave the uterotonic compound the name *ergotoxine* [45]. Combining the laboratories for preparative chemistry, chemical analysis, and physiology was the key to their rapid scientific success. In the same year, Burroughs, Wellcome & Co. introduced the drug into obstetrics under the trade name

Fig. 4.7 Scientists at the *Wellcome Physiological Research Laboratories*: Front row, 2nd from left George Barger, 3rd from left Henry Dale; photo 1914. (Wellcome Collection CC BY 4.0)

"Ernutin®". Their colleagues in the powerful marketing department rubbed their hands and knew exactly what their boss expected from their sales strategies to optimally position the new product. But around the corner lurked the notorious banana peel, which had so far brought down all researchers who had tried their hand at the pure ergot active component. Henry Wellcome's team of unsuspecting scientists, meanwhile, continued celebrating.

Info box 5: George Barger

George Barger was born in Manchester. As the son of a Dutch father and an English mother, he grew up bilingual. After his school days in Holland, he returned to England and began studying chemistry and botany at King's College, Cambridge. This was followed by two scientifically formative years at the University of Brussels, where he taught botany and worked on the isolation of natural substances and analytical methods. In 1903, he joined the Wellcome Chemical Research Laboratories to study cardiac glycosides of foxglove, before turning his attention to ergot substances together with the British physiologist Henry Dale. In 1909, Barger left industrial research and continued his academic career. In 1919, he became head of the new Chair of Medicinal Chemistry at the University of Edinburgh. His earlier choice of subject and his great interest in botany were ideal prerequisites for his later legendary chemical work in the field of plant alkaloids. In 1939, the passionate hiker traveled to visit friends in Switzerland, where he also took the opportunity to give lectures at the University of Basel. During an excursion near Aeschi on Lake Thun, Barger died of heart failure [46].

George Barger (1878 Manchester – 1939 Aeschi), British chemist. (© Mondadori Portfolio/Bridgeman Images)

References

1. J. Dietl, Ich kann kein Glück empfinden – die arme Frau hat so gelitten! – Schmerzvolle Geburtserfahrungen in historisch-literarischen Fallbeispielen, in *Die geburtshilfliche Anästhesie*, ed. by P. Kranke (Springer, Germany, 2018), pp. 9–10
2. J.C.G. Röhl, Geburtstrauma: "Es lebt und ist ein Prinz!", in *Wilhelm II: die Jugend des Kaisers, 1859–1888* vol 1. (Verlag C.H. Beck, Munich, 1993), p. 24
3. W.J. Mommsen, Aus Mangel strebte er zum Militär. *Frankfurter Rundschau*, July 24, 2004
4. F.W. Sertürner, Darstellung der reinen Mohnsäure (Opiumsäure) nebst einer chemischen Untersuchung des Opiums mit vorzüglicher Hinsicht auf einen darin neu entdeckten Stoff und die dahin gehörigen Bemerkungen. J Pharm Fuer Aerzte Apotheker Chem **14**(06), 47 (1805)

5. L.N. Vauquelin, Analyse du Seigle ergoté du bois de Boulogne, près Paris. Ann Chim Phys **3**, 337 (1816)

6. H.A.L. Wiggers, Untersuchung über das Mutterkorn, Secale cornutum. (Liebig's) Ann Pharm **1**, 129 (1832)

7. C.A. Ingenohl, Über das Ergotin und das Extractum Secalis cornuti, in *Archiv der Pharmacie, eine Zeitschrift des Apotheker-Vereins in Norddeutschland Reihe 2* vol 62., ed. by H. Wackenroder, L. Bley (Verlag der Hahn'schen Hofbuchhandlung, Hannover, 1850), p. 17

8. J. Althaus, A Lecture on the Prognosis of Cerebral Haemorrhage. BMJ **2**, 101 (1876)

9. H. Köhler, Vergleichend-experimentelle Untersuchungen über die physiologischen Wirkungen des Ergotin Bonjeans und des Ergotin Wiggers, in *Archiv f. pathol. Anat* vol 60., ed. by R. Virchow (Georg Reimer, Berlin, 1874), p. 384

10. J.W. Ross, Report upon Yellow Fever, in *Annual Report of the Surgeon-General of the United States Navy for the Year 1884* (Government Printing Office,, Washington, 1885), p. 316

11. J. Bonjean, *Ergotine gegen durch Verwundungen veranlaßte Blutungen aus Arterien und Venen* Notizen aus dem Gebiet der Natur- und Heilkunde Dritte Reihe, vol. 11 (ruck und Verlag des Landes-Industrie-Comptoirs, Weimar, 1849), pp. 201–208. Ed: R. Froriep

12. C.L. Diehl, Ergotin. How should Bonjean's ergotine be prepared and what advantage, if any, does it possess over the extract of ergot of the German Pharmacopoeia? Pharm J Trans 3rd Ser **12**, 519 (1882)

13. C. Löwig, *Chemie der organischen Verbindungen* vol. 2 (F. Schulthess, Zurich, 1840), p. 350

14. A.P. de Candolle, *Mémoire sur le genre Sclerotium, et en particulier sur l'Ergot des céréales* Mém. Mus. d'hist. nat, vol. 2 (G. Dufour, Paris, 1815), p. 401

15. C.C. Schmidt, *Encyklopädie der gesammten Medicin, im Vereine mit mehreren Aerzten Band*, 2nd edn. vol. 4 (Wigand, Leipzig, 1844), p. 667

16. F. von Berchtold, W.B. Seidl, *Oekonomisch-technische Flora Böhmens* vol. 1 (J.Ht. Pospíšil, Prague, 1836), p. 372

17. J. Smith, XXVII. Observations on the Cause of Ergot. Trans Linn Soc Lond **18**(3), 449 (1841)

18. E.J. Quekett, XXVIII. Observations on the Ergot of Rye, and of other grasses. Trans Linn Soc Lond **18**(3), 453 (1841)

19. F. Bauer, XXIX. On the Ergot of Rye. Trans Linn Soc **18**(3), 475 (1841)

20. E.J. Quekett, Origin of the ergot of rye. Lancet **827**, 542 (1839)

21. E.J. Quekett, Origin of the Ergot of Rye. Am J Pharm **5**(3), 237 (1840)

22. H.A.L. Wiggers, Untersuchung über das Mutterkorn, Secale cornutum, in *Annalen der Pharmacie* vol 1, 2., ed. by R. Brandes, Ph, L. Geiger, J. Liebig (Meyersche Hof-Buchhandlung Wintersche Universitäts-Buchhandlung, Lemgo Heidelberg, 1832), pp. 145–156

23. L.-R. Tulasne, Mémoire sur l'ergot des glumacées. Ann Sci Nat **20**, 5 (1853)

24. C. Tanret, Sur la presence d'un nouvel alcaloid, l'ergotinine, dans le seigle ergoté. CR hebd Séances Acad Sci **81**, 896 (1875)

25. C. Tanret, Sur l'ergotinine cristallisée. Bull Acad Med **6**, 919 (1877)

26. C. Tanret, De l'ergotinine. Ann Chim Phys **17**, 493 (1879)

27. G. Barger, The Alkaloids of Ergot, in *Ergänzungswerk. Handbuch der Experimentellen Pharmakologie*, ed. by W. Heubner, J. Schüller (Springer, Berlin Heidelberg, 1938), p. 84

28. L. Lestel, *Charles Tanret. Itinéraires de chimistes: 1857–2007: 150 ans de chimie en France avec les présidents de la SFC* (EDP Sciences, Les Ulis, 2021), p. 501

29. A. Stoll, A. Hofmann, Die Alkaloide der Ergotoxingruppe: Ergocristin, Ergokryptin und Ergocornin (7. Mitteilung über Mutterkornalkaloide). Helv Chim Acta **26**, 1570 (1943)

30. C. Tanret, A new base taken from rye ergot, ergothioneine. Ann Chim Phys **18**, 114 (1909)

31. C. Tanret, Sur un nouveau principe immédiat de l'ergot de seigle, l'ergostérine. CR hebd Séances Acad Sci **108**, 98 (1889)

32. G. Tanret, Sur un alcaloid retiré du Galega officinalis. C R Hebd Seances Acad Sci **158**, 1182 (1914)

33. G. Tanret, Sur quelques propriétés physiologiques du sulfate de galégine. CR hebd Séances Acad Sci **159**, 108 (1914)

34. F.J. Bové, The Pharmacology of Ergot, in *The Story of Ergot* (Karger, Basel, 1970), p. 252

35. C.M. Wenyon, Henry Solomon Wellcome, 1853–1936. Obit Not Biogr Mems Fell R Soc **2**, 229 (1936)

36. W. Hoffman, *The Long View from The Watonwan River: The Millenarian Odyssey of Pioneer Drug Yeast Henry Wellcome* (University of Minnesota Medical School, 1995). https://mbbnet.ahc.umn.edu/hoff/hsw_art.html

37. R. Church, The British Market for Medicine in the late Nineteenth Century: The Innovative Impact of S M Burroughs & Co. Med Hist **49**, 281 (2005)

38. N.E. Yorke-Davies, Thyroid Tabloids in Obesity. BMJ **2**, 42 (1894)

39. E.M. Tansey, Medicines and men: Burroughs, Wellcome & Co, and the British drug industry before the Second World War. J R Soc Med **95**, 411–416 (2002)

40. T. Tansey, *Celebrating 75 Extraordinary Years—A Wellcome man: Henry Dale and the early years of the Trust* (Wellcome Trust, London, 2011)

41. W.S. Feldberg, Henry Hallett Dale, 1875–1968. Biogr Mems Fell R Soc **16**, 77 (1970)

42. R.A. Kyle, M.A. Shampoo, Henry Hallett Dale—Chemical Transmissions of Nerve Impulses. Mayo Clin Proc **78**, 6 (2003)

43. A. Wickens, Sir Henry Hallet Dale (1875–1968). Resonance **24**, 833 (2019)

44. F. Kraft, Über das Mutterkorn. Arch Pharm **244**, 336 (1906)

45. G. Barger, F.H. Carr, Note on ergot alkaloids. Chem News **94**, 89 (1906)

46. H.H. Dale, Obituary George Barger, 1878–1939. Biogr Mems Fell R Soc **3**, 63 (1940)

5

Successful failures and accidental breakthroughs are changing the field of medicine

Something has gone wrong – Part 1: The "adrenaline reversal"

One of Dale's responsibilities, which bored him to tears, was the routine analysis of ergot and organ extracts from the production department at Wellcome's research laboratories. In 1906, he again had to determine the adrenaline activity of an adrenal extract administered to a cat, and he expected the usual rise in blood pressure. But he had obviously misstepped because, to his surprise, the cat's blood pressure dropped. Dale reported to his colleagues that the supplied preparation was inactive. A week later, a new batch arrived and, as before, the cat's blood pressure decreased. As the British physiologist reflected on this, it turned out that the animal had received ergot samples from Barger's laboratory prior to the administration of the adrenaline extract. The effect observed by chance, which entered pharmacological literature as *adrenaline reversal*, led Dale to two grandiose conclusions:

> *"(…) ergot contains a principle which has a paralytic action on the motor elements of that myotrophic structure or substance, which is excited by adrenaline and by impulses in fibres of the true sympathetic system; the inhibitor elements of the same being relatively or absolutely unaffected"* [1].

If ergotine and ergotoxine could selectively neutralize the blood pressure-raising component of adrenaline without affecting its blood pressure-lowering properties, there would have to be two different "receptive substances for adrenaline", which Dale suspected were in the arteries. Not only had he first observed the blocking of the α-receptors of adrenaline by ergotoxine, which increases blood pressure, but he had also discovered the blood pressure-lowering activity of the hormone, which is triggered via the β-receptors in the blood vessels. It was not until 1948 that the US physiologist Raymond Perry Ahlquist was able to confirm Dale's assumption that two different adrenaline receptors must exist and explain why one substance can have both excitatory and inhibitory activity [2, 3].

"The action (...) appears a somewhat complicated one."—Histamine

The ergot sclerotia were a chemical treasure trove that Barger watched over and from which he continually unearthed more and more biologically active molecules. In 1910, Dale, Barger and the British biochemist Patrick Playfair Laidlaw (1881–1940) extracted *histamine* from it (Fig. 5.1). In physiological studies on frogs and rodents, they recognized the "somewhat complicated" effect of the biogenic amine, which varied significantly depending on the animal or organ. They found that the molecule triggers contractions of the smooth muscles of the respiratory tract, uterus and intestines, dilates blood vessels, and increases heart rate and gastric acid secretion. In addition, Dale and Laidlaw recognized histamine as the agent that can cause allergic reactions and anaphylactic shock [4, 5].

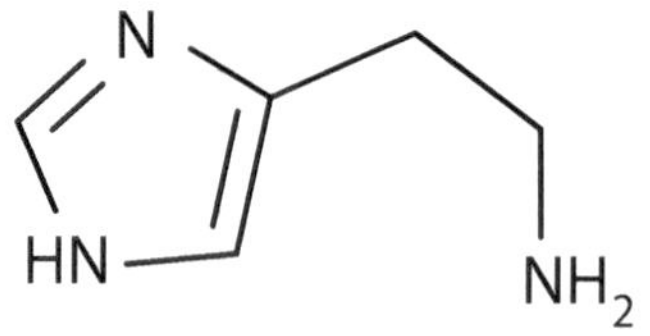

Fig. 5.1 Histamine

After Dale's working group identified histamine as an endogenous substance in mammals in 1927, their research results became the starting point for a drug discovery program at the *Institut Pasteur* in Paris [6]. The Swiss-Italian physiologist and pharmacologist Daniel Bovet (1907–1992) was looking for inhibitors of severe allergies. Among the compounds synthesized by his boss Ernest Fourneau, head of the Institute of Therapeutic Chemistry, and Bovet's doctoral student Anne-Marie Staub, he discovered a molecule from the *N,N-dimethylethylenediamine* class that suppressed allergies and intolerance reactions triggered by histamine. Staub and Bovet's research laid the foundation for the development of the first antihistamines *phenbenzamine* and *mepyramine*. The French pharmaceutical company Rhône-Poulenc introduced the two inhibitors of the histamine H_1-receptor into human therapy as *Antergan®* (phenbenzamine, 1942) and *Neo-Antergan®* (mepyramine, 1944). In 1957, Bovet was awarded the Nobel Prize in Physiology or Medicine "for his discoveries relating to synthetic compounds that inhibit the action of certain body substances, and especially their action on the vascular system and the skeletal muscles" [7].

Since neither of the two drugs blocked the histamine effect on the heart rate and gastric acid secretion, there had to be further receptors in addition to the histamine H_1-receptor. The British pharmacologist Sir James Black (1924–2010) predicted that their inhibitors must be very similar to the histamine molecule, unlike phenbenzamine and mepyramine. Black hit the bull's-eye with his assumption, and *cimetidine* emerged from the chemical modification of histamine as a selective inhibitor of the histamine H_2-receptor. In 1976, the drug substance of the British pharmaceutical company Smith Kline-Beecham was approved for the treatment of gastric and duodenal ulcers under the trade name *Tagamet®*. In 1988, Sir James Black was honored with the Nobel Prize in Physiology or Medicine for his "discoveries of important principles for drug treatment" [7].

Something has gone wrong – Part 2: Acetylcholine, or the discovery of the first neurotransmitter

In research, exciting scientific experimentation and lean periods of monotonous routine work are two sides of the same coin. Very rarely, however, the coin remains on the edge after a toss. For Henry Dale, such a moment of happiness came in 1913. He had to check the activity of a new ergot extract from the chemistry department, as he had done many times before, and administered it intravenously to a cat. Dale was startled when the animal's heart rate suddenly dropped dramatically. He initially believed that there had been a mistake during the injection. When the heart rate returned to normal, Dale repeated the experiment and observed the same reaction of the heart muscle. Without a doubt, he must have been dealing with a new molecule of the ergot fungus, because the inhibition of the heart rate had previously only been known by the vagus nerve of the parasympathetic nervous system, as well as by a substance synthesized in 1866 that had been obtained by the acetylation of the body's own choline: acetylcholine (Fig. 5.2).

Dale and the British chemist Arthur James Ewins (1882–1958) began to isolate the new active principle from the sclerotia and, to their astonishment, came across acetylcholine again, which had now been found for the first time in a biological source [8, 9].

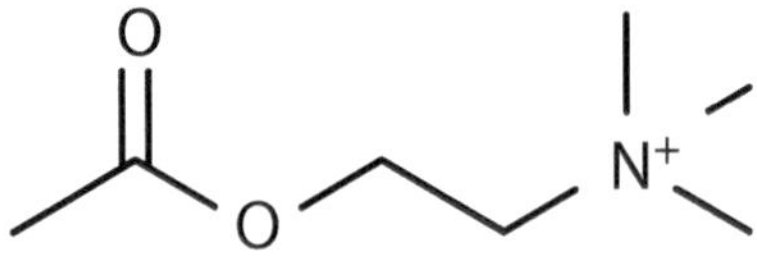

Fig. 5.2 Acetylcholine

Dale was fascinated by the molecule and wrote enthusiastically to his former lab colleague, Thomas Renton Elliott:

"We got that thing out of our silly ergot extract. It is acetylcholine, and a most interesting substance. (…) Here is a good candidate for the role of a hormone related to the rest of the autonomic nervous system. I am perilously close to wild theorizing… I shall be surprised, however, if this principle, once identified, does not turn up in all sorts of tissue extracts" [10].

The discovery of acetylcholine as a natural substance and its potent effect on the heart muscle was for Elliott grist to his mill. In 1904, during his experiments with the sympathetic nerve and adrenaline, he came up with the revolutionary idea that electrical impulses would release messenger substances at *myoneural junctions* (i.e. chemical synapses) that modulate the cell activity of their effector organs [11].

The central question of how the existence of such a signal transmission system could be experimentally proven had brought worry lines to the foreheads of all those involved. The problem had also preyed on the mind of Dale's friend from their days together at University College in London, the German-American physician Otto Löwi (Fig. 5.3). He racked his brains around it so intensively that his night's sleep began to suffer. On the night of Easter Monday 1920, he dreamt about the experimental setup for the key experiment that was to provide the missing proof. At the crack of dawn, Löwi jumped out of bed and rushed "head over heels" to his laboratory at the University of Graz. He prepared two isolated, spontaneously beating frog hearts, only one of which was connected to the vagus nerve, which is involved in the regulation of the heart rate. He filled the first beating heart with Ringer's solution and stimulated its vagus nerve. The frog's heart reacted as expected with a decrease in heart rate. Löwi then transferred the fluid from the ventricle into the second

Fig. 5.3 Otto Löwi (1875 Frankfurt a. M. – 1961 New York), German-American physician and pharmacologist. (© Wellcome Collection CC BY 4.0)

heart. Although this heart was not connected to the vagus nerve, the heart rate was also inhibited. This, however, could only have been possible if the nerve did not interact directly with the organ, but released substances that slowed down the heart rate. Löwi had demonstrated the chemical signal transmission of nerve impulses within two hours, after which his assistant merely remarked that his boss would receive the Nobel Prize as a result [12, 13].

Criticism of Löwi's legendary publication, which consisted of just four pages, did not take long to appear. Other working groups had considerable difficulty reproducing the results and also complained that Löwi had failed to answer the question of the chemistry of the *vagus substance*. At this point he had to pass, but at least he had been able to rule out the possibility that the signaling molecule was potassium, whose slowing effect on the heart rate had already been described. However, Otto Löwi had a sneaking suspicion as to which molecule he might be dealing with. He had noticed that atropine, the active ingredient in belladonna, inhibited the activity of the vagus substance but also that of acetylcholine [12, 13]. This commonality was certainly interesting, but was the finding relevant to solving his problem? Whether acetylcholine was present in vertebrates was unknown. Löwi needed precisely this missing chemical link to crown his research on the signal substance of the brain. He had to be patient for nine long years until his friend Henry Dale handed him the missing piece of the puzzle.

While Otto Löwi was brooding over his vagus substance in Austria, in England, Dale was still interested in histamine. In 1927, he and the British chemist Harold Ward Dudley (1887–1935) set out to prove that histamine is also found in mammals. Conveniently, there was a slaughterhouse near their research institute, from which they carried buckets of ox and horse organs to the laboratory from early in the morning until late at night. They succeeded in isolating the biogenic amine from ox liver, but in 1929 they also happened to find acetylcholine. Dudley needed 75 pounds of horse spleen to obtain 64 mg of the signal substance [6]. Dale and Dudley's lucky break was the conclusive evidence for Otto Löwi. Now the cautious scientist was sure that his vagus substance had to be acetylcholine or an "acetylcholine-like substance". Dale, on the other hand, asked himself the difficult question of whether acetylcholine only mediates the lowering of the heart rate or whether it could also be a general transmitter of the autonomic and peripheral nervous system. An exotic test organism helped provide the answer.

The German-British physiologist Wilhelm Feldberg (1900–1993) (Fig. 5.4) had spent two months at Dale's institute in the mid-1920s, where he was influenced by his teacher's mantra that "a scientific method must first be perfected over months or even years before an experiment can be started". Following Feldberg's subsequent escape from Nazi Germany, Dale immediately employed him again to help him detect acetylcholine in various body tissues. Feldberg succeeded in discovering the messenger substance, which is only released in trace amounts, using a method based on the contraction of the dorsal muscle of the Hungarian leech. In 1917, the German physiologist Hermann Fühner reported that the sensitivity of the parasite's dorsal muscle to acetylcholine was increased a million-fold by the addition of physostigmine, an inhibitor of the acetylcholine-cleaving esterase [14]. In an exuberant letter to Otto Löwi, Dale remarked:

> *"What a joy it is to have Feldberg back here, however, much one deplores the conditions, which have driven him out of his own country. His importation of the leech test (…) seems likely to be as stimulating for my own work on chemical transmission, as the expulsion of the Huguenots from France was for the British textile industry"* [15].

Fig. 5.4 *From left*: Wilhelm S. Feldberg, Sir Henry H. Dale, Sir John H. Gaddum (1960). (Credit: J. Donnerer and F. Lembeck; CC BY-SA 3.0 DE)

Wilhelm Feldberg was able to demonstrate the importance of acetylcholine as a neurotransmitter for signal transmission in the peripheral nervous system, and as a regulator of body's basic functions using the highly sensitive leech test [12, 16]. Now, Dale was also convinced that the acetylcholine from the sclerotia material was identical to Löwi's vagus substance of the frog heart and Feldberg's transmitter substance [17].

In 1936, Feldberg and the German-British pharmacologist Marthe Louise Vogt (Fig. 5.5) reported the release of acetylcholine from the motor neurons innervating the skeletal muscles. In 1948, they discovered the acetylcholine-forming enzyme in the central nervous system and, from the evidence, deduced the neurotransmitter function of the molecule at central synapses [16, 18]. Feldberg's and Vogt's research on acetylcholine and its involvement in the chemical transmission of stimuli to muscle cells was a scientific masterstroke, but met with fierce, though not entirely unexpected, resistance from neurophysiologists who adhered to direct bioelectrical signal transduction. The *War of the Sparks and the Soups* began [19, 20].

Fig. 5.5 Marthe Louise Vogt (1903 Berlin – 2003 La Jolla), German-British pharmacologist. (© Wellcome Images CC BY 4.0)

Two friends win the Nobel Prize for their discovery of chemical signal transmission—the dispute with neurophysiologists becomes even more bitter

In 1936, the two friends Henry Dale and Otto Löwi were jointly awarded the Nobel Prize in Physiology or Medicine "for their discoveries relating to chemical transmission of nerve impulses". Despite this most prestigious scientific recognition, their model of chemical signal transmission remained controversial, and the decades-long dispute entered a new round [21]. Although some neurophysiologists conceded that chemical substances could possibly regulate slow organ functions, the short reaction times that are essential for skeletal muscles could only be achieved by a completely bioelectrical transmission of nerve stimulation (some of their colleagues understood even this modest concession as an unacceptable break from their stubbornly held strongholds).

Furthermore, an extrapolation of the acetylcholine findings to the signal transduction of the rest of the organism had not been demonstrated experimentally. In addition to all the justified criticism, something else hardened their opinions even further: pharmacology had invaded the domain of neurophysiologists, whose professional pride had been hurt and who saw themselves scientifically challenged. Some had always been skeptical about pharmacologists' closeness to the industry, believing that, as a result, they had lost their scientific brilliance and were now spending their time "investigating sweat, spit, snot and urine" [22]. The conflict became increasingly heated.

* * *

The Australian neurophysiologist John Carew Eccles (1903–1997) and Henry Dale were the major proponents of bioelectric and chemical signal transmission, respectively. The two tough-as-nails paladins of the *Sparks* and *Soup Schools* went head-to-head with open visors and fielded their research data. Their followers did the same and welcomed any discussion, no matter how heated [23]. Eccles launched one attack after another against Henry Dale, Wilhem Feldberg, Otto Löwi, and their scientific comrades. When his opponents' nerves were once again on edge, Löwi got carried away with the insult: "Eccles is a creep" [24]. However, the lively correspondence between Eccles and Dale makes it clear that, despite their disagreement, they were close on a human level and had the greatest respect for each other's research work. Their humorous letters underline the fact that they thoroughly enjoyed their arguments. On November 28, 1937, Eccles wrote to Dale from Sydney:

> *"(. . .) your artillery will soon be ready, but I expect that by that time you will have constructed new lines of fortification for one to have a crack at. Of course, at this distance we will miss the short-range practice that we had at the Physiological meetings, but, if you don't make it too hot for me, I may venture over to England in a few years"* [25].

By crossing swords, the two great researchers became each other's best teacher. Dale saw himself and Eccles as *ideal sparring partners*, encouraging the other's associates to develop new ideas and to test them experimentally to fully answer open-ended questions in their research. In 1944, the conflict between the two camps took an unexpected turn: a philosopher had taken the floor.

Eccles had met the Austrian-British philosopher Karl Popper (1902–1994) in Cambridge. In their joint discussions on Popper's philosophy of science of *critical rationalism*, and the drawn conclusion that a hypothesis can only be refuted, but never be verified, the aggressive neuroscientist began to rethink epistemically his view of signal transmission. Influenced by his friend Popper, Eccles designed a "killer experiment" in 1952 to disprove the completely electrical stimulus conduction via the neurons of the central nervous system to the skeletal muscles. But things did not turn out as planned. Eccles rebutted his own hitherto unshakeable position and "converted to a passionate advocate" of chemical signal transduction [19, 26, 27].

In 1963, Sir John Carew Eccles was awarded the Nobel Prize in Physiology or Medicine together with Sir Alan Hodgkin and Sir Andrew Huxley "for their discoveries concerning the ionic mechanisms involved in excitation and inhibition in the peripheral and central portions of the nerve cell membrane".

Dale's discovery of "adrenaline reversal", based on which he postulated the existence of two types of adrenoreceptors, and his work with histamine and acetylcholine as "chemical bycatch" were essential contributions from his ergot period in the research laboratories at Burroughs, Wellcome & Co., and were the impetus for the establishment of new research fields in the medical sciences [28]. The molecules from the ergot sclerotia pointed subsequent physiologists in the direction of regulatory processes of the human body, and the understanding of chemical signal transmission from motor neurons to muscle cells. Medicinal chemistry and the pharmaceutical sciences transformed these findings into new therapeutic agents and fundamentally changed medical practice in the treatment of coronary and pneumological diseases, high blood pressure, allergic reactions, ulcers, reflux, anesthesia, and intensive care medicine.

Dale's ability to bring together outstanding scientists and win them over for his projects, his friendliness, infectious enthusiasm, professional brilliance, and scientific instinct made these groundbreaking successes possible. He had a close, lifelong friendship with Otto Löwi. When Löwi died in New York in 1961, Henry Dale wrote an obituary for his old friend and scientific companion, just as Dale had previously done for his fellow ergot campaigners Harold Ward Dudley, George Barger, Patrick Playfair Laidlaw, and Arthur James Ewins.

Another damp squib: ergotoxine and the disappointed gynecologists

Henry Wellcome should have been proud of the great achievements of his young ergot team, which had made the launch of ergotoxine into the market, under the drug name *Ernutin*®, possible—perhaps he was. But the assessment of the new drug by gynecologists thwarted the commercial plans of the com-

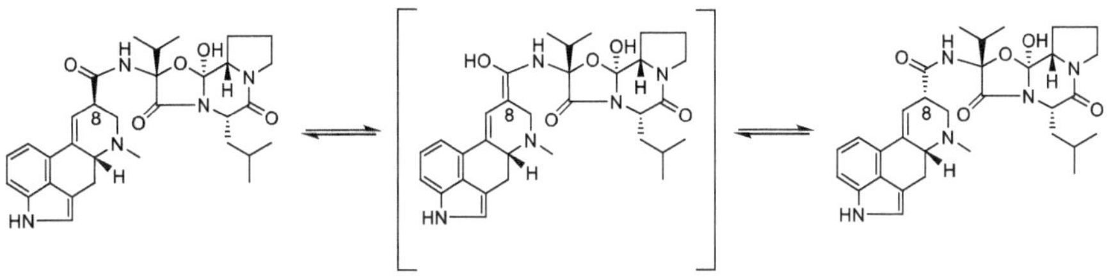

Fig. 5.6 Epimerization using the example of ergocryptine

pany's chief officer: they were not convinced of its uterotonic activity and also noted toxic side effects. It was not until 40 years after the isolation of ergotoxine that it was shown that Dale's, Barger's, Carr's and Kraft's crystallizates had also been substance mixtures. They contained the ergot alkaloids *ergocornine*, *ergocristine*, and *ergocryptine*, which were nothing other than the physiologically highly active conversion products of the almost inactive natural substances that Tanret had obtained 30 years earlier in his *Ergotinine cristallisée* (Fig. 5.6 and Fig. 8.7; [29, 30]).

From a chemical point of view, six ergot alkaloids were now known, even if they were only present in mixtures. In their search for the active principle of ergot, chemists had taken a new direction, but, ultimately, they had only gone round in circles. The gynecologists had rejected the drug from the Wellcome laboratories and at the same time demanded a *different* ergot substance [31]. But which one? Even more concerning: did it even exist? Were the ergot alkaloids really the pharmaceutically relevant compounds scientists were looking for, or was the complex mixture of alkaloids, uterotonic histamine and sympathomimetic tyramine the actual medicine [28, 32]? Once again, deep-seated doubts emerged. In the following ten years, ergot research made no headway.

References

1. H.H. Dale, On some physiological actions of ergot. J Physiol **34**, 163 (1906)
2. H.H. Dale, On the action of ergotoxine; with special reference to the existence of sympathetic vasodilators. J Physiol **46**, 291 (1913)
3. M.R. Lee, The history of ergot of rye (*Claviceps purpurea*) II: 1900–1940. JR Coll Physicians Edinb **39**, 365 (2009)
4. G. Barger, H.H. Dale, Chemical structure and sympathomimetic action of amines. J Physiol **41**, 19 (1910)

5. H.H. Dale, P.P. Laidlaw, The physiological action of β-iminazolylethylamine. J Physiol **41**, 318 (1910)
6. H.H. Dale, H.W. Dudley, The presence of histamine and acetylcholine in the spleen of the ox and the horse. J Physiol **68**, 97 (1929)
7. E. Tiligada, M. Ennis, Histamine pharmacology: from Sir Henry Dale to the 21st century. Brit J Pharmacol **117**, 469 (2020)
8. R. Hunt, R. de Mortemer Taveau, On the physiological action of certain choline derivatives and new methods for detecting choline. BMJ **2**, 1788 (1906)
9. A.J. Ewins, Acetylcholine, a new active principle of ergot. Biochem J **8**, 44 (1914)
10. E.M. Tansey, Chemical neurotransmission in the autonomic nervous system: Sir Henry Dale and acetylcholine. Clin Auto Res **1**, 63 (1991)
11. T.R. Elliott, The action of adrenaline. J Physiol **32**, 401 (1905)
12. A. Wickens, Sir Henry Hallet Dale (1875–1968). Resonance **24**, 840 (2019)
13. O. Loewi, Über humorale Übertragbarkeit der Herznervenwirkung. Pflugers Arch Gesamte Physiol Menschen Tiere **189**, 239 (1921)
14. H. Fühner, Ein Vorlesungsversuch zur Demonstration der erregbarkeitssteigernden Wirkung des Physostigmins. Naunyn-Schmiedeberger's Arch f exp Pathol u Pharmakol **82**, 81 (1917)
15. R.W. Kirk, N. Pemberton, *Leech* (Reaktion Books, London, 2013), p. 157
16. H.H. Dale, W. Feldberg, M. Vogt, Release of acetylcholine at voluntary motor nerve endings. J Physiol **86**, 353 (1936)
17. H.H. Dale, W. Feldberg, The chemical transmitter of vagus effects to the stomach. J Physiol **81**, 320 (1934)
18. W. Feldberg, M. Vogt, Acetylcholine synthesis in different regions of the central nervous system. J Physiol **107**, 372 (1948)
19. J.S. Cook, "Spark" vs. "soup": a scoop for soup. News Physiol Sci **1**, 206 (1986)
20. M.C. Fishman, Sir Henry Hallett Dale and the Acetylcholine Story. Yale J Biol Med **45**, 104 (1972)
21. E.S. Valenstein, The discovery of chemical neurotransmitters. Brain Cogn **49**, 73 (2002)
22. E.S. Valenstein, *The War of the Soups and the Sparks—The Discovery of Neurotransmitters and the Dispute Over How Nerves Communicate* (Columbia University Press, New York Chichester, 2005), pp. 121–122
23. E.S. Valenstein, *The War of the Soups and the Sparks—The Discovery of Neurotransmitters and the Dispute Over How Nerves Communicate* (Columbia University Press, New York Chichester, 2005), p. 123
24. K. Umrath, II. Rückblick – Ausblick: Die Entdeckung von Otto Loewi von der humoralen Übertragbarkeit der Vaguswirkung auf das Herz und ihr mutmaßlicher Einfluß auf die Arbeiten aus dem Grazer Kreis – Physiologische Befunde und psychologische Zusammenhänge. Mitt naturwiss Ver Steiermark **114**, 17 (1984)

25. E.S. Valenstein, *The War of the Soups and the Sparks—The Discovery of Neurotransmitters and the Dispute Over How Nerves Communicate* (Columbia University Press, New York Chichester, 2005), pp. 123–124

26. D. Todman, John Eccles (1903–1997) and the experiment that proved chemical synaptic transmission in the central nervous system. J Clin Neurosci **15**, 972 (2008)

27. L.G. Brock, J.S. Coombs, J.C. Eccles, The recording of potentials from motor neurons with an intracellular electrode. J Physiol **117**, 431 (1952)

28. K.J. Williams, *British Pharmaceutical Industry, Synthetic Drug Manufacture and the Clinical Testing of Novel Drugs 1895–1939* (University of Manchester, 2005), pp. 125–126

29. A. Stoll, A. Hofmann, Die Alkaloide der Ergotoxingruppe: Ergocristin, Ergokryptin und Ergocornin (7. Mitteilung über Mutterkornalkaloide). Helv Chim Acta **26**, 1570 (1943)

30. R. Köppen, T. Rasenko, S. Merkel, B. Mönch, M. Koch, Novel Solid-Phase Extraction for Epimer-Specific Quantitation of Ergot Alkaloids in Rye Flour and Wheat Germ Oil. J Agric Food Chem **61**, 10699 (2013)

31. E. Rothlin, The specific action of ergot alkaloids on the sympathetic nervous system. J Pharmacol Sci Exp Ther **36**, 657 (1929)

32. G. Barger, H.H. Dale, The water-soluble active principles of ergot. J Physiol **38**, 77 (1909)

6

Darn, the equation doesn't add up!

A Swiss natural products chemist enters the stage: the fearless Arthur Stoll

Before the First World War, German chemical companies controlled 85% of the global textile dye market, followed by the enterprises in Basel, Switzerland, which had a market share of 10%. The outbreak of war in 1914 shifted this relative strength within a very short space of time. The conversion of German industrial production to war-related goods, the export embargoes, and the British naval blockade struck at the heart of the German dye industry at the Main and Rhine rivers. Their deliveries to the foreign textile industry stopped. Companies in England, Italy, France, and the USA now turned to the Basel dye producers, primarily ordering three colors: field gray, field green, and bluish gray for their soldiers' uniforms. Sandoz AG profited the most from these market shifts. While sales of textile dyes reached six million Swiss francs in 1914, they rose to 37 million within four years. Melchior Böniger (Info box 1), one of the two company directors, expected that the German chemical companies would resume supplying the market at the end of the war and that the sales of Sandoz AG's dyestuffs division would collapse accordingly [1].

Info box 1: Melchior Böniger

Melchior Böniger was born in Nidfurn, Canton Glarus, Switzerland, the son of a xylographer. After training as a teacher, he studied chemistry at the University of Zurich and joined the chemistry department of textile dyes at Sandoz AG in

---

Basel in 1889. From 1895, Böniger was a director of the company and joined its Board of Directors in 1922. He significantly influenced the company's strategy of establishing a pharmaceutical drug research department, which began its work in 1917 under the direction of the natural products chemist Arthur Stoll. In 1924, Böniger was elected President of the Swiss Society of Chemical Industry where he promoted scientific societies and various welfare institutions for workers and employees [2]. He found a balance to his professional work by playing music: Böniger was a committed member of the Basler Liedertafel, a local male choir, and its president from 1901 to 1908.

Melchior Böniger (1866 Nidfurn – 1929 Kreuzlingen), around 1890, Swiss chemist and director of Sandoz AG. (© Novartis Company Archive)

To reduce the risky dependence on the booming textile dye business, and to balance the future company portfolio, Böniger proposed the establishment of a "Pharmaceutical Department". In search of a scientist who was up to the challenge, Böniger contacted the former President of Sandoz AG, Robert Gnehm. He recommended the Swiss natural products chemist Arthur Stoll (Info box 2), a young professor at the Ludwig Maximilian University in Munich, as exactly right candidate for this task [1].

Info box 2: Arthur Stoll

Arthur Stoll, born in Schinznach-Dorf in the Swiss canton of Aargau, began studying geology and botany at ETH Zurich in 1906. He attended the lectures of Richard Willstätter (1872–1942) in inorganic and organic chemistry, and was so fascinated by the subject matter and Willstätter's personality that he also began studying chemistry. In 1909, Willstätter took him on as an assistant in his private laboratory to investigate the isolation of chlorophylls and other plant pigments. In 1911, both moved to the Kaiser Wilhelm Institute for Organic Chemistry in Berlin. In 1915, Richard Willstätter was awarded the Nobel Prize in Chemistry "for his research on plant pigments, especially chlorophyll", to which Stoll had made significant contributions. In 1916, both moved to the Ludwig Maximilian University in Munich, where Willstätter succeeded Adolf von Baeyer as head of the Institute of Chemistry. At his request, Stoll was appointed professor of chemistry in the same year.

In 1917, Arthur Stoll returned to Switzerland to set up the "Pharmaceutical Department" of Sandoz AG in Basel by founding a natural product research group. During his drug discovery projects, he worked on the ergot and senna alkaloids, as well as the cardiac glycosides of foxglove plants, squill, and the large-leafed poison rope *Strophantus kombé* Oliv. Stoll's research resulted in numerous drugs being introduced into human medical treatments. Arthur Stoll rose rapidly in the corporate hierarchy of Sandoz AG and was appointed to the Board of Directors in 1933, where he was Chairman from 1964 to 1967. In 1939, he succeeded in obtaining an entry visa to Switzerland for his Jewish teacher Richard Willstätter, who had been subjected to harassment in Nazi Germany and had lost his assets and most of his art collection through expropriation. Stoll's personal interests were not limited to building up a renowned art collection, which included sculptures and paintings from the 19th and 20th centuries. He also played the organ and engaged with theological topics. His wide-ranging interests led to long-standing friendships with Albert Schweitzer and Hermann Hesse (personal communication by Dr. Beat Stoll, 2023) [3, 4].

Arthur Stoll (1887 Schinznach-Dorf – 1971 Dornach), Swiss natural products chemist and Chairman of the Board of Directors of Sandoz AG. (© Novartis Company Archive)

Against the advice of his university friends, Stoll applied to the Basel-based chemical company (the reservations about industrial pharmaceutical research had not changed since Henry Dale's day; they were to remain in place for a long time), and on March 15, 1917, the Board of Directors of Sandoz AG decided, under the agenda item "Miscellaneous", to commission the natural products researcher to set up a pharmaceutical research department [1, 5]. That summer, Stoll pulled up stakes in Bavaria and left behind the "laboratories of the chemical institute, which had been rather deserted by the second year of the war" [6].

Stoll's first day at work on October 1, 1917, was quite sobering and may have reminded him of how he had found the institute in the Isar metropolis outdated when he moved from Berlin-Dahlem. In contrast to the exquisite conditions under which Henry Dale and George Barger had begun their work at Burroughs, Wellcome & Co. in London, Stoll entered an "empty room without any installations or furniture, equipped with glassware and apparatuses in the simplest manner" (Figs. 6.1 and 6.2). However, the die was cast

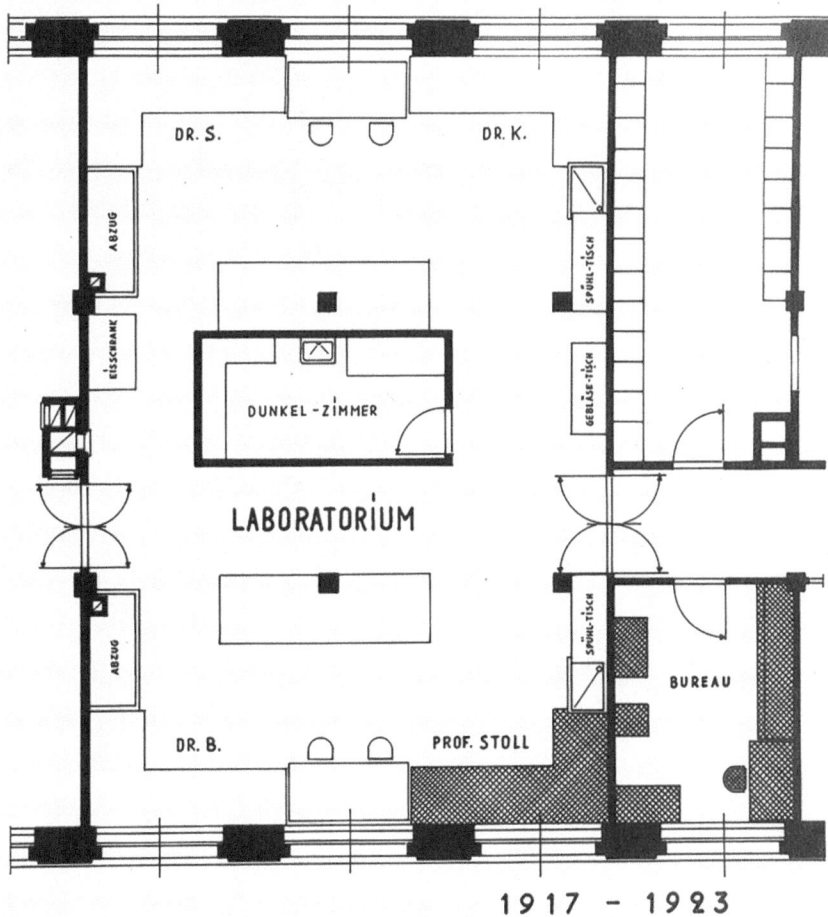

Fig. 6.1 Floor plan of Arthur Stoll's chemistry laboratory, 1917/23. (© Novartis Company Archive)

and now it was time to identify a promising project that offered the chance of rapid scientific success. Stoll threw his hat with verve into the ring and chose—almost unbelievably—the ergot alkaloids.

Although the best scientists had been trying their hand at the recalcitrant ergot substances for half a century, and physicians had always found fault with the pharmaceutical effect of the resulting preparations, Stoll gave three reasons why, of all things, he wanted to work on these alkaloids: on the one hand, he was fascinated by the scientific problems he had come across in 1917 in an article authored by the Bernese pharmacist Alexander Tschirch in the *Schwei-*

Fig. 6.2 First pharmaceutical research building of Sandoz AG with Arthur Stoll's laboratory on the first floor, 1917. (© Novartis Company Archive)

zerische Apotheker-Zeitung. On the other hand, he was looking for a medically relevant starting material with which to begin his research work at Sandoz. According to Stoll's assessment, the origin and storage time of the sclerotia, as well as the instability and heterogeneity of their biologically active ingredients were the reasons why the therapeutic effect of previous ergot preparations in gynecological and obstetrical indications was not convincing or had failed. Reliable and safe administration of the ergot medicine was simply impossible under such miserable circumstances. Only a pure substance could achieve this, but at this point all previous researchers had to lay down their arms. Stoll's third reason was his rock-solid conviction that the preparative methodology he had worked out and continuously refined during his research on plant pigments in Richard Willstätter's working group would lead to the isolation of the active principle of ergot [7].

It was an impressively detailed analysis of the problem, including a solution approach, that the thirty-year-old dreadnought put down on paper. After the crushing failure in England, Stoll's confidence was more important than ever, even refreshing, and had a convincing effect on his superiors. Stoll plunged into his ergot adventure.

Ergotamine crystallizes!

Only one year later, on December 8, 1918, Arthur Stoll observed the crystallization of an ergot substance from aqueous acetone. He made a note in his lab journal:

> *"In the stripped-off solution immediately and in the concentrated filtrate after about $\frac{1}{4}$ hour, a crystallization of splendid, extremely strongly refractive prisms and plates began, which were often bounded by domes and lateral pyramidal surfaces"* [8].

Stoll's *mild isolation method*, as he liked to call it, was the key to his success. He isolated 0.2% pure alkaloid from the sclerotia material, which he called *ergotamine* (Fig. 6.3; [8–10]). It was almost a miracle that the natural products chemist had reached his goal so quickly. His sparse laboratory equipment severely limited him, and he constantly had to improvise when procuring solvents. As neither ether nor chloroform, acetone or sulphuric acid were available for his work due to the war, Stoll was forced to gain the required solvents himself from impure by-product fractions from dye manufacturing. Decades later, with a twinkle in his eye, he summed up that "ergotamine was actually born as the child of poor people" [11].

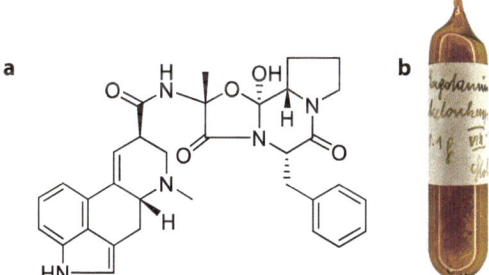

Fig. 6.3 a Structural formula of ergotamine; **b** Ampoule with ergotamine acetone crystallite, August 1920: Oldest active ingredient preparation of Novartis AG. (© Novartis Company Archive)

His project colleague was the German chemist and physician Karl Spiro. He had done research under Oswald Schmiedeberger and Franz Hofmeister at the University of Strasbourg and had to leave France after the end of the First World War. In 1919, he found a new job in Stoll's pharmaceutical department and set up the first pharmacological laboratories at Sandoz AG.

Spiro's task was to test Stoll's preparations on the guinea pig uterus. He was able to demonstrate the uterotonic activity of ergotamine in a dilution of 1:20,000,000, which had never been seen before in drugs. The alkaloid was even more active in a human uterus. When the life-threatening postpartum hemorrhage of a woman in labor at the Basel Women's Hospital could be stopped after the administration of 0.5 mg ergotamine, the pharmacologists calculated that the compound was still therapeutically effective at a dilution of 1:120,000,000 [12].

Following the company's decision to introduce ergotamine into medicine, things progressed quickly: in 1920, a construction permit application was submitted for the ergot extraction building, which was ready for operation in the same year (Figs. 6.4 and 6.5), and in 1921 the tartaric acid salt of the alkaloid

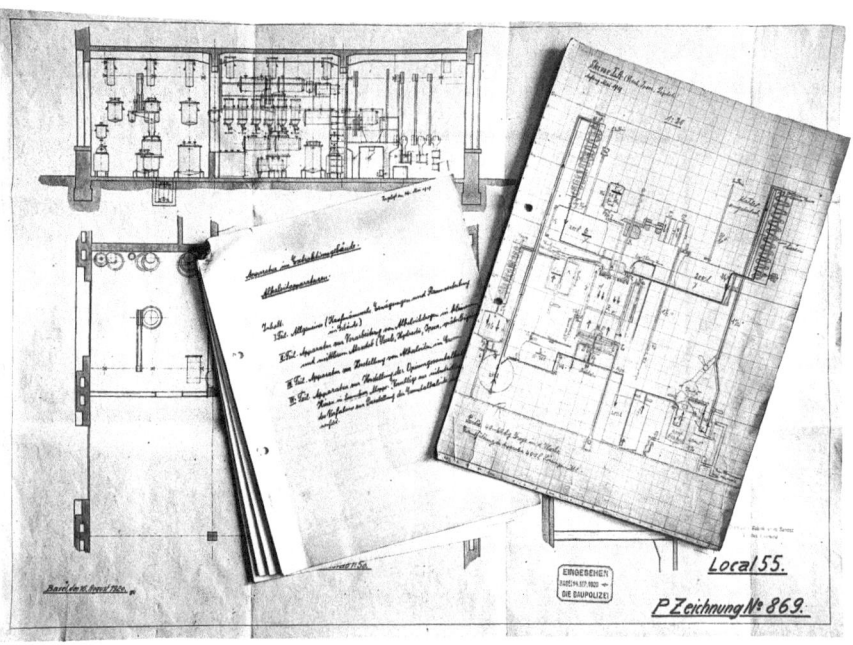

Fig. 6.4 Plans for the construction permit application for the ergot extraction building, 1920. (© Novartis Company Archive)

Fig. 6.5 Ergot extraction building, 1920. (© Novartis Company Archive)

was officially approved under the brand name *Gynergen*® (Fig. 6.6), to be used for the induction of labor and for the treatment of postpartum hemorrhage.

Everything seemed to be in perfect order, but right after the market launch, disaster almost struck. The obstetricians, who had no experience in administering the highly potent drug, dosed it too high: women experienced strong contractions too early, and during labor, they vomited and suffered from cramping pains. The doctors immediately stopped administering ergotamine; before sales of the alkaloid had taken off in Switzerland, they had already collapsed. Stoll's drug was on the rocks. Did this mean the end of the ergot program at Sandoz, as it did at Burroughs Wellcome? Despite the delicate situation, Karl Spiro forged ahead. In a very short time, he was able to convince clinicians to start new studies with lower doses. The results, which were published immediately afterwards, proved the therapeutic benefit and safety of ergotamine, and managed to save *Gynergen*® [13].

After the market launch, Arthur Stoll monitored the sales figures of his first drug and compiled the monthly income of the Sandoz AG pharmaceutical portfolio with a sharp eye (Fig. 6.7). After two years, the ergotamine income remained unremarkable, much to the chagrin of the company management. The initial expectations regarding the pharmaceutical department had been

Fig. 6.6 *Gynergen®* packaging, around 1930. (© Novartis Company Archive)

quite different, and soon the shameful term "expenditure multiplier" was doing the rounds.

In the meantime, Sandoz pharmacologists had begun to search for further indication areas in order to exploit the therapeutic potential of the drug. The new head of the pharmacology department, Ernst Rothlin, studied the phenomenon of the "adrenaline reversal" in particular. Henry Dale had described this effect for the first time during his ergotoxin research, but did not seem to consider using it therapeutically afterwards. Since ergotamine had the same effect, Rothlin saw the possibility of using ergotamine to treat diseases caused by an increased sympathetic tone, such as hyperthyroidism or Graves' disease [14–16]. During further research, Rothlin also came across the testimonials of a British doctor. In 1868, Edward Woakes (1837–1912) had shared the assumption of earlier physicians, who had seen the dilation of blood vessels, as the trigger for neuralgia and migraine attacks, and pursued the vasoconstrictive effect of the ergot extract as a new therapeutic approach for these pain disorders [17, 18]. Even if this connection is no longer supported today, Woakes' ergot medicine nevertheless became the first migraine treatment to target the causes of the disease—the inhibition of the hyperactivation of certain nerve cells of the "migraine center" in the brain stem, and an associated neurogenic inflammation triggered by an increased release of the neurotransmitter serotonin [19]. For patients who had previously been maltreated with potassium cyanide, strychnine, belladonna, hashish, opium, cocaine, chloroform, mercury compounds or with the complete extraction of their teeth, the innovative drug doubled their relief from suffering [20].

The sclerotia extract was only prescribed sporadically due to its strongly fluctuating content of active molecules. It was not until 1925, when the efficacy of ergotamine was demonstrated, that *Gynergen*® was granted marketing authorization for the treatment of migraines [21, 22]. The drug was restricted to the therapy of acute migraine attacks, as the necessarily longer administration times for migraine prophylaxis induced vasoconstriction and peripheral circulatory disorders. Sandoz later developed *methysergide*, the first migraine prophylactic, which was approved around 1960. Ergotamine and the new ergotalkaloid-based drug highlighted the crucial role of serotonin in the development of migraines. At the beginning of the 1970s, the British pharmaceutical company, GlaxoSmithKline, took up these findings. Its medicinal chemistry research focused on serotonin as the lead structure, from which *sumatriptan* (*Imigran*®) was synthetized. In 1992, the molecule was introduced into medicine as the first representative of the new class of *triptans* for the acute treatment of migraine attacks and cluster headaches [23].

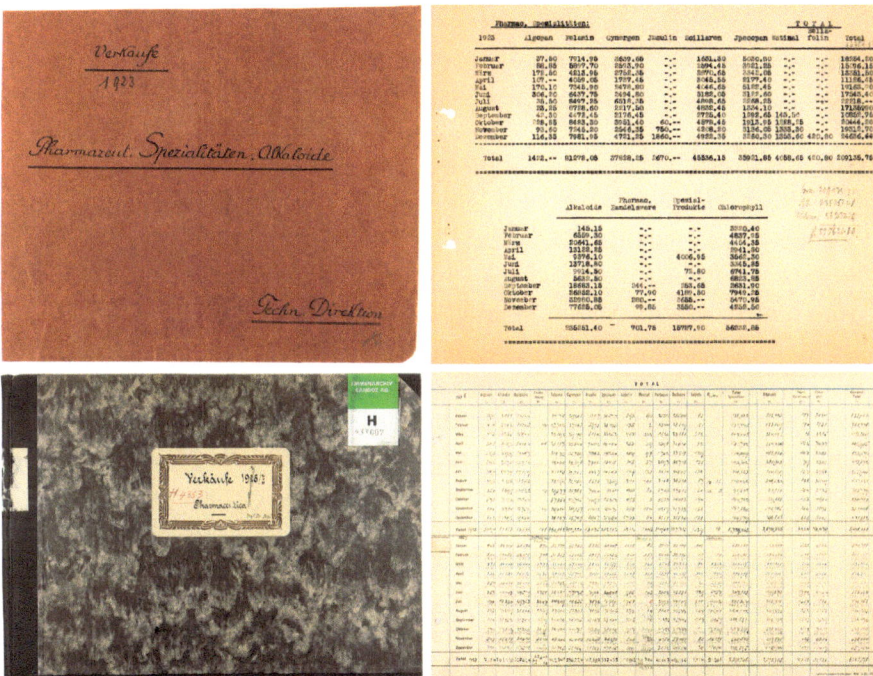

Fig. 6.7 Arthur Stoll's list of monthly sales figures for pharmaceutical specialties and alkaloids from 1923, 1926, and 1927. (© Novartis Company Archive)

At the end of 1927, Stoll again added up the monthly sales figures for San-doz pharmaceutical products and was able to report to management with great satisfaction that ergotamine had become their best-selling drug (Fig. 6.7).

Something is wrong! The *Dark Matter Molecule*

While Sandoz AG's *Gynergen*® sales slowly began to soar, something unusual happened in England. In 1922, Henry Dale took the floor at a Joint Meet-ing with the Section of Therapeutics and Pharmacology and unequivocally expressed the opinion that the continued adherence to ergot extracts in the official British Pharmacopoeia of 1914 "was something of a reproach to the scientific profession" [24]. Had they just misheard? What had happened?

Despite the marketing authorizations for ergotoxine and ergotamine, the majority of British gynecologists and obstetricians saw no reason to deviate from their previous practice and continued to administer the sclerotia extract. When, in 1914, the British Medicines Agency recommended that the alco-holic extract of ergot should no longer be used as a medicine, as had previously been the case, but that the aqueous extract should be used instead, the medical profession was not alarmed. The aqueous decoction still demonstrated its usual therapeutic effect. Chemists and pharmacologists reacted with less composure to this change, because their uterotonic and vasoconstrictive pharmaceuticals from *Secale cornutum* are insoluble in water and could therefore no longer be contained in the ergot medicine that had recently been recommended. The ex-perts of the British Pharmacopoeia had removed ergotoxine and ergotamine from human treatment canons *ex officio*, so to speak.

An irritating contradiction, but in Dale's eyes, a major, unacceptable mis-take. At the evening meeting, tempers flared noticeably. First, the authors of the Pharmacopoeia in question were heckled. They were accused of not having understood what they were doing when they officially decided to discard the alcohol-soluble medicinal substances of ergot and instead use water-soluble by-products or impurities therapeutically. Moreover, according to Dale, the authority's task was not to set the direction for pharmaceutical science, but to follow it. Otherwise, medical progress would be completely impossible. The respected Secretary of the Pharmacopoeia Committee of the General Medical Council, Sir Nestor Tirard, then mounted the barricades. He had been in-strumental in the 1914 issue and countered Dale by saying that not one of the nineteen drug authorities consulted had requested the removal of the former ergot medicine at the time. Tirard's retort hit the mark. For the sake of com-pleteness, Sir Nestor added that, according to an international agreement, his authority required all liquid extracts to be watery ones, and alcohol should be added subsequently. Only the American Pharmacopoeia would list the alcoholic ergot extract as a medication. Dale could not help but comment that "the American disobedience should have prevailed in this country also" [24].

Dale inferred: either the alkaloids studied in detail were the actual active ingredients, in which case the former method of producing the sclerotia extract had to be reintroduced, or, if the non-specifically active, simple degradation products histamine and tyramine were to be the carriers of the medicinal effect of ergot, then ergotoxine and ergotamine would have no place in the British Pharmacopoeia [24].

The following year, British gynecologists once again made their position clear, which they officially published for all to hear in the British Pharmaceutical Codex of 1923:

> *"Ergotoxine has been used clinically for its action on the uterus, but it is disappointing, and gynecologists are now generally agreed that it is not the active constituent of ergot they want"* [25].

Everyone now gazed spellbound at the two biogenic amines, histamine and tyramine, the last ingredients of the sclerotia that were still known. When they also failed to induce the hoped-for (or feared) contraction of the uterus, the experts shrugged their shoulders in dismay. Nothing of what could have been effective remained in the aqueous extract, and yet the ergot medicine served well in delivery rooms and women's wards. The story was becoming sinister [26].

Info box 3: Chassar Moir

Chassar Moir was born in Montrose, Angus, Scotland and grew up in a family who ran a local wine merchant and grocery store. Moir studied medicine at the University of Edinburgh and was awarded a gold medal for his doctoral thesis on the internal rotation of the fetus during birth. This was followed by periods of study in Vienna, Berlin, Leipzig and at Johns Hopkins Hospital in Baltimore.

In 1932 Moir took up his post at University College Hospital, London, where he became the first assistant in the obstetrics department. Here, together with the British chemist Harold Ward Dudley, he began his pioneering ergot alkaloid investigations, which led to the discovery of ergometrine. In 1937, he was awarded the first Nuffield Professorship of Obstetrics and Gynecology at the University of Oxford. Chassar Moir was later president of the obstetrics and gynecology section of the Royal Society of Medicine [27, 28].

John Chassar Moir (1900 Montrose, Angus – 1977 Oxford), British obstetrician and gynecologist. (© Courtesy of the Moir family)

How the Scottish gynecologist Chassar Moir gets Henry Dale to dance around the room

Henry Dale, who was appointed to the newly formed Therapeutic Trials Committee of the Medical Research Council in 1931, was at the end of his tether. At his instigation, the committee commissioned the University College Hospital in London to clarify the "anomalous effect" of the ergot extract and finally put an end to the unbearable confusion. The young Scottish physician Chassar Moir (Info box 3), who was in the middle of his specialist training in obstetrics at the hospital, was to fix this vexing issue [29, 30].

From the outset, he ruled out administering ergotamine and ergotoxine during the birth process to avoid the risk of uterine rupture. Moir conducted his measurements on uteruses seven days after delivery to minimize the additional risk of sepsis. He used an examination method that the German gynecologist Friedrich Schatz had developed in 1872 to measure intrauterine pressure. Schatz had inserted a small rubber balloon filled with water into the uterus and was able to follow the contractions of the muscle via a connected measuring device [31]. When Moir compared the data from the ergotamine and ergotoxine measurement series with that of the traditionally obtained, aqueous ergot extract, he found notable differences. The time between administration of the ergot extract and onset of action was considerably shorter, and the triggered uterine contractions were stronger and significantly more frequent. In addition, the aqueous drug was more potent than the two ergot alkaloid preparations when administered orally [30, 32].

Moir contacted Henry Dale and presented him with the results of his investigations. Dale pored over the data sheets—and looked up again with a beaming smile. It couldn't be any other way: the aqueous ergot extract had to contain an unknown highly active compound that imparted the real pharmaceutical effect of ergot. Dale had already suspected something like this in 1907, as the pharmacological activity of the starting material for his isolation work was always far too high compared to the amount of ergotoxine it contained [30, 33].

Dale later explained:

"To me, of course, after some 28 years of investigation on ergot and its principles, leading into all kinds of unexpected side issues (many of them more interesting than ergot itself), the emergence of this new evidence concerning what may well be the really important constituent of ergot from the clinical point of view, had a touch of humor, as well as of interest. (…) The result gave me some surprise, but still more satisfaction. I hope it may yet be possible to discover the substance responsible for the effect which can be demonstrated under such conditions" [29].

In 1957, Chassar Moir recalled their meeting in a letter to Dale:

"I well remember how delighted you were when the first evidence came to hand that the liquid extract contained a substance highly active but which had hitherto escaped detection. (…) 'delighted' was a gross understatement of what took place, as (you) 'jumped up', danced round the room like a ten-year-old boy, waved (your) arms and repeated again and again 'I told them so'" [29].

But why had the research groups at Burroughs, Wellcome & Co. and Sandoz AG completely overlooked the ultimate active ingredient in *Secale cornutum*? In extracting the substances from the sclerotia, they had all followed Charles Tanret's 1875 procedure and had used 95% alcohol for this step. However, unlike ergotinine, ergotoxine, and ergotamine, the "dark matter molecule" was insoluble in the solvent. As the alcoholic extract obtained had nevertheless been active, nobody had given a thought to the existence of water-soluble active substances. By retracing his steps, Moir found the fork in the road where science had taken a wrong turn in 1875. His *eureka moment* was stumbling across the forgotten *Dr. John Stearns's Effect*, as Moir called it.

In his 1808 report, the American physician had emphasized the rapid onset of action after administration of the aqueous ergot decoction:

"In most cases you will be surprised with the suddenness of its operation; it is, therefore, necessary to be completely ready before you give the medicine, as the urgency of the pains will allow you but a short time afterwards" [34].

Moir's findings were undoubtedly a scientific sensation, and perhaps for the first time everyone involved was rightly at united in their exuberant joy. The grumbling obstetricians had always known this and saw "their molecule" finally within reach. The young Dr. Moir was happy about his early success. The commission of the British Pharmacopoeia, whose 1914 edition had been the impetus that set everything in motion, was certainly also pleased. Henry Dale was delighted that his 1907 hunch had been confirmed, and that the dispute with the drug authorities had reached a happy conclusion. He, who had accompanied Moir's project with his typical infectious enthusiasm and warmth, was probably looking forward even more to the imminent publication of the clinic's striking data, which would wind up the ergot world to a fever pitch.

As Dale had predicted, it happened, and in England, Switzerland, and the USA the hunt was on for the molecule of *Dr. John Stearns's Effect*.

References

1. *Years of Novartis—250 Years of Innovation*, Profile Books Ltd, London, 2021, pp. 46–47
2. *Years of Novartis—250 Years of Innovation*, Profile Books Ltd, London, 2021, p. 52
3. L. Ruzicka, Arthur Stoll, 1887–1971. Biogr Mems Fell R Soc **18**, 566 (1972)
4. R. Willstätter, *Aus meinem Leben*. Ed: A. Stoll (Verlag Chemie, Weinheim, 1949), p. 401
5. H. Fritz, Die Mutterkornforschung bei der Sandoz AG. Gesch Pharm **44**, 32 (1992)
6. R. Willstätter, *Aus meinem Leben*. Ed: A. Stoll (Verlag Chemie, Weinheim, 1949), p. 289
7. K. Spiro, A. Stoll, Ueber die wirksamen Substanzen des Mutterkorns. Schweiz Med Wochenschr **23**, 525 (1921)
8. A. Stoll, *35 Jahre Ergotamin* (Privatdruck, Basel, 1953), p. 5
9. A. Stoll, Verfahren zur Isolierung eines hochwertigen Präparates aus Secale cornutum. Swiss Patent **79**, 879 (1918)
10. A. Stoll, Zur Kenntnis der Mutterkornalkaloide. Verhandl d Schweizer Naturf Gesellsch **101**, 190 (1920)

11. A. Stoll, *35 Jahre Ergotamin* (Privatdruck, Basel, 1953), pp. 13–14
12. A. Stoll, *35 Jahre Ergotamin* (Privatdruck, Basel, 1953), p. 12
13. A. Stoll, *35 Jahre Ergotamin* (Privatdruck, Basel, 1953), pp. 17–19
14. D. Adlersberg, O. Porges, Über die Behandlung des Morbus Basedow mit Ergotamin (Gynergen). Klin Wochenschr **4**, 1489 (1925)
15. P.S. Sándor, H. Isler, Aus der Geschichte der Migräne – Ein Rückblick zum Anlass des 100. Geburtstags der SNG, in *Geschichte, Meilensteine und Perspektiven – Jubiläumstagung* Montreux., ed. by M. Mumenthaler (Rosenfluh, Neuhausen, 2008), p. 10. Eine gemeinsame Sonderpublikation der Zeitschriften "*TMJ The Medical Journal* – Schweizer Zeitschrift für Innere Medizin", "Ars Medici" und "Schweizer Zeitschrift für Psychiatrie & Neurologie"
16. E. Rothlin, Über die Pharmakologische und Therapeutische Wirkung des Ergotamins auf den Sympathicus. Klin Wochenschr **4**, 1437 (1925)
17. E. Woakes, On ergot or rye in the treatment of neuralgia. BMJ **2**, 360 (1868)
18. E. Moretti, Storia di una cefalalgia scorbutica guarita mediante l'uso interno dell'estratto di segale cornuta. Gior di med mil Torino **10**, 392 (1862)
19. Neurologen und Psychiater im Netz – Das Informationsportal zur psychischen Gesundheit und Nervenerkrankungen 2022. https://www.neurologen-und-psychiater-im-netz.org/neurologie/erkrankungen/migraene/ursachen
20. P.J. Koehler, H. Isler, The early use of ergotamine in migraines. Edward Woakes' report of 1868, its theoretical and practical background and its international reception. Cephalalgia **22**(8), 686 (2002)
21. H.W. Maier, L'ergotamine, inhibiteur du sympathique étudié en clinique, comme moyen d'exploration et comme agent thérapeutique. Rev Neurol **1**, 1104 (1926)
22. M.J. Eadie, Ergot of rye—the first specific for migraine. J Clin Neurosci **11**, 4 (2004)
23. R. Ramachanderan, S. Schramm, B. Schaefer, Migraine drugs. ChemTexts **9**, 6 (2023)
24. H.H. Dale, The Value of Ergot in Obstetrical and Gynecological Practice; with Special Reference to its Present Position in the British Pharmacopoeia. Section of Obstetrics and Gynecology: Joint meeting with the section of Therapeutics and Pharmacology. Proc R Soc Med **1**, 1 (1922)
25. E. Rothlin, The specific action of ergot alkaloids on the sympathetic nervous system. J Pharmacol Sci Exp Ther **36**, 657 (1929)
26. J.H. Burns, Essential Pharmacology. Annu Rev Pharmacol **9**, 1 (1969)
27. D. Haskett, P. Ciardullo, *John Chassar Moir (1900–1977). Embryo Project Encyclopedia. ISSN: 1940–5030* 2017. http://embryo.asu.edu/handle/10776/11412
28. *Professor Chassar Moir—Biographical note*, Wellcome Collection, 2022
29. E.M. Tansey, Ergot to Ergometrine: An Obstetric Renaissance?, in *Women and Modern Medicine*, ed. by A. Hardy, L.I. Conrad (Editions Rodopi B.V., Amsterdam New York, 2001), p. 202
30. J.C. Moir, The Obstetrician Bids, and the Uterus Contracts. BMJ **2**, 1025 (1964)

31. F. Schatz, Beiträge zur physiologischen Geburtskunde. Arch Gynäkol **4**, 34 (1872)
32. C. Moir, H.H. Dale, The action of ergot preparations on the puerperal uterus. BMJ **1**, 1119 (1932)
33. G. Barger, H.H. Dale, Ergotoxine and some other Constituents of Ergot. Biochem J **2**, 287 (1907)
34. J. Stearns, Account of the Pulvis Parturiens, a remedy for quickening childbirth, in *New York Medical Repository, Hexade II* vol V. (T. & J. Swords, New York, 1808), p. 308

7

Albert Hofmann's path to psychotogenic LSD

When Henry Dale was asked who could tackle isolating the water-soluble, mysterious active ingredient from the *Claviceps purpurea* sclerotia, he immediately thought of his long-time colleague and chief chemist, Harold Ward Dudley (1887–1935), at the National Institute for Medical Research. He knew him well from their joint research work on histamine, acetylcholine, and insulin, when Dudley had some tough nuts to crack. In 1932, Dudley and Chassar Moir set to work and were undeterred by the harsh criticism and skepticism of Moir's clinical study results after his publication. They had to be quick, because three excellent scientific groups in Chicago, Baltimore, and Basel were hot on their heels. The two Britons soon realized that they had underestimated the quantities of sclerotia required in their study plans. As a result, they were repeatedly forced to interrupt the isolation process because their ergot stocks were depleted. The crippling waiting times until the delivery of new sclerotia, which only arrived intermittently from Spain, were almost unbearable. During these times, they anxiously wondered about the competing groups, who had breathed down their necks from the beginning. Had the Swiss and Americans already bypassed them, or could they defend their small lead?

Finally, on February 9, 1935, a crystalline substance showed the identical uterotonic activity profile as the *Dr. John Stearns's Effect* [1]. But were the London scientists really the first to cross the finish line in this legendary race for the new pure substance from *Claviceps purpurea*, which Dudley and Moir named *ergometrine* [2]? Within three months, the other groups also reported the isolation of their uterotonic compounds, which they named *ergobasine* [3], *ergotocin* [4], and *ergostetrine* [5]. When it transpired that all three working groups had discovered the same substance, the situation became uncomfortable. Marvin Thompson from Baltimore insisted that the name "ergostetrine" must have priority as he had already isolated the pharmaceutically active ergot alkaloid in 1934 and had patented the compound under this name, thus before Dudley and Moir. The British disagreed with Thompson's view and argued that at the time, his preparation contained even greater amounts of ergotoxine. Arthur Stoll, in turn, showed that Dudley's and Moir's ergometrine had been contaminated too, and only he had been the first to receive a pure substance with "ergobasine". After months of wrangling, the rivals agreed on a Solomonic judgment, which they published in 1936 in a joint statement that is still unique today:

> "The authors leave it to the scientific world to choose one of the previously proposed names for the alkaloid" [6].

Accordingly, ergobasine/ergostetrine/ergotocin is hereafter referred to as "ergometrine". The physicochemical and pharmacokinetic advantages of the new molecule over ergotamine and ergotoxine were obvious: good solubility in aqueous media, rapid absorption, and rapid onset of action when taken orally. Even with higher doses and repeated administration, neither side effects nor the induction of gangrene occurred. The two Britons decided against patenting the isolation process so that each company could produce and distribute ergometrine without restriction [7]. Harold Dudley underwent surgery after completing the research project and tragically passed away on the day of the publication of the scientific details of his groundbreaking work [8].

Moir and Dudley had come across a substance which had chemists, pharmacologists, and physicians once again reaching a fork in the road. One path traversed an already familiar landscape: the modulation of smooth muscle cell tone as a therapeutic principle to stop postpartum hemorrhage, the regulation of blood circulation, as a uterotonic, and in the treatment of migraine, which would long be explained by this mechanism of action. The other path unveiled a veritable *coup de théâtre* through which subsequent scientists arrived in an unknown country where they were to find something they had not been looking for and had not even dreamed of: the biochemistry of the psyche.

The discovery of lysergic acid

While Chassar Moir pharmacologically investigated the ergot preparations in the women's ward of his London hospital, the first attempts to explain the structure of ergot alkaloids began at the Wellcome Chemical Works, Dartford. The methods available at the time were very simple: applying chemical degradation reactions of an intact compound in the hope of obtaining

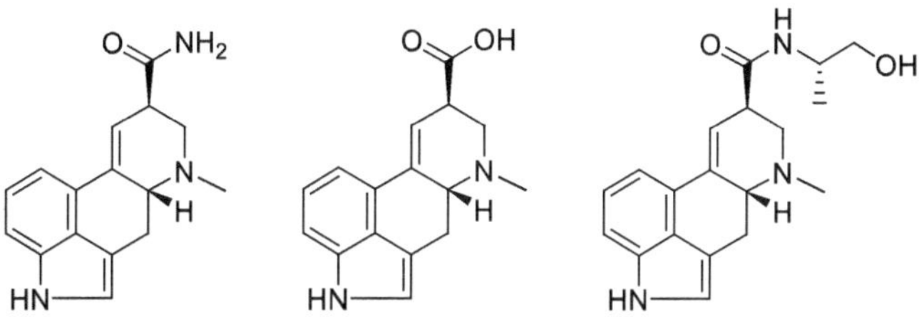

Fig. 7.1 Chemical Structures. *From left*: Ergine, lysergic acid, ergometrine

smaller building blocks whose elemental compositions could be determined. The molecular formulas of these substance fragments made it possible to develop initial structural ideas or to identify already known structural elements.

In 1932, the British chemists Sidney Smith and Geoffrey Millward Timmis isolated ergotinine, ergotoxine, and ergotamine using alcoholic potassium hydroxide solution. In all reaction mixtures, they always found a building block with the molecular formula $C_{16}H_{17}N_3O$ and named this characteristic degradation product *ergine* (initially, they had incorrectly calculated the gross formula of the molecule as $C_{17}H_{21}N_3O$) [9, 10]. The US chemists Walter Jacobs and Lyman Craig at the Rockefeller Institute for Medical Research in New York repeated the work from England and generated a fragment of ergine with the molecular formula $C_{16}H_{16}N_2O_2$ under slightly modified reaction conditions. They gave it the name *lysergic acid* (from the Greek *lysis* = dissolving, and ergine/ergotinine) [11, 12]. When they looked at Moir's and Dudley's ergometrine, they realized that it was composed of a small lysergic acid residue attached to a simple propanolamine group (Fig. 7.1; [13]).

Albert Hofmann starts lysergic acid chemistry at Sandoz

After the ergotamine success, Arthur Stoll completed research on the ergot alkaloids and focused on the processing of cardiac glycosides for the treatment of chronic heart failure. After Moir and Dudley published the uterotonic activity of an unknown molecule in the aqueous ergot decoction, Stoll also tried to get his hands on the new drug substance. In Stoll's department, the young Swiss natural products chemist Albert Hofmann (info box 1) had witnessed the feverish search for the actual active ingredient of ergot up close and had enthusiastically read the previous publication of the British research group on the pharmacology of ergometrine. It quickly became clear to him that Sandoz AG could risk losing its leading position in the field of ergot alkaloids due to the new active ingredient with its exquisite properties [14]. However, the compound had a glaring problem: in sclerotia, it was only present in trace amounts. No more than 60 mg of ergometrine could be isolated from 2 lbs of ergot. This made the production of sufficient drug substance quantities for the pharmaceutical market illusory.

Info box 1: Albert Hofmann

Albert Hofmann was born in Baden near Zurich, the son of a locksmith. The beauty of the meadows and forests and his childhood experiences in nature played a major role in his later career choice. In 1925, he began studying chemistry at the University of Zurich with Paul Karrer, the later Nobel Prize laureate. At the time, it was possible to start a doctoral thesis in Switzerland immediately after graduation without taking a course of study. Hofmann's task was to cleave chitin, the polymeric exoskeletal substance of insects and arachnids, into its monomers to analyze them chemically. With the help of the hepatopancreatic fluid of the vineyard snail, he degraded chitin and demonstrated its composition of N-acetylglucosamine building blocks [15].

In 1929, Hofmann switched to pharmaceutical research at Sandoz AG in Basel. Although the salary offered was more modest than the lucrative offers from Hoffmann-La Roche and Ciba, he had been drawn to Arthur Stoll's research group. There, Hofmann was able to pursue his great scientific interest in developing new medicines from natural substances found in medicinal plants. Until 1935, he did structural work on cardiac glycosides from squill (*Drimia maritima* (L.) Stearn), the woolly foxglove (*Digitalis lanata* Ehrh.) and skin gland secretions of toads. This was followed by his semi-synthetic derivatizations of lysergic acid [16]. Hofmann's medicinal chemistry work with the ergot alkaloids revealed not only the accidentally discovered psychoactive effect of *lysergic acid diethylamide*, abbreviated to *LSD-25*, but also an impressive number of drug substances for human therapy (Fig. 8.9 and Table 8.1). His chemical investigations of the hallucinogenic ingredients of the Mexican magic mushroom (*Psilocybe mexicana* R. Heim) led to the discovery of the psychotogenic molecules *psilocin* and *psilocybin*. Albert Hofmann took over as head of the natural products department in 1969, for which he was responsible until his departure from Sandoz AG in 1971.

Albert Hofmann (1906 Baden – 2008 Burg), Swiss natural substances chemist, 1942. (© Novartis Company Archive)

When the research group at the Rockefeller Institute for Medical Research published a structural proposal for lysergic acid in 1936, Hofmann saw the time had come to tackle the only weak point of the natural substance [12, 13, 17]. He intended to synthesize ergometrine by cleaving off the lysergic acid from ergotamine and then linking it to propanolamine. Hofmann was unsuspecting when he filled out an order form and requested 0.5 g of ergotamine from his colleagues in the production department. Stoll, whose approval was essential for such requests, immediately appeared in Hofmann's office and categorically prohibited him from touching the precious ergotamine for his synthesis work. But immediately afterwards, the twenty-nine-year-old chemist had nothing better to do than to organize ergotamine "through unofficial channels" (personal comment by Dr. Günter Engel, 2022; [14, 18]).

In his later five-step synthesis, Hofmann detached the lysergic acid from ergotoxine/ergotinine substance mixtures arising as waste products during ergotamine production. He first stabilized the resulting isolysergic acid mixture as a hydrazide and then converted it into the azide, which reacted with D-2-aminopropan-1-ol. After a rearrangement reaction and a fractional crystallization step, he finally obtained pure ergometrine (Fig. 7.2; [18]).

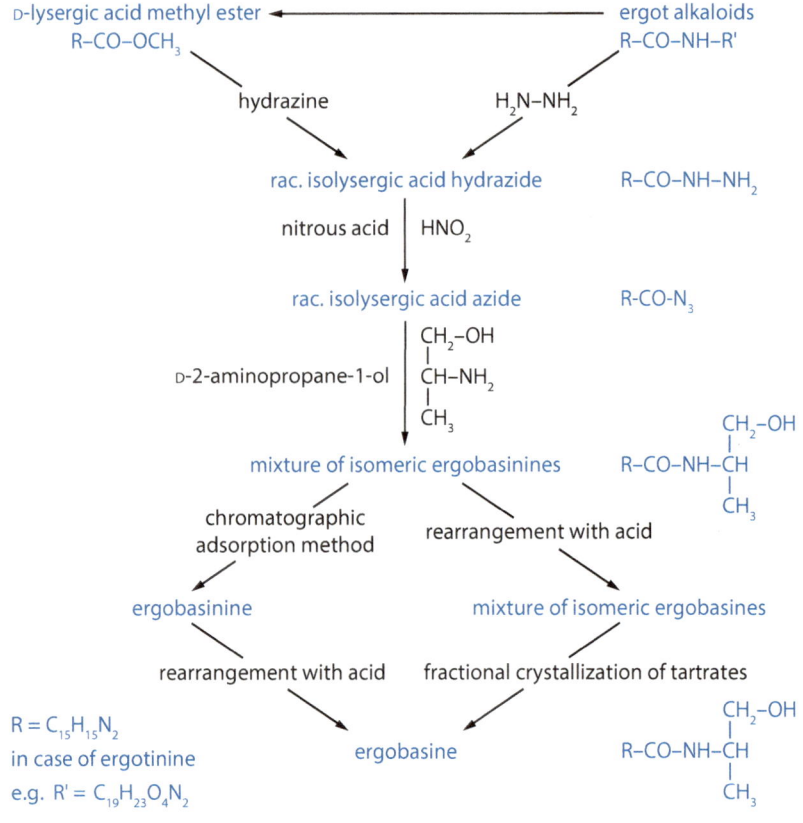

D-lysergic acid methyl ester ← ergot alkaloids
R–CO–OCH₃   R–CO–NH–R'

hydrazine   H₂N–NH₂

rac. isolysergic acid hydrazide   R–CO–NH–NH₂

nitrous acid │ HNO₂

rac. isolysergic acid azide   R–CO–N₃

                           CH₂–OH
                           │
D-2-aminopropane-1-ol   CH–NH₂
                           │
                           CH₃

                                            CH₂–OH
                                            │
mixture of isomeric ergobasinines   R–CO–NH–CH
                                            │
                                            CH₃

chromatographic   rearrangement with acid
adsorption method

ergobasinine   mixture of isomeric ergobasines

rearrangement with acid   fractional crystallization of tartrates

R = C₁₅H₁₅N₂   CH₂–OH
in case of ergotinine   ergobasine   │
e.g. R' = C₁₉H₂₃O₄N₂   R–CO–NH–CH
                                            │
                                            CH₃

Fig. 7.2 Hofmann's 1938 published partial synthesis of ergometrine (= ergobasine) [18]

The project idea of the young natural product chemist heralded a new phase of ergot alkaloid research at Sandoz. He had succeeded in the first partial synthesis of a naturally occurring ergot alkaloid, which would also be suitable for manufacturing the required amount of ergometrine after possible market approval. During his chemical research, Hofmann improved the activity and stability of the molecule by adding a methyl group to the propanolamine moiety. *Methylergometrine* was introduced to obstetrics and gynecology in 1946 as *Methergine®* (Fig. 7.3a; [19]). The drug is still on the World Health Organization's list of "Essential Medicines" (*WHO Model List of Essential Medicines 2021*) and is used medically to reduce postnatal blood loss, support labor and placental separation, and to promote uterine involution.

Hofmann had developed the methodology for the lysergic acid chemistry. Now he wanted to utilize the medicinal-chemical options to discover new pharmacological activities of the molecule class.

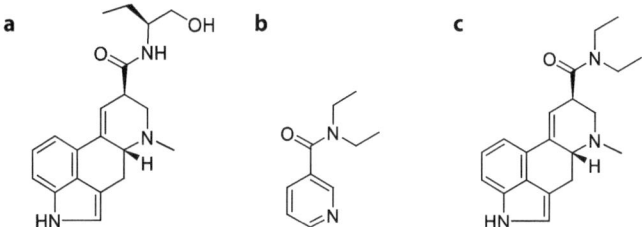

Fig. 7.3 Chemical structures. **a** Methylergometrine (Methergine®), **b** Nicotinic acid di-ethylamide (Coramine®), **c** Lysergic acid diethylamide (LSD-25)

A good idea doesn't work—LSD-25

On the other side of the Rhine, the Swiss chemist Max Hartmann, from the Basel-based pharmaceutical company Ciba, had synthesized the *diethylamide of nicotinic acid*, which was administered from 1924 under the name *Coramine®* (Fig. 7.3b) as a respiratory and circulatory stimulant for resuscitating drowned patients, in cases of circulatory weakness, or as an emergency medication for narcotic poisoning. In 1938, Hofmann was inspired by the structure of this drug and synthesized several lysergic acid substances to find a competitor compound to the successful Ciba drug. The 25th molecule in this series was the *diethylamide of lysergic acid, LSD-25* for short (Fig. 7.3c), which he handed over to the pharmacology department for *in vivo* profiling. Hofmann waited eagerly for the test results, but they were disappointing. The report from the head of the pharmacological department, Professor Ernst Rothlin, showed that the substance possessed only 70% of the uterotonic activity of ergometrine, and the anesthetized animals had been restless [19, 20]. A negative assessment by pharmacologists always entailed the end of further research on a substance, and so Hofmann was forced to give up his work on LSD-25.

Five years later, he synthesized LSD again. Why? It was a hunch, he said many decades later and added with a smile that the substance had probably found him rather than him finding the substance. Regardless, Albert Hofmann firmly believed in the pharmacological potential of his molecule and did not want to accept the pharmacologists' verdict.

On April 16, 1943, after the resynthesis of LSD's tartaric acid salt, a tiny amount of substance entered Hofmann's body despite exercising caution. When he began to feel uncomfortable, he went home. His notes on the physical and psychogenic effects of LSD and, above all, his self-experiment three days later, in which he took 0.25 mg of the active ingredient at 16:20, made history and are indispensable in the narrative of natural products re-

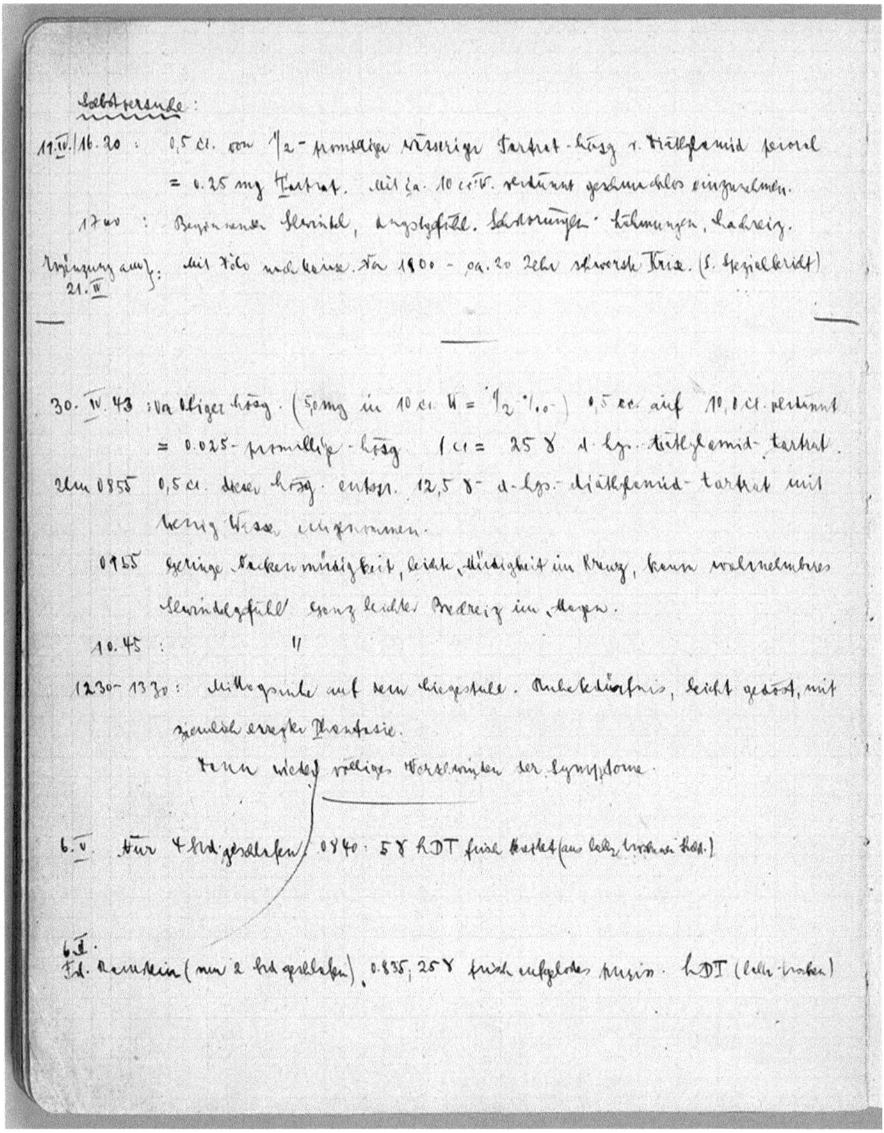

Fig. 7.4 Albert Hofmann's original note on his first LSD self-experiment on April 19, 1943 (Hofmann's "special report" of April 22, 1943: see appendix) (© Novartis Company Archive)

search. After 40 minutes, hallucinations, dizziness, and the urge to laugh set in (Fig. 7.4). He then asked his laboratory assistant Susie Ramstein (she was to become the first woman to take LSD a few weeks later) to accompany him home. His condition persisted during the bike ride home and could not be alleviated by two to three liters of milk, which a neighbor had rushed to him as a hoped-for detox. From 18:00, Hofmann endured a *severe crisis* that lasted for two hours. Three days later, he wrote a detailed *special report*, which he sent to Arthur Stoll and Ernst Rothlin (info box 2). When studying the letter, both faltered at the passage mentioning the administered substance amount. 0.25 mg? That couldn't be right.

Without further ado, Rothlin decided to double-check the reported LSD findings in a renewed self-experiment together with two employees. As a precaution, he reduced the dosage amount to one-third of the original amount. After the three Sandoz subjects had all come to their senses, Rothlin was able to confirm Hofmann's results in all respects [20, 22].

Info box 2: Ernst Rothlin

Ernst Rothlin was born in Lachen on Lake Zurich and had loved music since his youth. Before breakfast, he practiced the violin for two hours so that he could be with his school friends in the afternoon. Rothlin wanted to study chemistry, which his father forbade him on the grounds: "I know what a doctor is, but I don't know what a chemist should be good for!" Instead, he began studying medicine in Geneva, Berlin and Zurich and received his doctorate in 1914. But he was still drawn to chemistry. Rothlin went back to Geneva to Aimé Jules Pictet, who had impressed him during his studies, and deepened his knowledge of physiology and pharmacology. After his habilitation in Zurich, he accepted Arthur Stoll's job offer in 1922 and became head of pharmacology at Sandoz AG in Basel and successor to Karl Spiro, who had left him "three rather poorly equipped (...) labs in a dilapidated building". Rothlin was a key figure in the physiological and pharmacological investigations of ergotamine, cardiac glycosides, ergometrine/methylergometrine, and LSD, and in the identification of their medical indications. After leaving the company, he founded the International Society for Psychopharmacology (*Collegium Internationale Neuropsychopharmacologicum, CINP*) in 1956 [21].

Ernst Rothlin (1888 Lachen – 1972 Rigi Kaltbad), Swiss physician and pharmacologist. (© Novartis Company Archive)

Studies on a new *"phantasticum"*

The question remained: what should be done with such a substance? The fact that nature produces psychoactive and hallucinogenic substances was nothing new. Psychiatric examinations of induced symptoms, from which doctors hoped to find new methods of treating mental illness, had been part of medical practice for a hundred years [23].

* * *

The French psychiatrist Jacques-Joseph Moreau was one of the first physicians to study the hallucinogenic effects of the cannabis plant. In 1844, he assembled a group of volunteer test subjects in Paris, who called themselves *Le Club des Hachichins*. In monthly meetings, they gathered around Moreau at the *Hôtel Pimodan*, and he recorded their reactions to the administration of cannabis. The names of the club members read like a *who's who* of the then French cultural Olympus: Gustave Flaubert, Charles Baudelaire, Honoré de Balzac,

Honoré Daumier, Eugène Delacroix, and Théophile Gautier, or Alexandre Dumas the Elder [24–26]. In Vienna, the young psychiatrist Sigmund Freud investigated the effect of cocaine on the psyche. He administered the alkaloid to friends and patients to confirm the described stimulating effects of the coca plant drug, adding further experiences from self-experiments and his medical practice. In papers published between 1884 and 1887, Freud recommended cocaine for the treatment of depressive moods, digestive problems, alcoholism, morphinism and asthma, sexual asthenia and local anesthesia. From today's vantage point, he was not very careful in assessing the addictive potential of the drug and took the view that only those who were already prone to addiction would become dependent. The experts accused Freud of "wanting to unleash a third scourge on mankind after morphine and alcohol". In May 1884, he advised the Austrian physiologist Ernst Fleischl von Marxow to treat his morphine addiction with cocaine. Freud thus followed a therapeutic approach that he had become acquainted with in a scientific article from the USA. Fleischl von Marxow's (suspected) self-medication eventually made him a morpho-cocainist, a fate he shared with many other morphinists of his time who decided to replace one evil by another. It was probably due to seeing the suffering of his friend and teacher that Freud subsequently recanted his recommendation to treat alcohol and morphine addiction with cocaine [27, 28].

Likely at Freud's suggestion, the young Viennese ophthalmologist Karl Koller dealt with the numbing activity of cocaine. After detecting that the alkaloid made the cornea of the eye insensitive to pain, he successfully used it as a "surface anesthetic" in cataract surgery on September 11, 1884 [29, 30]. Koller's report influenced the American surgeon William Stewart Halsted, who recognized the possibility of administering the anesthetic locally by injection directly into the tissue. In 1885, by injecting cocaine around the *inferior alveolar nerve* and thereby switching off its conduction, for the first time he succeeded in the painless extraction of a tooth in the lower jaw at New York's Roosevelt Hospital. Halsted's method went down in the history of surgery as the first "nerve block anesthesia". The American neurologist James Leonard Corning, who frequently attended Halsted's courses, and the German surgeon August Bier went one step further and injected cocaine into the peridural space of the dura mater of the spinal cord or directly into the spinal canal to block the conduction of stimuli between the spinal cord and the extremities. Their pioneering anesthesia procedures made them the founders of "peridural and spinal anesthesia" [31].

Between 1896 and 1898, the German chemist Arthur Heffter isolated mescaline from the peyote cactus, which had become the subject of psychological studies in New York in 1912 [32]. When the drug became synthetically accessible in 1919, psychiatrist Kurt Beringer at the Psychiatric University Hospital in Heidelberg administered mescaline to induce "experimental psychoses" to better understand and relive the symptoms and nature of psychotic diseases [23, 33, 34]. At the same time, Leni Alberts, one of the first female doctors in the German Empire, analyzed the influence of mescaline on arithmetic or memory performance, as well as on linguistic expressiveness in the context of her doctoral thesis [35]. Alberts's professors Hans Gruhle and Willy Mayer-Groß, as well as Hans Prinzhorn, made themselves available as test subjects to support her in this pioneering work.

Against this background, the first clinical LSD examinations, initiated at the Psychiatric University Hospital Zurich Burghölzli in 1947, corresponded to a common procedure. The only unusual thing about it was that the Swiss psychiatrist Werner A. Stoll, who initially wanted to examine LSD in a self-experiment, was the son of the head of the pharmaceutical department of Sandoz AG. After Stoll had called in a medical technician to log the induced symptoms, he darkened his room. He knew that after taking the planned 0.06 mg of LSD, which he referred to in his 1947 publication as a "*phantasticum*", he would hardly be able to put anything evaluable or readable on paper [36].

The irritatingly novel feature and most significant aspect of Hofmann's LSD was something completely different and is easily overlooked: the molecule displayed extreme activity even in very small amounts, and its pharmacological potency was infinitely higher than all hallucinogens or other psychoactive substances known at the time.

What causes schizophrenia? LSD and the "autotoxin" dispute

"Are you sure you didn't make a mistake at the weigh-in? Is the dosage really correct?" Arthur Stoll was astonished after reading the information on the amount of LSD taken in Hofmann's report, and Ernst Rothlin's first thought was also that of a weighing error [22]. There was probably good reason for their doubts about the amount of substance ingested.

Since the end of the 19th century, there had been a fierce debate in medicine about what triggers schizophrenia. The doyen of psychiatry in Germany, Emil Kraepelin (1856–1926), and the Swiss physician, Carl Gustav Jung (1875–1961), were two advocates of a hypothesis that saw the reason for this mental illness as a kind of "self-poisoning". Accordingly, the body's own psychotogenic substances, so-called "autotoxins", would damage the brain and cause schizophrenia [23, 37–39]. In contrast to other supporters of the self-poisoning hypothesis, which localized the origin of the toxic metabolic products in the intestine, Kraepelin and Jung suspected that they were formed by the sex glands. For quite some time, however, these complex topics had made no headway. Kraepelin complained at every opportunity that the search for autotoxins had remained unsuccessful only because they had "never been seriously (…) searched for using reliable methods" [40]. In the midst of this ongoing dispute, the most influential psychiatrist in the USA, Adolf Meyer (1866–1950), raised his voice. Meyer came from a parish family in Niederweningen, Switzerland. After his medical studies, he had not found employment in Switzerland and had emigrated to the USA. There, Meyer had introduced Kraepelin's classification system of mental illnesses but had his fair share of trouble with the German's autotoxin hypothesis. When Kraepelin once again spoke out about self-poisoning in a new textbook, Meyer wrote a biting criticism, frustratedly concluding:

> "As long as chemistry cannot furnish more accurate data and methods, the theory of intoxication and auto-intoxication so often resorted to by Kraepelin will be a terminus technicus for our ignorance" [38].

Then, however, a molecule in LSD was discovered that had exactly these predicted properties, where even the slightest trace caused psychoses that resembled those of schizophrenia patients. Hofmann's active ingredient gave new wind to the wings of the autotoxin hypothesis followers. They now argued vehemently that if such highly potent substances existed, it could not be ruled out that comparable, endogenous trace metabolites could enter the brain and trigger mental diseases [23, 37, 39]. But how would these molecules ever be found? As so often happened, the doubters were in the majority, and the hope of success smacked suspiciously of losing touch with reality. The scientists succeeded nonetheless, but the paths to knowledge ahead of them were narrow, winding, and, at first, not even rudimentarily recognizable.

References

1. H.W. Dudley, C. Moir, The substance responsible for the traditional clinical effect of ergot. Br Med J **1**, 520 (1935)
2. J.C. Moir, The Obstetrician Bids, and the Uterus Contracts. Br Med J **2**, 1025 (1964)

3. A. Stoll, E. Burckhardt, L'ergobasine, un nouvel alcoloïde de l'ergot de seigle, soluble dans l'eau (The new water-soluble ergot alkaloid, ergobasine). Bull Sci Pharm **42**, 257 (1935)

4. M.S. Kharasch, R.R. Legault, Ergotocin. J Am Chem Soc **57**, 1140 (1935)

5. M.R. Thompson, Some properties of Ergostetrine. J Am Pharm Assoc **24**, 748 (1935)

6. M.S. Kharasch, H. King, A. Stoll, M.R. Thompson, The New Ergot Alkaloid. Nature **137**, 403 (1936)

7. P.M. Dunn, John Chassar Moir (1900–1977) and the discovery of ergometrine. Arch Dis Child Fetal Neonatal Ed **87**, F152 (2002)

8. H.H. Dale, Harold Ward Dudley, 1887–1935. Biogr Mems Fell R Soc **1**, 595 (1935)

9. S. Smith, G.M. Timmis, The alkaloids of ergot. Part III. Ergine, a new base obtained by the degradation of ergotoxine and ergotinine. J Chem Soc **0**, 763 (1932)

10. S. Smith, G.M. Timmis, The Alkaloids of Ergot. Part IV. A Complex Group common to Ergotoxine and Ergotamine. J Chem Soc **0**, 1543 (1932)

11. W.A. Jacobs, L.C. Craig, The Ergot alkaloids II. The degradation of ergotinine with alkali. Lysergic acid. JBC **104**, 547 (1934)

12. W.A. Jacobs, L.C. Craig, The Ergot Alkaloids. The Structure of Lysergic Acid. Science **83**, 38 (1936)

13. W.A. Jacobs, L.C. Craig, On an Alkaloid from Ergot. Science **82**, 16 (1935)

14. A. Hofmann, How LSD originated. J Psychedelic Drugs **11**, 53 (1979)

15. P. Karrer, A. Hofmann, Polysaccharide XXXIX. Über den enzymatischen Abbau von Chitin und Chitosan I. Helv Chim Acta **12**, 616 (1929)

16. N.S. Finney, J.S. Siegel, In Memoriam: Albert Hofmann (1906–2008). Chimia **62**, 444 (2008)

17. L.C. Craig, Th Shedlovsky, R.G. Gould Jr., W.A. Jacobs, The Ergot Alkaloids: XIV. The Positions of the Double bond and the Carboxyl group in Lysergic Acid and its Isomer. The Structure of the Alkaloids. JBC **125**, 289 (1938)

18. A. Stoll, A. Hofmann, Partialsynthese des Ergobasins, eines natürlichen Mutterkornalkaloids sowie seines optischen Antipoden (3. Mitteilung über Mutterkornalkaloide). Hoppe-Seylers Z Physiol Chem **251**, 155 (1938)

19. A. Stoll, A. Hofmann, Partialsynthese von Alkaloiden vom Typus des Ergobasins. (6. Mitteilung über Mutterkornalkaloide). Helv Chim Acta **26**, 944 (1943)

20. A. Hofmann, *LSD – Mein Sorgenkind. Die Entdeckung einer "Wunderdroge"*, 1st edn. (Ernst Klett – J.G. Cotta'sche Buchhandlung, Stuttgart, 1979), p. 24

21. E. Rothlin, Outlines of a pharmacological career. Annu Rev Pharmacol **4**, IX (1964)

22. A. Hofmann, *LSD – Mein Sorgenkind. Die Entdeckung einer "Wunderdroge"*, 1st edn. (Ernst Klett – J.G. Cotta'sche Buchhandlung, Stuttgart, 1979), pp. 31–36

23. N. Langlitz, Ceci n'est pas une psychose. Toward a Historical Epistemology of Model Psychoses. BioSocieties **1**, 159 (2006)

24. M.-A. Crocq, History of cannabis and the endocannabinoid system. Dialogues Clin Neurosci **22**, 223 (2020)
25. M. Tornay, Zugriffe auf das Ich – Psychoaktive Stoffe und Personenkonzepte in der Schweiz, 1945–1980, in *Historische Wissensforschung*, ed. by C. Arni, S. Gregory, B. Kleeberg, A. Langenohl, M. Sandl, R. Suter (Mohr Siebeck, Tübingen, 2016), p. 70
26. M. Fankhauser, *Haschisch als Medikament – Zur Bedeutung von Cannabis sativa in der westlichen Medizin*. Veröffentlichungen der Schweizerischen Gesellschaft für Geschichte der Pharmazie, vol. 23 (Verlag Schweizerische Gesellschaft für Geschichte der Pharmazie, Liebefeld, 1996), pp. 89–90
27. A. Springer, Kokain, Freud und die Psychoanalyse. Suchttherapie **3**, 18 (2002)
28. J. Daiber, Therapeutisches Scheitern. Freud, das Kokain und die Literatur, in *Hofmannsthal. Jahrbuch zur Europäischen Moderne* vol 26., ed. by M. Bergengruen, A. Honold, U. Renner-Henke, G. Schnitzler, G. Wunberg (Rombach, Freiburg, 2018), p. 261
29. C. Koller, Ueber die Verwendung des Cocain zur Anästhesirung am Auge. Protokoll der Sitzung vom 17. Oktober 1884, in *Anzeiger der k. k. Gesellschaft der Aerzte in Wien*, ed. by K.K. Gesellschaft der Aerzte (Wilhelm Braumüller, Wien, 1884), p. 7
30. C.C. Koller, Preliminary report on local anesthesia of the eye. Arch Ophthalmol **12**, 473 (1934)
31. P. Oehme, M. Goerig, Rückenmarksanästhesie mit Kokain: Die Prioritätskontroverse zur Lumbalanästhesie. Dtsch Ärztebl **95**, A-2556 (1998)
32. A. Heffter, Ueber Pellote. Beiträge zur chemischen und pharmakologischen Kenntniss der Cacteen. Zweite Mittheilung. Arch Exp Path Pharmakol **40**, 385 (1898)
33. J.G. Bruhn, B. Holmstedt, Early peyote research an interdisciplinary study. Econ Bot **28**, 353 (1973)
34. K. Beringer, Experimentelle Psychosen durch Mescalin. Z Ges Neurol Psychiat **84**, 426 (1923)
35. L. Alberts, *Einwirkungen des Mescalins auf komplizierte psychische Vorgänge* (University of Heidelberg, Heidelberg, 1921). Med. Diss
36. W.A. Stoll, Lysergsäure-diäthylamid, ein Phantastikum aus der Mutterkorngruppe. Schweiz Arch Neurol Psychiatr **60**, 279 (1947)
37. B.B. Quednow, M.A. Geyer, A.L. Halberstadt, Serotonin and Schizophrenia, in *Handbook of the Behavioral Neurobiology of Serotonin*, 1st edn., ed. by C.R. Müller, B. Jacobs (Academic Press, London, 2009), p. 585
38. R. Noll, Kraepelin's "lost biological psychiatry"? Autointoxication, organotherapy and surgery for dementia praecox. Hist Psychiatry **18**, 301 (2007)
39. M. Tornay, Zugriffe auf das Ich – Psychoaktive Stoffe und Personenkonzepte in der Schweiz, 1945–1980, in *Historische Wissensforschung*, ed. by C. Arni, S. Gregory, B. Kleeberg, A. Langenohl, M. Sandl, R. Suter (Mohr Siebeck, Tübingen, 2016), pp. 65–67

40. A. Heier, *Geschichte der Erherbung der Schizophrenie in Deutschland im Zeitraum 1890 bis 1970* (Medical faculty of the Westphalian Wilhelms University Münster, 2020), p. 63. Diss. Med

8

A *pas de deux* of molecules, or the discovery of the chemistry of the psyche

The initial spark for clarifying the daring hypothesis that existing endogenous molecules cause mental illnesses took place in a laboratory that dealt with completely different questions about the "biological universe". Around 1935, the Italian physician and physiologist Vittorio Erspamer (Fig. 8.1) focused on the gastrointestinal mucosa of the rabbit. From extracts of the enterochromaffin cells, he discovered that the activity of a certain substance caused the smooth muscles of the rat intestine and uterus to contract. When he was able to reverse the effects with ergot alkaloids, his interest in the unknown substance increased. Based on various color reactions, Erspamer suspected that his com-

Fig. 8.1 Vittorio Erspamer (1909 Malosco – 1999 Rome), Italian physiologist and physician [3]. (© Elsevier)

Fig. 8.2 Irvine H. Page (1901 Indianapolis, IN – 1991 Hyannis Port, MA), US physiologist. (Image Courtesy of the History of Medicine Division at the U.S. National Library of Medicine)

pound could be a phenylalkylamine, a phenol derivative or an indole, which he called *enteramine*. He was unable to find out more about the chemistry of the compound, which he subsequently found in tissue extracts from amphibians, molluscs, and tunicates, as well as in the spleens of cattle, sheep, pigs, and humans [1, 2].

On the other side of the Atlantic, the US physician Irvine Page (Fig. 8.2) pondered on two physiological phenomena: it had long been known that a substance released during blood coagulation constricts the blood vessels. In 1931, at the end of his three-year research stay in Berlin, Page stopped off at Franz Volhard's institute at the University of Frankfurt. Here he learned of a vasoconstrictor compound that could be extracted from the blood of hypertensive patients and that increased blood pressure [4]. When Page took over

Fig. 8.3 Maurice M. Rapport (1919 Atlantic City, NJ – 2011 Durham, NC), US biochemist

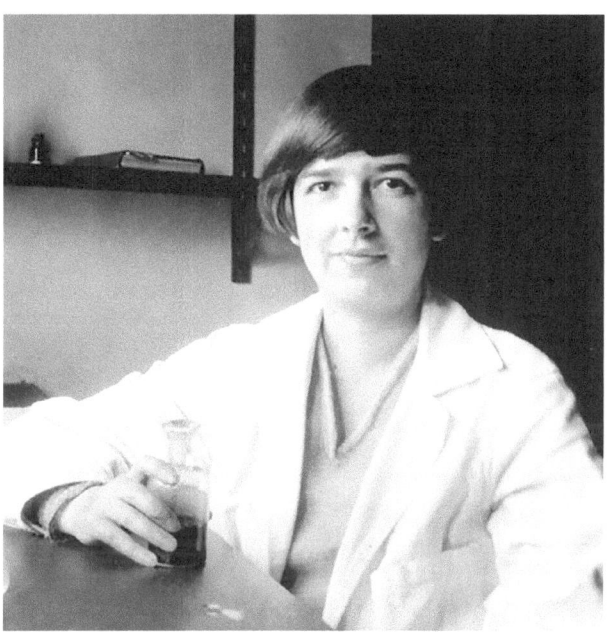

Fig. 8.4 Arda A. Green (1899 Prospect, PA – 1958 New York), US biochemist (1928). (Credit: Marine Biological Laboratory Archives, Univ. of Chicago, CC BY 4.0)

as head of research at the Cleveland Clinic Foundation in Ohio in 1945, he made the identification of this unknown messenger substance one of his first scientific priorities.

He entrusted the chemical-preparative part of the project to Maurice Rapport (Fig. 8.3), who had just completed his doctorate in biochemistry. The biochemist Arda Green (Fig. 8.4) was asked to search for the vasoconstrictive activity of the molecule in the resulting fractions, which she was able to detect based on changes in blood flow through a rabbit's ear artery [5]. Perhaps Rapport was not fully aware of the scale of the project, because he ultimately needed 450 liters of bovine blood, or 210 liters of serum, to isolate 103 mg of a substance called *serotonin*, which increased blood pressure by constricting the blood vessels. The research directorate was delighted with the happy outcome of the "bloodbath" and invited Rapport to dinner—at the time, an extraordinary gesture of recognition for a young scientist. After the structure elucidation of the messenger substance, it turned out that Rapport's serotonin from bovine blood was identical to Erspamer's enteramine from the rabbit's intestine and from molluscs (Info box 1; [3, 6–9]).

Info box 1: Enteramine, serotonin, and 5-hydroxytryptamine

The identity of enteramine and serotonin triggered a discussion about the naming of the molecule. Vittorio Erspamer named his compound enteramine, because it occurs in the intestine and is an amine. Arthur Corcoran, a colleague of Irvine Page, named it serotonin, because it was isolated from serum and increases the tone of the smooth muscles of the arteries.

In 1952, the Belgian physician Zénon Bacq discarded both names, as their basis in physiological effect and occurrence were too specific and imprecise. He suggested the neutral chemical name *5-hydroxytryptamine (5-HT)*. Erspamer immediately agreed with Bacq's reasoning, but Page could never come to terms with the compromise. Years later, he criticized the pharmacologist Sir John Gaddum for using the name 5-HT in his publications and said: "5-HTogenic was an abomination" [5].

5-Hydroxytryptamin (5-HT)

The US neurophysiologist at Harvard University, Betty Mack Twarog (Fig. 8.5), had carefully read Rapport's publications from 1948/49. Her research topic was the tone regulation of the byssus retractor muscle in the blue mussel (*Mytilus edulis* L.), with which the mollusc regulates its attachment to the substrate and adapts its orientation to changing water currents. Twarog

Fig. 8.5 Betty Mack Twarog (1927 New York – 2013 Damariscotta, ME), US neurophysiologist. (With permission by Prof. Patricia M. Whitaker-Azmitia, University of Toronto)

had been stuck for some time. Although she had identified the neurotransmitter acetylcholine, which triggers the contraction of the muscle, she was unable to find its counterpart for muscle relaxation. But the latest publications by Vittorio Erspamer in Italy made Twarog sit up and take notice. In the meantime, Erspamer had detected enteramine also in the salivary glands of the common octopus and in the skin of the Mediterranean painted frog and shown that the messenger substance increases the heart rate of molluscs [10].

If enteramine was found in mussels, cephalopods, and frogs, perhaps the substance was also effective in the smooth muscle cells of mussels? Twarog tested the biological messenger and observed how the rigor-like tone of the byssus retractor muscle released [3, 11].

Is the signaling substance 5-HT from molluscs also in the brain of vertebrates?

But that was not the end of the story for Betty Twarog. She now considered whether 5-HT, which has a neurotransmitter function in invertebrates, might also have an analogous function in higher vertebrates. She contacted Irvine Page to see if it would be possible to detect 5-HT in mammalian organs at his institute.

Page, however, thought her idea that the signaling molecule could possibly occur in the brain of vertebrates was nonsense—but immediately invited the scientist to work on this topic with him [3].

Twarog used the isolated heart of the quahog (*Mercenaria mercenaria* L) for their highly sensitive 5-HT observation system. When the pure substance was added, it reacted by increasing the pulse amplitude. However, Betty Twarog had difficulties in reliably detecting the activity of the transmitter in tissue extracts of vertebrate organs. The results were too volatile. But when she tested acetone extracts from the brain tissue of dogs, rats and rabbits, the quahog heart clearly displayed the presence of 5-HT [12]. There was no doubt: a large amount of the biological messenger was found in mammalian brains [3].

While Twarog and Page had been looking specifically for 5-HT in vertebrate brains, the British pharmacologist Sir John Henry Gaddum (Info box 2) at the University of Edinburgh chanced upon the molecule in the central nervous system. When analyzing the distribution of the antihypertensive *substance P* in a dog's brain, he had also discovered the vasoconstrictive activity of a compound, which turned out to be 5-HT, in comparative experiments [13].

Info box 2: Sir John Henry Gaddum

John Henry Gaddum came from a wealthy family of silk merchants whose company had been importing fabrics from China and India since 1875. He was extremely close to his father, who introduced John to the joys of horse riding and sailing, and hiking in Wales and Switzerland. Through his mother Phyllis Mary, he was related to Sir Samuel Hoare, who later became Britain's Foreign Secretary. His school reports state "gleams of intelligence only occasionally break through the mists" or "often flighty and dreamy though 'less in the clouds'", thus making clear that John had been a dreamy child. In 1919, Gaddum began studying mathematics and physiology at Trinity College, Cambridge, and in 1922 he started a medical degree at University College Hospital, London. In 1925, he took up a position in pharmacological research at the Wellcome Physiological Research Labs, where he was able to indulge his passion for data and statistics. After joining Henry Dale at the National Institute for Medical Research, Gaddum and his Swedish doctoral student, the later Nobel Prize winner, Ulf Svante von Euler, discovered the antihypertensive effect of *substance P*. His acetylcholine research helped clarify the function of the messenger substance in neuromuscular signal transmission. When his applications to British universities were unsuccessful, Gaddum took up the Chair of Pharmacology at the University of Cairo, where he established detection methods for histamine, and was the first to describe its concentration increase in the blood during the shock phase after severe burns. Back in England, he transferred the well-known principle of substrate competition from enzymology to pharmacology. From 1935 onwards, he developed his theory of "drug antagonism" and "competitive inhibition" at the Institute of Pharmacology at University College, London, which became calculable with the help of the mathematical models developed for this purpose. The view that activating and inhibitory substances, which bind to the same receptor, are in competition with each other still characterizes the interpretation of drug effects today. In 1942, Gaddum took over the chair of Materia Medica at the University of Edinburgh. Here he demonstrated the antagonism of 5-HT and LSD on the smooth muscles and deduced the chemical basis of mental processes and mental illnesses. From childhood, Gaddum had loved plants, insects, birds, and pond dwellers. In the spring of 1962, when he was already seriously ill, he spent his last vacation in the French Alps. When his landlord in the small town La Grave was later asked if he could remember Professor Gaddum, he simply said: *"Toujours dans les fleurs"* ("Always in the flowers") [14].

Sir John Henry Gaddum (1900 Hale, Cheshire – 1965 Cambridge), British pharmacologist. (© National Portrait Gallery, London)

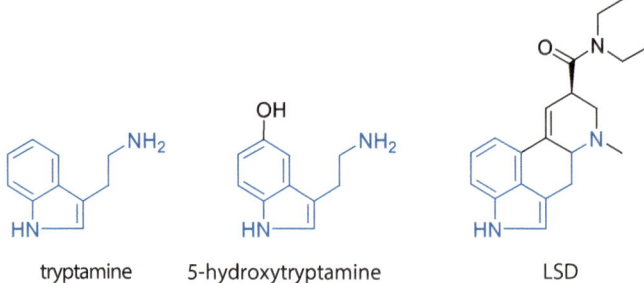

Fig. 8.6 Structural similarity of tryptamine, 5-hydroxytryptamine and LSD

Gaddum now remembered the earlier physiological tryptamine work of Arthur Ewins and Patrick Laidlaw, and step by step he put the pieces of the puzzle together to form a picture that gave him an incredible idea.

In 1912, Laidlaw had conducted physiological studies on the biogenic amine tryptamine at Henry Dale's Wellcome Research Laboratories. It caused the cats' blood pressures and heart rates to rise and dilated their pupils. While the animals had purred during the injection of the substance, they were extremely agitated shortly afterwards. But that was not all: Laidlaw had been able to reduce the antihypertensive activity of tryptamine by using ergotoxine [15].

Suddenly, everything made sense to Gaddum: the striking change in the cats' behavior, the increase in blood pressure caused by Ewins/Laidlaw's tryptamine, the presence of Rapport/Erspamer's 5-HT in the brain, and the structural similarity of both molecules to Hofmann's hallucinogenic LSD (Fig. 8.6). Gaddum, in a state of expectant excitement, suspected a functional connection between the three molecules and attempted to experimentally demonstrate the interaction of 5-HT and LSD on the smooth muscles of the blood vessels of a rabbit's ear and a rat's uterus [5, 15, 16]. The outcome was that the contracting activity of one compound was eliminated by the addition of the other substance. Shortly before, the Canadian biochemist Dilworth Wayne Woolley (Info box 3), at the Rockefeller Institute for Medical Research in New York, had achieved the same effect with plant compounds which were similar in structure to 5-HT [5, 13, 16, 17].

Info box 3: Dilworth Wayne Woolley

Dilworth Wayne Woolley was the son of a farmer, born in Raymond, Alberta, Canada. He finished school at the age of thirteen and completed his bachelor's degree in chemistry at the University of Alberta at the age of nineteen. Woolley then continued his studies at the Institute of Agrochemistry at the University of Wisconsin in the US.

At the age of 24, he attributed "black tongue" in dogs and pellagra-induced psychosis in humans, which was responsible for most admissions to psychiatric clinics at the time, to a niacin deficiency. In 1939, Woolley moved to the Rockefeller Institute in New York and became head of the Institute of Biochemistry.

Woolley had suffered from type 1 diabetes mellitus since childhood. When there was no doubt that he would soon go blind, he and his wife Janet took train journeys throughout the USA in order to absorb as many images as possible. Despite his complete blindness at the age of 43, Woolley worked in the laboratory and instructed his scientific colleagues in their experiments. In 1966, he wanted to take part in a research conference in Brazil. As he had been interested in archaeology all his life, he visited Cuzco in the Peruvian Andes on this trip. In the former Inca capital, Woolley succumbed to a heart attack [18, 19].

Dilworth Wayne Woolley (1914 Raymond – 1966 Cuzco), Canadian biochemist. (Image Courtesy of the History of Medicine Division at the U.S. National Library of Medicine)

But if 5-HT can be antagonized by the psychotropic LSD in the peripheral nervous system, would it not be conceivable that such conflict also takes place in the brain? Gaddum and Woolley's experimental data were reason enough for them to assume that the psychotogenic effect of Hofmann's molecule must be based on its interaction with 5-HT in the brain [13].

Dilworth W. Woolley turns psychiatry on its head

The analogy between the contraction of smooth muscle cells and the chemical basis of mental processes was too absurd for many of their colleagues [20, 21]. A few people considered it, but most shook their heads at the two scientists. Gaddum was not put off by the cautious response and even speculated:

> "It is possible that the HT (serotonin) in our brains plays an essential part in keeping us sane and that the effect of LSD is due to its inhibitory action on the HT in the brain" [16, 22].

Woolley, who now referred to LSD as *serotonin antimetabolite*, evolved the assumed interaction of both substances in the brain into the mould-breaking view that mental illnesses might be generally caused by the dysregulation of their biochemical basis [20].

He and Gaddum were the first to take this bold leap into a previously uncharted area of psychiatry. They must be credited with courage, as they formulated their idea at a time when the brain was still largely understood as a place of purely electrical processes [23]. Woolley and Gaddum's daring "5-HT hypothesis" notably put them in a precarious position, standing as they were on rather shaky ground. When they stirred up neurophysiologists and psychiatrists with their "abstruse" assumption, they could not show a single experiment on the involvement of chemical substances in mental processes that supported their theory in any way. They had no proof other than their observations on the smooth muscle cells from rabbits and rats.

Woolley summarized their ideas in a manuscript, which he submitted to the medical journal *The Lancet*, but this revolutionary disease model was too much of a good thing for the editors. They refused publication on the grounds that the considerations had to be proven by the "cure of a mental illness" [3, 18].

In this phase of the scientific debate, it was presumptuous to call for a clinical study. Woolley searched for another approach to reach his goal and developed a psychiatric animal model to prove the antagonism of 5-HT and LSD in the brain. His decision to work with mice posed a methodological problem: was it even possible for a mouse to experience a psychosis, and how could it be recognized? Woolley carried out behavioral studies with mice, to which he applied LSD. The drug triggered a typical behavioral pattern in the rodents, which repeatedly looked rapidly from left to right, spread their front toes and moved backwards as if they were sliding down a slippery slope. Woolley was able to almost completely eliminate this movement pattern, which is characteristic of hallucinogens, by administering 5-HT and cholinergic substances. At the same time, another research group was working with Siamese fighting fish. As soon as LSD was dripped into the aquarium, the fish also went into reverse [24].

Woolley's article, published in 1955, turned psychiatry on its head. Conversely, the demonstrated antagonism of LSD and 5-HT meant that the neurotransmitter must be involved in mental processes and that a disturbance of the messenger balance in the brain could be the cause of psychotic illnesses [3, 20]. Only this new understanding of the disease had a positive impact on the lives of affected families. Previously, parents were blamed if their children developed schizophrenia or autism. The mothers, in particular, were accused of not taking sufficient care of their children. If children suffered from autism, the "refrigerator mothers"—cold, uncaring mothers—had obviously not permitted them the necessary social contact. Parents worldwide suffered not only from their circumstances, but also from profound feelings of guilt and shame. Woolley's LSD research lifted this heavy burden from their shoulders. At the same time, he demonstrated to the pharmaceutical sciences the possibility of using small molecules to specifically modulate the biochemical processes that can underlie mental illness [25].

Thanks to Woolley's work, critical assessments of psychotropic substances—such as mescaline and LSD and their use in the induction of "model psychoses"—also changed in clinical psychiatry. In self-experiments, psychiatrists investigated "normal" and "pathological" feelings, behavior, and perceptions, thereby learning about and better understanding the mental illnesses of their patients [26, 27]. The "experimental psychosis" had long been controversial in basic psychiatric research. Clinical psychiatrists had argued that the course of an experimentally induced psychosis was not comparable with that of a psychotic illness [28]. However, when the accidentally discovered neuroleptic chlorpromazine was also able to eliminate symptoms of LSD-induced model psychosis, the skeptics had to admit defeat. It was now considered a relevant disease model in drug research and experimental psychiatry, and clinical research began to intensify its investigations into the psychotogenic agent [29–31]. This was a continuation of earlier work by psychiatrists and psychotherapists who had had positive experiences with LSD in the treatment of trauma and addiction patients, states of anxiety and severe depressions [32, 33].

In 1949, Sandoz AG received marketing authorization for LSD, which was made available to doctors as *Delyside*® for research purposes. However, when it left hospitals and psychiatric practices and was consumed as a hallucinogenic drug in the 1960s, the Swiss company stopped providing the psychotic on April 18, 1966, just a few months before it was banned in the United States. To this day, LSD has remained synonymous with drug abuse, which obscures its scientific significance as a biochemical tool and medical model substance: together with lithium, 5-HT and chlorpromazine, Hofmann's molecule pushed open the window to psychopharmacology.

The ergot treasure chest has not yet been emptied

Although ergotoxine was a medical and financial flop for Burroughs, Wellcome & Co, in 1943 the Basel researchers again undertook its investigation. Chief pharmacologist Ernst Rothlin had seen its fluctuating pharmacological activity as an indication that ergotoxine must be a mixture of substances. Albert Hofmann was able to confirm Rothlin's assumption and obtained the new alkaloids *ergocristine, ergocornine, and ergocryptine* from *Claviceps purpurea* (Fig. 8.7; [34]).

Along the lines of his lysergic acid research, Hofmann now also chemically modified the ergopeptides to expand their spectrum of activity. He hydrogenated ergotamine to *dihydroergotamine*, which was approved as *Dihydroergot*® (Table 8.1) for the treatment of orthostatic hypotension, acute migraine attacks, severe migraine, and the *status migrainosus*. He reduced ergotoxine to the respective dihydroderivatives. To the amazement of pharmacologists, the pharmacological profile of the resulting preparation shifted diametrically. If ergotoxine increased blood pressure by constricting the blood vessels, the hydrogenated compounds widened the diameter of the arteries and thus lowered blood pressure [35]. In 1951, the drug mixture was approved as *Hydergine*® (Table 8.1) for the treatment of hypertension, vasoconstriction, and circulatory disorders.

But this was not the end of ergotoxine's potential to surprise. In 1954, during his pioneering work on artificial insemination and contraception at the Weizmann Institute of Science in Rehovot, Israel, the US reproductive biologist Moses Shelesnyak discovered that in rats, ergotoxine inhibits the production of the corpus luteum hormone progesterone [36]. It became apparent that the alkaloid mixture did not directly affect the biosynthesis of the sex hormone but suppressed the release of prolactin in the anterior pituitary gland of the brain. In rats, the lack of prolactin prevents the formation of progesterone,

Table 8.1 Ergot alkaloid-based medications: mechanisms of action and indications

Name/Structure	Mechanism of action	Drug	Listing as an essential medicine	Indication
Ergotamine tartrate	Partial agonist of the α_1-adrenoreceptors, the D_2 receptor, 5-HT$_{1D}$ and 5-HT$_{2A}$ receptors; Partial agonist of the 5-HT$_{2B}$ and 5-HT$_{2C}$ receptors	Gynergen® 1921, 1925 Ergo-Kranit® Ergomar®	National Essential Medicines Lists, 2017	Oxytocic agent Postpartum hemorrhage Acute migraine attack
Ergometrine hydrogen maleate	Partial agonist of the α_1-adrenoreceptors; Agonist or partial agonist of the 5-HT$_1$ receptors; Agonist or partial agonist of the 5-HT$_2$ receptors of the smooth muscles of the uterus and blood vessels	Ergonovine® and others	Parenteral Model list of the essential medicines, WHO 2021, National Essential Medicines Lists, 2017	Postpartum hemorrhage Bleeding after miscarriage with uterine atony
Methylergometrine hydrogen maleate	Antagonist of the D_1 receptor; Partial agonist of the α_1-adreno- and 5-HT$_1$ receptors; Agonist or partial agonist of the 5-HT$_2$ receptors of the smooth muscles of the uterus and blood vessels	Methergine® and others 1946	National Essential Medicines Lists, 2017 Model list of the essential medicines, WHO 2021, *Médicaments essentiels, Médecins sans Frontières,* 2019 (for injection)	Uterotonicum Postnatal phase Postpartum hemorrhage

Table 8.1 (continued)

Name/Structure	Mechanism of action	Drug	Listing as an essential medicine	Indication
Methysergide hydrogen maleate	Antagonist of the 5-HT$_{1B}$ and 5-HT$_7$ receptors; Partial agonist of the 5-HT$_{1B}$ receptor	Sansert® Deseril® 1960		Cluster headache Migraine prophylaxis Migraine
Dihydroergotamine mesylate	Agonist of the 5-HT$_{1B}$, 5-HT$_{1D}$ and 5-HT$_{1F}$ receptors; Antagonist of α-adrenoreceptors	Dihydroergot® 1946, et al.	National Essential Medicines Lists, 2017	Severe migraine *Status migrainosus* Acute migraine attack Orthostatic circulatory disorders

Table 8.1 (continued)

Name/Structure	Mechanism of action	Drug	Listing as an essential medicine	Indication
Dihydroergotoxine mesylate is a mixture of three substances: Dihydroergocristine Dihydroergocornine Dihydroergocryptine 	Agonists of the D_1 and D_2 receptors and various 5-HT receptors; Antagonist of α-adrenoreceptors	Hydergine® 1951, et al.	National Essential Medicines Lists, 2017	Brain disorders in old age Mental performance Social interaction

Table 8.1 (continued)

Name/Structure	Mechanism of action	Drug	Listing as an essential medicine	Indication
2-Bromo-α-ergocryptine mesylate	Partial agonist of the D_2 receptor	Parlodel® 1975, et al.	National Essential Medicines Lists, 2017	Prolactin hypersecretion and correlated female infertility Parkinson's disease Acromegaly Accompanying symptoms of pituitary tumors
Lisuride hydrogen maleate	Antagonist of the D_1 receptor; Partial agonist of the D_2, D_3 and D_4 receptors; Partial agonist of $5\text{-}HT_{1A}$, $5\text{-}HT_{2A}$, $5\text{-}HT_{2C}$ receptors; Antagonist of $5\text{-}HT_{2B}$ receptor	Dopergin® 1970s	National Essential Medicines Lists, 2017	Parkinson's disease Migraine Prolactin hypersecretion

Table 8.1 (continued)

Name/Structure	Mechanism of action	Drug	Listing as an essential medicine	Indication
Cabergoline	Agonist of the D_2 and $5\text{-}HT_{2B}$ receptors	Dostinex® et al.	National Essential Medicines Lists, 2017 *Médicaments essentiels, Médecins sans Frontières,* 2019 (oral)	Prolactin hypersecretion Parkinson's disease
Dihydroergocristine mesylate	Antagonist of the 5-HT receptors; Partial agonist/antagonist of dopaminergic and adrenergic receptors	Brinerdine® et al.	National Essential Medicines Lists, 2017	Ménière's disease Cerebral and peripheral circulatory disorders

Table 8.1 (continued)

Name/Structure	Mechanism of action	Drug	Listing as an essential medicine	Indication
Nicergoline	Selective antagonist of the α_{1A}-adrenoreceptor; Antagonist of the 5-HT$_{1A}$ receptor	Sermion®	National Essential Medicines Lists, 2017	Migraine Raynaud's disease Age-related and circulatory disorders of the brain

https://global.essentialmeds.org/dashboard/medicines/581

which maintains the function of the corpus luteum and, among other things, prepares the uterine lining for the implantation of the fertilized egg.

The preclinical research department at Sandoz AG recognized in Shelesnyak's results the first chance to treat pathological prolactin hypersecretion triggering complex physiological dysregulations with an inhibitor. Ergocornine proved to be the most potent component in the ergotoxine mixture. However, the Sandoz pharmacologist Edward Flückiger saw ergocryptine as a more promising lead structure to circumvent the undesirable effect of ergocornine on the uterus and blood vessels. The development project resulted in *2-bromo-α-ergocryptine*, which received marketing authorization in 1975 under the name *Parlodel*® (Fig. 8.8 and Table 8.1). It is still used today as a therapeutic agent for Parkinson's disease and is administered to inhibit the flow of mother's milk after miscarriages. The drug was the first treatment used for female infertility, acromegaly, and other symptoms caused by prolactin or growth hormone-secreting pituitary adenomas [37–40].

During this time, the natural product group with Albert Hofmann completed the determination of the absolute configuration of ergotamine and lysergic acid in a sophisticated synthesis program, which is still regarded today

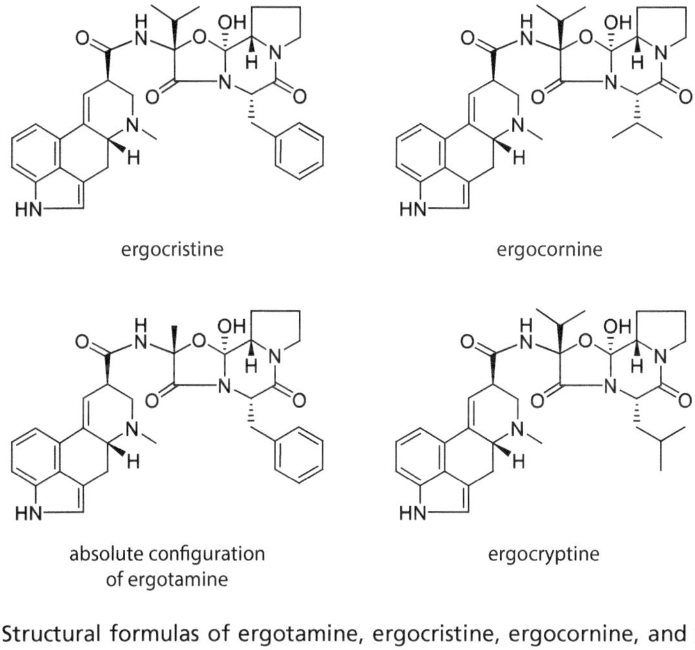

ergocristine

ergocornine

absolute configuration
of ergotamine

ergocryptine

Fig. 8.7 Structural formulas of ergotamine, ergocristine, ergocornine, and ergocryptine

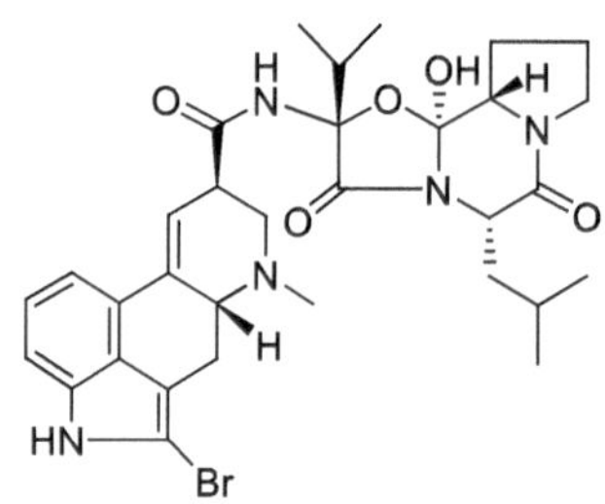

Fig. 8.8 2-Bromo-α-ergocryptine, *Parlodel*®

as a milestone in structure determination by chemical resynthesis (Fig. 8.7; [41–43]).

2-Bromo-α-ergocryptine was the last ergot alkaloid from the Basel-based company to be introduced into human therapy. This new molecule from the metabolite pool of the ergot fungus also gifted an unexpected, very last surprise. It was only after the launch of *Parlodel*® that, to everyone's astonishment, a specific interaction of the brominated drug with the brain's dopamine D2 receptor was discovered. Thus, the release of prolactin from the lactotropic cells and the secretion of the growth hormone from the somatotropic cells in acromegaly is inhibited. Sandoz AG had unintentionally developed a first-in-class representative of a novel class of drugs, the first specific D2 receptor agonists in medicine [40, 44].

Ergot medication: diversity of mechanisms of action and indications
Even today, the unusually high number of approved medicinal substances derived from ergot alkaloids is amazing (Fig. 8.9 and Table 8.1). Ultimately, this is due to the complex molecular mechanisms of action—the "polypharmacology" of these substances. Even the slightest changes in chemical structures lead to altered preferences and activities in relation to their adrenergic, dopaminergic, and serotonergic receptors, or influence the distribution of the molecules in the body. In a precisely coordinated interplay between pharmacology and clinical research, medicinal chemistry has been able to work out these subtle nuances and open up more and more indications for these metabolites. Their therapeutic relevance is reflected in the fact that all but one of them were included in the World Health Organization's *National Essential Medicines Lists* 2017 (Table 8.1).

However, this medical success created growing challenges in a completely different area: the provision of sufficient quantities of ergot, which could only be obtained by cultivating the fungus in the field and thus subject to unpredictable factors such as climatic conditions, insect or fungal infestation,

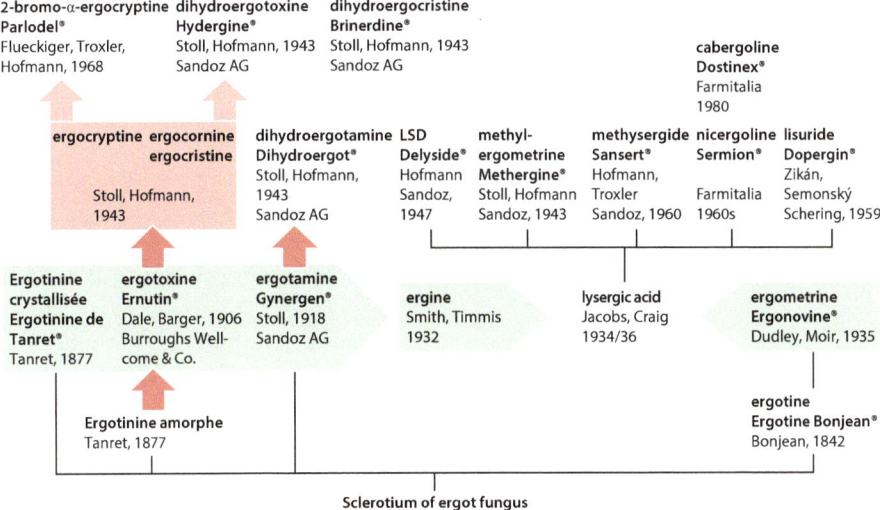

Fig. 8.9 "Family tree" of the medically relevant ergot alkaloids with their chemical derivatives and the year of their first publication/market launch

training and diligence of local workers, as well as the security situation in producing countries that influenced access to cultivation areas and reliable sclerotia supplies. All these factors made ergot production and logistics vulnerable. The fragility of this supply chain especially to the US became clear during the two world wars, when it was under ever-increasing tension, inevitably heading towards breaking point.

References

1. V. Erspamer, Pharmakologische Studien über Enteramin. I. Mitteilung: Über die Wirkung von Acetonextrakten der Kaninchenmagenschleimhaut auf den Blutdruck und auf isolierte überlebende Organe. Arch Exp Pathol Pharmakol **196**, 343 (1940)
2. V. Erspamer, Pharmakologische Studien über Enteramin III. Mitteilung: Über das Vorhandensein eines enteramin-ähnlichen Stoffes in Milzextrakten. Arch Exp Path Pharmakol **196**, 391 (1940)
3. P.M. Whitaker-Azmitia, The discovery of serotonin and its role in neuroscience. NPP **21**, 2S (1999)
4. H.P. Dustan, *Irvine Heinly Page 1901–1991* (National Academy of Sciences. National Academies Press, Washington D.C., 1995), p. 235

5. A.R. Green, Gaddum and LSD: the birth and growth of experimental and clinical neuropharmacology research on 5-HT in the UK. Br Journal Pharmacol **154**, 1583 (2008)

6. M.M. Rapport, A.A. Green, I.H. Page, Partial purification of the vasoconstrictor in beef serum. J Biol Chem **174**, 735 (1948)

7. M.M. Rapport, A.A. Green, I.H. Page, Serum vasoconstrictor (serotonin): IV. Isolation and characterization. J Biol Chem **176**, 1243 (1948)

8. M.M. Rapport, Serum vasoconstrictor (serotonin) the presence of creatinine in the complex; a proposed structure of the vasoconstrictor principle. J Biol Chem **180**, 961 (1949)

9. V. Erspamer, B. Asero, Identification of Enteramine, the Specific Hormone of the Enterochromaffin Cell System, as 5-hydroxytryptamine. Nature **169**, 800 (1952)

10. V. Erspamer, B. Asero, Isolation of enteramine from extracts of posterior salivary glands of Octopus vulgaris and of Discoglossus pictus skin. J Biol Chem **200**, 311 (1953)

11. B.M. Twarog, Responses of a molluscan smooth muscle to acetylcholine and 5-hydroxytryptamine. J Cell Comp Physiol **44**, 141 (1954)

12. B.M. Twarog, I.H. Page, Serotonin content of some mammalian tissues and urine and a method for its determination. Am J Physiol **175**, 157 (1953)

13. A.H. Amin, T.B.B. Crawford, J.H. Gaddum, The distribution of substance P and 5-hydroxytryptamine in the central nervous system of the dog. J Physiol **126**, 596 (1954)

14. W.S. Feldberg, John Henry Gaddum, 1900–1965. Biogr Mems Fell R Soc **13**, 1356 (1967)

15. P.P. Laidlaw, The Physiological Action of Indolethylamine. Biochem J **6**, 141 (1912)

16. J.H. Gaddum, Antagonism between lysergic acid diethylamide and 5-hydroxytryptamine. J Physiol **121**, 15P (1953)

17. E. Shaw, D.W. Woolley, Yohimbine and ergot alkaloids as naturally occurring antimetabolites of serotonin. J Biol Chem **203**, 979 (1953)

18. R. Turner, Wayne Woolley's Marvelously Equipped Mind—What drove a blind biochemist to experiment with LSD?, in *Distillations Magazine*, ed. by Science History Institute (Chemical Heritage Foundation, Philadelphia, 2021)

19. G.C. Wild, J.G. Hildebrand, Dilworth W. Woolley 1914–1966, in *Biogr. Mem. Natl. Acad. Sci*, ed. by National Academy of Sciences (National Academy Press, Washington D.C., 2014). https://www.nasonline.org/wp-content/uploads/2024/06/woolley-dilworth.pdf

20. D.W. Woolley, E. Shaw, A biochemical and pharmacological suggestion about certain mental disorders. PNAS **40**, 228 (1954)

21. C. Overy, E.M. Tansey (eds.), *Drugs affecting 5-HT systems* Wellcome Witnesses to Contemporary Medicine, vol. 47 (Queen Mary, University of London, London, 2013)

22. A. Sjoerdsma, C. Kornetsky, E.V. Evarts, Lysergic acid diethylamide in patients with excess serotonin. AMA Arch Neurol Psychiatry **75**, 488 (1956)

23. E.S. Valenstein, The Discovery of Chemical Neurotransmitters. Brain Cogn **49**, 73 (2002)

24. D.W. Woolley, Production of abnormal (psychotic?) behavior in mice with lysergic acid diethylamide, and its partial prevention with cholinergic drugs and serotonin. PNAS **41**, 338 (1955)

25. D.E. Nichols, Serotonin, and the past and future of LSD. Special Edition Psychedelics in Psychology and Psychiatry. Maps Bull **23**, 20 (2013)

26. K. Beringer, Experimentelle Psychosen durch Mescalin. Z Ges Neurol Psychiat **84**, 426 (1923)

27. D. de Gregorio, S. Comai, L. Posa, G. Gobbi, D-lysergic acid diethylamide (LSD) as a model of psychosis: Mechanism of action and pharmacology. Int J Mol Sci **17**, 1953 (2016)

28. N. Langlitz, Ceci n'est pas une psychose. Toward a historical epistemology of model psychoses. BioSocieties **1**, 159 (2006)

29. M. Tornay, Zugriffe auf das Ich – Psychoaktive Stoffe und Personenkonzepte in der Schweiz, 1945–1980, in *Historische Wissensforschung*, ed. by C. Arni, S. Gregory, B. Kleeberg, A. Langenohl, M. Sandl, R. Suter (Mohr Siebeck, Tübingen, 2016), p. 28

30. M. Tornay, Zugriffe auf das Ich – Psychoaktive Stoffe und Personenkonzepte in der Schweiz, 1945–1980, in *Historische Wissensforschung*, ed. by C. Arni, S. Gregory, B. Kleeberg, A. Langenohl, M. Sandl, R. Suter (Mohr Siebeck, Tübingen, 2016), p. 71

31. T.A. Ban, Fifty years chlorpromazine: a historical perspective. Neuropsychiatr Dis Treat **3**, 495 (2007)

32. E. Dyck, Flashback: Psychiatric Experimentation with LSD in Historical Perspective. Can J Psychiatry **50**, 381 (2005)

33. J.J. Fuentes, F. Fonseca, M. Elices, M. Farré, M. Torrens, Therapeutic Use of LSD in Psychiatry: A Systematic Review of Randomized-Controlled Clinical Trials. Front Psychiatry **10**, 943 (2019)

34. A. Stoll, A. Hofmann, Die Alkaloide der Ergotoxingruppe: Ergocristin, Ergokryptin und Ergocornin (7. Mitteilung über Mutterkornalkaloide). Helv Chim Acta **26**, 1570 (1943)

35. A. Stoll, A. Hofmann, Die Dihydroderivate der natürlichen linksdrehenden Mutterkornalkaloide. (9. Mitteilung über Mutterkornalkaloide). Helv Chim Acta **26**, 2070 (1943)

36. M.C. Shelesnyak, Ergotoxine inhibition of deciduoma formation and its reversal by progesterone. Am J Physiol **179**, 301 (1954)

37. G. Engel, R. Giger, Die Arbeiten von Dr. Albert Hofmann auf dem Gebiet der Mutterkornalkaloide und deren Einfluss auf die Medikamentenentwicklung der Firma ehemals Sandoz, heute Novartis, in *Grenzgänge – Albert Hofmann zum 100. Geburtstag*, ed. by G. Engel, P. Herrling (Schwabe, Basel, 2006), p. 8

38. R.K.A. Giger, G. Engel, Albert Hofmann's pioneering work on ergot alkaloids and its impact on the search of novel drugs at Sandoz, a predecessor company of Novartis. Chimia **60**, 83 (2006)

39. H.R. Schneider, P.A. Stadler, P. Stütz, F. Troxler, J. Seres, Synthese und Eigenschaften von Bromocriptin – Synthesis and properties of bromocriptine. Experientia **33**, 1412 (1977)

40. G.M. Besser, R.F. Pfeiffer, M.O. Thorner, 50 years since the discovery of bromocriptine. Eur J Endocrinol **179**, R69 (2018)

41. A. Stoll, A. Hofmann, Th Petrzilka, Die Konstitution der Mutterkornalkaloide. Struktur des Peptidteils. III. (24. Mitteilung über Mutterkornalkaloide). Helv Chim Acta **34**, 1544 (1951)

42. A. Hofmann, H. Ott, R. Griot, P.A. Stadler, A.J. Frey, Die Synthese und Stereochemie des Ergotamins (58. Mitteilung über Mutterkornalkaloide). Helv Chim Acta **46**, 2306 (1963)

43. P.A. Stadler, A. Hofmann, Chemische Bestimmung der absoluten Konfiguration der Lysergsäure (54. Mitteilung über Mutterkornalkaloide). Helv Chim Acta **45**, 2005 (1962)

44. R.S. Auriemma, R. Pirchio, D. de Alcubierre, R. Pivonello, A. Colao, Dopamine agonists: From the 1970s to today. Neuroendocrinology **109**, 34 (2019)

9

Urgently wanted: new paths to a stable ergot alkaloid production

Supply chains break!

The ergot-kernel was the only source for all ergot medicines and had to be grown on rye plants in an extremely labor-intensive process. The spore infection of each individual rye flower and the harvesting of the sclerotia were based on arduous manual work (Figs. 9.1–9.3). In the 1940s, cultivation of the Claviceps fungus, for which wild isolates were initially used, yielded around 880 pounds of ergot on 2.5 acres from which only 8.8 pounds of total alkaloids were obtained [1]. In addition to low-yield alkaloid production, there were also unpredictable and disruptive factors that could negatively impact the ergot harvest and jeopardize a stable supply to the pharmaceutical market. At the same time, demand for sclerotia continued to rise, further exacerbating the supply situation. Annual sclerotia imports to the United States alone doubled from 58 to 112 tons between 1913 and 1919, reaching a value of US$ 208,000 [2].

On the other side of the Atlantic, the availability of drugs for stopping postnatal bleeding was limited when the supply chains from Russia and Spain to the USA collapsed at the beginning of the First World War. Whereas a pound of Russian ergot was available for US$ 0.43 in 1914, the same amount cost US$ 5.00–6.00 in 1920. The commodity had become a significant economic factor. To end the United States' dependence on European suppliers, in 1919 the US company Eli Lilly & Co. commissioned its Botanical Research Laboratory to establish ergot alkaloid production on artificial culture media. In the laboratory of Walter W. Bonns, the microbiologist responsible for cultivating

Fig. 9.1 Infection of rye with inoculation boards, Switzerland (1943). (© Novartis Company Archive)

the fungus, it had grown well but it had not produced any ergotoxine. Bonns had come to the less than encouraging conclusion:

> "In the light of the present study, it appears extremely doubtful that the artificial culture of Claviceps possesses practical application" [2].

After the war, the USA's ergot imports slowly increased again. Eli Lilly & Co. had summarily discontinued its research program in 1922, and Spain, Portugal, the Soviet Union and Germany became the main suppliers of Claviceps sclerotia to the USA.

With the outbreak of the Second World War, European ergot deliveries to the USA once again faced severe interruptions. Poland and Germany had stopped exporting sclerotia due to the war. The Soviet Union had almost completely stopped its exports in order to meet domestic demand. Portugal, the

Fig. 9.2 Inoculated rye with protective caps, Emme Valley, Switzerland (1938). (© Novartis Company Archive)

main exporter to the USA at the time, had repeatedly reported poor crop yields, and Spain had still not recovered from the effects of the civil war on sclerotia cultivation. In 1940, the Wartime Requirements Committee of the Medical Research Council of the US government was forced to impose a "strict economy in prescribing ergot" on doctors [3, 4].

Sandoz AG in Basel had also suffered from supply problems and hardly received any sclerotia from abroad for its ergotamine production, which it had previously obtained from Spain, the Belgian Congo or Asia. Fortunately, the company had decided to begin domestic sclerotia production a few years earlier. While ergotamine had been isolated from wild sclerotia until the mid-1930s, the growing demand for medicines made new production strategies necessary in order to produce ergot more economically, make supply chains more robust, and become less dependent on foreign imports.

Fig. 9.3 Ergot harvest in the Emme Valley, Switzerland (1942). (© Novartis Company Archive)

The start of large-scale ergot farming in Switzerland

The Basel-based company searched the Alpine republic for suitable regions for ergot farming. The Emme Valley in the Bernese *Mittelland*, with its long peasant tradition of rye cultivation, offered excellent prerequisites: the cooler temperatures and more frequent rainfall in the hilly landscape were ideal conditions for sclerotia production. The Emme Valley farmers' concerns about cultivating the dreaded grain pest in their fields and spreading it in the region were soon dispelled—the prospect of lucrative business with the Basel pharmaceutical company possibly having tipped the scales. In 1935, the Swiss chemist and microbiologist Artur Brack took over the responsibility of producing sclerotia at Sandoz AG (Info box 1). Over the next few decades, he established, coordinated, and optimized all process steps from spore production and delivery to the farms, to inoculation of the grain, quality control, ergot harvesting, and ergot transport to Basel. In 1939, the Swiss War Office of Food granted the company permission to drastically expand the area under cultivation. The existing farmers in the Emme Valley were joined by others from the surrounding areas of Lucerne, Fribourg, Graubünden, Solothurn, and the Basel region, compensating the loss of ergot imports due to the war [5].

Info box 1: Artur Brack

Artur Brack was born in 1907, the son of a St. Gallen politician. In 1926, he began studying chemistry at ETH Zurich and completed his studies with a thesis in chemical physics. In 1930, he became a microanalysis assistant in the Laboratory for General and Analytical Chemistry under the later Nobel Prize winner Leopold Ruzicka and obtained his doctorate in 1933 with research work in the fields of cyclobutadiene synthesis and gentian root oil. Brack then deepened his knowledge in microbiology. This combination of subjects helped him to obtain his first commission, a chemical-microbiological analysis of the River Aare's water quality for the city of Bern. In 1935, he accepted a job offer from the pharmaceutical department of Sandoz AG in Basel, where he was in charge of the ergot fungus strain development, the inoculum production, and ergot field cultivation. From 1939, Brack was responsible for the resolute expansion of sclerotia production in Switzerland, involving around 1500 farmers in the Emme Valley region alone. In 1970, Artur Brack took early retirement to start a second academic career in Egyptology, along with his wife Annelies. At the time, the couple could already read hieroglyphics and speak the ancient Egyptian language. Now they were learning archaeological practices from scratch and doing hard physical labor on the excavation sites of the Swiss Institute for Architectural and Archaeological Research on Ancient Egypt. Thanks to their in-depth training in unearthing and surveying tombs and sites, the Bracks were able to examine the above-ground and underground tomb complex of the Scribe of the Recruits Tjanuni, who lived during the reign of Thutmose IV (1413–1403 BC). In 1980, the Bracks published a comprehensive scientific treatise on their three-year investigation of the tomb of the pharaoh Horemheb in Thebes. Their research and international publications made them renowned archaeologists, and Artur Brack a corresponding member of the German Archaeological Institute [6, 7].

Artur Brack (1907 St. Gallen – 1993 Riehen), Swiss chemist and microbiologist. (© Novartis Company Archive)

After the war, Sandoz AG's ergot alkaloid portfolio had changed fundamentally. In addition to Gynergen® the new drugs Methergine®, Dihydroergot®, Hydergine® and Brinerdine® had been approved, whose active ingredients were based on different alkaloids of the fungus. The therapeutics further drove up the ergot demand, so the company pulled out all the stops to increase production of the individual parent compounds. The cultivation fields were expanded and could be operated more economically with ergot inoculation and harvesting machines (Fig. 9.4). The "Kluser rye" was successfully bred on the Sandoz experimental farm "Klushof" in Aesch, Switzerland. Its characteristics, such as vertical stability, late-maturing, stalk length and thickness, ear length and glume closure, were specifically optimized for sclerotia cultivation and led to a significant rise in ergot yield [5]. Process chemists left no stone unturned to maximize the alkaloid yield of their isolation process. Brack's department unswervingly obtained new Claviceps isolates, which were tested in the company's trial fields and greenhouses to increase the content of individual active ingredients in the sclerotia. Developments in agricultural technology and progress in rye breeding, as well as the expansion of the farming area, were the success factors that made it possible to soar Swiss sclerotia produc-

Fig. 9.4 Mechanical ergot inoculation of rye, Switzerland (1942). (© Novartis Company Archive)

tion from 3.5 tons to 48.5 tons between 1939 and 1954 [5, 8]. The complex production process, which had developed from the integration of microbiological research, preparative chemistry, rye breeding, efficient infection rate of the grain, and field cultivation work, was an insurmountable hurdle for other companies, preventing their penetration of the Sandoz AG business segment. When the weather cooperated, Brack's production process ran like the finely honed gears of a Swiss watch.

However, the management of Sandoz AG was under no illusions that it would be able to guarantee a stable and economical supply of the future pharmaceutical market through field cultivation alone [9]. The Basel-based company, which had created a "natural monopoly" in its steadily growing ergot business segment over the past three decades, had to look for ways to avoid becoming a victim of its own success. Experts put their heads together and pondered new possibilities for ergot alkaloid production. After in-depth discussions and careful deliberation, their unanimous analysis was sobering. The first option was quickly taken off the table: a chemical synthesis route was futile. The exact molecular structures were unknown (they were not understood until the early 1960s), and the drugs from a hypothetical alkaloid synthesis would have been unaffordable [10, 11]. The cultivation of the fungus in artificial culture media was the only remaining production option. Everyone was now seeking a solution from the microbiologists, who turned away in dismay. Even if they did not know it at that moment, their time had come.

At the end of the 19th century, methods were developed to obtain pure isolates of the ergot fungus on bread that had been soaked in a nutrient solution. The research efforts at Eli Lilly & Co. to produce ergotoxine on agar cultures had ultimately failed, but at least it had been learned that the fungus also grew on something other than pieces of bread. In 1931, the American mycologist Adelia McCrea, from the University of Michigan, Ann Arbor, provided the first glimmer of hope. After three years, she succeeded in detecting the characteristic activity of the ergot alkaloids in extracts of the Claviceps fungus that had been cultivated on solid agar media, on the basis of the black coloration of the cockscomb. She did not attempt to present the isolated active compounds in her doctoral thesis—the alkaloid quantities that had formed were not sufficient for this. McCrea had nevertheless assumed that she had detected ergotoxine [12].

After a Japanese working group had isolated the first ergot alkaloid of the clavine group from a liquid culture of *Claviceps purpurea* in 1948, Sandoz scientists began to examine fermentative ergot alkaloid production from all angles and were a little more confident than their colleagues in chemistry. However, there was no relief just yet. The biological route was paved with problems and countless unknown pitfalls of microbial physiology.

Could the fungus even produce the medically relevant alkaloids under artificial culture conditions? Following the results from Japan, there were justifiable doubts. If at all, which fungal isolates might be suitable for this and where could these microorganisms be found? Was it mandatory to induce sclerotia formation for a significant alkaloid production, and how could this be achieved? Under what conditions did cultures of *Claviceps purpurea* have to be stored so that it would grow again later and produce its substances? What nutrients did the fungus need for good growth? Were they the same as those for optimal alkaloid production? Were these media components even available in sufficient quantities for industrial production? Everyone agreed that a future production process would have to be achieved in large-volume cultivation tanks, so-called fermenters. But the technical requirements, process management and cultivation conditions for the Claviceps fungus were a depressing *terra incognita*. The reason for this scientific void was simple: metabolites from microorganisms did not play a role in medicine until the mid-1940s, and so there was no need to produce a microbially-derived medicinal substance industrially. Regardless, for the overall project to be a success, it would have to navigate through all these complications. There was no other way forward.

With all these unanswered questions, it is not surprising that until 1960 there was no alternative but for Sandoz AG to infect rye with ergot spores. The solution to this complex problem was found in eastern England when a Scottish bacteriologist's summer vacation was coming to an end. He had packed his bags, perhaps a little wistfully, and made his way home to London.

Penicillin, the pacemaker for the fermentative production of ergot alkaloids

In August 1928, Alexander Fleming spent his usual vacation at his country house, *The Dhoon*, in Barton Mills, Suffolk. He loved family life in the countryside and working in the garden, as it reminded him of his childhood at Lochfield Farm in Scotland, where he had grown up in the great outdoors, fishing and bird watching. After returning from his summer retreat, on Friday, September 28, Dr. Fleming re-entered his cramped laboratory at St Mary's Hospital in London. In the evening, he began to tidy up. As he was sorting out older agar cultures on which he had cultivated staphylococcus bacteria from a wound before his vacation, his gaze fell on something that made him pause: "That's funny ..."—a penicillium mold had infected one of the culture plates and inhibited the growth of the bacteria. In that brief moment, "Flem" made the momentous decision *not to* throw away the contaminated agar plate, a flash of inspiration that would change medicine. He inoculated the fungal strain and began to study the antibacterial activity of the discovered substance, which he named *penicillin* after the genus name of the microbial producer *Penicillium* Link [13, 14].

A few years later, the Australian physician Howard Florey, the German-British biochemist Ernst Boris Chain, and the British biologist Norman Heatley continued Fleming's work at the Sir William Dunn School of Pathology at Oxford University and produced penicillin in larger quantities to study it chemically and medically. The first cultivation vessels that Heatley tested for growing the fungus were actually "ducks" (urine bottles for men), though metal biscuit containers or porcelain vessels were also used to produce penicillin.

In 1941, when the research team realized that penicillin could cure systemic bacterial infections, a large-scale production process for the antibiotic had to be developed as quickly as possible. Due to the war, British industry had neither the capacity nor the scientific and technological prerequisites for this [15]. However, the technical know-how and the urgently needed fermentation capacities were available in the USA, where the company Charles Pfizer & Co. had been producing citric acid in large fermenters since the 1920s, using the black mold *Aspergillus niger* van Tieghem. Without the decisive support of the US government, the investments in the fermentation infrastructure and the pooling of all available resources of several US pharmaceutical companies, including the results of the Oxford Group, would have been impossible. In

1944, after only two years of development work, the production of the life-saving antibiotic was produced on ton-scale in Brooklyn, New York.

The realization that microorganisms can produce therapeutically relevant antibiotics triggered a boom in research projects to identify further metabolites for the treatment of bacterial infections. Microbiological research groups at universities and in industry developed methods to isolate and to cultivate fungi and bacteria, investigated artificial culture media for the formation of microbial metabolites, and how a successful scale up from laboratory scale to a bioreactor is accomplished. The penicillin project had become the big bang of a dynamically emerging new research domain: pharmaceutical biotechnology.

From 1945 onwards, the Institute for Fermentation, Osaka, of the Japanese company Takeda Chemical Industries Ltd., based its work on these results. Its aim was to produce medically relevant ergot alkaloids in artificial culture media. The microbiologist Matazô Abe examined around 500 Claviceps isolates from various regions of Japan and in 1948 was able to produce with *agroclavine* an ergot alkaloid in liquid culture for the first time (Fig. 9.5; [16]). Thereafter, Abe went on to describe further ergot compounds, but he never succeeded in accessing a single pharmaceutically significant ergot compound by fermentation. Unfortunately, the strains studied had one thing in common: they lacked the complete genetic repertoire of lysergic acid biosynthesis (Fig. 10.3). Even though he was unable to realize his original plans, Abe's work is one of the pioneering achievements in biotechnological natural product research. The resulting alkaloids of the clavine group later were of great importance for the elucidation of ergot alkaloid biosynthesis. Abe's most important contribution, however, was the development of the first liquid media in which *Claviceps purpurea* forms ergot alkaloids.

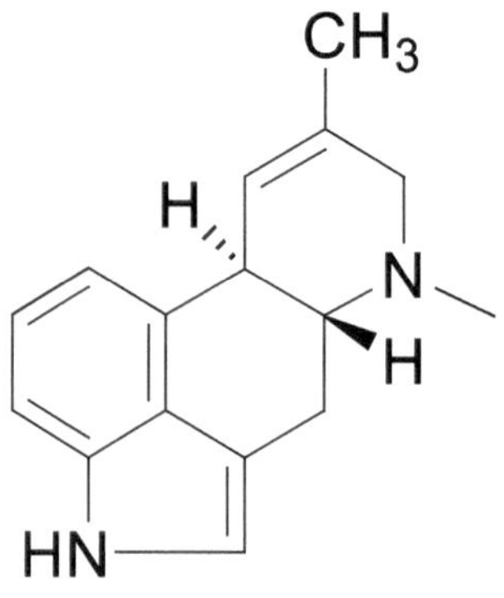

Fig. 9.5 Agroclavine

The breakthrough: Ernst Chain's research team in Italy succeeds in producing a lysergic acid compound in liquid cultures. Sandoz AG in Basel has to react quickly. But how?

The Japanese scientist's cultivation methodology was taken up by two research groups focusing on the development of lysergic acid production. It was the central parent compound for a number of ergot-derived drugs, the demand for which continued to grow unabated. In addition to Sandoz AG in Basel, a newly assembled team at the *Istituto Superiore di Sanità* in Rome also worked on this scientific problem. From 1948, Ernst Boris Chain was responsible for setting up a center for research on microbial active agents, the International Research Center for Chemical Microbiology [17].

Info box 2: Sir Ernst Boris Chain

Ernst Boris Chain was born in Berlin, the son of a Russian chemical manufacturer Michael Chain and his wife Margarete, née Eisner. Ernst was an excellent pianist, gave concerts, wrote music criticisms in the *Welt am Abend*, and seriously considered pursuing a career as a pianist. He gave up these musical dreams when he was repeatedly told by his father's cousin by marriage, Anna ("Nura") Sacharina, who was twenty years older than him, that there was no money in music. She cited the fate of an impoverished musician from their Russian relatives, and said that science would definitely offer better career opportunities. Chain left his career as a musician and studied chemistry and medicine at the Humboldt University in Berlin, where he was in contact with Walther Nernst, Fritz Haber, Max Planck, Otto Hahn and Otto Warburg. In April 1933, he fled from Nazi Germany to England with £10 in his pocket. In the early days, he was just able to keep his head above water thanks to financial support of £250 per year from the London Jewish Refugees Committee and the Liberal Jewish Synagogue. In 1935, Chain joined the working group of the Australian physician Howard Florey at Oxford University, where he continued the penicillin work of Alexander Fleming and worked on the production, isolation, and pharmacological profiling of the antibiotic. In 1945, together with Fleming and Florey, he was awarded the Nobel Prize in Physiology or Medicine "for the discovery of penicillin and its curative effect in various infectious diseases". After his research time at the *Istituto Superiore di Sanità* in Rome, in 1964 Chain founded the Department of Biochemistry at the Imperial College of the University of London. Aunt "Nura", who had already run Chain's household in Oxford and saw no reason to change this even after his marriage to the British biochemist Anne Beloff, always moved with him when he changed positions. After Chain was knighted in 1969—25 years after his colleagues Howard Florey and Alexander Fleming—he built a vacation home for himself and his family in Mulranny, Ireland. In 1971, he also had his beloved Steinway grand piano transported there [18, 19].

Sir Ernst Boris Chain (1906
Berlin – 1979 Mulranny,
Ireland), German-British
biochemist. (© National
Portrait Gallery, London)

Chain was the ideal person for the job, as he was able to contribute his wealth of experience from the penicillin projects in England and the USA. Until 1958, he worked on process improvements in penicillin manufacturing and the formation of semi-synthetic derivatives, after which he turned his attention to microbial lysergic acid production. Just one year later, the Italian microbiologist Antonio Tonolo isolated the strain *Claviceps paspali* F-550 (Stevens et Hall), which had been found at the gates of Rome and formed *D-lysergic acid α-hydroxyethylamide* in liquid culture (Fig. 10.2). In just a few reaction steps, the chemists were able to split off the desired lysergic acid from the new molecule. The Roman group sent the strain to the Milan-based pharmaceutical company *Farmitalia*, where Frederico-Maria Arcamone and Celestino Spalla worked out the large-scale production of the lysergic acid compound [20–22]. The Italian microbiologists optimized the fermentation process and finally achieved a production titer of 2 g/L, with improved mutants of the strain. In 1966, they transferred the fermentation parameters to the biotechnological production of ergotamine [22, 23]. In 1960, the popping of Prosecco corks in Rome and Milan could be heard as far away as Basel, where it alerted the scientists on the Rhine River bend—for good reason: the breakthrough threatened to shake Sandoz AG's previously unchallenged dominance in the field of ergot alkaloid production.

The Swiss company had been trying to cultivate Claviceps strains on solid culture media since 1952, with moderate success. The Basel researchers had isolated ergotamine, ergotaminine, and ergometrine from surface cultures of the fungus for the first time, but the already previously investigated approach had remained a dead end [24, 25]. It was useless for the development of an industrial production process, the alkaloid quantities were negligible and, last but not least, the ergot fungus degraded its active ingredients during cultivation. Sandoz AG had been forced to continue isolating the ergot substances from the sclerotia or to synthesize them semi-synthetically from the isolated lysergic acid. Now, however, Chain's research team and Farmitalia had left the Swiss pharmaceutical company in the production of the most important ergot alkaloid in the dust. In order to defend its important ergot business, Sandoz had to take up the gauntlet thrown by the Milan-based company. The Basel group was now well positioned for its *riposte*, and once again a great deal of luck was in play. Arthur Stoll's third son Christian had furthered the technology of natural product research at Sandoz AG. His working group searched for antibiotics from fungi and made them available in larger quantities for preclinical research in the newly installed fermentation plant. Microbiological expertise and modern biotechnological infrastructure were now available to work at full speed on lysergic acid production in liquid culture.

In 1960, Artur Brack and his laboratory assistant Hanni Gisi, and the Swiss microbiologist Hans Kobel (Fig. 9.7) set out on a feverish search for a lysergic acid producer that had to form the alkaloid, or closely related analogs, even more economically than Farmitalia's Claviceps isolate F-550. After trawling through hundreds of Claviceps sclerotia from all over the world, Hanni Gisi came to the rescue of her research team and most certainly also of the company management. The subsequent sigh of relief in Basel caused reciprocal disillusionment among the Italian research teams. She had isolated a fungus of the species *Claviceps paspali* Stevens & Hall from an ergot that had formed on a Dallis grass plant (*Paspalum dilatatum* Poir.) in Portugal, which produced the biosynthetic precursor of lysergic acid, *paspalic acid* (Fig. 9.6), in unusually high quantities. Paspalic acid differs from lysergic acid only in the position of a double bond, which is located between the carbon atoms C8/C9. Under mild alkaline conditions, it is shifted to the C9/C10 position resulting in the formation of lysergic acid (Fig. 9.6; [26]). The simple chemical rearrangement reaction and the strong improvements in productivity with further Claviceps isolates, achieved by Hans Kobel, René Germanier and Esther Segal, turned

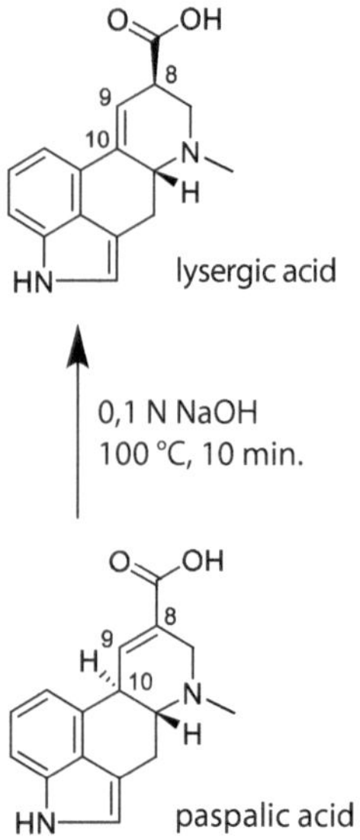

Fig. 9.6 Rearrangement reaction of paspalic acid into lysergic acid [26]

the tide in favor of the Basel company again (personal communication by Dr. Jean-Jacques Sanglier, 2023).

As Sandoz AG did not have any fermentation plants for the industrial production of paspalic acid, in 1965 it took over the Austrian antibiotic producer, Biochemie GmbH Kundl, and from 1966 became the market leader in fermentative lysergic acid production with an annual production volume of 2000 kg (personal communication by Dr. Andreas Friedrich and Julia Ager-Gruber, 2022). Following the success of paspalic acid, the Basel research group with the Belgian microbiologist Jean-Jacques Sanglier, developed the biotechnological processes for the peptide alkaloids ergocryptine, -cornine, -cristine, and -tamine, which were transferred to the Tyrolean plant. The parent compounds for the drugs *Hydergine*® and *Parlodel*® were produced there until the mid-1970s. After the completion of peptide alkaloid production, paspalic acid fermentation was continued for the synthesis of Methergine® and Sansert® (personal communication by Drs. Andreas Friedrich and Jean-Jacques Sanglier, 2022; [22, 27, 28]).

In 1999, the market volume of ergopeptides was 5–8 tons and that of lysergic acid 10–15 tons. The biotechnology production divisions of the former Sandoz AG and later Novartis (Austria), Farmitalia (Italy), Boehringer Ingelheim (Germany), Galena (Czech Republic), Gedeon Richter (Hungary), Lek (Slovenia) (now Sandoz), Poli (Italy), and Eli Lilly (USA) covered 60% of

Fig. 9.7 *From left*: Hans Kobel, Artur Brack, Albert Hofmann (1958). (© Novartis Company Archive)

global demand. Ergot alkaloids produced via traditional sclerotia cultivation on the grain variety *triticale*, a hybrid of wheat and rye, had a market share of 40%. The ergot yield was 1–2 tons per hectare, from which 10–20 kg of total alkaloids were isolated [1, 29].

References

1. H. Hulvová, P. Galuszka, J. Frébortová, I. Frébort, Parasitic fungus *Claviceps* as a source for biotechnological production of ergot alkaloids. Biotechnol Adv **31**, 79 (2013)
2. W.W. Bonns, A preliminary study of *Claviceps purpurea* in culture. Am J Bot **9**, 339 (1922)
3. News and Views: Shortage of ergot. *Nature* 1940, 146, 19
4. *World Trade Notes on Chemicals and Allied Products, July 8th*. Bureau of Foreign and Domestic Commerce, United States, 1939, 13, 27, p. 453
5. B. Bächi, Mutterkorn – Roggen zwischen Biotechnologie und LSD. Schweizer Z Ernährungsmedizin **5**, 10 (2017)
6. B. Hauser-Schäublin, Faszination Ägypten, in *Jahrbuch z' Rieche 1987*, ed. by Municipality Riehen (Friedrich Reinhardt, Basel, 1987)

7. A. Brack, *I. Versuche zur Darstellung des Cyclobutadiens. II. Über das Enzianwurzelöl* (ETH Zurich. Publishing House Fluntern, 1933). Doctoral thesis no. 755

8. H. Marti, Von Mutterkornanbau, Wolfszähnen, Kornzapfen und Kribbelkrankheit. Ein Stück Agrargeschichte ging zu Ende. Heimatkd Wiggertal **43**, 153 (1985)

9. H. Kobel, J.J. Sanglier, Ergot alkaloids, in *Biotechnology*, 2nd edn. vol 4., ed. by H.J. Rehm, G. Reed (VCH, Weinheim, 1986), pp. 598–601

10. P.A. Stadler, A. Hofmann, Chemische Bestimmung der absoluten Konfiguration der Lysergsäure (54. Mitteilung über Mutterkornalkaloide). Helv Chim Acta **45**, 2005 (1962)

11. A. Hofmann, H. Ott, R. Griot, P.A. Stadler, A.J. Frey, Die Synthese und Stereochemie des Ergotamins (58. Mitteilung über Mutterkornalkaloide). Helv Chim Acta **46**, 2306 (1963)

12. A. McCrea, The reactions of *Claviceps purpurea* to variations of environment. Am J Bot **18**, 50 (1931)

13. V.D. Allison, Personal recollections of Sir Almroth Wright and Sir Alexander Fleming. Ulst Med J **43**, 89 (1974)

14. E.W. Jones, R.G.W. Jones, Merlin Pryce (1902–1976) and Penicillin: An Abiding Mystery. Vesalius **8**, 6 (2002)

15. R. Bud, Innovators, deep fermentation and antibiotics: promoting applied science before and after the Second World War. Dynamics **31**, 323 (2011)

16. M. Abe, IX. Separation of an active substance and its properties. J Agric Chem Soc Japan **22**, 2 (1948)

17. B. Ernst, *Chain Biographical.* https://www.nobelprize.org/prizes/medicine/1945/chain/biographical/

18. E.P. Abraham, Ernst Boris Chain (19th June 1906 – August 12, 1979). Biogr Mems Fell R Soc **29**, 43 (1983)

19. R.W. Clark, *The life of Ernst Chain—penicillin and beyond* (Bloomsbury, London, 2011)

20. F. Arcamone, C. Bonino, E.B. Chain, A. Ferretti, P. Pennella, A. Tonolo, L. Vero, Production of lysergic acid derivatives by a strain of *Claviceps paspali* Stevens and Hall in submerged culture. Nature **187**, 238 (1960)

21. F. Arcamone, E.B. Chain, A. Ferretti, P. Pennella, A. Tonolo, L. Vero, Production of a New Lysergic Acid derivative in Submerged Culture by a Strain of *Claviceps paspali* Stevens & Hall. Proc R Soc Lond Ser B Biol Sci **155**, 26 (1961)

22. A. Minghetti, N. Crespi-Perellino, The history of ergot, in *Ergot: The Genus Claviceps*, 1st edn., ed. by V. Křen, L. Cvak (Harwood Academic Publishers, 1999), p. 7

23. A.M. Amici, A. Minghetti, T. Scotti, C. Spalla, L. Tognoli, Production of ergotamine by a strain of *Claviceps purpurea* (Fr.) Tul. Experientia **22**, 415 (1966)

24. A. Stoll, A. Brack, A. Hofmann, H. Kobel, *Process for production of ergotamine, ergotamine and ergobasin* Swiss Pat. No. 321.323 (1953)

25. A. Stoll, A. Brack, H. Kobel, A. Hofmann, R.D. Brunner, Die Alkaloide eines Mutterkornpilzes von Pennisetum typhoideum Rich. und deren Bildung in sapro-phytischer Kultur (36. Mitteilung über Mutterkornalkaloide). Helv Chim Acta **37**, 1815 (1954)

26. H. Kobel, E. Schreier, J. Rutschmann, 6-Methyl-Δ8,9-ergolen-8-carboxylic acid, a new ergoline derivative from cultures of a strain of Claviceps paspali STEVENS et HALL (60. Mitteilung über Mutterkornalkaloide). Helv Chim Acta **47**, 1052 (1964)

27. L. Cvak, Industrial Production of Ergot alkaloids, in *Ergot: The Genus Claviceps*, 1st edn., ed. by V. Křen, L. Cvak (Harwood Academic Publishers, Amsterdam, 1999), p. 376

28. H. Kobel, J.J. Sanglier, Ergot alkaloids, in *Biotechnology* vol 4., ed. by H.J. Rehm, G. Reed (VCH, Weinheim, 1986), pp. 601–604

29. P.L. Schiff Jr, Ergot and its alkaloids. Am J Pharm Educ **70**, 98 (2006)

10

Last secrets of ergot and its ingredients are revealed

The snake plant of the cloud people

Natural product research always assumed that only fungi could form lysergic acid and analogous compounds. This dogma was shaken when a manager at the bank J.P. Morgan & Co. and his wife became interested in psychedelic mushrooms and plants.

Info box 1: R. Gordon Wasson

R. Gordon Wasson was born in Great Falls, Montana, the son of a minister in the Episcopal Church. His father attached great importance to a comprehensive education, and before Gordon and his brother Thomas were even ten years old, they traveled alone to faraway New York for monthly museum visits. In 1914, his father sent his two teenagers on an educational trip to Europe. During their Grand Tour, the First World War broke out but somehow the boys managed to make it home safe and sound. After studying journalism, Gordon Wasson worked as a reporter in Argentina and London until he joined the public relations department of the bank J.P. Morgan & Co. in 1934. He first became acquainted with the world of fungi through his Russian-born wife, the pediatrician Valentina Pavlovna Guercken, and Gordon soon became fascinated by the importance of these microorganisms in the cultures of human beings. The Wasson couple pursued their shared hobby with great precision and scientific intent. Valentina and Gordon called their field of research "ethnomycology".

R. Gordon Wasson (1898 Great Falls, MT – 1986 Danbury, CT), (in his house in Connecticut c. 1972), American journalist and ethnomycologist. (© Photo by Janine Wiedel)

From 1941, Gordon Wasson (Info box 1) worked with *coaxihuitl* ("snake plant", Christmas vine *Turbina corymbosa* (L.) Raf.; syn. *Rivea corymbosa* (L.) Hallier f.) (Fig. 10.1), the cult plant of the Zapotecs in Oaxaca, which was also known to the Olmec, Aztec, and Maya peoples [1, 2].

The priests of the *Cloud People*, or Zapotecs, extracted a drug from *ololiúqui* ("round thing"), the seeds of the snake plant, which put them into a trance to contact the spirits of the dead or to look into the future as divine oracles. During Wasson's research visit to Mexico in the late summer of 1959, he undertook an expedition with the Austrian-Mexican anthropologist Robert Weitlaner, during which they collected 26 lbs (12 kg) of ololiúqui and sent them to Albert Hofmann in Basel for chemical analysis. Wasson had packed 21 g of seeds in an advance shipment to Hofmann and enclosed a letter, dated August 6, 1959:

> "(…) I am sending you (…) a small parcel of seeds that I take to be Rivea corymbosa, otherwise known as 'ololiuhqui', well-known narcotic of the Aztecs, called in Huautla 'la semilla de la Virgen'. This parcel (…) consists of two little bottles (…) and a larger batch of seeds, delivered to us by Francisco Bartolo

Fig. 10.1 Christmas vine (*Turbina corymbosa* (L.) Raf.)

Ortega (Chico), the Zapotec guide, who himself gathered the seeds from the plants at the Zapotec town of San Bartolo Yautepec (…)" [3].

Wasson had previously worked with the Swiss natural product chemist to identify the psychotogenic active ingredients of the magic mushroom *teonanácatl*. Like ololiúqui, the fungus *Psilocybe mexicana* R. Heim played a central role as a drug in religious or magical ceremonies of the Mayas and Aztecs. If the mushroom was not available for ritual acts, the shamans promptly switched to ololiúqui. In 1958, Albert Hofmann succeeded in isolating the hallucinogenic psilocybin and, later, the related psilocin from the fruiting bodies of Psilocybe mexicana, which is still used today in healing rites in a few villages in the Sierra Mazatec in Mexico [4].

Hofmann's first chemical analysis of the ololiúqui ingredients was unequivocal: the seeds contained several indoles. There was only one way for him and his laboratory assistant Hans Tscherter to find out whether they were also the carriers of the snake plant's psychotogenic activity: they ingested the substances of an enriched indole fraction and gradually increased the dose. At 2 mg, a dream-like state set in and their perception of colors and objects began to change. In addition to ergometrine, Hofmann and Tscherter also isolated the psychotogenic molecules ergine and D-lysergic acid-α-hydroxyethylamide from Wasson and Weitlaner's second, larger batch of ololiúqui (Fig. 10.2; [3, 5, 6]). Natural product researchers, phytochemists and ethnobotanists were perplexed: how was it possible for a plant to produce these substances in the

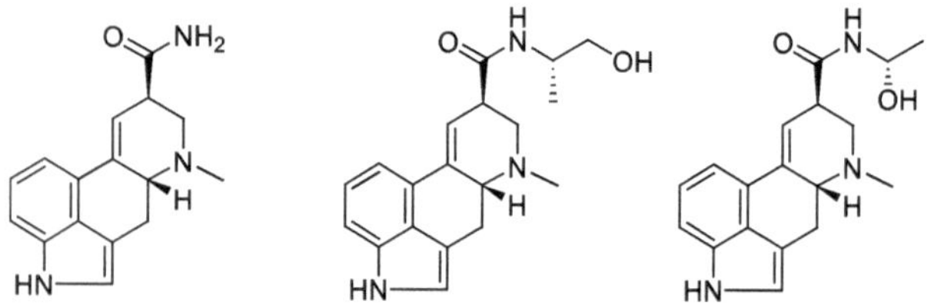

Fig. 10.2 Ololiúqui alkaloids, *from left*: Ergine, ergometrine, D-lysergic acid-α-hydroxyethylamide

same way as a fungus? The Coaxihuitl secret was only revealed fifty years later: the Christmas vine lives in symbiosis with fungi from the Claviceps family, which colonize the leaf surfaces of the plant. Here they form lysergic acid substances that protect the Christmas vine from insect infestation. After fertilization of the flower, the epibiontic microorganisms enter the maturing seeds in an as yet unknown way and are passed on to the next generation [7, 8].

How the ergot fungus builds its alkaloids

Mycologists had researched the life cycle of the ergot fungus, and pharmacists, chemists, and pharmacologists had isolated its active ingredients and described its physiological activities. Chemists had painstakingly explained the alkaloid structures in detail, thus creating the conditions for biochemists, microbiologists, and molecular geneticists to work on the biosynthesis of the microbial active ingredients. This mammoth project took almost sixty years to complete.

Work on this project began in 1953, with speculation on whether the amino acid tryptophan could be a building block of lysergic acid. To answer this question, the German pharmacist and botanist Kurt Mothes, at the Institute of Crop Plant Research in Berlin/Gatersleben, was one of the first natural product researchers to apply a method that was developed by the Hungarian chemist George de Hevesy (1885–1966). He used isotope-labeled molecules as tracers to study physiological processes in plants and animals. In 1923, de Hevesy was the first to track the transport of the radioactive lead isotope ^{210}Pb through a plant. In 1934, he leveraged non-radioactive heavy water to determine the residence time of D_2O in his body (or in that of his assistant?). For the first time in medical research, it was possible to measure the distribution of molecules in the human body [9–11]. In 1942, George de Hevesy was honored with the Nobel Prize in Chemistry "for his work on the use of isotopes as tracers in the study of chemical processes".

In 1957, Mothes took up de Hevesy's method and injected ^{14}C-labeled, radioactive tryptophan into the pith cavities of rye plants that he had previously inoculated with *Claviceps purpurea* spores. The isolation of ergot alkaloids with a radioactive lysergic acid residue proved that tryptophan must be a building block of their biosynthesis [12, 13].

The possibility of analyzing the formation of a natural substance by the incorporation of isotope-labeled building blocks fascinated the German chemist Heinz Floss (Info box 2), who deployed the method for elucidating the biochemical reactions of the ergot alkaloid biosynthesis and published his results in almost 100 scientific articles.

Info box 2: Heinz G. Floss

Heinz G. Floss was born in Berlin in 1934, the son of sales representative Friedrich Floss and his wife Annemarie. After a somewhat troubled childhood during the Second World War, he pursued so many interests that his father was worried that his boy would never amount to anything because he could not concentrate. Despite his father's fears, Floss obtained a high-school diploma and enrolled at the Technical University of Berlin. His choice of chemistry as a subject was largely a coincidence, as he had applied to study either chemistry or electrical engineering. After passing the one entrance exam for the chemistry course, he was not interested in taking another. Thus, chemistry gained a talented student, while electrical engineering lost out [the prelude to great scientific careers is sometimes refreshingly unspectacular]. The decision to write his doctoral thesis under Prof. Friedrich Weygand at the Technical University of Munich marked the beginning of Floss's formative years. He learned from his doctoral supervisor how to "lead" his future colleagues on a "long leash". The greatest influence on his scientific track, however, was Prof. Kurt Mothes in Halle, with whom he collaborated in the field of ergot alkaloids and their biosynthesis. After his postdoctoral year with Eric E. Conn at the University of California, Davis, he was so enthusiastic about the USA that he accepted an appointment to the Faculty of Pharmacy at Purdue University, Lafayette, Indiana, in 1966. In 1988, he became Chair of the Department of Chemistry at the University of Washington, Seattle, from which he retired in 2000. His scientific interest in the biosynthesis of natural substances (ergot alkaloids, and antibiotics) expanded in later years with studies on the stereochemistry of enzymatic reactions. Many of his former research assistants became renowned university professors all over the world. Heinz Floss remained true to his wide-ranging interests into old age: he loved traveling, visiting art museums and reading biographies and historical treatises (personal communication by Prof. Heinz Floss, 2022).

Heinz G. Floss, German chemist (1934 Berlin – 2022 Bellevue, WA). (© H.G. Floss)

Floss dedicated his important paper on the biosynthesis of ergot alkaloids, published in 1976, to the Japanese microbiologist Matazô Abe, in recognition of his pioneering Claviceps cultivation work, a wonderful gesture of scientific collegiality that has become rare [14]. In 1999, the research groups of Paul Tudzynski (University of Münster) and Ullrich Keller (Technical University of Berlin) completed this research topic when they dealt with the genetics and enzymatics of ergotamine biosynthesis. They identified the ergotamine biosynthesis genes on a 68,000-base pair DNA segment in the *Claviceps purpurea* genome, which comprises 30,000,000 base pairs.

The architecture and arrangement of the individual genes revealed that ergotamine is synthesized in three separate steps. First, D-lysergic acid is formed separately by a cascade of enzymatic reactions. The alkaloid is then activated by the multienzyme complex LPS2 and is docked to the enzyme complex LPS1, which transfers the amino acids alanine, phenylalanine and proline to D-lysergic acid. Lastly, the lysergyl-tripeptide lactam is uncoupled from the multienzyme complex LPS1. Oxidation of the alanine residue leads to the spontaneous formation of ergotamine in the final step (Fig. 10.3; [15–17]).

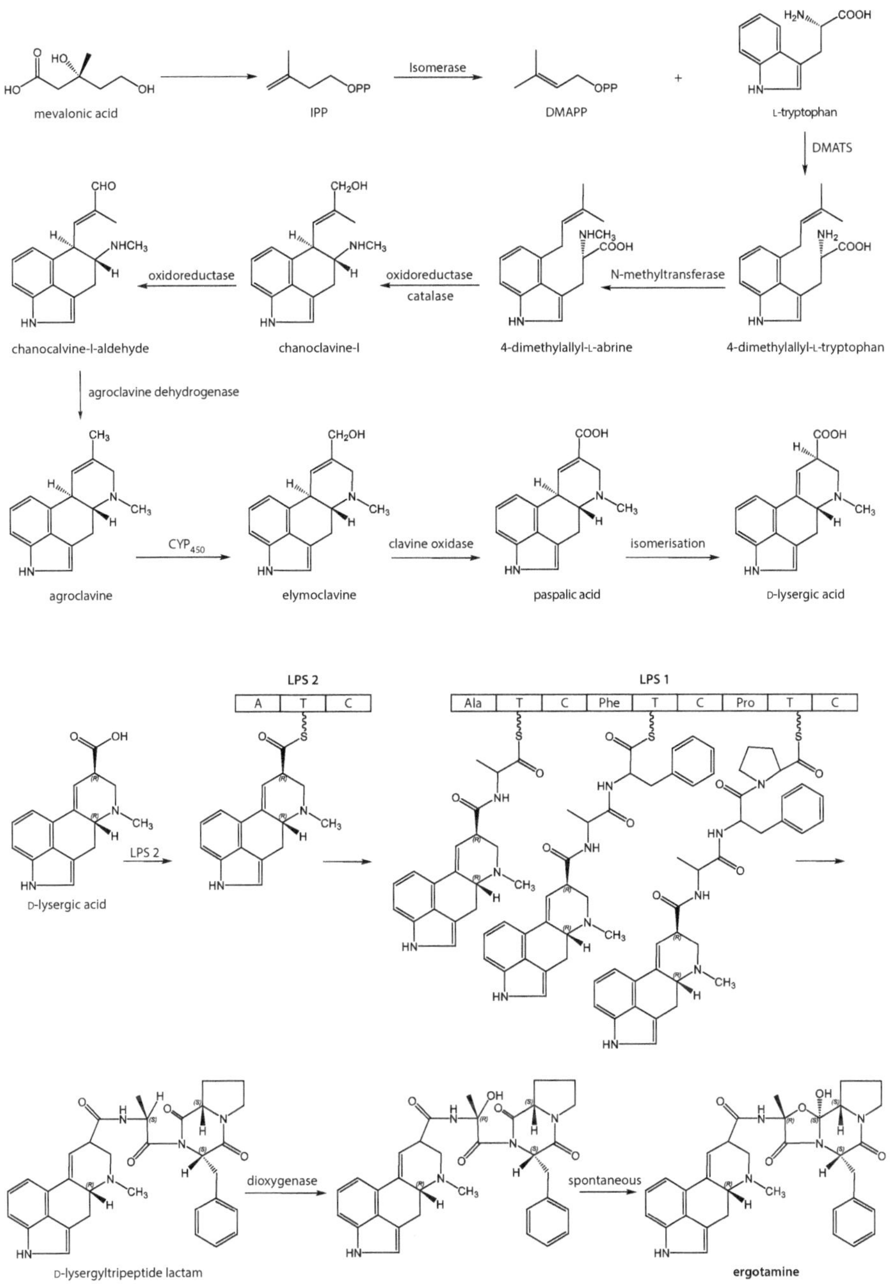

Fig. 10.3 Biosynthetic pathway of ergotamine: [15], *IPP* Isopentenyl pyrophosphate, *DMAP* Dimethylallyl pyrophosphate, *DMATS* Dimethylallyl tryptophan synthase, *CYP450* Cytochrom-P450 oxidoreductase, *LPS* D-lysergyl-peptide synthetase with the catalytic domains: *A* Adenylation of the amino acids, *ala* Alanine, *phe* Phenylalanine, *pro* Proline; *T* Thiolation; *C* Condensation

What biochemical processes trigger the crawly disease, and what does ergotism have to do with witchcraft?

Corresponding to the explanation of the alkaloid biosynthesis of the fungus, neurologists and historians shed light on ergot's remaining dark corners. Some of the features took their breath away ...

The physiological processes of gangrenous ergotoxicosis are now very well understood. The interactions of ergot alkaloids with α-adreno- and 5-hydroxytryptamine (5-HT) receptors lead to vasoconstriction and ischemia. Prolonged restriction of the blood flow eventually leads to gangrene. In contrast, the neurophysiological causes of convulsive ergotism are largely unknown. The Australian neurologist Mervyn J. Eadie developed a highly regarded working hypothesis about this second form of ergotism, which was published in the journal *The Lancet Neurology* in 2003. He found similarities between the symptoms of convulsive ergotism and the so-called "serotonin syndrome" and attributed them to comparable pathophysiologies of both forms of poisoning.

"Serotonin syndrome" is caused by an overdose, or the combined intake, of serotonergic drugs that inhibit the degradation of the neurotransmitter or increase its release. Interestingly, certain symptoms that affect the musculoskeletal system can also be triggered by excessive administration of dihydroergotamine. The alkaloid binds to the 5-HT_{1B} receptors of the posterior horn of the spinal cord, among others. In this anatomical area of the central nervous system, 19th-century pathologists had located characteristic neurotoxic damage in people who had once suffered from convulsive ergotism. These lesions may rationalize the motor seizures and neuromuscular transmission disorders in convulsive conditions.

The psychotic symptoms of this variant of ergotoxicosis require an increased concentration of ergot alkaloids in the brain. Under the influence of α-ergocryptine, molecules can enter the brain that cannot cross the blood-brain barrier under normal physiological conditions. The ergot substance could thus also enable the passage of various ergot alkaloids into the brain. A resulting central overstimulation of the 5-HT receptors could make the reported psychoses of the convulsive disorder plausible. However, this would require an increased content of α-ergocryptine in the sclerotia. Since the convulsive form of the disease occurred mainly east of the Rhine and in northern Europe, the weather and soil conditions there must have caused a significant increase in α-ergocryptine in the ergot kernels. Such an interplay of environmental factors and the natural substance content in plants and microorganisms is a frequently described phenomenon. However, environmental factors could also have caused the formation of an unknown ergot alkaloid, which was contained in the sclerotia east of the Rhine line and in Scandinavia, and which triggered the peripheral and central nervous symptoms [18, 19].

The crawly disease could also have played a fatal role in a completely different context.

The American psychologist, Linnda R. Caporael, analyzed the now famous events in a rye-growing region in the USA, where a terrible witch hysteria broke out in 1692. In January, two young girls in the town of Salem in Massachusetts suddenly experienced seizures. Writhing on the floor, screaming, they hid under furniture and reported hallucinations. During subsequent questioning, they accused women in their immediate environment of having bewitched them. Soon afterwards, more and more people reported similar symptoms. There was no doubt in the slightest that they were victims of black magic. The series of denunciations that were unleashed continued to spread until waves of arrests reached as far as Boston. Almost 200 people were arrested for witchcraft, and local prisons were full to bursting. The special court sitting in Salem imposed nineteen death sentences, all of which were carried out. After even the governor's wife had been accused of witchcraft, her husband Sir William Phips finally dissolved the special court he had convened and referred the proceedings to the Massachusetts Supreme Court in Boston. Only then did the religion-fueled mass hysteria in the New England state come to an end.

Linnda Caporael speculated that the girls' seizures resembled the symptoms of the crawly disease and published her analyses and conclusions in the scientific journal *Science* in 1976. The sensational new angle on the popular events in Massachusetts immediately "rushed" through the international gazette landscape [20]. However, psychologists Nicholas Spanos and Jack Gottlieb disagreed with Caporael's interpretation, as characteristic features of convulsive ergotism—such as vomiting, diarrhea, cravings after the seizures, seeing the environment in rainbow colors, or typical perceptual distortions—were lacking in the contemporary reports. Instead, they saw in the girls' behavior common, stereotypical images of "demonic obsession", which had always proved to be false in similar cases and explained them in terms of social-psychological factors. Shortly afterward, Spanos and Gottlieb presented their cogent counterarguments for discussion in the same journal [21]. The attention their pronouncement received was negligible.

Caporael's interpretation of the events in Salem would later fit seamlessly into US historian Mary K. Matossian's analyses, which she published in 1989.

According to her, since the mid-16th century, it had been common in Europe for witch hunts to occur mainly when existing climatic conditions favored ergot infections in rye-growing areas. In turn, a rapid rise in the price of rye forced poorer sections of the population to resort to grain of questionable quality. In Matossian's statistical models, the parameters of price development and temperature determined the frequency of witch hunts in Swabia, or Switzerland at the time. She found similar correlations for the winter temperatures in Russia and for the high dependence of Germany, Sweden, the Baltic states, and Poland on rye cultivation. In Poland, where 25 waves of ergotism were recorded between 1650 and 1800, the peaks of ergotoxicoses and the number of cases of witchcraft correlated. Documents from Essex, England, dating back to the 16th century, confirm the incidence chain of predominant rye cultivation, low summer temperatures, an increased incidence of ergotoxicoses, and a rise in witch trials [22, 23].

Decades later, the stupendous connection between ergotism and the persecution of witches and wizards in Europe was supported by new documentary findings. In Finnmark, a sparsely populated region in the Arctic Circle, interrogation records emerged that had been compiled in the 17th century during the local witch trials. They showed that the gangrenous ergotism, from which some defendants and plaintiffs had suffered, had often been noted during the taking of evidence. Many of the accused admitted to having acquired their magic powers after drinking beer. Hallucinations often occurred after eating cereal products. They had noticed black grains in porridge, bread, milk and viscous brew—as it was officially recorded. Of the 83 people who were tried for witchcraft between 1610 and 1692, 72 were sentenced to death—67 women and five men [24, 25].

Today's ergotism in medicine and pasture animal husbandry

Even though the hazard potential of ergot is known today, ergot infections and alkaloid contamination of grain cannot be completely avoided. Fungicides, the choice of plant variety, crop rotation measures, and appropriate field hygiene are effective methods of preventing widespread ergot infestation. The special care taken by farmers during cultivation, the subsequent removal of trimmings from the grain lots, and monitoring by state investigation offices minimize the alkaloid content in food and animal feed (Fig. 10.4).

Kantonslabor Basel findet giftiges Mehl

Verkaufsverbot Das kantonale Laboratorium Basel-Stadt hat in Mehl-Proben Spuren von giftigen Mutterkorn-Alkaloiden gefunden. Bei drei von 71 getesteten Getreideproben lag der Gehalt über dem Höchstwert und es wurden deshalb Verkaufsverbote für die Mehle ausgesprochen, wie das Kantonslabor gestern mitteilte. Alle drei Proben stammen aus der Schweiz. Der gelegentliche Konsum von Produkten mit Konzentrationen, wie man sie in den Proben festgestellt hat, habe kaum toxikologische Folgen, sagte Franz Dussy, Gruppenleiter beim Kantonalen Laboratorium, auf Anfrage von Keystone-SDA. Ein regelmässiger Verzehr könne aber gesundheitliche Folgen haben. *(SDA)*

Fig. 10.4 Article in the *Basler Zeitung* (July 13, 2023)

In the European Union, close monitoring of the sclerotia content in grain and the total alkaloid concentration in milled grain is required by law, with corresponding limit values. For example, the sclerotia value of 0.2 g/kg must not be exceeded in unprocessed cereals (this does not apply to rice and maize). A maximum content of 0.5 g/kg continues to apply to rye. Feed containing unground cereals must not contain more than 1 g/kg sclerotia. For milled cereals used in food production, the limit value for the total ergot alkaloid content is 50 µg/kg for spelt, oats and barley. From July 1, 2028, the respective maximum values for wheat will be reduced from the current 100 µg/kg to 50 µg/kg and for rye from 500 µg/kg to 250 µg/kg. The limit value for processed cereal products for infants and young children has been set at 20 µg/kg [26, 27].

This system of interlocking precautionary measures can only be implemented to a limited extent in countries with a precarious food situation and where grain cultivation is carried out by small-scale farmers in rural regions. The severe outbreaks of ergotism in India and Ethiopia in 1975, 1978 and

2001 are eloquent testimony to the fact that, to this day, ergotism has remained a disease associated with poverty [28, 29]. In the Western world, ergotoxicosis occurs primarily in migraine patients who erratically increase the dose of ergot alkaloid-based migraine medication. The case of ergotism that became known in Germany in 1985, in which a thirteen-year-old girl contracted chronic ergot poisoning from her morning muesli, has remained an exception to this day [28].

In contrast, ergot alkaloid-producing fungi, which live in a symbiotic community with forage grasses, are a worldwide problem in pasture animal husbandry [30]. Over the past forty years, ergotoxicoses have repeatedly occurred among grazing livestock in Australia (1987), the USA (1996), and Brazil (1999). South Africa was hit by three waves of ergotism in quick succession (1994, 1996, and 1997). In 1994, 2600 dairy cows on 29 farms were infected after eating stiff darnel (*Lolium rigidum* Gaudin). Endophytes, which produce ergot alkaloids and the neurotoxic lolitrem B, had infected the pasture grass [31, 32]. Animals that eat infested grasses—such as darnel (*Lolium temulentum* L.), perennial ryegrass (*Lolium perenne* L.) or tall fescue (*Festuca arundinacea* Schreber)—develop symptoms of poisoning after about two to eight weeks, which can first be seen on the hind legs. They become lame or stomp, or hardly move at all, or lose their balance. Circulatory disorders and the development of gangrene affect the extremities, as well as the muzzle, tail or ears. Convulsive ergotism rarely occurs and manifests itself in animals as twitching, muscle cramps, paralysis or hyperexcitability.

To reduce the ergot alkaloid concentration in pasture grasses, and their toxic effect, various approaches are being pursued in international research projects. Mixing clover-containing isoflavones into animal feed alleviates vasoconstriction, caused by ergot substances, in goats [33]. Alkaloids of endophytes from the genus *Epichloë* (Fr.) Tul. & C. Tul. protect their host plants from pest infestation and strengthen the plant's fitness against biotic and abiotic stress factors. Some forage grass-breeding programs aim to specifically remove the ergot alkaloid biosynthesis genes from these fungi without compromising the benefits for their plant hosts. Early taxonomic identification of fungi and analysis of the alkaloid composition and concentration in pasture grasses in paddocks are already reducing the risk of poisoning in pregnant mares, which are particularly sensitive to ergovaline in the later stages of pregnancy [34].

LSD in neurophysiology and as research substance for the treatment of mental diseases

From the mid-1950s, methodological advances in neurophysiology made it possible to biochemically characterize the dual function of 5-HT as a tissue hormone and as a neurotransmitter, as well as the target proteins of ergot alkaloids. At the University of Edinburgh, John Gaddum's experiments with 5-HT antagonists revealed the existence of two 5-HT receptor classes through which 5-HT as a hormone exerts its vasoconstrictive effect [35]. After the vasoconstrictor effect of ergot alkaloids had been attributed to their interaction with 5-HT receptors, the binding of ergotamine and ergometrine to the α-adrenoreceptors of smooth muscle, which contribute to the contraction of blood vessels and the uterus, was demonstrated in 1962 [36]. It took half a century to clarify with which target proteins of the brain 5-HT interacts as a neurotransmitter, and which 5-HT receptors are involved in an LSD-induced psychotic experience.

At the end of the 1970s, the two receptor classes 5-HT_1 and 5-HT_2 were identified in the cerebral cortex, which were used in a receptor binding study with LSD and other psychoactive molecules [37]. The biochemical results from this work, which was carried out with twenty-two substances, were compared with data sets indicating which of these molecules also induce a psychosis. The 5-HT_2 receptor thus had to be involved in the psychotogenic activity of the substances [38]. After subtypes of the 5-HT_2 receptor family had been identified, it became clear that LSD binds to most of them. However, since the specific psychotic 2,5-dimethoxy-4-iodamphetamine (DOI) has a pronounced affinity to the receptor subtypes $5\text{-HT}_{2A/2C}$, either both proteins or only one of them must also mediate the hallucinogenic activity of LSD. In 1996, LSD was recognized as a partial agonist of the 5-HT_{2A} receptor subtype. Its essential role in signal transmission and its involvement in the behavioral and perceptual changes elicited by LSD was described in 2003 using genetically modified mice from which the 5-HT_{2A} receptor had been removed [39–41]. It is the identical target protein that is also occupied by the psychotogenic substances, psilocin and psilocybin, from the magic mushroom teonanácatl and mescaline from the peyote cactus [42].

The exact molecular interaction of LSD with the membrane-bound 5-HT_{2A} receptor remained unclear for a long time. It was not until the development of cryo-electron microscopy that the structures of complex membrane proteins, with their bound ligands, could be determined. In this process, proteins are shock-frozen to approximately $-436\,°F$ and then bombarded with electrons.

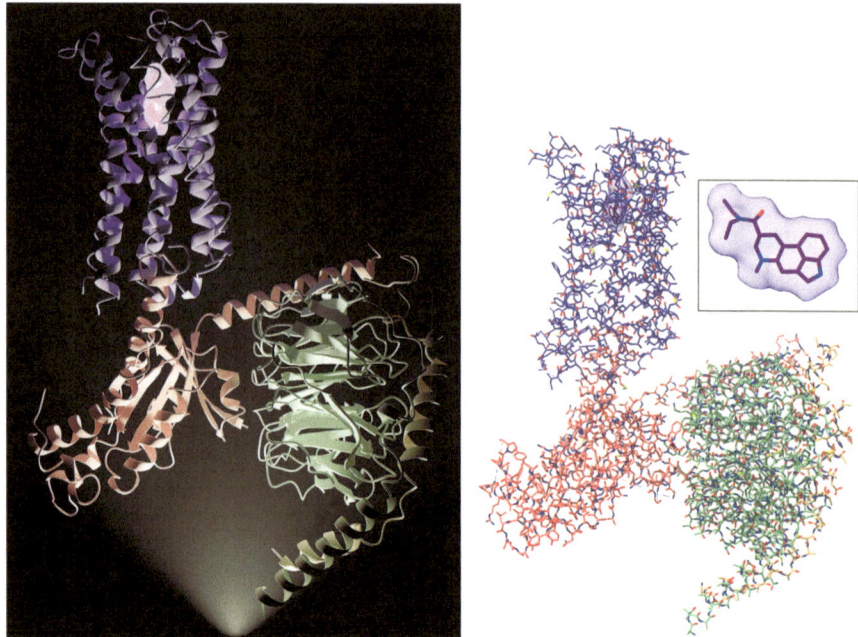

Fig. 10.5 Cryo-electron microscopic 3D-depictions of the entire 5-HT$_{2A}$ receptor complex bound to LSD (recalculated for this publication by Ryan Henry Gumpper and Bryan L. Roth, University of North Carolina). Resolution: 2.7 Å (1 Å = 10^{-10} m); 5-HT$_{2A}$ receptor complex with its subunits: *purple* 5-HT$_{2A}$ receptor; *pink* Mini Gαq; *green* Gβ; *yellow* Gγ. (© Ryan Henry Gumpper and Bryan L. Roth, University of North Carolina with kind permission [43])

From a data set of up to ten million microscopic "protein images", their three-dimensional structures are calculated at an almost atomic resolution.

In 2020, the US research groups of Bryan L. Roth and Georgios Skiniotis, from the University of North Carolina and Stanford University respectively, clarified the structure of the entire 5-HT$_{2A}$ receptor complex with a bound LSD derivative as ligand (Fig. 10.5 with LSD as ligand). This was followed in 2022 by their publication of the exact binding of LSD to the 5-HT$_{2B}$ receptor [43].

The "high-resolution" insight into the interaction of the hallucinogen with its target protein opened up the option for medicinal chemists to design anxiolytic and antidepressant 5-HT$_{2A}$ receptor modulators without hallucinogenic side effects. In 2022, this structure-guided synthesis of active ingredients was part of a successful research project at the University of the Chinese Academy of Science in Shanghai. The Chinese chemist Sheng Wang discovered a second, previously unknown binding domain of the 5-HT$_{2A}$ protein for 5-HT, psilocin and LSD, in addition to the first, already known domain. The research group then synthesized molecules that selectively interacted with the new binding pocket. To clarify whether the compounds had a hallucinogenic effect, the same animal model was used that D. Wayne Woolley designed seventy years earlier. At the time, Woolley had recognized the suspected LSD-induced psychosis by the characteristic turning of the mice's head. It must have been a special moment for the Chinese research group when some substances had the hoped-for anxiolytic and antidepressant effect, but the typical head movement pattern of the small rodents did not materialize [44].

The combination of hallucinogenic model substances, cryo-electron microscopy, disease relevant in-vivo model and structure-guided molecular design created the prerequisite for identifying this additional binding site, a narrow cleft in the outer protein subunit of the 5-HT$_{2A}$ receptor and characterizing it as a new therapeutically relevant binding domain.

At the same time as this extremely challenging work in neurophysiology and protein science, clinical psychiatry had resumed its earlier LSD research. Between 1988 and 1993, a small group of psychotherapists and psychiatrists in Switzerland were authorized to use LSD for *limited medical application* in psycholytic therapy. Since 2008, the molecule has been the subject of clinical studies investigating its therapeutic benefits in the treatment of depression, anxiety disorders, and anxiety states, life-threatening illnesses and cluster headaches [45, 46]. With an exceptional permit from the Federal Office of Public Health, doctors in Switzerland are allowed to administer LSD to patients who cannot be adequately treated with other drugs.

Final word

Fungi live as symbiotes and parasites, close nature's material cycle as aerobic decomposers of biomass, form active substances, some of which are toxic, and others are used as starting compounds for pharmaceuticals. The ergot fungus, a biotrophic microorganism that depends on living grasses, combines all these characteristics and has furthermore become the driving force behind a unique civilizing history of effects.

The people of the Middle Ages perceived the holy fire and crawly disease as an unmistakable sign of God's punishment or even the harbingers of the Fourth Horseman of the Apocalypse on his pale horse. The Order of St. Anthony was founded to care for the victims of ergotism alone, and its Europe-wide network of over 370 hospitals later developed into hospitals as part of municipal social institutions. By uncovering the cause of ergotoxicosis and thus creating the rationale for a safe and improved diet for the impoverished rural population, doctors and botanists also liberated people from their disbelief that infestation and healing from convulsive or gangrenous ergotism were indispensable elements of a divine plan of salvation.

For a long time, ergot was part of European folk medicine as a gynecological and obstetric therapeutic agent, and was introduced into scientific medicine in the 19th century. From this unusually rich source of active ingredients came medicines that, to this day, have changed the lives of billions of patients and their families for the better. The elucidation of their molecular mechanisms of action was of paramount importance.

The interaction of various ergot alkaloids with α_1-adreno-, 5-HT$_{2A}$ and D2 receptors is leveraged in the treatment of hyper- and hypotension, circulatory disorders, Parkinson's disease, Ménière's disease, acute migraine attacks and cluster headaches, acromegaly and diseases caused by prolactin hypersecretion. Between 1930 and 1952, ergot drugs, which reduces postnatal blood loss, and antibiotics decreased maternal mortality rate from 0.3 to 0.06 per 1000 births. Ergotamine and methysergide revealed 5-HT as the driving factor behind migraines. This understanding gave rise to the *triptan* drug class for significantly improved treatment of the pain of an acute migraine attack, and its accompanying symptoms such as nausea or vomiting [47, 48].

The ergotoxin-induced "adrenaline reversal" hinted at the existence of the α- and β-adrenoreceptors. The drug classes of *sympatholytics* and *sympathomimetics* emerged from the synthesis of specifically effective modulators of these receptors. They are administered in the treatment of coronary and pneumological diseases, high blood pressure or rhinitis, and are essential drugs in obstetrics to inhibit labor, in anesthesia, and in intensive care and emergency medicine.

The discovery of histamine led to the biochemical basis of allergic reactions and enabled the development of *antihistamines* for the treatment of allergies, stomach and duodenal ulcers, and sleep disorders.

Acetylcholine became the key substance with which the chemical transmission of nerve impulses between neurons, to muscle cells of the musculoskeletal system, and organs was demonstrated. The resulting *direct* and *indirect parasympathomimetics* act in the same way as acetylcholine, or prevent its degradation in the synaptic cleft. They are deployed in the treatment of glaucoma, post-operative bowel or bladder atony, *myasthenia gravis*, and *Alzheimer's disease*.

The active substances from the group of *parasympatholytics* competitively inhibit the activity of acetylcholine, through which bradyarrhythmia, intestinal colic, bronchospasms, and an overactive bladder can be treated. In ophthalmology, they are administered to dilate the pupil.

Natural product research and medicinal chemistry have developed new pharmaceuticals that inhibit the transmission of the nerve signal to the skeletal muscles by acetylcholine, thereby decreasing muscle tone. These *muscle relaxants* helped endotracheal intubation to secure the airway in anesthesiology, emergency and intensive care medicine to achieve a breakthrough, and improved operating conditions in thoracic and abdominal surgery.

The psychotogenic LSD, a molecule that took science and society's breath away like almost no other, revealed the chemistry of the psyche with 5-HT and chlorpromazine. Together with lithium, this molecular triad paved the way for the medical therapy of mental diseases with *psychotropic drugs*. The therapeutic benefits of the 5-HT$_{2A}$ receptor agonist LSD are currently being investigated in detail in psychiatric research for difficult-to-treat depression, trauma-induced disorders, and states of anxiety. In 2023, the Australian Health Authority approved psilocybin, another psychedelic agonist of the HT$_{2A}$-receptor, for the treatment of post-traumatic disorders.

The active substances from ergot have poisoned, killed, frightened, plunged people into misery, brought them together, healed them, made them curious, surprised them, taught them better, upset them, irritated them, overwhelmed them, fired their creativity—and revolutionized medical practice. They sharpened our view of the human body and changed our self-image forever. No other microbe has been able to launch such comparable developments.

These wheels are still in motion today.

The end?
… of course not.

References

1. R.G. Wasson, *The hallucinogenic fungi of Mexico: An inquiry into the origins of the religious idea among Primitive Peoples* vol. 19 (Botanical Museum Leaflets, Harvard University, Cambridge, 1961), p. 137
2. R.G. Wasson, *Notes on the present status of ololiuqui and other hallucinogens of Mexico* vol. 20 (Botanical Museum Leaflets, Harvard University, Cambridge, 1963), p. 161
3. A. Hofmann, *The active principles of the seeds of Rivea corymbosa and Ipomoea violacea* vol. 20 (Botanical Museum Leaflets, Harvard University, Cambridge, 1963), p. 194

4. A. Hofmann, R. Heim, A. Brack, H. Kobel, Psilocybin, ein psychotroper Wirkstoff aus dem mexikanischen Rauschpilz *Psilocybe mexicana* Heim. Experientia **14**, 107 (1958)

5. A. Prentner, Ololiuqui—*Turbina corymbosa* (LINNÉ) RAFINESQUE—*Convolvulaceae*, in *Bewusstseinsverändernde Pflanzen von A-Z*, 2nd edn. (Springer, Vienna, 2010), p. 209

6. A. Hofmann, H. Tscherter, Isolierung von Lysergsäure-Alkaloiden aus der mexikanischen Zauberdroge Ololiuqui (*Rivea corymbosa* (L.) Hall. f.). Experientia **XVI**, 414 (1960)

7. U. Steiner, E. Leistner, Ergoline alkaloids in convolvulaceous host plants originate from epibiotic clavicipitaceous fungi of the genus *Periglandula*. Fungal Ecol **5**, 316 (2012)

8. U. Steiner, M.A. Ahimsa-Müller, A. Markert, S. Kucht, J. Groß, N. Kauf, M. Kuzma, M. Zych, M. Lamshöft, M. Furmanowa, V. Knoop, Chr Drewke, E. Leistner, Molecular characterization of a seed transmitted clavicipitaceous fungus occurring on dicotyledoneous plants (Convolvulaceae). Planta **224**, 533 (2006)

9. G. Hevesy, The absorption and translocation of lead by plants: A contribution to the application of the method of radioactive indicators in the investigation of the change of substance in plants. Biochem J **17**, 439 (1923)

10. G. Hevesy, E. Hofer, Diplogen and fish. Nature **133**, 495 (1934)

11. G. Hevesy, E. Hofer, Elimination of water from the human body. Nature **134**, 879 (1934)

12. K. Mothes, F. Weygand, D. Gröger, H. Grisebach, Untersuchungen zur Biosynthese der Mutterkorn-Alkaloide. Z Naturforsch B **13**, 41 (1958)

13. D. Gröger, H.J. Wendt, K. Mothes, F. Weygand, Studies on the biosynthesis of ergot alkaloids. Z Naturforsch B **14**, 355 (1959)

14. H.G. Floss, Biosynthesis of ergot alkaloids and related compounds. Tetrahedron **32**, 873 (1976)

15. U. Keller, Biosynthesis of ergot alkaloids, in *Ergot: the genus Claviceps*, ed. by V. Křen, L. Cvak (Harwood Academic, Amsterdam, 1999), pp. 103–16337

16. T. Haarmann, C. Machado, Y. Lübbe, T. Correia, C.L. Schardl, D.G. Panaccione, P. Tudzynski, The ergot alkaloid gene cluster in *Claviceps purpurea*: Extension of the cluster sequence and intra-species evolution. Phytochemistry **66**, 1312 (2005)

17. N. Gerhards, L. Neubauer, P. Tudzynski, S.-M. Li, Biosynthetic pathways or ergot alkaloids. Toxins **6**, 3281 (2014)

18. M.J. Eadie, Convulsive ergotism: epidemics of the serotonin syndrome? Lancet Neurol **2**, 429 (2003)

19. A. Kodisch, M. Oberforster, A. Raditschnig, B. Rodemann, A. Tratwal, J. Danielewicz, M. Korbas, B. Schmiedchen, J. Eifler, A. Gordillo, D. Siekmann, F.J. Fromme, F.N. Wuppermann, F. Wieser, E. Zechner, M. Niewińska, Th Miedaner, Covariation of Ergot Severity and Alkaloid Content Measured by HPLC and One ELISA Method in Inoculated Winter Rye across Three Isolates and Three European Countries. Toxins **12**, 676 (2020)

20. L.R. Caporael, Ergotism: The satan loosed in Salem? Science **192**, 21 (1976)
21. N. Spanos, J. Gottlieb, Ergotism and the Salem village witch trials. Science **194**, 1390 (1976)
22. M.K. Matossian, Ergot and the Salem witchcraft affair, in *Poisons of the past: Molds, epidemics, and history* (Yale University Press, New Haven/London, 1989), p. 113
23. M.K. Matossian, Witch persecution in early modern Europe, in *Poisons of the past: Molds, epidemics, and history* (Yale University Press, New Haven/London, 1989), p. 70
24. T. Alm, The witch trials of finnmark, northern Norway, during the 17th century: evidence for ergotism as a contributing factor. Econ Bot **57**, 403 (2003)
25. T. Alm, B. Elnevåg, Ergotism in Norway. Part 1: The symptoms and their interpretation from the late Iron Age to the seventeenth century. Hist Psychiatry **24**, 15 (2013)
26. *Eurofins* 2024. https://www.eurofins.de/lebensmittel/food-news/food-testing-news/grenzwerte-ergotalkaloide-und-mutterkornsklerotien-in-getreide/
27. *Commission Regulation (EU) 2024/1808 of 1 July 2024 amending Regulation (EU) 2023/ 915 as regards the application date of lower maximum levels for ergot sclerotia and ergot alkaloids in food (Text with EEA relevance), pp. 1–3.* https://eur-lex.europa.eu/legal-content/EN/TXT/PDF/?uri=OJ:L_202401808
28. H.J. Pfänder, K.U. Seiler, A. Ziegler, Morgendliche "Müsli"-Mahlzeit als Ursache einer chronischen Vergiftung mit Secale-Alkaloiden. Dtsch Ärztebl **82**, A-2013 (1985)
29. K. Urga, A. Debella, Y.W. Medihn, N. Agata, A. Bayu, W. Zewdie, Laboratory studies on the outbreak of gangrenous ergotism associated with consumption of contaminated barley in Arsi, Ethiopia. Ethiop J Health Dev **16**, 317 (2002)
30. A.M. Craig, J.L. Klotz, J.M. Duringer, Cases of ergotism in livestock and associated ergot alkaloid concentrations in feed. Front Chem **3**, 8 (2015)
31. S. Belser-Ehrlich, A. Harper, J. Hussey, R. Hallock, Human and cattle ergotism since 1900: symptoms, outbreaks, and regulations. Toxicol Ind Health **29**, 307 (2013)
32. D.J. Schneider, C.O. Miles, I. Garthwaite, A. van Halderen, J.C. Wessels, H.J. Lategan, First report of field outbreaks of ergot alkaloid toxicity in South Africa. Onderstepoort J Vet Res **63**, 97 (1996)
33. B.E. Harlow, M.D. Flythe, J.P. Goodman, H. Ji, G.E. Aiken, Isoflavones Containing Legumes Mitigate Ergot Alkaloid-Induced Vasoconstriction in Goats (Capra hircus). Animals **12**, 750 (2022)
34. *Global impact of ergot alkaloids* (Ed: J.L. Klotz), MDPI Publisher, Basel, 2022
35. J.H. Gaddum, N.A. Hameed, Drugs which antagonize 5-hydroxytryptamine. Br J Pharmacol Chemother **9**, 240 (1954)
36. I.R. Innes, Identification of the smooth muscle excitatory receptors for the ergot alkaloids. Br J Pharmac Chemother **19**, 120 (1962)

37. S.J. Peroutka, S.H. Snyder, Multiple serotonin receptors: differential binding of [3H] 5-hydroxytryptamine [3H], lysergic acid diethylamide and [3H] spiroperidol. Mol Pharmacol **16**, 687 (1979)
38. R.A. Glennon, M. Titeler, J.D. McKenney, Evidence for 5-HT2 involvement in the mechanism of action of hallucinogenic agents. Life Sci **35**, 2505 (1984)
39. G.J. Marek, G.K. Aghajanian, LSD and the phenethylamine hallucinogen DOI are potent partial agonists at 5-HT2A receptors on interneurons in rat piriform cortex. J Pharmacol Exp Ther **278**, 1373 (1996)
40. F.X. Vollenweider, M.F. Vollenweider-Scherpenhuyzen, A. Babler, H. Vogel, D. Hell, Psilocybin induces schizophrenia-like psychosis in humans via a serotonin-2 agonist action. NeuroReport **9**, 3897 (1998)
41. J. Gonzalez-Maeso, T. Yuen, B.J. Ebersole, E. Wurmbach, A. Lira, M. Zhou, N. Weisstaub, R. Hen, J.A. Gingrich, S.C. Sealfon, Transcriptome fingerprints distinguish hallucinogenic and nonhallucinogenic 5-hydroxytryptamine 2A receptor agonist effects in mouse somatosensory cortex. J Neurosci **23**, 8836 (2003)
42. J.F. López-Giménez, J. González-Maeso, Hallucinogens and serotonin 5-HT2A receptor-mediated signaling pathways. Curr Top Behav Neurosci **36**, 45 (2018)
43. K. Kim, T. Che, O. Panova, J.F. DiBerto, J. Lyu, B.E. Krumm, D. Wacker, M.J. Robertson, A.B. Seven, D.E. Nichols, B.K. Shoichet, G. Skiniotis, B.L. Roth, Structure of a hallucinogen-activated Gq-coupled 5-HT2A serotonin receptor. Cell **182**, 1574 (2020)
44. D. Cao, J. Yu, H. Wang, Z. Luo, X. Liu, L. He, J. Qi, L. Fan, L. Tang, Z. Chen, J. Li, J. Cheng, S. Wang, Structure-based discovery of nonhallucinogenic psychedelic analogs. Science **375**, 403 (2022)
45. M. Liechti, *Experten-Bericht:Stand und Entwicklungsszenarien in Bezug auf die medizinische Behandlung und klinische Forschung mit Halluzinogenen und MDMA* (Federal Office of Public Health FOPH and interested professional associations/specialists, 2019)
46. F. Holze, P. Gasser, F. Müller, P.C. Dolder, M.E. Liechti, Lysergic acid diethylamide-assisted therapy in patients with anxiety with and without a life-threatening Illness: a randomized double-blind, placebo-controlled study. Biol Psychiatry **93**, 215 (2023)
47. M. Winkler, W. Rath, A risk-benefit assessment of oxytocics in obstetric practice. Drug Saf **20**, 323 (1999)
48. I. Loudon, Maternal mortality in the past and its relevance to developing countries today. Am J Clin Nutr **72** (suppl), 241S (2000)

Notes and further reading

Chapter 1

For [1] N. Forin, S. Nigris, S. Voyron, M. Garlanda, A. Vizzini, G. Casadoro, and B. Baldan: Next Generation Sequencing of Ancient Fungal Specimens: The Case of the Saccardo Mycological Herbarium. *Front. Ecol. Evol.* 2018, 6, 1.

For [11] Karl Böning, Deputy Director of the State Institute for Soil Culture, Crop Production and Protection, Munich, points out the connection between crop yields and the intensity of earlier waves of ergotism: "For example, it is reported from some places in Hesse-Darmstadt in the years 1770 and 1771 (according to Schröter, 1792) that a quarter, a third or even half of the rye harvest there consisted of ergot kernels. Although there are often reports of previous harsh winters, this may perhaps have been an indication of winter damage that caused a poor harvest and, under these circumstances, resulted in ergot being utilized to a considerable extent during the harvest, leading to poisoning. The fact that the major epidemics occurred precisely in the years when famine and inflation prevailed can be explained simply by the fact that in normal years the ergot kernels were picked out and thrown away, while in bad years they were left in the crop and eaten. The fact that weed seeds contaminated with ergot, especially rye brome, were also harvested and not cleaned out may also have played a role." (K. Böning: Die Auswirkungen der Hungerjahre 1770–1772 auf die letzte Großepidemie der Mutterkornseuche und die damals und in der Folgezeit veranlaßten Gegenmaßnahmen. *Nachrichtenbl. Deutsch. Pflanzenschutzd. Issue 8*, 1972, 24, p. 122).

For [17] In his book *From Ergot to "Ernutin"*, published in 1908 (Lit. 26), Henry Wellcome quoted a passage for which he cited the *Yasna* source of the *Avesta*. There was no doubt in his mind that this was a hint at the uterotonic effect of the ergot ingredients: "Among the evil things created by Angro Maynes [sic] are noxious grasses that cause pregnant women to drop the womb and die in child-bed". Prof. em. Dr. Philip G. Kreyenbroek, Institute of Iranian Studies at the Georg-August University of Göttingen, and Prof. Dr. Almut Hintze, Zartoshty Brothers Professor of Zoroastrianism at SOAS, University of London, who kindly searched the *Yasna* of the *Avesta* for the 1908 quotation, which is still widely cited today, were unable to find the passage. It was not possible to clarify whether Wellcome's English translation had moved too far away from the original Avestan text in terms of interpretation, so that it is no longer possible to identify it today, or whether the cited quote came from another source that was incorrectly stated. However, the common mention of the terms *evil grasses* and *Angra Mainyu* (destructive spirit) is correctly linked.

For [26] In his book *From Ergot to "Ernutin"* (1908), Henry Wellcome did not specify the source of the cuneiform script on which his translation of a "noxious pustule in the ear of grain", which is still often quoted today, is based. The Akkadian text of the Assyrian clay tablet, which according to Wellcome dates from around 660 BC, is therefore unknown. It is therefore not possible to judge how faithful Wellcome's translation is to the text or how far it has departed interpretatively from the original Akkadian cuneiform script. However, Wellcome's quote resembles the line of text of a magic formula from the extensive medical "Nineveh Treatise". It belongs to the library of the Assyrian king Aššur-bāni-apli (669–627 BC), comprising 31,000 cuneiform tablets, which was recovered in several British excavation expeditions between 1846 and 1855. The magical formula, which was spoken of for eye diseases, can be found on the Assyrian clay tablets "BAM 510" and "BAM 514", and belongs to a collection of medical prescriptions with the Akkadian title *Šumma amēlu īnāšu marṣā* (in English—"If a man's eyes are sick"):

(…)
194′ šiptu ina šurrî lām bašāmu alallû urda ana māti
195′ ittû šer'a ūlid šerhu habburra
196′ habburra kanna kannu kiṣra kiṣru šubulta šubultu
197′ mer'a Šamaš eṣṣid Sîn upahhar Šamaš ina eṣēdīšu Sîn ina puhhurīšu
198′ ana īn eṭli merhu īrub Šamaš u Sîn išizzānimma merhu lilâ [tê šipti]
199′ ka'inimma merhu ša libbi īnī šūlî
(…)

194′ In the beginning before creation, the shaduf descended (from heaven) to earth,

195′ the seeder-plough gave birth to the furrow, the furrow to the sprout,

196′ the sprout to the root-stock, the root-stock to the bud, the bud to the head-of-grain, (and) the head-of-grain to

197′ the merhu-kernel. The Sun-god was harvesting, the Moon-god was reaping. While the Sun-god was harvesting (and) the Moon-god was reaping,

198′ the merhu-kernel entered into the eye of the lad. O Sun-god and Moon-god stand by me, and let the merhu-kernel take off! [Incantation spell.]

199′ Invocation for removing merhu from the eyes.

(M. Geller and S.V. Panayotov: Mesopotamian eye disease texts—the Nineveh Treatise. In, *Die babylonisch-assyrische Medizin in Texten und Untersuchungen Volume 10* (W. de Gruyter, Berlin Boston, 2020), p. 105)

The cuneiform text passages BAM 510, 44, resp. BAM 514, 50, mention a mystical Akk. *merhu kernel*, which grows out of an Akk. *šubultu* (in English—ear of grain or barley) after a sequence of divine acts of creation, and produces a grain-like formation in the human eye, which presumably refers to a stye. Wellcome's quotation of "a noxious pustule in the ear of grain" and his mentioned allusion to ergot would therefore go back to an earlier interpretation of the *merhu kernel*. It is not only the textual similarities of the incantation that suggest that the clay tablets "BAM 510" and "BAM 514" are Wellcome's original sources. The date given for his clay tablet also agrees with the dating of both cuneiform tablets from the "Nineveh Treatise" (personal communication by M. Geller, I. Finkel, 2021). However, there is no causal link between an ergot kernel and the inflammation of the eyelid for which the magic formula was spoken. Thus, the stye would merely reflect the shape of the *merhu*/ergot kernel. The interpretation of this passage as the first evidence of mycotoxicosis in medicine should therefore be rejected (N. Benkerroum: Retrospective and prospective look at aflatoxin research and development from a practical standpoint. *Int. J. Environ. Res.* 2019, 16, 3633). The clarification of the question of whether Wellcome could have found out the translation of the magic formula and the cited allusion to ergot at all presupposes proximity to employees of the British Museum, who had scientifically processed these clay tablets in the second half of the 19th century. In fact, Wellcome was in contact with the leading Assyriologists R. Campbell Thompson and Theophilus Pinches of the British Museum. While Pinches had no specific interest in medical texts, Thompson was more interested in writings on Assyrian-Babylonian medicine, magic, astronomy and botany (personal communication by M. Geller, I. Finkel, 2021). First fragments of the clay tablet

BAM 510 (K. 2573) were put together by the German orientalist Carl Bezold at the British Museum, and translations of the first passages were published in 1891. Thompson had continued Bezold's work and edited further parts of the text of the "Nineveh Treatise". The cuneiform tablet BAM 510 was also the subject of his studies at the time, which Thompson said he had begun before 1906. Thus, Wellcome very likely obtained the translation of the magic formula and the interpretation of the *merḫu kernel* as ergot, which he published in his book in 1908, from Thompson. Independently, and very likely without being familiar with Thompson's *merḫu kernel/ergot* interpretation proposal, later Assyriologists came to the same conclusion: that the growth in the ear of grain could be ergot. Benno Landsberger and Thorkild Jacobsen had encountered the *merḫu* magic formula in a much older text (Ish. 35-T. 19 = IM31378) from the 2nd millennium BC. It was found in 1935 during excavations at the *Shamash Temple* near *Nērebtum* (today *Tell Iščāli/Iraq*). In 1955, they also translated the Akk. term *"merḫu"* as "ergot" or "stye", without mentioning the earlier translation proposal (B. Landsberger and Th. Jacobsen: An old Babylonian charm against merḫu. *JNES* 1955, 14, 14). Even if this interpretative equation is not uniformly supported today, the Assyriologists Prof. Mark Geller, Dr. Irving Finkel and Dr. Troels Pank Arbøll agree with the ergot translation. Geller and Finkel point out that *merḫu* can also spoil barley (S.V. Panayotov: Eye metaphors, analogies and similes within Mesopotamian magico-medical texts. In, *The comparable body* (Ed: J.Z. Wee), Brill Leiden, Boston, 2017, p. 204; for the ethymology of *"maraḫu/mirḫu"* see *Chicago Assyrian Dictionary* 10.1: 265–266 and *Chicago Assyrian Dictionary* 10.2: 106–107). The cuneiform tablets from the *Nērebtum* excavations are now in the Iraq Museum in Baghdad. Their content was published as a transcript by Thorkild Jacobson. Other cuneiform tablets (BAM 409, 11; BAM 494, 35, 38) from the library of King Aššur-bāni-apli mention the *samānu* disease, which is sometimes equated with ergotism. Humans, sheep, and barley contract the disease, which causes severe skin symptoms in humans (*Chicago Assyrian Dictionary* 15: 111–112). Today, *samānu* disease is more commonly seen as cutaneous leishmaniasis, *impetigo contagiosa*, boils or other diseases (S. Beck: Sāmānu as a human disease in Mesopotamia and Egypt. In, *Proceedings of the XI International Congress of Egyptologists, Florence* (Eds.: G. Rosati and M.C. Guidotti), Archaeopress Publishing Ltd, Oxford, 2017, p. 29; I. L. Finkel: A study in scarlet: Incantation against Samana. In, *Eine Festschrift Für Rykle Borger zu seinem 65. Geburtstag am 24. Mai 1994* (Ed: S.M. Maul), Styx Publications, Groningen, 1998, p. 71).

For [27] In his book *The Story of Ergot*, Frank James Bové cites the pharmacist Alexander Tschirch of the University of Bern as the source according to which the oldest reference to the medicinal effect of ergot is said to be documented in the Chinese dictionary *Erh ya* 爾雅 (also Erhya, Rh Ya, Rha Ya or Urh yà) of the early Han dynasty (206 BC – 9 AD) (Lit. 28); (W.S. Coblin: *Erh ya. Early Chinese texts: A bibliographical guide (Early China Special Monograph Series 2)* (Ed: M. Loewe), The Society for the Study of Early China and the Institute of East Asian Studies, University of California, 1993, p. 94). Tschirch's textbook, published in 1910, lists various medicinal plants of Chinese medicine from the *Erh ya*. In the paragraph in question, however, Tschirch does not write that *Secale cornutum* is also mentioned in *Erh ya*. Rather, Tschirch adopted almost word for word the corresponding sentence from Hermann Schelenz's 1904 *History of Pharmacy*, which did not mention *Erh Ya* at all. Schelenz refers to the translation of an ergot note by the French sinologist Stanislas Julien, which he had published in 1849 in *Journal Comptes rendus hebdomadaires des Séances de l'Académie des Sciences* (Lit. 29), and writes: "Secale cornutum *seems to have been used in obstetrics from the earliest times (Stanislas Julien)*". Schelenz had incorrectly stated the year of publication and the page number of Julien's publication, which Tschirch adopted without checking (H. Schelenz: China. In, *Geschichte der Pharmazie, (2. Reprint)*, Georg Olms Verlag, Hildesheim Zurich New York, 2005, p. 75; A. Tschirch: China. In, *Handbuch der Pharmakognosie. Erster Band – Allgemeine Pharmakognosie*, Christian Hermann Tauchnitz, Leipzig, 1910, p. 520). During his studies of the *Gu jin yi tong da quan* 古今医统大全 (1556), Stanislas Julien came across a plant recipe that was to be administered during a difficult birth. For him, this could only have been the effect of ergot.

For [33] Que mai 雀麦, was taxonomically determined by the Swedish botanist Carl Peter Thunberg during his time in Japan in 1775/76 as rye brome (*Bromus japonicus* Thunb.). It entered the German-language literature of Chinese medicine under the name "Japanese rye brome" (personal communication by Dr. U. Unschuld, 2022). The *Niu xi tang* 牛膝湯 formula contains rye brome, ox knee (*Achyranthes bidentata* flower), uterotonic Chinese angelica (*Angelica sinensis* (Oliv.) Diels), Chinese mallow (*Malva verticillata* L.), five-leave chocolate vine (*Akebia quinata* (Thunb.) Decne), and talcum.

For [39] The *Wai tai bi yao* 外台秘要 by the physician Wang Tao from 752 AD contains an exact indication of quantity for the preparation of the uterotonic: "*To abort a fetus during pregnancy … let her ingest one sheng of sprouted barley with one sheng of honey, and the fetus will be discharged.*"

For [40] Some authors thought that they could recognize the ergot of rye in *Mai nu* 麦奴 (B.E. Read: *Chinese medicinal plants from the Ben cao gang mu* 本草綱目 *3rd edition*, Beijing National History Bulletin, 1936, No. 851, 281). *Mai nu* is associated with the use of a wheat medicine that is included in the *Ming yi bie lu* 名医别录 ("Miscellaneous records of famous physicians") (around 500) by the physician Tao Hongjing (452–536). It mentions the healing powers of wheat (*Xiao mai*) without giving further details of possible indications (*BCGM* 2022, Vol. V, ch. 22-04, p. 633; *BCGM* 2022, Vol. V, ch. 22-04-09, p. 650; *BCGM* 2022, Vol. V, ch. 22-04 p. 633). In contrast, the physician of the Northern Song Dynasty (960–1127), Kou Zongshi, is somewhat more specific in his pharmacopoeia *Ben cao yan yi* 本草衍義 (1116). In it, he noted the medicinal use of the young wheat plant, flour, and wheat bran, and states that *Mai nu* 麦奴 (literally translated as wheat maid/slave, personal communication by Dr. Ulrike Unschuld, 2022) are *"black spots on a ripe ear of wheat"* (E. Bretschneider: Wheat. In, *Botanicon Sinicum. Notes on Chinese botany from native and Western sources Part III. Botanical investigations into the* materia medica *of the ancient Chinese*, Kelly & Walsh Ltd, Shanghai, Hong Kong, Yokohama & Singapore, 1895, p. 380). Li Shizhen describes the drug in *Ben cao gang mu* 本草綱目 (1593) under the monograph *Mai nu* as *"ears of wheat with black mold on the surface at the time of ripening"*. *Mai nu* is probably a smut or rust fungus of wheat (B.E. Read: *Chinese Medicinal Plants from the Pen Ts'ao Kang Mu* 本草綱目 *3rd edition*, Peking National History Bulletin, 1936, No. 851, p. 281; S. Li: *BCGM: Creeping herbs, water herbs, herbs growing on stones, mosses, cereals* (Ed and transl.: P.U. Unschuld), University of California Press, Oakland California, 2022. Vol. V, ch. 22-04-09, p. 650;). Li Shizhen also mentions *Da mai* 大麥, the common barley (*Hordeum vulgare* L.), which was first recorded in the pharmacopoeia *Ming yi bie lu* (*BCGM* 2022, Vol. V, ch. 22-05, p. 651). It mentions the medication *Da mai nu* 大麥奴, a *"mold on barley ears"*. The remedy was used for heat illnesses and poisoning by pharmaceutical drugs (*BCGM* 2022, Vol. V, ch. 22-05-03, p. 656). Whether the word *nu* 奴 (meaning slave, slave girl, servant) could possibly have been the Chinese name for ergot remains tenuous (personal communication by Dr. U. Unschuld, 2022).

Chapter 2

For [1] According to text analyses by the historian Heinz Löwe, the monk Gerward is now considered to be the author of the older part of the "Xanten Annals" (up to 860). He probably entered Lorsch Abbey as a young man, where he received his education. After Gerward's court career, he retired to the monastery in Ghent, which was part of the Lorsch possessions in Flanders. This would mean that the entries for the year 857 were written at Ghent Abbey (H. Löwe: Studies on the Annales Xantenses. In, *Deutsches Archiv für Erforschung des Mittelalters namens der Monumenta Germaniae Historica, 8th Year* (Eds.: F. Baethgen and W. Holtzmann), Simons Verlag, Marburg Lahn, 1951, pp. 87–92; H. Schefers: Zur Kulturgeschichte der karolingischen Königsabtei Lorsch. In, *Wandmalerei des frühen Mittelalters – Bestand, Maltechnik, Konservierung, Hefte des Deutschen Nationalkomitees XXIII* (Ed: M. Exner), K. Lipp Verlag, Munich, p. 12). The outbreak of gangrenous ergotism first documented in the annals is therefore likely to have taken place in the region around Ghent.

For [12] In the *Liber religionis Sancti Anthonii Viennensis Sacre Reformationis* (1478) the existence of 370 St. Antonine hospitals is mentioned.

For [21] The recipe of the St. Antony's balm:

> *"Take 4 pounds … 4 pounds tallow – 4 pounds lard – 4 pounds spruce resin – 4 ounces yellow wax – 4 ounces turpentine – 2 ounces verdigris – cabbage leaves – nut leaves – leafy goosefoot – lettuce – plantain, both kinds – elder leaves – wound sanicle or Pedis leonis – coltsfoot – leaves or grains of 'Satz' (?) growing on the walls – leaves of burning herb (nettle?) – blackberry and raspberry leaves and twig tips – Select 6 handfuls of these herbs, boil in a clean kettle and squeeze out the juice."*

Among the eleven remaining plant illustrations on the altarpieces are most probably the corn poppy or long-headed poppy (*Papaver rhoeas* L. or *Papaver dubium* L.) and the cross gentian (*Gentiana cruciata* L.). Corn poppy was used for diaphoretic poultices in the treatment of the plague (E. Wulfers: Medicinal plants as a remedy against the plague in the Middle Ages and early modern times. *Schweiz. Z. Ganzheitsmed.*, 2014, 26, 34). In septicemic plague, impaired blood clotting can lead to vascular occlusion. The resulting gangrene and black coloration of affected areas of skin and limbs are similar to the symptoms of gangrenous ergotism. It is therefore quite conceivable that corn poppy was also used in the treatment of *ergotism gangraenosus*.

The healing power of cross gentian is closely linked to folklore and superstition. Its magical powers against the plague were invoked in various magical formulas (R. Rothleitner: Enzian im Volksmund und Volksbrauch. In, *Jahrbuch des Vereins zum Schutze der Alpenpflanzen und Tiere 8th Year* (Ed: K. Boshart), Self-published, Munich, 1936, pp. 55–57). As its extracts were administered in the treatment of ulcers and abscesses, it can be assumed that they were also used to treat the St. Antony's fire (H. Will: *Vergleich der Indikationen des "Kleinen Destillierbuches" des Chirurgen Hieronymus Brunschwig (Straßburg 1500) mit den nach derzeitigem wissenschaftlichem Erkenntnisstand belegten Indikationen*, Diss. Universität Würzburg, 2009, p. 197). The fact that the cross gentian as a plant of the "dark forces" can be found on an altarpiece is probably due to its four cross-shaped blue petals. Their arrangement symbolizes the Holy Rood, and the color blue the sky and the divine.

Chapter 3

For [1] The German name "Weißwurz" was probably used for the tuber fleece-flower (*Polygonatum multiflorum* (L.) ALL.), the fragrant Solomon's seal "Sigillum Salomonis" (*Polygonatum odoratum* (MILL.) DRUCE) and for the gas plant (*Dictamnus albus* L.) collectively. The first two closely related plants were utilized in the treatment of period pains. The gas plant with its spasmolytic, mucolytic, and emmenagogic features was applied for these disorders too.

For [3] The "(...) rising and pain of womb ('mother')" was referred to by the medical terms *suffocatio uteri*, *suffocatio matricis* or *hysterica passio (affectio)*. The doctors blamed painful abdominal or uterine cramps, fainting spells, constipation or shortness of breath on the "wandering of the uterus". They suspected a connection between colicky, radiating pain and menstrual cramps with reduced menstruation. These symptoms rarely occurred before the age of sixteen and after the age of fifty. (J. Coler: Vom Auffsteigen der Mutter/uteri suffocatio genant. In, *Oeconomia oder Haußbuch: Zum Calendario Oeconomico & perpetuo gehörig. Pharmacopaeus, oder Haußapoteck genant*, P. Hellwig, Wittemberg, 1615, p. 579; *Grosses vollständiges Universal-Lexicon aller Wissenschaften und Künste: welche bisshero durch menschlichen Verstand und Witz erfunden und verbessert worden vol. 13*, J.H. Zedler, Leipzig and Halle, 1735, columns 1511–1518; J.A. Weber: *Lexicon encyclion: od. kurztzgefaßtes latein-teutsches u. teutsch-lateinisches Universal-Wörter-Buch*, Joh. Christoph and Joh. David Stößzeln, Chemnitz, 1745, p. 646; *Allgemeine Encyklopädie der Wissenschaften und Künste (Eds.: J.S. Ersch and J.G. Gruber), Section 2, H-N, vol. 13* (Ed: A.G. Hoffmann), F.A. Brockhaus, Leipzig, 1836, pp. 72–73).

For [7] It is doubtful whether Johannes Thal's brother Wendelin, who succeeded him as town physician in Nordhausen, recognized ergot as the cause of the St. Antony's fire. The search for the monograph mentioned by Kobert and Wright (Lit. 8), which Wendelin Thal is said to have written in 1588 or 1596, was unsuccessful. Rather, both authors seem to have confused the brothers. Kobert describes Wendelin as the author of the term *Mater Secalis*, which his brother Johannes had introduced in 1588 (Lit. 5). Johannes Thal only mentions the hemostatic activity but not the toxicity of ergot.

For [11] H.P. Fuchs-Eckert *Bauhinia* 1979, 6/3, 311 and *Bauhinia* 1982, 7/3, 135; P. Burckhardt: David Joris und seine Gemeinde in Basel. *Basler Zeitschrift für Geschichte und Altertumskunde* 1949, 48, pp. 37–39.

For [14] D. Dodart: *Mémoires pour servir à l'Histoire des Plantes*, De L'Imprimerie Royale, Paris, 1676.

The family backgrounds of Denis Dodart and Claude Perrault are strikingly similar. Perrault had also grown up in a family of lawyers whose members worked at the Paris Supreme Court and were supporters of Jansenism. His brother Nicolas, a professor at the Sorbonne, was one of the most courageous advocates of this doctrine of faith. The families presumably knew each other well and moved in the same circles, so that in addition to Dodart's scientific aptitude, this could also have been a reason, not to be underestimated, as to why Perrault was so resolutely in favor of his appointment to the Academy. Jean-Baptiste Colbert was certainly aware of these circumstances. The minister was very familiar with the Catholic movement, which the king saw as a threat: Colbert's younger brother Nicolas (1628–1676), Bishop of Luçon and Auxerre, his son Jacques-Nicolas (1655–1707), later Archbishop of Rouen, and also his nephew Charles-Joachim Colbert de Croissy (1667–1738), Bishop of Montpellier, were sympathizers or representatives of Jansenism (S. Caroll: The peace in the feud in sixteenth- and seventeenth-century France. *Past and Present* 2003, 178, 74; S. Blanchard: The "Friends of Truth": Ricci's Reforms and the "Republic of Grace". In, *The Synod of Pistoia (1786) and Vatican II: Jansenism and the struggle for Catholic reform. Oxford Studies in Historical Theology*, Oxford University Press, 2020, pp. 117–118; V. Durand: *Le Jansénisme au XVIIIe siècle et Joachim Colbert, évêque de Montpellier (1696–1738), Toulouse*: Private, 1907, XVI–372).

The fact that the Perrault brothers Claude and especially Charles, whom Jean-Baptiste Colbert entrusted with important tasks in his ministry for twenty years, were also influential advisors to the minister, indicates Colbert's pragmatic approach to supporters of the Jansenist movement. Françoise d'Aubigné, Marquise de Maintenon, remarked in a letter to the Comtesse de Saint-Géran that *"M. de Colbert only thinks about finances, but almost never about religion".* (A. Neymarck: *Colbert et son Temps, Tome Premier*, E. Dentu, Editeur, Paris, 1877, p. 460). Madame de Sévigné, an intimate connoisseur of life at the court of Louis XIV, gave the king's *opaque and maquiavelistic* servant the name "the North" because of his ice-cold charisma.

For [18] J.-B.H.R. Capefigue: *Richelieu, Mazarin, la Fronde et le règne de Louis XIV, Volume 6*, Dufey, Libraire, Paris, 1836, pp. 305–306.

For [45] Previously in J. Stockerus: The Haemorrhagia narium. In, *Comprobata et stabilita Empirica, sive Medicamentaria, Experientia Diuturna, etc.*, M. Hartmannus and N. Bassaeus, Francoforti, 1601, pp. 44–45.

For [48] Rudolph Jacob Camerarius recognized that a ripe seed only forms when the pollen pollinates the stigma. The transmission of the father's characteristics to the next generation was first demonstrated by Kölreuter in 1761.

The Swedish taxonomist Carl von Linné based his classification system of plants on the characteristics of their sexual organs, the stamens and carpels (*Systema Naturae*, 1735). However, modesty was not Linné's thing (*"Deus creavit, Linné disposuit"*; God created, but Linné sorted out). He also took pleasure in repeatedly emphasizing analogies between the processes of pollination and the sexual life of humans. By using sexualized clarifications, he wanted to popularize his taxonomic field of work in order to motivate as many plant hunters as possible to send him their new finds from all corners of the world. (S. Müller-Wille: The love of plants. *Nature* 2007, 446, 268). Linné's piquant reports inspired the naturalist and poet Erasmus Darwin (and grandfather of the founder of the modern theory of evolution Charles Darwin) to write his unique poem *The Loves of the Plants* (1789), while other scholars found the Swedish taxonomist's ambiguities simply obnoxious (L. Schiebinger: The private life of plants. In, *Nature's Body. Gender in the Making of Modern Science*, Rutgers University Press, New Brunswick New Jersey, 2004, pp. 11–39; T.M. Kelley: *Clandestine Marriage: Botany and romantic culture*, Johns Hopkins University Press, Baltimore, Maryland, 2012). The St. Petersburg physician and botanist Johann Georg Siegesbeck wrote in disgust:

> *"(…) Who would believe that God has instituted such despicable fornication in the plant kingdom? Who could present such an unchaste system to the academic youth without causing umbrage?"* (J.G. Siegesbeck: *Botanosophiae verioris brevis sciagraphia*, Typis Academiae, Petropoli, 1737, p. 49).

After Siegesbeck prevented the delivery of plant samples from Russia to Linné and his coworkers, the Swede responded with a *counter-attack* from a botanical systematist. He named a troublesome weed after his unscientifically arguing critic: the heart-leaved sigesbeckia (it is said that Linné deliberately misspelled the name).

The sexuality of plants, which Camerarius described for the first time, and the morphology of their sexual organs as the foundation of Linnaeus' systematics shook the church's understanding of nature. It had assumed asexual reproduction of plants as a symbol of their chastity and still rejected Camerarius' and Linné's findings in the 19th century (R. Schlegel: Sexuelles. In, *Phytotronik: Kurioses aus Botanik, Züchtung und Vererbung IV*, Books on Demand, 2017;

L. Taiz and L. Taiz: *Flora unveiled—The Discovery & Denial of Sex in Plants*, Oxford University Press, 2017; S. Vietor: *Astralis by Novalis: Handschrift, Text, Werk*, Verlag Königshausen & Neumann GmbH, Würzburg, 2001, p. 313; Discovery of Sexuality in Plants. *Nature* 1933, 131, 392; H. Funk: Adam Zalužanský's "De sexu plantarum" (1592): an early pioneering chapter on plant sexuality. *Arch. Nat. Hist.* 2013, 40, 244).

For [52] The information according to which the Dutch physician Jan Pieter Rathlauw had first stayed in the Marburg area or in the city itself, where "birthing powder" had been sold to doctors and midwives in Marburg pharmacies and had been available there for 30 years (Hecker, lit. 50, lit. 54), is not found in the cited article by Heinrich Felix Paulitzky (Lit. 53).

For [56] Desgranges' formula for labor remedies reads very simply: *"Boil a pinch of ground ergot in a little water for fifteen minutes and give the whole decoction (including the residue) to the women in labor to drink. After ten to twelve minutes, the effect sets in, and the child is born within a quarter of an hour."*

For [57] J. Fountaine: Further Observations on Ergot. *The United States Medical and Surgical Journal* 1835, 15, 469.

For [58] In Stearns' first publication of 1808 (Lit. 57), he let himself get carried away with the remark about ergot in obstetrics *"that it never produced any bad effects on the patient"*. After increasingly frequent reports of serious complications during birth, which Stearns attributed primarily to errors in the administration of the medication, he now corrected his earlier assessment and wrote: *"I solemnly retract it."*

For [63] John Stearn's article of 1822 (Lit. 58), in which he had compiled the contraindications of ergot medicine in obstetrics, was reprinted in this journal edition. Today's obstetricians agree with Hosack's assessment of the observed increase in the stillbirth rate and neonatal infant mortality: the induction of a tonic uterine contraction can interrupt the placental circulation so that the fetus suffocates during birth. Furthermore, the complex compound mixture of ergot, which contains other pharmacologically relevant substances in addition to the alkaloids, can lead to fatal poisoning of the fetus (P.A. Dargaville and N.T. Campbell: *Pulvis parturiens* and neonatal ergometrine poisoning in the 19th century. In, Abstract 707 Historical Perspectives Poster Symposium. *Pediatr. Res.* 1999, 45, 122).

Chapter 4

For [2] In the middle of the 19th century, the frequency of breech presentation was about 3% with a mortality rate of 98% (Prof. Johann Lucas Schönlein, lit. 2, pp. 31–32). Around 1900, the perinatal mortality rate for breech births was 20%. In 1970, it was still 15%, with 15% of those born suffering from respiratory problems or brain damage (ibid, p. 828). Against this background, it is nothing short of a miracle that Prof. Eduard Martin was able to give birth to Wilhelm, who was "already asphyxial". Using all the means described in medical books or by midwives, Martin and the midwife Miss Stahl saved Wilhelm's life. (T. Meissner: Wilhelm II.: Ein Geburtstrauma mit Folgen. In, *Der prominente Patient – Krankheiten berühmter Persönlichkeiten*, Springer Verlag GmbH Deutschland, 2019, p. 365)

For [21] F.B.: Mr. Smith's Discovery of the True Nature of the Ergot of Rye. *Lancet* 1838–1839, 2, 465.

For [33] C.J. Bailey: Metformin: its botanical background. *Pract. Diabetes* 2004, 21, 115; C.J. Bailey: Metformin: historical overview. *Diabetologia* 2017, 60, 1566.

For [36] When Henry Wellcome worked in his uncle's pharmacy, his talent in product advertising, which was later to play such an important role at Burroughs Wellcome and Co, was already evident. Here in Garden City, MN, the sixteen-year-old began manufacturing and marketing his first own product—a magic ink that he touted as follows (https://briandeer.com/septrin/henry-wellcome.htm):

Wellcome's Magic Ink
THE GREATEST WONDER OF THE AGE
This is something entirely New and Novel!
DIRECTIONS
Write with a quill or golden pen on white paper.
No trace is visible until held to the fire when it becomes very black.
Prepared only by
H.S. WELLCOME Garden City, Minn.

Chapter 5

For [2] R.P. Ahlquist: A study of the adrenotropic receptors. *Am. J. Physiol.* 1948, 153, 586.

For [4] While attending a physiological congress in Heidelberg in August 1907, Henry Dale became aware of the extraordinarily strong and immediate effect of some sclerotia extracts on the smooth muscle cells of the intestine and uterus, which differed from the previously described activities of ergot alkaloids. There was immediate speculation as to whether biogenic amines might be responsible for the pharmaceutical effects of the sclerotia decoction. Dale and Barger then isolated histamine from the ergot extract with its pronounced effect on the smooth muscle cells. The molecule was not new. Adolf Windaus and W. Vogt synthesized it in 1907 but did not investigate its physiological effects (J.F. Riley: Histamine and Sir Henry Dale. *BMJ* 1965,1, 1488; A. Windaus and W. Vogt: Synthese des Imidazolyläthylamins. *Ber. Dtsch. Chem. Ges.* 1907, 40, 3691). Today it is assumed that bacteria had infected Barger's sclerotia material and were the actual producers of the histamine.

For [6] O. Loewi: Nobel Prize Lecture 1936. https://www.nobelprize.org/prizes/medicine/1936/loewi/lecture/.

For [7] Sir James Black's drug research led to the development of cimetidine as a selective inhibitor of the histamine H2 receptor to reduce gastric acid production and propranolol as a non-selective β1/2-adrenoceptor blocker for the treatment of hypertension and various coronary diseases.

For [8] The authors explained the drop in blood pressure caused by acetylcholine with an "effect upon the terminations of the vagus in the heart" and discovered the characteristic antagonism of acetylcholine and atropine.

For [9] Ewins' isolated acetylcholine was most likely formed by a bacterial contaminant of the fungal material that had acetylated the choline of the ergot sclerotia. In 1938, A. Oury and Zénon M. Bacq contacted Henry Dale because they could not find acetycholine in their sclerotia batches. Dale replied that Ewins had isolated the signaling molecule from "*rotten ergot material*" that was to be discarded because it could no longer be used for therapeutic purposes (Y. Dunand: *Acetylcholine, a ubiquitous signaling substance*, Cambridge Scholar Publishing, 2021, p. 1). Following Hunt and Taveau (Lit. 8), Ewins also showed the antagonism of acetylcholine and atropine, which Otto Löwi established in 1921 for the "vagus substance" of the frog heart. The interaction of the two substances gave Löwi the idea that his vagus substance could possibly be acetylcholine or an *acetylcholine-like substance* (Lit. 13; A. v. Baeyer: Synthese des Neurins. *Liebigs Ann. Chem.* Vol. 140, 1866, p. 306; H. Teichmann: Cholin – Neurin – Betain: Ein Kapitel Naturstoff-Chemie aus der Gründungszeit der Deutschen Chemischen Gesellschaft. Gesellschaft Deutscher Chemiker/Fachgruppe Geschichte der Chemie. *Mitteilungen* 1994, 10, 31).

For [11] In his 1904 publication, Thomas Elliott formulated the principle of chemical signal transmission for the first time: "Adrenaline might then be the substance liberated when the nervous stimulus reaches the periphery" (T.R. Elliott: On the action of adrenalin. *J. Physiol. (Lond)* 1904, 31, 20). In 1905, he developed his idea further and wrote: "The specific reaction to adrenalin(e) marks the deep distinction between the myoneural junctions of the sympathetic nerves on the one hand, and of the cranial or sacral autonomic on the other together with all the preganglionic 'synapses'; which are rather related biochemically to the junctions of the skeletal nerves with the striated muscles." According to Henry Dale's comments, their mutual teacher John Newport Langley (1852–1925) rejected Elliott's theory of a "transmission" of nerve signals, just as he was skeptical of theories in general. Apparently, he also refused to discuss the transmitter concept at all. Dale was therefore surprised that, shortly after Elliott's publication, Langley followed it up with his own publication, in which he renamed the previous term "myoneural junctions" as "receptive substances" (J.N. Langley: On the reaction of cells and of nerve endings to certain poisons, chiefly as regards the reaction of striated muscle to nicotine and to curari. *J. Physiol.* 1905, 33, 374). In the end, Henry Dale left it open why Langley had written this publication, but pointed out "that this publication by Langley, carrying his very distinguished authority, was largely responsible for diverting attention from what should have been recognized as by far the most important result for physiological theory, of any of the work on adrenaline at that period". (H.H. Dale: Thomas Renton Elliott. 1877–1961. *Biogr. Mem. Fellows R. Soc.* 1961, 7, 52; A.-H. Maehle: "Receptive Substances": John Newport Langley (1852–1925) and his path to a receptor theory of drug action. *Med. Hist.* 2004, 48, 153).

For [13] A.N. McCoy and S.Y. Tan: Otto Loewi (1873–1961): Dreamer and Nobel laureate. *Singapore Med. J.* 2014, 55, 3.

For [16] Marthe Louise Vogt was able to leave Nazi Germany in 1935 with the help of a Rockefeller scholarship, and subsequently worked together with Wilhelm Feldberg on the chemical signal transmission of motor neurons. During the war, she and Feldberg found evidence that acetylcholine must also be a messenger substance of the brain. In 1954, Marthe Vogt recognized the role of "sympathin" (adrenaline and noradrenaline) as transmitter of the nerve cells of the brain (M. Vogt: The concentration of sympathin in different parts of the central nervous system under normal conditions and after the administration of drugs. *J. Physiol.* 1954, 123, 451; P. Wright: Obituary—Marthe Louise Vogt. *Lancet* 2003, 362, 1769).

For [27] John Eccles immediately informed Henry Dale that his experiments on the transmission of stimuli to motor neurons disproved the purely bioelectric mechanism and confirmed the chemical signal transduction advo-cated by Dale. Dale congratulated the Australian scientist on the beauty of his observations and said, with quiet British irony, "your new-found enthusiasm is certainly not going to cause any of us embarrassment." (In, F. Ashcroft: *The spark of life: Electricity in the human body*, Penguin Books, London, 2013.)

For [32] H.H. Dale and W.E. Dixon: The Action of Pressor Amines Pro-duced by Putrefaction. *J. Physiol.* 1909, 39, 25.

Chapter 6

For [1] Around 1886/7, both Durand & Huguenin in Basel and the salicylic acid factory Dr. F. von Heyden in Radebeul near Dresden started the produc-tion and sale of phenylsalicylic acid, or *salol*, at about the same time. While the drug from Basel was prescribed as an antiseptic and antirheumatic, the Saxon company marketed the compound as a deodorant, as an additive in mouth-washes, in bandages and as a therapeutic agent for urinary tract infections. From 1887, CIBA produced the antipyretic *antipyrine*, which had previously been introduced to medicine by "Farbwerke vorm. Meister Lucius & Brün-ing" in Frankfurt-Hoechst. This was soon followed by the production of other drugs that German pharmaceutical companies had successfully developed. In 1890, CIBA finally decided to research its own original preparations, which were approved for human therapy in the following years:

1900: *Vioform* (clioquinol, antiseptic), *Isarol "CIBA"* (ammonium bitumi-nosulfonate (from the distillation product of oil shale), skin diseases)
1904: *Phytin "CIBA"* (calcium-magnesium salt of plant-based inositol hexa-phosphoric acid, general tonic)
Fortossan "CIBA" (phytin lactose, infant formula, tonic)
Quinine-Phytin "CIBA" (tonic)
Salen "CIBA" (salicylic acid derivative (?), antirheumatic)
Peristaltin "CIBA" (anthraquinone glycosides of cascara, laxative)
1912: *Digifolin "CIBA"* (foxglove extract, heart failure)
1913: *Coagulen "CIBA"* (bovine blood extract, hemostatic agent)
Dial "CIBA" (barbiturate, epilepsy, insomnia, anxiety)
1915: *Orypan "CIBA"* (rice bran extract, tonic, beri-beri disease).

Since the beginning of the 20th century, several pharmaceutical companies have produced gonad extracts for hormone therapies. From 1914, CIBA con-centrated on research into female and male sex hormones. It acquired a license from doctors at the University of Erlangen to produce two corpus luteum extracts, which were approved for the treatment of hormonal disorders in 1918 (J. Süß and N. Simmer: Lipamin (Agomensin®) und Luteolipoid (Sistomensin®) – Tierexperimente und die vermeintliche klinische Erfahrung. *Geburtsh. u. Frauenheilk.*, 1987, 47, 351).

In 1898, Hoffmann-La Roche introduced the cough syrup *Sirolin "Roche"*, whose active ingredient *guaiacol* was extracted from the bark of guaiac trees. From 1905, the company also marketed first organ and gonad extracts for the treatment of hormonal disorders and menopausal complaints. In 1908, the standardized opium extract *Pantopon "Roche"* was launched for the treatment of pain, spasms, and colic, and the leaf extract of foxglove was developed as *Digalen "Roche"* for the treatment of heart failure. In 1914 Hoffmann-La Roche's *Veroglandol*, an extract of the corpus luteum, was approved for the treatment of amenorrhea and menorrhagia.

The pharmaceutical companies Merck in Darmstadt and Bayer in Leverkusen received marketing authorization for the sleeping pill *Veronal* in 1903. It is derived from the pharmacologically inactive barbituric acid first synthesized by Adolf von Baeyer in 1864. It was the introduction of two ethyl groups into the barbituric acid skeleton by his student Emil Fischer and the in-vivo studies by the physician Joseph von Mehring that made the molecule a highly potent hypnotic and narcotic. Due to its great financial success, CIBA wanted to develop its own barbiturate, which it succeeded in doing in 1913 with Dial "CIBA". Thanks to the transfer of barbiturate chemist Ernst Preiswerk from CIBA to Hoffmann-La Roche, medicinal chemistry work on the drug class could be started quickly. Hoffmann-La Roche introduced *Allonal "Roche"* (their first synthetically derived drug) in 1920 and *Somnifen "Roche"* in 1921 as a sleeping pill, painkiller and sedative (from: Chr. Ratmoko: Damit die Chemie stimmt – Die Anfänge der industriellen Herstellung von weiblichen und männlichen Sexualhormonen 1914–1938. *Interferenzen 16. ETH Zurich.* Chronos Verlag, Zurich, 2010; M. Bürgi: Pharmaforschung im 20. Jahrhundert – Arbeit an der Grenze zwischen Hochschule und Industrie. *Interferenzen 17. ETH Zurich.* Chronos Verlag, Zurich, 2011).

For [12] Even today, postpartum hemorrhage is responsible for 27% of maternal mortality worldwide, with a high prevalence in developing countries (A.H. James, J.J. Federspiel, and H.K. Ahmadzia: Disparities in obstetric hemorrhage outcomes. *Res. Pract. Thromb. Haemost.* 2022, 6, e12656).

For [29] G.L. Brown and H.H. Dale: The pharmacology of ergometrine. *Proc. R. Soc. Lond.* 1935, 118, 446.

Chapter 7

For [6] After it had become clear that all groups had isolated the identical substances, Marvin R. Thompson from Baltimore spoke up. Even before Dudley and Moir, he had recognized that the new active substance was an alkaloid, had initially called it *new X-alkaloid* and then, in May 1934, referred to it as ergostetrine (M. Thompson: *U.S. Pat.* No. 2,192,460 Title: Ergot Preparation and Process for making same (priority application filed Aug. 16, 1934; US application number 740,199; published as US 2,192, 460 on Mar. 5, 1940); M.R. Thompson: The active constituents of ergot: A pharmacological and chemical study. *J. Am. Pharm. Assoc.* 1935, 24, 24; M.R. Thompson: The new active principle of ergot. *Science* 1935, 81, 636). As late as March 1935, Thompson announced that he did not yet have a uniform crystalline pure substance and could not make any statements about its purity (M.R. Thompson: The active constituents of ergot: A pharmacological and chemical study. *J. Am. Pharm. Assoc.* 1935, 24, 185). In June 1935, Dudley and Moir did not rule out the possibility that Thompson had been the first to recognize the alkaloid character of the molecule. However, the two British supposed that due to its physiological profile his X-alkaloid was still heavily contaminated with ergotoxine. They pointed out that Thompson was the last to publish the name ergostetrine and rejected a discussion of names based on entries in "laboratory journals". (H.W. Dudley and J. Chassar Moir: *Science* 1935, 81, 559). Thompson now became furious and objected to his British colleagues dismissing his work as a "later success". He rejected Dudley and Moir's suggestion to agree on a uniform substance name because, "unfortunately, my name 'Ergostetrine' is not a mere matter of 'note-book record'. This name was both scientifically and legally assigned by me in May 1934". (M.R. Thompson: The new active principle of ergot. *Science* 1935, 81, 636). In August, Henry Dale joined the discussion and agreed with the London scientists' argument that the discussion should be conducted solely based on publication priority. This way, the case was easy to solve: The substance should be called "ergometrine" (H.H. Dale: The new ergot alkaloid. *Science* 1935, 82, 99). In November, Arthur Stoll from Basel announced that his analytical data with pure ergobasine (so called because of its relatively strong basic property in aqueous solution) and its comparison with Thompson's ergostetrine proved the identity of both compounds. However, the analytical data from Dudley and Moir's ergometrine preparation differed significantly from his ergobasine/ergostetrine measurement results, meaning that the British had either a completely different substance than ergobasine or a contaminated substance. He added that *the* "Council on Pharmacy and Chemistry of the American Medical Association disapproves of names in which therapeutic indications are suggested and prefers terms based on the chemical nature or on the origin of a substance (adrenalin, insulin, etc.). 'Ergobasine' indicates the origin and an important chemical property of the substance". (A. Stoll: The new ergot alkaloid. *Science* 1935, 82, 415). Now there was a great deal of confusion. Finally, all groups agreed *to* "leave to the world of science the choice of one of these names, for adoption into scientific literature as the recognized name of the one alkaloid". (*Note*: It is possible to assign a name to a preparation for mixtures. Fleming's penicillin was also a crude mixture in the beginning. The name priority results from the first publication of the name. Thompson's ergostetrine from his patent was not yet known in 1935, as his patent application of August 16, 1934, which was still in the examination phase at the US Patent Office, had not yet been published. Ergometrine was therefore the first name to be published. However, ergostetrine and ergometrine contradicted the guidelines of the American Medical Association for the designation of active medical ingredients in the USA. Only Arthur Stoll's ergobasine complied with this regulation. Whether the US guidelines at the time were also internationally binding could not be clarified. If not, ergometrine is also the scientifically correct name. On the fringes of the celebrations for his 100th birthday at Novartis AG, Albert Hofmann still spoke of ergobasine in conversation with F.P., although the Sandoz researchers had based their later synthesized methylergometrine on the British substance name).

For [10] S. Smith and G.M. Timmis: 141. The alkaloids of ergot. Part V. The nature of ergine. *J. Chem. Soc.* 1934, 674–675.

For [20] Susi Ramstein was born into a family of opticians in Basel in 1922. After completing her apprenticeship as a laboratory assistant in pharmaceutical research at Sandoz, she joined Albert Hofmann's laboratory team in 1942. After the psychotogenic activity of LSD was discovered, Susi Ramstein was the first woman to take the substance in a self-experiment on May 6, 1943. Two others followed on which the effect of the active substance was investigated in more detail (from: D. Hagenbach and L. Werthmüller: *Albert Hofmann und sein LSD*. AT Verlag, Aarau, 2011). The following pages: Hofmann's "special report" on his self-experiment to the research management of Sandoz AG.

1 + 3

S. d. Hofmann

Herrn Prof. Stoll.
_____

Betr. d-Lysergsäure-diäthylamid.

<u>Bericht über einen Selbstversuch mit einer toxischen
Dosis d-Lysergsäure-diäthylamid-tartrat.</u>

Vergangenen Freitag, den 16. April, musste ich mitten im
Nachmittag meine Arbeit im Laboratorium unterbrechen und mich
nach Hause in Pflege begeben, da ich von einer merkwürdigen Unruhe, verbunden mit einem leichten Schwindelgefühl, befallen
wurde. Zu Hause legte ich mich nieder und versank in einen
nicht unangenehmen rauschartigen Zustand, der sich durch eine
äusserst angeregte Phantasie kennzeichnete. Im Dämmerzustand
bei geschlossenen Augen (das Tageslicht empfand ich als unange-
nehm grell) drangen ohne Unterbruch phantastische Bilder von
ausserordentlicher Plastizität und mit intensivem, kaleidoskop-
artigem Farbenspiel auf mich ein. Nach etwa zwei Stunden ver-
flüchtigte sich dieser Zustand. Noch leicht benommen stand ich
wieder auf und nahm mit gutem Appetit mit meiner Familie das
Nachtessen ein. Anschliessend machte ich mit meiner Frau einen
kleinen Spaziergang, wonach ich mich wieder vollkommen frisch
und normal fühlte.

Art und Verlauf dieser Störung erweckten sogleich den
Verdacht einer von aussen erfolgten toxischen Einwirkung. Ich
hatte an jenem Tag mit zwei Verbindungen zum erstenmal in grösse-
ren Mengen gearbeitet. Es waren drei grosse Adsorptionssäulen
mit Methylenchlorid als Lösungsmittel im Betrieb. Ich hatte in
der Literatur keine Angaben über toxische Wirkungen dieses Leicht-
flüchtigen Stoffes (Kp. 41°), der zum Entwickeln von Chromatogram-
men von Mutterkornsubstanzen vorzüglich geeignet ist, gefunden.
Trotzdem schien es mir wahrscheinlich, dass der oben geschilderte
Zustand durch Einatmen von Methylenchlorid-Dämpfen verursacht
worden war, denn chlorierte Kohlenwasserstoffe besitzen bekanntlich

- 2 -

narkotische und zum Teil toxische Wirkung. Von meinem Labor-Personal hatte niemand etwas verspürt, was ich aber darauf zurückführte, dass ich allein über die Mittagspause durchgearbeitet hatte.

Als weitere ausserordentliche Substanz hatte an jenem Freitag das d-Lysergsäure-, bezw. Isolysergsäure-diäthylamid im Laboratorium figuriert. Ich hatte nach verschiedenen Methoden versucht, das aus den beiden Isomeren bestehende Kondensationsprodukt XXX zu reinigen und in die Komponenten zu zerlegen. Es waren aber erst Vorversuche mit wenigen Milligrammen Substanz und es war mir eben gelungen, das d-Lysergsäure-diäthylamid als gut kristallisierendes, spielend wasserlösliches, neutrales Tartrat zu fassen. Es schien mir aller-dings unerklärlich, auf welche Weise ich eine, die oben geschilderte Wirkung ermöglichende genügend grosse Menge dieses Stoffes hätte erwischt haben können. Auch die Art der Wirkung schien weder mit den Symptomen der Ergotamin-Ergotoxin- noch der Ergobasin-Gruppe verwandt zu sein. Ich wollte aber der Sache auf den Grund gehen, und ich beschloss mit dem kristallisierten d-Lysergsäure-diäthyl-amid-tartrat einen Selbstversuch zu machen. Da, wenn dieser Stoff als Ursache in Frage kam, er in sehr kleiner Dosis wirksam sein musste, begann ich mit der kleinsten Menge, von der, verglichen mit den Verhältnissen beim Ergotamin oder Ergobasin, noch eine feststellbare Wirkung zu erwarten war. Nachstend das Protokoll dieses Versuches:

19.IV.43.-Herstellung einer 0,5-promill. wässerigen d-Lysergsäure-
diäthylamid-tartrat-Lösung. 5,0 mg kristallisiertes, luft-
trockenes Tartrat wurden in 10,0 ccm Wasser gelöst. Die
Substanz löste sich spielend.   (entspr. 0,25 mg Tartrat)/
Um 16.20 Uhr 0,5 ccm dieser Lösung peroral eingenommen. Mit
etwas Wasser nachgespült. Die Lösung war vollkommen ge-
schmacklos, wie reines Wasser einzunehmen.
Um 16.50 Uhr noch keine Spur einer Wirkung. Auch im Magen
völliges Fehlen von Brechreiz, wie er nach Einnahme von
Ergotamin oder Ergobasin beobachtet werden kann.
Um 17.00 leichtes Schwindelgefühl, Unruhe, Gedanken nur
noch schwer zu konzentrieren, Sehstörungen, Lachreiz,

Hier hören die Aufzeichnungen im Laborjournal auf. Die letzten Worte konnten nur noch mit Mühe niedergeschrieben werden. Meine Laborantin war über den Versuch orientiert. Ich bat sie, mich sofort nach Hause zu begleiten, da ich glaubte, die Sache nehme den gleichen

- 3 -

Verlauf wie die Störung am vergangenen Freitag. Aber schon auf
dem Heimweg per Velo nach Bottmingen zeigte es sich, dass alle
Symptome stärker waren als das erstemal. Ich hatte bereits grösste
Mühe klar zu sprechen und mein Gesichtsfeld schwankte und war verzerrt wie ein Bild in einem verkrümmten Spiegel. Auch hatte ich das
Gefühl nicht vom Fleck zu kommen, während mir nachher meine Laborantin sagte, dass wir ein scharfes Tempo gefahren seien.

　　Da meine **Familie** an jenem Tag nach Luzern verreist war, liess
ich durch Frl. Ramstein (meine Laborantin) meine Nachbarn rufen,
während ich das Haus öffnete und mich sogleich auf einem Sofa nieder-
legte. Als die Nachbarsfrau, Frau Dr. Ruch, nach ungefähr 5 Minuten
erschien, hatte sich mein Zustand derart verschlechtert, dass ich
kaum mehr richtig Auskunft geben konnte. Ich veranlasste Frl.
Ramstein, nach Ihnen zu telephonieren. Da Sie aber abwesend waren
und mein Zustand immer bedrohlicher wurde, alarmierten wir den
nächsten Arzt, Herrn Dr. Schilling in Bottmingen, bezw. seinen
Stellvertreter. In der Zwischenzeit trank ich alle irgendwie
beschaffbare Milch, im Verlaufe des Abends insgesamt 2½ -3 Liter.

　　Soweit ich mich erinnern kann, waren während dem Höhepunkt
der Krise, der bereits überschritten war als der Arzt ankam, folgende
Symptome am ausgeprägtesten: Schwindel, Sehstörungen, die Gesichter
der Anwesenden erschienen mir wie farbige Fratzen; starke motorische
Unruhe, wechselnd mit Lähmungen; der Kopf, der ganze Körper und die
Glieder dünkten mich zeitweise schwer, wie mit Metall gefüllt; in den
Waden Krämpfe, Hände zeitweise kalt empfindungslos; auf der Zunge
metallischer Geschmack; Kehle trocken, zusammengezogen; Erstickungs-
gefühl; abwechselnd betäubt, dann wieder klares Erkennen der Lage,
wobei ich zeitweise als ausserhalb mir selbst stehender neutraler
Beobachter feststellte, wie ich halb wahnsinnig schrie oder un-
klares Zeug schwatzte.

　　Der Arzt, der wie gesagt erst nach dem Höhepunkt der Krise
erschien, stellte fest, dass der Puls etwas schwach, der Kreislauf
im Uebrigen aber normal war. Auf mein Ersuchen und auf Anraten von
Herrn Prof. Staub, den er telephonisch konsultierte, verzichtete er
in Anbetracht der völligen Unklarheit über die Wirkungsweise des
d-Lysergsäure-diäthylamids auf die Gabe irgend eines Pharmakons, das als

- 4 -

mögliches Gegengift hätte in Frage kommen können.

Als gegen elf Uhr abends meine Frau von Luzern eintraf, hatte sich mein Zustand bereits weitgehend gebessert. Ausgeprägt waren noch die Sehstörungen. Alles schien zu wanken und war in den Proportionen verzerrt, ähnlich dem Spiegelbild auf einer bewegten Wasserfläche. Dazu war alles in wechselnde, unangenehme, giftig grüne und blaue Farbtöne getaucht. Bei geschlossenen Augen drangen ständig farbige, sehr plastische und phantastische Gebilde auf mich ein. Besonders merkwürdig war, wie alle akustischen Wahrnehmungen etwa das Geräusch eines vorbeifahrenden Autos, in optische Empfindungen transponiert wurden, so dass durch jeden Ton und jedes Geräusch ein entsprechendes farbiges Bild, in Form und Farbe kaleidoskopartig wechselnd, ausgelöst wurde.

Von ungefähr 1 Uhr nachts bis 8 Uhr morgens konnte ich ruhig schlafen und fühlte mich dann wieder vollkommen gesund, wenn auch etwas müde und blieb auf Anraten des Arztes den ganzen Tag noch im Bett. Tags darauf konnte ich vollkommen normal und frisch die Arbeit im Laboratorium wieder aufnehmen.

Auf Grund dieses leider etwas dramatisch ausgefallenen Selbstversuches kann gesagt werden, dass das d-Lysergsäure-diäthylamid eine der physiologisch wirksamsten, wenn nicht die wirksamste bis anhin bekannte Substanz darstellt. Bei den giftigsten Substanzen wie Strychnin, Nicotin, HCN führen erst Dosen von einigen mg beim Menschen zu toxischen Erscheinungen. Beim wirksamsten Schlangengift, beim Cobratoxin, werden 0,01 bis 0,1 mg als therapeutische Dosierung angegeben.

Bemerkenswert ist auch, dass die stark toxische Dosis des d-Lysergsäure-diäthylamids, 0,25 mg Tartrat, das entspricht 0,20 mg freie Base, durch den Geschmack nicht im geringsten feststellbar ist und dass sie sich auch im Magen in keiner Weise bemerkbar machte. Ein Irrtum in der Dosierung im obigen Selbstversuch ist ausgeschlossen, da ich die 5,0 mg selbst abgewogen und damit die 0,5-promill. Lösung hergestellt habe.

Die beschriebenen Vergiftungserscheinungen gleichen am ehesten

– 5 –

den Symptomen, wie sie nach übermässigem Gebrauch von Pervitin
oder anderen Weckaminen beobachtet worden sind. Wie mir der
mich behandelnde Arzt, Herr Dr. Beerle, der zufällig selbst
Versuche mit Pervitin durchgeführt hat, mitteilte, werden dabei
auch motorische Unruhe, Sehstörungen, Farbensehen, usw. beobachtet.
Die toxische Dosis von Pervitin liegt allerdings in der Grösse
von Zehntelgrammen (nach Angaben von Herr Dr. Beerle), ist also
etwa 1000-mal grösser als beim d-Lysergsäure-diäthylamid.

22. April 1943   A. Hofmann.

For [26] Gustave Flaubert and Honoré de Balzac were sometimes present at the meetings, but they did not consume hashish.

For [30] C. Koller: Nachträgliche Bemerkungen über die ersten Anfänge der Lokalanästhesie. *Wien. Med. Wochenschr.* 1935, 1, 7–8; P. Heilig: Coca, Freud und (Coca-)Koller. Van Swieten Blog. University Library Medical University of Vienna 2020, https://ub.meduniwien.ac.at/blog/?p=35839.

For [31] R. Larsen: Spinalanästhesie. *Anästhesie und Intensivmedizin für die Fachpflege* 2016, 197. William Stewart Halsted (1852–1922) shaped surgery in the 20th century in many ways, perfected the radical mastectomy and developed a new training program for prospective surgeons in the USA. In 1884, he read about the use of cocaine as a "surface anesthetic" in eye operations by the Viennese ophthalmologist Carl Koller in a report on the Ophthalmology Congress in Heidelberg. In the search for further areas of application for the anesthetic, Halsted recognized that the alkaloid could block the conduction of every peripheral nerve, making the innervated tissue insensitive to pain. During the development of "conductive anesthesia", he, his medical students, and assistants took cocaine to study the administration and dosage of the drug for subsequent operations. Halsted developed a cocaine dependence, for which he repeatedly sought treatment in addiction clinics. In 1886, Halsted's doctors medicated his cocaine addiction with morphine and made him a morphine-cocaine addict. Many of his colleagues, who had also become dependent on drugs during the research work, died of their addiction (W.G. MacCallum: *Biographical Memoir of William Stewart Halsted 1852–1922*. National Academy of Sciences of the United States of America Vol. XVII—Seventh Memoir. 1935, P. 149; J.L. Cameron: William Stewart Halsted, M.D. Our Surgical Heritage. *Ann. Surg.* 1997, 225, 445).

For [32] In 1896, Arthur Heffter had isolated mescaline from the peyote cactus. Two years later, he proved that this was also the psychotogenic drug of the plant by examining the activities of the substance fractions prepared during isolation (A. Heffter: Ueber Cacteenalkaloïde. *Ber. Dtsch. Chem. Ges.* 1896, 29, 216).

For [33] T. Passie: Meskalinforschung in Deutschland 1887–1950: Grundlagenforschung, Selbstversuche und Missbrauch. (https://psychedelic-science.net/substanzen/halluzinogene/meskalin/meskalinforschung-in-deutschland-1887-1950/); I.A. Vamvakopoulou, A.D.K. Narine, I. Campbell, J.R.B. Dyck, and D.J. Nutt: Mescaline: The forgotten psychedelic. *Neuropharmacol.* 2023, 222, 109294.

For [35] Leni Alberts's test person Hans Prinzhorn (who was also a test subject in Kurt Beringer's mescaline studies for some time) took over works of art from Emil Kraepelin, the former director of the Psychiatric University Clinic in Heidelberg, that people had created during their stay in his clinic. By 1921, Prinzhorn had collected further art objects in Heidelberg from patients in psychiatric hospitals in Germany, Austria, and Switzerland. Today, the "Prinzhorn Collection" is a unique museum with a collection of 5000 artifacts.

Chapter 8

For [1] V. Erspamer: Pharmakologische Studien über Enteramin II. Mitteilung: Über einige Eigenschaften des Enteramins, sowie über die Abgrenzung des Enteramins von den anderen kreislaufwirksamen Gewebsprodukten. *Arch. Exp. Path. Pharmak.* 1940, 196, 366; V. Erspamer: Il sistema enterocromaffine ed i suoi rapporti con il sitema insulare. *Z. Anat. Entwickl. Gesch.* 1939, 109, 586.

For [3] M. Göthert: Serotonin discovery and stepwise disclosure of 5-HT receptor complexity over four decades. Part I. General background and discovery of serotonin as a basis for 5-HT receptor identification. *Pharmacol. Rep.* 2013, 65, 771.

For [4] I.H. Page: Serotonin (5-hydroxytryptamine). *Physiol. Rev.* 1954, 34, 563.

For [5] The 5-HT detection method established by Irvine Page was based on an experimental setup developed by John Gaddum for his adrenaline research (J.H. Gaddum and H. Kwiatkowski: The action of ephedrine. *J. Physiol.* 1938, 94, 87; I.H. Page: A method for perfusion of rabbits' ears, and its application to study of the renin-angiotonin vasopressor system, with a note on angiotonin tachyphylaxis. *Am. Heart J.* 1942, 23, 336).

For [11] Betty Twarog's physiological work at Harvard University was only published after her serotonin research with Irvine Page. The Journal of Cellular and Comparative Physiology "had not bothered to review an article on an unknown neurotransmitter by an unknown author" (Lit. 3).

For [14] Henry Gaddum reached pharmacology via a bumpy detour. He did not turn up for months during his medical studies on the ward at University College Hospital in London. It was to be expected: in 1924, he flunked the bachelor's examination twice. After that, his career went up in smoke. At a ball, he learned by chance from his dance partner Barbara Holmes, the daughter of future Nobel Prize winner Sir Frederick Hopkins, that the Wellcome Physiological Research Labs were looking for "someone". In 1925, Gaddum received his first position with the pharmacologist John William Trevan (who introduced the concept of the "lethal dose" to pharmacology in 1927). When Gaddum wanted to apply for a job with Henry Dale, Trevan advised him to read Dale's recent publications before the interview to find out about the physiologist's scientific interests and then think of experiments that Dale might enjoy—it was good advice! After six years in Dale's group, Gaddum tried to set up an independent research group to step out of his boss's shadow. But no British university wanted to hire him. Only his application to head the Institute of Pharmacology at Cairo University was successful. He pusillanimously admitted to his friend there, Gleb von Anrep, head of physiology, that he was a physiologist rather than a pharmacologist. Von Anrep cheered him up and wrote back that all it takes to become a pharmacologist is to learn dosages. Gaddum spent the ten-day voyage to the city on the Nile familiarizing himself with the science of dosing. It was his research and analytical work with histamine and acetylcholine in Egypt that made him of interest to an institute in Great Britain. In 1935 he was appointed professor at the Institute of Pharmacology at University College, London.

For [16] In 1955, Sandoz pharmacologists Aurelio Cerletti and Ernst Rothlin reported on the activity of *2-bromo-LSD* BOL 148. The potent antagonist of 5-HT had no psychotogenic effect. Their findings were in stark contrast to Gaddum's assumption that the antagonism of LSD and 5-HT at the 5-HT receptor in the brain was the reason for the induced psychotic experience. The conclusion of the Sandoz experts could not have been clearer: "The mere fact of a pharmacological antagonism between lysergic acid diethylamide and 5-hydroxytryptamine, however, no longer provides evidence for the hypothesis that inhibition of the latter in the brain is the cause of the mental disturbance." (A. Cerletti and E. Rothlin: Role of 5-hydroxytryptamine in mental diseases and its antagonism to lysergic acid derivatives. *Nature* 1955, 176, 785). The evidence presented by the two pharmacologists was conclusive, but it was based on the activity profile of a substance which, as was recently reported, differs significantly from that of LSD: BOL 148, which binds to HT-2A, and is not psychotogenic. Why this is the case is still the subject of scientific research (V. Lewis, E.M. Bonniwell, J.K. Lanham, A. Ghaffari, H. Sheshbaradaran, A.B. Cao, M.M. Calkins, M.A. Bautista-Carro, E. Arsenault, A. Telfer, F.F. Taghavi-Abkuh, N.J. Malcolm, F. El Sayegh, A. Abizaid, Y. Schmid, K. Morton, A.L. Halberstadt, A. Aguilar-Valles, J.D. McCorvy: A non-hallucinogenic LSD analogous to therapeutic potential for mood disorders. *Cell Rep.* 2023, 42, 112203).

For [20] D.W. Woolley: Serotonin in mental disorders. In, *Hormones, brain function and behavior: Proceedings of a Conference on Neuroendocrinology Held at Arden House, Harriman, New York, 1956* (Ed: H. Hoagland). Academic Press Inc, New York, 1957, p. 127.

For [40] R.M. MacLeod and J.E. Lehmeyer: Studies on the mechanism of the dopamine-mediated inhibition of prolactin secretion. *Endocrinology* 1974, 94, 1077.

For [44] E. Flückiger: The pharmacology of bromocriptine. In, *Pharmacological and clinical aspects of bromocriptine (Parlodel)* (Eds.: R.I.S. Bayliss, P. Turner, W.P. Maclay). Tunbridge Wells, Kent: Medical Congresses Symposia Consultants, 1976, p. 12.

Chapter 9

For [5] B. Bächi: *LSD auf dem Land: Produktion und kollektive Wirkung psychotroper Stoffe*. Konstanz University Press, 2020.

"Sandoz AG entered the agricultural business at the end of the 1930s. As the project was initially conceived on a fairly modest scale—the agrochemical department for pesticides was only to comprise around three to four specialists—this diversification step was the responsibility of the chemicals department. The Board of Directors was merely informed, and its approval was just a formality. A similar approach was taken with the plan to affiliate an own experimental farm to the new division: Hans Leemann (1882–1967), then Vice Chairman and Delegate of the Board of Directors, informed the Board of Directors in December 1944 about the intended purchase of Unterer Klushof near Aesch in the canton of Basel-Landschaft. The sales negotiations between the then owner of Unterer Klushof and Sandoz were laborious and were only concluded in February 1945. After Sandoz had already purchased part of the Vordere Klus, the company also acquired the Obere Klus estate in 1957. The primary task of the Klushof complex was to test the newly developed agrochemical products under natural conditions. The Klushof's original field of work was significantly expanded through the cultivation of medicinal plants. The aim was to breed plants with the highest possible content of active ingredient" (personal communication by W. Dettwiler, 2024). Rye varieties, such as the "Kluser rye", were also bred here in order to increase the ergot yield on the grain plant. In 1996, the Basel-based companies Ciba and Sandoz merged to form today's Novartis AG and integrated their two agricultural businesses. In 2000, the merger of Novartis Agribusiness with the agribusiness division of the British-Swedish company AstraZeneca created the agribusiness company Syngenta.

For [16] M. Abe: XI. Separation of Agroclavine from Natural Ergot. *J. Agric. Chem. Soc. Japan* 1948, 22, 61; M. Abe: XI. Position of Agroclavine in the group of Ergot. *J. Agric. Chem. Soc. Japan* 1948, 22, 85.

For [26] J. Rutschmann, H. Kobel, E. Schreier: Heterocyclic carboxylic acids and their production. 1964 *U.S. Patent* 3, 314, 961.

For [28] From 1935, Artur Brack headed the ergot group in the production division of Sandoz AG. In 1964, the three independent natural product groups "alkaloids" (Hans Kobel), "antibiotic fungal metabolites" (Christian Stoll), and "natural product chemistry" (Hans-Peter Sigg) existed in preclinical research. They reported directly to the Head of Pharmaceutical Research, Jürg Rutschmann. In 1967, the Swiss chemist Hans Peter Sigg became responsible for all natural product groups in research. When Sigg was appointed Head of Agricultural Research in 1969, Albert Hofmann succeeded him along with the Swiss chemist Albert von Wartburg as Deputy Head. In 1971, Hofmann retired, and von Wartburg became head of the natural product research department (personal communication by Dr. Jean-Jacques Sanglier, 2023).

Chapter 10

For [6] A. Hofmann and A. Cerletti: Die Wirkstoffe der dritten aztekischen Zauberdroge oder Die Lösung des "Ololiuiqui-Rätsels". *Dtsch. Med. Wochenschr.* 1961, 86, 885.

For [10] In 1933, the Hungarian chemist George de Hevesy showed a strong interest in a new molecule that had just been described. The American Harold Urey discovered "heavy hydrogen", deuterium or diplogen, and published his findings under the title "A hydrogen isotope of mass 2". After Gilbert N. Lewis produced "heavy water" at the University of California a year later, de Hevesy recalled a long past encounter with the British physicist Henry Moseley (1887–1915). During his visit to Ernest Rutherford at the Physics Laboratory at Manchester University in 1913, they had met for a cup of tea. During the conversation, the somewhat crazy speculation arose as to whether it would one day be possible to follow the path of the water molecules in the tea through the body. Now, after thirty years, the time had come for such an experiment. De Hevesy asked Urey to send him some of the precious water for his research. De Hevesy obtained a few liters of 0.5 mol% heavy water. He then let 20 goldfish "glide around" in 60 ml of D_2O for 15 hours to measure the exchange of the heavy water molecules with the light water molecules. In the preface to the publication in the journal *Nature* in 1934 (Lit. 11), he returned to the cup of tea with Moseley. In 1933, when all the goldfish were apparently in perfect condition after the experiment, de Hevesy or his laboratory assistant Erich Hofer, a descendant of the Tyrolean freedom fighter Andreas Hofer, drank several glasses of heavy water to calculate its retention time in the human body (Lit. [11]).

For [17] P. Tudzynski, K. Hölter, T. Correia, C. Arntz, N. Grammel, and U. Keller: Evidence for an ergot alkaloid gene cluster in *Claviceps purpurea*. *Mol. Gen. Genet.* 1999, 261, 133; J.-J. Chen, M.-Y. Han, T. Gong, J.-L. Yang, and P. Zhu: Recent progress in ergot alkaloid research. *RSC Adv.* 2017, 7, 27384; G. Wong, L.R. Lim, Y.Q. Tan, M.K. Go, D.J. Bell, P.S. Freemont, and W.S. Yew: Reconstituting the complete biosynthesis of D-lysergic acid in yeast. *Nat. Commun.* 2022, 13, 712.

For [27] Bundesgesetzblatt part 1 no 15, 2005, p. 630.

For [35] J.H. Gaddum and Z.P. Picarelli: Two kinds of tryptamine receptor. *Br. J. Pharmacol.* 1957, 12, 323.

For [38] M. Titeler, R.A. Lyon, and R.A. Glennon: Radioligand binding evidence implies the brain 5-HT2 receptor as a site of action for LSD and phenylisopropylamine hallucinogens. *Psychopharmacology* 1988, 94, 213; D. Hoyer: Functional correlates of serotonin 5-HT1 recognition sites. *J. Recept. Res.* 1988, 8, 59.

For [41] J. Gonzalez-Maeso, N.V. Weisstaub, M. Zhou, P. Chan, L. Ivic, R. Ang, A. Lira, M. Bradley-Moore, Y. Ge, Q. Zhou, S.C. Sealfon, and J.A. Gingrich: Hallucinogens recruit specific cortical 5-HT (2A) receptor-mediated signaling pathways to affect behavior. *Neuron* 2007, 53, 439.

For [43] C. Cao, X. Barros-Álvarez, S. Zhang, K. Kim, M.A. Dämgen, O. Panova, C.-M. Suomivuori, J.F. Fay, X. Zhong, B.E. Krumm, R.H. Gumpper, A.B. Seven, M.J. Robertson, N.J. Krogan, R. Hüttenhain, D.E. Nichols, R.O. Dror, G. Skiniotis, and B.L. Roth: Signaling snapshots of a serotonin receptor activated by the prototypical psychedelic LSD. *Neuron* 2022, 110, 3154.

For [48] I. Loudon: Deaths in childbed from the eighteenth century to 1935. *Med. Hist.* 1986, 30, 1.